FAMILY THERAPY

Concepts, Process and Practice

Second Edition

Alan Carr

University College Dublin and Clanwilliam Institute Dublin, Ireland

John Wiley & Sons, Ltd

Chichester · New York · Weinheim · Brisbane · Singapore · Toronto

Copyright © 2006 John Wiley & Sons Ltd, The Atrium, Southern Gate, Chichester,
West Sussex PO19 8SQ, England

Telephone (+44) 1243 779777

Email (for orders and customer service enquiries):
cs-books@wiley.co.uk
Visit our Home Page on www.wiley.com

While every effort has been made to contact the owner of copyright of 'At Swim-two-birds'
by Flann O'Brien, we have been unable to obtain his formal copyright permission for the
use of material.

Reprinted February 2008

Other Wiley Editorial Offices

John Wiley & Sons Inc., 111 River Street, Hoboken, NJ 07030, USA

Jossey-Bass, 989 Market Street, San Francisco, CA 94103-1741, USA

Wiley-VCH Verlag GmbH, Boschstr. 12, D-69469 Weinheim, Germany

John Wiley & Sons Australia Ltd, 42 McDougall Street, Milton, Queensland 4064, Australia

John Wiley & Sons (Asia) Pte Ltd, 2 Clementi Loop #02-01, Jin Xing Distripark, Singapore 129809

John Wiley & Sons Canada Ltd, 22 Worcester Road, Etobicoke, Ontario, Canada M9W 1L1

Wiley also publishes its books in a variety of electronic formats. Some content that appears
in print may not be available in electronic books.

Library of Congress Cataloging-in-Publication Data

Carr, Alan, Dr.
  Family therapy: concepts, process and practice / Alan Carr.— 2nd ed.
    p. cm. — (The Wiley series in clinical psychology)
  Includes bibliographical references and index.
  ISBN-13: 978-0-470-01454-7 (cloth : alk. paper)
  ISBN-10: 0-470-01454-7 (cloth : alk. paper)
  ISBN-13: 978-0-470-01455-4 (pbk. : alk. paper)
  ISBN-10: 0-470-01455-5 (pbk. : alk. paper)
  1. Family psychotherapy.   I. Title.   II. Series.
  RC488.5.C367 2006
  616.89'156—dc22   2005035562

British Library Cataloguing in Publication Data

A catalogue record for this book is available from the British Library

ISBN-13 978-0-470-01454-7(HB) ISBN-13 978-0-470-01455-4 (PB)

Typeset in 10/12 pt Palatino by Thomson Press (India) Limited, New Delhi
Printed and bound in Great Britain by TJ International, Padstow, Cornwall

CONTENTS

ABOUT THE AUTHOR

Professor Alan Carr is the director of the Doctoral training programme in clinical psychology at University College Dublin and Consultant Martial and Family Therapist at the Clanwilliam Institute for Marital and Family Therapy in Dublin. He has published over a dozen books and 200 academic papers and conference presentations in the fields of family therapy and clinical psychology. His work has been translated into a number of languages including Korean, Polish and Chinese. He has extensive experience in family therapy and clinical psychology, having worked in the field in the UK, Ireland and Canada.

FOREWORD

I have never met Alan Carr, and really know nothing about him (except that his parents showed eminently good taste in choosing his forename). But I have been familiar with his writings for a long time, and for several years, in fact, have required the psychiatric residents I teach to read his earliest work on the Formulation Model. The reason for this is clear and simple. In the Psychiatry Department in which I teach, residents have such demanding clinical responsibilities that they can allot only minimal time to their reading. So, seminar readings must be concise, relevant and use-able. For my values, they must also be conceptually well grounded. On all these criteria, Alan Carr's writings have easily passed the test. So, when he invited me to write this Foreword, I thought, 'What a remarkably good clinician he must be to know intuitively how highly I regard his work!'

Now that he has fully elaborated the Formulation Model in this book, I regard his contribution even more, and so should the reader, who really is getting 'two for the price of one' in this volume. The 'first book' in this book is a highly readable and accessible introductory account of the major approaches to family therapy, one which will be very well received by teachers of family therapy and their students. This new edition has been well updated with important new material on cutting-edge attachment-based therapies and integrative approaches, and a concise presentation of recent clinically relevant research on couple and family therapy. Moreover, it seems to me that Carr has actually revised more of the original text than second edition authors usually do, and, of course, the reader is the benefi-ciary of the work of such a responsible author! As in the first edition, the numerous comparative tables Carr includes are pedagogical gold mines for instructors. The second 'book-within-a-book' is Alan Carr's singular contribution, The Formulation Model of family therapy treatment plan-ning and intervention. This is how Carr's book sets itself apart from other introductory texts, which usually explicate all the extant clinical theories, but leave (especially) the novice reader hanging as to what to do with them. Carr never leaves such matters unattended to, and consistently suc-ceeds at showing the reader how to make theory practical. I like to think of Carr's book as news you can use, rather than views that confuse.

Carr's central contribution is his Formulation Model. As an empiri-cally oriented clinical theoretician, Carr is appropriately respectful of purportedly disparate points of view. He demonstrates his integrative conceptual open-mindedness through his 'three-column' method of formulating clinical problems and exceptions to problems. These levels or domains of behaviour appear at first blush roughly to parallel the time-honoured tripartite division of human experience into 'behaviour', 'cognition' and 'affect', but, in fact, they are far more inclusive of practical possibilities than such traditional categories would statically suggest. Carr's model politely but powerfully reminds us that intrapersonal factors, whether biochemical or intrapsychic, belong just as much in the domain of the real-life practice of couple and family therapy as the interpersonal factors with which the field of family therapy seemed to have been obsessed until just a few years ago. This is the power of his model, that change can potentially be initiated within any functionally relevant domain of experience, and still be systemically meaningful. Carr's Formulation Model is family therapy, but more important, it is wise therapy.

Alan Carr's writing is consistently crisp, clear and cogent. I am very pleased with the very positive reception with which the first edition of this book has been met, and I truly hope this new edition's exposure will not be limited to students, colleagues and practitioners in Great Britain and Europe. It certainly has much to commend it as an introductory textbook for students of couple and family therapy everywhere. As noted, it is an introduction-with-a-twist, and that 'twist' is that it presents an eminently teachable and learnable clinical model that leads to effective action. I hope Alan Carr's important contribution to the family therapy field will soon be more visible on this side of the Atlantic.

Alan S. Gurman PhD
Professor of Psychiatry, University of Wisconsin Medical School, Madison,
Wisconsin, USA
October 2005

PREFACE

One beginning and one ending for a book was a thing I did not agree with. A good book may have three openings entirely dissimilar and inter-related only in the prescience of the author, or for that matter one hundred times as many endings.... One book, one opening, was a principle with which I did not find it possible to concur.

Flann O'Brien (1939, *At Swim-two-birds*, pp. 9, 13.)

The end lies concealed in the beginning. All bodies grow around a skeleton. Life is a petticoat about death. I will not go to bed.

James Stephens (1912, *The Crock of Gold*, p. 16)
(Reproduced by permission of the Society of Authors as the Literary Representative of the Estate of James Stephens.)

New worlds for old.

James Joyce (1922, *Ulysses*, p. 462)

It is not easy to learn either the graceful skills required for practicing family therapy or the complex theoretical heritage on which this practice rests. Some of the central challenges of teaching, learning and practicing family therapy are well expressed in the words of O'Brien, Stephens and Joyce that open this Preface. Certainly it is not possible to encapsulate the story of family therapy in a book with one beginning and one ending. So you may find that this book reads like a number of volumes condensed into one. A central idea of family therapy is that many important human processes involve cycles where the end lies concealed in the beginning. You will find that this book opens with a discussion of the lifecycle and that the concept of circularity is a core feature of the formulation model presented in the heart of the book. Family therapy is built on a bedrock of hope. Family therapy is not just about problems. It is also about exceptions to problems. It does not focus exclusively on deficits and disability, but also is concerned with resilience and resourcefulness. Family therapy is a process through which we exchange new and better worlds for old.

This second edition of *Family Therapy: Concepts, Process and Practice* retains the same overall structure, style and content of the first edition but includes a number of important revisions that make it more useful for postgraduates, trainers and experienced therapists.

- The content and references in each chapter have been updated to take account of significant developments that have occurred during the past six years.
- An additional chapter on integrative models of practice has been added to Part I.
- Attachment theory and therapy have been addressed more fully in Part I.
- Developments in the formulation model have been added to Part II.
- Parts III and IV have been revised in light of relevant new theoretical and empirical material on each of the child- and adult-focused problems addressed in these sections.
- The research review in Chapter 18 has been brought up to date and expanded to include a section on common factors in effective therapy.
- The final chapter on resources has been expanded to include lists of relevant websites; a section on ethics; and a series of practical exercises for developing family therapy skills.

The book retains all of the features of the first edition that have made it popular among postgraduates and experienced clinicians alike.

Family Therapy: Concepts, Process and Practice was written both as a textbook for use in marital and family therapy professional postgraduate training programmes and as a sourcebook for experienced clinicians. The book offers a critical evaluation of the major schools of family therapy, an integrative model for the practice of marital and family therapy, and examples of how this model may be used with a range of common child-focused and adult-focused problems. Findings from research on the effectiveness of family therapy are reviewed and the implications of these for evidence-based practice outlined.

The first part of this volume contains a critical evaluation of the major schools of family therapy. The major traditions are grouped together in terms of their central focus of therapeutic concern, and in particular with respect to their emphasis on (1) problem-maintaining behaviour patterns; (2) problem-related belief systems and narratives; and (3) historical, contextual and constitutional predisposing factors.

Family therapy schools that highlight the role of repetitive patterns of family interaction in the maintenance of problem behaviour and advocate practices that aim to disrupt these patterns of interaction include: the MRI brief therapy approach; strategic therapy; structural therapy; cognitive-behavioural approaches; and functional family therapy.

Traditions that point to the centrality of belief systems and narratives that subserve repetitive interaction patterns include: constructivism; Milan systemic family therapy; social-constructionist family therapy approaches; solution-focused therapy; and narrative therapy.

Traditions that highlight the role of historical, contextual and constitutional factors in predisposing family members to adopt particular belief systems and engage in particular problematic interaction patterns include: transgenerational family therapy; psychoanalytic family therapy traditions; attachment theory-based approaches; experiential family therapy; multisystemic therapy; and psychoeducational approaches.

This organisation of schools of therapy in terms of their emphases on three particular themes is a useful learning device, but is an oversimplification. Most schools of family therapy address problem-maintaining behaviour patterns, constraining beliefs and broader historical, contextual and constitutional factors. However, the classification of schools according to the degree to which they emphasize these three themes, offers a backdrop against which a number of integrative models are presented, including the integrative approach to family therapy advocated in this volume.

A three-column model for formulating both problems and exceptions to these is presented in the second part of this book. The formulation model uses the three themes by which the schools of family therapy were classified to organise information about a particular problem. That is, it is argued that for any problem, a formulation may be constructed using ideas from many schools of family therapy in which the pattern of family interaction that maintains the problem is specified; the constraining beliefs and narratives that underpin each family member's role in this pattern are outlined; and the historical, contextual and constitutional factors that underpin these belief systems and narratives are specified. In parallel with this, a similar formulation may be constructed to explain why the problem does not occur in exceptional circumstances, which, while similar to problematic situations, differs in important key respects.

In light of these formulations, a range of interventions that address factors within each column of these three-column formulations may be considered. Some interventions aim primarily to disrupt problem-maintaining behaviour patterns or amplify exceptional non-problematic patterns. Others aim to help family members re-author their constraining narratives and develop more liberating and flexible belief systems that underpin exceptions to the problem. Still others aim to modify the negative impact of historical, contextual and constitutional factors or to draw on family strengths in these domains. Thus, while it is accepted that the classification of schools of family therapy according to three themes is an oversimplification, it is a particularly useful oversimplification insofar as it may facilitate a coherent, integrative and flexible approach to the practice of family therapy.

In the third part of this book, the way in which the integrative model may be used in the treatment of common child-focused problems, including child abuse, conduct problems and drug abuse, is outlined. The application of the model with common adult-focused problems is considered in the fourth part. The focus here is on marital distress, depression and anxiety, alcohol problems and schizophrenia.

In the final part, evidence for the effectiveness of family therapy and family-based interventions with a range of child and adult-focused problems is addressed and the implications of this research for evidence-based practice is set out. Also, useful resources for the training, practice and research are presented.

While this volume is intended as a sourcebook for experienced clinicians, it has also been written as a textbook for newcomers to the field of family therapy and systemic consultation. I have probably erred on the side of oversimplifying many complex ideas in an attempt to make the family therapy literature accessible to the newcomer. I hope that experienced clinicians can bear with this shortcoming. A glossary of new terms is provided at the end of theoretical chapters. In addition, reading lists that include references to original sources, overview chapters from major handbooks and important journal articles are given.

The integrative model and approach to practice described here evolved in two particular contexts. The ground work for the model was laid over a seven-year period during the 1980s and early 1990s while I was working in a UK National Health Service Child and Family Clinic (Carr, 1995, 1997). During this period there was a national emphasis on cooperation between health service professionals and their colleagues in social services and education. There was also an emphasis on liaison between district hospital departments offering services to children such as child psychology, child psychiatry and paediatrics. In addition, many hospitals within the NHS became privately run trusts. These factors created a climate which favoured the development of models of assessment and intervention that were time-limited, that took account of the wider professional network of which the child and therapist were part, that clearly addressed the overlap between the roles of therapist and agent of social control, and that could be evaluated or audited in a relatively objective way. The model was extended for use with adult-focused problems, as well as child-focused problems from 1992 to the present at the Clanwilliam Institute in Dublin.

Many of us who work in the field of systemic consultation and family therapy at some time during our professional development held the view that there is a *true formulation* of the client's problems and exceptions to these and a related correct set of solutions. In the approach described in the heart of this book, it is assumed that the formulations that emerge from talking with families about the presenting problem and exceptions to these are no more than social constructions. Since it is possible to construct multiple formulations to explain any problem or exception, it is important to have a criterion by which to judge the merit of any particular one.

In the approach to practice presented in the heart of this volume, it is the *usefulness* of formulations in suggesting a variety of feasible solutions that are acceptable to the family which is the sole criterion for judging the merit of one formulation over another. Because of its emphasis on the socially constructed nature of problem and exception formulations and the choice of usefulness as a criterion for selecting between different formulations, the approach described in this volume may be viewed as falling within the tradition of social-constructionism.

In deciding about the usefulness of formulations and interventions, clinicians using the approach to practice set out in this volume are invited to take account of the results of empirical research on the effectiveness of family therapy. Indeed, a thorough review of the more rigorous family therapy outcome research is given in Chapter 18. Due to the social-constructionist positioning that is taken in this book, and because treatment outcome research results are used to inform clinical practice, this text will be of interest to both postmodern practitioners and empirically oriented clinicians.

A distinction has been made within the field between first- and second-order approaches to practice, with first-order approaches using observed systems as a central explanatory concept and second-order approaches using the metaphor of observing systems as the principal theoretical frame. The integrative approach set out in this volume attempts to reap a harvest from both of these fields and – for want of a better metaphor – may be called an 'integrative third-order approach to family therapy' although I have reservations about the usefulness of such labels.

Alan Carr
University College Dublin & Clanwilliam Institute Dublin, Ireland
October 2005

ACKNOWLEDGEMENTS

I am grateful to the many colleagues, friends and relatives who have helped me develop the ideas presented in this book. In particular I would like to thank the group who introduced me to family therapy at the Mater Hospital in Dublin in the late 1970s: Dr Imelda McCarthy, Dr Jim Sheehan, Dr Nollaig Byrne, Koos Mandos and Dr Paul McQuaid.

I am also grateful to Dr Chris Cooper, Peter Simms and Carol Elisabeth Burra in Kingston, Ontario, with whom I worked while living in Canada.

In the UK, my gratitude goes to the group with whom I practiced at Thurlow house and the Queen Elisabeth Hospital in King's Lynn during the 1980s and early 1990s: Dr Dermot McDonnell, Dr Chris Wood, George Gawlinski, Sheila Docking, Sue Grant, Nick Irving, Shahin Afnan, Dr Jonathan Dossetor, Dr Dennis Barter, Denise Sherwood and Mike Cliffe.

Thanks are due to Dr Ivan Eisler, Dr Eddy Street, Professor John Carpenter, Bebe Speed and Professor Bryan Lask at the editorial office of the *Journal of Family Therapy*; to Professor Terry Trepper, Editor of *Journal of Family Psychotherapy*; to Professor Peter Stratton, Editor of *Human Systems: The Journal of Systemic Consultation and Management*; to Max Cornwall, Editor of *The Australian Journal of Family Therapy*; to Professor Doug Sprenkle, past Editor of the *Journal of Marital and Family Therapy*; and to Professor Michael Nichols, Editor of *Contemporary Family Therapy* for challenging me to articulate my ideas more clearly. I am grateful to Professor Martin Herbert at Exeter University and Dr Arlene Vetere at the University of Surrey for their collegial support.

Thanks to Mike Coombs, Senior Publishing Editor with John Wiley & Sons, Ltd, for guidance throughout the production of the first edition of this book and to Deborah Egleton for her support with the production of the second edition.

The second edition of this book was completed at the Psychology Institute, Aarhus University in Denmark, where I was a visiting professor in the autumn of 2005. I am especially grateful to Professors Aegen Trillingsgaard and Ask Elklit, who arranged funding and support for this sabbatical leave and for their generosity and hospitality during my time in Denmark.

Past and present colleagues at UCD, especially Professor Ciarán Benson, Dr Gary O'Reilly, Dr Muireann McNulty, Dr Barbara Dooley, Muriel Keegan, Dr Suzanne Guerin, Dr Jennifer Edgeworth, Dr Patricia Noonan Walsh, Fíona Kelly Meldon and Frances Osborne, have been very supportive of my efforts to write the two editions of this book and I am grateful to them for their patience and encouragement.

A special word of thanks is due to past and present colleagues at the Clanwilliam Institute in Dublin, particularly Dr Ed McHale, Phil Kearney, Aileen Tiernery, Dr Bernadette O'Sullivan, Declan Roche, Clive Garland, Cory deJong, Innes Collins, Noreen Dennehy, Breda McGee, Linda Finnegan, Dr Gregor Lange, Carl Murphy and Adele McGrath.

Postgraduates at UCD and the Clanwilliam have offered useful feedback, which has been helpful in writing the second edition and I am grateful to them for this.

Much of what I know about family life, I have learned from my own family and to them I owe a particular debt of gratitude.

Go raibh míle maith agaibh go léir.

Alan Carr,
University College Dublin & Clanwilliam Institute Dublin, Ireland
October 2005

ENDORSEMENTS OF THE FIRST EDITION

This is an excellent basic text in family therapy.

Journal of Child Psychology and Psychiatry

The book is an encyclopaedic achievement and will be of use both to trainees and more experienced practitioners.

Clinical Psychology Forum

This volume's scope and approach set it apart from other introductory texts in family therapy.

Contemporary Family Therapy

As Alan Gurman writes in his foreword, the reader is getting 'two for the price of one'. The first book is a highly readable introductory account of the major approaches to family therapy. The second book details the author's formulation model. What impressed me was the comprehensiveness of this volume.

Journal of Family Therapy

The key to Carr's book may well lie in his early quotations from James Joyce, James Stephens and Flann O'Brien, in that, like them, his project is an attempt to tame the untameable, to marry the many differences. It is a bold project.

Clinical Child Psychology and Psychiatry

Part I

CENTRAL CONCEPTS IN FAMILY THERAPY

Chapter 1

GOALS OF FAMILY THERAPY ACROSS THE LIFECYCLE

Family therapy is a broad term given to a range of methods for working with families with various biopsychosocial difficulties. Within the broad cathedral of family therapy there is a wide variety of views on what types of problems are appropriately addressed by family therapy; who defines these problems; what constitutes family therapy practices; what type of theoretical rational undepins these practices; and what type of research supports the validity of these practices.

Some family therapists argue that all human problems are essentially relational and so family therapy is appropriate in all instances. Others argue that marital and family therapy are appropriate for specific relationship problems or as an adjunct to pharmacological treatment of particular conditions, such as schizophrenia.

Some family therapists argue that problems addressed in therapy are defined by clients, that is, parents, children or marital partners seeking help. Others argue that problems are best defined by professionals in terms of psychiatric diagnoses or statutory status, such as being a family in which child abuse has occurred and on an at-risk register, or being a person with an alcohol problem on probation.

With respect to practices, some family therapists invite all family members to all therapy sessions. Others conduct family therapy with individuals, by empowering them to manage their relationships with family members in more satisfactory ways. Still others have broadened family therapy so that it includes members of the wider professional and social network around the family, and may refer to this approach as 'systemic practice'.

There are many theories of family therapy. Some focus on the role of the family in predisposing people to developing problems or in precipitating their difficulties. Others focus on the role of the family in problem maintenance. But all family therapists highlight the role of the family in problem resolution. There is also considerable variability in the degree to which theories privilege the role of family patterns of interaction, family belief systems and narratives, and historical contextual and constitutional factors in the aetiology and maintenance of problems.

With respect to research, some family therapists argue that case studies or descriptive qualitative research provides adequate support for the efficacy of family therapy. On the other hand, some family therapists highlight the importance of quantitative results from controlled research trials in supporting the degree to which family therapy is effective in treating specific problems.

Within this volume, an integrative and developmental approach will be taken to family therapy, and where better to start than with a consideration of family problems across the lifecycle. Family problems occur across all stages of the lifecycle. Here are some examples:

- A six-year-old child whose parents cannot control him and who pushes his sister down the stairs.
- A 13-year-old girl who worries her parents because she will not eat and has lost much weight.
- A 19-year-old boy who believes he is being poisoned and refuses to take prescribed antipsychotic medication.
- A couple in their mid-30s who consistently argue and fight with each other.
- A blended family in which the parents have both previously been married and who have difficulties managing their children's unpredictable and confusing behaviour.
- A family in which a parent has died prematurely and in which the 13-year-old has run away from home.
- A family in which a child is terminally ill and will not follow medical advice.
- A family with traditional values in which a teenager 'comes out' and declares that he is gay.
- A family in which both parents are unemployed and who have difficulty managing their children without getting into violent rows.
- A black family living in a predominantly white community, where the 16-year-old boy is involved in drug abuse in a delinquent peer group.

These are all complex cases that involve or affect all family members to a greater or lesser degree. A number of these cases also involve or affect members of the community in which the family lives. In some of the cases listed, other agencies, including schools, hospitals, social services, law enforcement, juvenile justice or probation, may be involved. Family therapy is a broad psychotherapeutic movement that offers conceptual frameworks for making sense of complex cases such as those listed here and entails approaches to clinical practice for helping families resolve complex problems.

The lifecycle is a particularly useful framework within which to conceptualise problems that may be referred for family therapy. In this chapter, normative models of the family and individual lifecycles will be described. Gender development; lifecycle issues unique to lesbian and gay people; and issues of culture and class will also be discussed. The aim of the chapter is to sketch out some of the problem areas that may be addressed by family therapy across the lifecycle.

THE FAMILY LIFECYCLE

Families are unique social systems insofar as membership is based on combinations of biological, legal, affectional, geographic and historical ties. In contrast to other social systems, entry into family systems is through birth, adoption, fostering or marriage and members can leave only by death. Severing all family connections is never possible. Furthermore, while family members fulfil certain roles, which entail specific definable tasks such as the provision of food and shelter, it is the relationships within families which are primary and irreplaceable.

With single-parenthood, divorce, separation and remarriage as common events, a narrow and traditional definition of the family is no longer useful (Parke, 2004; Walsh, 2003a). It is more expedient to think of a person's family as a network of people in the individual's immediate psychosocial field. This may include household members and others who, while not members of the household, play a significant role in the individual's life. For example, a separated parent and spouse living elsewhere with whom a child has regular contact; foster parents who provide relief care periodically; a grandmother who provides informal day-care, and so forth. In clinical practice the primary concern is the extent to which this network meets the individual's needs.

Leaving Home

Having noted the limitations of a traditional model of family structure, paradoxically, the most useful available models of the family lifecycle are based on the norm of the traditional nuclear family with other family forms being conceptualised as deviations from this norm (Carter & McGoldrick, 1999). One such model is presented in Table 1.1. This model delineates the main developmental tasks to be completed by the family at each stage of development. In the first two stages, the principal concerns are with differentiating from the family of origin by completing school, developing relationships outside the family, completing one's education and beginning a career. Problems in developing emotional autonomy from the family of origin may occur at this stage and may find expression in many ways, including depression, drug abuse and eating disorders such as anorexia and bulimia. Problems in developing economic independence may also occur where young adults have not completed their education or

Table 1.1 Stages of the family lifecycle

Stage	Tasks
1. Family of origin experiences	Maintaining relationships with parents, siblings and peers Completing school
2. Leaving home	Differentiation of self from family of origin and developing adult-to-adult relationship with parents Developing intimate peer relationships Beginning a career
3. Premarriage stage	Selecting partners Developing a relationship Deciding to marry
4. Childless couple stage	Developing a way to live together based on reality rather than mutual projection Realigning relationships with families of origin and peers to include spouses
5. Family with young children	Adjusting marital system to make space for children Adopting parenting roles Realigning relationships with families of origin to include parenting and grandparenting roles Children developing peer relationships
6. Family with adolescents	Adjusting parent–child relationships to allow adolescents more autonomy Adjusting marital relationships to focus on midlife marital and career issues Taking on responsibility of caring for families of origin
7. Launching children	Resolving midlife issues Negotiating adult-to-adult relationships with children Adjusting to living as a couple again Adjusting to including in-laws and grandchildren within the family circle Dealing with disabilities and death in the family of origin
8. Later life	Coping with physiological decline Adjusting to the children taking a more central role in family maintenance Making room for the wisdom and experience of the elderly Dealing with loss of spouse and peers Preparation for death, life review and integration

Source: Adapted from Carter and McGoldrick (1999). *The Expanded Family Lifecycle. Individual, Family and Social Perspectives*, 3rd edn. Boston: Allyn & Bacon.

where limited career options are available. In these circumstances some young adults become involved in crime.

Forming a Couple

In the third stage of the family lifecycle model, the principal tasks are those associated with selecting a partner and deciding to marry or co-habit. In the following discussion, the term marriage is used to cover both traditional marriage or the more modern arrangement of long-term co-habitation. Adams (1995) views mate selection as a complex process that involves four stages. In the first phase, partners are selected from among those available for interaction. At this stage, people select mates who are physically attractive and similar to themselves in interests, intelligence, personality and other valued behaviours and attributes. In the second phase, there is a comparison of values following revelation of identities through self-disclosing conversations. If this leads to a deepening of the original attraction then the relationship will persist. In the third phase, there is an exploration of role compatibility and the degree to which mutual empathy is possible. Once interlocking roles and mutual empathy have developed the costs of separation begin to outweigh the difficulties and tensions associated with staying together. If the attraction has deepened sufficiently and the barriers to separation are strong enough, consolidation of the relationship occurs. In the fourth and final phase, a decision is made about long-term compatibility and commitment. If a positive decision is reached about both of these issues, then marriage or long-term cohabitation may occur. When partners come together they are effectively bringing two family traditions together, and setting the stage for the integration of these traditions, with their norms and values, rules, roles and routines into a new tradition. Decision making about this process is not always easy, and couples may come to a marital and family therapist to address this complex issue.

Marriage

In the fourth stage of the family lifecycle model, the childless couple must develop routines for living together that are based on a realistic appraisal of the other's strengths, weaknesses and idiosyncrasies rather than on the idealized views (or mutual projections) which formed the basis of their relationship during the initial period of infatuation. Coming to terms with the dissolution of the mutual projective system, which characterizes the infatuation so common in the early stages of intimate relationships, is a particularly stressful task for many couples and may lead to a referral for marital or family therapy (Savage-Scharff & Bagini, 2002).

Contextual Factors Associated with Marital Satisfaction

The following demographic factors are associated with marital satisfaction (Newman & Newman, 2003):

- high level of education
- high socioeconomic status
- similarity of spouses interests, intelligence and personality
- early or late stage of family lifecycle
- sexual compatibility
- for women, later marriage.

The precise mechanisms linking these factors to marital satisfaction are not fully understood. However, the following speculations seem plausible. Higher educational level and higher socioeconomic status probably lead to greater marital satisfaction because where these factors are present people probably have better problem-solving skills and fewer chronic life stresses, such as crowding. Although there is a cultural belief that opposites attract, research shows that similarity is associated with marital satisfaction, probably because of the greater ease with which similar people can empathise with each other and pursue shared interests. Marital satisfaction drops during the child-rearing years and satisfaction is highest before children are born and when they leave home. During these periods, it may be that greater satisfaction occurs because partners can devote more time and energy to joint pursuits and there are fewer opportunities for conflict involving child management. Most surveys find wide variability in the frequency with which couples engage in sexual activity but confirm that it is sexual compatibility rather than frequency of sexual activity that is associated with marital satisfaction. Couples may come to marital and family therapy to find ways to cope with marital dissatisfaction and sexual difficulties, often arising from incompatibility.

Belief Systems and Interactional Patterns Associated with Marital Satisfaction

Studies of belief systems and interaction patterns of well-adjusted couples show that they have distinctive features (Gottman & Notarius, 2002; Gurman & Jacobson, 2002). These include:

- respect
- acceptance
- dispositional attributions for positive behaviour
- more positive than negative interactions
- focusing conflicts on specific issues
- rapidly repairing relationship ruptures
- addressing needs for intimacy and power.

Well-adjusted couples attribute their partners' positive behaviours to dispositional rather than situational factors. For example, 'She helped me because she is such a kind person', not 'She helped me because it was convenient at the time'. The ratio of positive to negative exchanges has been found to be about five to one in happy couples (Gottman, 1993). Even though well-adjusted couples have disagreements, this is balanced out by five times as many positive interactions. When well-adjusted couples disagree, they focus their disagreement on a specific issue, rather than globally criticising or insulting their partner. This type of behaviour is a reflection of a general attitude of respect that characterises happy couples. Well-adjusted couples tend to rapidly repair their relationship ruptures arising from conflict and they do not allow long episodes of non-communication, sulking or stonewalling to occur. Sometimes well-adjusted couples resolve conflicts by agreeing to differ. The specific process of agreeing to differ reflects a general attitude of acceptance.

Distressed couples, in contrast, have difficulties in many of the areas listed above and these may find expression in disagreements about communication and intimacy on the one hand; and the power balance or role structure of the relationship on the other. With respect to intimacy, usually males demand greater psychological distance and females insist on greater psychological intimacy. With respect to power, males commonly wish to retain the power and benefits of traditional gender roles while females wish to evolve more egalitarian relationships. Such disagreements may lead to a referral for marital therapy. In well-adjusted couples, partners' needs for intimacy and power within the relationship are adequately met, and partners have the capacity to negotiate with each other about modifying the relationship if they feel that these needs are being thwarted.

Types of Marriages

Fitzpatrick (1988) and Gottman (1993) have both identified three types of stable marriage, in questionnaire and observational studies, respectively. I have termed these 'traditional', 'androgynous' and 'avoidant' couples. Characteristics of these types of marriage are summarised in the first part of Table 1.2. Traditional couples adopt traditional sex roles and lifestyles and take a low key approach to conflict management. Androgynous couples strive to create egalitarian roles and take a fiery approach to conflict resolution. Avoidant couples adopt traditional sex-roles but live parallel lives and avoid conflict. Two types of unstable couples were identified in Gottman's study. In Table 1.2, I have labelled these conflictual and disengaged couples. The former engage in conflict but without resolution and the latter avoid conflict for much of the time. Gottman found that in all three stable types of couples the ratio of positive to negative verbal exchanges during conflict resolution was 5:1. For both unstable types

Table 1.2 Five type of couples

Stability	Type	Characteristics
Stable	Traditional couples	They adopt traditional sex roles They privilege family goals over individual goals They have regular daily schedules They share the living space in the family home They express moderate levels of both positive and negative emotions They tend to avoid conflict about all but major issues They engage in conflict and try to resolve it At the outset of an episode of conflict resolution, each partner listens to the other and empathises with their position In the later part there is considerable persuasion
	Androgynous couples	They adopt androgynous egalitarian roles They privilege individual goals over family goals They have chaotic daily schedules They have separate living spaces in their homes They express high levels of positive and negative emotions They tend to engage in continual negotiation about many issues Partners disagree and try to persuade one another from the very beginning of episodes of conflict resolution They have a high level of both positive and negative emotions
	Avoidant couples	They adopt traditional sex roles They have separate living space in their homes They avoid all conflict They have few conflict resolution skills Partners state their case when a conflict occurs but there is no attempt at persuasion or compromise They accept differences about specific conflicts as unimportant compared with their shared common ground and values Conflict-related discussions are unemotional
Unstable	Conflictual couples	They engage in conflict without any constructive attempt to resolve it Continual blaming, mind-reading and defensiveness characterise their interactions High levels of negative emotion and little positive emotion are expressed There is an attack–withdraw interaction pattern

Stability	Type	Characteristics
	Disengaged couples	They avoid conflict and have few conflict resolution skills
		Brief episodes of blaming, mind-reading and defensiveness characterise their interactions
		Low levels of negative emotion and almost no positive emotion is expressed
		There is a withdraw–withdraw interaction pattern

Source: Based on Gottman (1993). The roles of conflict engagement, escalation and avoidance in marital interaction: A longitudinal view of five types of couples. *Journal of Consulting and Clinical Psychology*, **61**, 6–15, and Fitzpatrick (1988). *Between Husbands and Wives: Communication in Marriage*. Newbury Park, CA: Sage.

of couples the ratio of positive to negative exchanges was approximately 1 : 1. Gottman and Fitzpatrick's work highlights the fact that there are a number possible models for a stable marital relationship. Their work also underlines the importance of couples engaging in conflict with a view to resolving it rather than avoiding conflict. Negativity is only destructive if it is not balanced out by five times as much positivity. Indeed, negativity may have a prosocial role in balancing the needs for intimacy and autonomy and in keeping attraction alive over long periods.

Marital Violence

In the UK, 23% of assaults occur within domestic relationships (British Crime Survey, 2000). In the USA, 12% of couples experience serious marital violence each year (Straus & Gelles, 1990). Marital violence is a multifactorial phenomenon and characteristics of the abuser, the victim, the marital relationship and the wider social context have all been found to contribute to the occurrence and maintenance of the cycle of violence (Frude, 1990; Holtzworth-Munroe, Meehan, Rehman & Marshall, 2002). A personal history of abuse; a high level of the personality trait of aggressiveness; strong conservative attitudes; beliefs in traditional sex roles; low self-esteem; poor social skills; depression; antisocial personality disorder; alcohol abuse; and morbid jealousy have all been found to characterise abusers. Victims, quite understandably have been found to be retaliative and to use verbal and physical abuse during conflict resolution. The majority of couples who seek therapy for domestic violence have engaged in reciprocal violence, but the negative physical and psychological consequences of domestic violence is greater for women than for men. Marriages in which domestic violence occur are typically characterised by a history of multiple separations, a low level of commitment and little marital satisfaction. There is commonly conflict about intimacy, with women demanding more psychological intimacy and men demanding more physical intimacy. Many rows are about not enough 'talking and empathy' from the woman's perspective and 'not enough sex' from the man's. There is also conflict about power, with the woman having higher status than the man and the man believing in a model of marriage where the male has more power. Many marital disagreements are about money, and this reflects the disagreement about power. Poor communication and negotiation skills characterise these couples, so they cannot resolve their conflicts about intimacy and power. Because they cannot communicate about what they want from each other, they make negative inferences and assumptions about their partners intentions and respond to their partners as if these inferences were accurate. This results in a blaming stance rather than an understanding stance. They also believe that arguments must involve winners and losers and therefore in all conflicts they escalate the exchange so that they can win. They believe in a win–lose model of conflict resolution, not a win–win model. They work on a short-term *quid pro quo* system, not a long-term goodwill system. This results in attempts to control each other by punishment not reward.

This destructive relational style is more likely to escalate into violence if certain broader contextual factors are present. Violence is more likely where couples live in crowded living conditions; are unemployed; live in poverty; have a low educational level; are socially isolated and have experienced many life changes and stresses recently. With crowding, unemployment and poverty, couples struggle for access to their own limited resources and displace aggression towards societal forces that have trapped them in poverty onto each other. Better educated couples use more sophisticated negotiation skills to prevent conflict escalation. Social isolation increases stress and reduces social support. This stress may lead to heightened arousal and so increase the risk of violence. Also, abusive families may isolate themselves so that the abuse is not uncovered. Major life changes may lead to increased cohesion in some families and increased conflict in others. Moving house, the birth of a baby and redundancy are examples of transitions that may lead to marital violence. Family therapy for couples involved in violence focuses on both risk assessment and helping couples evolve alternatives to violence (Cooper & Vetere, 2005; Holtzworth-Munroe et al., 2002). Multicouple therapy, a recent innovation for the treatment of violent couples, is particularly effective (Stith, McCollum, Rosen, Locke & Goldberg, 2005).

Families with Children

In the fifth stage of the family lifecycle model, the main tasks are for couples to adjust their roles as marital partners to make space for young children; for couples' parents to develop grandparental roles; and for children, as they move into middle childhood, to develop peer relationships.

Parenting Roles

The development of parenting roles involves the couple establishing routines for meeting children's needs for:

- safety
- care
- control
- intellectual stimulation.

Developing these routines is a complex process. Difficulties in meeting each of these needs may lead to specific types of problems, all of which may become a focus for family therapy (Reder & Lucey, 1995; Reder, McClure & Jolley, 2000; Reder, Duncan & Lucey, 2004). Routines for meeting children's needs for safety include protecting children from accidents by, for example, not leaving young children unsupervised and also developing skills for managing frustration and anger that the demands of parenting young children often elicit. Failure to develop such routines may lead to accidental injuries or child abuse. Routines for providing children with food and shelter, attachment, empathy, understanding and emotional support need to be developed to meet children's needs for care in these various areas. Failure to develop such routines may lead to a variety of emotional difficulties. Routines for setting clear rules and limits; for providing supervision to ensure that children conform to these expectations; and for offering appropriate rewards and sanctions for rule following and rule violations meet children's need for control. Conduct problems may occur if such routines are not developed. Parent–child play and communication routines for meeting children's needs for age-appropriate intellectual stimulation also need to be developed if the child is to avoid developmental delays in emotional, language and intellectual development.

Attachment

Children who develop secure attachments to their caregivers fare better in life than those who do not (Cassidy & Shaver, 1999). Children develop secure emotional attachments if their parents are attuned to their needs and if their parents are responsive to children's signals that they require their needs to be met. When this occurs, children learn that their parents are a secure base from which they can explore the world. John Bowlby (1988), who developed attachment theory, argued that attachment behaviour, which is genetically programmed and essential for survival of the species, is elicited in children between six months and three years when faced with danger. In such instances children seek proximity with their caregivers. When comforted they return to the activity of exploring the immediate environment around the caregiver. The cycle repeats each time the child perceives a threat and their attachment needs for satisfaction, safety and security are activated. Over multiple repetitions, children build internal working models of attachment relationships based on the way these episodes are managed by caregivers in response to children's needs for proximity, comfort and security. Internal working models are cognitive relationship maps based on early attachment experiences, which serve as a template for the development of later intimate relationships. Internal working models allow people to make predictions about how the self and significant others will behave within relationships. In their ground-breaking text, *Patterns of Attachment*, Mary Ainsworth and colleagues (1978) described three patterns of mother–infant interaction following a brief episode of experimentally contrived separation and further research with mothers and children led to the identification of a fourth category (Cassidy & Shaver, 1999). The four attachment styles are as follows:

1. *Securely attached* children react to their parents as if they were a secure base from which to explore the world. Parents in such relationships are attuned and responsive to the children's needs. While a secure attachment style is associated with autonomy, the other three attachment styles are associated with a sense of insecurity.
2. *Anxiously attached* children seek contact with their parents following separation but are unable to derive comfort from it. They cling and cry or have tantrums.
3. *Avoidantly attached* children avoid contact with their parents after separation. They sulk.
4. *Children with a disorganised attachment* style following separation show aspects of both the anxious and avoidant patterns. Disorganised attachment is a common correlate of child abuse and neglect and early parental absence, loss or bereavement.

Research on intimate relationships in adulthood confirms that these four relational styles show continuity over the lifecycle (Cassidy & Shaver, 1999). Significant adult relationships and patterns of family organisation may be classified into four equivalent attachment categories, which will be discussed further in Chapter 5, in the section on attachment-based therapies. Difficulties associated with insecure attachment may lead to referrals for marital or family therapy.

Parenting Styles

Reviews of the extensive literature on parenting suggest that by combining the two orthogonal dimensions of warmth or acceptance and control, four parenting styles may be identified, and each of these is associated with particular developmental outcomes for the child (Darling & Steinberg, 1993). These four styles are presented in Figure 1.1.

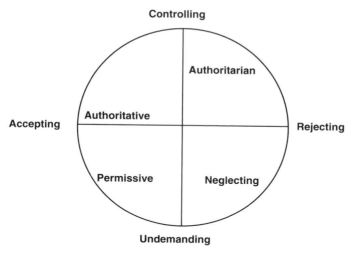

Figure 1.1 Patterns of parenting

Authoritative parents, who adopt a warm, accepting child-centred approach coupled with a moderate degree of control that allows children to take age-appropriate responsibility, provide a context which is maximally beneficial for children's development as autonomous confident individuals. Children of parents who use an authoritative style learn that conflicts are most effectively managed by taking the other person's viewpoint into account within the context of an amicable negotiation. This set of skills is conducive to efficient joint problem-solving and the development of good peer relationships and consequently the development of a good social support network. Children of *authoritarian parents,* who are warm and accepting but controlling, tend to develop into shy adults who are reluctant to take initiative. The parents' disciplinary style teaches them that unquestioning obedience is the best way to manage interpersonal differences and to solve problems. Children of *permissive parents,* who are warm and accepting but lax in discipline, in later life lack the competence to follow through on plans and show poor impulse control. Children who have experienced little warmth or acceptance from their parents and who have been either harshly disciplined or had little or inconsistent supervision develop adjustment problems which may become a focus for family therapy. This is particularly the case with corporal punishment. When children experience corporal punishment, they learn that the use of aggression is an appropriate way to resolve conflicts and tend to use such aggression in managing conflicts with their peers. In this way children who have been physically punished are at risk for developing conduct problems and becoming involved in bullying (Olweus, 1993).

Grandparental Roles

In addition to developing parental roles and routines for meeting children's needs, a further task of the fifth stage of the family lifecycle is the development of grandparental roles and the realignment of family relationships that this entails. Neugarten and Weinstein (1964) identified six types of grandparental roles. First, there were those that adopted a formal role and were not involved in childcare but loving and emotionally involved with the grandchildren. The second role was essentially fun-seeking and these grandparents acted as playmates for the grandchildren. The third type of grandparental role was that of a distant figure who had little contact with grandchildren. The fourth role-type was that of parental surrogate and these grandparents assume the role of parent to the grandchildren so that the mother could work outside the home. The final grandparental role was that of a reservoir of family wisdom who occupied a powerful patriarchal or matriarchal position within the extended family. Where grandparents adopt roles that are supportive of parents and grandchildren, they contribute to family resilience. Where they adopt roles that greatly increase the demands on parents and grandchildren, without offering support, then they may contribute to the development of adjustment problems that become a focus for family therapy.

Children's Peer Group Roles

Peer group membership is a central part of children's lives (Dunn, 2004; Kupersmidt & Dodge, 2004; Malik & Furman, 1993). Over the first five years, with increasing opportunities for interaction with others and the development of language, interaction with other children increases. Cooperative play premised on an empathic understanding of other children's viewpoints gradually emerges and is usually fully established by middle childhood. Competitive rivalry (often involving physical or verbal aggression or joking) is an important part of peer interactions, particularly among boys. This allows youngsters to establish their position of dominance within the peer group hierarchy. There are important sex differences in styles of play adopted, with girls being more cooperative and relationship-focused, and boys being more competitive and activity-focused. Boys tend to play in larger peer groups whereas girls tend to play within small groups characterised by emotionally intimate exclusive friendships. Sex segregated play is almost universal in middle childhood.

Peer friendships are important because they constitute an important source of social support and a context within which to learn about the management of networks of relationships. Children who are unable to make and maintain friendships, particularly during middle childhood and early adolescence, are at risk for the development of psychological difficulties. Children who have developed secure attachments to their parents are more likely to develop good peer friendships. This is probably because their experience with their parents provides them with a useful cognitive model on which to base their interactions with their peers. Children reared in institutions have particular difficulty with peer relationships in their teens.

Popular children are described by their peers as helpful, friendly, considerate and capable of following rules in games and imaginative play. They also tend to be more intelligent and physically attractive than average. They accurately interpret social situations and have the social skills necessary for engaging in peer group activities. About 10–15% of children are rejected by their peer-group. In middle childhood two main types of unpopular child may be distinguished: the aggressive youngster and the victim. Victims tend to be sensitive, anxious, have low self-esteem and lack the skills required to defend themselves and establish dominance within the peer-group hierarchy. They are often the targets for bullies (Olweus, 1993). Unpopular aggressive children are described by peers as disruptive, hyperactive, impulsive and unable to follow rules in games and play. Their aggression tends to be used less for establishing dominance or a hierarchical position in the peer group and more for achieving certain instrumental goals. For example, taking a toy from another child.

Popular children are effective in joining in peer group activities. They hover on the edge, tune-in to the groups activities and carefully select a time to become integrated into the groups activities. Unpopular children, particularly the aggressive type, do not tune-in to group activities. They tend to criticize other children and talk about themselves rather than listening to others. Warmth, a sense of humour and sensitivity to social cues are important features of socially skilled children. Unpopular children, particularly the aggressive type, are predisposed to interpreting ambiguous social cues negatively and becoming involved in escalating spirals of negative social interaction.

Unpopularity is relatively stable over time. A child who is unpopular this year is likely to remain so next year and this unpopularity is not wholly based on reputation. For the aggressive unpopular child, inadequate cognitive models for relationships, difficulties in interpreting ambiguous social situations and poor social skills appear to be the main factors underpinning this stability of unpopularity. For the unpopular victim the continued unpopularity is probably mediated by low self-esteem, avoidance of opportunities for social interaction and a lack of pro-social skills. Also, both types of unpopular children miss out on important opportunities for learning about cooperation, team work and the management of networks of friendships. While unpopularity is not uniformly associated with long-term difficulties, it appears to put such youngsters at risk for developing academic problems, dropping out of school, conduct problems in adolescence, mental health problems in adulthood and criminality. Multisystemic family therapy (described in Chapter 5), which includes school-based consultations and social skills training, is a useful approach when working with unpopular children.

Families with Adolescents

In the sixth stage of the family lifecycle model, which is marked by children's entry into adolescence, parent–child relationships require re-alignment to allow adolescents to develop more autonomy. Concurrently, demands of caring for ageing grandparents may occur. This is an extremely complex and demanding stage of the family lifecycle, particularly for parents.

Facilitating the Growth of Adolescent Autonomy

Good parent–child communication and joint problem-solving skills facilitate the renegotiation of parent–child relationships and the growth of adolescent autonomy. Skills deficits in these areas may underpin referrals for family therapy. Results of empirical studies of adolescent relationships with parents, peers and partners contradict many commonly held misconceptions (Coleman & Hendry, 1999; Rice & Dolgin, 2004). Psychoanalytic writers, on the basis of clinical observations of distressed adolescents, argued that parent–child conflict is the norm in adolescence. Epidemiological studies of adolescents show that this is not the case. While one in five families experience some parent–child conflict, only one in 20 experience extreme conflict. A traditional view of adolescence is one where a visionary adolescent confronts conservative parental values. Epidemiological studies show that in most families parent–adolescent quarrels are about mundane topics such as untidiness, music, clothing and curfew-time. They are rarely about values or ethics. A traditional view of adolescence posits a gradual erosion of the quality of parent–adolescent relationships with a complementary increase in the quality of the adolescent–peer relationships. Studies of attachment suggest that this is not the case. Secure attachments to parents are correlated with secure attachments to peers.

Promiscuity in adolescence is not the norm. Most surveys show that a majority of older teenagers view premarital sex between committed partners as acceptable. Premarital sex with multiple partners is viewed as unacceptable. Teenage pregnancy is a risk factor for later adjustment primarily because it may interfere with education and compromise the career prospects of the teenager. Adolescent marriages resulting from unplanned pregnancies run a high risk of dissolution, and these young families often develop multiple life problems and require particularly intensive multisystemic intervention.

Resilience in Adolescence

Adolescence is a risky period (Coleman & Hendry, 1999; Rice & Dolgin, 2004). Opportunities for developing a wide variety of psychological problems abound. A central concern for many parents and practitioners is knowing the degree to which the dice is loaded in favour of the adolescent emerging from adolescence relatively unscathed. Factors that characterise adolescents and children who are resilient in the face of adversity are summarised in Table 1.3 (Carr, 2004; Luthar, 2003). Adolescents are more likely to show good adjustment if they have an easy temperament and a high level of intellectual ability. A high level of self-esteem, a general belief in control over one's life and a specific belief that factors related to specific stresses may be controlled are all associated with good adjustment. Adolescents will be less adversely affected by life stresses if they have good planning skills, if they can elicit social support from family and peers, if they have a sense of humour and if they can empathise with others. Better adjustment to life stress occurs when adolescents come from higher socioeconomic-groups, have good social support networks comprising family members and peers, and attend schools that provide a supportive yet challenging educational environment. Secure attachment relationships to primary caregivers, the use of an authoritative parenting style and the involvement of both mothers and fathers in parenting are the

Table 1.3 Factors associated with resilience in adolescence

Domain	Factors
Family factors	Absence of early separation or losses Secure attachment Authoritative parenting Father involvement

Community factors	Positive educational experience
	Good social support network
	    (including good peer relationships,
	    and involvement in organised
	    religious activity)
	High socioeconomic status

Psychological traits	High ability level Easy temperament
Self-evaluative beliefs	High self-esteem Internal locus of control Task-related self-efficacy
Coping skills	Planning skills Skill in seeking social support Sense of humour Empathy skills

major positive family factors associated with adolescents' adjustment to life stress. The absence of childhood separations, losses, bereavements, parental mental health problems, criminality and marital discord also characterise the families of children who are resilient in the face of stress.

Grandparental Care

Increasingly, with the lengthening of the average lifespan, the responsibility of caring for ageing parents is becoming a routine responsibility for men and women in midlife. The stress associated with this role and the impending death of the ageing parent tends to be most acutely felt by daughters of ageing parents. Social support from family and friends and periodic relief custodial care are important coping resources for such daughters to employ in managing the stresses of caring for ageing parents. Family therapists have a role to play in helping families manage this important task of sharing the stresses associated with caring for ageing family members (Richardson, Gilleard, Lieberman & Peeler, 1994).

Launching

The seventh stage of the family lifecycle model is concerned with the transition of young adult children out of the parental home. Ideally this transition entails the development of a less hierarchical relationship between parents and children. During this stage, the parents are faced with the task of adjusting to living as a couple again, to dealing with disabilities and death in their families of origin and of adjusting to the expansion of the family if their children marry and procreate. However, the process of midlife re-evaluation, which began in the previous life-cycle stage, takes on a particular prominence as the nest empties.

Midlife Re-evaluation

As adolescents grow up and begin to leave home parents must contend not only with changes in their relationships with their maturing children but also with a midlife re-evaluation of their marital relationship and career aspirations. Just as the notion of the universality of adolescent rebellion has not been supported by the results of carefully conducted community-based surveys, so also the popular conception of the midlife crisis has been found to be a relatively rare phenomenon (Papalia, Wendkos-Olds, Duskin & Feldman, 2001; Santrock, 2003). Longitudinal studies show that many men and women in their 40s become more introspective and re-evaluate their roles within the family and the world of work. For men, there may be a shift in values with an increased valuing of family life over work life. For women, there may be an increased emphasis on work over family. However, these changes in values rarely lead to changes that assume crisis proportions.

Gould (1981) has shown in an extensive study of clinical and non-clinical populations that the assumptions and belief systems learned within the family of origin are challenged in a gradual way over the course of adulthood, and this process reaches a resolution in midlife. Gould's findings are summarised in Table 1.4. The assumptions of childhood give a sense of safety and security. They include a belief in omnipotent thought; a belief in omnipotent protective parents; a belief in the absoluteness of the parents' world view; and defences against a rage reaction to separation.

Table 1.4 False assumptions challenged in adulthood

Period	False assumption	Belief systems
Late teens	I will always belong to my parents and believe in their world	If I get any more independent it will be a disaster I can only see the world through my parents' assumptions Only they can guarantee my safety They must be my only family I don't own my body
20s	Doing it their way will bring results and they will guide me through difficulties	If I follow the rules, I will be rewarded There is only one right way to do things Rationality, commitment and effort will always prevail over other forces My partner will do those things for me that I cannot do for myself (i.e. give me a love-cure)
30s	Life is simple and controllable. There are no significant coexisting contradictory forces within me	What I know intellectually, I know emotionally I am not like my parents in ways that I don't want to be I can see the reality of those close to me clearly I can realistically identify and deal with threats to my security
40s	There is no evil in me or death in the world. The sinister has been expelled	My work or my relationships grant me immunity from death and danger There is no life beyond this family I am innocent

Source: Based on Gould (1981). *Transformations: Growth and Change in Adult Life.* New York: Simon & Schuster.

Adult consciousness on the other hand is governed by an acceptance that we create our own lives according to beliefs and values that are different from those internalised in childhood.

In the late teens, if the adolescent is to be liberated from the family, the parents' world view must be appraised. The parents' roles as protectors must be evaluated and their command over the youth's sexuality and body must be challenged. The conflict is between retaining a childhood role and trying out new roles.

In the 20s, within the work arena, the idea that life is fair and if you stick to the rules you will win, is challenged. With relationships, the idea that our partners can make up for our deficiencies and we can make up for theirs is also challenged at this time. The idea that love can cure personal deficiencies must be given up during the 20s. For example, a talkative partner can't make up for a quiet partner's style nor can a nurturent partner fulfil all their partner's dependency needs. When these assumptions have been challenged, the person is in a position to differentiate sufficiently to establish a family separate from the family of origin.

The assumptions that are challenged up to the 20s relate to the outer world. In the 30s, assumptions about our inner selves or our relationships with ourselves are challenged. The person realises that one can know something intellectually such as 'this row with my partner can be resolved through patient negotiation', and yet lack the emotional knowledge to work through the process of negotiation. In the 30s people realise that they have many characteristics of their parents, which they dislike. For example, they may treat their children unfairly. This has to be recognised if patterns are not to be repeated across generations. There must be an acceptance of a partner's evolution and growth, and the fact that we cannot assume that we see their point of view today just because we saw it a year ago. There are many threats to security in midlife both within marriage and the workplace. Perceived threats within marriage are often projections, rather than realistic threats.

People in their 30s assume that the feelings of being mistreated or taken for granted are real threats from their partners rather than projections onto their partners of ways in which they were treated as children by their parents or significant others. The belief that we can always identify and deal with threats accurately must be challenged in midlife.

In the 40s illusions of safety are challenged. For men, the most common illusion is 'If I am successful I will never be frightened again'. For women, the most widespread illusion is 'I cannot be safe without a man to protect me'. When these illusions are challenged, both men and women are freed from slavish adherence to career or marital roles to make the best use of their remaining years with an awareness of their mortality in mind. Within marriage, both husbands and wives must challenge the belief that there is no life outside the marriage. This may lead to them choosing to separate or choosing consciously to live together. The choice to remain married enriches the marriage. In midlife there must be a reappraisal of the idea that we are innocent, since this is usually a defence against the childhood tendency to label certain emotional states as bad or unacceptable. There is an examination of how we label these emotional experiences rather than a continued attempt to try to deny them. For example:

- anger need not be labelled destructiveness
- pleasure need not be labelled as irresponsibility
- sensuality need not be labelled as sinfulness
- wicked thoughts need not entail wicked actions
- dissatisfaction need not be labelled as greed
- love need not be labelled as weakness
- self-concern need not be labelled as selfishness.

When these aspects of the self are relabelled rather than denied and integrated into the conscious self a process of liberation and increased psychological vitality occurs. For Gould (1981), at the end of the midlife period the adult experiences a consciousness where the guiding belief is 'I own myself' rather than 'I am theirs'. The sense of self-ownership gives life meaning.

Couples who seek marital and family therapy in midlife are often preoccupied with the consolidation of an adult consciousness, as described by Gould.

Later Life, Illness and Death

In the final stage of the family lifecycle model, the family must cope with the parents' physiological decline, and approaching death, while at the same time developing routines for benefiting from the wisdom and experience of the elderly. A central issue for all family members in this stage as parents move into later life is coping with their approaching death, possible terminal illness and the inevitability of death and ultimately bereavement. Following bereavement or during adjustment to life-threatening illness, families may be referred for therapy because one or more of their members display adjustment difficulties, such as those listed in Table 1.5. All of these types of problems typically reflect involvement in the following grief processes:

- shock
- denial or disbelief
- yearning and searching
- sadness
- anger
- anxiety
- guilt and bargaining
- acceptance.

Table 1.5 Behavioural expressions of themes underlying grief processes following bereavement or facing terminal illness

Grief process	Bereavement		Terminal Illness	
	Underlying theme	Adjustment problems arising from grief processes that may lead to referral	Underlying theme	Adjustment problems arising from grief processes that may lead to referral
Shock	I am stunned by the loss of this person	Complete lack of affect and difficulty engaging emotionally with others Poor concentration	I am stunned by my prognosis and loss of health	Complete lack of affect and difficulty engaging emotionally with others Poor concentration
Denial	The person is not dead	Reporting seeing or hearing the deceased Carrying on conversations with the deceased	I am not terminally ill	Non-compliance with medical regime
Yearning and searching	I must find the deceased	Wandering or running away Phoning relatives	I will find a miracle cure	Experimentation with alternative medicine
Sadness	I am sad, hopeless and lonely because I have lost someone on whom I depended	Persistent low mood, tearfulness, low energy and lack of activity Appetite and sleep disruption Poor concentration and poor work	I am sad and hopeless because I know I will die	Giving up the fight against illness Persistent low mood, tearfulness, low energy and lack of activity Appetite and sleep disruption Poor concentration and poor work

Anger	I am angry because the person I needed has abandoned me	Aggression Conflict with family members and others Drug or alcohol abuse Poor concentration	I am angry because it's not fair. I should be allowed to live	Non-compliance with medical regime Aggression Conflict with medical staff, family members and peers Drug or alcohol abuse Poor concentration
Anxiety	I am frightened that the deceased will punish me for causing their death or being angry at them. I am afraid that I too may die of an illness or fatal accident	Separation anxiety, agoraphobia and panic Somatic complaints and hypochondriasis Poor concentration	I am frightened that death will be painful or terrifying	Separation anxiety and regressed behaviour Agoraphobia and panic
Guilt and bargaining	It is my fault that the person died so I should die	Suicidal behaviour	I will be good if I am allowed to live	Overcompliance with medical regime
Acceptance	I loved and lost the person who died and now I must carry on without them while cherishing their memory	Return to normal behavioural routines	I know that I have only a short time left to live	Attempts to live life to the full for the remaining time

There is not a clear-cut progression through these processes from one to the next (Stroebe, Hansson, Stroebe & Schut, 2001; Walsh & McGoldrick, 2004). Rather, at different points in time, one or other process predominates when a family member has experienced a loss or faces death. There may also be movement back and forth between processes.

Shock and Denial

Shock is the most common initial reaction, it can take the form of physical pain, numbness, apathy or withdrawal. The person may appear to be stunned and unable to think clearly. This may be accompanied by denial, disbelief or avoidance of the reality of the bereavement, a process can last minutes, days, even months. During denial people may behave as if the dead family member is still living, albeit elsewhere. Thus, the bereaved may speak about future plans that involve the deceased. Terminally ill people may talk about themselves and their future as if they were going to live indefinitely.

Yearning and Searching

A yearning to be with the deceased, coupled with disbelief about their death, may lead younger family members to engage in frantic searches for the dead person, wandering or running away from the home in a quest for the person who has died. Children or grandchildren within the family may phone relatives or friends trying to trace the person who has died. During this process, those who have lost family members may report seeing them or being visited by them. Some children carry on full conversations with what presumably are hallucinations of the deceased person. Mistaking other people for the deceased is also a common experience during the denial process. With terminal illness, the yearning for health may lead to a frantic search for a miracle cure and to involvement in alternative medicine.

Sadness

When denial gives way to a realisation of the reality of death, family members may experience profound sadness, despair, hopelessness and depression. The experience of sadness may be accompanied by low energy, sleep disruption, a disturbance of appetite, tearfulness, an inability to concentrate and a retreat from social interaction. Young children or grandchildren experiencing the despair process may regress and begin to behave as if they were a baby again wetting their beds and sucking their thumbs, hoping that by becoming a baby, the dead person may return to comfort them. With terminal illness, despair, hopelessness and depression finds expression in an unwillingness to fight the illness.

Anger

Complementing the despair process, there is an anger process associated with the sense of having been abandoned. Aggression, conflict within the family and the wider social system, and drug and alcohol abuse are some of the common ways that grief-related anger finds expression. With terminal illness, the anger may be projected onto family members or members of the medical team. Destructive conflicts within these relationships may occur, such as refusal to adhere to medical regimes, to take medication or to participate in physiotherapy.

Anxiety

The expression of such anger, may often be followed by remorse or fear of retribution. Young children or grandchildren may fear that the deceased family member will punish them for their anger and so it is not surprising that they may want to leave the light on at night and may be afraid to go to bed alone. In adolescents and adults anxiety is attached to reality-based threats. So, where a family member has been lost through illness or accident, those grieving may worry that they too will die from similar causes. This can lead to a belief that one is seriously ill and to a variety of somatic complaints, such as stomach aches and headaches. It may also lead to a refusal to leave home, lest a fatal accident occur. Referral for assessment of separation anxiety, recurrent abdominal pain, headaches, hypochondriasis and agoraphobia may occur in these cases.

Guilt and Bargaining

The guilt process is marked by self-blame for causing or not preventing the death of the deceased. Family members may also find themselves thinking that if they died this might magically bring back the deceased. Thus, the guilt process may underpin suicidal ideation or self-injury, which invariably leads to referral for mental health assessment. With terminal illness, the illness may be experienced as a punishment for having done something wrong. This sense of guilt underpins the bargaining process in which people facing death engage. The bargaining process may be carried out as imagined conversations with a deity, where the dying person makes promises to live a better life if they are permitted to live longer.

Acceptance

The final grief process is acceptance. With bereavement, the surviving family members reconstruct their view of the world so that the deceased person is construed as no longer living in this world, but a benign and accessible representation of them is constructed that is consistent with the family's belief system. For example, a Christian may imagine that the deceased is in heaven. Atheists may experience the deceased as living on in their memory or in projects or photographs left behind. In terminal illness, acceptance involves a modification of the world view so that the future is foreshortened and therefore the time remaining is highly valued and is spent living life to the full rather than searching in vain for a miracle cure. For bereaved families, new lifestyle routines are evolved as part of the process of accepting the death of a family member and the family is reorganised to take account of the absence of the deceased person. With terminal illness, once the family accept the inevitability of imminent death, routines that enhance the quality of life of the dying person may be evolved. A summary of the grief processes and related adjustment problems that may lead to referral is presented in Table 1.5.

Variability in Grief Responses

Reviews of empirical studies of bereavement confirm that there is extraordinary variation in grief processes and the following points have been well substantiated (Kissane & Bloch, 2002; Shackleton, 1983; Stroebe et al., 2001; Walsh & McGoldrick, 2004; Wortman & Silver, 1989). First, not everyone needs to work through their sense of loss by immediate intensive conversation about it. Second, depression following bereavement is not universal. Only about a third of people suffer depression following bereavement. Third, failure to show emotional distress initially does not necessarily mean that later adjustment problems are inevitable. It appears that different people use different coping strategies to cope with loss. Some use distraction or avoidance, while others use confrontation of the grief experience and working through. Those that effectively use the former coping strategy may not show emotional distress. Fourth, extreme distress following bereavement commonly occurs in those who show protracted grief reactions. Fifth, many people who work through their sense of loss early have later problems. Sixth, a return to normal functioning does not always occur rapidly. While the majority of people approximate normal functioning within two years, a substantial minority of bereaved people continue to show adjustment difficulties even seven years after bereavement. Seventh, resolution and acceptance of death does not always occur. For example, parents who loose children or those who loose a loved one in an untimely fatal accident show protracted patterns of grief. Eighth, grief may have a marked effect on physical functioning. Infections and other illnesses are more common among bereaved people and this is probably due to the effect of loss-related stress on the functioning of the immune system. However, with the passage of time immune-system functioning returns to normal. Ninth, children's grief reactions tend to be similar in form to those of adults but to be briefer and less intense, probably because in comparison with adults, children do not tend to focus for a protracted time period on memories or lost possibilities concerning the bereaved person. Tenth, the quality of family relationships may change in response to bereavement or terminal illness, with discordant relationships becoming more discordant and supportive relationships remaining so. Finally, bereavement, particularly loss of a parent, leaves young children vulnerable to depression in adult life. Adults bereaved as children have double the risk of developing depression when faced with a loss experience in adult life compared with their non-bereaved counterparts. Bereaved children most at risk for depression in adulthood are girls who were young when their parents died a violent or sudden death, and who subsequently received inadequate care associated with the surviving parent experiencing a prolonged grief reaction.

Having considered a family lifecycle model that assumes lifelong monogamy, lifecycle models that address other types of family arrangements deserve attention, particularly those that evolve when separation, divorce and remarriage occurs.

LIFECYCLE STAGES ASSOCIATED WITH SEPARATION AND DIVORCE

Divorce is no longer considered to be an aberration in the normal family lifecycle, but a normative transition for a substantial minority of families (Greene, Anderson, Hetherington, Forgatch & DeGarmo, 2003; Haskey, 1999). In the USA and the UK, between a third and a half of marriages end in divorce. Family transformation through separation, divorce and remarriage may be conceptualised as process involving a series of stages. Carter and McGoldrick's (1999) model of the stages of adjustment to divorce is presented in Table 1.6. This model outlines tasks that must be completed during various stages of the transformation process that involves separation and remarriage. Failure to complete tasks at one stage, may lead to adjustment problems for family members at later stages and referrals for couples or family therapy (Emery & Sbarra, 2002).

Decision to Divorce

In the first stage, the decision to divorce occurs and accepting one's own part in marital failure is the central task. However, it is useful to keep in mind that many contextual factors contribute to divorce including socioeconomic status (SES), urban/rural geographical location, age at marriage, premarital pregnancy, psychological adjustment and parental divorce (Faust & McKibben, 1999; Raschke, 1987). Divorce is more common among those from lower socioeconomic groups with psychological problems who live in urban areas and who have married before the age of 20. It is also common where premarital pregnancy has occurred and where parental divorce has occurred. Divorce is less common among those from higher socioeconomic groupings without psychological problems who live in rural areas and who have married after the age of 30. Where

Table 1.6 Extra stages in the family lifecycle entailed by separation or divorce and remarriage

Stage	Task
1. Decision to divorce	Accepting one's own part in marital failure
2. Planning separation	Cooperatively developing a plan for custody of the children, visitation and finances
	Dealing with the families of origin's response to the plan to separate
3. Separation	Mourning the loss of the intact family
	Adjusting to the change in parent–child and parent–parent relationships
	Avoiding letting marital arguments interfere with parent-to-parent cooperation
	Staying connected to the extended family
	Managing doubts about separation and becoming committed to divorce
4. Post-divorce period	Maintaining flexible arrangements about custody, access and finances without detouring conflict through the children
	Ensuring both parents retain strong relationships with the children
	Re-establishing peer relationships and a social network
5. Entering a new relationship	Completing emotional divorce from the previous relationship
	Developing commitment to a new marriage
6. Planning a new marriage	Planning for cooperative co-parental relationships with ex-spouses
	Planning to deal with children's loyalty conflicts involving natural and step-parents
	Adjust to widening of extended family
7. Establishing a new family	Realigning relationships within the family to allow space for new members
	Sharing memories and histories to allow for integration of all new members

Source: Adapted from Carter and McGoldrick (1999). *The Expanded Family Lifecycle. Individual, Family and Social Perspectives*, 3rd edn. Boston: Allyn & Bacon.

premarital pregnancy has not occurred and where the couples' parents are still in their first marriage divorce is also less common. The economic resources associated with high SES, the community integration associated with rural living, the psychological resources associated with maturity and the model of marital stability offered by non-divorced parents are the more common explanations given for the associations among these factors associated with divorce. The relationship between these various factors and divorce while consistent, are moderate to weak. That is, there are significant subgroups of people who show some or all of these risk factors but do not divorce.

Separation

In the second stage of the lifecycle model of divorce, plans for separation are made. A cooperative plan for custody of the children, visitation, finances and dealing with families of origin's response to the plan to separate must be made if positive adjustment is to occur. Mediation may facilitate this process (Folberg, Milne & Salem, 2004). The third stage of the model is separation. Mourning the loss of the intact family; adjusting to the change in parent–child and parent–parent relationships; preventing marital arguments from interfering with interparental cooperation, staying connected to the extended family and managing doubts about separation are the principal tasks at this stage.

Divorce leads to multiple life changes that affect parental well-being, and the impact of these changes on parental well-being is mediated by a range of personal and contextual factors (Amato, 2000; Anderson, 2003; Hetherington & Kelly, 2002). Divorce leads custodial parents to experience major changes in their lives, including a change in residential arrangements, economic disadvantage, loneliness associated with social network changes, and role-strain associated with the task overload that results from having to care for children and work outside the home. Non-custodial parents experience all of these changes with the exception of role-strain. Changes in divorced couples' residential arrangements, economic status, social networks and role demands lead to a deterioration in physical and mental health for the majority of individuals immediately following separation. Mood swings, depression, identity problems, vulnerability to common infections, and exacerbation of previous health problems are all common sequalae for adults who have separated or divorced. However, for most people these health problems abate within two years of the separation.

Post-divorce Period

The fourth stage of the lifecycle model of divorce is the post-divorce period. Here couples must maintain flexible arrangements about custody, access and finances without detouring conflict through the children; retain strong relationships with the children; and re-establish peer relationships. The stresses and strains of residential changes, economic hardship, role changes and consequent physical and psychological difficulties associated with the immediate aftermath of separation may compromise parents' capacity to cooperate in meeting their children's needs for safety, care, control, education and relationships with each parent (Amato, 1993, 2000, 2001; Amato & Gilbreth, 1999). Authoritarian–punitive parenting, lax *laissez-faire* or neglectful parenting, and chaotic parenting, which involves oscillating between both of these extreme styles, are not uncommon among both custodial and non-custodial parents who have divorced. Couples vary in the ways in which they coordinate their efforts to parent their children following divorce. Three distinct coparenting styles have been identified in studies of divorced families (Bray & Hetherington, 1993). With *cooperative parenting*, a unified and integrated set of rules and routines about managing the children in both the custodial and non-custodial households is developed. This is the optimal arrangement but only occurs in about one in five cases. With *parallel parenting*, each parent has his or her own set of rules for the children and no attempt is made to integrate these. Most children show few adjustment problems when parallel parenting occurs and this is the most common pattern. When *conflictual parenting* occurs, the couple do not communicate directly with each other. All messages are passed through the child and this go-between role, forced on the child, is highly stressful and entails sustained adjustment problems.

Parental separation and divorce are major life stressors for all family members. For children, the experiences of separation and divorce may lead to short- and longer-term adjustment reactions (Amato, 2000, 2001; Amato & Gilbreth, 1999; Hetherington & Kelly, 2002; Kelly, 2000; Leon, 2003; Reifman, Villa, Amans, Rethinam & Telesca, 2001; Rogers, 2004; Wallerstein, 1991). During the two-year period immediately following divorce, most children show some adjustment problems. Boys tend to display conduct or externalising behaviour problems and girls tend to experience emotional or internalising behaviour problems. Both boys and girls may experience educational problems and relationship difficulties within the family, school and peer group. The mean level of maladjustment has consistently been found to be worse for children of divorce in comparison with those from intact families on a variety of measures of adjustment, including conduct difficulties, emotional problems, academic performance, self-esteem and relationships with parents. This has led to the erroneous conclusion by some interpreters of the literature that divorce always has a negative effect on children. When the impact of divorce on children is expressed in terms of the percentages of maladjusted children, it is clear that divorce leads to maladjustment for only a minority of youngsters. A small proportion of individuals from families where divorce has occurred have difficulty making and maintaining stable marital relationships, have psychological adjustment difficulties and attain a lower socioeconomic level in comparison with adults who have grown up in intact families.

Certain characteristics of children and certain features of their social contexts mediate the effects of parental divorce on their adjustment

(Amato, 2000, 2001; Amato & Gilbreth, 1999; Anderson, 2003; Faust & McKibben, 1999; Hetherington & Kelly, 2002; Greene et al., 2003; Kelly, 2000; Leon, 2003; Reifman et al., 2001; Rogers, 2004; Visher, Visher & Pasley, 2003; Wallerstein, 1991). In terms of personal characteristics, males between the ages of three and 18 years are particularly at risk for post-divorce adjustment problems, especially if they have biological or psychological vulnerabilities. Biological vulnerabilities may result from genetic factors, prenatal and perinatal difficulties, or a history of serious illness or injury. Psychological vulnerabilities may be entailed by low intelligence, a difficult temperament, low self-esteem, an external locus of control, or a history of previous psychological adjustment problems. Specific features of children's families and social networks may render them vulnerable to adjustment difficulties following parental separation or divorce. Children are more likely to develop post-separation difficulties if there have been serious difficulties with the parent–child relationship prior to the separation. Included here are insecure attachment, inconsistent discipline and authoritarian, permissive or neglectful parenting. Exposure to chronic family problems including parental adjustment problems, marital discord, domestic violence, family disorganisation, and a history of previous separations and reunions also place children at risk for post-separation adjustment problems. Early life stresses, such as abuse or bereavement, may also compromise children's capacity to deal with stresses entailed by parental separation. In contrast to these factors that predispose children to post-separation adjustment difficulties, better post-separation adjustment occurs where youngsters have a history of good physical and psychological adjustment and where their families have offered a stable parenting environment.

Following parental separation, adjustment difficulties may be maintained by a variety of psychological factors within the child and a range of psychosocial factors within the child's family and social network (Amato, 2000, 2001; Amato & Gilbreth, 1999; Anderson, 2003; Faust & McKibben, 1999; Hetherington & Kelly, 2002; Greene et al., 2003; Kelly, 2000; Leon, 2003; Reifman et al., 2001; Rogers, 2004; Visher et al., 2003; Wallerstein, 1991). At a personal level, adjustment problems may be maintained by rigid sets of negative beliefs related to parental separation. These beliefs may include the view that the child caused the separation and has the power to influence parental reunification, or a belief that abandonment by parents and rejection by peers is inevitable. Within the child's family and social network, adjustment problems following separation may be maintained by sustained parental conflict and routine involvement of the child in this ongoing parental acrimony. The use of non-optimal parenting styles, a lack of consistency in parental rules and routines across custodial and non-custodial households, a lack of clarity about new family roles and routines within each household, and confused family communication may all maintain children's post-separation adjustment problems. These parenting and coparenting problems that maintain children's adjustment difficulties are in turn often a spin-off from parents' personal post-separation adjustment problems. The degree to which parental post-separation problems compromise their capacity to provide a coparenting environment that minimises rather than maintains their children's adjustment reactions is partially determined by the stresses that parents face in the aftermath of separation. These include the loss of support, financial hardship and social disadvantage.

In contrast to these factors that maintain post-separation adjustment difficulties, better post-separation adjustment occurs in youngsters who have psychological strengths, such as high self-esteem, an internal locus of control, realistic beliefs about their parents separation and divorce, good problem-solving skills and good social skills. In terms of the child's family and social network, better adjustment occurs usually after a two-year period has elapsed, where parental conflict is minimal and not channelled through the child, and where an authoritative parenting style is employed. Where parents cope well with post-separation grief, have good personal psychological resources, and a high level of satisfaction within their new relationships, children show better post-separation adjustment. Parental commitment to resolving child-management difficulties and a track record of coping well with transitions in family life may be viewed as protective factors. The availability of social support for both parents and children from the extended family and peers and the absence of financial hardship are also protective factors for post-separation adjustment. Where the school provides a concerned student-centred, achievement-oriented ethos with a high level of student contact and supervision, children are more likely to show positive adjustment following separation. The factors discussed above have a cumulative effect, with more predisposing and maintaining factors being associated with worse adjustment and more protective factors being associated with better adjustment.

New Relationships

Establishing a new relationship occurs in the fifth stage of the divorce life-cycle model. For this to occur, emotional divorce from the previous relationship must be completed and a commitment to a new marriage must be developed. The sixth stage of the model is planning a new marriage. This entails planning for cooperative coparental relationships with ex-spouses and planning to deal with children's loyalty conflicts involving natural and step-parents. It is also important to adjust to the widening of the extended family. In the final stage of the model establishing a new family is the central theme. Realigning relationships within the family to allow space for new members and sharing memories and histories to allow for integration of all new members are the principal tasks of this stage.

Step-families have unique characteristics that are, in part, affected by the conditions under which they are formed (Hetherington & Kelly 2002; Raschke, 1987; Visher et al., 2003). On the positive side, surveys of step-families have found them to be more open in communication, more willing to deal with conflict, more pragmatic, less romantic and more egalitarian with respect to childcare and housekeeping tasks. On the negative side, compared with intact first marriages, step-families are less cohesive and more stressful. Step-parent–child relationships on average tend to be more conflictual than parent–child relationships in intact families. This is particularly true of step-father–daughter relationships and may be due to the daughter's perception of the step-father encroaching on a close mother–daughter relationship.

Children's adjustment following remarriage is associated with age, gender and parents' satisfaction with the new marriage (Greene et al., 2003; Hetherington & Kelly, 2002; Visher et al., 2003). Good adjustment occurs when the custodial parent remarries while children are pre-adolescent, in their late adolescence or in early adulthood. All children in divorced families resist the entry of a step-parent. But during the early teenage years (10–15) this resistance is at a maximum. Divorced adults with children in middle childhood and early adolescence who wish to remarry should try to wait until after the children have reached about 16–18 years, if they want their new relationship to have a fair chance of survival. Remarriage is more disruptive for girls than for boys. Marital satisfaction in the new relationship has a protective effect for young boys and it is a risk factor for preadolescent girls. Young boys, benefit from their custodial mothers forming a satisfying relationship with a new partner. Such satisfying relationships lead step-fathers to behave in a warm, child-centred way towards their step-sons and to help them learn sports and academic skills. These skills help young boys become psychologically robust. Preadolescent girls feel that the close supportive relationship they have with their divorced mothers is threatened by the development of a new and satisfying marital relationship. They usually respond with increased conduct problems and psychological difficulties. In adolescence, when the remarriage has occurred while the children were pre-adolescent, a high level of marital satisfaction is associated with good adjustment and a high level of acceptance of the step-parent for both boys and girls.

Adjustment problems arising from difficulties with managing the developmental tasks associated with family transformation through separation, divorce and remarriage may lead to a referral for family therapy.

THE INDIVIDUAL LIFECYCLE

In practising family therapy, the lifecycle of the family offers one important developmental framework within which to conceptualise problems.

However, it is also useful for therapists to conceptualise the dilemmas faced by each individual at various lifecycle stages. For this reason, a cursory review of a model of the individual lifecycle follows. Newman and Newman's (2003) modification of Erik Erikson's (1959) model of identity development is presented in Table 1.7. The model has been selected because it pinpoints personal dilemmas that must be resolved at various stages of development, which have particular relevance for participating in family life. In this model it is assumed that at each stage of social development the individual must face a personal dilemma. The ease with which successive dilemmas are managed is determined partly by the success with which preceding dilemmas were resolved and partly by the quality of relationships within the individual's family and social context.

Trust vs Mistrust

The main psychosocial dilemma to be resolved during the first two years of life is trust versus mistrust. If parents are responsive to infants' needs in a predictable and sensitive way, the infant develops a sense of trust. In the long term, this underpins a capacity to have hope in the face of adversity and to trust, as adults, that difficult challenges can be resolved. If the child does not experience the parent as a secure base from which to explore the world, the child learns to mistrust others and this underpins a view of the world as threatening. This may lead the child to adopt a detached position during later years and difficulties with making and maintaining peer relationships may occur (Cassidy & Shaver, 1999).

Autonomy vs Shame and Doubt

The main psychosocial dilemma in the pre-school years is autonomy versus shame and doubt. During this period children become aware of their separateness and strive to establish a sense of personal agency and impose their will on the world. Of course, sometimes this is possible, but other times their parents will prohibit them from doing certain things. There is a gradual moving from the battles of the 'terrible twos' to the ritual orderliness that many children show as they approach school-going age. Routines develop for going to bed or getting up, mealtimes and playtimes. The phrase 'I can do it myself ' for tying shoelaces or doing their buttons are examples of the appropriate channelling of the desire to be autonomous. If parents patiently provide the framework for children to master tasks and routines, autonomy develops together with a sense of self-esteem (Darling & Steinberg, 1993). As adults, such children are patient with themselves and have confidence in their abilities to master the challenges of life. They have high self-esteem and a strong sense of will and self-efficacy. If parents are unable to be patient with the child's

Table 1.7 Newman's revision of Erikson's psychosocial stage model

Stage (years)	Dilemma and (main process)	Virtue and (positive self-description)	Pathology and (negative self-description)
Infancy (0–2)	Trusty vs mistrust (Mutuality with caregiver)	Hope (I can attain my wishes)	Detachment (I will not trust others)
Early childhood (2–4)	Autonomy vs Shame & doubt (Imitation)	Will (I can control events)	Compulsion (I will repeat this act to undo the mess that I have made and I doubt that I can control events, and I am ashamed of this)
Middle childhood (4–6)	Initiative vs guilt (Identification)	Purpose (I can plan and achieve goals)	Inhibition (I can't plan or achieve goals, so I don't act)
Late childhood (7–11)	Industry vs inferiority (Education)	Competence (I can use skills to achieve goals)	Inertia (I have no skills, so I won't try)
Early adolescence (12–18)	*Group identity vs alienation (Peer pressure)	Affiliation (I can be loyal to the group)	Isolation (I cannot be accepted into a group)
Adolescence (19–22)	Identity vs role confusion (Role experimentation)	Fidelity (I can be true to my values)	Confusion (I don't know what my role is or what my values are)
Young adulthood (23–34)	Intimacy vs isolation (Mutuality with peers)	Love (I can be intimate with another)	Exclusivity (I have no time for others, so I will shut them out)
Middle age (34–60)	Productivity vs stagnation (Person-environment fit and creativity)	Care (I am committed to making the world a better place)	Rejectivity (I do not care about the future of others, only my own future)
Old age (60–75)	Integrity vs despair (Introspection)	Wisdom (I am committed to life but I know I will die soon)	Despair (I am disgusted at my frailty and my failures)
Very old age (75–death)	*Immortality vs extinction (Social support)	Confidence (I know that my life has meaning)	Diffidence (I can find no meaning in my life, so I doubt that I can act)

Source: Adapted from Erikson (1959) *Identity and the Life Cycle*. New York: International University Press. and Newman and Newman (2003). Development Through Life, 8th edn. Pacific Grove, CA: Brookes/Cole.

*Stages marked with * are Newman's additions to Erikson's original model.

evolving wilfulness and need for mastery and criticise or humiliate failed attempts at mastery, the child will develop a sense of self-doubt and shame. The lack of patience and parental criticism will become internalised and children will evolve into adults who criticise themselves excessively and who lack confidence in their abilities. In some instances this may lead to the compulsive need to repeat their efforts at problem solving so that they can undo the mess they have made and so cope with the shame of not succeeding.

Initiative vs Guilt

At the beginning of school-going years the main psychosocial dilemma is initiative versus guilt. When children have developed a sense of autonomy in the preschool years, they turn their attention outwards to the physical and social world and use their initiative to investigate and explore its regularities with a view to establishing a cognitive map of it. The child finds out what is allowed and what is not allowed at home and at school. Many questions about how the world works are asked. Children conduct various experiments and investigations, for example by lighting matches, taking toys apart, or playing doctors and nurses. The initiative versus guilt dilemma is resolved when the child learns how to channel the need for investigation into socially appropriate courses of action. This occurs when parents empathise with the child's curiosity but establish the limits of experimentation clearly and with warmth (Darling & Steinberg, 1993). Children who resolve the dilemma of initiative versus guilt, act with a sense of purpose and vision as adults. Where parents have difficulty empathising with the child's need for curiosity and curtail experimentation unduly, children may develop a reluctance to explore untried options as adults because such curiosity arouses a sense of guilt.

Industry vs Inferiority

At the close of middle childhood and during the transition to adolescence, the main psychosocial dilemma is industry versus inferiority. Having established a sense of trust, of autonomy and of initiative, the child's need to develop skills and engage in meaningful work emerges. The motivation for industry may stem from the fact that learning new skills is intrinsically rewarding and many tasks and jobs open to the child may be rewarded. Children who have the aptitude to master skills that are rewarded by parents, teachers and peers emerge from this stage of development with new skills and a sense of competence and self-efficacy about these.

Unfortunately, not all children have the aptitude for skills that are valued by society. Youngsters who have low aptitudes for literacy skills, sports and social conformity are disadvantaged from the start. This is compounded by the fact that in our culture, social comparisons are readily made through, for example, streaming in schools and sports. In our society, failure is ridiculed. Youngsters who fail and are ridiculed or humiliated develop a sense of inferiority and in adulthood lack the motivation to achieve (McEvoy & Walker, 2000).

Group Identity vs Alienation

The young adolescent faces a dilemma of group identity versus alienation. There is a requirement to find a peer group with which to become affiliated so that the need for belonging will be met. Joining such a group, however, must not lead to sacrificing one's individuality and personal goals and aspirations. If young adolescents are not accepted by a peer group they will experience alienation. In the longer term they may find themselves unaffiliated and have difficulty developing social support networks, which are particularly important for health and well-being. To achieve group identity, their parents and school need to avoid over-restriction of opportunities for making and maintaining peer relationships. This has to be balanced against the dangers or overpermissivness since lack of supervision is associated with conduct problems and drug dependence (Burke, Loeber & Birmaher, 2002; Crome, Ghodse, Gilvarry & McArdle, 2004; Loeber, Burke, Lahey, Winters & Zera, 2000).

Identity vs Role Confusion

While the concern of early adolescence is group membership and affiliation, the establishment of a clear sense of identity – that is, a sense of who I am – is the major concern in late adolescence. Marcia (1981) has found that adolescents may achieve one of four identity states. With identity diffusion there is no firm commitment to personal, social, political or vocational beliefs or plans. Such individuals are either fun-seekers or people with adjustment difficulties and low self-esteem. With foreclosure, vocational, political or religious decisions are made for the adolescent by parents or elders in the community and are accepted without a prolonged decision-making process. These adolescents tend to adhere to authoritarian values. In cases where a moratorium is reached, the adolescent experiments with a number of roles before settling on an identity. Some of these roles may be negative (delinquent) or non-conventional (drop-out/commune dweller). However, they are staging posts in a prolonged decision-making process on the way to a stable identity. Where adolescents achieve a clear identity following a successful moratorium, they develop a strong commitment to vocational, social, political and religious values, and usually have good psychosocial adjustment in adulthood. They have high self-esteem, realistic goals, a stronger sense of independence and are more resilient in the face of stress. Where a sense of identity is achieved following a moratorium in which many roles have been explored, the adolescent avoids the problems of being aimless, as in the case of identity diffusion, or trapped, which may occur with foreclosure. Parents may find allowing adolescents the time and space to enter a moratorium before achieving a stable sense of identity difficult and referral for psychological consultation may occur.

Intimacy vs Isolation

The major psychosocial dilemma for people who have left adolescence is whether to develop an intimate relationship with another or move to an isolated position. People who do not achieve intimacy experience isolation. Isolated individuals have unique characteristics (Newman & Newman, 2003). Specifically, they overvalue social contact and suspect that all social encounters will end negatively. They also lack the social skills, such as empathy or affective self-disclosure, necessary for forming intimate relationships. These difficulties typically emerge from experiences of mistrust, shame, doubt, guilt, inferiority, alienation or role confusion associated with failure to resolve earlier developmental dilemmas and crises in a positive manner. A variety of social and contextual forces contribute to isolation. Our culture's emphasis on individuality gives us an enhanced sense of separateness and loneliness. Our culture's valuing of competitiveness (particularly among males) may deter people from engaging in self-disclosure. Men have been found to self-disclose less than women, to be more competitive in conversations and to show less empathy.

Productivity vs Stagnation

The midlife dilemma of is that of productivity versus stagnation. People who select and shape a home and work environment that fits with their needs and talents are more likely to resolve this dilemma by becoming productive. Productivity may involve procreation, work-based productivity or artistic creativity. Those who become productive focus their energy into making the world a better place for further generations. Those who fail to select and shape their environment to meet their needs and talents may become overwhelmed with stress and become burnt out, depressed or cynical on the one hand, or greedy and narcissistic on the other.

Integrity vs Despair

In later adulthood the dilemma faced is integrity versus despair. A sense of personal integrity is achieved by those who accept the events that make up their lives and integrate these into a meaningful personal narrative in a way that allows them to face death without fear. Those who avoid this introspective process or who engage in it and find that they cannot accept the events of their lives or integrate them into a meaningful personal narrative that allows them to face death without fear develop a sense of despair. The process of integrating failures, disappointments, conflicts, growing incompetencies and frailty into a coherent life story is very challenging and is difficult to do unless the first psychosocial crisis of trust versus mistrust was resolved in favour of trust. The positive resolution of this dilemma in favour of integrity rather than despair leads to the development of a capacity for wisdom.

Immortality vs Extinction

In the final months of life the dilemma faced by the very old is immortality versus extinction. A sense of immortality can be achieved by living on through one's children; through a belief in an afterlife; by the permanence of one's achievements (either material monuments or the way one has influenced others); by viewing the self as being part of the chain of nature (the decomposed body becomes part of the earth that brings forth new life); or by achieving a sense of experiential transcendence (a mystical sense of continual presence). When a sense of immortality is achieved the acceptance of death and the enjoyment of life, despite frailty, becomes possible. This is greatly facilitated when people have good social support networks to help them deal with frailty, growing incompetence and the possibility of isolation. Those who lack social support and have failed to integrate their lives into a meaningful story may fear extinction and find no way to accept their physical mortality while at the same time evolving a sense of immortality.

Erikson's model has received some support from a major longitudinal study (Valliant, 1977). However, it appears that the stages do not always occur in the stated order and often later life events can lead to changes in the way in which psychosocial dilemmas are resolved.

It is important for therapists to have a sensitivity to the personal dilemmas faced by family members who participate in marital and family therapy. The individual lifecycle model presented here and summarised in Table 1.7 offers a framework within which to comprehend such persona dilemmas.

SEX-ROLE DEVELOPMENT

One important facet of identity is sex role (Vasta, Haith & Miller, 2003). This area deserves particular consideration because a sensitivity to gender issues is essential for the ethical practice of family therapy. From birth to five years of age, children go through a process of learning the concept of gender. They first distinguish between the sexes and categorise themselves as male or female. Then they realise that gender is stable and does not change from day to day. Finally they realise that there are critical differences (such as genitals) and incidental differences (such as clothing) that have no effect on gender. It is probable that during this period they develop gender scripts, which are representations of the routines associated with their gender roles. On the basis of these scripts they develop gender schemas, which are cognitive structures used to organise information about the categories male and female (Levy & Fivush, 1993).

Extensive research has shown that in western culture sex-role toy preferences, play, peer group behaviour and cognitive development are different for boys and girls (Serbin, Powlishta & Gulko, 1993). Boys prefer trucks and guns. Girls prefer dolls and dishes. Boys do more outdoor play with more rough and tumble, and less relationship-oriented speech. They pretend to fulfil adult male roles, such as warriors, heroes and firemen. Girls show more nurturent play involving much relationship conversation and pretend to fulfil stereotypic adult female roles, such as homemakers. As children approach the age of five years they are less likely to engage in play that is outside their sex role. A tolerance for cross-gender play evolves in middle childhood and diminishes again at adolescence. Boys play in larger groups, whereas girls tend to limit their group size to two or three.

There are some well-established gender differences in the abilities of boys and girls (Halpern, 2000). Girl's show more rapid language development than boys and earlier competence at maths. In adolescence, boys competence in maths exceeds that of girls and their language differences even out. Males perform better on spatial tasks than girls throughout their lives.

While an adequate explanation for gender differences on cognitive tasks cannot be given, it is clear that sex-role behaviour is influenced by parents' treatment of children (differential expectations and reinforcement) and by children's response to parents (identification and imitation) (Serbin et al., 1993). Numerous studies show that parents expect different sex-role behaviour from their children and reward children for engaging in these behaviours. Boys are encouraged to be competitive and activity oriented. Girls are encouraged to be cooperative and relationship oriented. A problem with traditional sex roles in adulthood is that they have the potential to lead to a power imbalance within marriage, an increase in marital dissatisfaction, a sense of isolation in both partners and a decrease in father involvement in child care tasks (Gelles, 1995).

However, rigid sex roles are now being challenged and the ideal of androgyny is gaining in popularity. The androgynous youngster develops both male and female role-specific skills. Gender stereotyping is less marked in families where parents' behaviour is less sex typed; where both parents work outside the home; and in single-parent families. Gender stereotyping is also less marked in families with high socioeconomic status (Vasta et al., 2003).

GAY AND LESBIAN LIFECYCLES

A significant minority of individuals have gay or lesbian sexual orientations. When such individuals engage in family therapy, it is important that frameworks unique to their sexual identity be used to conceptualise their problems, rather than frameworks developed for heterosexual people and families (Laird, 2003).

Gay and Lesbian Identity Formation

Lifecycle models of the development of gay and lesbian identities highlight two significant transitional processes: self-definition and 'coming out' (Laird, 2003; Laird & Green, 1996; Malley & Tasker, 1999; Stone-Fish & Harvey, 2005; Tasker & McCann, 1999). The first process – self-definition as a gay or lesbian person – occurs initially in response to experiences of being different or estranged from same-sex heterosexual peers and later in response to attraction to and/or intimacy with peers of the same gender. The adolescent typically faces a dilemma of whether to accept or deny the homoerotic feelings he or she experiences. The way in which this dilemma is resolved is in part influenced by the perceived risks and benefits of denial and acceptance. Where adolescents feel that homophobic attitudes within their families, peer groups and society will have severe negative consequences for them, they may be reluctant to accept their gay or lesbian identity. Attempts to deny homoerotic experiences and adopt a heterosexual identity may lead to a wide variety of psychological difficulties including depression, substance abuse, running away and suicide attempts, all of which may become a focus for family therapy. In contrast, where the family and society are supportive and tolerant of diverse sexual orientations, and where there is an easily accessible supportive gay or lesbian community, then the benefits of accepting a gay or lesbian identity may outweigh the risks, and the adolescent may begin to form a gay or lesbian self-definition. Once the process of self-definition as gay or lesbian occurs, the possibility of 'coming out' to others is opened up. This process of coming out involves coming out to other lesbian and gay people; to heterosexual peers; and to members of the family. The more supportive the responses of members of these three systems, the better the adjustment of the individual.

In response to the process of 'coming out' families undergo a process of destabilisation. They progress from subliminal awareness of the young person's sexual orientation, to absorbing the impact of this realisation and adjusting to it. Resolution and integration of the reality of the youngster's sexual identity into the family belief system depends on the flexibility of the family system, the degree of family cohesion and the capacity of core themes within the family belief system to be reconciled with the youngster's sexual identity. Individual and family therapy conducted within this frame of reference, aim to facilitate the processes of owning homoerotic experiences, establishing a gay or lesbian identity and mobilising support within the family, heterosexual peer group, and gay or lesbian peer group for the individual.

Gay and Lesbian Couple Lifecycles

While there is huge variability in the patterns of lives of gay and lesbian couples, a variety of models of normative lifecycles have been proposed (Laird, 2003). Slater (1995) has offered a five-stage lifecycle model for lesbian couples. In the first stage of couple formation, the couple are mobilised by the excitement of forming a relationship but may be wary of exposing vulnerabilities. The management of similarities and differences in personal style so as to permit a stable relationship occurs in the second stage. In the third stage, the central theme is the development of commitment, which brings the benefits of increased trust and security and the risks of closing down other relationship options. Generativity, through working on joint projects or parenting, is the main focus of the fourth stage. In the fifth and final stage the couple learn to cope jointly with the constraints and opportunities of later life, including retirement, illness and bereavement on the one hand, and grandparenting and acknowledging life achievements on the other.

McWhirter and Mattison (1984) developed a six-stage model for describing the themes central to the development of enduring relationships between gay men. The first four stages, which parallel those in Slater's model, are 'blending', 'nesting' 'maintaining' and 'building'. McWhirter and Mattison argue that the fifth stage, which they term 'releasing', in the gay couple lifecycle is characterised by each individual within the couple pursuing his own agenda and taking the relationship for granted. This gives way to a final stage or 'renewal', in which the relationship is once again privileged over individual pursuits.

Research on children raised by gay and lesbian couples shows that the adjustment and mental health of children raised in such families does differ significantly from that of children raised by heterosexual parents (Laird, 2003).

Difficulties in managing progression through the lifecycle stages may lead gay and lesbian couples to seek family therapy (Coyle & Kitzinger, 2002; Green & Mitchell, 2002; Laird & Green, 1996; Stone-Fish & Harvey, 2005).

CLASS, CREED AND COLOUR

The models of family and individual development and related research findings presented in this chapter have all been informed by a predominantly western, white, middle-class, Judeo-Christian sociocultural tradition. However, in westernised countries, we now live in multicultural, multiclass context. A significant proportion of clients who come to family therapy are from ethnic minority groups. Also, many clients are not from the affluent middle classes, but survive in poverty and live within a subculture that does not conform to the norms and values of the white, middle-class community. When such individuals engage in family therapy, a sensitivity to these issues of race and class is essential (Falicov, 1995, 2003; Hardy & Laszloffy, 2002; Ingoldsby & Smith, 2005; McGoldrick, 2002).

This type of sensitivity involves an acceptance that different patterns of organisation, belief systems, and ways of being in the broader sociocultural context may legitimately typify families from different cultures. Families from different ethnic groups and subcultures may have differing norms and styles governing communication, problem-solving, rules, roles and routines. They may have different belief systems involving different ideas about how family life should occur, how relationships should be managed, how marriages should work, how parent–child relationships should be conducted, how the extended family should be connected, and how relationships between families and therapists should be conducted. Most importantly, family therapists must be sensitive to the relatively economically privileged position that most therapists occupy with respect to clients from ethnic minorities and lower socioeconomic groups. We must also be sensitive to the fact that we share a responsibility for the oppression of minority groups. Without this type of sensitivity we run the risk of illegitimately imposing our norms and values on clients and furthering this oppression.

SUMMARY

Families are unique social systems insofar as membership is based on combinations of biological, legal, affectional, geographic and historical ties. In contrast to other social systems, entry into family systems is through birth, adoption, fostering or marriage, and members can leave only by death. It is more expedient to think of the family as a network of people in the individual's immediate psychosocial field. The family lifecycle may be conceptualised as a series of stages, each characterised by a set of tasks family members must complete to progress to the next stage. Failure to complete tasks may lead to adjustment problems. In the first two stages of family development, the principal concerns are with differentiating from the family of origin by completing school, developing relationships outside the family, completing one's education and beginning a career. In the third stage, the principal tasks are those associated with selecting a partner and deciding to marry. In the fourth stage, the childless couple must develop routines for living together, which are based on a realistic appraisal of the other's strengths, weaknesses and idiosyncrasies. In the fifth stage, the main task is for couples to adjust their roles as marital partners to make space for young children. In the sixth stage, which is marked by children's entry into adolescence, parent–child relationships require realignment to allow adolescents to develop more autonomy. The demands of grandparental dependency and midlife reevaluation may compromise parents' abilities to meet their adolescents' needs for the negotiation of increasing autonomy. The seventh stage is concerned with the transition of young adult children out of the parental home. During this stage, the parents are faced with the task of adjusting to living as a couple again, to dealing with disabilities and death in their families of origin and of adjusting to the expansion of the family if their children marry and procreate. In the final stage of this lifecycle model, the family must cope with the parents' physiological decline and approaching death, while at the same time developing routines for benefiting from the wisdom and experience of the elderly.

Family transformation through separation, divorce and remarriage may also be viewed as a staged process. In the first stage, the decision to divorce occurs and accepting one's own part in marital failure is the central task. In the second stage, plans for separation are made. A cooperative plan for custody of the children, visitation, finances and dealing with families of origin's response to the plan to separate must be made if positive adjustment is to occur. The third stage of the model is separation. Mourning the loss of the intact family; adjusting to the change in parent–child and parent–parent relationships; preventing marital arguments from interfering with interparental cooperation; staying connected to the extended family; and managing doubts about separation are the principal tasks at this stage. The fourth stage is the post-divorce period. Here couples must maintain flexible arrangements about custody, access and finances without detouring conflict through the children; retain strong relationships with the children; and re-establish peer relationships. Establishing a new relationship occurs in the fifth stage. For this to occur, emotional divorce from the previous relationship must be completed and a commitment to a new marriage must be developed. The sixth stage of the model is planning a new marriage. This entails planning for cooperative coparental relationships with ex-spouses and planning to deal with children's loyalty conflicts involving natural and step-parents. It is also important to adjust to the widening of the extended family. In the final stage of the model, establishing a new family is the central theme. Realigning relationships within the family to allow space for new members and sharing memories and histories to allow for integration of all new members are the principal tasks of this stage.

The development of individual identity, within a family context, may also be conceptualised as a series of stages. At each stage the individual must face a personal dilemma. The ease with which successive dilemmas are managed is determined partly by the success with which preceding dilemmas were resolved and partly by the quality of relationships within the individual's family and social context. The dilemmas are: trust vs mistrust; autonomy vs shame and doubt; initiative vs guilt; industry vs inferiority; group identity vs alienation; identity vs role confusion; intimacy vs isolation; productivity vs stagnation; integrity vs despair; and immortality vs extinction.

Lifecycle models of the development of gay and lesbian identities highlight two significant transitional processes: the process of self-definition as a gay or lesbian person and the process of coming out to other lesbian and gay people, to heterosexual peers, and to members of the family. The more supportive the responses of others, the better the adjustment of the individual. Stage models for the development of lesbian and gay couple relationships have been developed which take account of their unique life circumstances.

When working with individuals from ethnic minorities and lower socioeconomic groups in family therapy, a sensitivity to issues of race and class is essential if the illegitimate imposition of norms and values from the dominant culture is to be avoided.

FURTHER READING

Carter, B. & McGoldrick, M. (1999). *The Expanded Family Lifecycle. Individual, Family and Social Perspectives*, 3rd edn. Boston: Allyn & Bacon.
Walsh, F. (2003). *Normal Family Processes*, 3rd edn. New York: Guilford.

Chapter 2

ORIGINS OF FAMILY THERAPY

Family therapy is a relatively recent development. As a movement, family therapy began in the early 1950s. It is a highly flexible psychotherapeutic approach, applicable to a wide range of child-focused and adult-focused problems. The central aim of family therapy is to facilitate the resolution of presenting problems and to promote healthy family development by focusing primarily on the relationships between the person with the problem and significant members of his or her family and social network. Family therapy is a broad psychotherapeutic movement that contains many constituent schools and traditions. These many schools and traditions may be classified in terms of their emphasis on: (1) problem-maintaining behaviour patterns; (2) problematic and constraining belief systems and narratives; and (3) historical and contextual predisposing factors. In this chapter, the origins of family therapy are first outlined, with reference to important contributions from various movements, professional disciplines, psychotherapeutic approaches and research traditions. Detailed consideration is given to the unique contribution of Gregory Bateson to the emergence of family therapy. The scope and goals of family therapy are then considered with reference to the three central themes, outlined above, which underpin various approaches to family therapy theory and practice.

Family therapy emerged simultaneously in the 1950s in a variety of different countries, and within a variety of different movements, disciples, therapeutic and research traditions. The central insight that intellectually united the pioneers of the family therapy movement was that human problems are essentially interpersonal not intrapersonal, and so their resolution requires an approach to intervention that directly addresses relationships between people. This insight contravened the prevailing view held by mental health professionals at the time. This view was that all behavioural problems are manifestations of essentially individual disorders and so require individually-focused therapy. In the 1950s and 1960s, psychodynamic, client-centred and biomedical individually-focused interventions dominated mainstream mental health practice. It was within this relatively hostile environment that the family therapy movement evolved. Family therapy emerged partly in response to the genuine limitations of exclusively individually-based treatment approaches. The failure of individually-based therapies to promote the resolution of marital and parent–child problems; the observation that relapses sometimes occurred when patients who had successfully been treated on an inpatient individual basis returned to their families; and the observation that sometimes following the successful treatment of one family member, another would develop problems, all contributed to a growing disillusionment in an exclusively individual approach to psychotherapy. Detailed scholarly accounts of the history of the couples and family therapy movement are given in Broderick and Schrader (1991), Guerin (1976), Gurman and Fraenkel (2002), Guttman (1991), Hecker, Mims and Boughner (2003), Hoffman, 2001, Kaslow (1980) and Wetchler (2003b). The following sketch of some of the more important aspects of the development of family therapy owes much to these scholarly sources.

MOVEMENTS: CHILD GUIDANCE, MARRIAGE COUNSELLING AND SEX THERAPY

Couples and family therapy in the USA and the UK emerged from a number of movements and services including child guidance clinics, the marriage counselling movement and, later, the sex therapy movement.

Child Guidance

Within child guidance clinics, the traditional model of practice was for the psychiatrist to conduct individual psychodynamically-based play therapy with the child (who had been psychometrically and projectively assessed by the psychologist), while the mother received concurrent counselling from the social worker. Family therapy evolved within child guidance clinics when experimental conjoint meetings involving parents and children began to be held by pioneering practitioners, including John Bowlby (the originator of attachment theory) in the UK and John Bell in the USA. For example, Bell described the case of a boy expelled from school for behaviour problems. In the face of strong resistance from established practice and the parents of the boy, who saw the difficulties as intrinsic to the child, Bell conducted a series of family sessions. From these he found that the boy, an adopted child, had developed behaviour problems as his parents' relationship had gradually deteriorated. The deterioration occurred when the father developed an alcohol problem and this in turn arose because of the father's disappointment in the difficulty his wife had in accepting and caring for the child. She was perfectionistic and harboured strong feelings of hostility towards the boy because of his failure to meet her perfectionistic standards. Bell's therapy focused on ameliorating the family's relationship problems, not on interpreting the boy's intrapsychic fantasies, the standard approach that would have been taken by most clinicians in the late 1950s (Broderick & Schrader, 1991).

Marriage Counselling

The practice of conducting conjoint meetings with marital partners evolved within the marriage counselling movement (Gurman & Fraenkel, 2002). In the USA, the American Association of Marriage Counsellors, which was founded in 1945, eventually became the American Association for Marital and Family Therapy in 1978, the largest family therapy organisation in the world. In the UK, Henry Dicks (1967) at the Tavistock Clinic pioneered the development of object relations-based marital therapy, and today the Tavistock continues to be a major centre for family therapy research and training in the UK.

Sex Therapy

Sex therapy developed out of the work of Masters and Johnson (1970), which was conducted in the USA during the 1960s. Masters and Johnson developed a conjoint approach to conducting therapy to deal with a wide variety of psychosexual problems. This essentially behavioural approach to psychosexual difficulties became integrated subsequently with psychodynamic and systemic marital therapy in the work of Helen Singer Kaplan (1974, 1995) and others (e.g. Leiblum & Rosen, 2001; Levine, Risen & Althof, 2003; Schnarch, 1991).

DISCIPLINES: SOCIAL WORK, PSYCHIATRY AND CLINICAL PSYCHOLOGY

Family therapy emerged relatively independently within the three disciplines of social work, psychiatry and clinical psychology. It was, therefore an approach adopted by a number of disciplines. This was in contrast to psychoanalysis, which, in the USA, was dominated by psychiatry. It also was in stark contrast to the humanistic client-centred therapy movement and the behaviour therapy movement, which were dominated by clinical and counselling psychologists.

Social Work

Social work has historically privileged family work and home-visiting as an important part of clinical practice (Guerin, 1976; Kaslow, 1980). A central guiding idea behind social casework has been that the family provides the social context within which children develop. Therefore, interventions that focus on supporting parents, either psychologically through counselling or materially through organising state benefits were seen as important because they would have a knock-on effect and benefit the child. Prominent social workers in the history of family therapy have included Virginia Satir, Lynn Hoffman, Betty Carter and Monica McGoldrick in the USA; Michael White in Australia; John Burnham, Gill Gorell Barnes and Barry Mason in the UK; and Imelda McCarthy, Phil Kearney and Jim Sheehan in Ireland.

Psychiatry

Within psychiatry, Alfred Adler and Harry Stack Sullivan pioneered the development of social psychiatry with its emphasis on the importance of ongoing family relationships in the development and maintenance of symptomatic behaviour (Broderick & Schraeder, 1991). Alfred Adler was one of the first psychoanalysts to conduct conjoint family meetings and his protégé Rudolph Dreikurs, who worked in a US child guidance clinic, laid the foundations for Adlerian family therapy. Sullivan's clinical work with schizophrenia inspired the development of Murray Bowen's and Don Jackson's systemic approaches to family therapy. Prominent psychiatrists in the development of family therapy include Nathan Ackeerman, Carl Whitaker, Salvadore Minuchin and Nathan Epstein in the USA; Robin Skynner, John Byng-Hall, Brian Lask, Arnon Bentovim, Alan Cooklin, and Eia Asen in the UK; Mara Selvini Palazolli, Luigi Boscolo, Gianfranco Cecchin and Guiliana Prata in Italy; and Nollaig Byrne in Ireland.

Psychology

Within clinical psychology, the involvement of parents in behaviour therapy programmes with their children and the application of the principles of social learning theory to marital therapy laid the foundations for the development of family and marital therapy within the discipline, although these were relatively late developments within the history of family therapy (Dattilio & Epstein, 2003; Epstein, 2003). Psychologists have also made a significant contribution to developing the evidence base for marital and family therapy (Sprenkle, 2002). Prominent psychologists in the development of family therapy include Neil Jacobson, Alan Gurman, Frank Dattilio, Normal Epstein, James Alexander and Scott Henggeler in the USA; Ivan Eisler, Arlene Vetere, Peter Stratton, David Campbell, Eddy Street, Rudi Dallos and Elsa Jones in the UK; and Ed McHale in Ireland.

GROUP THERAPY: GROUP ANALYSIS, ENCOUNTER GROUPS, PSYCHODRAMA AND GESTALT THERAPY

Ideas and practices from a variety of group therapy traditions have been imported into family therapy, notably group analysis, encounter groups, psychodrama and Gestalt therapy.

Group Analysis

In the UK, Robin Skynner (1981) drew on the insights of a number of group analysts including Foulkes, Bion, Ezriel and Anthony, who developed their ideas within the psychodynamic tradition. Group analysts focused their attention primarily on the interpretation of recurrent group processes as a way of helping patients understand their own self-defeating behaviour patterns. Skynner imported this technique into family therapy.

Encounter Groups

Carl Rogers's (1970) client-centred approach to group counselling – encounter groups – included two practices that were imported whole-sale into family therapy (Bott, 2001). First, group members were required to speak for themselves (but not others) within therapy and to use language such as 'I-statements', which promoted taking responsibility for one's own behaviour and priviledging personal narratives. Second, therapists facilitated clients' expression of their immediate emotional experience; empathised with these phenomenological accounts; and expressed warm and genuine acceptance of clients when they gave such accounts. Within the family therapy field, Virginia Satir, Carl Whitaker, and Bunny and Fred Duhl adopted these practices as central to their therapeutic style.

Psychodrama

Enactment and sculpting are two techniques that were imported into family therapy from psychodrama (Moreno, 1945). With enactment, a technique popularised by Salvador Minuchin (1974), family members are helped to show the therapist their interpersonal problems by engaging in routine patterns of problematic behaviour and problem solving within the therapeutic session. The therapist may at critical junctures disrupt these habitual processes by requiring family members to change places, alter alliances, or modify their problem-solving strategies. With sculpt-ing, a technique favoured by Virginia Satir (1983), the therapist invites one family member at a time to arrange the positioning of family mem-bers, so their spatial arrangement reflects the family member's emotional experience of the pattern of family organisation. Discrepancies between differing family members' sculpts are used as an impetus for helping family members change their repetitive patterns of problematic behaviour. Satir also evolved a psychodrama-based technique, which she termed a 'parts party'. Here, different family members, under the direction of one specific family member, act out positions or roles that represent various aspects of a specific family member's personality. This enhances family members' understanding of, and empathy for, the specific family member in question.

Gestalt Therapy

The empty chair technique, developed by Fritz Perls (1973), the originator of Gestalt therapy, offers a forum within which clients may address two sides of a dilemma or deal with unfinished (emotional) business in instances where the other party is unavailable or deceased. When Perls used this technique in a group therapy context he would invite one client to express in a forceful and emotionally congruent way their sense of hurt, anger or fear and to direct this address to an empty chair, which represented either the part of themselves that reflected the other side of the conflict (in the case of processing a dilemma) or the deceased or unavailable person (in the case of processing unfinished business). Other members of the group would observe the process and support the person engaging in the 'empty chair work'. This technique has been used by a number of family therapists, notably Schwartz (1995), to help individuals resolve problems in their internalized family systems.

RESEARCH TRADITIONS: WORK GROUPS, ROLE THEORY AND SCHIZOPHRENIA

Discoveries within a number of research traditions have contributed to the development of family therapy. In particular, ideas from research on work-group dynamics, functionalism and role theory, and family factors in the development of schizophrenia have been particularly important.

Work Group Dynamics

Kurt Lewin (1951), a Gestalt psychologist interested in the performance of work groups, developed field theory to account for a number of experimental observations of groups. First, he observed that it was not possible to predict group performance on the basis of information about the individual performance of group members. That is, he showed that a group is more than the sum of its parts. Second, he observed that group discussions were more effective than individual instruction in changing group behaviour. Thus, he showed that interventions involving all significant members of a social system were more effective than individually-based interventions. Third, he noted that groups displayed a *quasi-stationary equilibrium*, and that this force resists change. For change in group behaviour patterns to occur there must be an *unfreezing* of group behaviour patterns, a process of transition, and a *refreezing*. Fourth, he made a distinction between content and process, and noted that the group process (how group members discuss and manage issues), as well as the content of group discussions, had a significant effect on group performance. All four ideas have been incorporated into family therapy theory and practice. Within systems-based family therapy it is assumed that the whole is more than the sum of the parts; that homeostatic forces within families make them resistant to change; that change is more likely to occur when significant family members are involved in therapy; that effective therapy addresses family processes as well as content issues; and that therapy involves disrupting family homeostasis, facilitating the development of new behaviour patterns, and consolidation of these new and more adaptive behavioural routines.

Bion (1948) observed that most groups become diverted from their primary tasks by engaging in three classes of repetitive and unproductive patterns; that is, *fight-flight, dependency* and *pairing*. Within the family therapy field, it has been noted that many families in therapy engage in these three processes rather than in effective problem solving. Some families engage in continued fighting and conflict, or skirt around central issues that need to be addressed. Others develop a strong dependency relationship with the therapist, who may reinforce this through overactivity. Under stress many families become segregated into pairs or factions. For example, a mother and daughter may develop a cross-generational coalition from which the father and other siblings are excluded.

Functionalism and Role Theory

A central assumption of functionalism is that within any social system enduring roles are adaptive because they serve particular functions. For example, Emile Durkheim argued that individuals who adopt deviant or pathological roles within society serve the function of uniting the remainder of society. Talcott Parsons (Parsons & Bales, 1955) argued, much to the anger of later feminists, that a mother's proper role within the family is expressive and nurturing, while the father's is instrumental and managerial. These roles were viewed by Parsons as reciprocal, complementary and mutually reinforcing. According to Parsons, the survival of the family unit in society would be jeopardised if people did not conform to these roles. Of course, later feminists argued that this said more about the problematic society families were trying to adapt to rather than the usefulness of these chauvinistic role specifications (e.g., Leupnitz, 1988; Schwoeri, Sholevar & Vilarose, 2003). Functionalism, had an impact on family therapy insofar as many schools of family therapy viewed the symptomatic member as serving some useful function for the family that aided family adaptation within society. A problem with this view is that often symptoms have no such function and are just one more hassle for a stressed family to cope with. Functionalism provided family therapists with the construct of roles as a useful device for describing regularities in family functioning. Virginia Satir (1983), one of the pioneers of family therapy, proposed that within families four dysfunctional roles could be identified: the blamer, the placater, the distractor and the super-reasonable person. Structural family therapy highlighted the importance of clear and flexible roles for healthy family functioning (Fishman & Fishman, 2003; Wetchler, 2003a).

Family Origins of Schizophrenia

Scientific investigations into the family origins of schizophrenia, which were carried out by Theadore Lidz and Lyman C. Wynne in the USA and R.D. Laing in the UK, contributed to the emergence of family therapy by highlighting the role of family dynamics in the aetiology and maintenance of abnormal behaviour. In a developmental study of the families of people with schizophrenia, Lidz (1957a, 1957b) found that these families were characterised by problematic marital relationships and poor paternal adjustment. Lidz described two types of problematic marital relationships. In instances where *marital schizm* occurred, Lidz noted that couples failed to develop reciprocal cooperative roles. In situations where *marital skew* occurred, one partner, often with serious personal adjustment difficulties, adopted an extremely dominant role and the other a dependent role within which they accommodated to the dominant partner's demands. In families characterised by both types of discordant marriages, parents consistently vied for their children's loyalty and the children in turn felt torn between their parents' conflicting demands for exclusive loyalty. This systemic account of the family origins of schizophrenia opposed simplistic prevailing theories, espoused by analysts such as Frieda Fromm-Reichmann, which attributed the development of schizophrenia to maternal rejection.

Lyman Wynne, influenced by the ideas of the sociologist Talcott Parsons, believed that an individual's personality could be conceptualised as a subsystem within the larger family system. Thus, the ongoing transactions between the individual and the family, if particularly deviant or abnormal, could initiate and maintain psychopathology. Wynne observed that families containing members with schizophrenia were characterised by unusual emotional transactions, peculiar family boundaries and deviant communication styles (Singer, Wynne & Toohey, 1978; Wynne, 1961; Wynne, Ryckoff, Day & Hirsch, 1958). With respect to emotional transactions, he noted that some families where characterised by *pseudomutuality* and others were characterised by *pseudohostility*. Pseudomutuality is an overt display of positive emotion, togetherness, loyalty and apparent enmeshment. This facade masks underlying conflict, hostility, anger, needs for autonomy, separateness and divergent interests and opinions. With pseudohostility, there is an overt display of negative emotion played out in a series of shifting alliances and splits within the family. However, this facade masks an underlying and rigid set of alignments and splits, such as a coalition between a mother and child and a split between this alignment and other family members. Wynne used the term 'rubber fence' to refer to the impermeable boundary that characterised families with a schizophrenic member. Such families permit professionals to have superficial contact with them bur resist interactions that would significantly alter the way in which the family is organised. Wynne also noted that families with schizophrenic members showed *communication deviance*, characterised by difficulties in maintaining a shared focus when problem solving and attempting to communicate directly and clearly in a goal-directed way.

R.D. Laing (1965), in clinical and experimental studies of people with schizophrenia, was impressed by the observation that patients' parents commonly denied, distorted or relabelled the patients' experiences so as to compel the patient to conform to the parents' expectations. Laing used Karl Marx's term 'mystification' to refer to this process. He argued that mystification led to the development of an overtly displayed *false self* and a private *real self*. When the split between these two selves exceeded a critical level, Laing believed that schizophrenia occurred. In this sense, madness for Laing was a sane response to an insane situation.

The idea central to this early research, that dysfunctional families cause schizophrenia, has not been supported by later more sophisticated research. Current evidence suggests that in many instances individuals are genetically or constitutionally vulnerable to schizophrenia; that psychotic episodes are precipitated by acute life stresses; and that stressful family interaction patterns that occur in response to psychotic symptoms may maintain these symptoms (as outlined in Chapter 17 of this volume).

GREGORY BATESON

Gregory Bateson, a Cambridge anthropologist, is probably the single most influential individual in the history of family therapy. He never personally practised family therapy, nor was he centrally interested in its development as a psychotherapeutic movement. His interests were far broader, and his family-based work was only a single aspect of an extraordinary research programme that addressed phenomena as diverse as tribal rituals; animal learning; communication in porpoises; and the analysis of paradoxes (Bateson, 1972, 1979, 1991; Bateson & Bateson, 1987; Bateson & Ruesch, 1951). The central aim of his research programme was to develop a unified or ecosystemic framework within which mind and material substance could be coherently explained. Bateson's work with families began when he formed the Palo Alto group in the early 1950s. The group included Jay Haley, founder of strategic therapy (1963, 1967a, 1967b, 1973, 1976a, 1976b, 1984, 1985a, 1985b, 1985c, 1996, 1997; Haley & Richeport-Haley, 2003), Don Jackson (1968a, 1968b; Watzlawick, Beavin & Jackson, 1967), John Weakland (Fisch, Weakland & Segal, 1982; Watzlawick & Weakland, 1977; Watzlawick, Weakland & Fisch, 1974; Weakland & Fisch, 1992; Weakland & Ray, 1995) and John Fry, all of whom went on to set up the Mental Research Institute and develop MRI brief therapy. Among the many conceptual contributions that this group made to the development of family therapy, three were particularly influential and these concerned the double-bind theory of schizophrenia; the conceptualisation of communication as a multilevel process; and the use of general systems theory and cybernetics as a framework for conceptualising family organisation and processes. In the following sections an account of each of these areas will be given.

The Double-bind Theory

In the *double-bind theory*, Bateson's (1972) group proposed that schizophrenic behaviour occurs in families characterised by particular rigid and repetitive patterns of communication and interaction, referred to as 'double binds'. In such families, double binds involve parents issuing the symptomatic child with a primary injunction, which is typically verbal (e.g. 'Come here and I will hug you'); concurrently the parents issue a secondary injunction that contradicts the primary injunction and which is typically conveyed non-verbally (e.g. 'If you don't hug me I will be disappointed in you or be angry with you'); there is also a tertiary injunction prohibiting the child from escaping from the conflictual situation or commenting on it and this is often conveyed non-verbally (e.g. 'If you comment on these conflicting messages or try to escape from this relationship, I will punish you'). Once children have been repeatedly exposed to double-binding family process, they come to experience much of their interactions with their parents as double binding even if all of the conditions for a double bind are not met. This theory was extremely important for the development of family therapy because it offered a sophisticated and coherent explanation for the links between family process and abnormal behaviour, and an account that pointed to the importance of considering communication occurring simultaneously at multiple levels. Of course there were problems with the double-bind theory. Subsequent research has shown that other types of problematic communication characterise families containing children with schizophrenia, notably criticism and overinvolvement, and these affect the course of the disorder, particularly the relapse rate, more than its onset (Kopelowicz, Liberman & Zarate, 2002). The double-bind theory was also a dyadic and linear formulation that did not take the role of fathers or other family members into account, and which did not consider the reciprocal influence of children on parents.

Levels of Communication

The second major contribution of Bateson's (1972) group, was their conceptualisation of communication as a multilevel process and their highlighting of the way that this conceptualisation can account for paradoxical communications which may maintain abnormal behaviour. They pointed out the parallels between the distinction made in computer science between *digital* and *analogical* communication, and *verbal* and *non-verbal* behaviour in humans, and noted that every message has a *report* and *command* function. Thus, the actual words in a message (e.g. 'It's time for dinner') are a verbal report and similar to digital communication in computer science insofar as each word is a discrete sign, arbitrarily signifying a particular meaning. In contrast, each message entails a *metacommunication* about the relationship between speakers, which is usually conveyed non-verbally (e.g. 'I am in a hierarchically superior position to you and am commanding you to sit down and eat your dinner'). This non-verbal command function is similar to analogical communication in computer science insofar as the non-verbal aggression and force with which the words are said are directly proportional to the degree to which the speaker is asserting their hierarchically superior position. Also, there is nothing arbitrary about the relationship between the non-verbal display of aggression and force and the meaning of the command (i.e. 'I am hierarchically superior to you and expect you to obey me'). Bateson's group noticed that abnormal behaviour and psychological problems commonly occurred in families where there were frequent inconsistencies between report and command functions of messages about significant issues. The double-bind theory is one example of this process.

Inspired by the philosophical writings of Whitehead and Russell (1910–1913), Bateson's group argued that report and command functions of messages belong to different logical levels. If report and command functions are inconsistent, one way out of the paradox is to metacommunicate about the inconsistencies between the report and command functions. Whitehead and Russell had used a similar device to solve the paradox posed by the proposition, '*This statement is false*'. If you draw a box around the proposition, you may then outline the implications of the 'proposition in the box' being either true or false. That is, you may metacommunicate about both the meaning of the proposition, which occupies one logical level, and statements about the truth or falsity of the 'proposition in a box', which occupies a different logical level.

At Bateson's suggestion, Jay Haley in the 1950s visited the hypnothera-pist Milton Erickson who was noted for his broad interpretation of the concept of trance and his wide-ranging and creative use of hypnother-apy to work with individuals, couples and families. Subsequently Haley interpreted Erickson's work for the field of family therapy and became his major expositor and biographer (Haley, 1967b, 1973, 1985a, 1985b, 1985c; Lankton & Lankton, 1991). Haley noted that Erickson often delt with apparent resistance in therapy, by communicating with clients in trance at multiple levels. Haley argued that Erickson's multilevel commu-nications were therapeutic double binds, which promoted therapist–client cooperation and problem resolution. These often involved referring to the conscious and unconscious minds as separate recipients of therapeutic communications. For example, 'Your conscious mind might be ready to make progress but your unconscious mind might be wary of the dangers of this; the wisdom of both the conscious and unconscious minds must be respected'. In this example, no matter what the client does, he or she will be cooperating with the therapist, and so a cooperative relationship will be established to provide a foundation for cooperative problem solving.

Systems Theory and Cybernetics

A third major contribution of Bateson's group was the idea that general systems theory combined with insights from cybernetics could offer a framework within which to conceptualise family organisation and pro-cesses and thereby offer an explanation for abnormal behaviour (Guttman, 1991; Hecker et al., 2003; Robbins, Mayorga & Szapoznick, 2003). Bateson's familiarity with general systems theory stemmed from his interest in his father's work as a biologist. His interest in cybernetics stemmed from his involvement in the Macy Foundation conferences in the 1940s where he met Norbert Wiener, founder of cybernetics, and others interested in the area. *General systems theory* was developed by Ludwig von Bertalanfy and others as a framework within which to conceptualise the emergent prop-erties of organisms and complex non-biological phenomena that could not be explained by a mechanistic summation of the properties of their con-stituent parts (Bertalanffy, 1968; Buckley, 1968). General systems theory addresses the question:

How is it that the whole is more than the sum of it parts?

One characteristic of viable systems is their capacity to use feedback about past performance to influence future performance. Norbert Wiener

(1948–1961) coined the term cybernetics to refer to the investigation of feedback processes in complex systems. Cybernetics addresses the question:

How do systems use feedback to remain stable or to adapt to new circumstances?

General systems theory and cybernetics when applied to families, suggested a series of theoretical propositions or hypotheses to Bateson's group. What follows is a selection of some of the more important propositions entailed by a systems view of families. Some of these were quite explicitly stated by Bateson, Jackson, Haley and members of Bateson's team. Others were implicit in their work, but were made explicit at later points in the development of family therapy. I have organised these propositions in as coherent an order as possible and stated each of them as simply as possible. In doing so, there is a risk that the relatively disorganised way in which these propositions entered the family therapy literature is obscured and subtleties of meaning entailed by the propositions may be oversimplified.

1. *The family is a SYSTEM WITH BOUNDARIES and is organised into SUBSYSTEMS.* Within the structural family therapy tradition, distinctions have been made between parental and child subsystems, male and female subsystems, and so forth (Fishman & Fishman, 2003; Wetchler, 2003a).

2. *The boundary around the family sets it apart from the wider social system of which it is one subsystem.* This broader system includes the extended family, the parents' work organisations, the children's schools, the children's peer groups, the involved health care professionals, and so forth. Within multisystemic family therapy, it is routine practice to work with the wider social system if it is involved in problem maintenance or could potentially be involved in problem resolution (Sheidow, Henggeler & Schoenwald, 2003). Bateson (1979) took the view that ultimately everything is part of a single system.

3. *The boundary around the family must be SEMIPERMEABLE to insure adaptation and survival.* That is, a family's boundary must be impermeable enough for the family to survive as a coherent system and permeable enough to permit the intake of information and energy required for continued survival. Isolated families have impermeable boundaries and chaotic families have boundaries that are too permeable (Fishman & Fishman, 2003).

4. *The behaviour of each family member, and each family subsystem, is determined by the pattern of interactions that connects all family members.* Bateson (1972, 1979) referred to this as *the pattern that connects* and it is his most acclaimed insight. Everybody in a family is connected to everybody else and a change in one person's behaviour inevitably leads to a change in all family members. Bateson took the view

that this pattern of organisation must be respected. Therapists may use observation and interviewing processes to understand it and describe their insights to family members, but attempts to change the pattern through the unilateral exercise of power may lead to unintended consequences, which may threaten the integrity of the system. This position has been adopted by social construction-ist therapists, such as Anderson, Cecchin, Boscolo and Hoffman (Anderson, 2003; Campbell, Draper & Crutchley, 1991; Rambo, 2003). In contrast, the MRI group (Fisch, 2004; Segal, 1991) and strategic therapists (Browning & Green, 2003; Rosen, 2003), particularly Jay Haley, have argued that once problem-maintaining patterns are un-derstood, they may be altered through the use of carefully designed direct or paradoxical interventions. These two extreme positions have been referred to as 'aesthetic' and 'pragmatic' approaches to systemic family therapy (Keeney & Sprenkle, 1982).

5. *Patterns of family interaction are rule governed and RECURSIVE. These rules may be inferred from observing repeated episodes of family interaction.* Identifying these recursive patterns, particularly those associated with episodes of problematic behaviour, is a core fam-ily therapy skill common to many family therapy traditions. Many schools of family therapy focus their interventions on disrupting these recursive problem-maintaining patterns of family interaction.

6. *Because these patterns are of the form 'A leads to B leads to C leads to A', the idea of circular causality should be used when describing or explaining family interaction. Descriptions and explanations of families that involve linear (or lineal) causality, of the form 'A leads to B', are probably incomplete and inaccurate.* The idea of circular causality has been used to remove the concept of blame from family therapy discourse. For example, if a family with a child who displays behaviour problems is referred for therapy, the notion of circular causality allows the family therapist to avoid blaming the child's problems on parental mismanagement of the child. Rather, the therapist may view the parents' ineffective management of the child's problems as a legitimate response to the child's frustrating behaviour, and the child's behaviour problems as a response to parental frustration. This use of the concept of circu-larity is therapeutically expedient for many difficulties. However, it becomes problematic when dealing with cases of family violence and abuse. It is clearly unethical and unjust to argue that a child provoked parental abuse or a wife provoked spouse abuse. The dif-ficulty with the concept of circularity is that while members of sys-tems exert mutual influence on each other, they do not all have the same degree of influence. That is, within family systems members are organised hierarchically with respect to the amount of power they hold, and this notion of hierarchy must be coupled with the con-cept of circularity, when working with cases involving the abuse of

power. Bateson (1972) did not include the concept of hierarchy within his consideration of circular causality in family systems. He believed that the concept of unilateral power was flawed and argued that all family members exerted mutual influence on each other. Haley (1976a) and later feminist family therapists (Leupnitz, 1988) argued that mutuality of influence does not entail equality of influence and so the concept of circularity is only clinically useful in family therapy when considered in conjunction with the concepts of hierarchy and power.

7. *Within family systems there are processes which both prevent and promote change. These are referred to as 'morphostasis' (or 'homeostasis') and 'morphogenesis'.* For families to survive as coherent systems, it is critical that they maintain some degree of stability or homeostasis. Thus, families develop recursive behaviour patterns that involve relatively stable rules, roles and routines, and mechanisms that prevent disruption of this stability, a point highlighted particularly in the work of Don Jackson (1968a, 1968b). It is also essential that families have the capacity to evolve over the course of the lifecycle and meet changing demands necessary for the healthy development, adaptation and survival. Thus families require mechanisms for making transitions from one stage of the lifecycle to the next and for dealing with unpredictable and unusual demands, stresses and problems (Carter & McGoldrick, 1999). Often families who lack such morphogenetic forces come to the attention of clinical services. A central feature of family therapy is promoting morphogenesis.

8. *Within a family system one member – the identified patient – may develop problematic behaviour when the family lack the resources for morphogenesis. The symptom of the identified patient serves the positive function of maintaining family homeostasis.* Members of Bateson's group argued that when the integrity of the family system is threatened by the prospect of change, in certain instances one family member may develop problematic behaviour that serves an important function in maintaining family homeostasis or stability. For example, Haley (1997) argued that in some families characterised by covert marital discord, older teenagers develop problematic behaviour that prevents them from developing autonomy and leaving home, because to do so might lead to the covert marital discord becoming overt and to a dissolution of the family. This idea, that an identified patient's symptoms serve a positive function for the family as a whole, gave rise within the strategic therapy tradition and within the original Milan systemic family therapy group to paradoxical interventions (Adams, 2003; Campbell et al., 1991). With the original Milan group's paradoxical interventions, the function of the symptom for the integrity of the system are described to the family; the dangers of change and problem-resolution are highlighted; each family member is advised

to continue to play his or her role in the recursive interaction pattern of which the symptom is part; and finally the identified patient is advised to continue to engage in symptomatic behaviour until some alternative is found. For example, a family with an anorexic girl was informed that the teenage girl's refusal to eat was a generous self-sacrificing gesture vital for holding the family together. It offered the girl a way of ensuring that her parents would remain together, since it was clear she suspected that their loyalties to their own families of origin would force them to separate. It offered each of the parents a way of jointly expressing love for their daughter, while showing loyalty to their own families of origin. As long as the daughter starved herself, the father, like his own father could express his paternal love by being stern with his daughter and disagreeing with his wife's permissive approach. As long as the daughter starved herself, the mother, like her own mother could express her maternal love by being gentle and understanding of her daughter, while disagreeing with her husband's sternness. It, therefore, seemed important for the girl to continue to starve herself, and for the parents to hold to their positions until some alternative way of dealing with these complex family issues became clear.

9. *Negative feedback or deviation reducing feedback, maintains homeostasis and subserves morphostasis.* In families referred for treatment, if it is assumed that the symptom serves a positive function in maintaining the integrity of the family system, then it may also be assumed that when the identified patient begins to improve and this is noticed by family members, this feedback may lead to patterns of family inter-action that intensify the patient's problem and so maintain the status quo (Jackson, 1968a, 1968b). The Milan group's paradoxical interven-tions capitalised on this insight (Adams, 2003; Campbell et al., 1991). The MRI brief therapy group developed a practice of advising clients not to change their symptoms or problematic behaviour too rapidly as this might have negative consequences (Fisch, 2004; Segal, 1991). This was a way of preventing clients from reacting too quickly and extremely to negative feedback.

10. *Positive feedback or deviation amplifying feedback, subserves morphogen-esis. If too much deviation amplifying feedback occurs, in the absence of deviation reducing feedback, then a runaway effect or a snowball effect oc-curs.* In some forms of family therapy, notably that evolved by the MRI group, attempts are made to initiate small instances of deviation amplifying feedback by asking clients to set small achievable goals (Fisch, 2004; Segal, 1991). The assumption is that if these are reached, a snowball effect may occur.

11. *Individuals and factions within systems may show symmetrical behaviour patterns and complementary behaviour patterns.* Bateson (1972) described a process called 'schizmogenesis' in which pairs of individuals or

pairs of factions within a social system develop recursive patterns of behaviour over time thorough repeated interaction. Within these recursive behaviour patterns, the role of each member becomes quite distinct and predictable until the system fragments. He described two types of schizmogenesis, which he termed 'symmetrical' and 'complementary' patterns. With symmetrical behaviour patterns, the behaviour of one member (or faction) of a system invariably elicits a similar type of behaviour from another member (or faction) and over time the intensity of symmetrical behaviour patterns escalate until the members (or factions) separate. For example, a marital couple may become involved in a symmetrical pattern of blaming each other for their marital dissatisfaction and ultimately separate. With complementary behaviour patterns, the increasingly dominant behaviour of one member (or faction) of a system invariably elicits increasingly submissive behaviour from another member (or faction), and over time the intensity of the complementary behaviour pattern increases until the members (or factions) separate. For example, over time an increasingly caregiving husband and an increasingly depressed wife may eventually reach a stage where the relationship is no longer viable because of the mutual anger and disappointment experienced by partners. Healthy and viable family systems and relationships are characterised by a mix of symmetrical and complementary behaviour patterns. Where pairs of members (or factions) within family systems engage exclusively in symmetrical or complementary behaviour patterns, the integrity of the system will be threatened. In such instances, the introduction of even a small amount of the missing behaviour pattern may increase the viability of the system. For example, a couple engaged in a symmetrical process of mutual blaming may become more viable, if each partner makes a caring gesture towards the other on a small number of occasions. In a similar fashion, if a couple engaged in a complementary process of illness and caregiving engage in a few transactions where the roles are reversed, then the viability of the relationship may be enhanced. Within the therapeutic relationship, complementary client–therapist relationships, in which the more the therapist helps the more debilitated the client becomes, may in some instances be productively altered by the therapist taking a one-down position. That is, the therapist may point out that he or she is puzzled by the problem and at loss to know how to proceed at this point and he or she may then speculate that a period of observation without intervention may be most appropriate. Strategic therapists have used Bateson's concepts of symmetrical and complementary schizmogenesis to develop practices such as these (Haley, 1963; Madanes, 1991). Schizmogenesis (either symmetrical or complementary) may be halted by factors that unite the two people or factions engaged in the process. This may explain the development and maintenance of some types of problems in families and their resolution in the face of particular interventions. For example, a child who develops emotional, psychosomatic or behavioural symptoms; a child hospitalized for these or other types of problems; or a child taken into care for abuse or neglect may become a united focus for concern in a family and halt the parents' involvement in either a symmetrical process of mutual blaming or a complementary process of caregiving and illness.

12. *Positive and negative feedback is new information, and new information involves news of difference.* Bateson (1972) argued that information is news of difference and that this is commonly provided through a process of double description. That is, if two descriptions are given of the same events, then the difference in perspectives provides news of difference and this may help family systems to change so as to adapt to their problematic circumstances. Bateson referred to such information as the *difference that makes a difference.* The Milan group and others, particularly Karl Tomm, have developed a variety of types of circular questions that are explicitly designed to introduce news of difference into family systems (Adams, 2003; Campbell et al., 1991). These included asking each family member to describe an interaction between another two family members; asking each family member to rank-order other family members in terms of a particular characteristic; asking each family member to describe the difference between episodes within which the problem occurs and does not occur; or asking each family member how the future (when the problem is resolved) will differ from the past and the present.

13. *Within systems, a distinction may be made between first-order change and second-order change.* With first-order change, the rules governing the interaction within the system remain the same but there may be some alteration in the way in which they are applied. First-order change is continuous or graded. With second-order change, the rules governing relationships within the system change and so there is a discontinuous step-wise change in the system. For example, a family in which a 13-year-old boy who walked to school, was regularly late and was scolded by both teachers and parents for this tardiness, might solve this problem by the parents asking the child to walk to school more quickly on pain of further scolding. This solution would represent first-order change, because the rules about the pattern involving the child's tardiness and the parents' scolding remain essentially unchanged. If however, the parents and teachers jointly invited the boy to take responsibility for getting himself to school on time and offered a prize at the end of the month if he was on time 75% of the time, this would represent second-order change because the rules about the pattern involving the child's tardiness and the parents' response to this would have been radically altered. In most cases, family therapy is concerned with facilitating second-order change.

When families move from one stage of the lifecycle to the next they have to engage in second-order change. That is, they have to replace many of the rules, roles and routines of the earlier stage with new ones. In the example just given, the first-order change solution might be appropriate for a family with a preadolescent boy, but the second-order change solution is more suited to a family containing an adolescent child, since in adolescence youngsters need to learn to take more responsibility for self-management.

14. *Within systems theory, a distinction may be made between first- and second-order cybernetics.* This distinction was implicit in Bateson's work and made explicit by Heinz von Foerster (Howe & von Foerster, 1974). In family therapy based on first-order cybernetics, it is assumed that a therapist independently may observe, assess and intervene in a family system without joining and becoming part of a new system that includes the family and the therapist. In second-order cybernetics, it is assumed that when a therapist engages in family therapy with a family, a new therapeutic system is formed, which includes the therapist and the family. Within this system patterns of mutual influence develop and these may subserve morphostasis or morphogenesis. That is, therapists and families may engage in patters of interaction that maintain the problem as well as patterns that lead to problem resolution. Structural (Fishman & Fishman, 2003), strategic (Rosen, 2003) and MRI brief therapy (Fisch, 2004; Segal, 1991) approaches to family therapy have been based more on first-order rather than second-order cybernetics. Social-constructionist approaches, have been based more on second-order cybernetics (Anderson, 2003; Rambo, 2003).

15. *Within social systems recursive patterns, present in one part of the system, replicate isomorphically in other parts of the system.* This issue, implicit in the work of Bateson, has been made explicit and relevant to the practice of family therapy, systemic consultation and family therapy supervision by others. Transgenerational family therapists have noted that patterns of family interaction may be replicated across generations (Kerr, 2003; Nelson, 2003). For example, a pattern involving marital violence and child behaviour problems may occur across three or more generations (Browne & Herbert, 1997). Multisystemic family therapists have observed that problem-maintaining patterns of interaction within the family may be replicated within the wider social system (Sheidow, Henggeler & Schoenwalt et. al., 2003). For example, in a case of school refusal, a family-based pattern, involving a strong mother–child coalition and a peripheral father, may be replicated in the wider system with a strong coalition between a school counsellor and the family and a peripheral relationship with the class teacher. Within family therapy supervision (Sprenkle & Wilkie, 1996; Storm, McDowell & Long, 2003), in the same case the triadic pattern

involving the parents and child may be replicated in the supervisory system with a strong coalition between the parents and the therapist to which the supervisor becomes peripheral. On the positive side, adaptive patterns of family interaction, such as secure attachment, may be intergenerationally transmitted (Byng-Hall, 1995). In families involved with multiple agencies, where there are well-articulated procedures for interagency cooperation, this pattern of cooperation may come to be replicated within the family (Imber-Black, 1988, 1991). In supervision, where there is a collaborative relationship between the supervisor and the therapist, this may become to be replicated in the therapist's relationship with the family (White & Russell, 1997).

A summary of these 15 propositions drawn from systems theory and cybernetics on which family therapy was based is given in Table 2.1.

16. *Only probabilistic statements may be made about the impact of interventions on social systems.* We can never know with absolute certainty what impact an intervention will have on a family. This is because according to systems theory, in some instances different interventions may have the same impact, because systems have the property of equifinality. It is also because, according to systems theory, in some instances the same intervention leads to different outcomes, because systems have the property of equipotentiality.

Table 2.1 Propositions from systems theory and cybernetics on which family therapy was based

Domain	Propositions
Boundaries	1. The family is a *system with boundaries* and is organised into *subsystems*.
	2. The boundary around the family sets it apart from the wider social system of which it is one subsystem.
	3. The boundary around the family must be *semipermeable* to ensure adaptation and survival.
Patterns	4. The behaviour of each family member, and each family subsystem, is determined by the pattern of interactions that connects all family members.
	5. Patterns of family interaction are rule governed and *recursive*. These rules may be inferred from observing repeated episodes of family interaction.
	6. Circular causality should be used when describing or explaining family interaction.
Stability and change	7. Within family systems there are processes that both prevent and promote change. These are morphostasis (or homeostasis) and morphogenesis.

(Continued on next page)

Table 2.1 (*Continued*)

Domain	Propositions
Stability	8. Within a family system, one member – the identified patient – may develop problematic behaviour when the family lack the resources for morphogenesis. The symptom of the identified patient serves the positive function of maintaining family homeostasis.
	9. Negative feedback or deviation reducing feedback, maintains homeostasis and subserves morphostasis.
Change	10. Positive feedback or deviation amplifying feedback, subserves morphogenesis and may lead to a runaway or snowball effect.
	11. Individuals and factions within systems may show symmetrical behaviour patterns and complementary behaviour patterns, which, if left unchecked, may fragment the system.
	12. Positive and negative feedback is new information, and new information involves news of difference.
	13. A distinction may be made between first-order change and second-order change; between behaving differently according to the system's rules and changing the rules.
Complexity	14. Within systems theory, a distinction may be made between first- and second-order cybernetics; between observed and observing systems.
	15. Within social systems, recursive patterns, present in one part of the system, replicate isomorphically in other parts of the system.
	16. Only probabilistic statements may be made about the impact of interventions on social systems.

THREE ORGANISING THEMES: BEHAVIOUR PATTERNS, BELIEFS AND CONTEXTS

A central theme within the field of family therapy is the belief that therapy targeting family relationships should be grounded in theoretical frameworks that privilege interpersonal factors over personal characteristics and which take account of the family as a social organisation.

The many family therapy schools and traditions may be classified in terms of their central focus of therapeutic concern and in particular with respect to their emphasis on (1) problem-maintaining behaviour patterns; (2) problematic and constraining belief systems and narratives; and (3) historical, contextual and constitutional predisposing factors.

With respect to the first theme, some family therapy schools highlight the role of repetitive patterns of family interaction in the maintenance of problem behaviour and advocate practices that aim to disrupt these patterns of interaction. Schools that fall into this category include the MRI brief therapy approach (Fisch, 2004); strategic therapy (Rosen, 2003); structural therapy (Fishman & Fishman, 2003; Wetchler, 2003a); cognitive-behavioural approaches (Dattilio & Epstein, 2003; Epstein, 2003); and functional family therapy (Sexton & Alexander, 2003).

With respect to the second theme, some schools of family therapy point to the centrality of belief systems and narratives that subserve repetitive interaction patterns that maintain presenting problems. Practices that facilitate the emergence of new belief systems and narratives which liberate family members from problem-maintaining interaction patterns are espoused by these schools. Traditions that fall into this category include constructivism (Feixas, 1995a, 1995b); the original Milan school (Adams, 2003); social-constructionist family therapy approaches (Anderson, 2003; Rambo, 2003); solution-focused family therapy (Duncan, Miller & Sparks, 2003); and narrative therapy (Browning & Green, 2003).

With respect to the third theme, a number of family therapy traditions highlight the role of historical, contextual and constitutional factors in predisposing family members to adopt particular belief systems and engage in particular problematic interaction patterns. Such schools advocate using practices that specifically address these historical, contextual and contextual predisposing factors, including working with members of the extended family and wider social network as well as coaching individuals to manage historical, contextual and constitutional constraints. This category contains transgenerational family therapy (Kerr, 2003; Nelson, 2003); psychoanalytic family therapy traditions (Savage-Scharf & Scharf, 2003); attachment theory-based approaches (Byng-Hall, 1995; Johnson, 2003a); experiential family therapy (Volker, 2003); multisystemic consultation, which includes reference to the wider system (Imber-Black, 1991; Sheidow et al., 2003); and psychoeducational approaches (McFarlane, 1991; Schwoeri & Sholevar, 2003). A summary of this triadic classification system is given in Table 2.2.

This organisation of schools of therapy in terms of their emphases on three particular themes is a useful learning device, but an oversimplification. Most schools of family therapy address problem-maintaining behaviour patterns, constraining beliefs and broader historical, contextual and constitutional factors. However, the classification of schools according to the degree to which they emphasize these three themes, offers a backdrop against which the integrative approach to family therapy set out in Part 2 may be understood.

In the second part of this text a three-column model for formulating cases in family therapy will be presented that uses the three themes mentioned in this part to organise information about a particular case. That is,

Table 2.2 Classification of schools of family therapy according to their emphasis on three themes

Predisposing historical, contextual and constitutional factors	Belief systems and narratives	Problem-maintaining behaviour patterns
Transgenerational	Constructivist	MRI brief therapy
Psychoanalytic	Original Milan school	Strategic therapy
Attachment based	Social constructionist	Structural therapy
Experiential	Solution focused	Cognitive-behavioural
Multisystemic	Narrative	Functional
Psychoeducational		

it will be argued that for any problem, a formulation may be constructed using ideas from many schools of family therapy in which the pattern of family interaction that maintains the problem is specified; the constraining beliefs and narratives which underpin each family members role in this pattern are outlined; and the historical and contextual factors that underpin these belief systems and narratives are specified. In parallel with this, a similar formulation may be constructed to explain why the problem does not occur in exceptional circumstances, which, while similar to problematic situations, differ in important key respects. In light of these formulations, a range of interventions that address factors within each column of these three-column formulations may be considered. Some interventions aim primarily to disrupt problem-maintaining behaviour patterns or amplify exceptional non-problematic patterns. Others aim to help family members re-author their constraining narratives and develop those more liberating and flexible belief systems that underpin exceptions to the problem. Still others aim to modify the negative impact of historical, contextual and constitutional factors or to draw on family strengths in these domains. Thus, while it is accepted that the classification of schools of family therapy according to three themes is an oversimplification, it is a particularly useful oversimplification insofar as it may facilitate a coherent, integrative and flexible approach to the practice of family therapy.

SUMMARY

Family therapy emerged simultaneously in the 1950s in a variety of different countries, services, disciples and therapeutic traditions. The central insight that intellectually united the pioneers of the family therapy movement was that human problems are essentially interpersonal not intrapersonal and so their resolution requires an approach to intervention that directly addresses relationships between people. Family relationships became the focus for intervention since these are of greater significance than most other relationships in people's social networks. The pioneers of family therapy agreed that therapy targeting family relationships should be grounded in theoretical frameworks, which privileged interpersonal factors over personal characteristics and which took account of the family as a social organisation.

A combination of ideas from communications theory, systems theory and cybernetics were used by Gregory Bateson and his colleagues to offer an overarching theoretical framework for family therapy. Within this framework communication was viewed as a complex multilevel process. The family was viewed as a system with semipermeable boundaries comprising constituent subsystems and capable of using negative and positive feedback to promote stability and change respectively. Within this context symptomatic behaviour was viewed as functional insofar as it subserved family stability. Causality within family systems was viewed as circular and involving patterns of mutual influence. The wide variety of family therapy practices that evolved from these ideas addressed the whole family system and took account of both morphostatic and morphogenic forces within the family. The double-bind theory of schizophrenia represents an early application of systems theory and cybernetics to the etiology and maintenance of psychopathology, and so is of historical significance.

Different schools of family therapy accorded differing levels of prominence to the role of family relationships in problem formation, the maintenance of problems, and problem resolution. Some theorists focused predominantly on problem-maintaining interaction patterns and methods of disrupting these rigid repetitive cycles of interaction. Others addressed family members' belief systems, scripts and narratives that underpinned the problem-maintaining interaction patterns. A third focus of therapeutic concern within the field of family therapy was the broader historical and social context out of which problem-related belief systems, scripts and narratives had emerged. In Chapters 3, 4 and 5, these three themes will be used to organise the presentation of theoretical ideas and clinical practices from the major schools of family therapy.

GLOSSARY

Analogical and digital communication. These approximate to non-verbal and verbal communication or to the command and report functions of a message or to the process and content of a conversation. Digital communications are verbal and entail a report of events, for example 'Its time to go'. Analogical communications are non-verbal, entail commands and may be metaphorical in meaning. For example by saying, 'Its time to go', a mother may be non-verbally communicating that she is in charge in this situation, is commanding her daughter to go, and this command may be a metaphor for maternal authority over the daughter's other situations.

Complementary behaviour patterns. Bateson's term for a process of schizmogenesis in which the increasingly dominant behaviour of one member (or faction) of a system invariably elicits increasingly submissive behaviour from another member (or faction), and over time the intensity of the complementary behaviour pattern increases until the members (or factions) separate. For example, over time an increasingly caregiving husband and an increasingly depressed wife may eventually reach a stage where the relationship is no longer viable because of the mutual anger and disappointment experienced by partners.

Cybernetics. A term coined by Norbert Wiener to refer to the study of the way biological and mechanical systems use feedback to maintain stability.

Double-bind theory. A theory developed by Bateson's team to explain how, over extended time periods, conflicting verbal and non-verbal messages given by parents to children with prohibitions against comment or escape lead to schizophrenia.

Double description. Bateson's term for the process by which the discrepancy between two separate accounts of the same event provide information or news of difference.

Equifinality. A property of systems whereby different interventions may have the same impact and similar developmental outcomes may arise from different family processes.

Equipotentiality. A property of systems whereby similar interventions lead to different outcomes and different developmental outcomes may arise from the same family processes.

Feedback. Within cybernetics, information about change in the system that produces action. Negative feedback leads to self-correction and stability. Positive feedback produces change.

First- and second-order change. First-order change involves a change in the relationship among elements in a system without an alteration in the rules governing these relationships. An alteration in these relationship rules is entailed by second-order change.

First- and second-order cybernetics. In therapy based on first-order cybernetics it is assumed that a therapist (or observer) can change a family system while remaining separate and unaffected by the system. Heinz Von Foerster refered to second-order cybernetics as the cybernetics of observing systems, which entails the view that therapists and families become involved in a process of mutual influence.

Homeostasis. A term introduced into family therapy by Don Jackson to refer to the tendency for families to develop recurrent patterns of interaction that help them to maintain stability, particularly under stress.

Isomorphism. The replication of patterns across subsystems of a larger system.

Marital schism and marital skew. Terms coined by Lidz to refer to marriages characterised by chronic conflict (schism) or power imbalance (skew).

Morphogenesis and morphostasis. The processes by which systems change and evolve (genesis) or retain stability (stasis).

Mystification. A process described by Laing where parents distort and relabel a child's experiences.

Pseudomutuality and pseudohostility. Terms coined by Wynne to describe enmeshed and conflictual families respectively.

Rubber fence. Wynne's term for impermeable family boundaries that prevent therapists' interventions from having a sustained influence on patterns of family interaction.

Schizmogenesis. Bateson's term for a process in which pairs of individuals or factions within social systems develop recursive patterns of behaviour over time thorough repeated interaction, which result in fragmentation of the system. He described two types of schizmogenesis, which he termed 'symmetrical' and 'complementary'.

Subsystem. A system within a system, separated from other subsystems by a boundary.

Symmetrical behaviour patterns. Bateson's term for a process of schizmogenesis in which the behaviour of one member (or faction) of a system invariably elicits a similar type of behaviour from another member (or faction), and over time the intensity of symmetrical behaviour patterns escalate until the members (or factions) separate. For example, a marital couple may become involved in a symmetrical pattern of blaming each other for their marital dissatisfaction and ultimately separate.

System. A complex rule-governed organisation of interacting parts, the properties of which transcend the sum of the properties of the parts, and which is surrounded by a boundary that regulates the flow of information and energy in and out of the system. Family systems are complex rule-governed organisations of family members and their interrelationships. The properties of a family cannot be predicted from information about each of the family members only. Family relationships are central to the overall functioning of the family.

FURTHER READING

History of Family Therapy

Broderick, C. & Schrader, S. (1991). The history of professional marital and family Therapy. In A. Gurman & D. Kniskern (Eds), *Handbook of Family Therapy, Vol. 11*, pp. 3–41. New York: Brunner Mazel.

Guerin, P. (1976). Family therapy: The first twenty-five years. In P. Guerin (Ed.), *Family Therapy: Theory and Practice*, pp. 1–30. New York: Gardner Press.

Gurman, A. & Fraenkel, P. (2002). The history of couple therapy: A millennial review. *Family Process*, **41**, 199–259.

Guttman, H. (1991). Systems theory, cybernetics and epistemology. In A. Gurman & D. Kniskern (Eds), *Handbook of Family Therapy, Vol. 11*, pp. 41–64. New York: Brunner Mazel.

Hecker, L., Mims, G. & Boughner, S. (2003). General systems theory, cybernetics and family therapy. In L. Hecker & J. Wetchler (Eds), *An Introduction to Marital and Family Therapy*, pp. 39–62. New York: Haworth.

Hoffman, L. (2001). *Family Therapy: An Intimate History*. London: Karnack.

Kaslow, F. (1980). History of family therapy in the united states: A kaleidoscopic view. *Marriage and Family Review*, **3**, 77–111.

Wetchler, J. (2003). The history of marital and family therapy. In L. Hecker & J. Wetchler (Eds), *An Introduction to Marital and Family Therapy*, pp. 3–38. New York: Haworth.

Key Reference Works

Barker, P. (1998). *Basic Family Therapy*, 4th edn. Oxford: Blackwell.

Becvar, D. & Becvar, R. (2003). *Family Therapy: A Systemic Integration*, 5th edn. New York: Allyn & Bacon.

Dallos, R. & Draper, R. (2000). *An Introduction to Family Therapy*. Buckingham, UK: Open University Press.

Gladding, S. (2001). *Family Therapy: History, Theory, and Practice*, 3rd edn. New York: Prentice Hall.

Goldenberg, I. & Goldenberg, H. (2003). *Family Therapy: An Overview*, 6th edn. New York: Brooks-Cole.

Gorell-Barnes, G. (2004). *Family Therapy in Changing Times*, 2nd edn. London: Palgrave Macmillan.

Gurman, A. & Kniskern, D. (1981). *Handbook of Family Therapy*, New York: Brunner/ Mazel.

Gurman, A. & Kniskern, D. (1991). *Handbook of Family Therapy, Vol. 11*. New York: Brunner/Mazel.

Gurman, A. & Jacobson, N. (2002). *Clinical Handbook of Couple Therapy*, 3rd edn. New York: Guilford.

Hecker, L. & Wetchler, J. (2003). *An Introduction to Marital and Family Therapy*. New York: Haworth.

Nichols, M. & Schwartz, R. (2004). *Family Therapy: Concepts and Methods*, 6th edn. Boston: Rearson.

Piercy, F., Sprenkle, D., Wetchler, J. & Associates (1996). *Family Therapy Sourcebook*, 2nd edn. New York: Guilford.

Sexton, T., Weeks, G. & Robbins, M. (2003). *Handbook of Family Therapy*. New York: Brunner-Routledge.

Speed, B. & Carpenter, J. (Eds) (1998). *Journal of Family Therapy: Twentieth Anniversary Issue*. **20**(2) (complete issue).

Street, E. & Dryden, W. (1988). *Family Therapy in Britain*. London: Harper & Row.

Vetere, A. & Dallos, R. (2003). *Working Systemically with Families. Formulation, Intervention and Evaluation*. London: Karnac.

Books by Bateson

Bateson, G. (1936/1958). *Naven*. Stanford: Stanford University Press.

Bateson, G. & Mead, M. (1942). *Balinese Character. A Photographic Analysis*. New YorK: Academy of Sciences.

Bateson, G. & Ruesch, J. (1951). *Communication: The Social Matrix of Psychiatry*. New York: Norton.

Bateson, G. (1972). *Steps to an Ecology of Mind*. New York: Ballentine. (Republished in 2000 by University of Chicago Press with a new foreword by Catherine Bateson.)

Bateson, G. (1974). *Perceval's Narrative: A Patient's Account of his Psychosis 1830–1832*. New York: William Morrow.

Bateson, G. (1979). *Mind and Nature: A Necessary Unity*. New York: Dutton.

Bateson, G. & Bateson, C. (1987). *Angels Fear*. New York: Macmillan.

Bateson, G. (1991). *A Sacred Unity*. New York: Harper Collins.

Chapter 3

THEORIES THAT FOCUS ON BEHAVIOUR PATTERNS

It has already been noted in Chapter 2 that family therapy schools and traditions may be classified in terms of their central focus of therapeutic concern. That is they may be classified with respect to their emphasis on problem-maintaining behaviour patterns; problematic and constraining belief systems; and historical, contextual and constitutional predisposing factors. This chapter is concerned with family therapy traditions that highlight the role of repetitive patterns of family interaction in the maintenance of problem behaviour. Schools that fall into this category include the MRI brief therapy approach; strategic family therapy; structural family therapy; cognitive-behavioural family therapy; and functional family therapy. A summary of their main characteristics is given in Table 3.1.

MRI BRIEF THERAPY

The principal figures in this tradition include Don Jackson, John Weakland, Paul Watzlawick, Lynn Segal, Arthur Bodin, Robert Fish and Wendel Ray (Cade & O'Hanlon, 1993; Duncan et al., 2003; Fisch & Schlanger, 1999; Fisch et al., 1982; Green & Flemons, 2004; Hoyt, 2001; Ray, 2004; Segal, 1991; Shoham & Rohbaugh, 2002; Watzlawick et al., 1974; Weakland & Fisch, 1992; Weakland & Ray, 1995). The Mental Research Institute, was founded by members of Bateson's group in the late 1950s as the Bateson project came to a close and in 1967, the Brief Therapy project at MRI was set up. The MRI brief approach to family therapy is a pragmatic integration of Bateson's (1972) ideas on cybernetics and systems theory; Milton Erickson's unique approach to hypnotherapy (Haley, 1973); and Heinz Von Foerster's (1981) constructivism.

The central organising idea of the MRI approach is that ineffective attempts to solve problems eventually come to maintain these problems, and so are aptly called 'ironic processes'. Assessment should therefore focus on tracking repetitive behaviour patterns involving problems and ineffective attempted solutions. Treatment, in turn, should disrupt

Table 3.1 Key features of family therapy schools and traditions that emphasise the role of problem-maintaining behaviour patterns

Domain	MRI	Strategic	Structural	Cognitive-behavioural	Functional
Key figures	Don Jackson John Weakland Paul Watzlawick Lynn Segal Arthur Bodin Robert Fish Wendel Ray	Jay Haley Cloe Madanes	Salvador Minuchin Charles Fishman Braulio Montalvo Jorge Colapinto	Gerry Patterson Neil Jacobson Richard Stuart Frank Dattilio Donald Baucom Norman Epstein Ian Falloon	James Alexander Cole Barton Bruce Parsons Thomas Sexton
Healthy family functioning	Absence of recursive problem-maintaining behaviour patterns	Clear intergenerational hierarchies Flexible management of lifecycle transitions Mix of complementary and symmetrical transactions in family relationships Love rather than violence as main value	Clear boundaries between parental and child subsystems Flexible roles Moderate level of emotional engagement between family members	Parents work cooperatively to set clear rules for children. They reinforce prosocial behaviour but not antisocial behaviour and have positive cognitions about their children Marital partners engage in high rates of mutually reinforcing behaviour, high rates of emotional acceptance of relationship incompatibilities, have good problem solving and communication skills, and have positive cognitions about each other	The functions of regulating relational connection and hierarchy are fulfilled by non-problematic behaviour patterns

(Continued on next page)

Table 3.1 (*Continued*)

Domain	MRI	Strategic	Structural	Cognitive-behavioural	Functional
Unhealthy functioning	Presence of recursive problem-maintaining behaviour patterns	Pathological triangles involving incongruous intergenerational hierarchies Difficulty making lifecycle transitions Some family relationships exclusively symmetrical or complementary The presenting problem is a metaphor for the actual problem Problems with giving and receiving love or control	Rigid or diffuse boundaries between parental and child subsystems Excessively chaotic or rigid roles Extreme family enmeshment or disengagement	Parent–child relationships are characterised by coercive cycles of interaction, unclear rules, little reinforcement of prosocial behaviour, and parents and children have negative cognitions about each other Marital relationships are characterised by little mutual reinforcement, coercive cycles of interaction, little emotional acceptance of incompatibilities, poor problem solving and communication skills and partners have negative cognitions about each other	The functions of regulating relational connection and hierarchy are fulfilled by problematic behaviour patterns
Assessment	Identification of recursive problem-maintaining behaviour patterns	Identification of pathological triangles Lifecycle transition problems Symmetrical and complementary relationships	Mapping out family structure including boundaries, role flexibility and degree of family engagement	Functional analysis of problem behaviour to identify problem-maintaining interaction patterns	Clarifying the function of the problematic behaviour for all family members, the pattern of interaction and set of relationships

			within which it is embedded and the personal characteristics of family members that serve as constraints or aids to family change	Help the family replace problematic behaviour with non-problematic behaviour to fulfil the same function of regulating relational connection and hierarchy	
Scope of treatment goals	Disruption of recursive problem-maintaining behaviour Small goals	Problems with giving and receiving love and control	Disruption of problem-maintaining behaviour patterns associated with pathological triangles, avoidance of making lifecycle transition, complementary and symmetrical relationships, and managing issues of love and control	Promoting a healthy family structure by disrupting chaotic, rigid, enmeshed or disengaged problem-maintaining interaction patterns	Disrupt coercive cycles of interaction and emotional non-acceptance and restructure negative cognitions
Therapy	Restraining interventions Paradoxical interventions Stop doing more of the same interventions Reframing	Changing parental roles in pathological triangles Empowering parents with late adolescent leaving-home problems	Restructuring the family Joining Enactments Reframing Unbalancing Boundary making	Contingency contracting Time out Problem-solving and communication training Cognitive restructuring Emotional acceptance training Self-control training	Treatment involves an engagement phase of therapy in which reframing is used to help family members move from blaming and making personal attributions for

(Continued on next page)

Table 3.1 (*Continued*)

Domain	MRI	Strategic	Structural	Cognitive-behavioural	Functional
		Rituals for family violence and abuse Paradoxical interventions and pretending intervention with specific symptoms Reframing in terms of symptom function	Challenging family assumptions		problems to viewing problems as situationally determined This is followed by a behaviour changed phase of therapy in which contingency contracting communication and problem-solving training occurs Generalisation and relapse prevention is occurs in the third phase of therapy
Special areas of applicability	Focal behavioural problems Relationship problems	Child behaviour problems Adolescent leaving home problems Sexual abuse Marital problems	Multiproblem families with delinquent adolescents Families with children who have psychosomatic complaints	Childhood conduct problems Marital discord	Delinquency

these problem-maintaining behaviour patterns or ironic processes, by paradoxically (or counter-intuitively) inviting clients to stop trying to solve their problems.

For example, Watzlawick et al. (1974) describe how a wife's concern about her husband's lack of openness led her to continually enquire about his whereabouts, his thoughts and feelings and his plans. However, he perceived his wife's concern as overly intrusive and became secretive. In turn his wife became more inquisitive. Assessment focused on clarifying this vicious cycle of demanding and withdrawing behaviour. Treatment aimed to disrupt the cycle and replace it with the seeds of a behaviour pattern that would become a virtuous cycle of mutually satisfying encounters.

The MRI approach does not entail a well-articulated model of the functional and dysfunctional family, but does involve the view that families who repeatedly use ineffective solutions for problems will be less well adjusted than those that show greater flexibility and avoid becoming trapped in cycles that involve doing 'more of the same'.

Assessment and the MRI Approach

Assessment is typically conducted by interview, and it is only essential for the 'customers' – that is, the people who most wants change to occur – to be present. The MRI model distinguishes between 'customers' who are committed to resolving the problem and 'window-shoppers' who are attending treatment to satisfy someone else. For example, a person with a drink problem who denies the difficulty but attends therapy at their spouse's request is a 'window-shopper'. There is no requirement for the whole family to attend brief therapy. Indeed, MRI brief marital and family therapy is often conducted with individuals, but the conceptual framework for this individual work involves identifying others who are trapped in a repetitive cycle of interaction around a specific clearly defined presenting problem. The identification of this repetitive cycle, which includes the problem and ineffective attempted solutions or ironic processes, is the core assessment task. Historical, constitutional and broader contextual predisposing and precipitating factors are of little concern in the assessment of problems from an MRI perspective. The cycle of interaction around the presenting problem is identified by inviting clients to describe recent episodes of the problem and attempts to solve it. The therapist probes about the details of who was involved and what they did. A typical assessment question is 'If I had a video of a problematic episode, what would I see?'. During the assessment process, the emphasis is on developing a step-by-step description of the way episodes begin, progress and conclude. Such accounts clarify the nature of problem-maintaining factors and these typically involve ineffective solutions.

Ineffective solutions, or ironic processes, fall into four main categories:

1. Attempts at making the self or others deliberately be spontaneous. For example, trying to force another family member to spontaneously feel love or respect towards oneself.
2. Using solutions that do not entail risk when some risk taking is inevitable. For example, trying to cope with anxiety by avoiding the anxiety-provoking situation.
3. Trying to resolve conflict through oppositional arguing.
4. Confirming an accuser's suspicions by defending oneself. When accused of being distant, a spouse who responds defensively confirms the accuser's suspicions that the spouse is being distant.

As part of assessment, the smallest noticeable change that would be required for the client to believe that therapeutic progress has occurred is identified. This is then set as the treatment goal. A typical goal identification question is, 'When things take a small turn for the better, what will be happening that is different from the current situation?' This idea of setting minimalist goals rests on the assumption that once a small change occurs, provided it is noticeably different from the status quo, then this will be maintained and expand through positive feedback.

The quality of the therapist–client relationship is also an important focus for assessment. Clients may engage in predominantly compliant or predominantly defiant relationships with therapists and interventions should be designed to fit with clients' predominant styles. So, tasks requiring compliance should be offered to complaint clients and, for defiant clients, tasks requiring resistance should be offered.

Clients' explanations of their problems and their expectations concerning treatment also deserve assessment. These reflect the clients' framing of their problems, and quite often MRI interventions involve offering alternative reframings of the problem which fit to some degree with clients' original framing. For example, a parent who describes her daughter as extremely bad and needing punishment may be offered a reframe, that the extremely bad behaviour reflects the extent of an underlying insecurity, which requires very clear rules concerning acceptable behaviour and very predictable daily routines involving reassurance that she is loved and cherished. Reframing derives from the constructivist epistemology of Heinz Von Foerster, which underpins the MRI approach. According to this epistemology, there is not a single true way to construe events. Rather, any set of events is open to multiple punctuations and reframings, which differ in their usefulness.

Treatment and the MRI Approach

The overall aim of MRI brief therapy is to help clients resolve their presenting problems. MRI brief therapy is not concerned with restructuring the organisation of the family or facilitating personal growth. Furthermore, brief therapy sessions are a forum within which clients and therapists work towards developing and reviewing tasks that are carried out between sessions. It is these intersession tasks that are the main avenue through which change occurs. The process within the therapy sessions is of less importance in promoting change.

Treatment is typically conducted in under 10 sessions and relies for its effectiveness on designing interventions that will help clients break out of problem-maintaining interaction patterns. The therapist's positioning is not collaborative but strategic. That is, the therapist carefully plans to maintain a high level of control over the therapeutic process and dictate the terms of the therapeutic contract. This positioning involves therapists not committing themselves to a premature statement of the nature of the problem or the ideal solution, even if these are apparent to the therapist. MRI therapists may also strategically withhold information about the cybernetic and systemic rationale underpinning their interventions. Finally, to encourage clients to work harder at resolving their problems, MRI therapists may take a one-down position with respect to their clients, and claim temporary puzzlement or helplessness in response to their clients' effective or ineffective solution-oriented behaviour. Thus, MRI brief therapists may say, 'I am mystified by the improvement you describe. I do not understand it', or 'Your problems seem deeply entrenched and I am uncertain about how to advise you to proceed at this point'.

The most commonly used MRI intervention involves describing the clients' problem-maintaining pattern, which covers the problematic behaviour and their unsuccessful attempted solutions or ironic processes, and then using therapeutic restraint. Clients are invited 'to go slow'; 'to avoid making things worse by impulsively rushing for simple but inappropriate solutions for complex difficult problems'; and 'to make step-by-step changes gradually because these rest on a firmer foundation than large sudden changes'. With couples involved in demand-withdraw interaction patterns, where the complaint is the husband's lack of openness, the therapeutic invitation would be to not try to increase the husband's openness too rapidly, because this might actually make things worse. Therapeutic restraint, typically has the paradoxical effect of accelerating change, probably because the therapist places him- or herself in a complementary relationship with the client. The therapist's increasingly cautious invitations to exercise restraint are met with clients' increasingly bolder strides towards problem resolution. When rapid changes occur in response to invitations to 'go slow', further cautious invitations to 'go slow' are typically given rather than congratulations for making major changes. Therapists may express puzzlement about the changes, doubt about their permanence, explore the dangers of rapid improvement and predict a relapse. These therapeutic restraints may further accelerate positive changes. All credit for positive changes is attributed to the client, not the therapist. Termination occurs without celebration, and often with the therapist expressing puzzlement at the rate of the client's improvement. When clients request further work for other problems, therapists suggest postponing a further episode of therapy to allow for consolidation of changes that have already been made.

A related MRI intervention is to invite clients to list negative consequences of change. Some common negative consequences of change are: new habits are unfamiliar; change is scary; change requires risk taking; change involves greater intimacy; negotiation will be necessary; change requires new and difficult skills; and 'if it doesn't work it will be my fault'. On the basis of these negative consequences, clients may be advised to make haste slowly. Later in treatment, if clients show resistance or reluctance to improve, they may be invited to explore those negative consequences of change that they initially listed as preventing them from improving. They may be asked to consider going slow because the negative consequences are too great.

Problem-maintaining interaction patterns may be disrupted by directly inviting clients, who are judged to be compliant, to do 'less of the same', or to stop doing 'more of the same'. The rationale for these invitations often involves reframing the client's views about the problem in terms that the client can accept. For example, parents of a non-compliant asthmatic who continually remind him to take his medication, may be invited to view his non-compliance as a statement about his need for independence. They may be invited to offer him the opportunity of developing independent control of his health, by asking him about his medication once and once only each day at 7 p.m.

Problem-maintaining interaction patterns may be disrupted by paradoxically inviting clients, who are judged to be defiant, to do 'more of the same' and offering a plausible reframing of the problem, a rationale for the paradoxical task. For example, couples whose problem is repetitive arguments may have these reframed as a sign of strong commitment to getting the relationship right, and be invited to engage in 15 minutes of arguing each day at a specified time.

In MRI brief therapy, unique interventions are constructed in each case to disrupt problem-maintaining attempted-solutions or ironic processes. However, for the different types of attempted solutions listed in the earlier section on assessment, templates for developing interventions have been developed. What follows is a sketch of these.

Where clients' attempted solutions involve attempts at making themselves improve spontaneously by resisting an urge or controlling an involuntary action, they may be invited to practise the problem under specified conditions, to improve control over the problem and closely monitor what happens. For example, children with motor tics or men with premature ejaculation may be invited to conduct daily practice sessions.

Where clients' attempted solutions involve trying to make others behave spontaneously, effective MRI interventions involve arranging for the client to agree that when the other person agrees to do the required act voluntarily in response to a request, the problem has shown the first sign of improving. For example, a man who wants his partner to express love spontaneously may be invited to consider, as a minimum treatment goal, his partner agreeing to take a daily walk with him voluntarily, in response to an open request. That is, the minimum goal is not, 'She wants to go for a walk with me', but rather 'She agrees voluntarily to go for a walk with me'.

Where problems are maintained by solutions that do not entail risk when some risk taking is inevitable, clients may be invited to take small controllable risks and, once they have done this, to be cautious about making further progress. Clients with exam anxiety, for example, may be invited to deliberately not complete a question on the exam paper.

Where conflict is maintained through oppositional arguing, clients may be invited within the context of an appropriate reframe to take a one-down position. For example, members of a conflictual couple whose arguments have been reframed as an expression of concern, connectedness and commitment to the relationship, may be invited after each fight to apologise to each other for not arguing harder and longer and to thank each other for these apologies.

Where an accuser's suspicions are repeatedly confirmed by the other person defending him- or herself, the defender may be invited to agree with the accuser or to not take the criticism seriously. For example, a husband accused of being secretive, may be invited to accept that this is his true nature and he must confess, whenever accused, that he is indeed secretive.

There is a risk that this brief sketch of interventions misrepresents the extraordinary respect and thoughtfulness with which MRI brief therapists practise, and if this is the case it is a reflection on the brevity of the account rather than nature of MRI practice.

STRATEGIC FAMILY THERAPY

Jay Haley (Grove & Haley, 1993; Haley, 1963, 1973, 1976a, 1984, 1996, 1997; Haley & Richeport-Haley, 2003), the founder of strategic family therapy, was initially a member of Bateson's group, an interpreter of the works of the hypnotherapist Milton Erickson (Haley, 1985a, 1985b, 1985c; Lankton & Lankton, 1991), a colleague in Philadelphia of Salvador Minuchin, founder of structural family therapy and subsequently a co-founder with Cloe Madanes (1981, 1984, 1990, 1991, 1994; Madanes, Keim & Smelser, 1995) of the Washington Family Therapy Institute. Because of Haley and Minuchin's association, it is not surprising that their strategic and structural approaches to family therapy are often blended together into coherent practice models (Behar-Mitrani & Perez, 2000; Keim & Lappin, 2002).

A central underlying theme of strategic family therapy is that families are ambivalent about change, usually because family problems serve some important interpersonal protective function for some family members, and so therapists must carefully design specific directives to undermine this ambivalence or resistance and so help families resolve their presenting problems, while also providing the family with an opportunity to deal with the complex interpersonal problem that the symptom was designed to solve. For example, the misbehaviour of a depressed unemployed father's son may distract the father from his depression. Managing the misbehaviour gives the father a focus for his attention and in this sense serves the function of keeping the father from sinking into depression. In this instance, requesting both parents to spend exclusive private time with each other planning how best to manage the son, would address both the father's need for support and the boy's need for security and structure.

The Healthy Family and Strategic Therapy

Within strategic therapy it is assumed that healthy families have clearly defined intergenerational hierarchies, so that it is quite clear that for important issues, parents are in charge and have the final veto on major family decisions. It is also assumed that when healthy families move from one stage of the family lifecycle to the next, they are flexible enough to modify their rules, roles and routines sufficiently to meet the demands of the new lifecycle stage. For example, when families move from having preadolescent children to having adolescents, there is usually a requirement for the teenager to have increased autonomy and privacy, and also to take on more age-appropriate responsibilities. Healthy families manage such changes flexibly, solving problems and negotiating new arrangements as required and without excessive difficulty. A third assumption of strategic therapy is that within family relationships there is a mix of complementary and symmetrical transactions (which have been defined in Chapter 2). A final assumption is that healthy families select love rather than violence as the central value and distribute love within the family in a non-intrusive, non-violent way.

The Problematic Family and Strategic Therapy

In contrast to this profile of the healthy family, within strategic therapy it is assumed that problems occur when the hierarchical structure of the family is unclear; when there is a lack of flexibility in moving from one lifecycle stage to the next; and when family relationships are characterised exclusively by complementary or symmetrical transactions.

Haley argues that when there are differing overt and covert hierarchical structures within a family or social system and this difference is denied, problems occur. For example, if it is overtly accepted that both parents set rules for all the children in a family, but covertly this agreement is undermined by, for example, the son breaking the rules and the mother not bringing this to the father's attention or sanctioning the son for his misbehaviour, and this arrangement between the mother and son is denied, then it is probable that the son will develop behaviour problems and the couple will experience marital conflict. Haley also argues that when these types of 'pathological triangles' occur, they prevent families from moving smoothly from one stage of the family lifecycle to the next. For example, they may make it difficult for young adults to leave home and develop a lifestyle independent of their family of origin, because to do so would entail the risk that the parents would separate and the family as a whole would disintegrate. Incongruous hierarchies may also occur within marital relationships; for example, in a couple where one member is depressed, overtly it may appear that the depressed person is hierarchically subordinate to their partner but covertly the depressed person may be hierarchically superior since the depression may play a dominant role in organising the relationship. It is also assumed within strategic therapy that relationships, particularly marital relationships, which are characterised exclusively by symmetrical transactions (such as persistent oppositional arguments) and relationships characterised by exclusively complementary transactions (such as caregiving and caretaking) inevitably become seriously problematic.

Within problematic families, symptoms may be conceptualised as metaphorical messages about problems in other domains. For example, a conflict between a child and parents about school attendance may reflect a metaphorical communication about a conflict between a husband and wife about the woman working.

Family difficulties are conceptualised within Madanes's (1991) formulation of strategic therapy as arising from attempts to dominate and control; to be loved; to love and protect; or to repent and forgive. Problems associated with domination and control include aggression, delinquency and some forms of drug abuse. Those associated with the wish to be loved include depression, anxiety and eating disorders. Problems associated with the desire to love and protect include intrusive domination of a partner or child, and consequent excessive guilt, suicide threats and gestures, and thought disorder. Problems associated with the wish to repent and to forgive include sexual and physical abuse.

Assessment in Strategic Therapy

Assessment in strategic therapy involves identifying the specific problem with which the family want help; clarifying the pattern of interaction around the problem; and clarifying the role of hierarchical incongruities, lifecycle stage 'stuckness', and exclusive reliance on symmetrical or complementary transactions in this cycle. The way the family manage the issues of power, the need to be loved, to love and protect, and to repent and forgive is also addressed.

The assessment interview is segmented into four parts (Haley, 1976a), opening with a brief social stage where the therapist as host welcomes family members, often starting with the most peripheral member, usually the father. In the second stage of the assessment interview, each member gives an account, from his or her perspective, of the problem and the sequences of events that typically precede and follow it. Family members' explanations of the problems, previous attempted solutions and the effects of these are also clarified. In this second stage of assessment, the therapist by implication conveys that the problem is embedded in a pattern of interaction involving some or all family members, but is careful not to offer any interpretation or reframing of the problem at this stage. In the third stage of the assessment interview, family members are invited to discuss the problem among themselves. During the second stage, it typically has become apparent that different family members hold different views of the problem, different explanations for it and advocate different solutions. During the third interactional stage, family members may be encouraged to discuss these differing views and the therapist observes the interaction noting the overt and covert hierarchies and problem-solving sequences within the family. Following the interactional stage, in the fourth and final stage of the assessment interview, the therapist helps family members define the problem in solvable terms and specify their therapy goals in concrete, visualisable terms. Vague goals, like 'To get in touch with our feelings', are not acceptable within strategic therapy. Goals must be concrete, such as 'To have a game of family scrabble together for 30 minutes every night for a week without fighting'. It is vital that the problem be defined this way so that later it will be clear whether or not therapy has been successful in helping clients reach their goals. The assessment session may close with the agreement of a goal and agreeing to work towards that goal over a limited number of sessions.

Treatment in Strategic Family Therapy

Treatment in strategic family therapy involves conceptualising or formulating problems within the therapeutic team; reframing problems for clients; and giving directives to clients that will disrupt the pattern of interaction which maintains the presenting problem. Therapy sessions are largely devoted to reframing, giving directives and reviewing progress. Therapeutic change in strategic therapy is assumed to arise from responding to directives between sessions, since it is between sessions that problem-maintaining behaviour patterns occur. These problem-maintaining behaviour patterns, as has been noted, often involve hierarchical incongruities.

With pre-adolescent children with behaviour problems maintained by a denied covert alliance between the mother and child to which the father is subordinate, Haley typically corrects such hierarchical incongruities by directing the father to exclusively take charge of the child and give the child's mother a well-earned rest from dealing with the youngster's misbehaviour (Haley, 1976a). Once the child's behaviour problems abate, the parents may be directed to manage conjointly the child as a team.

With late adolescent conduct problems, drug abuse and psychiatric difficulties maintained by a denied covert alliance between the mother and child to which the father is subordinate, Haley directs both parents to cooperate in treating the adolescent as a disobedient pre-adolescent, with strictly enforced house rules until the adolescent begins to behave more responsibly. The adolescent's difficulties are reframed as controllable, rather than uncontrollable (especially in the case of psychotic symptoms) and as a reflection of irresponsibility and immaturity, rather than illness. When parents unite in the management of their adolescent, problem-maintaining interaction patterns entailing the incongruous hierarchies are disrupted and the adolescent's problems resolve. In such, instances, Haley cautions against addressing marital discord directly, even if clients bring this issue up. Rather, he suggests that dealing with such issues be postponed until the child-focused difficulty is resolved.

Haley, inspired by the work of Milton Erickson, the hypnotherapist, has used the prescription of ordeals as a way of disrupting problem-maintaining interaction patterns. Ordeals involve inviting clients to complete a difficult task each time they have an urge to behave symptomatically. For example, a bulimic may be invited to flush binge food that they have hand-mixed down the toilet with the family watching when a binge urge occurs.

Prescribing the symptom under specified conditions can disrupt symptom-maintaining interaction patterns. For example, a child with a problem of fire-setting was directed to light fires regularly under parental supervision. Prescribing the symptom is an apparently paradoxical or counter-intuitive intervention.

Madanes has used pretending tasks to disrupt problem-maintaining interaction patterns. With pretending tasks, clients are invited to pretend to behave symptomatically some of the time, while other family members are invited to see if they can distinguish between real and pretend symptoms or to behave as if the symptoms were genuine. For example, a husband may be invited to pretend to be depressed some of the time when he is not truly depressed and his wife may be invited to give the support and care she typically offers when he is genuinely depressed, regardless of whether he is pretending or not.

Reuniting the family is an approach used when family members become estranged. For example, where an adolescent makes a suicide gesture, this may be framed as a need for love and protection, and the parents, older siblings and extended family may be organised into a 24 hours-a-day suicide watch, offering the self-injurious adolescent constant monitoring, supervision and protection until their will to live and sense of being accepted by the family returns.

When sexual abuse occurs within the family and is maintained by a pattern of interaction involving denial and secrecy, Madanes (1990), has developed a 16-step intervention programme that disrupts this cycle of abuse and secrecy. The intervention involves facilitating acknowledgement of the abuse by the whole family; contextualising the abuse, since it is often part of a multigenerational pattern; facilitating repentance and reparation; organising continued protection; and opening up the possibility of forgiveness.

STRUCTURAL FAMILY THERAPY

Structural family therapy was developed in New York at the Wiltwyck school for delinquent boys and later at the Philadelphia Child Guidance Clinic in the late 1950s and 1960s by Salvador Minuchin and his colleagues Braulio Montalvo, Charles Fishman, Bernice Rosman and others (Colapinto, 1991; Elizur & Minuchin, 1989; Fishman, 1988, 1993; Fishman & Fishman, 2003; Minuchin, 1974, 1984; Minuchin & Fishman, 1981; Minuchin, Lee & Simon, 1996; Minuchin, Montalvo, Guerney, Rosman & Schumer, 1967; Minuchin & Nichols, 1993; Minuchin, Rosman & Baker, 1978). Minuchin's background was in Harry Stack Sullivan's tradition of social or interpersonal psychiatry, and during the early 1950s Minuchin was mentored by Nathan Ackerman, a founding father of family therapy in the USA. Both Jay Haley and Cloe Madanes (the strategic therapists described in the previous section) worked with Minuchin's team at Philadelphia during the 1960s. Minuchin initially developed his active family-based approach because his working-class clients at the Wyltwick school were unresponsive to verbal passive psychoanalytically-based individual therapy. Structural family therapy is now the most widely practiced and influential approach to family therapy in the world. Although Minuchin retired in 1995, the Minuchin Centre for the Family in New York continues the structural family therapy tradition.

The central idea underlying structural family therapy is that problematic family organisational structures may compromise their capacity to meet the demands of lifecycle changes or unpredictable intrafamilial or extrafamilial stresses. Structural family therapists join with families, come to understand their structure and the demands that the family are having difficulty meeting; facilitate enactment of their problem-solving attempts; and, through unbalancing and boundary making, help the family use its own latent resources to modify its structure so that it can meet the demands it faces. For example, in helping families with anorexic children, Minuchin noted the lack of parental coalitions and the diffuse intergenerational boundaries. He unbalanced these family systems by asking the parents to feed their daughters in the early stages of therapy and later once weight gain had begun by inviting the girls to take control of their own weight. He drew boundaries by insisting that, once out of the danger zone, the girls' weight be monitored away from the parents, and the parents engage in joint problem solving and decision making about managing routine aspects of family life.

Healthy and Unhealthy Families and Structural Family Therapy

Within structural family therapy, healthy families are assumed to have a structure that permits them to meet lifecycle demands which is characterised by clear intergenerational boundaries between parent and child subsystems. These should be neither rigid nor diffuse and entail neither rigid nor chaotic family functioning. In terms of emotional closeness, they are neither enmeshed nor disengaged.

In contrast, family structures characterised by diffuse or rigid boundaries and extreme enmeshment or disengagement, and excessively weak or rigid and arbitrary hierarchies make it difficult for families to respond to environmental or developmental stresses. Disengaged families are slow to mobilise support when needed, whereas enmeshed families have difficulty permitting the development of autonomy. Both disengagement and enmeshment are strategies for conflict avoidance. They allow couples to avoid the pain entailed by conflict resolution, which would lead to modification of the rules governing the family structure. Disengaged parents avoid conflict by cutting off conversations about change. Enmeshed parents avoid conflict by denying differences, and in some instances by detouring conflict through a child. Parents may submerge their own differences and express either joint concern about the child or joint anger at the child. These triangulations tend to lead to aggressive or psychosomatic responses respectively. In families with weak hierarchies, parents fail to offer joint leadership and executive functions may be taken by so called parental-children, who behave as if they are parents. In families with rigid arbitrary hierarchies, parents may inappropriately abuse their power without taking account of children's needs. A dysfunctional family, according to structural family therapists, is one that cannot fulfil its functions of nurturing the growth of its members.

Assessment and Treatment in Structural Family Therapy

Assessment and treatment occur concurrently in structural family therapy. Those members of the family and wider social system thought to be most relevant to the resolution of the problem are invited to the first session. Where schools and other agencies are involved, staff from these settings may be invited. The process of assessment and therapy begins with joining, when the therapist and clients unite to form a therapeutic system. During the joining process, the therapist develops a working alliance with family members. The therapist tracks each person's description of the problem in a blow-by-blow manner and notes differences between differing accounts. Through enactment, the therapist encourages family members to jointly attempt problem solving in the consultation room. The therapist may coach family members to persist with particularly difficult transactions or try different ways of discussing the problem during an enactment. The enactment reveals the family structure and also its strengths and flexibilities. These structural problems and strengths are continually fed back to the family in sessions through the process of reframing. For example, the therapist may say to an enmeshed parent who answers for a teenager, 'You have become your daughter's voice'.

In structural family therapy, the therapist and clients agree overtly to the goal of eliminating the symptom. Inevitably there is an underlying tension between the therapist and the family about this goal. This is because families typically wish to loose symptoms while retaining their dysfunctional structure. In contrast, structural therapists believe that the family structure, which entails problem-maintaining interaction patterns, will also have to change in order for symptoms to be lost and this will be resisted by clients. Unlike MRI brief therapy and strategic therapy where this resistance is dealt with by prescribing carefully designed tasks to be conducted between sessions, in structural family therapy, resistance is addressed in therapy sessions by enactment, reframing, boundary marking and unbalancing. Boundary marking involves regulating the flow of information between family members by, for example, asking each person to speak for themselves and no one else, or by blocking a parental child from joining the parental subsystem. With unbalancing the therapist supports one family member more than another to challenge the prevailing family structure. When this is done with extreme intensity a family crisis may be purposely precipitated. Minuchin used this unbalancing technique when he conducted family lunch sessions with anorexic girls and asked the parents to make the child eat their lunch in the family session.

Structural family therapists also try actively to avoid being inducted into the problem-maintaining interactional patterns that are part of the dysfunctional family structure. For example, structural therapists attempt to avoid becoming triangulated into defusing conflicts between two family members. They also try to avoid becoming centralised into listening to huge volumes of content from all family members in every session because this leaves little time to comment on process, to unbalance, make boundaries and restructure.

COGNITIVE-BEHAVIOURAL MARITAL AND FAMILY THERAPY

Cognitive-behavioural family therapy for child-focused problems evolved from the pioneering work of Gerry Patterson (1971) on behavioural parent training, where the central emphasis was on training parents to use the principles of social learning theory to modify their children's aggressive behaviour. Cognitive-behavioural marital therapy evolved from Richard Stuart's (1969) early work on contingency contracting with distressed couples. Interventions in both the parent training and marital therapy domains of this tradition have grown in sophistication over the years and more empirical research has been published on the effectiveness of interventions within this tradition than any other (Atkins, Dimidjian & Christensen, 2003; Baucom & Epstein, 1990; Dattilio, 1997; Dattilio & Padesky, 1990; Dimidjian, Martell & Christensen, 2002; Epstein, Schlesinger & Dryden, 1988; Falloon, 1988, 1991; Falloon, Laporta, Fadden & Graham-Hole, 1993; Jacobson & Christensen, 1996; Jacobson & Margolin, 1979; Mueser & Glynn, 1995; Sanders & Dadds, 1993). In recent times, leaders in the field include Frank Dattilio, Donald Baucom, Norman Epstein and Ian Falloon (Baucom, Epstein & La Taillade, 2002; Dattilio & Epstein, 2003; Epstein, 2003; Falloon, 2003).

The central assumption of cognitive behavioural family therapy is that problematic behaviour and cognitions are learned and maintained by particular types of repetitive patterns of interaction. These patterns of interaction may involve imitation, operant conditioning, classical conditioning, or some combination of these. Cognitive-behavioural marital and family therapists help clients disrupt problem-maintaining interaction patterns by coaching them in the skills required to shape and reinforce non-problematic behaviours in other family members and by challenging their negative cognitions. For example, in behavioural parent training, parents learn to positively reinforce prosocial behaviour and to extinguish antisocial behaviour by arranging for the child to have time-out from reinforcement when it occurs. In traditional behavioural marital therapy, couples learn to reinforce each other for engaging in positive rather than negative interpersonal behaviour.

Differences between Distressed and Non-distressed Family Relationships

Research conducted within the cognitive-behavioural tradition has shown that relationships within distressed and non-distressed couples and families are different. Compared with non-distressed family relationships, family members in distressed relationships engage in more negative interpersonal behaviour patterns, which are mutually reinforcing and view each other in more negative terms. Patterson (1982) described a coercive family process in which the negative behaviours of two family members are maintained by mutual negative reinforcement. For example, if every time a child screams 'No' when asked to go to bed and after an escalating battle the parent withdraws to another room, the child's screaming is negatively reinforced because it leads to a cessation of parental nagging, and the parental withdrawal is negatively reinforced because it leads to an escape from the child's screaming. Coercive family processes maintain defiant and aggressive behaviour problems in children and also within distressed couples.

Negative cognitive schemas dominate the thought processes of family members in distressed relationships. Negative cognitive schemas underpin negative selective attention, and involve particular types of attributions, expectancies, assumptions and standards concerning family relationships that maintain negative family-based behaviour patterns. Negative cognitive schemas are associated with selectively attending to negative aspects of others; making personal attributions for negative behaviour and situational attributions for positive behaviour; holding negative expectations of other family members; holding assumptions about how to conduct family relationships that fit with those of other family members; and holding standards of conduct which other family members do not accept.

Assessment in Cognitive-behavioural Marital and Family Therapy

Assessment in cognitive behavioural marital family therapy begins with conducting a functional analysis in specific problematic domains. This involves monitoring the duration, frequency and intensity of problematic or positive behaviours and their antecedents, related cognitions and consequences. In addition, behavioural checklists may be used to assess overall patterns of positive and negative behaviours. Psychometric questionnaires may be used to evaluate cognitive aspects of family relationships. Typically, goals are framed in terms of increasing positive and reducing negative interactions, behaviours, feelings and cognitions.

Treatment in Cognitive-behavioural Family Therapy

In behavioural family therapy for children, a range of procedures based on social learning theory are used to help parents modify their children's behaviour. These include using reward systems, such as star charts and token economies, to increase positive behaviour and time-out procedures to reduce the frequency of negative behaviour.

With adolescents and in couples therapy, contingency contracts are used for the same purposes. These involve an agreement between parents and adolescents or members of a couple about the consequences of specific behaviours. With couples a distinction is made between *quid pro quo* and good faith contracts. With *quid pro quo* contracts, the consequences for both parties of engaging in target positive behaviours are specified and linked. For example, 'If you make dinner, I'll wash up the dishes afterwards'. With good faith contracts, the consequences for both parties of engaging in target positive behaviours are specified but are not linked. For example, 'If you make dinner, you may go sailing; if I do the shopping, I may go out with friends'. Good faith contracts are more commonly used.

Problem-solving and communication-skills training is an essential element of cognitive-behavioural therapy with families containing adolescents and couples. In communication-skills training, clients are coached through modelling and role play in communicating messages clearly, directly and congruently to their partners; checking that one has been understood; listening in an empathic manner; paraphrasing partners' messages; and checking the accuracy of such paraphrases. In problem-solving skills training clients are coached in defining large daunting problems as a series of small solvable problems and for each problem: brainstorming solutions; evaluating the pros and cons of these; selecting one; jointly implementing it; reviewing progress; and modifying the selected solution if it is ineffective or celebrating success if the problem is resolved.

Cognitive restructuring is the principal intervention used to challenge negative cognitions. Family members are invited to monitor and record the antecedent situations which gives rise to particular cognitions, and their subsequent impact on mood and interpersonal behaviour. When negative cognitions are identified in this way, clients are coached in challenging these by finding tangible evidence to support or refute them. When negative cognitions are not supported, clients are invited to revise them so that the new cognitions fit the evidence. They are also invited to record the impact of revised cognitions on mood and interpersonal behaviour.

Within integrative behavioural couples therapy acceptance building is used to help couples adapt to unchangeable aspects of their relationship. It involves empathic joining around the couple's problem; detachment from the problem; tolerance building; and self-care.

A variety of self-regulatory procedures for controlling anxiety, anger and depression have been developed within the cognitive-behavioural tradition. These include, for example, relaxation training, pleasant event scheduling and graded task assignment. Within behavioural couples therapy, where the regulation of negative mood states in one partner with a diagnosis of anxiety or depression is the principal aim, the non-symptomatic partner may be invited to assist with the other partner's self-regulatory behavioural exercises.

Where children with intellectual disabilities have skills deficits, parents may be trained to use complex behavioural procedures for shaping new skills such as backward chaining. For example, in training a child to help with housework, begin by rewarding them for putting the vacuum cleaner away and next time for switching it off until finally he is rewarded for taking it out, using it and putting it away.

FUNCTIONAL FAMILY THERAPY

Functional family therapy evolved from the observation that often families find it difficult to cooperate in behavioural family therapy (Alexander & Parsons, 1982; Alexander, Pugh, Parsons & Sexton, 2000; Barton & Alexander, 1981; Morris, Alexander & Waldron, 1988; Sexton & Alexander, 2003). James Alexander and colleagues integrated aspects of structural and strategic family therapy with behavioural family therapy and found that this led families to cooperate more fully in implementing behavioural programmes in cases of delinquency. They refer to this integrative model as functional family therapy and it is of particular significance because its efficacy is empirically well supported.

The central assumption of functional family therapy is that many problematic behaviours and symptoms that lead families to be referred to treatment serve important relational functions. There are two main dimensions of relational functions: relational connection and relational hierarchy. Problem behaviours may serve the function of regulating relational connection by creating distance and independence or intimacy and interdependence within relationships. Problem behaviours that serve the function of regulating relational hierarchy create a power structure within relationships where one member has more economic, physical or social power than another.

The aim of functional family therapy is to help families replace problematic behaviours with non-problematic behaviours that fulfil the same relationship functions. That is, functional family therapy helps families find less problematic ways to regulate the relational distance and relational hierarchy between people.

For example, if a mother and child are involved in a relationship characterised by separation anxiety, which prevents school attendance, an intervention such as coaching the mother to teach the child anxiety-management skills would be appropriate, since this fulfils the function of creating relational intimacy within the mother–child relationship, a function also fulfilled by the problematic behaviour. A second example concerns relational hierarchy. If a father and son are involved in a relationship that often escalates into shouting matches and inappropriate parental punishment of the adolescent, an intervention where the child can earn points for adhering to house rules and exchange these for items on a reinforcement menu would be appropriate because this fulfils the function of creating relational hierarchy within the father–son relationship, a function also fulfilled by the problematic behaviour.

In functional family therapy it is assumed that well-adjusted families have adaptive routines for regulating relational connection and hierarchies within the family.

Assessment and Treatment in Functional Family Therapy

During assessment family relationship processes are evaluated by interview and observation. The function of problematic behaviour on regulating relational connection and hierarchy is clarified. The degree to which family members' personal styles, strengths and weaknesses act as constraints or aids to problem resolution are also evaluated.

Therapy is conducted in a series of three main stages: (1) engagement and enhancing motivation, (2) behaviour change, and (3) generalisation. The process of functional family therapy is guided by four principles:

1. Creating positive alliances between family members and between the family and therapist enhances motivation to change.
2. Changing the family's belief system and the meaning of problematic transactions through reframing enhances motivation to change.
3. Therapeutic goals should be observable, obtainable and consistent with a family's abilities, cultural values and overall social context.
4. Therapeutic strategies should match and respect the family's profile of risk and protective factors and other characteristics.

In the first stage of therapy, the priority is helping families move from a position of hopelessness where they attribute blame to individual family members and are unmotivated to make positive changes, to a more hopeful position where they see the problem as shared and are motivated to engage in problem resolution. Establishing a good therapeutic alliance with each family member is central to this task. The usual joining procedures of showing warmth, empathy and genuineness on the one hand and structuring therapy sessions coherently on the other are important in this regard.

However, alliance building must be coupled with reframing to enhance motivation. Reframing is essential for helping family members reduce blaming, develop positive alliances with each other and being able to conceptualise their difficulties as a shared solvable problem. In functional family therapy, reframing involves three steps, which are described below and illustrated with an example.

1.   Empathise with a family member's current framing of the problem: 'It seems like he's always in trouble and that's a real difficulty. You get scared he will end up in prison and so you give him a good talking to.'
2.   Reattribute the problem to the family situation rather than the child, with reference to positive attributes of family members and point to a positive way forward: 'You and he get into a lot of rows about this. Your are both strong willed. You want him to follow the rules. He wants to be more grown up and independent. The challenge is for us to explore other ways to do this. For you to be able to keep a level head and set clear rules and consequences and for him to be grown up and fit in with these.'
3.   Check if the reframe is acceptable, and if not reformulate.

Reframing is not a discrete intervention. Throughout functional family therapy, one reframe leads to another. However, in the first phase of therapy it is the central intervention that helps families become motivated to work together to resolve a shared problem.

Once the family have moved to a stage where they have stopped blaming each other and view the problem as situationally determined, the second phase of treatment occurs. Here the focus is on behaviour change. Well-validated cognitive behavioural change strategies are used here to help families reduce risk factors associated with maintaining problem behaviours and to fulfil the interpersonal functions previously fulfilled by the problematic behaviour that led to the referral. The risk factors of problematic parenting practices, communication difficulties, chaotic problem solving, and poor self-regulation may be addressed through behavioural parent training, contingency contracting, communication and problem-solving skills training and coping skills training.

Once families have sufficient mastery experiences in dealing with problem situations to have developed self-efficacy for problem-management skills, the final stage of therapy occurs. Here the focus is on generalising skills learned during the second phase to a wider range of problems including potential relapse situations. There is also an emphasis on using community resources such as schools, other agencies and the extended family as an aid to problem-solving.

CLOSING COMMENTS

All five of the family therapy approaches described in this chapter focus predominantly on identifying problem-maintaining interaction patterns and disrupting these. To a lesser degree they all acknowledge the role of belief systems as a basis for these patterns. Both the structural and strategic models highlight the importance of the organisational structure of the family in contributing to the development of problem-maintaining interaction patterns. For all of the models reviewed here, with the exception of structural family, the only treatment goal is the resolution of the presenting problem. None of the models reviewed in this chapter is concerned with personal growth as a main goal. All five approaches to treatment are brief.

A substantial body of empirical evidence supports the effectiveness of strategic (Szapocznik & Williams, 2000), structural (Behar-Mitrani & Perez, 2003), behavioural (Dattilio & Epstein, 2003) and functional family therapy (Sexton & Alexander, 2003) in treating child and adolescent conduct problems, and drug abuse particularly, and this is reviewed in Chapter 18. There is also considerable evidence for the effectiveness for behavioural marital therapy (Byrne, Carr & Clark, 2004b). One of the distinguishing features of functional family therapy is that comprehensive fidelity and adherence programmes and clinical service systems have been developed for this therapy model. These allow the degree to which the model is being faithfully implemented in new settings to be monitored. There is now good evidence that functional family therapy may be successfully 'exported' to new sites and effectively implemented (Sexton & Alexander, 2003).

Process studies show that functional family therapy increases the amount of supportive family communication, decreases the amount of defensive communication and helps family members move from personal to situational attributions for problems (Sexton & Alexander, 2003). Process studies have also shown that effective functional family therapists have well-developed structuring and relationship skills. Structuring skills are necessary for confidently and clearly coaching family members in behavioural skills, such as contingency contracting. Relationship skills are required to maintain a good working alliance with all family members.

The models reviewed in this chapter focus predominantly on identifying problem-maintaining interaction patterns and disrupting these. The approaches described in the next chapter emphasise the role of belief systems in subserving these patterns and the importance of addressing these belief systems in family therapy.

GLOSSARY

MRI Brief Therapy

'Customers' and 'window-shoppers'. 'Customers' are committed to use therapy to resolve their problems, whereas 'window-shoppers' reluctantly attend therapy at the request of another person who may be the 'customer' for change.

Ironic processes. Problem-maintaining ineffectual attempted solutions. The MRI theory is that clients' ineffective attempted solutions, ironically, are usually the problem.

Punctuation. A number of starting points may be selected in describing repetitive patterns of family interaction and these different descriptions are alternative punctuations of the same set of events. For example, one partner may say, 'I shout because you don't listen', but the other partner may offer the following punctuation of the same events: 'I don't listen because you shout'.

Reframing. The positive redescription of a complex behaviour pattern, described originally by clients in negative terms. For example, 'He always fights with me because he hates me' may be reframed as, 'The passion with which you fight about important issues, shows how much you both care about this relationship working'.

Relabelling. Ascribing a new meaning to a discrete event. For example, in response to the statement, 'He *pesters* me', a therapist might ask, 'When did you first notice this *curiosity?*'.

Strategic Therapy

Hierarchy. Power structure within a system. In many families with pre-adolescent children, parents are in charge and children are hierarchically subordinate to them, but this hierarchy becomes reversed when children enter middle age and parents enter old age.

Metacommunication. A comment about the processes underpinning a conversation, such as 'When you argue about sex, you are at your most passionate'.

Ordeals. Inviting clients to complete a difficult task each time they have an urge to behave symptomatically. A bulimic may be invited to flush binge food down the toilet with the family watching when a binge urge occurs.

Paradoxical intervention. A directive given to a client, which initially appears to be counter-intuitive and to contradict the client's therapeutic goals, such as prescribing the symptom or inviting clients to change very slowly.

Pathological triangle. A common problem-maintaining pattern of family organisation characterised by a cross-generational coalition between a parent and a child to which the other parent is hierarchically subordinate.

The pattern of alliances is covert or denied, and lip-service is paid to a strong parental coalition to which the child is hierarchically subordinate.
Pretending. Inviting clients to pretend to behave symptomatically some of the time, while asking other family members to see if they can distinguish between real and pretend symptoms.
Therapeutic double-bind. A message (usually paradoxical) that contains two conflicting injunctions, given by a therapist to a client on which the client is prohibited from commenting within the context of a strong working alliance. For example, a couple who have agreed their therapeutic goal is to reduce the frequency of their fights may be told, 'You must continue to fight passionately and regularly to show that you care about each other'.

Structural Family Therapy

Boundaries. The conceptual social border around a family system or subsystem that regulates the flow of information and energy in and out of the system or subsystem. Boundaries manage proximity and hierarchy. Families that have diffuse boundaries between subsystems are enmeshed and those with rigid boundaries are disengaged.
Boundary marking. Regulating the flow of information between family members by, for example, asking each person to speak for themselves and no one else, or blocking a parental child from joining the parental subsystem.
Coalition. An alliance, either overt or covert, between two system members, the boundary around which usually excludes a third system member or subsystem.
Detouring. The re-routing of interparental conflict through the child to avoid overt interparental conflict. In a detouring-attacking triad, the parents express joint anger at the child and this is associated with conduct problems. In a detouring-protecting triad, parents express joint concern about the child, who may present with a psychosomatic complaint.
Enactment. Inviting a family to engage in problem-maintaining or problem-resolving interactions within the session.
Enmeshed and disengaged families. Enmeshed families are emotionally very close and do not tolerate high levels of individual autonomy. In disengaged families, members are emotionally distant.
Family lunch. The enactment of a family's way of coping with an eating disorder involving all members (including the member with an eating disorder) eating lunch with the therapist.
Family structure. A set of predictable family rules, roles and routines.
Hierarchy. The difference in power between people on either side of a boundary. Parents are commonly hierarchically superior to children within the family structure.

Intensity. Intensity may be created by increasing the duration or emotional forcefulness of a message or interaction, or by repetition.

Intergenerational boundary. A conceptual social border between generations that segregates parental and child roles.

Joining. Developing a working alliance with family members.

Parental child. A child who, by virtue of having a cross-generational coalition with one parent, is permitted (usually inappropriately) to have parental authority over siblings.

Proximity. The emotional distance between family members on either side of a boundary. There is normally greater proximity between family members than between the members of a family and those outside the family.

Restructuring. Using interventions, such as enactments, boundary making, unbalancing, creating intensity or reframing, to challenge the prevailing family structure.

Triangulation. A pattern of organisation in which the triangulated individual (usually a child) is required to take sides with one of two other family members (usually the parents).

Mimesis. Fitting in with the mood and tone of the family to strengthen the working alliance.

Unbalancing. Supporting one family member more than another to challenge the prevailing family structure.

Cognitive-behavioural Family Therapy

Acceptance building. In integrative behavioural couples therapy, a process involving empathic joining around couples problem; detachment from the problem; tolerance building; and self care.

Assumptions. Beliefs about how people generally behave in family relationships, for example, 'give them an inch and they'll take a mile'.

Attributions. Explanations for specific actions or events. Attributions for the actions of family members may be classified as personal (where the person is blamed) or situational (where the circumstances are blamed).

Backwards chaining. Shaping a complex behavioural response pattern by beginning with reinforcing the last step in the sequence and successively working backwards. For example, in training a child to help with housework, begin by rewarding them for putting the vacuum cleaner away and next time for switching it off until finally they are rewarded for taking it out, using it and putting it away.

Baseline. A record, usually established through monitoring, of problematic and positive behaviours prior to intervention.

Caring days. In discordant couples, increasing the amount of noncontingent reinforcement within their relationships by inviting couples to *concurrently* increase the rate with which they engage in behaviours their spouse has identified as enjoyable.

Classical conditioning. Learning to produce a response in reaction to a conditioned stimulus or cue, as a result of frequent pairing of the cue with other stimuli that produce the response. For example, having an urge to argue when a family member clears their throat a particular way because in the past this has been a cue for arguing.

Coercion. A process where the behaviours of two family members are maintained by mutual negative reinforcement. If every time a child screams 'No' when asked to go to bed and after an escalating battle the parent withdraws to another room, the child's screaming is negatively reinforced because it leads to a cessation of parental nagging and the parental withdrawal is negatively reinforced because it leads to an escape from the child's screaming.

Cognitive factors in family relationships. Selective attention, attributions, expectancies, assumptions and standards are the main classes of cognitive factors that affect family relationships. These may be organised into schemas.

Communication skills training. This involves coaching clients through modelling and role play in communicating messages clearly, directly and congruently to their partners; checking that one has been understood; listening in an empathic manner; paraphrasing partners' messages; and checking the accuracy of such paraphrases.

Contingency contract. An agreement between a parent and child or members of a couple about the consequences of specific behaviours. Parent–child contracts typically specify the consequences for the child of target positive and negative behaviours.

Cue. A stimulus that elicits a conditioned response. For example, through classical conditioning many cues come to elicit a craving for alcohol and cigarettes. Cue exposure training is the process of learning to be in such situations, without experiencing the craving as strongly and without satisfying the craving.

Expectancies. Beliefs about how specific people will behave and specific events will unfold in the future, for example, 'he'll grow out of it'.

Exposure and response prevention. A procedure where clients with obsessive compulsive disorder are exposed to obsession and anxiety-provoking stimuli (such as dirt) and are prevented from engaging in anxiety-reducing compulsive rituals (such as hand washing).

Extinction. The reduction in frequency of a behaviour, as a result of non-reinforcement.

Flooding. A procedure where phobic clients habituate to anxiety-provoking stimuli through sustained exposure to maximally anxiety-provoking stimuli.

Functional analysis. An assessment procedure where the antecedents and consequences of problem behaviours are pinpointed.

Good faith contract. A contingency contract for couples in which the consequences for both parties of engaging in target positive behaviours are specified but are not linked. For example, 'If I make dinner, I may go sailing; if you do the shopping, you may go out with friends'.

Graded task assignment. For depressed inactive patients, gradually increasing clients' activity levels by successively assigning increasingly larger tasks and activities.

Love days. In discordant couples, increasing the amount of non-contingent reinforcement within their relationships by inviting couples, *on alternate days*, to increase the rate with which they engage in behaviours their spouse has identified as enjoyable.

Modelling. Learning by observing others.

Monitoring. Regularly observing and recording information about specific behaviours or events. These include the duration, frequency and intensity of problematic or positive behaviours and their antecedents and consequences.

Negative reinforcement. Increasing the probable frequency of a response by rewarding it with the removal of an undesired stimulus. For example, increasing the child's use of the word 'please' by stopping things they do not like when they say 'please'.

Operant conditioning. Learning responses as a result of either positive or negative reinforcement. For example, working hard because of praise for doing so in the past, or bullying others because in the past it has stopped them annoying you.

Pleasant event scheduling. For depressed clients with constricted lifestyles, increasing the frequency with which desired events occur by scheduling their increased frequency.

Positive reinforcement. Increasing the probable frequency of a response by rewarding it with a desired stimulus. For example, increasing good behaviour by praising it.

Problem-solving skills training. This involves coaching clients through modelling and role play in defining large daunting problems as a series of small solvable problems and, for each problem: brainstorming solutions; evaluating the pros and cons of these; selecting one; jointly implementing it; reviewing progress; and modifying the selected solution if it is ineffective or celebrating success if the problem is resolved.

Punishment. Temporarily suppressing the frequency of a response by introducing an undesired stimulus every time the response occurs. Punished response recurs once punishment is withdrawn and if aggression is used as a punishment, the punished person may learn to imitate this aggression through modelling.

***Quid pro quo* contract.** A contingency contract for couples in which the consequences for both parties of engaging in target positive behaviours are specified and linked. For example, 'If you make dinner, I'll wash up'.

Reinforcement menu. A list of desired objects or events.

Relaxation training. Training clients to reduce physiological arousal and anxiety by systematically tensing and relaxing all major muscle groups and visualising a tranquil scene.

Reward system. A systematic routine for the reinforcement of target behaviours.

Schemas. Hypothetical complex cognitive structures (involving biases, attributions, beliefs, expectancies, assumptions and standards) through which experience is structured and organised.

Selective attention. An automatic (often unconscious) process of preferentially directing attention to one class of stimuli rather than others, for example, noting and responding only to negative behaviour in family members.

Shaping. The reinforcement of successive approximations to target positive behaviour.

Standards. Beliefs about how people generally should behave in family relationships, for example family members should be honest with each other.

Star chart. A reward system where a child receives a star on a wall chart each time they complete a target behaviour such as not bedwetting. A collection of stars may be cashed in for a prize from a reinforcement menu.

Systematic desensitisation. A procedure based on classical conditioning where phobic clients learn to associate relaxation with increasingly anxiety-provoking concrete or imaginal stimuli.

Time-out (from reinforcement). A system for extinguishing negative behaviours in children by arranging for them to spend time in solitude away from reinforcing events and situations if they engage in these negative behaviours.

Token economy. A reward system where a child or adolescent receives tokens, such as poker chips or points, for completing target behaviours and these may be accumulated and exchanged for items from a reinforcement menu.

Functional Family Therapy

Attributional style. The explanatory style used by family members to account for positive and negative behaviours. Under stress, family members tend to attribute negative behaviour to personal factors and positive behaviours to situational factors.

Education. The second stage of treatment which involves training family members to use routines from behaviour therapy, such as contingency contracts, to replace problematic with non-problematic behaviour patterns that fulfil similar relationship functions.

Functions. Problematic and non-problematic behaviour patterns serve relationship functions, including distancing, creating intimacy and regulating distance.

Relationship skills. These include clarifying how family members' emotional responses force them unwittingly into problem-maintaining behaviour patterns; adopting a non-blaming stance involving the use of relabelling fair turn taking in family sessions; using warmth and humour to defuse conflict; and engaging in sufficient self-disclosure to promote empathy.

Structuring skills. These include directives in maintaining a therapeutic focus, clear communication and self-confidence.

Therapy. The first stage of treatment which involves helping family members change their attributional styles so that they attribute positive behaviours to personal factors and negative behaviours to situational factors.

FURTHER READING

MRI Brief Marital and Family Therapy

Cade, B. & O'Hanlon, W. (1993). *A Brief Guide to Brief Therapy*. New York: Norton.

Duncan, B., Miller, S. & Sparks, J. (2003). Interactional and solution-focused brief therapies: Evolving concepts of change. In T. Sexton, G. Weeks & M. Robbins (Eds), *Handbook of Family Therapy*, pp. 101–124. New York: Brunner-Routledge.

Fisch, R. & Schlanger, R. (1999). *Brief Therapy with Intimidating Cases. Changing the Unchangeable*. San Francisco, CA: Jossey Bass.

Fisch, R., Weakland, J. & Segal, L. (1982). *The Tactics of Change: Doing Therapy Briefly*. San Francisco, CA: Jossey Bass.

Green, S. & Flemons, D. (2004). *Quickies: The Handbook of Brief Sex Therapy*. New York: Norton

Hoyt, M. (2001). *Interviews with Brief Therapy Experts*. Philadelphia, PA: Brunner-Routledge.

Segal, L. (1991). Brief therapy: The MRI Approach. In A. Gurman & D. Kniskern (Eds), *Handbook of Family Therapy, Vol. 11*, pp. 171–199. New York: Brunner-Mazel.

Shoham, V. & Rohbaugh, M. (2002). Brief strategic couple therapy. In A. Gurman & N.Jacobon (Eds), *Clinical Hanbook of Couples Therapy*, 3rd edn, pp. 5–21. New York: Guilford.

Watzlawick, P. Weakland, J. & Fisch, R. (1974). *Change. Principles of Problem Formation and Problem Resolution*. New York: Norton.

Weakland, J. & Fisch, R. (1992). Brief therapy: MRI style. In S. Budman, M. Hoyt & S. Friedman (Eds), *The First Session in Brief Therapy*, pp. 306–323. New York: Guilford.

Weakland, J. & Ray, W. (1995). *Propagations: Thirty Years of Influence from the Mental Research Institute*. Binghampton, NY: Haworth.

Strategic Marital and Family Therapy

Behar-Mitrani, V. & Perez, M. (2000). Structural-strategic approaches to couple and family therapy. In T. Sexton, G. Weeks & M. Robbins (Eds), *Handbook of Family Therapy*, pp. 177–200. New York: Brunner-Routledge.

Browning, S. & Green, R. (2003). Constructing therapy: From strategic to systemic to narrative models. In G. Sholevar (Ed.), *Textbook of Family and Couples Therapy: Clinical Applications*, pp. 55–76. Washington, DC: American Psychiatric Press.

Grove, D. & Haley, J. (1993). *Conversations on Therapy*. New York: Norton.

Haley, J. & Richeport-Haley, M. (2003). *The Art of Strategic Therapy*. New York: Brunner-Routledge.

Haley, J. (1963). *Strategies of Psychotherapy*. New York: Grune & Stratton.

Haley, J. (1967). *Advanced Techniques of Hypnosis and Therapy: Selected Papers of Milton H. Erickson, MD*. New York: Grune & Stratton.

Haley, J. (1973). *Uncommon Therapy*. New York: Norton.

Haley, J. (1976). *Problem Solving Therapy*. San Francisco: Jossey Bass.

Haley, J. (1984). *Ordeal Therapy*. San Francisco: Jossey Bass.

Haley, J. (1985a). *Conversations with Milton H. Erickson, MD: Volume 1. Changing Individuals*. New York: Norton.

Haley, J. (1985b). *Conversations with Milton H. Erickson, MD: Volume 2. Changing Couples*. New York: Norton.

Haley, J. (1985c). *Conversations with Milton H. Erickson, MD: Volume 3. Changing Children and Families*. New York: Norton.

Haley, J. (1996). *Learning and Teaching Therapy*. New York: Guilford.

Haley, J. (1997). *Leaving Home: The Therapy of Disturbed Young People*, 2nd edn. Philadelphia, PA: Brunner-Mazel.

Keim, J. & Lappin, J. (2002). Structural-strategic marital therapy. In A. Gurman & N. Jacobon (Eds), *Clinical Handbook of Couples Therapy*, 3rd edn, pp. 86–117. New York: Guilford.

Lankton, S. & Lankton, C. (1991). Ericksonian family therapy. In A. Gurman & D. Kniskern (Eds), *Handbook of Family Therapy, Vol. 11*, pp. 239–283. New York: Brunner Mazel.

Madanes, C. (1981). *Strategic Family Therapy*. San Francisco, CA: Jossey-Bass.

Madanes, C. (1984). *Behind the One-way Mirror: Advances in the Practice of Strategic Therapy*. San Francisco, CA: Jossey Bass.

Madanes, C. (1990). *Sex, Love and Violence*. New York: Norton.

Madanes, C. (1994). *The Secret Meaning of Money*. San Francisco, CA: Jossey-Bass.

Madanes, C. Keim, J. & Smelser, D. (1995). *The Violence of Men*. San Francisco, CA: Jossey-Bass.

Madanes, C. (1991). Strategic Family Therapy. In A. Gurman & D. Kniskern (Eds), *Handbook of Family Therapy, Vol. 11*, pp. 396–416. New York: Brunner-Mazel.

Rosen, K. (2003). Strategic family therapy. In L. Hecker & J. Wetchler (Eds), *An Introduction to Marital and Family Therapy*, pp. 95–122. New York: Haworth.

Structural Family Therapy

Behar-Mitrani, V. & Perez, M. (2003). Structural-strategic approaches to couple and family therapy. In T. Sexton, G. Weeks & M. Robbins (Eds), *Handbook of Family Therapy*, pp. 177–200. New York: Brunner-Routledge.

Colapinto, J. (1991). Structural family therapy. In A. Gurman & D. Kniskern (Eds), *Handbook of Family Therapy, Vol. 11*, pp. 417–443. New York: Brunner-Mazel.

Elizur, J. & Minuchin, S. (1989). *Institutionalising Madness. Families, Therapy and Society*. New York: Basic Books.

Fishman, C. & Fishman, T. (2003). Structural family therapy. In G. Sholevar (Ed.), *Textbook of Family and Couples Therapy: Clinical Applications*, pp. 35–54. Washington, DC: American Psychiatric Press.

Fishman, C. (1988). *Treating Troubled Adolescents: A Family Therapy Approach.* New York: Basic Books.

Fishman, C. (1993). *Intensive Structural Family Therapy: Treating Families in their Social Context.* New York: Basic Books.

Keim, J. & Lappin, J. (2002). Structural-strategic marital therapy. In A. Gurman & N. Jacobon (Eds), *Clinical Handbook of Couples Therapy*, 3rd edn, pp. 86–117. New York: Guilford.

Minuchin, S. & Fishman, H.C. (1981). *Family Therapy Techniques.* Cambridge, MA: Harvard University Press.

Minuchin, S. & Nichols, M. (1993). *Family Healing: Tales of Hope and Renewal from Family Therapy.* New York: Free Press.

Minuchin, S. (1974). *Families and Family Therapy.* Cambridge, MA: Harvard University Press.

Minuchin, S. (1984). *Family Kaleidoscope.* Cambridge, MA: Harvard University Press.

Minuchin, S., Rosman, B. & Baker, L. (1978). *Psychosomatic Families: Anorexia Nervosa in Context.* Cambridge, MA: Harvard University Press.

Minuchin, S., Lee, W. & Simon, G. (1996). *Mastering Family Therapy: Journeys of Growth and Transformation.* New York: Wiley.

Minuchin, S., Montalvo, B., Guerney, B., Rosman, B. & Schumer, F. (1967). *Families of the Slums.* New York: Basic Books.

Wetchler, J. (2003). Structural family therapy. In L. Hecker & J. Wetchler (Eds), *An Introduction to Marital and Family Therapy*, pp. 39–62. New York: Haworth.

Behavioural Marital and Family Therapy

Atkins, D., Dimidhian, S. & Christensen, A. (2003). Behavioural couple therapy: Past, present and future. In T. Sexton, G. Weeks & M. Robbins (Eds), *Handbook of Family Therapy*, pp. 281–302. New York: Brunner-Routledge.

Baucom, D. & Epstein, N. (1990). *Cognitive Behavioural Marital Therapy.* New York: Brunner-Mazel.

Baucom, D., Epstein, N. & LaTaillade, J. (2002). Cognitive behavioural couple therapy. In A. Gurman & N. Jacobon (Eds), *Clinical Handbook of Couples Therapy*, 3rd edn, pp. 86–117. New York: Guilford.

Dattilio, F. & Epstein, N. (2003). Cognitive-behavioural couple and family therapy. In T. Sexton, G. Weeks & M. Robbins (Eds), *Handbook of Family Therapy*, pp. 147–176. New York: Brunner-Routledge.

Dattilio, F. & Padesky, C. (1990). *Cognitive Therapy with Couples.* Sarasota, FL: Professional Resource Exchange.

Dattilio, F. (1997). *Integrative Cases in Couples and Family Therapy. Cognitive-Behavioural Perspective.* New York: Guilford.

Dimidjian, S., Martell, C. & Christensen, A. (2002). Integrative behavioural couple therapy. In A. Gurman & N. Jacobon (Eds), *Clinical Handbook of Couples Therapy*, 3rd edn, pp. 251–280. New York: Guilford.

Epstein, N. (2003). Cognitive behavioural therapies for couples and families. In L. Hecker & J. Wetchler (Eds), *An Introduction to Marital and Family Therapy*, pp. 203–254. New York: Haworth.

Epstein, N., Schlesinger, S. & Dryden, W. (1988). *Cognitive Behavioural Therapy with Families*. New York: Brunner-Mazel.

Falloon, I. (1988). *Handbook of Behavioural Family Therapy*. New York: Guilford.

Falloon, I. (1991). Behavioural family therapy. In A. Gurman & D. Kniskern (Eds), *Handbook of Family Therapy, Vol. 11*, pp. 65–95. New York: Brunner-Mazel.

Falloon, I. (2003). Behavioural family therapy. In G. Sholevar (Ed.), *Textbook of Family and Couples Therapy: Clinical Applications*, pp. 147–172. Washington, DC: American Psychiatric Press.

Falloon, I., Laporta, M., Fadden, G. & Graham-Hole, V. (1993). *Managing Stress in Families*. London: Routledge.

Jacobson, N. & Christensen, A. (1996). *Integrative Behavioural Couple Therapy*. New York: Norton.

Jacobson, N. & Margolin, G. (1979). *Marital Therapy; Strategies Based on Social Learning and Behavioural Exchange Principles*. New York: Brunner-Mazel.

Mueser, K. & Glynn, S. (1995). *Behavioural Family Therapy for Psychiatric Disorders*. Boston: Allyn & Bacon.

Sanders, M. & Dadds, M. (1993). *Behavioural Family Intervention*. New York: Pergammon Press.

Sayers, S. (1998). Special issue on behavioural couples therapy. *Clinical Psychology Review*, **18**(6).

Functional Family Therapy

Alexander, J., Pugh, C., Parsons, B. & Sexton, T. (2000). *Functional Family Therapy*, 2nd edn. Golden, CO: Venture.

Sexton, T. & Alexander, J. (2003). Functional family therapy: A mature clinical model for working with at-risk adolescents and their families. In T. Sexton, G. Weeks & M. Robbins (Eds), *Handbook of Family Therapy*, pp. 323–350. New York: Brunner-Routledge.

Alexander, J. & Parsons, B. (1982). *Functional Family Therapy*. Montereny, CA: Brooks Cole.

Barton, C. and Alexander, J. (1981). Functional family therapy. In A. Gurman & D. Kniskern (Eds), *Handbook of Family Therapy*, pp. 403–443. New York: Brunner-Mazel.

Morris, S., Alexander, J. & Waldron, H. (1988). Functional family therapy. In I. Falloon (Ed.), *Handbook of Behavioural Family Therapy*, pp. 130–152. New York: Guilford.

Chapter 4

THEORIES THAT FOCUS ON BELIEF SYSTEMS

Family therapy schools and traditions, it was noted in Chapter 2, may be classified in terms of their emphasis on problem-maintaining behaviour patterns; constraining belief systems and narratives; and historical, contextual and constitutional predisposing factors. While Chapter 3 was concerned with traditions that highlight the role of problem-maintaining behaviour patterns, this chapter is primarily concerned with approaches that focus on belief systems and narratives which subserve these interaction patterns. Traditions that fall into this category, and which are summarised in Table 4.1, include constructivism; the Milan School; social-constructionist family therapy approaches; solution-focused family therapy; and narrative therapy. These traditions share a rejection of positivism and a commitment to some alternative epistemology, so it is with a consideration of these epistemologies that this chapter opens.

EPISTEMOLOGY: POSITIVISM, CONSTRUCTIVISM, SOCIAL CONSTRUCTIONISM, MODERNISM AND POSTMODERNISM

Bateson (1972, 1979) was fond of the word epistemology and referred to what he described as an 'ecosystemic epistemology'. This, for Bateson, was a world view or belief system that entailed the idea that the universe – including non-material mind and material substance – is a single ecological system made up of an infinite number of constituent subsystems. However, in the strictest sense, epistemology is a branch of philosophy concerned with the study of theories of knowledge. Following Bateson's idiosyncratic use of the term, epistemology within the family therapy field is used more loosely to mean a specific theory of knowledge or world view. Using this definition, within the family therapy field, distinctions are made between three main epistemologies: positivism, constructivism and social constructionism.

Table 4.1 Key features of family therapy schools and traditions that emphasise the role of belief systems and narrative

Domain	Constructivism	Milan	Social constructionism	Solution focused	Narrative
Key figures	Harry Procter Rudy Dallos Guillem Feixas Greg and Robert Neimeyer	Mara Selvini Palazzoli Gianfranco Cecchin Luigi Boscolo Giuliana Prata	Gianfranco Cecchin Luigi Boscolo Karl Tomm Imelda McCarthy Nollaig Byrne Phil Kearney Tom Andersen Harlene Anderson Harry Goolishan	Steve deShazer Insoo Kim Berg	Michael White David Epston
Healthy family functioning	Members of healthy families have personal and family construct systems that are sufficiently complex, flexible and congruent to promote adaptation to the changing demands of the family lifecycle and the wider ecological system	Each family system develops a unique set of relationships, patterns of interactions and belief systems. In healthy families these are sufficiently flexible to promote adaptation to the changing demands of the family lifecycle and the wider ecological system	Healthy families hold belief systems that are sufficiently flexible to promote adaptation to the changing demands of the family lifecycle and the wider ecological system	Family members attend to exceptional circumstances in which common problems do not recur and learn to recreate these circumstances when they need to resolve specific problems	In healthy families, the dominant narratives subserve the liberation of family members and their empowerment Also healthy families open space for creating narratives about personal competence

(Continued on next page)

Table 4.1 (*Continued*)

Domain	Constructivism	Milan	Social constructionism	Solution focused	Narrative
Unhealthy functioning	Members of unhealthy families have personal and family construct systems that are too rigid and simple and disparate to allow adaptation to the changing demands of the family lifecycle and the wider ecological system	In unhealthy families the relationships, interaction patterns and belief systems are not sufficiently flexible to promote adaptation to the changing demands of the family lifecycle and the wider ecological system	Unhealthy families hold belief systems that are not sufficiently flexible to promote adaptation to the changing demands of the family lifecycle and the wider ecological system	Family members engage in recursive problem-maintaining behaviour patterns and do not recreate exceptions	In unhealthy families, the dominant narratives subserve the entrapment of family members, the equation of people with problems, and the closing down of possibilities for new narratives to emerge
Assessment	Triadic questioning; constructing perceived element grids; laddering; circular questioning; bow-tie mapping; completing paper and pencil or computer versions of the repertory grid; self- and family characterisation; completing an autobiographical table of contents; and	Circular questioning asked from a position of neutrality is used to progressively modify hypotheses about belief systems, interaction patterns (family games), and family relationships	Circular questions asked from positions of curiosity and irreverence to bring forth the family's construction of the problem	Clarifying if clients are customers, complainants or visitors. Identification of exceptional circumstances under which the problem does not occur	The identification of the problem and unique outcomes where the problem does not occur

	defining the self and the family through metaphor are used to clarify family members individual and shared construct systems				
Scope of treatment goals	Elaborating personal and family construct systems so they make more accurate predictions	Challenging the family belief system that underpins problem-maintaining interaction patterns	Co-constructing or bringing forth a new and more adaptive belief system	Facilitate the occurrence of exceptional episodes in which the problem does not recur	Re-authoring personal narratives so they no longer equate the person with the problem and so they include a view of the self as competent
Therapy	Use construct articulation and fixed role therapy to elaborate more complex and flexible individual and family construct systems	Circular questioning within sessions and end of session interventions are used to promote change End of session interventions include positive connotation of family members intentions; split-team messages empathising with beliefs, feelings and	Circular questions asked from a position of curiosity and irreverence along with reflections of the therapist and team opens up space for co-constructing a new belief system The therapist uses strategising and interventive interviewing to help	Goal setting using the miracle question Deconstructing the complaint Exploring differences between problematic and exceptional episodes Use scaling questions, questions about presession change and questions about coping	Externalise the problem Enquire about unique outcomes in the past Thicken the plot about competence Extend the story into the future Recruit family members to act as outsider witnesses

(Continued on next page)

Table 4.1 (Continued)

Domain	Constructivism	Milan	Social constructionism	Solution focused	Narrative
		behaviours of different family factions or sides of a family dilemma; paradoxical prescriptions of each family members role in the problem-maintaining behaviour pattern to challenge family belief system; prescriptions of rituals to challenge family belief systems; the invariant prescription for parents to engage in repeated secret meetings without the children to disrupt problem-maintaining parent–child interactions	the family develop new constructions of the problem The therapist dissolves the problem in conversation	Giving compliments to visitors Give complainants the tasks of observing and predicting exceptions Give customers tasks of recreating exceptions	Invite clients to engage in bringing it back practices
Special areas of applicability	Alcohol and drug problems	Adolescent psychosis Anorexia nervosa			Encopresis Coping with hallucinations Anorexia

Positivism

Positivists argue that our perceptions are a true reflection of the world as it is (Gergen, 1994). For positivists, there is therefore a single true reality which may be directly perceived. When family therapy is conducted from a positivist position, it is assumed that there is a single true definition of the problem, which may be discovered through rigorous assessment and resolved though the application of techniques that have been shown to be effective through rigorous scientific evaluation. Disputes about definitions of the problem may be resolved by the therapist offering his or her expert opinion on the true nature of the problem. Behavioural and psychoeducational approaches to family therapy are explicitly rooted in positivism.

A problem with positivism is that our sensations and perceptions are conscious non-material experiences and we cannot know exactly what relationship exists between these non-material experiences and the material objects and events they represent. Neither can we know if this relationship between perceptions and objects is the same for everyone.

Positivism has been useful because it has led to the development of family assessment and intervention packages, the usefulness of which has been tested in rigorous scientific studies. However, my opinion is that the outcome of these studies are useful social constructions, not the objective truth.

Positivism, is associated with a number of other related positions including empiricism, representationalism, essentialism and realism. Empiricism argues that true knowledge comes through the senses rather than being innately acquired. Representationalism argues that perceptions are accurate representations of the world, rather than personal or social constructions. Essentialism argues that each object or event has an essential nature that may be discovered, as opposed to the view that multiple meanings may be given to objects and events by individuals and communities. Realism argues that there is one real world that may be known rather than multiple personal or social constructions.

Constructivism

Constructivists argue that individuals construct their own representations of the world and these representations are determined, in part, by the nature of their sense organs, nervous systems, information processing capabilities and belief systems, and, in part, by the objects and events of the world (Neimeyer & Mahoney, 1995). Thus, for each individual, the world is actively constructed not passively perceived. This personal construction of the world is influenced to a greater or lesser extent by innate and acquired characteristics of the person and characteristics of the environment. Radical constructivists accord a major role to the characteristics of the person in determining what is perceived and known. In contrast, constructive alternativism (or perspectivism) argues that the world out there may be construed in multiple possible ways, so the characteristics of both the environment and the person contribute to what is perceived and known.

Radical constructivism as espoused, for example, by Maturana (1991) is a problematic position. It entails the view that each person's knowledge of the world is determined predominantly by his or her personal characteristics and that the environment (including encounters with other people) are of negligible importance. If this were the case, meaningful communication and coordinated cooperation, the hallmarks of human society and indeed family therapy, would be impossible.

Constructive alternativism, a position advocated by George Kelly (1955), in contrast, may be a more useful position for family therapists. Constructive alternativists argue that a person's view of the world is similar to that of others insofar as it is influenced by a common environment but differs from that of others insofar as a person's interpretation of events is influenced by his or her unique perspective and interpretation.

Within the family therapy field, radical constructivism is endorsed by the MRI brief therapy group (discussed in Chapter 3) who have been influenced by Heinz von Foerster (1981). Milan systemic family therapy, during its evolution, has been influenced by the radical constructivist Humberto Maturana (Campbell et al., 1991). Maturana (1991) argued that therapists could not instruct clients in how to resolve their problems and be certain that they would follow instructions. The only certainty, he argued is that they would use the instructions to adapt to their problematic situation in a way that was consistent with their physiological and psychological structure. According to this position all a therapist may do is perturb the client's system, but not direct it to change in a predictable manner. Of course, if this were wholly accurate, skilled therapy and family therapy training programmes would not be viable.

George Kelly's (1955) personal construct psychology; the constructivist family therapy based on it; and, in some instances, the position taken by cognitive therapists within the cognitive-behavioural tradition are grounded in constructive alternativism. Adherence to this type of constructivist epistemology affects therapeutic practice in a number of important ways. Such constructivists privilege each family member's view of the problem equally since each is a unique and valid account that is true for that family member. They accept that some ways of construing the world are more useful than others for problem solving, and capitalise on the possibility that changing a family member's way of construing a problematic situation from a less useful to a more useful alternative may lead to problem resolution. Thus, sequences may be repunctuated, reframed and relabelled. Situations may be construed in more complex and flexible ways. Self-defeating attributions and beliefs may be replaced by more adaptive and empowering attributions and beliefs. Another valuable contribution of constructivism is that it allows us as therapists to self-reflectively question the degree to which our beliefs about a particular family are determined by the behaviour they have shown us or by our own theories, professional belief systems and prejudices.

This type of constructivism is true to Korsybski's (1933) dictum, which Bateson and others in the field have been so fond of quoting: 'A map is not the territory it represents, but, if correct, it has a similar structure to the territory, which accounts for its usefulness'.

Social Constructionism

Social constructionists argue that an individual's knowledge of the world is constructed within a social community through language (Gergen, 1994). Like constructivists, social constructionists accept that an individual's perceptions of objects and events are determined in part by the objects and events themselves; in part by a person's physiological constitution (including sense organs, nervous system, etc.) and psychological make-up (including information-processing capacity, belief systems, etc.); but they highlight that an individual's belief system is strongly influenced by social interaction within the person's community. This interaction occurs through the medium of language (including both verbal and non-verbal communication processes) in conversations (including the spoken and written word).

For social constructionists, truth is not discovered but constructed. However, it is not constructed by isolated individuals; rather, it is co-constructed by communities of people in conversation. Useful constructions of objects and events and useful explanations of the relationships between them are retained by communities in conversation. Constructions that are not useful are discarded. The usefulness of a construction is judged by a community in terms of the degree to which it facilitates problem solving, adaptation to the environment, need fulfilment and survival.

Social constructionism was endorsed by the male Milan systemic therapists, Cecchin and Boscolo (Campbell, 1999); Lynn Hoffman (1993); Karl Tomm (Tomm, 1987a, 1987b, 1988); Tom Andersen's (1987, 1991) reflecting team group; Harlene Anderson's Houston Galveston group (Anderson, 2003); the solution-focused tradition founded by Steve deShazer and Insoo Kim Berg (Duncan et al., 2003; Hoyt, 2002; Lethem, 2002); and by the narrative therapy tradition founded by Michael White and David Epston (Anderson, 2003; Freedman & Combs, 2002).

With respect to therapy, social constructionists argue that they co-construct with clients more useful ways of describing their problematic situation, ways that open up new possibilities. Particular attention is paid to using language to co-construct new definitions of problematic situations. Social constructionism is the most coherent epistemology for family therapists, in my opinion. It is also a coherent position for family therapy researchers to take, since it may be argued that the results of their research are not objectively true but are, rather, useful social constructions developed by communities of researchers in conversation (through the printed word in peer-reviewed journal articles and through the spoken work in conference presentations and workshops).

Modernism and Postmodernism

Positivism, as a theory of knowledge, was an integral part of a broad movement referred to as modernism. In contrast, constructivism and social constructionism are both identified with postmodernism, a movement that arose in response to the perceived failure of modernism to deliver a brave new world (Sarup, 1993). Because postmodernism has received frequent mention within the family therapy literature a brief statement on modernism and postmodernism is given below (Flaskas, 2002).

Modernism, which began with the enlightenment, promised liberation from the tyranny of superstition, religion and monarchy through science and reason. Modernism assumed the existence of a knowable world whose universal laws could be discovered through systematic empirical investigation. The modernist vision entailed the view that rigorous research would lead to the gradual accumulation of value-free knowledge. A further assumption of the modernist view was that language was representational and that scientific reports were therefore accurate accounts of the world as it is. Modernism privileged the rational individual in its world view. Finally, it was assumed that the modernist movement, through scientific progress, would lead to a better world.

In contrast to this noble vision, modernism and related scientific progress led to a world threatened by nuclear holocaust, environmental crises, widespread economic inequality and political injustice. In addition, developments within the philosophy of science, notably Kuhn's (1962) demonstration of the role of non-rational factors in the emergence of new scientific paradigms cast a shadow over modernism. Kuhn showed that often scientists suppress or disregard data that does not fit with their theories, so science is not rational and value free, but strongly influenced by scientists' values, emotions and other non-rational factors. Paradigm shifts from one major world view or theory to another occur when an individual, or a small group of scientists, propose a new framework that can accommodate all of the data that has been suppressed or ignored by mainstream scientists because it did not fit with the prevailing old paradigm or world view.

Postmodernism is a broad cultural transformation that is occurring in response to the failure of the modernist programme to fulfil its promise. In many fields, including the social sciences, modernist discourse has been deconstructed by postmodernists. That is, the historically conditioned assumptions and blind spots entailed by the modernist grand narrative of value-free scientific objectivity and cumulative progress have been identified. Postmodernists believe that they have shown that modernist discourses are no more than ungrounded, historically situated rhetoric.

Postmodernism rejects the idea that a single objective and rational account of the world can be reached. It accepts the existence of a world, but this can never be accurately known. Rather, through perception and language the world is socially constructed by communities.

From the perspective of family therapy as a scientific movement, postmodernism has the following implications (Gergen, 1994). First, no single true overarching theoretical model may be constructed. Rather, more or less useful models for particular problems and contexts may be identified. Second, empirical research results from therapy outcome studies are not reflections of the truth, but socially-constructed statements by scientists in conversation that may throw light on the usefulness of particular therapies with particular problems in particular contexts. Third, contextual variables, such as gender, class, ethnicity and culture, must be incorporated into useful models of therapy, because there are no universal principles for good practice or for the perfectly adjusted family. Models of good practice and of family functioning are local, not global and take account of salient contextual and cultural factors.

Postmodernism also has implications for practice (Pocock, 1995). Postmodern therapy rejects the idea of true diagnoses; the idea that one family member's definition of the problem or the solution is more valid than another's; and the idea that therapists' views should be privileged over those of clients. Postmodern practice favours the exploration of multiple views of problems and their resolution; the idea that therapy is about finding useful rather than true definitions of problems and solutions; the idea that ways of construing problems and solutions are always provisional, temporary and tentative; the idea of collaborative partnership between therapists and clients; and the idea that all attempts to help clients define their problems in useful ways and search for solutions are ethical rather than value-free practices.

In light of these cursory accounts of positivist, constructivist and social constructionist epistemologies, and this description of postmodernism, let us turn to a discussion of those family therapy traditions that have looked to constructivist, social constructionist and postmodern ideas as a basis for practice, and which have highlighted the centrality of helping clients construct new belief systems and narratives in family therapy.

A CONSTRUCTIVIST APPROACH TO FAMILY THERAPY

A constructivist approach to family therapy grounded in George Kelly's (1955) personal construct theory (PCT) has been articulated by Harry

Procter (1981, 1985a, 1985b, 1995, 2003) and Rudi Dallos (1991, 1997; Dallos & Aldridge, 1985) in the UK; by Guillem Fexias (1990a, 1990b, 1995a, 1995b; Feixas, Proctor & Neimeyer, 1993) in Spain; and by Greg and Robert Neimeyer (Alexander & Neimeyer, 1989; Neimeyer, 1985, 1987; Neimeyer & Hudson, 1985; Neimeyer & Neimeyer, 1994) in the USA; and by Vince Kenny (1988) formerly in Ireland, but now in Italy.

Personal Construct Theory

The core assumption of George Kelly's theory is that people develop construct (or belief) systems to help them accurately anticipate events. Kelly argues that people are like scientists and they develop belief systems that are like scientific theories about how the world operates. They test out the validity of these belief systems though behavioural experiments, much as the scientist tests out scientific theories through laboratory experiments.

A person's construct system changes as repeated experiences suggest modifications that may lead to more accurate predictions. The degree to which constructs change is determined by their permeability, that is the degree to which they will permit new elements into their range of convenience. Change in construct systems is likely where new experiences make new elements available, and where validating data throw light on the how accurately the old construct made predictions about new situations. Threatening situations, preoccupation with old experiences and a lack of opportunity for new experiences all inhibit the elaboration of new construct systems. When construct systems change, peripheral and permeable constructs change first. Core constructs used to define a person's identity change later.

Personal Construct Theory and the Family

Neimeyer (1985, 1987; Neimeyer & Hudson, 1985; Neimeyer & Neimeyer, 1994) has shown that people choose marital partners whom they believe will help them elaborate their construct systems so that their world will become more predictable and understandable. Procter (1995, 2003), Dallos (1991,1997) and Feixas (1990a; 1990b) argue that families develop shared construct systems that are validated or invalidated by the collective behaviour, interactions and conversations of family members within and outside therapy. Family construct systems, that is, shared family belief systems, play a central role in organising patterns of family interactions. Family construct systems are implicitly negotiated by the marital couple. Any specific family construct system may be traced to the parents' interpretation of the construct systems shared by their families of origin and by their idiosyncratic interpretation of the prevailing construct system within their society and culture.

Symptoms may occur when family construct systems are too tight (e.g. in rigid enmeshed families), too loose (e.g. in chaotic families), or where lifecycle transitions lead one family member to behave in a way that invalidates the family construct system (Procter, 1981). For example, an adolescent may be construed by his parents as having behaviour problems when the youngster's requirement for increased privacy and autonomy invalidates the family's belief that emotional closeness and unquestioning openness and obedience are the characteristics of a happy family.

Family Assessment Based on Personal Construct Theory

The positioning of the therapist in PCT is both expert and collaborative. Since all people are viewed as scientists, the task on which clients and therapists collaborate is that of articulating construct systems and their predictions. They also test out the accuracy of the predictions entailed by construct systems by talking about the probability of these predictions being accurate. In some instances, clients are invited to carry out behavioural experiments to check the accuracy of predictions entailed by construct systems. Within this process, the clients are the experts on the content of their own construct systems and the types of situations in which they wish their construct systems to make accurate predications. The therapist, on the other hand is an expert on the processes of facilitating the articulation of constructs and designing useful ways for testing and revising construct systems. The therapist takes an invitational approach and invites clients to articulate their construct systems and test their validity.

In the initial interview, Kelly advises that seven key questions be addressed to determine: what the problem is; when the client first noticed the problems; under what conditions the problems occurred; corrective measures that were taken; the effects of these; the conditions under which the problems is most noticeable; and the conditions under which the problem is least noticeable.

The line between assessment and intervention in family therapy based on personal construct psychology is blurred. Assessment techniques that clarify individual and family construct systems also challenge family members to consider the usefulness of these systems in making accurate predictions. Such challenges may lead to revisions of clients' construct systems. Having said that, the following are the main techniques that are oriented to some degree toward assessment more than therapy: triadic questioning; laddering; circular questioning; completing paper and pencil or computer versions of the repertory grid; self- and family characterisation; completing an autobiographical table of contents; and defining the self and the family through metaphor.

Triadic questioning is the main technique for identifying constructs and it involves asking a family member to list a series of elements (people, objects, events or relationships), and then to indicate how each pair are the same and different from a third. For example, if two people are the same because they are warm but different from a third because he or she is cold, the construct identified is cold–warm. Once each family member's constructs have been identified, he or she may be invited to rate the status of each member of the family or each significant relationship within the family on that construct. For example, a therapist may ask, 'Can you rate your father/mother/sibling on a 10-point scale where 10 is warm and 1 is cold?'

Laddering is a method for discovering the hierarchical way in which constructs are organised and the core constructs used to define a person's values and identity by repeatedly asking which of two poles of a construct the client is at (or would prefer to be at) and why that is the case.

> *Therapist:* You said your mother and yourself are the same because you are soft but you are different from your father who is hard. Why is that?
>
> *Client:* It's because we like to let people do what they want and he wants to control everyone.
>
> *Therapist:* Why is that?
>
> *Client:* It's because we think everyone has a right to be their own person and he thinks everyone should be like him.
>
> *Therapist:* Why is that?
>
> *Client:* It's because we believe being friends is the most important thing and he believes doing your duty is the most important thing.

This laddering interview segment shows that 'Being friends versus doing one's duty' is a core construct which defines the client's identity.

Circular questions, described below in the discussion of Milan systemic family therapy, may be used to asses family construct systems and the construct systems of individual family members (Feixas et al., 1993). Such questions may enquire about the problem ('What do you see as the main problem?'); the pattern of interaction around the problem ('What happens before during and after the problem?'); and comparisons of differences between family member's constructions of the problems ('What are the main differences between your own views and those of your partner and children?'). In each of these domains, questions about the past, present and future may be asked. So family members may be asked about the problem, the pattern of interaction around it and their explanation for it prior to therapy, right now and then they may be invited to project into the future and speculate on how things may evolve. The limitations of the family construct system becomes apparent when it entails a lack of problem resolution in the future. For example, if the overriding theory of the problem behaviour is that it's caused exclusively by genetic factors and so is unalterable, this way of construing the family's difficulties will require revision.

The *Repertory Grid Test* (REP) is a paper-and-pencil or computerized method for eliciting constructs using the triadic questioning technique. Computer REP tests can elicit element lists in many areas of life, elicit constructs, position elements along scales, factor analyse constructs into dimensions, hierarchically organise these construct-based dimensions, position elements accurately along these dimensions, and cluster analyse elements in terms of dimensions. Computer-based REP tests are a useful way of mapping out individual and family construct systems and print-outs of these construct systems may be used as basis for therapeutic conversations about the revision of construct systems.

Self-characterisation is an assessment procedure in which a person writes an account of themselves from the perspective of a close friend. Family characterisation is a similar process in which family members write an account of the family from the perspective of a close friend (Alexander & Neimeyer, 1989). Self- and family characterisations may be used as basis for identifying core constructs.

Couples may be invited to imagine they are planning go write an autobiography of their relationship and then be asked to write out a list of the chapter headings and a brief sketch of the contents of each of these chapters. This autobiographical table of contents of a couple's relationship throws light on the way in which couples construe the evolution of their relationship over time and may highlight significant stages, transitions and turning points. Similarities and differences between partners' tables of contents may reveal how the differing ways that partners have of construing the relationship underpins both strengths and problems within the relationship.

Family members may be invited to select a metaphor that best fits their view of the family or the presenting problem and to write a paragraph elaborating this. For example: A family is like a boat. It provides security on the sea of life. You can travel farther in a boat than you can swim without it. You can land a boat and explore new lands, but return to your boat for supplies. Even if a boat sinks or capsizes, it can always be righted or repaired. Similarities and differences between differing metaphors may then be discussed and the implications of this for individual and family construct systems.

Family Therapy Based on Personal Construct Theory

Therapy techniques in personal construct family therapy all hinge on the positioning of the therapist. The therapist's position is primarily that of facilitating constructive revision by helping clients develop construct systems that lead to accuracte predictions.

Fixed role therapy is an intervention unique to PCT. In light of an assessment of a client's construct systems, through the various techniques outlined above, the therapist and team (if one is available) design a new role or set of roles for one or more family members. These fixed roles are defined in terms of their construct systems. Clients are invited to play out these fixed roles for a period of a couple of weeks and then they are interviewed to determine the impact of the behaviours, entailed by the roles, have for their construct systems. If aspects of the fixed roles lead to more accurate anticipations, then clients may wish to incorporate the relevant constructs into their systems. For example, a parent who construed her child's apparent fearfulness as the expression of a need for reassurance decided, after fixed-role therapy, to construe it as a need to develop self-reliance and bravery.

Within therapy sessions, where it is clear that family member's construe each other in ways that are not accurate, they may be invited to listen carefully to other family members' positions and check the discrepancies between their beliefs and the views expressed by relevant family members. For example, family members who believe the other family members care little for them may be invited to listen to the other family members' expressing care and commitment in an emotionally congruent way.

Within therapy sessions, family members may be invited to try out new constructs by having conversations in which they talk *as if* the new or suggested constructs were true, looking at evidence from the past to support them, and guessing at how the future might be if these new ways of construing the world were used. For example, a couple who construed their relationship as fundamentally cold and distant, were invited to talk as if they had a fundamentally close relationship, but had got out of the habit of expressing affection.

Within PCT, it is assumed that all clients do all things for good reasons and underlying these is the need to elaborate their construct systems so they can predict the future more accurately, although this reason is not always conscious. Thus, when clients appear to be uncooperative, to show resistance and so forth, the PCT therapist attempts to understand how this behaviour fits with the client's construct system. Resistance as a concept within traditional psychotherapy, according to PCT, is a product of a flawed therapeutic construct system, which entails the idea that clients should show certain types of cooperative behaviours under certain conditions.

MILAN SYSTEMIC FAMILY THERAPY

Milan systemic family therapy is an umbrella term for a clinical tradition founded by Mara Selvini-Palazzoli, Luigi Boscolo, Gianfranco Cecchin and Guiliana Prata, which has now divided into at least two main subtraditions (Campbell, 1999; Campbell et al., 1991; Pirrotta, 1984; Jones, 1993). The original Milan team, influenced by the writing of Gregory Bateson (1972,1979) and the practice of the MRI brief therapy team as outlined to them by Watzlawick in a series of consultations conducted in Italy in the 1970s developed their own unique style. This involved the use of five-part therapy sessions; the use of co-therapy and a team behind a screen; a commitment to the guidelines of hypothesising, circularity and neutrality; circular questioning; end of session interventions involving positive connotation and the prescription of rituals, some of which were apparently paradoxical; long gaps between sessions; and the idea that the goal of therapy was altering the family belief system so as to end the symptom -maintaining interactional patterns (Selvini-Palazzoli, 1988; Selvini-Palazzoli, Boscolo, Cecchin & Prata, 1978, 1980; Tomm, 1984a, 1984b).

The original four-member Milan team divided into two traditions, with one committed to the original, essentially strategic approach to practice with its emphasis on designing interventions to challenge family belief systems and disrupt family games (Prata, 1990; Selvini-Palazzoli et al., 1989), and the other committed to a collaborative social-constructionist approach with an emphasis on the use of positioning and circular questioning to co-construct new belief systems (Boscolo & Bertrando, 1992, 1993; Boscolo, Cecchin, Hoffman & Penn, 1987; Cecchin, 1987; Cecchin, Lane & Ray, 1992, 1993, In Press). It is this social constructionist group that has had greatest influence in North America (Papp, 1983; Penn, 1982; 1985; Tomm, 1987a, 1987b, 1988), the UK (Burnham, 1986; Campbell, 1999; Campbell & Draper, 1985; Campbell, Draper & Huffington 1988a, 1989a, 1989b; Campbell, Reder, Draper & Pollard, 1988b; Jones, 1993) and Ireland (Young, 2002).

In the original Milan team, the approach to practice began with a telephone interview in which the family composition and the role of the referring agent was clarified. The Milan team took the view that in some instances the referring agent may occupy a homeostatic position with respect to the family problem, and in making a referral be inadvertently inviting the therapist to take on this homeostatic role. If there was any suspicion that this was the case, the Milan team would invite the referring agent to the initial session. This possibility was commonly considered when the referrer was a family member or a close friend of the family who had played a long-standing and supportive role in helping the family deal with the presenting complaint or some other problem.

Before the initial session, the team would meet to hypothesise on the basis of available information, about possible links between the presenting problems; problem-maintaining interaction patterns; and family belief systems.

Once a set of hypotheses had been drawn up, two of the team members would interview the family and two would observe this interview from behind a one-way screen. An interviewing style was used that allowed the hypotheses or hunches formed before the interview to be tested or checked out. For example, the Milan team in their 1980 paper described a case where they hypothesised that a psychotic daughter's discharge from a long-stay institution, the family's ambivalence about the acceptance of this, and their confusion about how to manage it served the function of maintaining family cohesion at a time when another sibling was about to leave home. Each person was asked to describe their views of this predicament. Beliefs underpinning discrepancies between these accounts were examined by asking one family member to give their beliefs about the reasons for the discrepancies between accounts of another two members, and so forth. In addition to providing the team with information about the fit between their hypothesis and the observed patterns of family interaction, circular questioning was thought to provide family members with new information about their situation, information that challenged their prevailing belief systems and which trapped them into repetitive problem-maintaining interaction patterns.

Throughout this circular interviewing process the therapist adopted a position of neutrality or impartiality, siding with no one family member or faction against another. (This is in stark contrast to the use of unbalancing in structural family therapy to restructure the family.)

Following the first part of the interview, the original Milan team would meet and discuss the implications of the information that arose from circular questioning for the original hypotheses, synthesise available information into a new systemic hypothesis about the way the symptom was maintained by recursive patterns of family behaviour and underlying beliefs, and then design an intervention. Typically such interventions positively connoted the behaviour of all family members by empathising with their reasons for engaging in problem-maintaining behaviour. For example, to an anorexic girl and her parents it may be said, 'It is good that you do not eat at this point in your life because it makes your parents talk together about how to help you. When you have grown up and left home they will need to be practiced at talking to each other. It is good that you, her parents, explore many ways to help your daughter because you want her to be healthy'.

In addition to positive connotation the Milan team commonly asked families to complete rituals between sessions. For example, parents who regularly disqualified each other's attempts to manage their children's behaviour problems were invited to alternate the days on which they took exclusive charge of the children, with the father being in charge on odd days and the mother being in charge on even days.

Following the team's mid-session meeting, the family interview would be resumed and in this final part of the family interview the message developed by the team in the mid-session team meeting, including the positive connotation and prescription of a ritual or task, would be given to the family. Discussion of the message would be kept to a minimum. In some instances, families would be sent a written version of the message following the session.

After this final part of the interview, the team would meet once again to discuss the family's reaction to the message, to hypothesise about this, and to make tentative plans for the next session. This five-part session structure involving a pre-session meeting, the first part of the interview, the mid-session break, the final phase of the interview and the post-interview discussion was central to the Milan team's style of practice.

When resistance occurred in the form of disagreements between some family members and the therapist, the original Milan team adopted a practice of offering a split message, such as 'Some of my colleagues on the team disagree strongly with your position and think X, but having thought about this and listened to your position I am inclined to agree with your position, which is Y'. This split message approach allowed resistant families to remain engaged with the therapist while their problem-maintaining beliefs were challenged. Where family members completely opposed the treatment team and engagement was jeopardised, the Milan therapists commonly took a one-down position to mobilise the family to engage in therapy. For example, the team would express puzzlement and therapeutic impotence by, for example, noting that the family's problems were so complex and baffling and that they would probably be unresponsive to therapy. In some instances they referred to therapy sessions as preliminary meetings and described the possibility of family therapy as too risky an option to consider because it might jeopardise the integrity of the family or lead to unpredictable negative consequences for family members.

By about 1980, the original Milan four-member team had crystallised the model of practice just described. At this point the team split. Selvini-Palazzoli and Prata developed the strategic aspects of the original model further by outlining the development of particular types of problem-maintaining interaction patterns that they referred to as family games. Selvini Palazzoli et al. (1989) found that roles in families with a psychotic member entail a series of steps where the symptomatic child sides with the perceived loser against the winner in a discordant marriage, but the loser and winner eventually unite against the child, whose bizarre behaviour escalates and this interaction pattern maintains the psychotic process.

Prata (1990) with Selvini-Palazzoli has also experimented with the use of a highly standardised intervention with all cases, rather than designing different interventions for each case. They refer to this as the invariant prescription. With this prescription the parents are invited to hold a series of joint meetings in private, away from the home, and to make a point of not discussing the contents of these meetings with children or other family members. Over the course of therapy, the impact of this intervention of the beliefs and behaviour of the family is tracked. The therapeutic style of this branch of the original Milan team became highly directive and therapy could be terminated in instances where families did not comply with the invariant prescription.

SOCIAL CONSTRUCTIONIST DEVELOPMENTS

In contrast to the strategic Milan tradition and the way in which Selvini-Palazzoli and Prata developed this aspect of the work, Cecchin and Boscolo have evolved a non-interventionist style premised on social constructionism where the therapist's use of circular questioning opens up space for the client and therapist to co-construct multiple new perspectives on the problem situation (Boscolo et al., 1987). These multiple new perspectives contain the seeds of problem resolution. For Cecchin and Boscolo, the emphasis has been on elaborating the positioning of the therapist and developing approaches to circular questioning.

Cecchin argued that the concept of neutrality must be expanded to include the ideas of curiosity and irreverence: curiosity about the construction of multiple possible ways of thinking about the situation and irreverence toward therapist's favoured frames of reference, pet theories, biases and cherished ideas (Cecchin, 1987; Cecchin et al., 1992, 1993).

Boscolo has evolved a system of circular questioning that is future-oriented, and so focuses client's attention on the development of new belief systems about problems and solutions and how these will be in the future when the problem resolves (Boscolo & Bertrando, 1992, 1993).

Developments within the social constructionist movement have been documented by Hoffman (2002) and McNamee and Gergen (1992). Among the more important are Karl Tomm's (1987a, 1987b, 1988) interventive interviewing; the Fifth Provence associates' approach to enquiring about polarities (McCarthy & Byrne, 1988); Tom Andersen's (1987, 1991) reflecting team approach; and Harlene Anderson's collaborative language approach (Anderson, 1997, 2003). These developments will be considered next. Solution-focused and narrative approaches to family therapy are also premised predominantly on a social-constructionist world-view, but these are sufficiently large-scale and well-developed approaches to warrant consideration as separate schools and will be discussed in later sections of this chapter.

Interventive Interviewing

Karl Tomm (1987a; 1987b; 1988), in Calgary, Canada, has developed new ways of conceptualising the positioning of the therapist and therapeutic uses of particular types of questioning. He highlighted the fact that every question is a mini-intervention, and he refers to circular questioning guided by specific strategies as 'interventive interviewing'. Strategising is the process that guides such interviewing. When strategising, therapists, according to Tomm, clarify their intentions about why they are asking particular questions. Tomm identifies four main types of intent: investigative (to find out more facts); exploratory (to uncover patterns); corrective (to direct clients to act in a particular way); and facilitative (to open up new possibilities). He distinguished between four different types of questions that correspond to each of these four different types of intent. *Lineal* questions enquire about problem definitions and explanations (e.g. 'What is the problem?'). *Circular* questions enquire about patterns of interaction (e.g. 'Tell me what happens before, during and after the problem?'). *Strategic* questions are leading or confrontative (e.g. 'What if you did X? What prevents you from doing Y?'). *Reflexive* questions suggest new possibilities ('Imagine X were the case, how would the problem situation be different?'). Peggy Penn (1985) also developed a future-oriented or feed-forward approach to questioning.

Fifth Province Interviewing about Polar Positions

In Ireland the Fifth Province associates (McCarthy & Byrne, 1988) have developed a style of interviewing in which circular questions are asked to compare, amplify and eventually bridge polarities within systems. Diamond-shaped structural maps are used to map alliances within systems, and themes on which system members in polar positions hold different viewpoints. The therapist adopts a neutral, curious position, which is not aligned with any particular faction within the system. From this non-aligned 'dis-position' the therapist opens up a conversational space where extreme polarities and new possibilities may be explored. The disposition adopted by Fifth Province associates at the imaginal centre of conflicted networks and the name of this therapy team is taken from Celtic mythology. It refers to an imaginal place where oppositions were resolved and unrelated things coincided. In this style of therapy, pairs of significant bipolar constructs may be crossed at right angles to form diamond-shaped maps. For example, in a case of school refusal, bad versus mad and organic aetiology versus non-organic aetiology might be identified as two constructs organising parents' and involved professionals' conversations about a girl's non-attendance at school. A diamond-shaped map, based on crossing these two constructs at right angles, may be used as a basis for questioning network members in a way that moves the network towards a position where less polarisation occurs. Two approaches to questions developed by the Fifth Province team deserve particular mention: (1) questioning at the extremes; and (2) juxtapositioning. In questioning at the extremes, network members are asked to imagine what would happen if one of the extreme positions on the diamond were to form the basis for future actions. Here are a couple of examples of these types of questions: (1) 'If her behaviour was an act of defiance for which she required some form of punishment, what sort of things should the family do and say if she continued to appear defiant over the next couple of years?'; (2) 'Let us imagine that her behaviour reflects some underlying mental illness, how would you treat her over the next year or two?'. Questioning at the extremes allows network members to explore what would happen if a process of continual amplification occurred with respect to opposing constructions of the problem. With juxtapositioning, network members are asked to compare opposing constructions of the problem. For example, 'How would you see the main differences between what would happen to your child over the next year if she were treated as if she were delinquent or if she were treated as if she were ill?' Juxtapositioning allows network members to consider in an uncensored way, the contrasting implications of extreme or amplified positions.

Reflecting Team

While Karl Tomm, Peggy Penn, and the Fifth Province Associates have elaborated the Milan team's interviewing techniques, others, notably Tom Andersen, developed new ways of giving families the team's message arising from the mid-session team discussion. The reflecting team approach was developed by Tom Andersen (1987, 1991) in Norway. With this approach, during the mid-session break the family and therapist observe the team behind the one-way screen discussing the family interview. Members of the reflecting team comment on the interview process in a way that highlights family strengths and opens up new possibilities for problem resolution. After this the family and therapist resume the session and discuss useful ideas that have come from listening to the observations of the reflecting team. This is a highly collaborative approach to the use of a team behind the screen and contrasts starkly with the competitive frame that dominated the early Milan approach to using a team and screen in family therapy. For the original Milan team, the mid-session discussion was a secretive, competitive affair in which the team reconsidered their initial hypotheses in light of the information that arose from circular questioning to revise their map of the family game. They then devised a counterparadoxical, positively connoted description of the family game and a ritual to disrupt the game. This intervention was delivered to the family without opportunity for clarification or discussion. In contrast, with the reflecting team approach there is complete openness about the process and ample opportunity for clarification.

Tom Andersen highlights the importance of reflections being given by a small number of team members (no more than three) and that they be speculative, given in the style of the family's normal speech, that they be relevant to the preceding conversation, and that they not differ too much from the family's current views. He classifies reflections as those which comment on the picture of the problem situation; explanations for it; alternative possible solutions or hypothetical future scenarios; ways in which family members have constructed their picture of the problem, explanations for it and alternative solutions; and ways in which family members might construct new pictures of the problem, explanations for it and alternative solutions in the future. Thus, his reflections tap into the same areas as Tomm's linear, circular and reflexive questions mentioned earlier. Andersen also presents multiple reflections in both/and or neither/nor formats to help the family escape from limiting either/or conversations. Reflections on non-verbal processes which may introduce threatening information that is outside of awareness are made only if there is good reason to believe that the family is ready to hear it. When the therapist resumes the interview with the family, he or she explores positive and negative reactions of family members to the reflections. Throughout the process the team takes a positive, respectful, non-critical attitude towards the family.

The reflecting team process was to some degree foreshadowed by Peggy Papp's (1982) strategic practice of offering family members multiple differing messages from the team after the mid-session break and the original Milan team's use of split messages from the therapist and team to maintain engagement while challenging the family's belief system.

While Karl Tomm and Peggy Penn elaborated the Milan team's interviewing techniques, and Tom Andersen, developed new ways of giving families the team's message arising from the mid-session team discussion, Harlene Anderson and Harry Goolishian elaborated the idea of a collaborative positioning of the therapist with respect to clients.

Collaborative Language Systems

Harlene Anderson and Harry Goolishian at the Houston Galveston Institute developed a unique social-constructionist approach to family therapy (Anderson, 1995, 1997, 2000, 2001, 2003; Anderson & Goolishan, 1988; Anderson & Levine, 1998; Anderson, Goolishan & Windermand, 1986; Goolishian & Anderson, 1987). They abandoned systems theory and cybernetics as explanatory frameworks and replaced these with the extreme social-constructionist notion of collaborative language systems. They argued that systems of central concern were not families but groups of people in conversation about problems. Within these collaborative language systems, problems were co-constructed or dissolved in language.

They distinguished between problem-determined systems and problem dissolving systems. Problem-determined systems include people who agree that a problem exists and whose beliefs about the problem maintain its existence. Such systems may include some or all members of a family, but may also include other significant members of the social network, such as school teachers and involved health or social service professionals. Problem dissolving systems, in contrast, include a therapist and members of the problem-determined system. This system is organised by a belief that there is a problem and it dissolves the problem through conversation. Within this conversation, the therapist adopts a non-hierarchical, non-expert, not-knowing collaborative position with respect to clients, privileging the clients' views as much as the therapist's. The therapist engages in respectful listening to the clients' views, asking respectful questions without consciously hypothesising or strategising. Such generative conversations are used to explore multiple possible co-constructions of the problem and possible solutions. Therapists avoid the use of technical jargon, diagnoses and therapeutic directives since these may limit possibilities for co-constructing new solutions. Therapeutic conversations and new co-constructions of the clients' situation are all conducted in terms from the clients' language, not technical terms and jargon from the mental health or family therapy literatures.

SOLUTION-FOCUSED THERAPY

Solution-focused therapy was developed by Steve deShazer (1982, 1985, 1988, 1991, 1994; deShazer et al., 1986), Insoo Kim Berg (Berg, 1994; Berg, & Dolan 2000; Berg & Kelly, 2000; Berg & Miller, 1992; Berg & Reuss, 1997; DeJong & Berg, 2000; Miller & Berg, 1995), and their colleagues at the Milwaukee Brief Family Therapy Centre. Bill O'Hanlon (Hudson & O'Hanlon, 1994; O'Hanlon & Bertolino, 2002; O'Hanlon & Weiner-Davis, 2003; Rowan & O'Hanlon, 1999), Eve Lipchik (2002) and a team including Miller, Hubble and Duncan (1996) have made significant contributions to the development of solution-focused brief therapy in North America. Solution-focused centres have been established in the UK by Evan George, Chris Iveson and Harvey Ratner (1999), and in Ireland by John Sharry, Brendan Madden and Melissa Darmody (2003). Brief therapy is now a major international therapeutic movement (Carpenter, 1997; Duncan et al., 2003; Hoyt, 2002; Lethem, 2002).

Before developing the model, Steve deShazer worked with the MRI group and was strongly influenced by their idea of focusing on current interactional patterns rather than historical predisposing factors. However, his approach is distinct from the MRI approach in the following way. MRI brief therapy aims to identify problem-maintaining interaction patterns and then disrupt these patterns or ironic processes, while solution-focused therapy aims to identify infrequent exceptional interaction patterns in which the problem behaviour is expected to occur but does not, and arrange for clients to increase the frequency of these exceptional behaviour patterns. For example, a family in which the main complaint is the children's sleep difficulties would be asked to note occasions on which an exceptional, normal sleep pattern occurred and then to take particular steps to try to recreate this situation. This process of recreating exceptions is technically deceptively simple and is described in the texts *Keys to Solutions in Brief Therapy* and *Clues: Investigating Solutions in Brief Therapy* to solutions (deShazer, 1985, 1988). Amplifying exceptions always involves talking about problems differently, and here deShazer has been influenced by the philosopher Wittgenstein in his assertion that problems are constituted and not reflected in language. This idea is expanded in his book *Words were Originally Magic* (deShazer, 1994).

Solution-focused therapy has little to say about differences between 'normal' families and those in which problems occur, but the implicit message is that non-problematic families do not become entrenched in problem-maintaining interaction patterns. Rather, they notice exceptional circumstance where the expected problem does not occur and try to learn from these how to avoid or solve the problem in future.

Assessment and Treatment in Solution-Focused Therapy

Distinctions between assessment and therapy are not clearly drawn in solution-focused therapy. Assessment (insofar as it may be distinguished) begins with enquires about the problem; the position of the clients with respect to their problems; and their views of the role of the therapist with respect to problem resolution. Distinctions are made between visitors, complainants and customers. Clients who are sent to therapy by another person but do not view themselves as having a problem or requiring therapy are referred to as visitors. Clients who accept that they have problems but are unwilling or believe they are unable to resolve them in therapy are called complainants. Clients who accept that they have problems and want to change them through engaging in therapy are customers. These three positions are not fixed and clients may move from one to another over the course of therapy. For example, after a couple of sessions a previously despondent complainant may become a more hopeful customer. Also, different family members may occupy differing positions at different times. For example, an adolescent with a drug problem may be a visitor, his concerned mother may be a customer and his stepfather may be a complainant, wishing the problem would resolve but not willing to act on this wish.

Given this analysis of differing positions that clients may take with respect to their problem and therapy, it is not surprising that de Shazer takes the view that the idea of resistance is based on misunderstanding the fact that all clients have unique ways of cooperating, only some of which conform to traditionally trained therapists' expectations. These are the cooperative styles that typify customers, but not visitors or complainants. To promote continued cooperation, tasks must be selected to fit with clients' readiness to change. Compliments for attending therapy are more likely to ensure continued cooperation from visitors. Observational tasks such as noting the occurrence of exceptions promote increased cooperation from complainants. Behavioural tasks, such as the recreation of exceptions are best suited to customers.

In addition to assessing the positioning of clients, solution-focused therapists also assess exceptions. This may be done by enquiring about pre-session change. That is, by asking questions such as, 'Between the time you made the appointment to come here and today has the problem got better or worse? If it got better, what exactly was it about these past few days that led to improvement?'. Enquires about pre-session change in a majority of instances lead to recent vivid accounts of exceptions. However, where such accounts are not forthcoming, clients may simply be asked exception-finding questions, such as, 'Can you tell me about instances where the problem did not occur or occurred and was coped with effectively?'. DeShazer's formula first session task may also be used to identify exceptions. This involves an invitation for clients between the first and second session to observe family life so they can tell the therapist what they want to continue to have happen in future.

Beyond client positioning and exceptions, a third important aspect of assessment in solution-focused therapy is helping clients articulate their vision of problem resolution and therapeutic goals. For this deShazer uses Milton Erickson's miracle question: 'Supposing one night there was a miracle while you were asleep and the problem was solved, how would you know? What would be different. How would X know without you saying a word about it?' The more concrete and visualisable this vision, the better. Progress towards this vision may be articulated as more frequent exceptions and less frequent problems. For example, if the vision was 'We would have dinner each night as a family without fighting', then progress may be assessed by counting the number of nights on which fight-free family dinners occur.

However, not all problems and exceptions may be defined in concrete terms. For vague problems, particularly those that include statements about feelings and moods, clients may be asked to express changes in terms of a scale from 1 to 10, e.g. 'On a scale of 1 to 10 where 10 is how you want to feel when the problem is resolved, how good do you feel now?' Where scaling questions reveal improvements between one session and the next, exception questions may be asked, such as 'How do you explain the improvement that occurred between then and now, what exactly was different?'.

It has already been noted that in solution-focused therapy, compliments, observational tasks and behavioural tasks are given to visitors, complainants and customers respectively. Compliments are empathic statements about clients' positive qualities and are typically given to all clients to enhance cooperation, and the only class of intervention given to visitors.

With observational tasks, clients may be invited to observe the occurrence of successful coping with the problem, exceptions to the problem, factors that prevent deterioration, or to predict whether more or less exceptions than have previously occurred will occur between one session and the next and to check their prediction through observation. With behavioural tasks, clients may be invited, when exceptions are identified, to 'do more of what works' or, if it is difficult to specify the nature of exceptions, to simply 'do something different'.

When clients become despondent and have difficulties recreating solutions, the solution-focused therapist continually helps clients to give accounts of exceptions and make plans to recreate these. A positive hopeful perspective concerning problem resolution, a respect for clients' problem-solving resources, and an elegantly simple view of therapeutic technique are the corner stones of solution-focused therapy.

NARRATIVE THERAPY

Michael White, David Epston and their colleagues (Epston, 1989, 1998; Epston & White, 1992; Freeman, Epston & Lobovits, 1997; Jenkins, 1990; Monk, Winslade, Crocket & Epston, 1997; Morgan, 2000; White, 1989, 1995, 1997, 2000, 2005; White & Epston, 1989) are the originators of the narrative approach to family therapy. Michael White practices at the Dulwich Centre in Adelaide, which is run by Michael and his partner Cheryl White. David Epston practices in Auckland, New Zealand. Inspired by White's seminal work, other practitioners have begun to write about narrative therapy in the USA (Freedman & Combs, 1996, 2002; Parry & Doane, 1994; Zimmerman & Dickerson, 1996) and in the UK (Byng-Hall, 1995; McLeod, 1997). White and Epston have been influenced by the postmodern movement within philosophy, anthropology and psychology, and in particular by Michael Foucault (1965, 1975, 1979, 1980, 1982, 1984); Jacques Derrida (1981); Clifford Geertz (1983); Barbara Myerhoff (1982, 1986); Irving Goffman (1961, 1986); and Jerome Bruner (1986, 1987, 1991).

Problem Development and Narrative Therapy

While narrative therapy has little to say about normal and problematic family development, a clear theory of problem development is set out. Within a narrative frame, human problems are viewed as arising from, and being maintained by, oppressive stories that dominate the person's life. Human problems occur when the way in which people's lives are storied by themselves and others does not significantly fit with their lived experience. Indeed, significant aspects of their lived experience may contradict the dominant narrative in their lives.

Developing therapeutic solutions to problems, within the narrative frame, involves opening space for the authoring of alternative stories, the possibility of which have previously been marginalised by the dominant oppressive narrative which maintains the problem. These alternative stories typically are preferred by clients, fit with, and do not contradict significant aspects of lived experience and open up more possibilities for clients controlling their own lives.

The narrative approach rests on the assumption that narratives are not representations of reflections of identities, lives and problems. Rather, narratives constitute identities, lives and problems. According to this social-constructionist position, the process of therapeutic re-authoring changes lives, problems and identities because personal narratives are constitutive of identity (Bruner, 1986, 1987, 1991).

Rejection of Both Individual Diagnostic Systems and Systems Theory

White rejects both traditional individually-based conceptualisations of human problems and also, like Harlene Anderson, the use of a systemic framework that has been central to almost all forms of family therapy. Drawing on the work of Foucault (1965, 1975, 1979, 1980, 1982, 1984), White refers to the process of applying psychiatric diagnoses to clients and construing people exclusively in terms of these diagnostic labels as 'totalising techniques'. Totalising techniques such as diagnostic classification turn people (subjects) into things (objects). Related practices such as keeping files (to which clients have no access) written within the context of a pejorative pathological deficit-discourse promote the construction of *global* knowledges and undermine *local* knowledges. In this sense, using mainstream mental health practices that are founded in scientific knowledge inevitably entails exerting power or social control over clients. Michael White's approach to narrative therapy invites us to accept that knowledge and power are two sides of the same coin, and to question the ethics of traditional practices that privilege global knowledges and totalising techniques. Ultimately, the pathologising mainstream mental health narrative, which permeates our culture, leads people to identify themselves with their problems and develop *problem-saturated identities* (Gergen, 1991, 1994).

Drawing on the work of the anthropologist Clifford Geertz (1983), the narrative analogy and development of *thick descriptions* of multistranded stories has been distinguished by Michael White (1989) from the systems and game analogies so widely favoured within the family therapy field. According to White, when couples and families are conceptualised as systems or quasi-biological organisms, then interpersonal problems are construed as serving a particular function, such as maintaining family homeostasis (Guttman, 1991). The goal of therapy, within this frame, is the discovery of the function of the symptom and replacing the problematic symptom with a less destructive set of routines that fulfil the same function as the symptom. This systems analogy entails the view that certain families are dysfunctional and, because of this, problems are required for them to remain intact and stable. Furthermore, the systems analogy disqualifies the personal agency of individual family members, by interpreting individual behaviours as arising, not from personal intentions, but from the requirements of the system. Narrative therapy, in contrast, privileges the power of the individual to choose the narrative by which he or she lives.

When the analogy of a game is used to make sense of problematic patterns of family interaction, then problem behaviours of family members are understood as moves and countermoves that are undertaken to win the game. Within this frame, therapy involves mapping out the moves and countermoves of the game and using this map to develop a strategic plan for ending the game so that the moves and countermoves are no longer necessary. The therapist inevitably becomes a player in the game and uses secrecy and deception (in the form of paradoxical injunctions or taking a one-down position) as a powerbase from which to end the game. This type of approach underpins strategic therapy (Madanes, 1991) and the early work of the Milan Team (Campbell et al., 1991). In contrast, narrative therapy requires the therapist to form an open collaborative partnership with clients and avoids the use of power practices such as secrecy and deception.

Assessment and Treatment in Narrative Therapy

A central goal of narrative therapy is to help people re-author their lives so that they define themselves in non-pathologising non-problem saturated ways. The process of 're-authoring', a term drawn from the work of the anthropologist Myerhoff (1982, 1986), is essentially collaborative and requires therapists and clients to engage in particular practices that lead to clients doing what Myerhoff refers to as 'performing new meanings'. To facilitate re-authoring, the narrative therapist adopts a collaborative co-authoring consultative position. Externalisation is used to help clients view themselves as separate from their problems. For example, a client may be asked how depression has been oppressing them. The narrative therapist helps clients pinpoint times in their lives when they were not oppressed by their problems by finding 'unique outcomes' (a term coined by Goffman (1961, 1986)). Unique outcomes include exceptions to the routine pattern within which some aspect of the problem normally occurs. Unique outcomes may be identified by asking questions such as, 'Can you tell me about a time when you prevented this problem from oppressing you?'. Descriptions of these unique outcomes are then elaborated by posing landscape-of-action and landscape-of-consciousness questions. The terms for these twin 'landscapes' were coined by Bruner (1986, 1987, 1991). Landscape-of-action questions address sequences of events, for example, 'Give me a step-by-step account of that episode?'. Landscape-of-consciousness questions in contrast are concerned primarily with the meaning of events and enquire about motives, purposes, intentions, hopes, beliefs and values, for example, 'What does this story say about you as a person?'. Narrative therapists link unique outcomes to other events in the past and extend the story into the future to form an alternative and preferred self-narrative in which the self is viewed as more powerful than the problem. For example, links with the past may be established through asking question like this: 'If I were watching you earlier in your life, what do you think I would have seen that would have helped me to understand how you were able recently to achieve X?' Links with the future may be made with such questions as: 'If you were to keep these ideas in mind over the next while, how might they have an effect on your life?'.

Through the use of outsider witness groups, significant members of the client's social network are invited to witness this new self-narrative. Outsider witnesses let clients know what they are up against and what to expect in overcoming problems and taking charge of their lives. Michael White has also drawn on Tom Andersen's (1987) practice of using a reflecting team in narrative therapy as a format for a particular type of outsider witness group.

New knowledges and practices that support the new self-narrative established in therapy are documented using literary means. Letters of invitation, redundancy letters, letters of prediction, counter-referral letters, letters of reference, letters of special occasions, self-stories, certificates and declarations may be used to facilitate and document changes in narrative therapy.

Finally, clients are encouraged to let others who are trapped by similar oppressive narratives benefit from their new knowledge through bringing -it-back practices. They may be invited to allow the therapist to share their new personal narratives, knowledges, skills or literary records of these with other clients facing similar difficulties. Alternatively, they may agree to meet with other clients and let other clients know directly about their experiences.

CLOSING COMMENTS

All of the family therapy approaches described in this chapter focus predominantly on belief systems that underpin problem-maintaining interaction patterns. These constructivist, constructionist, solution-focused and narrative approaches all involve helping clients develop new ways of making sense of their problems so that they become more resolvable. All of these approaches share some common ground with cognitive techniques associated with cognitive-behavioural therapy described in the previous chapter, insofar as they aim to alter problem-maintaining belief systems. The style of practice used by the original four-member Milan team prior to 1980 shares much in common with strategic and MRI brief therapy, particularly the competitive use of paradoxical interventions to disrupt problem-maintaining interaction patterns and to undermine problem-maintaining belief systems. There are notable similarities between the solution-focused and narrative approaches. Both privilege the importance of amplifying exceptions to problems, privileging solution-talk over problem-talk in therapeutic consultations and generating hope.

For all of the models reviewed here the only treatment goal is the resolution of the presenting problem. None of the models reviewed in this chapter is concerned with personal growth as a main goal. For all of the approaches described in this chapter treatment is brief.

There is a small body of empirical evidence to support the effectiveness of the original Milan approach to family therapy with common child- and adult-focused mental health problems (Carr, 1991). There is also evidence from controlled trials for the effectiveness of solution-focused therapy (Gingerich & Eusengart, 2000). However, for narrative therapy, constructivist or social constructionist approaches to family therapy, although some exploratory qualitative studies have been conducted, clear demonstrations of their effectiveness are lacking (e.g. Anderson, 2003; Sexton, Robbins, Hollimon, Mease & Mayorga, 2003).

The strength of the models overviewed in this chapter is way in which they highlight the importance of multiperspectivism for clinical practice and the many creative techniques based on this idea that may be used to transform or marginalise problem-maintaining belief systems and enhance solution-developing belief systems. A problem with constructivist and constructionist positions, however, is that they entail the paradoxical view that the one underlying truth is that there is no one underlying truth. Social constructionists who have abandoned general systems theory and cybernetics are left with a very flimsy therapeutic framework and set of practices with which to empower therapists in training. Without any of the insights and practices of structural, strategic, MRI, cognitive-behavioural and functional family therapy, therapists in training may easily be inducted into problem-maintaining behaviour patterns without being aware of this. Equipped only with the ideas of co-constructing new alternatives, amplifying solutions, or re-authoring, they may never be able to break out of counter-therapeutic positions. Also, from an empirical perspective, it is not ethically justifiable to abandon practices entailed by structural, cognitive-behavioural and functional family therapy that have been shown to be very effective in many treamtent outcome studies, and to adopt practices for which there is virually no empirical support.

My view is that an attempt should be made to integrate the insights and practices from the models reviewed in this chapter with those from the models in the preceding and following chapters. One way of forging such an integration is given in Chapters 7–9.

The models reviewed in this chapter focus predominantly on modifying belief systems that underpin problem-maintaining interaction patterns. The approaches described in the next chapter are primarily concerned with historical, contextual and constitutional factors that predispose family members and others to hold particular belief systems and so engage in problem-maintaining behaviour.

GLOSSARY

Bateson's ecosystemic epistemology. The idea that the universe – including mind and nature – is a single ecological system.

Constructivism. The theory that each individual's world view is determined more by his or her physiological and psychological make-up than the world out there.

Epistemology. A branch of philosophy concerned with the study of theories of knowledge, but in family therapy the term is used loosely to refer to a world view or belief system, such as Bateson's ecosystemic epistemology, constructivism, social constructionism and positivism.

Modernism. A movement that began with the enlightenment and entailed the view that the underlying nature of the world would be revealed through rigorous and rational scientific enquiry.

Positivism. The theory that perceptions are reflections of the world-as-it-is and that, through rigorous scientific observation and experiment, we may acquire true knowledge about this world.

Postmodernism. Postmodernism entails a rejection of positivism and representationalism in favour of constructivism or social constructionism; an acceptance of the idea that there may be multiple accounts of events over the idea that there is a single knowable underlying truth; a favouring of marginalised discourse over the dominant discourse; a favouring of local accounts over global accounts; and a commitment to the idea that all accounts entail an ethical dimension over the idea that there are value-free facts.

Social-constructionism. The theory that each individual's world view is determined more by social consensus within the community, expressed in language, than the world out there.

Constructivism

Autopoiesis. Maturana's term 'autopoesis' literally means self-creating (auto = self; poiesis = creating). Such self-creating processes distinguish living from mechanical systems and are subject to structural determinism.

Complex and simple construct systems. Complex construct systems may contain many constructs that are interrelated in many ways. Simple construct systems contain few constructs with limited relationships to one another. People with complex construct systems are better able to empathise with others and form workable relationships.

Construct. The simplest hypothesis that a person can hold about a group of elements (persons, objects, events or relationships). A construct defines how two things are alike and different from a third. Constructs have similarity and contrast poles, a range or application to a set of elements and focus of convenience to a subset of elements to which they may be easily applied.

Core and peripheral constructs. Core constructs are vital for the survival of a person's construct system and peripheral constructs are not.

Cycle of experience. A cycle that maps out how construct systems are revised through experiential feedback. The cycle includes the following stages: (1) anticipation of an event; (2) investment in the outcome; (3) encounter with the event; (4) confirmation or disconfirmation of the initial anticipation; and (5) constructive revision of the construct if disconfirmation occurred.

Family characterisation. An assessment procedure in which a family member writes an account of the family from the perspective of a close friend.

Fixed role therapy. An intervention to help clients evolve more adaptive construct systems, where they are invited to play a fixed role, which entails constructs that are different from their own, for a period of days and then to comment on the impact of this on their construct system.

Laddering. A method for discovering the hierarchical way in which constructs are organised and pinpointing core constructs by repeatedly asking clients, after a construct has been elicited, which pole of a construct they prefer and why.

Objectivity in parenthesis. Maturana's term for the idea that we cannot claim that a reality out there exists independently of ourselves as observers.

Personal construct psychology. The constructivist psychology of George Kelly, in which he articulated a set of propositions outlining how personal belief systems could be viewed as made up of a set of personal bipolar constructs, and how these construct systems determined behaviour and relationships.

Repertory grid test (REP). A paper and pencil or computerised method for eliciting constructs. Computer REP tests can elicit element lists in many areas of life, elicit constructs, position elements along construct scales, factor analyse constructs into dimensions, hierarchically organise these construct-based dimensions, and position elements accurately along these dimensions, and cluster-analyse elements in terms of dimensions.

Self-characterisation. An assessment procedure in which a person writes an account of themselves from the perspective of a close friend.

Structural coupling. Maturana's idea that when two systems (such as therapist and family) come together a process of mutual influence occurs and the changes that occur in each system are structurally determined and so, to a large degree, unpredictable.

Structural determinism. Maturana's constructivist proposition that the structure of an organism's nervous system or the structure of the family's systemic organisation determine its actions, not external stimuli, information or instructions. According to this viewpoint, therapists cannot instruct clients to act and predict the outcome, they can only structurally couple with them, perturb the system and await an unexpected outcome according to this view.

Superordinate and subordinate constructs. A superordinate construct includes subordinate constructs in the system.

Tight (impermeable) and loose (permeable) construct systems. Construct systems that are tight lead the person to make precise and rigid predictions in every situation. Loose construct systems do not allow the person to make useful predictions.

Triadic questioning. A process for identifying constructs, which involves asking a person to list a series of elements (people, objects, events or relationships), and then asking them to indicate how each pair are the same and different from a third. For example, if two relationships are the same because they are close but different from a third because it is distant, the construct identified is close–distant.

Verbal and pre-verbal constructs. Pre-verbal constructs are not easily verbalised, for example a vague feeling of abandonment versus a feeling of attachment.

Milan Systemic Family Therapy

Circular causality. The idea that, within (observed) family systems, problem behaviours typically occur within the context of repetitive interactional patterns in which event A leads to B leads to C leads to A. This is distinguished from linear (or lineal) causality, which characterises non-systemic theories and takes the form: event A leads to event B.

Circular questioning. A style of interviewing used to check out the validity of hypotheses about family and therapeutic systems. Information brought forth by circular questions is used to modify successive hypotheses so that they gradually come to account for more and more of the available information. This is a recursive process of the therapist–family (observing) system. There are many types of circular questions including questions about sequences of interaction, such as, 'What happened next?'; questions about comparisons, such as, 'Who was the most concerned?'; questions about agreement, such as, 'Who would agree and who would disagree with this view?'; questions about explanations, such as, 'What explanation do you think you (or some other family member) would give for this?'; and questions about the future, such as, 'Suppose X happens, then how will the situation be different in 6 months?'.

Circularity. An umbrella term used to refer to both circular causality in observed systems and the recursive processes of the therapist–family observing system in circular questioning.

Counter-paradox. An invitation for each family member to persist, for the time being, in their roles in a pattern of problem-maintaining interaction, because these afford an avenue for the expression of positive intentions and to do otherwise would lead to negative consequences for the family. However, the possibility of future change is left open.

Family games. The historical steps involved in the development of problem-maintaining interaction patterns and the repetitive roles entailed by these patterns. Selvini-Palazzoli argues that psychotic family roles entail a series of steps where the symptomatic child sides with the perceived loser against the winner in a discordant marriage, but the loser and winner eventually unite against the child and this interaction pattern maintains the psychotic process.

Five-part session. A session plan that includes: (1) a pre-session team discussion, which focuses on hypothesising; (2) the first part of the family interview in which circular questioning is used to check out hypotheses; (3) the mid-session break and team discussion where the implications on hypotheses of new information arising from circular questioning are clarified and an end-of-session intervention is developed; (4) the final part of the family interview, which may include an end-of-session intervention; and (5) a post-session team discussion in which further hypothesising occurs and planning for the next session.

Hypothesising. Developing a tentative systemic mini-theory about some aspect of a system, the validity of which is subsequently checked out through interviewing and observation. Information from interviewing and observation may lead to successive modifications and refinements of hypotheses to improve the degree to which the hypotheses correspond with available information about the system.

Invariant prescription. A ritualistic intervention developed by Selvini-Palazzoli and Prata to disrupt rigid problem-maintaining interaction patterns in the families of psychotic individuals. The parents are invited to form an alliance, the details of which are kept secret from other family members by requesting the parents to hold a series of joint meetings in private, often away from the home, and making a point of not discussing the contents of these with children or other family members.

Neutrality. An interviewing position of impartiality, characterised by an openness to the validity of each system member's viewpoint and an openness to multiple possible hypotheses to account for available information. Neutrality as an interviewing position does not entail an ethically neutral position with respect to intrafamilial abuses of power.

Odd days and even days. A ritual in which on odd days one person is given unilateral control over a particular family problem and on even days the other person is given such control. This may be used to help parents whose inability to agree on how to manage child behaviour problems makes such problems worse.

Positive connotation. The practice of ascribing positive intentions to each family member concerning their role in a pattern of problem-maintaining interaction.

Problem of the referring person. The idea that siblings or professionals who have a long-standing relationship with a patient, who make referrals for family therapy, may inadvertently be inviting the therapist to become inducted into a specific role in the problem-maintaining interaction pattern.

Rituals. Interventions designed to disrupt repetitive problem-maintaining interaction patterns in which specific behaviours and the circumstances under which they should occur are specified for one or more family members.

Social Constructionism

Curiosity. An interviewing position of impartiality, characterised by an openness not only to the validity of each system member's viewpoint but also an openness to multiple possible constructions of clients' situations and a respect for the integrity of the system and its way of operating. Cecchin offered curiosity as a social constructionist refinement of the therapeutic position of neutrality.

Hermeneutics. The art of analysing texts or therapeutic conversations by recursively interpreting successive levels of meaning. The hermeneutic circle is a recursive loop of successive interpretations.

Interventive interviewing. A term coined by Karl Tomm to refer to an orientation where every question the therapist asks in a session is thought of as an intervention.

Irreverence. An interviewing position characterised by an openness to multiple possible constructions of clients' situations and a scepticism about personal pet theories and prejudices. Cecchin offered irreverence as an expansion of the therapeutic position of curiosity.

Juxtapositioning. Asking about the contrasting implications of extreme or amplified positions.

Karl Tomm's four classes of questions. Karl Tomm distinguished between lineal questions, which enquire about problem definitions and explanations, e.g. 'What is the problem?'; circular questions, which enquire about patterns of interaction, e.g. 'Tell me what happens before during and after the problem?'; strategic questions, which are confrontative, e.g. 'What prevents you from doing X?'; and reflexive questions, which suggest new possibilities, e.g. 'Imagine X were the case, how would the problem situation be different?'.

Languaging. Carol Anderson and Harry Goolishian's term for talking about a problem with a view to exploring new and more useful co-constructions.

Multiversa. Tom Andersen's term for the multitude of possible ways to think about clients' problems and solutions.

Not-knowing approach. Harlene Anderson and Harry Goolishian's term for taking a non-expert collaborative position where clients and therapist explore multiple possible co-construction of the problem and possible solutions. In the not-knowing approach, therapists avoid the use of diagnoses and therapeutic directives since these may limit possibilities for co-constructing new solutions.

Problem-determined system. Harlene Anderson and Harry Goolishian's term for a group of people who agree in conversation that a problem exists and whose beliefs about the problem maintain its existence.

Problem organising, problem dissolving system. Harlene Anderson and Harry Goolishian's term for the therapeutic system that includes the therapist and members of the problem-determined system. This system is organised by a belief that there is a problem and dissolves the problem through conversation.

Questioning at the extremes. Inviting speculation about what would happen if a process of continual amplification occurred with respect to opposing constructions of the problem.

Reflecting team. A practice developed by Tom Andersen where, after watching an interview, the team discuss their observations and ideas about the interview, the problem, explanations for it and alternative solutions, while the therapist and clients observe them. The clients and therapist then discuss the team's conversation with the therapist.

Reflexive time. Boscolo's idea that in systemic therapy and consultation the construction of both past and future problems and their resolution may be changed by the way they are co-constructed in the present. Multiple possible futures may be created in the present and this may influence the way the past is constructed. This may be achieved by asking future questions, such as, 'If you decided not to behave like a person with schizophrenia what would the future be like?'.

Strategising. A term coined by Karl Tomm to refer to the process of interviewing with particular intentions in mind. Tomm identifies four main types of intent: investigative (to find out more facts); exploratory (to uncover patterns); corrective (to direct clients to act in a particular way); and facilitative (to open up new possibilities).

Stuck systems. Systems become stuck when they focus on one or a limited number of possible ways of thinking about problems and solutions and are closed to multiple possibilities (multiversa).

Solution-Focused Therapy

Compliments. Empathic statements of clients' positive qualities, typically given to all clients to enhance cooperation, and the only class of intervention given to visitors.

Cooperation and resistance. DeShazer takes the view that the idea of resistance is based on misunderstanding the fact that all clients have unique ways of cooperating, only some of which conform to therapists' expectations. These are the cooperative styles which typify customers, but not visitors or complainants.

Do more of what works tasks. When exceptions are identified, if clients believe they have control over them they may be asked to do more of what works and if they believe such exceptions occur spontaneously they may be asked to do them randomly at the flip of a coin.

Do something different task. To disrupt routine problematic responses clients may be invited simply to do something different in situations where problems typically occur.

Exceptions. Instances where the problem does not occur, or occurs and is coped with effectively.

Fitting tasks to clients. To promote continued cooperation, tasks must be selected to fit with clients' readiness to change. Compliments for attending therapy are more likely to ensure continued cooperation from visitors. Observational tasks, such as noting the occurrence of exceptions, promote increased cooperation from complainants. Behaviour tasks, such as the recreation of exceptions, are best suited to customers.

Formula first session task. Clients are invited between the first and second session to observe family life so they can tell the therapist what they want to continue to have happen in future.

Identify factors that prevent deterioration. Clients are invited to identify factors that prevent complex or volatile problematic situations from deteriorating further.

Miracle question. An Ericksonian goal-setting question used by deShazer: 'Supposing one night there was a miracle while you were asleep and the problem was solved, how would you know? What would be different. How would X know without you saying a word bout it?'

Observation of successful coping task. Clients are invited between one session and the next to pay attention to what they do when they cope successfully with the problem, overcome the urge to do something problematic, or resist the temptation to do something problematic.

Observe exceptions task. Clients are invited to keep a log of exceptional episodes in which the problem should occur but does not.

Prediction task. Clients are invited to make a predication about whether between one session and the next there will be more or fewer exceptions to the problem.

Pre-session change. Positive changes and the exceptional circumstances surrounding them that occur between making an appointment and attending a first session.

Scaling question. For vague problems and feelings, clients may be asked to express changes in problems and feeling in terms of a scale from 1 to 10. For example, 'On a scale of 1 to 10 where 10 is good, how good do you feel now and how did you feel then?'. Where scaling questions reveal improvements, exception questions may be asked, such as, 'How do you explain the improvement that occurred between then and now?'.

Visitors–complainants–customers. Within the therapist–client relationship, clients who are sent to therapy by another person but do not view themselves as having a problem or requiring therapy are referred to as 'visitors'. Clients who accept that they have problems but are unwilling or believe they are unable to resolve them are 'complainants'. Clients who accept they have problems and want to change them are 'customers'.

Narrative Therapy

Bringing-it-back practices. Practices that involve clients letting others who are trapped by similar oppressive narratives benefit from their new knowledge and skills.

Dominant narratives. Typically, clients' dominant narratives entail problem-maintaining ideas and practices, especially the idea that the dominant narrative is the truth or the most valid world view.

Externalising the problem. Helping clients view themselves as separate from their problems and then inviting the clients and their families to deal with this externalised problem.

Landscape of action questions. Questions (about unique outcomes) that enquire about sequences of behaviour and interaction, such as, 'What happened next?'.

Landscape of consciousness questions. Questions (about unique outcomes) that enquire about meaning, intentions, beliefs and values, such as, 'What does that say about you as a person?'.

Narrative. A story that usually involves characters and a plot. Most people have dominant and subjugated personal narratives, with the former having greater influence on their lives than the latter.

Outsider witness groups. Significant members of clients' social networks who are invited to witness new self-narratives.

Positioning. In narrative therapy a collaborative co-authoring consultative position is adopted.

Re-authoring. The process of helping clients develop new and liberating self-narratives that promote problem resolution.

Relative influence questioning. Clients are invited to consider the influence of the problem on their lives and relationships and the influence that they exert on the problem. For example, 'In that situation were you stronger than the problem or was the problem stronger than you?'.

Subjugated narratives. The infinite number of alternatives to the dominant narrative, some of which entail world views, which open up possibilities for resolving presenting problems. Useful subjugated narratives may include accounts of exceptional circumstances where the problem did not occur, or occurred and was dealt with effectively.

Therapeutic certificates. In narrative therapy, clients may be issued with certificates to indicate that they have resolved their problems and they may use these certificates to substantiate their new self-narratives.

Therapeutic letters. In narrative therapy, therapists may send clients letters which consolidate new self-narratives by, for example, referring to unique outcomes mentioned in therapy and the implications of these for the clients' self-narratives.

Thickening new plots. Linking unique outcomes to other events in the past and extending the story into the future to form an alternative and preferred self-narrative in which the self is viewed as more powerful than the problem.

Unique outcomes. Exceptional circumstances under which problems did not occur but were expected to occur.

FURTHER READING

Constructivist Systemic Practice

Alexander, P. & Neimeyer, G. (1989). Constructivism and family therapy. *International Journal of Personal Construct Psychology*, **2**, 111–121.

Dallos, R & Aldridge, D. (1985). Handing it on: Family constructs, symptoms and choice. *Journal of Family Therapy*, **8**, 45–49.

Dallos, R. (1991). *Family Belief Systems, Therapy and Change*. Milton Keynes, UK: Open University Press.

Dallos, R. (1997). *Interacting Stories: Narratives, Family Beliefs and Therapy*. London: Karnac.

Feixas, G. (1990a). Approaching the individual, approaching the system: A constructivist model for integrative psychotherapy. *Journal of Family Psychology*, **4**, 4–35.

Feixas, G. (1990b). Personal construct theory and the systemic therapies. Parallel or convergent trends? *Journal of Marital and Family Therapy*, **16**, 1–20.

Feixas, G. (1995a). Personal construct approaches to family therapy. In G. Neimeyer & R. Neimeyer (Eds), *Advances in Personal Construct Psychology, Vol. 2*, pp. 215–255. Greenwich, CT: JAI Press.

Feixas, G. (1995b). Personal constructs in systemic practice. In R. Neimeyer & M. Mahoney (Eds), *Constructivism in Psychotherapy*, pp. 305–337. Washington, DC: APA.

Feixas, G., Procter, H. & Neimeyer, G. (1993). Convergent lines of assessment: Systemic and constructivist contributions. In G. Neimeyer (Ed.), *Casebook in Constructivist Assessment*, pp. 143–178. Newbury Park, CA: Sage.

Kelly, G. (1955). *The Psychology of Personal Constructs*, Vols 1 and 2. New York: Norton.

Kenny, V. (Ed.) (1988). Special edition on Constructivism. *Irish Journal of Psychology*, **9**.

Neimeyer, G. (1985). Personal constructs and the counselling of couples. In F. Epting & A. Landfeld (Eds), *Anticipating Personal Construct Psychology*, pp. 201–215. Lincon: University of Nebraska Press.

Neimeyer, G. (1987). Marital role reconstruction through couples group therapy. In R. Neimeyer & G. Neimeyer (Eds), *A Casebook of Personal Construct Therapy*. New York: Springer.

Neimeyer, G. & Neimeyer, R. (1994). Constructivist methods of marital and family therapy: a practical precis. *Journal of Mental Health Counseling*, **16** (1), 85–104.

Procter, H. (1981). Family construct psychology: An approach to understanding and treating families. In S. Walrond-Skinner (Ed.), *Developments in Family Therapy: Theories and Applications since 1948*, pp. 350–366. London: Routledge.

Procter, H. (1985a). A construct approach to family therapy and systems intervention. In E. Button (Ed.), *Personal Construct Theory and Mental Health*, pp. 327–350. London: Croom Helm.

Procter, H. (1985b). Repertory grids in family therapy and research. In N. Beail (Ed.), *Repertory Grid Techniques and Personal Constructs: Applications in Clinical and Educational Settings*, pp. 218–239. London: Croom Helm.

Procter, H. (1995). The family construct system. In D. Kalekin-Fishman & B. Walker (Eds), *The Construct on of Group Realities. Culture and Society in the Light of Personal Construct Theory*, pp. 161–180. New York: Krieger.

Procter, H. (2003). Family therapy. In F. Fransella (Ed.), *International Handbook of Personal Construct Psychology*, pp. 431–434. Chichester: Wiley.

Milan Systemic Family Therapy

Boscolo, L. & Bertrando, P. (1992). The reflexive loop of past present and future in systemic therapy and consultation. *Family Process*, **31**, 119–133.

Boscolo, L. & Bertrando, P. (1993). *The Times of Time: A New Perspective in Systemic Therapy and Consultation*. New York: Norton.

Boscolo, L., Cecchin, G., Hoffman, L. & Penn, P. (1987). *Milan Systemic Family Therapy*. New York: Basic Books.

Campbell, D. (1999). Family therapy and beyond. Where is the Milan systemic approach today. *Child Psychology and Psychiatry Review*, **4** (2), 76–84.

Campbell, D. & Draper, R. (1985). *Applications of Systemic Therapy: The Milan Approach*. London: Grune Stratton.

Campbell, D., Draper, R. & Huffington, C. (1988a). *Teaching Systemic Thinking*. London: Karnack.

Campbell, D., Reder, P. Draper, R. & Pollard, D. (1988b). *Working With the Milan Method: Twenty Questions*. London: Institute of Family Therapy.

Campbell, D., Draper, R. & Huffington, C. (1989a). *A Systemic Approach to Consultation*. London: Karnack.

Campbell, D., Draper, R. & Huffington, C. (1989b). *Second Thoughts on the Theory and Practice of the Milan Approach*. London: Karnack.

Campbell, D., Draper, R. & Crutchley, E. (1991). The Milan systemic approach to family therapy. In A. Gurman & D. Kniskern (Eds), *Handbook of Family Therapy, Vol. 11*, pp. 325–362. New York: Brunner Mazel.

Cecchin, G. (1987). Hypothesizing, circularity and neutrality revisited: An invitation to curiosity. *Family Process,* **26**, 405–413.

Cecchin, G., Lane, G. & Ray, W. (1992). *Irreverence: A Strategy for Therapist Survival.* London: Karnac.

Cecchin, G., Lane, G. & Ray, W. (1993). From strategising to non-intervention: Toward irreverence in systemic practice. *Journal of marital and Family Therapy,* **2**, 125–136.

Cecchin, G., Ray, W. & Lane, G. (In Press). *Power Struggles: Managing Escalations in Psychotherapy.* London: Karnac.

Gelcer, E., McCabe, A. & Smith-Resnick, C. (1990). *Milan Family Therapy: Variant and Invariant Methods.* Northvale, NJ: Aronson.

Jones, E. (1993). *Family Systems Therapy: Developments in the Milan Systemic Therapy.* Chichester: Wiley.

Papp, P. (1983). *The Process of Change.* New York: Guilford.

Penn, P. (1982). Circular questioning. *Family Process,* **21**, 267–280.

Penn, P. (1985). Feedforward: Further questioning future maps. *Family Process,* **24**, 299–310.

Pirrotta, S. (1984). Milan Revisited: A comparison of the two Milan Schools. *Journal of Strategic and Systemic Therapies,* **3**, 3–15.

Prata, G. (1990). *A Systemic Harpoon into Family Games: Preventative Interventions in Therapy.* New York: Brunner Mazel.

Selvini Palazzoli, M. (1981). *Self Starvation: From the Intrapsychic to the Transpersonal Approach to Anorexia.* New York: Jason Aronson.

Selvini Palazzoli, M. (1988). *The Work of Mara Selvini Palazzoli.* New York: Jason Aronson.

Selvini-Palazzoli, M., Boscolo, L., Cecchin, G. and Prata, G. (1978b). *Paradox and Counterparadox.* New York: Aronson.

Selvini-Palazzoli, M., Boscolo, L., Cecchin, G. & Prata, G. (1980). Hypothesizing–circularity–neutrality: Three guidelines for the conductor of the session. *Family Process,* **19**, 3–12.

Selvini-Palazzoli, M., Cirillo, Selvini, M. & Sorrentino, A. (1989). *Family Games: General Models of Psychotic Processes within the Family.* New York: Norton.

Tomm, K. (1984a). One perspective on the Milan Systemic Approach: Part I. Overview of development theory and practice. *Journal of Marital and Family Therapy,* **10**, 113–125.

Tomm, K. (1984b). One perspective on the Milan Systemic Approach: Part II. Description of session format, interviewing style and interventions. *Journal of Marital and Family Therapy,* **10**, 253–271.

Social Constructionist Family Therapy

Andersen, T. (1987). The Reflecting team: Dialogue and meta-dialogue in clinical work. *Family Process,* **26**, 415–428.

Andersen, T. (1991). *The Reflecting Team: Dialogues and Dialogues about the Dialogues.* New York: Norton.

Anderson, H. (1995). Collaborative language systems: Toward a postmodern therapy. In R. Mikesell, D. Lusterman & S. McDaniel (Eds), *Integrating Family Therapy. Handbook of Family Psychology and Systems Theory*, pp. 27–44. Washington, DC: APA.

Anderson, H. (1997). *Conversation, Language and Possibilities. A Postmodern Approach to Therapy.* New York: Basic Books.

Anderson, H. (2000). Becoming a postmodern collaborative therapist: A clinical and theoretical journey, Part I. *Journal of the Texax Association for Marriage and Family Therapy,* **5** (1), 5–12.

Anderson, H. (2001). Becoming a postmodern collaborative therapist: A clinical and theoretical journey, Part II. *Journal of the Texax Association for Marriage and Family Therapy,* **6** (1), 4–22.

Anderson, H. (2003). Postmodern, social construction therapies. In T. Sexton, G. Weeks & M. Robbins (Eds), *Handbook of Family Therapy,* pp. 125–146. New York: Brunner-Routledge.

Anderson, H. & Goolishan, H. (1988). Human systems as linguistic systems: Preliminary and evolving ideas about the implications for clinical theory. *Family Process,* **27**, 371–394.

Anderson, H. & Levine, S. (1998). *Collaborative Conversations with Children: Country Clothes and City Clothes. Narrative Therapy with Children.* New York: Guilford.

Anderson, H., Goolishan, H. & Windermand, L. (1986). Problem determined systems: Toward transformation in family therapy. *Journal of Strategic and Systemic Therapies,* **5** (4), 1–14.

Friedman, S. (1993). *The New Language of Change: Constructive Collaboration in Psychotherapy.* New York: Guilford.

Friedman, S. (1995). *The Reflecting Team in Action: Collaborative Practice in Family Therapy.* New York: Guilford.

Gergen, K. (1994). *Realities and Relationships. Soundings in Social Constructionism.* Cambridge, MA: Harvard University Press.

Gergen, K. (1999). *An Invitation to Social Construction.* Newbury Park, CA: Sage.

Gergen, K. (2001). *Social Construction in Context.* Newbury Park, CA: Sage.

Goolishian, H. & Anderson, H. (1987). Language systems and therapy: An evolving idea. *Psychotherapy,* **24**, 529–538.

Hoffman, L. (1990). Constructing realities: The art of lenses. *Family Process,* **29**, 1–12.

Hoffman, L. (1991). A reflexive stance for family therapy. *Journal of Strategic and Systemic Therapies,* **10** (3–4), 4–17.

Hoffman, L. (1993). *Exchanging voices: A Collaborative Approach to Family Therapy.* London: Karnac.

Hoffman, L. (2002). *Family Therapy: An Intimate History.* New York: Norton.

McNamee, S. & Gergen, K. (1992). *Therapy as Social Construction.* Newbury Park, CA: Sage.

Pearce, B. (1992). A 'campers guide' to constructionisms. *Human Systems: The Journal of Systemic Consultation and Management,* **3**, 139–161.

Rambo, A. (2003). The collaborative language-based models of family therapy: When less is more. In L. Hecker & J. Wetchler (Eds), *An Introduction to Marital and Family Therapy,* pp. 149–172. New York: Haworth.

Tomm, K. (1987a). Interventive Interviewing Part I. Strategising as a fourth guideline for the therapist. *Family Process,* **25**, 4–13.

Tomm, K. (1987b). Interventive Interviewing Part II. Reflexive questioning as a means to enable self healing. *Family Process*, **26**, 167–183.

Tomm, K. (1988). Interventive Interviewing Part III. Intending to ask linear, circular, strategic or reflexive questions. *Family Process*, **27**, 1–15.

Solution Focused Marital and Family Therapy

Berg, I. (1994). *Family Based Services: A Solution-Focused Approach.* New York: Norton.

Berg, I. & Dolan, Y. (2000). *Tales of Solutions. A Collection of Hope Inspiring Stories.* New York: Norton.

Berg, I. & Kelly, S. (2000). *Building Solutions in Child Protective Services.* New York: Norton.

Berg, I. & Miller, S. (1992). *Working with the Problem Drinker: A Solution Focused Approach.* New York: Norton.

Berg, I. & Reuss, N. (1997). *Solutions Step-by-Step: A Substance Abuse Treatment Manual.* New York: Norton.

Carpenter, J. (1997). Special Issue on Brief Solution Focused Therapy. *Journal of Family Therapy*, **19**, (2) (whole issue).

DeJong, P. & Berg, I. (2000). *Interviewing for Solutions*, 2nd edn. New York: Brooks Cole.

deShazer, S. (1982). *Patterns of Brief Family Therapy.* New York: Norton.

deShazer, S. (1985). *Keys to Solutions in Brief Therapy.* New York: Norton.

deShazer, S. (1988). *Clues: Investigating Solutions in Brief Therapy.* New York: Norton.

deShazer, S. (1991). *Putting Difference to Work.* New York: Norton.

deShazer, S. (1994). *Words were Originally Magic.* New York: Norton.

deShazer, S., Berg, I., Lipchik, E., Nunnally, E., Molnar, A., Gingerich, W. & Weiner-Davis, M. (1986). Brief therapy, Focused solution Development. *Family Process*, **25**, 207–222.

Duncan, B., Miller, S. & Sparks, J. (2003). Interactional and solution-focused brief therapies: Evolving concepts of change. In T. Sexton, G. Weeks & M. Robbins (Eds), *Handbook of Family Therapy*, pp. 101–124. New York: Brunner-Routledge.

George, E., Iveson, C. & Ratner, H. (1999). *Problem to Solution. Brief Therapy with Individuals and Families*, revised edn. London: Brief Therapy Press.

Hoyt, M. (2002). Solution focused couple therapy. In A. Gurman & N. Jacobon (Eds), *Clinical Hanbook of Couples Therapy*, 3rd edn, pp. 335–373. New York: Guilford.

Hudson, P. & O'Hanlon, W. (1994). *Rewriting Love Stories: Brief Marital Therapy.* New York: Norton.

Lethem, J. (2002). Brief solution focused therapy. *Child and Adolescent Mental Health*, **7**, 189–192.

Lipchik, E. (2002). *Beyond Technique in Solution-Focused Therapy.* New York: Guilford.

Miller, D., Hubble, A., Duncan, B. (1996). *Handbook of Solution Focused Brief Therapy: Foundations, Applications and Research.* San Francisco, CA: Jossey-Bass.

Miller, S. & Berg, I. (1995). *The Miracle Method.* New York: Norton.

O'Hanlon, W. & Bertolino, B. (2002). *Even from a Broken Web: Brief, Respectful Solution-Oriented Therapy for Sexual Abuse and Trauma.* New York: Norton.

O'Hanlon, W. & Weiner-Davis, M. (2003). *In Search of Solutions. A New Direction in Psychotherapy.* New York: Norton.

Rowan, T. & O'Hanlon, B. (1999). *Solution-Oriented Therapy for Chronic and Severe Mental Illness.* New York: Wiley.

Sharry, J., Madden, B. & Darmody, M. (2003). *Becoming a Solution Detective. Identifying Your Clients' Strengths in Practical Brief Therapy.* New York: Haworth.

Narrative Therapy

Byng-Hall, J. (1995). *Rewriting Family Scripts. Improvisation and Change.* New York: Guilford.

Epston, D. & White, M. (1992). *Experience, Contradiction, Narrative and Imagination.* Adelaide: Dulwich Centre Publications.

Epston, D. (1989). *Collected Papers.* Adelaide: Dulwich Centre Publications.

Epston, D. (1998). *Catching up with David Epston: A Collection or Narrative Practice Based Papers Published Between 1991 and 1996.* Adelaide: Dulwich Centre.

Freedman, J. & Combs, G. (1996). *Narrative Therapy: The Social Construction of Preferred Realities.* New York: Norton.

Freedman, J. & Combs, G. (2002). Narrative couple therapy. In A. Gurman & N. Jacobon (Eds), *Clinical Hanbook of Couples Therapy*, 3rd edn, pp. 308–334. New York: Guilford.

Freeman, J., Epston, D. & Lobovits, D. (1997). *Playful Approaches to Serious Problems: Narrative Therapy with Children and Families.* New York: Norton.

Jenkins, A. (1990). *Invitations to responsibility: The Therapeutic Engagement of Men who are Violent and Abusive.* Adelaide: Dulwich Centre Publications.

McLeod, J. (1997). *Narrative and Psychotherapy.* London: Sage.

Monk, G., Winslade, J., Crocket, K. & Epston, D. (1997). *Narrative Therapy in Practice: The Archeology of Hope.* San Francisco, CA: Jossely-Bass.

Morgan, A. (2000). *What is Narrative Therapy: An Easy-to-Read Introduction.* Adelaide: Dulwich Centre.

Parry, A. & Doane, R. (1994). *Story Re-visions. Narrative Therapy in the Postmodern World.* New York: Guilford.

White, M. (1989). *Selected Papers.* Adelaide: Dulwich Centre Publications.

White, M. (1995). *Re-authoring Lives.* Adelaide: Dulwich Centre Publications.

White, M. (1997). *Narrative Therapists' Lives.* Adelaide: Dulwich Centre Publications.

White, M. (2000). *Reflections on Narrative Practice: Essays and Interviews.* Adelaide: Dulwich Centre Publications.

White, M. (2005). *Narrative Practice and Exotic Lives: Resurrecting Diversity in Everyday Life.* Adelaide: Dulwich Centre Publications.

White, M. & Epston, D. (1989). *Literate Means to Therapeutic Ends.* Adelaide: Dulwich Centre Publications. (Republished in 1990 as *Narrative Means to Therapeutic Ends.* New York: Norton.)

Zimmerman, J. & Dickerson, V. (1996). *The Problem Speaks: Adventures in Narrative Therapy.* New York: Guilford.

Chapter 5

THEORIES THAT FOCUS ON CONTEXTS

It has already been noted in Chapter 2 that family therapy schools and traditions may be classified in terms of their central focus of therapeutic concern and, in particular, with respect to their emphasis on problem-maintaining behaviour patterns; problematic and constraining belief systems; and historical, contextual and constitutional predisposing factors. This chapter is concerned with family therapy traditions that highlight the role of historical, contextual and constitutional factors in predisposing family members to adopt particular belief systems or engage in particular problematic interaction patterns. Such schools advocate using practices that specifically address these historical, contextual and constitutional predisposing factors, including working with members of the extended family and wider social network, as well as coaching individuals to manage historical, contextual and constitutional constraints. Schools that fall into this category include: transgenerational family therapy; psychoanalytic family therapy; practices based on attachment theory; experiential family therapy; multisystemic therapy; and psychoeducational approaches. Transgenerational family therapy; psychoanalytic family therapy; practices based on attachment theory; and experiential family therapy are concerned predominantly with historical predisposing factors. Multisystemic therapy pays particular attention to the role of contextual predisposing factors. Managing constitutional predisposing factors is a central concern for psychoeducational approaches. A summary of the main features of these models is given in Table 5.1.

TRANSGENERATIONAL FAMILY THERAPY

Transgenerational family therapy rests on the assumption that clients' family-of-origin relationships and events, which occurred and continue to occur in clients' families of origin, predispose them to developing current life problems in their families of procreation (Nelson, 2003; Nichols, 2003). Murray Bowen (Bowen, 1978; Friedman, 1991; Kerr, 2003; Kerr & Bowen, 1988; McGoldrick & Carter, 2001; Papero, 1990; Roberto, 1992;

Table 5.1 Key features of family therapy schools and traditions that emphasise the role of predisposing historical and contextual factors

Domain	Transgenerational family therapy	Psychoanalytic family therapy	Attachment-based therapies	Experiential family therapy	Multisystemic approaches	Psychoeducational approaches
Key figures	Murray Bowen Ivan Boszormenyi-Nagy	Nathan Ackerman Henry Dicks David Scharff and Jill Savage-Scharff Samuel Slipp	Susan Johnson Leslie Greenberg John Byng-Hall Guy Diamond	Carl Whittaker Virginia Satir	Scott Henggeler	William McFarlane Elizabeth Kuipers Ian Falloon
Healthy family functioning	Members of healthy families, individuals are differentiated from their families of origin They are not bound to repeat parental problems by a legacy of invisible loyalties	Members of healthy marriages over time move from emotionally experiencing their partners (in terms of part-object relations) as all-good or all-bad to experiencing them as they are with	In healthy marriages, attachment needs are met within the context of flexible interactional patterns that facilitate emotional engagement Healthy families provide sufficiently secure	Healthy families communicate congruently, permit a wide range of positive and negative emotional expression, interact spontaneously, are not bound by rigid rules, roles routines and power structures, are open to the	Healthy families include well-adjusted individual members, an appropriate intergenerational hierarchy, a strong parental subsystem, prosocial peer relationships outside the family; supportive and well-resourced educational	Healthy families have good communication and problem-solving skills and coping strategies for dealing with ill family members These skills and strategies minimise the risk of relapse or poor illness management on the part of the ill family member

(Continued on next page)

Table 5.1 (*Continued*)

Domain	Transgenerational family therapy	Psychoanalytic family therapy	Attachment-based therapies	Experiential family therapy	Multisystemic approaches	Psychoeducational approaches
		strengths and weaknesses	attachment relationships to permit improvising new scripts when required	non-rational playful side of life, and foster personal growth and the growth of family relationships	placements for children, and good community support from a stable non-deviant community	
Unhealthy functioning	Members of unhealthy families are not differentiated from the family of origin and this is maintained by children and parents becoming emotionally cut-off They repeat parental problems by a legacy of invisible loyalties	Members of unhealthy marriages respond to their partners (in terms of part object relations) as all-good or all-bad and over time these mutual splitting and projection processes become rigidly entrenched	In unhealthy marriages, attachment needs are not met because of rigid interactional patterns that block emotional engagement Unhealthy families do not provide sufficiently secure attachment relationships	Unhealthy families have communication problems, a restricted range of emotional expression, a rigid set of rules, roles and routines, little space for non-rational play, and obstruct personal growth and the growth of family relationships	Unhealthy families include poorly adjusted individual members, little intergenerational hierarchy, a weak parental subsystem, antisocial peer relationships outside the family; unsupportive and poorly resourced educational placements for children, and	Unhealthy families have emotionally charged critical or overinvolved relationships with their ill family members and the stress associated with this increases the risk of relapse or poor illness management on the part of the ill family member

			to permit improvising new scripts and so old scripts are repeated	These difficulties are imported into the family from the family of origin	little community support from a mobile deviant community	Identification of critical or overinvolved relationships and evaluation of communication and problem-solving skills and coping strategies
Assessment	Genogram construction and identification of multigenerational problem-maintaining patterns	Family, couple and individual interviews to assess couples' suitability for long-term therapy	Identification of negative interactional cycles and underlying unmet attachment needs and related emotions. Clarification of family attachment style and family scripts and myths underlying problem-maintaining interactions	None	Identification of systemic strengths and problems or needs associated with individual family members; the family as a whole; the children's peer groups; school placements; and community agencies	

(Continued on next page)

Table 5.1 (*Continued*)

Domain	Transgenerational family therapy	Psychoanalytic family therapy	Attachment-based therapies	Experiential family therapy	Multisystemic approaches	Psychoeducational approaches
Scope of treatment goals	Differentiation from the family of origin and develop non-hierarchical person-to-person relationships with parents Exoneration of parents	Facilitate insight into mutual projective processes and enhance the couples' capacity to contain conflict and meet each other's needs for autonomy and attachment	Help couples develop a secure attachment and view the marriage as a safe base from which to solve family problems Help family improvise new scripts and develop interactional awareness	Facilitate the development of clear communication, spontaneity, expression of positive and negative emotions, flexible rules, roles and routines, non-rational playfulness, the personal growth and self-actualisation of family members and the family as a whole	To help family members resolve identified problems and behave responsibly over the long term and in multiple contexts	To help family members develop communication and problem-solving skills and coping strategies for managing ill family members and to avoid emotionally charged patterns of family interaction
Therapy	Help family members develop self-observation skills, skills required to	Marital therapy is long-term therapy, 100 sessions over two years,	Short-term therapy Disrupting negative interactional	Establish family meetings as the structure for therapy but place the	Individual, family, peer group-based, school-based and community-based interventions	Single family or multiple family meetings are used for psychoeducation

reduce emotional reactivity and detriangle from emotional family situations
Uncover invisible loyalties and facilitate exoneration

family therapy may be briefer
Therapy is relatively non-directive and involves creating therapeutic space, listening, following affect, empathy, interpretation of defences, and confronting basic anxiety

cycles by facilitating mutual expression and acceptance of disowned unmet attachment needs and related emotions
Help family use therapy as a secure base for improvisation

responsibility for initiating therapeutic work on the family
Encounter the family at an emotional level
Use the therapist's 'self' to facilitate change
Within sessions use sculpting, psychodrama, Gestalt methods to promote emotional experiencing and expression
Use co-therapy teams in which one member regresses to the level of the identified patient and the other coordinates the therapy process

are employed to harness systemic strengths to alter risk factors that underpin deviant behaviour and to disrupt problem-maintaining behaviour patterns

about illness management, communication and problem-solving skills training and reduction of emotionally charged family interaction patterns

(Continued on next page)

Table 5.1 (*Continued*)

Domain	Transgenerational family therapy	Psychoanalytic family therapy	Attachment-based therapies	Experiential family therapy	Multisystemic approaches	Psychoeducational approaches
Special areas of applicability	Marital discord Child behaviour problems Multigenerational patterns of abuse and violence	Marital discord Bereavement	Marital discord Child emotional and behaviour problems		Delinquency Drug abuse Child abuse	Schizophrenia Bipolar disorder Chronic illness

Roberto-Forman, 2002) and Ivan Boszormenyi-Nagy (Boszormenyi-Nagy, 1987; Boszormenyi-Nagy & Krasner, 1987; Boszormenyi-Nagy & Spark, 1973; Boszormenyi-Nagy, Grunebum & Ulrish, 1991; Ducommun-Nagy & Schwoeri, 2003) are central figures in this broad tradition. All transgenerational therapists are united by their belief that family problems are multigenerational phenomena and that often this is because patterns of family interactions or relationships are replicated from one generation to the next.

Murray Bowen

For Murray Bowen (Bowen, 1978; Friedman, 1991; Kerr, 2003; Kerr & Bowen, 1988; McGoldrick & Carter, 2001; Papero, 1990; Roberto, 1990, 1992; Roberto-Forman, 2002), families are fundamentally emotional systems. When threatened, family anxiety occurs and families engage in recursive emotionally-driven problematic interaction patterns. Families differ in the amount of anxiety they contain. Some families are relatively unthreatened and show little anxiety, while others feel extremely threatened and consistently experience high levels of anxiety. The amount of anxiety a family experiences determines the degree to which family members may become differentiated. Highly anxious families, Bowen argues, are characterised by an undifferentiated ego mass. That is, they have extremely emotionally close relationships characterised by enmeshment or fusion. In contrast, families containing little anxiety facilitate a high level of differentiation and autonomy in family members. There is some empirical support for the relationship between differentiation and chronic anxiety, marital satisfaction and psychological distress (Miller, Anderson & Kaulana-Keala, 2004).

Psychopathology occurs because of what Bowen terms' family projection and multigenerational transmission processes'. The family projection process occurs when parents project part of their immaturity onto one of their children, who in turn becomes the least differentiated family member and the most likely to become symptomatic. Children who are most involved in their families' emotional processes and the least differentiated select marital partners who share an equivalently low level of differentiation. Consequently they pass the problems of limited differentiation from the family of origin on to the next generation by inadvertently organising family rules, roles and routines in rigid enmeshed and fused ways that prevent differentiation.

In Bowenian multigenerational family therapy, couples are helped to recognise the degree to which they are experiencing fusion or lack of differentiation from their family of origin. They also gain insight into how this is affecting their capacity to manage current life problems in their family of procreation. The Bowenian therapist coaches clients in strategies that promote differentiation of self. Differentiation of self involves separation of intellectual and emotional systems. This intrapsychic differentiation of intellect and emotion facilitates the concurrent differentiation of self from others within the family of origin. When intrapsychic differentiation occurs, the individual does not impulsively act out strong feelings, but rather reflects on these feelings and chooses a course of action. This frees the person to avoid repeating problematic, emotionally-driven interaction patterns associated with the family of origin.

Bowenian therapists help clients understand their degree of differentiation or fusion within the family of origin by mapping out the family and its relationship patterns in a genogram, and considering these patterns within the context of the demands of the family lifecycle. (Genogram construction is described in detail in Chapter 7.) In mapping out family relationships, clients' attention is drawn to the way in which family triangles develop when the family faces anxiety associated with life cycle transitions. According to Bowen, the smallest stable relational system is a triangle. When anxious, dyads involve a third party to form a triangle. Larger systems are composed of a series of interlocking triangles. Clients' difficulties in their current life may stem from recurrently being inadvertently inducted into family triangles. Alternatively, clients may have evolved a way of coping with this continual family pressure to become involved in a triangle by emotionally cutting off from one or more family members. Emotional cut-offs with parents in the family of origin underpin many later parenting problems in the family of procreation. Emotional cut-off may involve physically making little contact and/or psychologically denying the significance of the unresolved family-of-origin relationship problems. One of Bowen's hypotheses is that the greater the degree of cut-off, the greater the probability of replicating the problematic family of origin relationship in the family of procreation.

Bowen helps clients understand these family-of-origin patterns and processes and then arranges for clients to use this understanding to change the way that they are involved in relationships in their families of origin. The goals of this therapy are for clients to become differentiated so their understanding of family of origin processes prevent them from being inducted into recursive emotionally driven interaction patterns. A second goal is for clients to develop person-to-person relationships in which they can talk to other family members about each other, and avoid impersonal discussion or gossip. In Bowenian therapy, these goals may be achieved by inviting clients to bring their parents or siblings to therapy sessions or by coaching clients in how to set up meetings outside therapy with members of their family of origin to renegotiate triangular relationships and replace fused or cut-off relationships with person-to-person relationships. Bowenian family therapy may be conducted in many formats. In some instances it may involve family of procreation meetings followed by couples sessions and finally couples sessions that are attended by members of the family of origin. In other instances, it may be conducted on an individual basis. In some professional family therapy training programmes, trainee family therapists undergo Bowenian therapy in a group format as part of their training. It is a paradox of Bowenian therapy that it aims to enhance family relationships primarily not by focusing on relationship building but by focusing on the opposite: the promotion of autonomy and the differentiation of self.

Ivan Boszormenyi-Nagy

Ivan Boszormenyi-Nagy (Boszormenyi-Nagy, 1987; Boszormenyi-Nagy et al., 1991; Boszormenyi-Nagy & Krasner, 1987; Boszormenyi-Nagy & Spark, 1973), the founder of contextual family therapy, argues that family life may be described in terms four main dimensions: facts (such as ethnicity or family size); psychology (such as thoughts and emotions); transactions (such as interaction patterns); and relational ethics (the balance of fairness among people). Contextual family therapy focuses largely on relational ethics – establishing fairness – as the central way of helping families to resolve problems. This is because contextual therapists argue that many problems develop because there is an imbalance of fairness or lack of justice within the family across generations. For each family member, each family relationship entails an unconscious ledger of accumulated accounts of entitlements and debts that reflects the balance of what has been given and what is owed. Where there is a significant imbalance in such ledgers, across generations, problems may occur. That is, invisible loyalties may predispose families to developing problems. Invisible loyalties are the unconscious commitments that children make to meet debts to parents or entitlements arising from their interactions with them. Invisible loyalties balance relational ledgers.

For example, an adult who was neglected by his parents may feel that he is entitled to be neglectful in relationships with his children because he did not receive care himself and to do otherwise would be disloyal to his parents. Split loyalties, where a child is forced through parental conflict to side with one parent against another may generate a sense of entitlement at having lost a parent. The youngster may replicate this pattern in adult life, and feel entitled to separate from a spouse despite its effects on his or her children. If parents instil a sense that the sacrifices they have made for their children make the children feel eternally indebted to them, then it may be difficult for such children to form intimate relationships in adult life because loyalty to the spouse may be construed as disloyalty to the parent to whom an eternal debt is owed.

Contextual therapists adopt a position of multidirected impartiality that is marked by an openness to communication from all family members, a duty to ensure open communication between family members, an accountability to all family members affected by interventions, and a duty to facilitate solutions that are in the best interests of all affected family members. The central aim is to establish fairness within the present family and fairness for future generations. However, this involves dealing with legacies that may be unfair.

Contextual therapists disrupt the intergenerational transmission of destructive interaction patterns by facilitating exoneration. That is, they help clients understand the positive intentions and intergenerational loyalty underpinning actions of family members who have hurt them. When clients develop such understanding they are less likely to replicate the hurtful behaviour they have experienced. For example, an abused child may come to understand that their abuse was in part due to their parents' abusive experiences and so exonerate them. In doing so, they may be empowered to make a commitment not to abuse their own children when they procreate. Through exoneration individuals earn entitlement.

Fairness within the parent–child relationship is delt with in the following way in contextual therapy. It is assumed that children are entitled to receive more than they give to their parents, but the ledger is balanced when they in turn give more to their own children than they receive. Thus, relational ethics spans three generations when considering fairness and justice within parent–child relationships.

PSYCHOANALYTIC FAMILY THERAPY

Many of the pioneers of family therapy were psychoanalytically trained and some used psychoanalytic theory as the basis for family therapy practice, for example, Nathan Ackerman (1958, 1966, 1970, 1984) in the USA and Robin Skynner (1981) in the UK. Frameworks that integrate systemic and psychodynamic concepts have also emerged in the UK (Bentovim & Kinston, 1991) and the USA (Friedman & Pearce, 1980; Kirschner & Kirschner, 1986). One particularly sophisticated psychodynamic approach to marital and family therapy has developed from Ronald Fairburn's (1952, 1963) object relations theory, beginning with the work of Dicks (1963, 1967) at the Tavistock on mutual projective systems within marriage. This object relations-based marital and family therapy tradition has been evolved by David Scharff and Gill Savage-Scharff (Savage-Scharf, 1989,1992; Savage-Scharff & Bagini 2002; Savage-Scharff & Scharff, 1994, 2003; Scharff, 1982; Scharff & Savage-Scharff, 1987, 1991) and Slipp (1984, 1988).

Object relations-based family therapy rests on the assumption that people are predisposed to engage in problem-maintaining interaction patterns because they conduct current relationships on the basis of unconscious primitive relationship maps that were developed during early life. These unconscious primitive relationship maps of self and others based on early parent–child relationships, which are replicated in current significant relationships, are referred to as 'object relations'. For example, an 'angry child'–'frustrating parent' relationship map may be partially replicated in a discordant marital relationship.

According to object relations theory, by using the defence mechanism of splitting, infants come to view the mother figure as two separate people: the good object whom they long for and who satisfies their needs, and the bad object with whom they are angry because she frustrates them. They engage in splitting to defend against the anxiety they feel when their mother frustrates their needs. They become so angry that they fantasise they may annihilate the mother on whom they are totally dependent. To destroy the mother would involve destroying themselves. By splitting, they may protect the good object from the threat of annihilation and direct their intense anger exclusively at the bad object.

Fairburn argued that the bad object was further split into a need-exciting object, which was craved by the infant, and a need-rejecting object towards which the infant experienced rage. He further argued that these two object relations systems were repressed. So the personality in object relations theory contains three distinct subsystems: (1) a central conscious self attached with feelings of security and satisfaction to an ideal good object; (2) a repressed craving self attached with feeling of dissatisfaction and longing to an need-exciting object (or craved object); and (3) a repressed rejecting self attached with feelings of anger and rage to need-rejecting object.

According to object relations-based marital and family theory, in romantic relationships partners project internal craved objects onto each other and induce their partners to conform to these through the process of projective identification. In healthy relationships, partners conform partially, but not completely, to these projections so that they partially, but not excessively frustrate, each others' needs. Gradually partners learn to respond to the reality of their spouses rather than their projections. So, for example, partners may project an image of an extremely caring and sensitive person into each other and treat each other as if they were these projections. Each in response may feel compelled to behave in an extremely considerate manner, and mange to do so much, but not all, of the time. As the relationship matures and exceptions to these mutual projections become apparent, the projection process is gradually replaced by accurate perception. Partners come to accept the reality of each other as sometimes considerate and sometimes not, and to have a sense of humour about their initial idealisations of each other.

In problematic relationships, partners either completely conform to the demands of each other's projections or do not conform sufficiently. Both of these options, lead to disappointment, conflict and the mutual projection of rejecting objects. In distressed marriages, partners induce each other, through projective identification, to conform to these rejecting roles. That is, they project images onto each other of being intentionally critical, rejecting and frustrating and treat each other as if this were the case. Inevitably this leads to mutual hurt. However, the couple remain bound together because the mutual projective system allows each person to view themselves as 'all good' and to disown negative aspects of the self by viewing the partner as 'all bad'. Also, the mutual projective system is maintained by the unconscious wish to recover and integrate the good and bad objects in themselves.

These mutual projective systems are not unlike transference–countertransference systems that occur in individual psychotherapy. Psychodynamic psychotherapists deal with transference through containment, interpretation and working through. In couples therapy, the same processes are used and clients are coached in using containment and interpretation for managing mutual projections in their own relationships.

Containment involves privately reflecting on another's action, its effect on oneself, and its meaning within the context of relationship where it occurred, and then responding by supportively outlining one's under-standing of the situation. In object relations-based psychotherapy, two types of interpretations, based on the triangle of person and the triangle of conflict, may be distinguished (McCullough et al., 2003). Interpreta-tions based on the triangle of person draw parallels between the trans-ference relationship between client and therapist; the family-of-origin relationship between client and parent; and the current life relationship between client and partner. Interpretations based on the triangle of con-flict link the present defence mechanisms with the underlying anxiety about expressing an unacceptable hidden sexual or aggressive impulse or feeling. For example, it may be pointed out that the tendency to view the partner as 'all bad', allows the person to avoid the anxiety associ-ated with accepting that they may in fact be angry with a person who is imperfect, both good and bad, and who may never fully meet all their needs.

Object relations-based marital and family therapy modifies the impact of historical predisposing factors, notably unconscious relationship maps or object relations, acquired in early life.

Object relations-based couples therapy is a long-term intervention in which couples learn to use containment and interpretation within their relationship to become free of their mutual projective system and to learn to accept each other as they are.

In object relations-based family therapy, parents are helped to avoid projecting bad objects onto their children and inducing them to behave in problematic ways or projecting good objects onto them and requiring that they act as a go-between in a conflictual marital relationship charac-terised by mutual negative projections.

ATTACHMENT-BASED THERAPIES

John Bowlby (1969, 1973, 1980, 1988), in addition to being one of the first family therapists in the UK, was the founding father of attachment theory, a complex ethologically-based formulation that explains the development of significant family relationships and relationship problems from the initial bonds between children and their caregivers (Cassidy & Shaver, 1999). In recent times, attachment theory has provided the basis in the UK for John Byng-Hall's (1995) approach to family therapy and in the USA to Susan Johnson and Leslie Greenberg emotionally-focused approach to couples therapy (Greenberg & Johnson, 1988; Johnson, 1996, 2002a, 2003a, Johnson & Denton, 2002; Johnson & Whiffen, 2003). Other important attachment-based approaches to family therapy include Doane and Diamond's (1994) system for classifying and treating families of people with severe psychiatric disorders, and Diamond, Siqueland and Diamond's (2003) approach to treating adolescent depression.

Attachment Theory

Bowlby (1969, 1973, 1980, 1988) argued that attachment behaviour, which is genetically programmed and essential for survival of the species, is elicited in children between six months and three years when faced with danger. In such instances, children seek proximity with their caregivers. When comforted, they return to the activity of exploring the immediate environment around the caregiver. The cycle repeats each time the child perceives a threat and their attachment needs for satisfaction, safety and security are activated. Over multiple repetitions, the child builds an internal working model of attachment relationships based on the way these episodes are managed by the caregiver in response to the child's needs for proximity, comfort and security. Internal working models are cognitive relationship maps based on early attachment experiences, which serve as templates for the development of later intimate relationships. Internal working models allow people to make predictions about how the self and significant others will behave within relationships. Empirical research with mothers and children has shown that child–parent attachments may be classified into four distinct categories. Later work on intimate relationships in adulthood confirms that these four relational styles show continuity over the individual lifecycle and significant adult relationships may be classified into four equivalent categories (Cassidy & Shaver, 1999). John Byng-Hall (1995) has argued that patterns of family organisation may also be classified into the four attachment style categories. A summary of these four attachment styles is given in Figure 5.1.

Securely attached children and marital partners react to their parents or partners as if they are a secure base from which to explore the world.

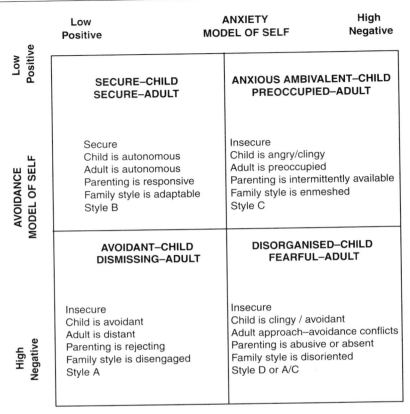

Figure 5.1 Characteristics of four attachment styles in children and adults

Parents and partners in such relationships are attuned and responsive to the needs of the children or partners. Families with secure attachment relationships are adaptable and flexibly connected. While a secure attachment style is associated with autonomy, the other three attachment styles are associated with a sense of insecurity. *Anxiously attached* children seek contact with their parents following separation but are unable to derive comfort from it. They cling and cry or have tantrums. Marital partners with this attachment style tend to be overly close but dissatisfied. Families characterised by anxious attachment relationships tend to be enmeshed and to have blurred or highly permeable boundaries between family subsystems. *Avoidantly attached* children avoid contact with their parents after separation. They sulk. Marital partners with this attachment style tend to be distant and dissatisfied. Families characterised by avoidant relationships tend to be disengaged and to have impermeable boundaries between family subsystems. Children with a *disorganised attachment* style following separation show aspects of both the anxious and avoidant patterns. Disorganised attachment is a common correlate of child abuse and neglect and early parental absence, loss or bereavement. Disorganised marital and family relationships are characterised by approach–avoidance conflicts, disorientation and alternate clinging and sulking.

Emotionally-Focused Couples Therapy

Within emotionally-focused couples therapy (Greenberg & Johnson, 1988; Johnson, 1996, 2002a, 2003a; Johnson & Denton, 2002; Johnson & Whiffen, 2003), it is assumed that marital conflict arises when partners are unable to meet each other's attachment needs for safety, security and satisfaction. That is, marital distress represents the failure of a couple to establish a relationship characterised by a secure attachment style. Members of the couple do not view each other as a secure base from which to explore the world. Initially, partners' failure to meet each other's attachment needs gives rise to primary emotional responses of fear, sadness, disappointment, emotional hurt and vulnerability. These primary emotional responses are not fully expressed and the frustrated attachment needs are not met within the relationship. The frustration that occurs leads these primary emotional responses to be supplanted by secondary emotional responses such as anger, hostility and the desire for revenge or to induce guilt. These secondary emotional responses find expression in attacking or withdrawing behaviour. Couples become involved in rigid repetitive attack–withdraw or pursuer–distancer behaviour patterns. These may eventually evolve into attack–attack or withdraw–withdraw patterns. These rigid mutually reinforcing patterns of conflict-maintaining behaviour persistently recur because partners desperately want their genetically programmed attachment needs to be met. Unfortunately their behavioural attempts to elicit caregiving from their partners is (mis-) guided by internal working models based on insecure attachment styles. Consequently, they inadvertently prompt their partners to relate to them in ways that ensure that their attachment needs will be persistently frustrated. These problematic internal working models for self and others in close relationships have derived from insecure attachments to primary caregivers in early life.

Emotionally-focused couples therapy aims to help couples find ways to meet each other's attachment needs and develop a relationship based on a secure attachment style. Thus, the goal of therapy is for partners to be able to declare their needs for safety, security and satisfaction in ways that predictably elicit caregiving within the relationship.

Emotionally-focused couples therapy begins by asking couples to identify the issues over which they have conflicts and to describe their rigid patterns of interaction around these which involve attacking and withdrawing. When this pattern is clarified, the underlying feelings that led to this behaviour is explored. First the secondary emotional responses of anger and hostility are clarified. These are distinguished from the primary emotional experiences of fear, sadness disappointment, emotional hurt and vulnerability that arise when attachment needs for safety, security and satisfaction are not met in a predictable way. The couple's problem is then reframed as one involving the miscommunication of primary attachment needs and related disappointments. Members of the couple are facilitated to fully and congruently express their attachment needs and related primary emotional responses, but not to give vent to their secondary emotional responses through blaming or guilt induction. For example, a woman who regularly attacks her husband for being distant, and whose husband withdraws, would be facilitated to emotively state her need for her husband's companionship without guilt inducing embellishments. The husband, would be facilitated to respond by congruently hearing this need and meeting his partner's need for companionship. This accessing and expressing primary emotional responses and needs has two functions. First, it provides an opportunity for the partner hearing the expression (uncontaminated by secondary emotional responses) to respond in an appropriate caregiving manner. Second, it allows the person expressing the primary emotional responses and receiving care from their partner to revise their internal working models of self and others in close relationships. In this respect, emotionally-focused couples therapy modifies the impact of historical predisposing factors, i.e. internal working models of self and others based on early life experiences. Once partners modify their internal working models of each other, they can abandon their attack–withdraw interactional patterns and openly state their attachment needs and respond to these without persistent conflict. A series of controlled trials support the effectiveness of emotionally-focused couple therapy (Byrne et al., 2004b).

John Byng-Hall's Approach Based on Attachment Theory and Script Theory

John Byng-Hall (1995), who originally trained with John Bowlby at the Tavistock in London, has proposed a model of family therapy based on attachment theory and script theory. He argues that the predictable rules, roles and routines of family life are governed and guided by family scripts, which have been learned in repeated scenarios within the family of origin. Scenarios are significant episodes of family interaction, which occur in a specific context, entail a specific plot, and involve specific roles and motives for participants. For example, how to deal with loss or how to manage disobedience. A distinction may be made between replicative, corrective and improvised scripts. Replicative scripts underpin the repetition of scenarios from the family of origin in the current family.

Corrective scripts underpin the playing out of scenarios in the current family which are the opposite of those that occurred in similar contexts within the family of origin. Improvised scripts underpin the creation of scenarios in the current family which are distinctly different from those that occurred in similar contexts within the family of origin.

Byng-Hall argues that, to manage family lifecycle transitions, extra-familial stresses and other challenges, in some instances replicative or corrective family scripts are inadequate and an improvised script may be required. However, a secure family base is necessary for the effective development of an improvised script. A secure family base provides a reliable network of attachment relationships so that all family members can have sufficient security to explore and experiment with improvised scripts. For Byng-Hall, when families come to therapy, they often have had difficulty developing a secure enough family base to permit the develop-ment of an improvised script. The therapist's responsibility is to provide a secure base and containment of family affect for the family as a whole, so they can avoid repeating an unhelpful family script and reflect on their situation before improvising a new script. Techniques from structural family therapy are used to help families explore improvised scripts. Im-provisation involves abandoning the rules, roles and routines prescribed in replicative and corrective family scripts and exploring new possibili-ties, options and solutions. This process of abandoning the familiar may raise anxiety, especially in instances where, in addition to family scripts, there are family myths and legends that warn about the calamitous con-sequences for particular courses of action.

It is therefore not surprising that families exert strong emotional pres-sure on therapists to abandon their impartial position of containment and provision of a secure base, and emotionally pressurise the therapists into taking up a partisan role in the enactment of the family script. If therapists become stuck in such roles they are unable to be therapeuti-cally effective. To avoid recruitment into such roles, therapists may use live supervision to track and comment on the process, reflect on their emotional experience of the recruitment process and try to understand it. In indirect supervision, therapists may explore the links between their family-of-origin issues and the issues in the client family, and use in-tervention strategies that have been carefully planned in light of their understanding of the role in the family script into which they are being inducted.

Byng-Hall's approach to family therapy modifies the impact of histori-cal predisposing factors, notably family scripts and attachment styles. It facilitates the development of a system of secure family attachments and an improvised script so that the family can manage its immediate problems. A wider therapeutic goal is to facilitate the development inter-actional awareness. This is the capacity of family members to track pat-terns of family interaction; understand their own and others' roles in such patterns; understand the meaning of the patterns for all involved; and the predict the probable outcome of such patterns.

Attachment-based Family Therapy for Depressed Adolescents

Guy Diamond in the USA has developed a brief, manualised attachment-based treatment model for depressed adolescents and their families (Diamond, Siqueland & Diamond, 2003). In this model, attachment theory serves as the main theoretical framework for repairing relational ruptures and rebuilding relationships between depressed adolescents and their parents. Within the model a distinction is made between parent and adolescent problem states. Parent problem states include criticism, personal distress and parenting skills deficits. Adolescent problem states include lack of motivation, negative self-concept and poor affect regulation. Within the parent–adolescent relationship, these parent and adolescent problem states subserve a gradual process of disengagement. Attachment-based family therapy addresses this disengagement process and aims to enhance parent–adolescent attachment. Therapy involves the following sequence: (1) relational reframing; (2) building alliances with the adolescent first and then with the parents; (3) repairing parent–adolescent attachment; and (4) building family competency. Evidence from a series of treatment process studies supports the importance of the sequence of therapeutic tasks and there is evidence from a controlled trial for the effectiveness of this form of family therapy in alleviating adolescent depression (Diamond et al., 2003).

Attachment-based Family Therapy for Psychosis

Doane and Diamond (1994), in a study of families of people with diagnoses of seriously debilitating psychotic disorders, developed a family typology based on attachment theory and a therapeutic model that focuses on remediating attachment problems. The three family types are: (1) low-intensity families characterised by secure parent–child attachments and low-key patterns of family interaction with little criticism or over-involvment; (2) high-intensity families characterised by either secure or insecure attachments, but also by intense critical or over-involved patterns of interaction; and (3) disconnected families in which one or both parents have no significant attachment to the child with psychosis. According to Diamond and Doane these family types evolved because of parents' family-of-origin attachment experiences. Parents in low-intensity families had predominantly secure attachment experiences in their families of origin, while the family-of-origin experiences of disconnected families were predominantly insecure. Families-of-origin experiences of high-intensity families, in some cases, involved secure attachments and, in others, the attachments were insecure. Diamond and Doane have developed a set of family interventions tailored to the attachment styles of the different types of families in their typology. For disconnected families, the focus is primarily on facilitating the development of parent–child attachments, and secondary goals include the improvement of parent–child communication and the facilitation of joint problem solving. Commonly, in disconnected families, parents project negative aspects of themselves onto their children, who in turn display these negative attributes, and this in turn reinforces parents' negative and disconnected stance with respect to their children. Addressing these projective processes is central to facilitating the development of more secure parent–child attachments. For high-intensity families, the focus is on helping families regulate affect within family interactions by reducing hostility and overinvolvment, and developing more low-key approaches to communication and problem solving. For low-intensity families, the focus is mainly on psychoeducation and pointing out the value of the parents' low-key approach to communication and problem solving.

Family therapy for all types of families involves helping parents understand the intergenerational transmission of attachment styles. This aspect of therapy is especially important for disconnected and high-intensity families in which parents had insecure attachments in their families of origin. In conducting this intergenerational work, the therapist interviews the parents in the presence of the symptomatic child, who is invited to listen to their parents' account of their families of origin. The therapists asks the parents about their experiences growing up and the degree to which each of their parents met their attachment needs for safety, security, acceptance, warmth and esteem with reference to specific detailed examples. Such examples heighten affective experiencing of memories of parent–child attachment. Parents are helped to identify parallels between their problematic parenting style and the parenting style to which they were exposed as children. This, in turn, helps them to empathise with the distress their parenting style may be inducing in their children. Concurrently, their children, who witness their parents achieving these insights, may develop empathy for their parents' shortcomings. A major challenge of this type of work is avoiding inadvertently exposing recovering psychotic children to overly intense parental affect as they recall episodes of unfulfilled attachment needs in their families of origin.

EXPERIENTIAL FAMILY THERAPY

Experiential approaches to family therapy highlight the role of experiential impediments to personal growth in predisposing people to developing problems and problem-maintaining behaviour patterns. People within this tradition have drawn on Carl Rogers's (1951) client-centred approach, Fritz Perls's (1973) Gestalt therapy, Moreno's (1945) psychodrama, and a variety of ideas from the human potential and personal growth movements as inspirations for evolving their approaches to practice. Important figures in the experiential family therapy tradition include Virginia Satir (Banmen, 2002; Banmen & Banmen, 1991; Brothers, 1991; Grinder et al., 1976; Satir, 1983, 1988; Satir & Baldwin, 1983, 1987; Satir & Banmen, 1983; Satir, Banman, Gerber & Gomori, 1991; Suhd, Dodson & Gomori, 2000; Woods & Martin, 1984), Carl Whittaker (Mitten & Cinnell, 2004; Napier, 1987a; 1987b; Napier & Whitaker, 1978; Neill & Kniskern, 1982; Roberto, 1991; Whitaker & Bumberry, 1988; Whitaker & Malone, 1953; Whitaker & Ryan, 1989), Bunny and Fred Duhl (Duhl, 1983; Duhl & Duhl, 1981), and Walter Kempler (1973; 1991).

Healthy and Problematic Family Development from an Experiential Perspective

Experiential family therapists work within a humanistic tradition which assumes that, if given adequate support and a minimum of repressive social controls, children will develop in healthy ways because of their innate drive to self-actualise. According to this viewpoint, healthy families cope with stress, handle differences in personal needs, and acknowledge differences in personal styles and developmental stages by communicating clearly and without censure and by pooling resources to solve problems, so everyone's needs are met.

Within the experiential family therapy tradition it is assumed that problems occur when children or other family members are subjected to rigid, punitive rules, roles and routines that force them to deny and distort their experiences. According to this viewpoint, to be good and avoid the calamity of rejection, a family member must not think, feel or do certain things. To try to conform to family rules, roles and routines, prohibited aspects of experience are denied. In such instances, an incongruity develops between self and experience.

When people who have a major incongruity between self and experience form a family and have their own children, the prohibitions and injunctions that they have internalised from their parents (such as 'don't be angry'; 'don't be frightened'; 'don't be sad'; 'be good'; 'put a brave face on it'; 'be happy') may force them to deny strong emotions associated with their marital and parental relationships. Denied aspects of experience – often strong emotions such as anger, sadness or fear – may be projected onto one child through the process of scapegoating. In such instances the child is singled out, labelled as 'bad', 'sad', 'sick' or 'mad', and becomes the recipient of denied anger, fear or sadness. Carl Whitaker's use of the concept of scapegoating will be elaborated below. Virginia Satir highlighted how problematic styles of communicating may evolve in families where strong emotions are avoided by, for example, distracting others from unresolved issues, or blaming others for difficulties to avoid having to take responsibility for them. These styles will be elaborated below. Most experiential family therapists argue that, in adulthood, unfinished business from childhood must be resolved if self-actualisation is to occur. Unfinished business, in this context, refers to unresolved feelings about relationship difficulties with parents or significant others and unresolved feelings about disowned aspects of the self.

Treatment in Experiential Family Therapy

Experiential family therapists focus on the growth of each family member as a whole person rather than the resolution of specific problems as the main therapeutic goal. Personal growth entails increasing self-awareness, self-esteem, self-responsibility and self-actualisation. With increased self-awareness, there is a more realistic and undistorted appreciation of strengths, talents and potential, as well as vulnerabilities, shortcomings and needs. Increased self-esteem involves positive evaluation of the self in significant relationships; work situations; leisure situations; and within a spiritual context. Increased self-responsibility involves no longer denying or disowning personal experiences or characteristics, which may be negatively evaluated by clients or their parents, but accepting these and being accountable for them. Self-actualisation refers to the process of realising one's full human potential; integrating disowned aspects of experience into the self; resolving unfinished business; being fully aware of moment-to-moment experiences; taking full responsibility for all one's actions; valuing the self and others highly; and communicating in a congruent, authentic, clear direct way. From this brief account, it is clear that for experiential therapists, the goals of therapy are wide-ranging and far-reaching, but difficult to state in specific terms. Experiential therapy aims to help people change or modify the impact of broad developmental contextual factors that may underpin more specific belief systems and problem-maintaining interaction patterns.

Experiential family therapists share a commitment to using emotionally intense, action-oriented, highly creative, apparently non-rational methods to help individual family members overcome developmentally-based obstacles to personal growth so that problems and related problem-maintaining behaviour patterns may be modified. There are two key factors that are assumed to facilitate therapeutic change in experiential family therapy: (1) the authenticity of the therapeutic alliance; and (2) the depth of clients' emotional experiencing within therapy. The more authentic the relationship between the therapist and clients, the more effective therapy is assumed to be. It is not enough for the therapist to be technically skilled, as with all other forms of therapy described in this text. Rather, the therapist must relate to clients in a warm, non-judgemental way, offering clients unconditional positive regard. Therapists' responses to clients must also be emotionally congruent, with no mismatch between the words, actions and emotional experiences of the therapist. Where appropriate, experiential therapists disclose aspects of their own lives to clients to deepen the therapeutic alliance and facilitate clients' personal growth. The second factor that promotes change in experiential therapy is the degree to which the therapist can help clients to experience deeply a wide range of emotional responses concerning significant aspects of their past and present life within the therapy sessions. These new emotional experiences, often concerning earlier life experiences, are used by clients to re-evaluate their current problem-maintaining belief systems and behavioural patterns and so promote both problem resolution and broader personal growth.

It is because of their seminal importance in the emergence of family therapy that the work of Carl Whitaker and Virginia Satir deserve particular mention. Both founded their experiential approaches to family therapy quite independently of each other in the late 1950s and both highlighted the ineffectiveness of individual therapy as an important factor in their transition to family therapy.

Carl Whitaker

Carl Whitaker, although sceptical of the value of rigid theoretical formulations in facilitating good therapy, nevertheless held an implicit theory concerning the central role of the scapegoating process in problem development (Mitten & Cinnell, 2004; Napier, 1987a; 1987b; Napier & Whitaker, 1978; Neill & Kniskern, 1982; Roberto, 1991; Whitaker & Bumberry, 1988; Whitaker & Malone, 1953; Whitaker & Ryan, 1989). He believed that when a patient developed symptoms and was referred for therapy, the patient was a scapegoat onto whom anger, criticism and negative feeling within the family had been displaced, to avoid some imagined and unspoken calamity. For example, denied parental conflict, if acknowledged, might lead to interparental violence, and so negative affect associated with the denied conflict is displaced onto a child. Whitaker assumed that all families would actively resist engaging in family therapy since this would entail accepting that the identified patient was a flag-bearer for wider family difficulties. They would also resist family therapy because it opened up the possibility that denied difficulties would be discussed and possibly lead to the feared calamity. A further implication of Whitaker's scapegoating theory is that families, if they attended therapy, would actively avoid taking responsibility for resolving their own problems and look to the therapist to solve their problems for them.

Within this framework, Whitaker argued that for family therapy to be effective, two confrontative interventions were essential in the first stage of therapy. These were the battle for structure and the battle for initiative.

With the battle for structure, the therapist offers an uncompromising therapeutic contract which specifies that sessions must be attended by all family members. With the battle for initiative, the therapist places the primary responsibility for the content, process, and pacing of therapy sessions on the family. These two interventions maximise the opportunities for confronting and undoing the role of the scapegoating process in helping the family avoid resolving other denied difficulties.

Once therapy was underway, Whitaker relied more on 'being with' families than using any particularly techniques to help them resolve unfinished business, which prevented them from changing their rigid problematic interaction patterns and underlying belief systems. His 'being with' families involved the intuitive use of self-disclosure and what he termed 'craziness'. His self-disclosure and craziness were highly creative, non-rational, playful, lateral thinking-like, yet non-directive processes. They created a context within which family members experienced new ways of being and so they opened up new possibilities for them. However, they typically did so by increasing uncertainty and ambiguity, and forcing family members to take risks to explore new ways of being together and accepting denied aspects of their experience. To maximise the degree to which he could permit himself to be non-rational and 'crazy' in therapy, Whitaker commonly worked with a co-therapist who took on a more rational role within the co-therapy team. Some co-authors of his books and articles worked with Whittaker as co-therapists, and, through these younger more academically oriented therapists, Whittaker's insights continue to have a significant impact on the development of family therapy.

Virginia Satir

The aim of therapy for Virginia Satir was personal growth (Banmen, 2002; Banmen & Banmen, 1991; Brothers, 1991; Grinder et al., 1976; Satir, 1983, 1988; Satir & Baldwin, 1983, 1987; Satir & Banmen, 1983; Satir et al., 1991; Suhd et al., 2000; Woods & Martin, 1984), and this involved raising clients' self-esteem; helping clients become their own choice makers; helping clients become more responsible; helping clients become more congruent so they experienced harmony between feelings, thought and behaviour; helping clients resolve unfinished business; and helping clients achieve freedom in their current lives from the impact of past negative events.

According to Satir, movement towards these goals involved progression through a series of stages of therapy. These included: (1) the status quo; (2) introducing a foreign therapeutic element; (3) chaos arising from disrupting the status quo; (4) integration of experiences arising from the foreign element into a new way of being; (5) practice of a new way of being; and (6) consolidation of the new status quo.

While Satir's approach to family therapy addressed interaction within the current family system, it also focused on facilitating change in the intra-psychic system and current family members' relationships with members of their families of origin. To understand family of origin relationships, Satir used genograms (described in Chapter 7) and family histories. Satir used an 'iceberg metaphor' for conceptualising the intrapsychic system. Satir conceptualised behaviour or current patterns of family interaction as the observable tip of a metaphorical iceberg. Beneath this, she argued, are six hierarchically organised layers, which are not so apparent. These include: (1) immediate feelings, such as joy or sadness; (2) feelings about feelings, such as being worried about being sad; (3) perceptions including belief-systems and values; (4) expectations of self and others; (5) yearnings for belonging, freedom and creativity; and (6) the self. When exploring clients' problems Satir asked questions about all of these layers since it is private feelings, beliefs, expectations, yearnings and so forth, that under-pin publicly observable problematic behaviour patterns.

Virginia Satir highlighted how much of observable problem behaviour may be conceptualised as four problematic communication styles, which may evolve in families where strong emotions are denied and not clearly communicated. These are blaming, placating, distracting and computing. *Blaming* is a communication style used to avoid taking responsibility for resolving conflict, and is characterised by judging, comparing, complain-ing and bullying others while denying one's own role in the problem. *Placating* is a non-adaptive communication style used to consistently de-fuse rather than resolve conflict, and is characterised by pacifying, cover-ing up differences, denying conflict, and being overly 'nice'. *Distracting* is a communication style used consistently to avoid rather than resolve con-flict, and is characterised by changing the subject, being quiet, feigning helplessness or pretending to misunderstand. *Computing* is Satir's term for a non-adaptive communication style used to avoid emotionally engaging with others and communicating congruently. It is characterised by taking an overly intellectual and logical approach; lecturing; taking the higher moral ground; and using outside authority to back up intellectual argu-ments without concurrently and congruently expressing the emotions that go with these arguments.

Satir prized a communicational style she referred to as 'levelling'. This is an adaptive communication style which involves emotional engagement with others in a way that promotes conflict resolution. It is characterised by congruence between verbal and non-verbal messages, fluency, clarity, directness and authenticity. When levelling, people use 'I' statements, like 'I'm happy to see you', not 'Its good you're here'. They also infuse their verbal statements with emotional expressiveness, so that the logical con-tent of their statements is accompanied by a congruent emotional mes-sage conveyed by the style of speech and non-verbal gesures. Satir argued that if family members could be helped to evolve a culture within which levelling was the main way of communicating then the personal growth of all members would be fostered.

Much of Satir's therapy involved subtly modelling and coaching family members in levelling with each other. She frequently invited families to set aside time each day to connect with each other by expressing appreciation; talking about achievements; asking questions; making complaints; solving problems; and talking about hopes and wishes for the future. This task was referred to as taking a temperature reading.

Besides enhancing verbal communication, Satir also used touch- and movement-based techniques to facilitate personal growth within family therapy. With family sculpting, each family member conveys his or her psychological representation of family relationships by positioning other family members spatially so that their positions and postures represent the sculpting member's inner experience of being in the family. Family sculpts of how a member perceives the family to be now and how he or she would like it to be in future may be completed by all members. Then similarities and differences between these may be discussed. However, often the most powerful therapeutic feature of this technique is not the post-sculpting discussion, but the process of each family member 'experiencing' other family members' sculpts. For example, it is a powerful message for a father, if his son in a family sculpt places him a long distance away from the rest of the family and facing a wall. This says, more clearly than a thousand words, that the son views the father as uninvolved in family life.

Metaphors, story telling and externalising internal process were central to Satir's therapeutic style and these 'micro techniques' permeated her use of the broader 'macro techniques', such as family reconstruction and the parts party.

Satir used family reconstruction as the central technique for addressing unresolved family-of-origin issues. This technique was used by Satir in training groups, where individuals (with the help of group members who sculpt and role-play members of the family of origin) reconstruct and re-experience significant formative events from their families of origin. Family reconstruction typically activates strong emotions of which the individual was previously unaware. Experiencing and owning these may promote personal growth.

A related technique is the 'parts party', which was also used by Satir in training groups. An individual doing this exercise directs some group members to role-play different parts of their personality and to interact in a way that metaphorically reflects the way these different aspects of the self typically co-exist inside the person. In parts parties, often the differing parts represent internalisations of parental figures or aspects of parental figures and archaic aspects of the self, like the 'frightened child', 'punitive parent' and so forth. Parts parties, like family reconstruction, typically activate strong emotions of which the individual was previously unaware. Experiencing and owning these may promote personal growth.

In both family reconstruction and parts parties, clients become aware of internalised relations rules learned in childhood. These rules typically are articulated in extreme terms, for example, 'I should never ask questions', and such rules compromise successful adaptation in adulthood. Satir used a three-step procedure to help clients transform maladaptive relational rules into adaptive guidelines. First, change 'should' to 'can'. Second, change 'never' or 'always' to 'sometimes'. Third, identify possibilities. For example, 'I should never ask questions' becomes 'I can sometimes ask questions when I want to know something'.

Satir emphasised the importance of the therapist's use of 'self' as critical for therapeutic change. Satir represented aspects of the self in the 'self-mandala' as a set of concentric circles moving from the physical aspects of self at the centre, through the sensual, nutritional, intellectual, emotional, interactional, and contextual to the spiritual at the outer circle. The self-mandala may be used to help clients or therapists in training to identify their personal strengths and reflect on the interconnectedness of different aspects of the self. Self-actualised clients and therapists, according to Satir, exercise self-care in all of these areas and achieve self-esteem, autonomy, responsibility and congruence by maintaining a harmony between the eight aspects of self. Personal therapy involving family reconstruction, sculpting, exploration of typical communication styles using the iceberg metaphor and other processes can facilitate the personal growth of the therapist.

Experiential approaches to family therapy, like psychodynamic and attachment-based approaches focus on modifying the impact of historical predisposing factors. Multisystemic therapy, which will be described in the next section, in contrast, aims to modify the role of predisposing contextual factors in the wider network around the family.

MULTISYSTEMIC FAMILY THERAPY

The central premise of the multisystemic tradition is that family members may be predisposed to engage in problem-maintaining interaction patterns within the family because of their involvement concurrently in particular types of extrafamilial systems. Scott Henggeler has developed a sophisticated multisystemic model for individual, family and network intervention grounded in structural and strategic family therapy (Henggeler, 1999; Henggeler & Borduin, 1990; Henggeler, Schoenwald, Bordin, Rowland & Cunninghan, 1998; Henggeler, Schoenwald, Rowland & Cunninghan, 2002; Sheidow et al., 2003; Swenson, Henggeler, Taylor & Addison, 2005). The effectiveness of multisystemic therapy with multiproblem families containing youngsters involved in delinquency and drug abuse has been particularly well supported by his team's painstaking empirical research (Curtis et al., 2004). The approach has also been adapted for use with adolescents with a range of other psychiatric and paediatric disorders.

Multisystemic therapy is grounded in Urie Bronfenbrenner's (1979) theory that a youngster's behaviour is influenced by his or her social ecology, which is like a set of Russian dolls with the individual at the centre contained first within the family system. Beyond this, the family is contained within the extended family, which in turn is contained within the wider community. This includes the peer group, neighbourhood, school or work context, and health, social services and other agencies. Finally the community is contained within society with its institutions and culture. Multisystemic assessment involves evaluating the youngster's problems; factors that contribute to and maintain them; and potential problem-resolving resources, within the youngster's multiple systemic contexts. Assessment includes interviews with the child, the family, school staff, and involved agencies and professionals. It may also involve observations of the child and the use of paper and pencil checklists, inventories and psychometric assessment procedures.

Multisystemic intervention programmes are present-focused and action-oriented. They target specific problem-maintaining interaction patterns identified during assessment and aim to disrupt or alter these so that they no longer maintain the problem. These problem-maintaining interaction patterns may involve the child, family, peer group, school, or community. Interventions must fit with the child's social ecology and stage of development and be based on empirically validated pragmatic therapeutic practices. Individually-focused components of treatment programmes commonly include cognitive-behavioural therapy to improve self-regulation of anxiety, depression and impulsivity. Structural, strategic and behavioural family therapy interventions are used to enhance family functioning. Individual cognitive-behavioural interventions are used to enhance children's social skills so they can avoid deviant peer group influences. Remedial tuition and study skills training are used to promote academic attainment. Systemic consultations are used to enhance cooperative interagency working where multiple agencies from the child's wider community are involved.

Multisystemic programmes empower key figures within the child's multiple social contexts including the family, school, peer group and involved agencies to understand and resolve future problems. This ensures generalisation and maintenance of treatment effects.

Effective multisystemic therapy is delivered by small teams of three or four professionals with case loads of no more than six families per therapist. Frequent (often daily) home-based therapy sessions are offered at flexible times over a five-month period. Usually there is a 24-hour on-call crisis intervention service. Frequent therapist supervision, which promotes flexible adherence to manuals, is offered and treatment integrity is monitored by reviewing videotapes of sessions. Empirical evaluation of individual cases and entire service programmes is routinely conducted in multisystemic practice.

Experiential approaches to family therapy, like psychodynamic and attachment-based approaches focus on modifying the impact of historical predisposing factors. Multisystemic therapy aims to modify predisposing contextual factors in the wider network around the family. In contrast, psychoeducational approaches equip family members with the skills required to manage constitutional vulnerabilities that predispose a particular family member to developing psychological problems, such as schizophrenia.

PSYCHOEDUCATIONAL FAMILY THERAPY

Psychoeducational family-based interventions have developed from a tradition of empirical research, which has shown that certain individuals are genetically or constitutionally predisposed to developing psychological problems, such as schizophrenia or mood disorders, and the course of these disorders is affected by the levels of stress and support available in the immediate psychosocial environments of such vulnerable individuals. Psychoeducational family-based interventions help family members understand the factors that affect the aetiology and course of a particular psychological problem faced by a family member, and train family members in the skills required to offer their vulnerable child or spouse an optimally supportive home environment. The most striking feature of psycho-educational models that have emerged in many different centres around the world is their remarkable similarity (Anderson et al., 1986; Atkinson & Coia, 1995; Barrowclough & Tarrier, 1992; Falloon et al., 1993; Hatfield, 1994; Jewell, McFarlane, Dixon & Milkowitz, 2005; Kuipers, Leff & Lan, 2002; McFarlane, 1991, 2002; Milkowitz & Goldstein, 1997). Psychoeducational family therapy has also been used with families in which members have predominantly physical (rather than psychological) symptoms, and this is sometimes referred to as medical family therapy (McDaniel, Hepworth & Doherty, 1997; Ruddy & McDaniel, 2003).

Psychoeducation involves making psychological difficulties of patients understandable to them and their family by providing a coherent theoretical framework; giving families a coherent action plan to follow by training them in problem solving, communication, and medication management skills; and providing social support by arranging for families who face similar problems to meet and discuss common concerns.

Psychoeducational programmes explain major psychological problems, such as schizophrenia; bipolar disorder; and major depression in terms of a diathesis-stress model. Within such models, the occurrence of an episode of a major psychological disorder is attributed to the exposure of a genetically vulnerable person to excessive stress, in the absence of sufficient protective factors, such as social support, coping strategies and medication.

Psychoeducational family interventions arose from research on expressed emotion in the families of patients with schizophrenia and depression. Expressed emotion is an emotive disposition of a relative or caregiver towards a patient characterised by the expression of many critical comments, much hostility, or emotional over-involvement and is assessed in research trials with the Camberwell Family Interview (Vaughan & Leff, 1976) or the Five Minute Speech Sample (Magna et al., 1986). High levels of expressed emotion (probably due to confusion about how to cope with patients' unusual behaviour) are stressful for patients and are associated with higher relapse rates. One aim of psychoeducational programmes is to reduce expressed emotion (criticism, hostility and over-involvement) by helping family members develop supportive attitudes to patients and coaching them in handling potentially emotive situations in a low-key way.

Major stressful life events and changes, such as moving house, financial difficulties or changes in family composition, that place excessive demands on psychologically vulnerable people and which outstrip their coping resources, like exposure to high levels of expressed emotion, may also precipitate relapses or exacerbate psychotic and mood disorders. Psychoeducational programmes train families to recognise this and view the occurrence of stressful events as important opportunities for providing vulnerable family members with social support and facilitating effective coping. A distinction is made between problem-focused and emotion-focused coping. For controllable stress, problem-focused coping strategies, such as planning, soliciting instrumental help and problem-solving, are appropriate. For uncontrollable stresses, emotion-focused strategies, such as distraction, relaxation, seeking social support and reframing are appropriate. Psychoeducational family therapy programmes provide training in both sets of coping strategies and help families to pinpoint situations where one or other set of strategies may appropriately be used.

CLOSING COMMENTS

All of the family therapy approaches described in this chapter focus predominantly on predisposing factors, either historical, contextual or constitutional. They all acknowledge that problems are maintained by repetitive interaction patterns, which may be subserved by underlying belief systems. However, they highlight the fact that people may be predisposed to developing such behavioural patterns and belief systems because of factors in their history; factors in the wider social network outside the family; or personal constitutional factors such as a genetic vulnerability.

Transgenerational, psychoanalytic, attachment-based, and experiential models all highlight the key role of formative early experiences in the family of origin in predisposing people to developing problematic belief systems and behaviour patterns. Of these models, experiential family therapy includes both problem resolution and personal growth as therapeutic goals. In this respect, experiential therapy differs from other models reviewed in this chapter and in Chapters 3 and 4 models. For these, the primary goal of therapy is problem resolution.

Multisystemic therapy addresses predisposing factors within the wider social system around the family and also predisposing factors within the individual, such as skills deficits. Psychoeducational models are concerned with constitutional and genetic predisposing factors. Multisystemic therapy aims to modify the impact of contextual and personal predisposing factors by intervening in the wider system and at the individual level. However, psychoeducational family therapy focuses on helping families to accept and manage biological predisposing factors in more effective ways.

A substantial body of empirical evidence supports the effectiveness of multisystemic family therapy in the treatment of delinquency and related problems (Curtis et al., 2004) and the effectiveness of psychoeducational family therapy in reducing relapse rates following schizophrenia (McFarlane, Dixon, Lukens & Lucksted, 2003). There is also good empirical evidence for the effectiveness of emotionally-focused couples therapy, an attachment-based intervention (Byrne et al., 2004b). This evidence is reviewed in Chapter 18. However, there is little or no published empirical evidence, due to lack of investigations, for the effectiveness of transgenerational, psychoanalytic, or experiential family therapy. Obviously, research in these domains is an important requirement for the field of family therapy.

Process studies have shown that the maintenance of treatment integrity through the use of flexible manuals and regular video review and supervision is associated with a positive outcome in multisystemic therapy (Henggeler, 1999). Process studies of psychoeducational approaches have shown that family intervention makes families more tolerant of low-level psychotic symptoms and allows patients to take lower doses of antipsychotic medication and so suffer fewer side effects (McFarlane et al., 2003).

The models reviewed in this and the previous two chapters represent some of the most influential 'pure' clinical traditions within the field of family therapy. I have attempted to show how these traditions may be grouped with respect to their focus on problem-maintaining interaction patterns; subserving belief systems; and underlying predisposing factors.

However, not all models of family therapy fit neatly into this three-category system. There is a growing trend towards integration within the field of marital and family therapy, and integrative models often span two or more categories and focus equally on these. Within integrative models, aspects of two or more 'pure' models are brought together to provide a more complex framework for understanding the therapy process and to facilitate the use of a more comprehensive range of interventions.

In the next chapter some of the more influential integrative models are considered.

GLOSSARY

Transgenerational Therapy

Coaching. Bowen's term for supervising clients in the process of differentiation of self from the family of origin.

Debt. Boszormenyi-Nagy's term for costs accumulated as a result of failing to meet ethical obligations to other family members.

Detriangling. Bowen's term for the process of using the intellect to avoid the emotional pull to enter the emotional field of two others involved in an anxiety charged relationship.

Differentiation of self. Psychological separation of intellectual and emotional systems within the self which, according to Bowen, permits the concurrent separation of self from others within the family of origin and elsewhere. The opposite of fusion.

Emotional cut-off. Bowen's term for distancing from an unresolved family-of-origin attachment relationship. Distancing may involve physically making little contract and/or psychologically denying the significance of the unresolved family-of-origin relationship. The greater the degree of cut-off, the greater the probability of replicating the problematic family-of-origin relationship in the family of procreation.

Emotional system. Bowen's term for the recursive emotionally-driven problematic interaction patterns which occur is families, particularly those containing high levels of anxiety.

Entitlement. Boszormenyi-Nagy's term for merit accumulated as a result of meeting ethical obligations to other family members.

Exoneration. In contextual therapy, helping clients understand the positive intentions and intergenerational loyalty underpinning actions of family members who have hurt them. When clients develop such understanding they are less likely to replicate the hurtful behaviour they have experienced.

Family lifecycle. The stages of separation from parents, marriage, child rearing, ageing, retirement and death. Additional stages may occur in alternative family forms including same-gender couples, separated couples, non-coupled individuals, people with chronic life-threatening illness, and so forth.

Family of origin. This includes the parents and siblings of an adult client and is distinct from their family of procreation which includes their partners and children.

Family projection process. A process in which the parents project part of their immaturity onto one or more children, who in turn become the least differentiated family members and the most likely to become symptomatic.

Fusion. Extreme emotional enmeshment in one's family of origin.

Genogram. A family tree diagram. Details of how to construct a genogram are given in Chapter 7.

Genogram construction. In Bowenian therapy, conjointly drawing a family tree with one or more family members, identifying intergenerational patterns, speculating about their significance for current problems, and exploring new ways of understanding family relationships.

Invisible loyalties. Boszormenyi-Nagy's term for unconscious commitments that children take on to help their families.

Ledger. Boszormenyi-Nagy's term for the accumulated accounts of entitlements and debts within family relationships; the balance of what has been given and what is owed.

Legacy. Boszormenyi-Nagy's term for expectations associated with the parent–child relationships arising from the family's history.

Multidirected impartiality. The therapeutic position at the core of Boszormenyi-Nagy's contextual therapy, which involves an openness to communication from all family members, a duty to ensure open communication between family members, an accountability to all family members affected by interventions, and a duty to facilitate solutions that are in the best interests of all affected family members.

Multigenerational transmission process. Bowen's theory that the child who is most involved in the family's emotional process becomes the least differentiated, selects a marital partner who shares an equivalently low level of differentiation, and passes the problems of limited differentiation from the family of origin on to the next generation.

Person-to-person relationships. A relationship in which two (differentiated) family members talk to each other about each other, and avoid impersonal discussion or gossip about others.

Relational ethics. Boszormenyi-Nagy's term for the idea that within a family, members are responsible for the consequences of their behaviour and have a duty to be fair in their relationships by meeting their obligations.

Triangle. The smallest stable relational system is a triangle and, under stress, dyads involve a third party to form a triangle. Larger systems are composed of a series of interlocking triangles.

Undifferentiated ego mass. Bowen's term for extremely emotionally close relationships, enmeshment or fusion in certain families, particularly those containing people with schizophrenia.

Psychoanalytic Therapy

Containment. Privately reflecting on another's action, its effect on oneself, and its meaning within the context of the relationship where it occurred, and then responding by supportively outlining one's understanding of the situation.

Countertransference. Therapists' emotional reactions to client's transference which are coloured by therapists' relationships to their parent figures in early life.

Depressive position. Klein's term for the tendency to react to mother figures in infancy or significant others in adulthood as complex individuals having both good and bad characteristics.

Good and bad objects. According to object relations theory, infants, by using the defence mechanism of splitting, come view the mother figure as two separate people: the good object whom they long for and who satisfies their needs, and the bad object with whom they are angry because they long for her and she frustrates them. By splitting, infants may protect the good object from the threat of annihilation, by directing their intense anger exclusively at the bad object.

Identification. Integration of characteristics of an admired parental figure (such as kindness or athleticism) into one's own personality or identity.

Interpretations based on the triangle of conflict. These are interpretations that link the present defence mechanisms, with the underlying anxiety, about an unacceptable impulse or feeling, often involving sex, aggression or grief.

Interpretations based on the triangle of person. Interpretations that draw parallels between the client and therapist transference relationship, the family-of-origin relationship between client and parent, and the current life relationship between client and partner or significant other.

Introject. A primitive mental representation of part of a person, for example, 'good objects' and 'bad objects' are introjects.

Introjection. A primitive form of identification in which simplified representations of major aspects of parental figures (such as the 'good parent (object)' or the 'bad parent (object)') are incorporated completely into the child's psyche.

Mutual projective systems. According to object relations theory, in romantic relationships partners project internal craved objects onto each other and induce their partners to conform to these. In healthy relationships, partners conform partially, but not completely, to these projections so that they partially frustrate each other's needs. Gradually partners learn to respond to the reality of their spouses rather than to their projections. In problematic relationships, partners either completely conform to the demands of each other's projections or do not conform sufficiently and the resulting disappointment leads to relationship conflict and the mutual projection of rejecting objects. In distressed marriages, partners induce each other to conform to these rejecting roles.

Need-exciting and need-rejecting objects. According to object relations theory, the bad object is split into a need-exciting object, which is craved by the infant, and a need-rejecting object towards which the infant experiences rage. These two object relations systems are repressed and are distinct from the central conscious self, which is attached with feelings of security and satisfaction to an ideal good object.

Object relations. Unconscious primitive relationship maps of self and others based on early parent–child relationships that may be partially replicated in current significant relationships. For example an *angry child – frustrating parent* relationship map may be partially replicated in a discordant marital relationship.

Object relations theory. Psychoanalytic theory, developed by Fairburn, which explains current psychological difficulties in terms of the influence of unconscious primitive relationship maps of self and others.

Paranoid-schizoid position. Klein's term for the tendency to respond to mother figures in infancy or significant others in adulthood as all-good or all-bad.

Projection. Attributing an aspect of the self, either positive or negative, to another person.

Projective identification. A defence mechanism where person A attributes positive or negative aspects of themselves to person B, and person B is induced, by the benign or critical way in which they are treated by person A, to behave in accordance with these positive or negative characteristics.

Splitting. A primitive defence mechanism used to reduce anxiety due to an imagined threat, which involves viewing a person as being either completely good or completely bad.

Transference. Clients' emotional reactions to therapists, which mirror their relationships to their parent figures in early life.

Unconscious. Thoughts, memories, feelings and impulses that are outside awareness.

Attachment-based Therapies

Attachment. The emotional bond between a mother and child or between two adults in an intimate relationship.

Attachment needs. The need of children and adults to be involved in relationships that provide safety, security and satisfaction.

Attachment style. There are four attachment styles and most parent–child or marital relationships fall into one of these four categories: secure, insecure-ambivalent, insecure-avoidant and disorganised.

Corrective scripts. These underpin the playing out of scenarios in the current family, which are the opposite of those that occurred in similar contexts within the family of origin.

Disorganised attachment. Children with this attachment style following separation show aspects of both the avoidant and ambivalent patterns. Disorganised attachment is a common correlate of child abuse and neglect and early parental bereavement. Marital and family relationships are characterised by approach-avoidance conflicts, clinging and sulking.

Family myths. Family belief systems, based on distorted accounts of historical events within the family of origin, that underpin expectations about rules, roles and routines within the current family in various contexts. Family myths may stipulate injunctions against particular courses of action because they entail calamitous consequences.

Family scripts. Family belief systems, based on scenarios within the family of origin, that underpin expectations about rules, roles and routines within the current family in various contexts.

Improvisation. Byng-Hall's term for abandoning the rules, roles and routines prescribed in the family script and exploring new possibilities, options and solutions.

Improvised scripts. These underpin the creation of scenarios in the current family which are distinctly different from those that occurred in similar contexts within the family of origin.

Insecure-ambivalent attachment. Children with this attachment style seek contact with their parents following separation but are unable to derive comfort from it. They cling and cry or have tantrums. Marital partners with this attachment style tend to be overly close but dissatisfied. Families characterised by insecure-ambivalent relationships tend to be enmeshed and to have blurred boundaries.

Insecure-avoidant attachment. Children with this attachment style avoid contact with their parents after separation. They sulk. Marital partners with this attachment style tend to be distant and dissatisfied. Families characterised by insecure-avoidant relationships tend to be disengaged and to have impermeable boundaries.

Interactional awareness. Byng-Hall's term for the capacity of family members to track patterns of family interaction; understand their own and other's roles in such patterns; understand the meaning of the patterns for all involved; and predict the probable outcome of such patterns.

Internal working models. Cognitive relationship maps based on early attachment experiences, which serve as a template for the development of later intimate relationships. Internal working models allow people to make predictions about how the self and significant other will behave within the relationship.

Primary emotional responses. In emotionally focused couples therapy (EFCT), the initial emotional responses that occur in immediate response to unmet attachment needs, such as emotional hurt, loss, sadness and loneliness. Facilitating the expression of these is central to EFCT and is thought to promote therapeutic change.

Recruitment into family scripts. Families exert strong emotional pressure on therapists to abandon their impartial position of containment and provision of a secure base and to take up a partisan role in the enactment of the family script. If therapists become stuck in such roles they are unable to be therapeutically effective, hence the importance of reflection and supervision.

Replicative scripts. These underpin the repetition of scenarios from the family of origin in the current family.

Scenarios. Significant episodes of family interaction that occur in a specific context, entail a specific plot, and involve specific roles and motives for participants.

Secondary reactive emotions. In emotionally focused couples therapy, emotional responses that occur as a reaction to primary emotional responses when attachment needs are frustrated. They include anger, hostility, revenge and guilt induction. Preventing the full expression of these and promoting the expression of primary emotional responses is central to EFCT and is thought to promote therapeutic change.

Secure attachment. Securely attached children and marital partners react to their parents or partners as if they are a secure base from which to explore the world. Parents and partners in such relationships are attuned and responsive to the children's or partners' needs. Families with secure attachment relationships are flexibly connected.

Secure base. In secure attachment relationships the parent or partner is viewed as a secure base from which to explore the world.

Secure family base. According to John Byng-Hall, a secure family base provides a reliable network of attachment relationships so that all family members can have sufficient security to explore relationships within and outside the family.

Therapy as a secure base. For Byng-Hall, the therapist provides a secure base and containment of family affect for the family as a whole, so its members can avoid repeating an unhelpful family script, and reflect on their situation before improvising a new script.

Experiential Family Therapy

Battle for initiative. Whitaker's term for placing the primary responsibility for the content, process, and pacing of therapy sessions on the family.

Battle for structure. Whitaker's term for establishing a therapeutic contract that specifies the importance of all family members attending therapy sessions and the timing and venue for these.

Blaming. Satir's terms for a non-adaptive communication style used to avoid taking responsibility for resolving conflict characterised by judging, comparing, complaining and bullying others while denying one's own role in the problem.

Computing. Satir's terms for a non-adaptive communication style used to avoid emotionally engaging with others and communicating congruently, characterised by taking an overly intellectual and logical approach, lecturing, taking the higher moral ground, and using outside authority to back up intellectual arguments.

Craziness. Whitaker's term for the non-rational, creative and often playful processes that therapists and families engage in as part of experiential therapy.

Distracting or avoiding. Satir's terms for a non-adaptive communication style used to avoid consistently rather than resolve conflict characterised by changing the subject, being quiet, feigning helplessness or pretending to misunderstand.

Family reconstruction. A psychodrama technique used by Satir in training groups, where individuals (with the help of group members who role-play members of the family-of-origin) reconstruct and re-experience significant formative events from earlier stages in the family lifecycle. Family reconstruction typically activates strong emotions of which the individual was previously unaware, and experiencing and owning these may promote personal growth.

Family sculpting. An experiential technique where a family member conveys his or her psychological representation of family relationships by positioning other family members spatially so that their positions and postures represent the sculpting member's inner experience of being in the family.

Levelling. Satir's terms for an adaptive communication style which maximises appropriate emotional engagement with others and conflict resolution characterised by the use of emotionally expressive 'I statements' and congruence between verbal and non-verbal messages, fluency, clarity, directness and authenticity.

Parts party. A psychodrama technique used by Satir in training groups. An individual doing this exercise directs some group members to role-play different parts of their personality and to interact in a way that metaphorically reflects the way these different aspects of the self typically co-exist inside the person. Parts parties typically activate strong emotions of which the individual was previously unaware and experiencing and owning these may promote personal growth.

Personal growth. The primary goal of experiential therapies is personal growth, which includes increasing self-awareness, self-esteem, self-responsibility and self-actualisation. Solving the presenting problem is secondary to this primary goal.

Placating. Satir's term for a non-adaptive communication style used to consistently defuse rather than resolve conflict characterised by pacifying, covering up differences, denying conflict, and being overly nice.

Primary family triad. Satir's term for the mother–father–child system. Within this the child learns about parent–child relationships, intimate spouse relationships and communication.

Scapegoat. A family member (often the identified patient) onto whom anger, criticism and negative felling within the family are displaced.

Self-actualisation. Realising one's full human potential; integrating disowned aspects of experience into the self; resolving unfinished business; being fully aware of moment-to-moment experiences; taking full responsibility for all one's actions; valuing the self and others highly; and communicating in a congruent, authentic, clear direct way.

Self-awareness. The realistic and undistorted appreciation of one's strengths, talents and potential, on the one hand, and one's vulnerabilities, shortcomings and needs, on the other.

Self-disclosure. Therapists telling clients about their own experiences to let clients view them an accessible people rather than distant professionals. Self-disclosure is also used to promote trust, deepen the therapeutic alliance with the clients, and suggest possible solutions to family problems.

Self-esteem. The positive evaluation of the self and this may include the evaluation of the self in significant relationships, work situations, leisure situations, and self as an existential or spiritual being.

Self-responsibility. Not denying or disowning personal experiences or characteristics which may be negatively evaluated by the self or others, but accepting these and being accountable for them.

Temperature reading. Satir's term for the family task of setting aside time each day to connect with each other by expressing appreciation, talking about achievements, asking questions, making complaints, solving problems, and talking about hopes and wishes for the future.

Unfinished business. Fritz Perls' term for unresolved feelings about relationship difficulties with parents or significant others or unresolved feelings about disowned aspects of the self.

Multisystemic Approaches

Multisystemic assessment. This includes interviews with the child, the family, school staff, and involved agencies and professions; observations of the child; and the use of paper and pencil checklists, inventories and psychometric assessment procedures.

Multisystemic intervention programmes. These are present-focused, action-oriented and target specific problem-maintaining interaction patterns identified during assessment within relevant systemic contexts including the child, family, peer group, school and community.

Multisystemic therapy service delivery. Effective multisystemic therapy is delivered by small teams of three or four professionals; with case loads of no more than six families per therapist; with frequent (often daily) home-based therapy sessions offered at flexible times over a five-month period; with a 24-hour on-call crisis intervention service; with frequent therapist supervision involving promoting flexible adherence to manuals and monitoring by reviewing videotapes of sessions; and with empirical evaluation of individual cases and entire service programmes.

Social ecology. Bronfenbrenner likens a child's social ecology to a set of Russian dolls with the child at the centre contained first within the family system; beyond this within the extended family; then within the peer group, neighbourhood, school, supportive health, social services and other agencies; and finally within the wider community.

Psychoeducational Approaches

Coping strategies. These are methods for reducing stress. For controllable stress, problem-focused strategies such as planning, soliciting instrumental help and problem-solving are appropriate. For uncontrollable stresses, emotion-focused strategies such as distraction, relaxation, seeking social support and reframing are appropriate.

Diathesis-stress model. A model of recurrent debilitating psychological problems (particularly psychotic, mood and anxiety disorders) in which the occurrence of an episode of the disorder is attributed to the exposure of a genetically vulnerable person to excessive stress, in the absence of sufficient protective factors such as social support, coping strategies and medication. Most psychoeducational programmes for psychological problems are based on diathesis-stress models.

Expressed emotion. An emotive disposition of a relative or caregiver towards a person with a debilitating psychological problem characterised by the expression of many critical comments, much hostility, or emotional overinvolvement on the Camberwell Family Interview. High levels of expressed emotion (probably due to confusion about how to cope) are stressful for patients and are associated with higher relapse rates.

Psychoeducation. Making the psychological difficulties of patients understandable to family members by providing a coherent theoretical framework; giving them a coherent action plan to follow by training them in problem solving, communication, and medication management skills; and providing social support by arranging for families who face similar problems to meet and discuss common concerns.

Social support. Effective social support is provided within the context of a sustained confiding relationship where a person has considerable control over the frequency of contact and the issues discussed.

Stressful life events. Life changes that place demands on the person that outstrip their coping resources. Most stressful life events fall into four categories: (1) the formation of new significant relationships (entrances); (2) the loss of important relationships through separation or bereavement (exits); (3) lifecycle transitions; and (4) illness or injury within the family.

FURTHER READING

Transgenerational Marital and Family Therapy

Boszormenyi-Nagy, I. (1987). *Foundations of Contextual Therapy: Collected Papers of Ivan Boszormenyi-Nagy*. New York: Brunner Mazel.

Boszormenyi-Nagy, I. & Krasner, B. (1987). *Between Give and Take: A Clinical Guide to Contextual Therapy.* New York: Brunner Mazel.

Boszormenyi-Nagy, I. & Spark, G. (1973). *Invisible Loyalties: Reciprocity in Intergenerational Family Therapy.* New York: Harper & Row.

Boszormenyi-Nagy, I., Grunebum, J. & Ulrish D. (1991). Contextual therapy. In A. Gurman & D. Kniskern (Eds), *Handbook of Family Therapy, Vol. 11*, pp. 200–238. New York: Brunner Mazel.

Bowen, M. (1978). *Family Therapy in Clinical Practice.* Northvale, NJ: Jason Aronson.

Ducommun-Nagy, C. & Schwoeri, L. (2003). Contextual therapy. In G. Sholevar (Ed.), *Textbook of Family and Couples Therapy: Clinical Applications*, pp. 127–146. Washington, DC: American Psychiatric Press.

Framo, J. (1982). *Explorations in Marital and Family Therapy. Selected Papers of James L Framo, PhD.* New York: Springer.

Framo, J. (1992). *Family of Origin Therapy: An intergenerational Approach.* New York: Springer.

Freeman, D. (1992). *Family Therapy with Couples: The Family-of-Origin Approach.* Northvale, NJ: Jason Aronson.

Freeman, D. (1992). *Multigenerational Family Therapy.* Binghampton, NY: Haworth.

Friedman, E. (1991). Bowen theory and therapy. In A. Gurman & D. Kniskern (Eds), *Handbook of Family Therapy, Vol. 11*, pp. 134–170. New York: Brunner Mazel.

Guerin, P., Fogarty, T., Fay, L. & Kautto, J. (1996). *Working with Relationship Triangles. The One-Two-Three of Psychotherapy.* New York: Guilford.

Kerr, M. (2003). Multigenerational family systems theory of Bowen and its application. In G. Sholevar (Ed.), *Textbook of Family and Couples Therapy: Clinical Applications*, pp. 103–126. Washington, DC: American Psychiatric Press.

Kerr, M. & Bowen, M. (1988). *Family Evaluation.* New York: Norton.

McGoldrick, M. & Carter, B. (2001). Advances in coaching: Family therapy with one person. *Journal of Marital and Family Therapy*, **27**, 281–300.

Nelson, T. (2003). Transgenerational family therapy. In L. Hecker & J. Wetchler (Eds), *An Introduction to Marital and Family Therapy*, pp. 255–296. New York: Haworth.

Nichols, W. (2003). Family-of-origin treatment. In T. Sexton, G. Weeks & M. Robbins (Eds), *Handbook of Family Therapy*, pp. 83–100. New York: Brunner-Routledge.

Papero, D. (1990). *Bowen Family Systems Theory.* Needham Heights, MA: Allyn & Bacon.

Roberto, L. (1992). *Transgenerational Family Therapies.* New York: Guilford.

Roberto-Forman, L. (2002). Transgenerational marital therapy. In A. Gurman & N. Jacobon (Eds), *Clinical Hanbook of Couples Therapy*, 3rd edn, pp. 118–150. New York: Guilford.

Williamson, D. (1991). *The Intimacy Paradox: Personal Authority in the Family System.* New York: Guilford.

Psychoanalytic Marital and Family Therapy

Ackerman, N. (1958). *The Psychodynamics of Family Life: Diagnosis and Treatment of Family Relationships.* New York: Basic Books.

Ackerman, N. (1984). *A Theory of Family Systems*. New York: Gardner.

Ackerman, N. (1966). *Treating the Troubled Family*. New York: Basic Books.

Ackerman, N. (1970). *Family Therapy in Transition*. Boston, MA: Little Brown.

Bentovim, A. & Kinston, W. (1991). Focal family therapy. Joining systems theory with psychodynamic understanding. In A. Gurman & D. Kniskern (Eds), *Handbook of Family Therapy, Vol. 11*, pp. 284–324. New York: Brunner Mazel.

Box, S., Copley, B., Magagna, J. & Mustaki, E. (1981). *Psychotherapy with Families*. London: Routledge.

Dicks, H. (1963). Object relations theory and marital status. *British Journal of Medical Psychology*, **36**, 125–129.

Dicks, H. (1967). *Marital Tensions: Clinical Studies Toward a Psychoanalytic Theory of Interaction*. London: Routledge.

Fairburn, W. (1952). *An Object Relations Therapy of Personality*. New York: Basic Books.

Fairburn, W. (1963). Synopsis of an object relations theory of personality. *Journal of Psychoanalysis*, **44**, 224–225.

Friedman, L. & Pearce, J. (1980). *Family Therapy: Combining Psychodynamic and Family Systems Approaches*. New York: Grune & Stratton.

Kirschner, D. & Kirschner, S. (1986). *Comprehensive Family Therapy: An Integration of Systemic and Psychodynamic Models*. New York: Brunner Mazel.

Nichols, M. (1987). *The Self in the System: Expanding the Limits of Family Therapy*. New York: Brunner Mazel.

Savage-Scharff, J. (1989). *Foundations of Object Relations Family Therapy*. Northvale, NJ: Jason Aronson.

Savage-Scharff, J. (1992). *Projective and Introjective Identification and the Use of the Therapists Self*. Northvale, NJ: Jason Aronson.

Savage-Scharff, J. & Bagini, C. (2002). Object-relations couple therapy. In A. Gurman & N. Jacobon (Eds), *Clinical Handbook of Couples Therapy*, 3rd edn, pp. 59–85. New York: Guilford.

Savage-Scharff, J. & Scharff, D. (1994). *Object Relations Therapy of Physical and Sexual Trauma*. Northvale, NJ: Jason Aronson.

Savage-Scharf, J. & Scharf, D. (2003). Object relations and psychodynamic approaches to couple and family therapy. In T. Sexton, G. Weeks & M. Robbins (Eds), *Handbook of Family Therapy*, pp. 59–82. New York: Brunner-Routledge.

Scharff, D. (1982). *The Sexual Relationship: An Object Relations view of Sex and the Family*. Boston: Routledge.

Scharff, D. & Savage-Scharff, J. (1987). *Object Relations Family Therapy*. Northvale, NJ: Jason Aronson.

Scharff, D. & Savage -Scharff, J. (1991). *Object Relations Couple Therapy*. Northvale, NJ: Jason Aronson.

Skynner, R. (1981). An open-systems, group-analytic approach to family therapy. In A. Gurman & D. Kniskern (Eds), *Handbook of Family Therapy*, pp. 39–84. New York: Bruner Mazel.

Slipp, S. (1984). *Object relations: A Dynamic Bridge Between Individual and Family Treatment*. New York: Jason Aronson.

Slipp, S. (1988). *The Technique and Practice of Object Relations Family Therapy*. New York: Jason Aronson.

Marital and Family Therapies Based on Attachment Theory

Bowlby, J. (1988). *A Secure Base: Clinical Implications of Attachment Theory.* London: Routledge.

Byng-Hall, J. (1995). *Rewriting Family Scripts. Improvisation and Change.* New York: Guilford.

Cassidy, J. & Shaver, P. (1999). *Handbook of Attachment.* New York: Guilford.

Diamond, G., Siqueland, L. & Diamond, G. (2003). Attachment-based family therapy for depressed adolescents: programmatic treatment development. *Clinical Child and Family Psychology Review,* **6** (2), 107–127.

Doane, J. & Diamond, D. (1994). *Affect and Attachment in the Family: A Family Based Treatment of Major Psychiatric Disorder.* New York: Basic Books.

Greenberg, L. & Johnson, S. (1988). *Emotionally Focused Therapy for Couples.* New York: Guilford.

Johnson, S. (1996). *The Practice of Emotionally Focused Marital Therapy: Creating Connection.* New York: Brunner Mazel.

Johnson, S. (2002). *Emotionally Focused Couple Therapy with Trauma Survivors: Strengthening Attachment Bonds.* New York: Guilford.

Johnson, S. (2003). Emotionally focused couple therapy: Empiricism and art. In T. Sexton, G. Weeks & M. Robbins (Eds), *Handbook of Family Therapy*, pp. 263–280. New York: Brunner-Routledge.

Johnson, S. & Denton, W. (2002). Emotionally focused couple therapy: Creating secure connections. In A. Gurman & N. Jacobson (Eds), *Clinical Handbook of Couple Therapy*, 3rd edn, pp. 221–250. New York: Guilford.

Johnson, S. & Whiffen, V. (2003). *Attachment Processes in Couple and Family Therapy.* New York: Guilford.

Experiential Family Therapy

Banmen, J. (2002). *Special issue: Satir Today. Contemporary Family Therapy,* **24** (1).

Banmen, A. & Banmen, J. (1991). *Meditations of Virginia Satir: Peace Within, Peace Between, and Peace Among.* Palo Alto, CA: Science and Behaviour Books.

Brothers, D. (1991). *Virginia Satir: Foundational Ideas.* Binghampton, NJ: Haworth.

Duhl, B. & Duhl, F. (1981). Integrative family therapy. In A. Gurman & D. Kniskern (Eds), *Handbook of Family Therapy*, pp. 483–516. New York: Bruner Mazel.

Duhl, B. (1983). *From the Inside Out and Other Metaphors: Creative and Integrative Approaches to Training in Systems Thinking.* New York: Bruner Mazel.

Grinder, J., Bandler, R. & Satir, V. (1976). *Changing with Families.* Palo Alto, CA: Science and Behaviour Books.

Kempler, W. (1973). *Principles of Gestalt Family Therapy.* Salt Lake City: Dessert Press.

Kempler, W. (1991). *Experiential Psychotherapy within Families*, 2nd edn. Norway: Kempler Institute.

Mitten, T. & Cinnell, G. (2004). The core variables of symbolic-experiential family therapy. *Journal of Marital and Family Therapy,* **30**, 467–478.

Napier, A. (1987a). Early stages in experiential marital therapy. *Contemporary Family Therapy,* **9**, 23–41.

Napier, A. (1987b). Later stages in experiential marital therapy. *Contemporary Family Therapy*, **9**, 42–57.

Napier, A. & Whitaker, C. (1978). *The Family Crucible*. New York: Harper Row.

Neill, J. & Kniskern, D. (1982). *From Psyche to System: The Evolving Therapy of Carl Whitaker*. New York: Guilford.

Roberto, G. (1991). Symbolic-experiential family therapy. In A. Gurman & D. Kniskern (Eds), *Handbook of Family Therapy, Vol. 11*, pp. 444–478. New York: Brunner Mazel.

Satir, V. (1983). *Conjoint Family Therapy*, 3rd edn. Palo Alto, CA: Science and Behaviour Books.

Satir, V. (1988). *The New Peoplemaking*. Palo Alto, CA: Science and Behaviour Books.

Satir, V. & Baldwin, M. (1983). *Satir Step-by-Step. A Guide to Creating Change in Families*. Palo Alto, CA: Science and Behaviour Books.

Satir, V. & Baldwin, M. (1987). *The Use of Self in Therapy*. Binghampton, NY: Haworth.

Satir, V. & Banmen, J. (1983). *Virginia Satir Verbatim*. North Delta, BC: Delta Psychological Associates.

Satir, V., Banmen, J., Gerber, J. & Gomori, M. (1991). *The Satir Model: Family Therapy and Beyond*. Palo Alto, CA: Science and Behaviour Books.

Suhd, M., Dodson, L. & Gomori, M. (2000). *Virginia Satir: Her Life and Circle of Influence*. Palo Alto, CA: Science and Behaviour Books.

Whitaker, C. & Bumberry, W. (1988). *Dancing with the Family. A Symbolic-Experiential Approach*. New York: Brunner Mazel.

Whitaker, C. & Malone, T. (1953). *The Roots of Psychotherapy*. New York: Blakinson.

Whitaker, C. & Ryan, M. (1989). *Midnight Musings of a Family Therapist*. New York: Norton.

Woods, M. & Martin, D. (1984). The work of Virginia Satir: Understanding her theory and technique. *American Journal of Family Therapy*, **11** (1), 35–46.

Multisystemic Therapy

Henggeler, S. (1999). Multisystemic therapy; An overview of clinical procedures, outcomes and policy implications. *Child Psychology and Psychiatry Review*, **4** (1), 2–10.

Henggeler, S. & Borduin, C. (1990). *Family Therapy and Beyond: A Multisystemic Approach to Treating the Behaviour Problems of Children and Adolescents*. Pacific Grove, CA: Brooks Cole.

Henggeler, S., Schoenwald, S., Bordin, C., Rowland, M. & Cunningham, P. (1998). *Multisystemic Treatment of Antisocial Behaviour in Children and Adolescents*. New York: Guilford.

Henggeler, S.W., Schoenwald, S.K., Rowland, M.D. and Cunningham, P.B. (2002). *Serious Emotional Disturbance In Children And Adolescents: Multisystemic Therapy*. New York: Guilford Press.

Sheidow, A.J., Henggeler, S.W. & Schoenwald, S.K. (2003). Multisystemic therapy. In T.L. Sexton, G.R. Weeks & M.S. Robbins (Eds), *Handbook of Family Therapy*, pp. 303–322. New York: Brunner-Routledge.

Swenson, C.C., Henggeler, S.W., Taylor, I.S. and Addison, O.W. (2005). *Multisystemic Therapy And Neighborhood Partnerships: Reducing Adolescent Violence And Substance Abuse*. New York: Guilford Press

Psychoeducational Family Therapy

Anderson, C. Reiss, D. & Hogarty, G. (1986). *Schizophrenia and the Family*. New York: Guilford.

Atkinson, J. & Coia, D. (1995). *Families Coping with Schizophrenia: A Practitioners Guide to Family Groups*. New York: Wiley.

Barrowclough, C. & Tarrier, N. (1992). *Families of Schizophrenic Patients – Cognitive Behavioural Intervention*. London: Chapman Hall.

Falloon, I., Laporta, M., Fadden, G. & Graham-Hole, V. (1993). *Managing Stress in Families*. London: Routledge.

Hatfield, A. (1994). *Family Interventions in Mental Illness*. San Francisco, CA: Jossey Bass.

Jewell, T., McFarlane, W., Dixon, L. & Milkowitz, D. (2005). Evidence-based family services for adults with severe mental illness. In C. Stout & R. Hayes (Eds), *The Evidence-Based Practice: Methods, Models, And Tools For Mental Health Professionals*, pp. 56–84. New York: Wiley.

Kuipers, L., Leff, J. & Lam, D. (2002). *Family Work for Schizophrenia*, 2nd edn. London: Gaskell.

McDaniel, S. Hepworth, J. & Doherty, W. (1997). *Medical Family Therapy*. New York: Basic Books.

McFarlane, W. (1991). Family psychoeducational treatment. In A. Gurman & D. Kniskern (Eds), *Handbook of Family Therapy, Vol. 11*, pp. 363–395. New York: Brunner Mazel.

McFarlane, W. (2002). *Multifamily Groups in The Treatment of Severe Psychiatric Disorders*. New York: Guilford Press.

Miklowitz, D. J. & Goldstein, M. J. (1997). *Bipolar Disorder: A Family-Focused Treatment Approach*. New York, NY: Guilford Press.

Ruddy, N. & McDaniel, S. (2003). Medical family Therapy. In T. Sexton, G. Weeks & M. Robbins (Eds), *Handbook of Family Therapy*, pp. 365–379. New York: Brunner-Routledge.

Chapter 6

INTEGRATIVE MODELS

When therapists, trained within a particular model of family therapy practice, find that their usual therapeutic approach is not helpful in a particular case, they often improvise and 'borrow' concepts and interventions from other models to try to help clients who have not responded to their usual style of therapy. That is, they adopt an eclectic approach to practice. Most experienced clinicians are somewhat eclectic in their practice, using concepts and interventions from a range of theories when faced with complex clinical problems. Eclectic practitioners base their choice of concepts and interventions on clinical judgment about the appropriateness of the concept or intervention for a specific case. In contrast to eclecticism, integration aims to provide a broad overarching theoretical framework to guide the selection of concepts and interventions from a range of less complex theories for use with a range of cases rather than with a single case. Integrative models of practice afford therapists far greater flexibility, especially when working with complex cases.

There is a movement within the field of psychotherapy generally towards the integration of multiple therapeutic models (Norcross & Goldfried, 2005), and family therapy is no exception (Lebow, 2003). In this chapter, four such integrative models will be presented Models reviewed in Chapters 3–5 were grouped with respect to their focus on problem-maintaining interaction patterns; subserving belief systems or narratives; and underlying contextual factors. The integrative models reviewed in this chapter, focus even-handedly on behaviour, beliefs and contextual factors, and attempt to bring together at least three 'pure' models reviewed in Chapters 3–5 in a coherent way. The four integrative models chosen for review have been selected because they are leading examples of how insights from multiple models may be coherently synthesised.

METAFRAMEWORKS

The metaframeworks model was developed by Douglas Breunlin, Richard Schwartz and Betty MacKune-Karrer (1997). The aim of the metaframeworks model is to provide therapists with an integrative system for assessing and treating couples and families, which brings together key insights from multiple simpler approaches. Within this metaframeworks model, it is assumed that, for any problem an individual, couple or family brings to therapy, hypotheses may be formulated in terms of six meta frameworks: (1) internal family systems; (2) sequences or patterns of interaction; (3) family organisation; (4) development; (5) multicultural issues; and (6) gender issues. The process of therapy involves: (1) hypothesising in terms of metaframeworks; (2) planning how to check out these hypotheses by conversing with clients; (3) conversing with clients; and (4) reading feedback in a way that allows hypotheses to be refined or discarded. Hypotheses derived from one or two metaframeworks may be used as a point of entry for working with the clients initially, depending on the clients' central concerns.

With the internal family system's metaframework, it is assumed that each person has a central self and an internal family system composed of various introjects or 'parts'. This self has the potential to coordinate the activities and influence of these 'parts' on an individual's experience and behaviour within the external family system. Problems may be maintained by conflict or disorganisation among 'parts' of the individual, or where the 'self' is not taking a leadership role in coordinating and organising the influence that the 'parts' have on experience and behaviour. For example, angry, sad, frightened, dismissive or oppressive parts within the internal family system may have a primary influence on an individual's experience and behaviour. This in turn may lead to problem-maintaining interaction patterns within the external family system. Intervention based on internal family systems hypotheses involve helping individuals understand and modify the organisation of their internal family system, so the self adopts a leadership role over the parts. The internal family systems metaframework draws on Schwartz's (1995) model by the same name, but also has roots in Satir's (Satir et al., 1991) experiential model and object-relations family therapy (Savage-Scharf & Scharf, 2003).

With the sequences metaframework, it is assumed that, in any family, clinically useful distinctions may be made between four classes of sequences or patterns of interaction. The first class (S1) includes brief sequences of face-to-face interaction, such as those directly observed in a therapy session. The second class of sequences (S2) includes family routines that may span periods from a day to a week. The third class (S3) includes sequences such as those involved in the development, resolution and relapse of a problem, which may span periods from a few weeks to a year. The fourth class (S4) includes transgenerational sequences, where events in the family of origin are repeated in the current family of procreation. Any problem a family brings to therapy may be conceptualised as occurring within the context of one or more of these four classes of sequences, which maintain the problem and place constraints on the family resolving the problem. For example, a woman may show sadness and withdrawal each time her husband criticises her (S1), and this may typically happen when he comes home late from work (S2), although not during the summer months (S3), a pattern that was common in both of their families of origin (S4). Interventions based on the sequences metaframework aim to disrupt problem-maintaining sequences of interaction, starting with the most salient or most accessible. The sequences metaframework draws on a range of models including MRI (Segal, 1991), strategic (Madanes, 1991), structural (Fishman and Fishman, 2003) and transgenerational (Kerr, 2003).

With the organisation metaframework, it is assumed that for optimal family functioning the family must be organised so that it has clear effective leadership, a balance of power and a degree of cooperative harmony among members. Problems may arise when there is an absence of effective leadership, power imbalances and conflictual disharmony. Interventions based on the organisation metaframework involve collaborating with the family to identify and remove constraints that prevent leadership, balance and harmony. The organisation framework draws on Minuchin's structural family therapy (Fishman and Fishman, 2003) and Haley's strategic family therapy (Madanes, 1991).

With the developmental framework, it is assumed that family development over the lifecycle involves development at the biological, individual, relational and family levels in a way that is consistent with societal norms and values about development. In adaptive families, development at each level fosters development at other levels. Difficulties making developmental transitions at one level, however, may lead to disruption at other levels. Interventions based on the developmental metaframwork involve helping families successfully make individual, relational and family developmental transitions and adapt to biological constraints (such as disabilities) that impede development. The developmental metaframework draws on the work of family lifecycle theorists such as Carter and McGoldrick (1999) and also on developmental psychology.

With the multicultural framework, it is assumed that optimal family adjustment occurs when there is good fit between the ethnic culture of the family and the predominant culture of the community and society in which the family resides. Difficulties occur when there are significant discrepancies between the cultural norms, values and practices of mainstream society and a family from an ethnic minority. Interventions based on the multicultural metaframework involve helping families, especially those from ethnic minorities, successfully adapt to mainstream culture, while still retaining their unique ethnic minority cultural identity. The multicultural framework draws on a wide range of multicultural influences within family therapy (McGoldrick, 2002).

With the gender metaframework, it is assumed that optimal functioning occurs when power is fairly balanced within a family and members of both genders adopt flexible roles. Problems arise when narrowly defined traditional gender roles create a power imbalance between males and females within a family. Families vary in the degree to which their members adhere to traditional dominant male breadwinning and submissive female caregiving roles. Interventions based on the gender metaframework help families move along the continuum from traditional towards more egalitarian gender roles. The gender metaframework draws on the feminist critique of family therapy (Leupnitz, 1988).

The six metaframeworks in this integrative model are linked. In any family, all members have internal family systems of 'parts' that affect the sorts of sequences of interaction in which families engage. Internal family systems and external sequences of interaction affect family organisation and development. Sequences of interaction, family organisation and family development are affected by gender and culture-based norms and values. The metaframeworks model therefore provides a rich and complex way for hypothesising about client problems and planning interventions at multiple levels. Much of the therapy with complex cases involves modifying constraints that prevent families resolving their difficulties. These constraints typically occur at the multiple levels defined by the metaframeworks model (internal family systems, sequences of interaction, family disorganisation, developmental issues multicultural issues and gender issues).

INTEGRATIVE PROBLEM-CENTRED THERAPY

The integrative problem-centred therapy (IPCT) model was developed by William Pinsof (1995, 2005). The aim of the model is to integrate a range of therapeutic approaches and provide therapists with a framework for interrelating family, individual and biological approaches to treatment, particularly when working with complex cases that do not respond to routine family therapy.

In IPCT, it is assumed that the patient system includes all those involved in maintaining the presenting problem and those who could potentially be involved in its resolution. A distinction is made between the direct patient system with whom the therapist has face-to-face contact (for example, a couple), and the indirect patient system with whom the therapist does not have contact, but who nevertheless influence the maintenance or resolution of the problems (for example, a couple's parents). The therapy system includes all those providing therapy (the therapist, colleagues, supervisors and other professionals involved in treating the patient). Fragmentation in the patient system or the therapist system may prevent problem resolution. So a key intervention in IPCT is facilitating the development of good working alliances within the patient system and the therapist system.

It is also assumed that in addition to presenting problems (for example, panic attacks), typically in complex cases there are non-presenting problems (for example, infidelity or work difficulties), which often play a role in maintaining the presenting problem. Within IPCT, therapists focus exclusively on the resolution of the presenting problem, unless the non-presenting problem is clearly linked to the presenting problem or endangers the safety of someone. Thus, a second important intervention in IPCT is helping members of the patient system understand links between the presenting problems and the non-presenting problems that may be maintaining them.

Within IPCT, the therapist also invites clients to describe an adaptive solution to the presenting problem that specifies in detail the actions members of the patient system would need to take to resolve the presenting problem. The role of the therapist is to coach members of the patient system to enact the adaptive solution. The ease or difficulty with which adaptive solutions can be implemented is in part determined by problem-maintenance structures. These include the set of constraints that prevent members of the patient system from implementing the adaptive solution. Within IPCT it is assumed that these constraints are organised into six levels: (1) social organisational factors, such as family rules; (2) biological constraints, such as disabilities, illnesses and genetic vulnerabilities; (3) meaning constraints, such as problematic belief systems; (4) transgenerational constraints, such as family-of-origin legacies that influence functioning in the current family of procreation; (5) object relations constraints, including problematic internal representations of the self and significant attachment figures; and (6) self-constraints arising from the failure of attachment figures to meet patients' needs in early life. Within any problem-maintenance structure, the number of constraints and the power of these is determined in IPCT by attempting to facilitate clients' implementation of their adaptive solutions. Thus, assessment and intervention are ongoing inseparable processes.

Within IPCT distinctions are made between three therapeutic modalities: (1) individual therapy; (2) couples therapy; and (3) family or community therapy. Distinctions are also made between six therapeutic orientations, which correspond to the six levels of constraints listed above: (1) behavioural; (2) biobehavioural; (3) experiential; (4) family of origin; (5) psychodynamic; and (6) self-psychology. These three modalities and six orientations form a 3 × 6 matrix. They are presented in Figure 6.1 in the order in which IPCT recommends they first be used from left to right and top to bottom. The big arrow in the matrix indicates the way in which modalities and orientations are most commonly blended. For example, the behavioural orientation is most commonly blended with the family modality. The self-psychology orientation is most commonly used with the individual therapy modality.

The behavioural orientation assumes behavioural constraints maintain problems and so problems can be resolved by helping clients to behave differently. This orientation subsumes behavioural (Epstein, 2003),

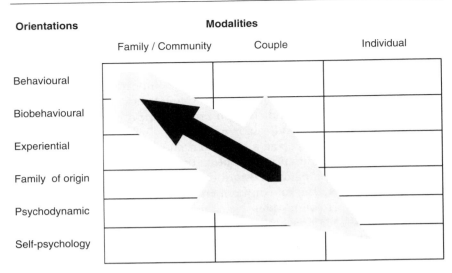

Orientations   **Modalities**

Source: Adapted from Pinsof (2005). Integrative problem-centred therapy. In J. Norcross & M. Goldfried (Eds.), *Handbook' of Psychotherapy Integration* (Second Edition, p. 389.). New York: Oxford University Press.

Figure 6.1 Problem-centred orientation-modality matrix

structural (Fishman & Fishman, 2003), strategic (Madanes, 1991), and solution-focused (Miller et al., 1996) approaches to family therapy. The biobehavioural orientation assumes that biological constraints such as disability, illness and genetic vulnerability play a central role in problem maintenance and effective treatment must address these constraints. Interventions within this orientation include medication, psychoeducation (McFarlane, 1991), meditation and massage. The experiental orientation assumes that cognitive and emotional constraints maintain problems and, hence, addressing belief systems and emotions is central to problem resolution. This orientation subsumes cognitive therapy (Epstein, 2003), narrative therapy (Freedman & Combs, 1996), post-modern approaches to therapy (Anderson, 2003) and emotionally-focused couple therapy (Johnson, 2003a). The family-of-origin orientation assumes that constraints from the family of origin maintain problems in the current family of procreation, and so these constraints must be addressed for the presenting problem to be resolved. This orientation subsumes Bowen's (1978) transgenerational therapy and Boszormenyi-Nagy's contextual therapy (Ducommun-Nagy & Schwoeri, 2003). The psychodynamic orientation assumes that problematic internal representations of the self and significant attachment figures, and the dysfunctional defence mechanisms associated with these constrain problem resolution and so these must be addressed for the adaptive solution to be implemented (Savage-Scharf &

Scharf, 2003). Psychodynamic psychotherapy is the principal intervention in this orientation. The self-psychology orientation assumes that problems are maintained by constraints arising from failure of attachment figures to meet patients' needs in early life. Psychotherapy based on Kohut's (1984) work is the main intervention associated with this orientation.

The IPCT matrix in Figure 6.1 lets the therapist know what category of intervention to use if the current category is not working, by moving down and right in the matrix, as indicated by the big downward pointing arrow. For example, if work involving a behavioural or biobehavioural orientation with the whole family is not working, then it may be useful to try experiential work with couples. If this does not work, the next intervention may be individual family of origin or psychodynamic work. The small upward pointing arrow indicates that at regular intervals, when working with clients in the lower, righ-hand part of the matrix, it is important to test their readiness to engage in constrained behaviours with members of the patient system that would lead to adaptive solutions. This overall approach involves therapists assuming that the problem-maintenance structure is simple until proved complex and that it is more cost effective to do therapy within an interpersonal than an individual modality.

Within IPCT, the therapeutic alliance is essential for effective therapy. It is conceptualised as involving tasks, goals and bonds. Alliances are conceptualised as being formed with individuals, family subsystems, whole family systems and within the family system. Family, couple, individual and therapy alliance scales, and revised versions of them, have been developed (Pinsof, 1994; Pinsof & Catherall, 1986). Pinsof et al. (2004a) have also developed the Systemic Therapy Inventory of Change to assess family functioning and progress through therapy. It assesses adult symptoms and well-being, child symptoms and well-being, adult family-of-origin experiences, current marital functioning and current family functioning. The Integrative Therapy Session Report (Pinsof et al., 2004a) has been developed to assess the major clinical foci and therapeutic techniques that therapists have used during each session.

BRIEF INTEGRATIVE MARITAL THERAPY

Alan Gurman's (2002) brief integrative marital therapy (BIMT) involves an integration of behavioural (Atkins et al., 2003), psychodynamic (Savage-Scharff & Bagini, 2002) and systemic (Keim & Lappin, 2002; Shoham & Rohbaugh, 2002) models. He has most recently referred to it as a depth-behavioural approach because of its explanation of marital distress in terms of behavioural patterns of interaction, on the one hand, and the psychodynamic factors that subserve these, on the other.

Within BIMT, it is assumed that distressed couples have essentially behavioural difficulties. These difficulties include communication, problem solving, engaging in positive exchanges, making positive attributions for their partner's behaviour, repairing conversational ruptures and staying calm when discussing differences. These problems arise not because couples have 'skills deficits' but because they find it challenging to use their relationship skills within their marriage.

Couples have difficulties using their relationship skills within their marriage because they experience their marital relationship as fundamentally unfair. They experience the basic systemic rule essential for a fair marriage as being violated. For couples to feel that their marriage is fair there must be an equitable marital quid pro quo governing the marital system (Jackson, 1965). This is not a conscious tit-for-tat bargain. It is an unconscious arrangement (in that it occurs outside awareness) where both partners conduct themselves in ways that allow them to be confident that they are equals and equally valued by each other as loveable people.

The reason couples do not maintain a fair marital quid pro quo is because they no longer see each other as they actually are, for reasons that may be explained psychodynamically. Partners view each other in distorted ways and as possessing negative attributes, such as being needy and likely to ask for too much, or angry and likely to abandon the marriage. This distorted image of partners occurs because individuals project aspects of themselves that they find unacceptable onto their partners. They do this because in infancy and early childhood, through neglectful or punitive parenting they learned that certain aspects of the self, such as neediness or anger, were unacceptable to the parent. They split off these aspects of the self to make themselves acceptable to their parents.

Within most distressed marriages, both partners are involved in a collusive arrangement where each projects negative split-off aspects of the self onto the other and responds to this distorted image of the partner negatively, but usually neither partner is conscious of this mutual projective system and so it cannot be modified by open discussion. This collusion usually involves individuals inadvertently eliciting and reinforcing the very behaviours in their partners, about which they complain, for example pursuer–distancer exchanges or escalating aggressive interactions. Also, within distressed marriages, splitting, projection and expressing hostility or fear are reinforced because these defences allow partners to avoid having to accept unacceptable aspects of the self, which would entail the anxiety-provoking expectation of punishment, abandonment or other catastrophes.

Marital distress is precipitated by violations of the unconscious marital quid pro quo rules, which exceed individuals' tolerance, as well as by explicit violations of marital agreements (e.g. infidelity) and life stresses (e.g. work-related stress). Individuals who have had more problematic early attachments and who are more vulnerable to splitting and projection probably have lower tolerance for violations of marital quid pro quo rules. There are also certain normative violations of such rules which may sow the seeds of marital distress. These include discovering that the reality of one's partner falls far short of the idealised version experienced during infatuation; realising that one's partner cannot meet all one's needs; observing a decrease in those attributes that initially made one's partner attractive; and finding that previously unknown and unacceptable aspects of oneself are elicited by one's partner.

Within BIMT hypotheses about the behavioural patterns associated with martial distress, the quid pro quo systemic rule violations, the underlying mutual projective system, and salient predisposing and precipitating factors are formed during the assessment phase. Treatment typically spans about 15 sessions. Within conjoint sessions, the therapists adopts three roles: (1) fostering systemic awareness of how partners behaviour is interconnected; (2) coaching couples in the use of relationships skills; and (3) challenging dysfunctional relationship rules. The three main categories or interventions are: (1) linking individual experience to relational experience; (2) setting therapeutic tasks; and (3) interrupting and modifying collusive processes. These three categories of interventions may include specific techniques drawn from many models of couples and family therapy.

PLURALISTIC COUPLES THERAPY

Douglas Snyder's approach to couples therapy (Snyder & Schneider, 2002) involves an integration of a wide range of different approaches including psychodynamic (Savage-Scharff & Bagini, 2002), systemic (Keim & Lappin, 2002; Shoham & Rohbaugh, 2002) and cognitive-behavioural (Atkins et al., 2003) models. It has previously been referred to as insight-oriented marital therapy (Snyder & Wills 1989; Snyder, Wills & Grady-Fletcher 1991) and most recently as affective reconstruction: a pluralistic developmental approach (Snyder & Schneider, 2002).

These different names reflect aspects of the central assumptions on which Snyder's approach rests. Snyder assumes that marital distress is maintained by a lack of emotional intimacy arising from the use of defensive strategies. These are employed to deal with interpersonal vulnerabilities that have their historic roots in early-life parent–child relationship injuries. A second assumption is that interpreting the persistent use of maladaptive defences and problem-maintaining interactional behaviour patterns, as arising from challenging developmental experiences, leads to both insight and affective reconstruction. A third assumption is that when distressed couples come to therapy, their immediate crises, relationship skills deficits and defensive postures prevent them from engaging in interpretative therapy. Because of this, insight-oriented techniques are offered strategically within a hierarchical, pluralistic model incorporating structural, behavioural and cognitive interventions earlier in the therapy process.

Within Snyder's hierarchical model for a pluralistic approach to couples therapy there are six levels. For each level there are therapeutic tasks that must be completed before progressing to the next level. At the first level, the therapist develops a collaborative alliance within which relationship distress can be safely discussed, develops a formulation and offers a treatment contract. At the second level, the therapist contains disabling relationship crises. This is done by facilitating more adaptive attributions and promoting intermediate solutions. It may also involve developing no-harm contracts where domestic violence has occurred. In some instances it may be necessary to facilitate the management of psychopathology and substance abuse. Interventions at this level draw on cognitive-behavioural and structural-strategic interventions. At the third level, the therapist helps couples to re-establish regular positive exchanges by setting positive-behavioural exchange contracts. Positive exchanges have typically become eroded through marital distress and crises. Behavioural marital therapy procedures are used here and at the fourth level, where the therapist promotes the development of relevant relationship skills. These include problem-solving and communication skills, but also parenting, financial management and time management skills where the lack of such skills are preventing the resolution of relationship distress. At the fifth level, the therapist challenges cognitive components of relationship distress, especially negative attributions and misconceptions, using the techniques of cognitive therapy. At the sixth level, the therapist explores and interprets the developmental sources of relationship distress. This process of affective reconstruction involves exploring how current problematic relationship themes and coping strategies have their roots in partners' family-of-origin experiences and early attachments. Strategies for emotional gratification and anxiety containment in current marital and past early-attachment relationships are explored. Strategies that may have been appropriate in early attachment relationships, but which are inappropriate in current marital relationship, are identified and alternatives explored.

Snyder has developed the revised Marital Satisfaction Inventory (MSI-R, Snyder, 1997), which is used along with clinical interviewing for couple assessment. This 150-item self-report measure of marital satisfaction yields scores for affective communication, role orientation, problem-solving communication, aggression, family history of distress, time together, dissatisfaction with children, disagreement about finances, conflict over child rearing, sexual dissatisfaction and global distress.

Snyder's approach to marital therapy has been shown in one treatment outcome study to be as effective as behavioural marital therapy at six-months follow-up and to be significantly more effective at four-years follow-up. Four years after treatment only 3% of couples in insight-oriented couples therapy had divorced compared with 38% of those in behavioural couples therapy (Snyder & Wills, 1989; Snyder et al., 1991).

INTEGRATIVE APPLICATIONS WITHIN SPECIFIC PROFESSIONS

Family therapy ideas have been 'packaged' for accessibility to specific professional groups including physicians, psychiatrists, psychologists, social workers and multidisciplinary groups. In these types of 'packages', ideas from multiple schools of family therapy are presented in a way that is tailored to the conceptual and practical needs of specific professionals.

Medicine

In medical family therapy, systemic ideas and practices are applied to the treatment of distress and adjustment problems that occur when family members have significant medical problems or illnesses (McDaniel, Hepworth & Doherty, 1992). Medical family therapy rests on a biopsychosocial model of illness and a family approach to medical care. Family therapy in this context aims to help families understand and adjust to the stresses of chronic illness and related medical regimes in a way that optimises quality of life. It does this by changing destructive transactional behaviour patterns, modifying unhelpful beliefs and narratives, and addressing significant contextual factors that underpin such beliefs and behaviour patterns. While medical family therapy evolved in North America as a service offered by specialist therapists in specialist settings, in the UK some family physicians are now offering medical family therapy, using a 10-minute consultation model in primary care settings (Asen, Tomson, Young & Tomson, 2004).

Psychiatry

Integrative family therapy textbooks have been written by psychiatrists for psychiatrists in training as the target market (Barker, 1998; Sholevar, 2003). In such texts a general overview of multiple models is given along with an integrative or eclectic approach to practice. This is coupled with an emphasis on conducting marital and family therapy with families containing members with specific psychiatric diagnoses.

Clinical Psychology

Family therapy textbooks written by clinical psychologists for clinical psychologists in training have also been produced in the UK (Vetere & Dallos, 2003) and the USA (Mikesell, Lusterman & McDaniel, 1995). These volumes are distinctly integrative in their approach. They also have a distinctive focus on assessment and evaluation, consistent with the ethos of clinical psychology. For example, Vetere & Dallos (2003) place a strong emphasis on linking intervention to preliminary formulation and on evaluating the effects of interventions.

Social Work

In the UK, some of the most widely-used basic family therapy texts, which adopt broad integrative approaches, while not exclusively for social workers, are written by leading family therapists with a primary training in social work (Burnham, 1986; Gorrell-Barnes, 2004).

Multidisciplinary – Multiple Family Therapy

Multiple family therapy is a systemic practice in which a number of families are concurrently treated, often within the context of intensive multidisciplinary day-hospital programmes (Asen, Dawson & McHugh, 2001). Typically these programmes are offered to multiproblem families, such as those in which child abuse or drug and alcohol abuse has occurred, or to families in which a member has suffered chronic debilitating conditions, such as psychosis or an eating disorder. These programmes involve multiple family group meetings; meetings exclusively for parents; meetings exclusively for symptomatic children; and meetings exclusively for siblings. These relatively large meetings are usually convened by multidisciplinary teams of co-therapists. Often the meetings involve an integration of systemic practices with therapeutic activities, such as art, life skills, parent craft, academic work, psychoeducation, and so forth. For example, parents may attend a session where the focus is on psychoeducation about the key problem of the child; youngsters with anorexia may attend occupational therapy sessions on buying and cooking food for normal meals; and siblings may concurrently attend art classes focusing on the experience of family living and sibling starvation. Multiple family therapy programmes are carefully designed and tailored to the needs of the clients they aim to help, so activities from occupational therapy, psychiatry, speech and language therapy, and so forth, are integrated within the context of an overall systemic plan. In multiple family therapy programmes, families benefit from the mutual support and learning that occurs between families.

CLOSING COMMENTS

The models reviewed in Chapters 3 to 5 represent some of the most influential 'pure' clinical traditions within the field of family therapy. These traditions were grouped with respect to their focus on problem-maintaining interaction patterns; subserving belief systems; and underlying predisposing factors. Each of the integrative models reviewed in this chapter spanned all three of these categories (patterns, beliefs and contexts) and attempted to bring together three or more 'pure' models in a coherent way. (Blends involving two models and less sophisticated eclectic models where theories are not coherently synthesised have not been addressed.)

The four integrative models reviewed in this chapter are leading examples of how insights from a number of simpler models may be coherently synthesised into a new model that is more than the sum of its parts. On the positive side, such integrative models allow therapists a far greater degree of flexibility in dealing with complex cases. However, they also involve a cost. Highly detailed comprehensive integrative models are difficult for therapists to keep in mind when conducting therapy in complex cases.

Integrative family therapy texts have been produced for specific professional groups including physicians, psychiatrists, psychologists, social workers and multidisciplinary groups. In these, ideas from multiple schools of family therapy are presented in a way that is tailored to the conceptual and practical needs of specific professionals.

In the remainder of this book an integrative approach will be presented which attempts to synthesise insights and clinical techniques from the many different models presented in Part I, but which I hope is not too complex to keep in mind when conducting therapy.

At the heart of this approach is a three-column formulation model. The formulation model allows clients' problems (and exceptions to these) to be conceptualised as being embedded within behaviour patterns, subserved by belief systems or narratives, and underpinned by broad contextual factors. This three-column model also allows clinicians to bring insights from all models described in Part I of this volume to bear on their clinical work.

GLOSSARY

Eclecticism. The selection of concepts or interventions from a range of theories based on clinical judgment without attempting to provide an coherent integrative overarching theoretical framework to explain or guide the selection of concepts or interventions.

Integration. The development of a broad overarching theoretical framework to explain and guide the selection of concepts and interventions from a range of less complex theories.

FURTHER READING

Breunlin, D., Schwartz, R. & MacKune-Karrrer, B. (1997). *Metaframeworks: Transcending the Models of Family Therapy* (Revised and updated). San Francisco, CA: Jossey Bass.

Pinsof, W. (1995). *Integrative Problem-Centred Therapy. A Synthesis of Biological, Individual and Family Therapies*. New York: Basic Books.

Snyder, D. & Schneider, W. (2002). Affective reconstruction: A pluralistic, developmental approach. In A. Gurman & N. Jacobon (Eds), *Clinical Handbook of Couples Therapy*, 3rd edn, pp. 151–179. New York: Guilford.

Gurman, A. (2002). Brief integrative marital therapy: A depth behavioural approach. In A. Gurman & N. Jacobon (Eds), *Clinical Handbook of Couples Therapy*, 3rd edn, pp. 180–120. New York: Guilford.

Part II

PROCESSES IN FAMILY THERAPY

Chapter 7

THE STAGES OF FAMILY THERAPY

The framework, set out in Figure 7.1. outlines the stages of family therapy from the initial receiving of a referral letter to the point where the case is closed. In the first stage, a plan for conducting the intake interview is made. The second stage is concerned with engagement and contracting for assessment; assessment and formulation; and alliance building. In the third stage, the focus is on setting goals, forming a therapeutic contract, and the management of resistance. In the final stage, disengagement or recontracting for further intervention occurs. In this chapter, principles of good clinical practice for each of these stages will be given.

At each developmental stage, key tasks must be completed before progressing to the next stage. Failure to complete the tasks of a given stage before progressing to the next stage may jeopardise the consultation process. For example, attempting to conduct an assessment without first contracting for assessment may lead to cooperation difficulties if family members find the assessment procedures arduous or threatening. Therapy is a recursive process insofar as it is possible to move from the final stage of one episode to the first stage of the next. What follows is a description of the stages of therapy and the tasks entailed by each, a description that builds on past descriptions of this approach (Carr, 1995, 1997, 2000d; Carr & McNulty, In Press, a).

STAGE 1 – PLANNING

In the first stage of therapy the main tasks are to plan who to invite to the first session, or series of sessions, and what to ask them. If there is confusion about who to invite, a network analysis may be conducted. In planning an agenda, a routine intake interview may be supplemented with lines of questioning that take account of the specific features of the case and hypotheses developed about these.

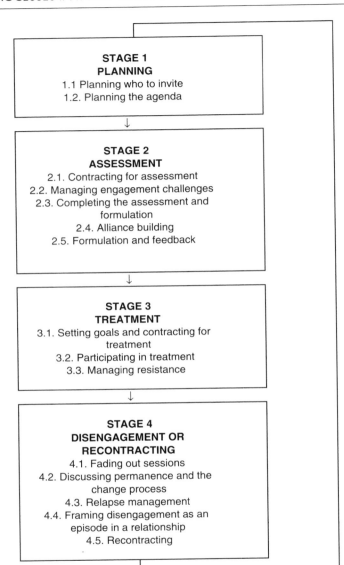

Figure 7.1 Stages of family therapy

Planning Who to Invite: Network Analysis

To make a plan about who to invite to the sessions, the therapist must find out from the referral letter or through telephone contact with the referrer who is involved with the problem and tentatively establish what roles they play with respect to it. With some cases this will be straightforward.

For example, where parents are concerned about a child's sleep, bedwetting, mood or behaviour, it may be sufficient to invite the child and the parents. In other cases, where probation, school, hospital or social services personnel are most concerned about the case, the decision about who to invite to the first interview is less straightforward. In complex cases, it is particularly important to analyse network roles accurately before deciding who to invite to the first session. Most network members fall into one or more of the following categories:

- The *referrer*, to whom correspondence about the case should be sent.
- The *customer*, who is most concerned that the referral be made.
- The *identified patient*, who is viewed by the customer as the problem person.
- The *legally responsible person*, or people. In child-focused cases, this is usually the parents but may be a social worker or other representative of the state where referred children are in care. In adult-focused cases, usually clients are responsible for themselves unless they are involuntarily detained under mental health legislation. With older adults, their middle-aged children may have power of attorney over their parents' estates.
- The *primary supportive figures* in the immediate social network. With children these are usually the parents but may be foster parents, residential childcare staff or nursing staff. With adults, typically partners fill this role.
- The *social control agents*. These are professionals with statutory powers who act as representatives of the state, such as social workers or probation officers. In some cases they may be already involved, while in others there may be a possibility of them becoming involved if clients do not engage in treatment.
- *Other involved professionals*. These may include school staff, medical professionals, social service professionals, law enforcement professionals, and so forth.
- *Change promoters*. Any members of the referred person's immediate family or wider social network may be potential change promoters insofar as they may be able to contribute to resolving the presenting problems.
- *Change preventers*. Any members of the referred person's immediate family or wider social network may be potential change preventers insofar as they may adopt positions that maintain the presenting problems.

Certain key network members constitute the minimum sufficient network necessary for effective therapy. These include the customer, the legally responsible persons, the primary supportive figures and the identified patient. It is difficult for family therapists to work effectively without engaging with these key network members. Ideally, all members of the minimum sufficient network and the household (which often includes important change promoters and preventers) should be invited to an intake meeting. If there are reasons to believe that this may be problematic it is good practice to suggest that the referrer or customer ask the key people to attend an initial appointment to give the therapist the benefit of their views on how they think the problem may best be solved and what they see as the main obstacles to this. If the customer or referrer cannot use this type of invitation to engage key network members effectively in therapy, then individual meetings or telephone calls may be used to connect with these key members of the network. Alternatively, the initial sessions may be used to help those family members who attend take steps to engage other significant network members in the therapy process. Other engagement difficulties will be dealt with below.

Planning What to Ask: Agenda Setting

Planning what questions to ask in a first session will depend on the problem posed in the referring letter, the preliminary hypothesis that the therapist or therapy team have about the case and the routine interviewing procedures typically used for such cases.

If the referrer's concerns are vague, much time may be saved by phoning the referrer and requesting clarification. In short, by asking

What is the main problem that needs to be solved, who is involved, and who is most concerned that the problem be addressed now?

Family therapists have a responsibility to educate those that use their services about types of cases that may be referred to them and the types of assessment, therapy and consultation services that they offer. Clarifying referral questions is one way of educating referrers about these issues.

It is important to acknowledge that family therapists do not typically begin intake interviews with a completely open mind about the presenting problems. The referrer's question along with the information provided by the referrer will give rise to certain hunches or hypotheses. These are typically informed by experience with similar cases and a knowledge of the relevant literature. The more explicit these hypotheses are made, the better, since these hypotheses will inform some of the lines of questioning followed in a preliminary interview.

For any problem, an initial hypothesis may be constructed using ideas from the many schools of family therapy reviewed in Chapters 1 to 6, in which the pattern of family interaction that maintains the problem is specified; the constraining beliefs and narratives that underpin each family member's role in this pattern are outlined; and the historical and contextual factors that underpin these belief systems and narratives are specified. In Chapter 8 a method for generating such hypotheses about both problems and exceptional circumstance in which problems do not occur is outlined, and methods for interviewing families to check out these hypotheses are given. However, in addition to specific lines of questioning that follow from hypotheses, therapists may also have a routine set of enquiries that elicit information about problems and the contexts within which they occur. Some such routine assessment procedures will be outlined below.

STAGE 2 – ASSESSMENT

In the second stage of the therapeutic process there are three main tasks:

- engagement and establishing a contract for assessment
- completing the assessment and formulation
- building a therapeutic alliance.

Contracting for Assessment

Contracting for assessment involves the therapist and clients clarifying expectations and reaching an agreement to work together. The first task is to explain the route of referral. For example:

Hello, I'm XYZ. You're very welcome. I thought to start I would explain my understanding of how you were referred here and check if that fits with your understanding. Dr PQR wrote to me and said that you were all concerned about ABC. She took the view that everyone in the family was affected by this and might be able to help with solving this problem so she referred you here. Is that your understanding of how the referral came about?

The next priority is to outline what the assessment involves and offer relevant members of the network a chance to accept or reject the opportunity to complete the assessment. The way in which the interviews will be conducted, their duration, and the roles of the team (if a team is involved) should be explained. For example:

What we had in mind for today was to invite each of you to give your views on the problem: how you see it; what you think makes it worse or better; who is most affected by it; how you think it might be solved. When each of you has given your view, we will take a break. During the break, I will take some time to think about all that you have said (or to talk with the team about their views of the situation) and then we can finish up by discussing what to do next. That is, I will be in a position to tell you if you have the type of problem with which we can help you and if so how we think it would be best to proceed. These meetings usually take about two hours altogether. Can I check with each of you if you wish to have this meeting right now and if you wish give your views on the problems that led to you coming here today?

If a team is involved in the assessment process, their roles need to be clarified. Also, if a one-way screen is being used, it is important to mention its function. For example:

In our clinic we have found that it's useful in helping families solve problems if more than one therapist is involved. But it can be distracting if more than one of us is here in the interviewing room. So our practice is to work in teams, and for the rest of the team to watch the interview silently from the other side of that screen. It looks like a mirror, but the team can see us from the other room. Their job is to keep track of each person's different view of the situation and think about how best to solve the problem. Some members of the team are very experienced and some (like me) are in training. I will introduce you to them after the break (or now) if that's OK with you?

If videotaping is used, a written consent form should be signed by family members. It may also be useful to give a verbal explanation. For example,

In our clinic we have found that we can get a clearer understanding of each person's different view of the situation if we video each session and then review it later. This is a bit like using an X-ray to see how badly a bone is broken or how well it is healing. To get this service, you must sign a consent form. The form simply says that you want the video-review service and understand that the video is confidential and will not be shown to anyone except the clinical team here in the Family Centre.

If after a course of therapy, a therapist wants to use a tape for training purposes, then it is good practice to request written consent specifically for this. The audience to which the tape will be shown must be specified on the consent form, with reference to local, national or international training events.

It is important, in the contracting meeting, to highlight the voluntary nature of the assessment. It is also important to clarify the limits of confidentiality. Normally, the contents of sessions are confidential unless there is evidence that a family member is a serious threat to themselves or to others. For example, where there is evidence of suicidal intent or child abuse, confidentiality may be breached.

With children and teenagers, in the contracting stage of the first session misconceptions need to be dispelled. Some children come to their first family therapy session believing that they will be involuntarily admitted to hospital, placed in a detention centre, or subjected to a variety of other coercive procedures. It is important to say that at the end of the first session a decision about whether to meet again for one or more times will be made and that these session do not involve coercion.

An information and consent form, which covers most of these contracting points, is given in Figure 7.2. Literate families may be sent an information and consent form like this before the first session. Non-literate families may be invited to sign the form at the first session after the therapist has read it to them.

SERVICE INFORMATION & CONSENT FORM

Please read the information below and then sign the form to indicate that you consent to these conditions of service.

Voluntary attendance. Our clinic offers help to families with problems of living. Attendance at this clinic is voluntary. You may attend if you wish.

Qualifications of therapists. All of our senior staff and supervisors are qualified marital and family therapists, and some have other additional qualifications. Details of these are available at reception. Other therapists on the staff are in professional training and work on teams under the supervision of senior staff.

If the main problem involves your children parents are invited. We find that it is most helpful if the young person with the problem and both parents attend the first appointment. Fathers (or step-fathers) have a particularly important contribution to make to our understanding of young people's problems and to their resolution.

If the main problem involves an adult in the family or if there are marital difficulties it is most helpful if both partners attend the first appointment.

First appointments. Your first appointment will last about 2 hours. During this meeting family members will be invited to give their view of the problem, the things that you have tried to do in the past to solve it, and information about family development. You may also be invited to fill out a questionnaire.

Other appointments. At the end of the first appointment we will let you know if our service can offer you help with the problem of living that led you to visit us. We will offer you further appointments at times that are convenient to you at that point. If we offer you a service, it is only fair to let you know that marital and family therapy is only effective in about two out of three cases. Most families know after about six sessions if therapy is helping. About 1 in 10 families find therapy makes their difficulties worse. If the service you are offered does not help you, please let your therapist know this and if you require a referral elsewhere please request this.

Fees and cancellations. Fees are payable at each session. There is no fee for cancelled appointments provided you cancel the appointment at least two days before the appointment so we can book in another client.

Confidentiality. In our clinic all staff work as part of team. The team includes experienced senior staff and in some cases staff in training who work under the supervision of senior staff. Everything that you say to your therapist is confidential to your team.

The only circumstances under which we are obliged to give information to other people about your case is where there is a risk that a member of your family may cause themselves or others serious harm.

We will not give information about your case to others, such as the young person's school or your family doctor, without your consent.

(Continued on next page)

The team and screen. As a routine part of our service, one member of your team will interview you and the other members of the team including the supervisor will view the therapy sessions from another room through a viewing screen. The therapist will occasionally consult with the team to give your family the benefit of their expertise. You will be introduced to the other team members if you wish.

Routine videotaping of therapy sessions. All therapy sessions are routinely videotaped and reviewed by therapists and their supervisors to ensure that you are provided with a high-quality service. Reviewing tapes of sessions also helps with therapist training. All videotapes are confidential to your team.

Annonymised case reports. As a routine part of staff training, therapists are required to write case reports for examination at the institute or university where they are training. All identifying details of your family will be omitted from such reports.

Professional reports. If you would like a professional report sent to your family doctor or to some other professional, discuss this with your therapist. There is a fee for such reports.

Crises and emergencies. If a crisis occurs while you are attending our service, please contact us in the first instance and we may be able to offer an appointment on short notice. If this is not possible, we will advise you, in the event of an emergency, to contact your family doctor or the accident and emergency department of the general hospital in your catchment area.

Questions. If you have questions about any of the points made in this box, please ask your therapist who will be happy to answer them.

Please sign the next line to indicate that you consent to the conditions of service outlined in this box.

Signature of parent/Partner _____

Signature of parent/Partner _____

Signature of young person_____

Signature of young person_____

Signature of young person_____

Signature of young person_____

Figure 7.2 Service information and consent form

Managing Engagement Challenges

The process of contracting for assessment does not always run smoothly. Engagement challenges are to be expected. The issue of partial family attendance has been mentioned already. Refusal to participate in assessment, non-attendance and receiving grossly inaccurate referral information are some of the more important obstacles to engagement and establishing a contract for assessment.

In some instances, where the whole family attend for an intake interview, children may not wish to complete the assessment, but their parents may be insistent. One strategy for managing this is to invite the parents to participate and the children to watch but not participate in the process. At various junctures the therapist can invite the parents to speculate about their children's views, while respecting the children's right not to participate in the assessment. For example:

> *Mr and Mrs XYZ, your understanding of this problem is very clear now and it does suggest a number of possible solutions such as ABC. We must respect the right of your children not to give us their views until they are ready. In the meantime, it would be unfair to completely disregard their positions. So, one option is for you both to guess or speculate about what you believe they would say about the problem and its solution if they were ready to discuss it. What do you think your son would say?*

Sometimes, when parents respond to invitations like these, their children spontaneously join in the conversation to agree or disagree with their parents speculations.

In some instances, the family may attend for assessment but the parents may not wish to cooperate with the assessment interview. At the same time, they may also not wish to earn the reputation of being a non-attender because of possible negative consequences of doing so, such as violating a probation order or risking having children taken into care. In these cases, the main customer for treatment is usually a professional such as a probation officer, social worker or physician who has forcefully recommend attendance. In such situations, the therapist should include the referring agent or professional most concerned about the case (i.e. the customer) in the contracting session.

When none of the people invited to the intake interview attend, the referrer should be contacted immediately to clarify why the family have not shown up. Non-attendance, in our experience, may be due to failure to identify the true customer or to practical difficulties. Where non-attendance is due to failure to identify the main customer, a meeting with the referrer may be arranged to clarify who the primary customer is. Non-attendance due to practical problems occurs most frequently with chaotic families invited to attend a public clinic. In these instances, intake interviews may best be conducted in clients' homes.

Sometimes, the information contained in the referral letter, or indeed through a referral phone call, is wildly inaccurate. For example, a child-focused referral problem may be a *red flag* to mark a profound adult-focused or marital difficulty. It is good practice to acknowledge the validity of clients using a small child-focused problem as a way of checking out the therapist's trustworthiness before mentioning more profound difficulties with which they want assistance. Recontracting for personal or marital work is usually deferred until after the child-focused problems have been dealt with.

The contracting for assessment is complete when family members have been adequately informed about the process and have agreed to complete the assessment. Cooperation problems or resistance may occur when therapists proceed to conduct an assessment interview without first establishing a contract for assessment.

Completing the Assessment 1. Enquiring about the Presenting Problem

Once a contract for assessment has been established, each person may be invited to give their view of the presenting problem. This typically involves questions about the nature, frequency and intensity of the problems; previous successful and unsuccessful solutions to these problems; and family members' views on the causes of these problems and possible solutions that they suspect may be fruitful to explore in future. In listening to replies to these enquires and requesting elaboration about the social context within which the problems have been occurring, particular attention should be paid to possible problem-maintaining interaction patterns. Account may be taken of the list of common problem-maintaining factors discussed in Chapter 8. Here are some questions that may be useful when enquiring about the presenting problem.

Everybody has their own view of the problem. What we are interested in finding out is each person's view. These may all be quite different. That's, OK. We are not looking for the right answer or the absolute truth, just each person's view of the problem. So, ABC, can you tell us how you see it?

How did it start?

How is it now?

Can you describe in detail a specific episode of the problem?

What has made it better or worse?

What different things have been tried to solve it and what were the effects of these attempts to solve it?

How do you think the problem will be in a year if you keep going as you have been?

Just say the problem got solved in the next few months, and I met you in a year's time and asked you what exactly had happened, what story would you tell me?

Completing the Assessment 2. Constructing a Genogram

The genogram is a family tree that contains clinical information about the people in a family and their pattern of organisation. The process of genogram construction may be routinely incorporated into initial family assessment sessions. Genogram symbols are given in Figure 7.3

and a checklist of areas to cover in genogram construction is given in Table 7.1.

It is useful to construct a genogram in a way that allows all family members to see it as it is drawn. A flip-chart or whiteboard may be used to facilitate this. Here is one way to introduce the genogram, after each person has given their views on the presenting problem.

You have each mentioned other family members, friends, teachers and professionals who are affected by the problem or who have tried to help solve it. It would help us to understand the roles of everyone involved, if we drew a family tree. Let's start by drawing a map of who is here today.

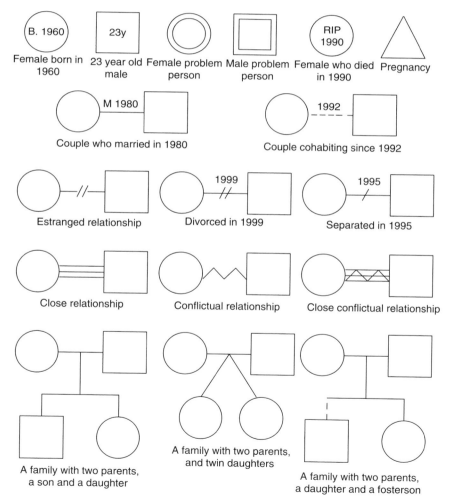

Figure 7.3 Genogram symbols

Table 7.1 Information to include in genograms

People	Demographics	Name Age Occupation
	Transitions	Births Deaths Marriages, cohabiting relationships Changing households Leaving home Foster care Anniversaries of transitions
	Strengths	Examples of having coped well with problems in the past Work and school performance Making and maintaining friendships Sports and leisure Special personal achievements
	Vulnerabilities	Illnesses and hospitalizations Psychological adjustment problems Substance abuse Anger control, violence and abuse Criminality
Patterns	Dyadic	Supportive alliances and coalitions Stressful conflicts
	Triadic	Triangulation where a child is required to take sides with one of two other family members (usually the parents) Pathological triangles with denied cross-generational coalitions Detouring-attacking triads where the parents express joint anger at the child, associated with conduct problems Detouring-protecting triads where parents express joint concern about the child who presents with a psychosomatic or emotional complaint
	Complex	Multigenerational dyadic patterns (e.g. mothers and daughters are close in three generations) Multigenerational triadic patterns (e.g. triangulation occurs in two generations)

It may be explained that squares stand for males and circles for females. The names and ages go inside these symbols. Sketch the nuclear family and invite family members to extend the genogram upwards by filling in the grandparents, and outwards by filling in aunts and uncles. From time to time, families will need more rules to help them code information on the genogram. Most of the genogram rules are contained in Figures 7.3. Once the genogram contains all important family members along with their names, ages and occupations, invite family members to include other important details following the checklist in Table 7.1.

When constructing a genogram, there are three common pitfalls. The first is to ask too many questions about negative or trivial details. The second is to miss the opportunity to use genogram construction as a chance to label family members' strengths. The third is not to ask enough questions about significant family patterns. If family members can not remember ages, dates, occupations or details about other problems, unless you have reason to believe that these omissions have a particular significance that is relevant to the presenting problem and their way of coping with it, ignore the omissions.

Genogram construction is a good opportunity to pinpoint and label family members' strengths. When asking about strengths, focus largely on the family members in the session and invite them to identify and label their own and each other's positive attributes. This often has the impact of raising morale, diminishing hopelessness and allowing families to develop more hopeful narratives about themselves. Here are some examples of how to enquire about and label strengths:

Can you describe the last time you noticed your son/daughter/mother/father doing X effectively? Would you agree that doing X well is one of their strengths?

Does your son or daughter go to school regularly? If so, would you say that being conscientious and reliable is one of their strengths?

Does you husband/wife work hard on some occasions? If so, would you say that being hardworking is one of their strengths?

Does your husband/wife/son/daughter help at home from time to time? If so, would you say that being kind and helpful are two of their strengths?

Has your husband/wife/son/daughter got a friend that they see from time to time. If so, would you say that they are a loyal friend?

How long have you been in this family? How many times have you run away or felt like running away but not done so? Does this mean that you are loyal to your family, that family loyalty is one of your strengths?

You have lived with this problem a long time but you still get up every day and keep going. Does this mean that that you have great stamina, like a long distance runner?

This problem would have caused other families to break up, but you are still together. Does this mean that you are a strong united family?

While it is useful to spend a lot of time asking questions which lead to strengths being labelled, when asking about vulnerabilities, illnesses, adjustment problems, it is less demoralising if these enquires are brief. One way of keeping such enquiries brief is to ask the question about each generation or the family as a whole, rather than each individual. For example:

> *Has anyone in this generation had a serious illness or been hospitalised (pointing to the grandparents' generation)?*
>
> *Do you know if anyone in this generation had bad nerves or a problem with drink?*
>
> *Has anyone in the family got a really short fuse?*
>
> *Has anyone in the family been in serious trouble with the police?*

Triangles and complex multigenerational patterns may be identified by first asking questions about alliances. Each family member may be asked to point out on the nuclear family part of the genogram:

> *Which member of the family is closest to which other member?*

and

> *Which family member is in disagreement with which other member?*

Multigenerational patterns may be identified by asking about similarities between relationships. For example:

> *What relationship in the wider family is most like the relationship between the father and son in your own household?*
>
> *It looks like sometimes a triangle happened in your house with A and B joining forces against C. If we go back a generation or across to the households of aunts and uncles, is there anywhere else that this triangle pattern happens?*

Significant supportive or stressful members of the family's social network should be identified and included on the genogram. In the following question, the term 'family map' is used for this type of extended genogram:

> *Outside of the family are there any close friends (neighbours/doctors/ teachers etc.) that are important because they are very helpful to you and so should be on the family map?*
>
> *Are there any people that are important because they cause your family a lot of hassle and so should be on the map?*

To explore the amount of support or stress associated extrafamilial relationships some questions are useful in keeping this process brief:

Which people in the family or wider network do you see on a daily basis and which do you see infrequently, like just at Christmas and Easter?

Are these contacts a hassle or are they something you look forward to?

If some family members look forward to these contacts more than others, each family member may be asked of these contacts:

Who looks forward to them the most ?

Who looks forward to them the least?

The management of developmental issues at an individual and family level may be enquired about with reference to the developmental frameworks outlined in Chapter 1. Questions may focus on how well individuals and the family as a whole managed particular lifecycle stages and transitions from one stage to the next. Once again, enquiring about individual and family development offers an opportunity to pinpoint and label strengths. For example:

When X was a preschooler/preadolescent/adolescent/young adult/middle aged/a mature adult, how well did he/she manage the tasks of that life stage? Does this mean that he/she was a competent person at that time?

When you were a family with no children/young children/preadolescents/ adolescents/ young adults how well did you manage the tasks of that life stage? Does this mean that you were a competent couple/family at that time?

When you were a family with no children/young children/ preadolescents/ adolescents/ young adults how supportive were you of each other at that life stage? Does this mean that you were a close supportive family/family that cared about each other at that time?

Genograms may be used to engage family members who have found it difficult to become involved in the earlier part of the interview. For example, children and teenagers who have had little to say in the early part of the interview may be given the task of drawing the genogram after the rules for using the symbols have been explained to them. The therapist may invite the youngster to write in specific details as they emerge in the interview.

An example of a genogram for the Byrnes is presented in Figure 7.4. The Byrnes were referred because Miles, aged 9 years, was having multiple problems. From this genogram, it is apparent that Miles is soiling, has literacy difficulties and tantrums. He is a middle child living with his mother, father and siblings. His father, like Miles has a history of literacy problems. Miles' tantrums date back two years to the birth of his brother and his soiling dates back a year to his older sister's departure to boarding

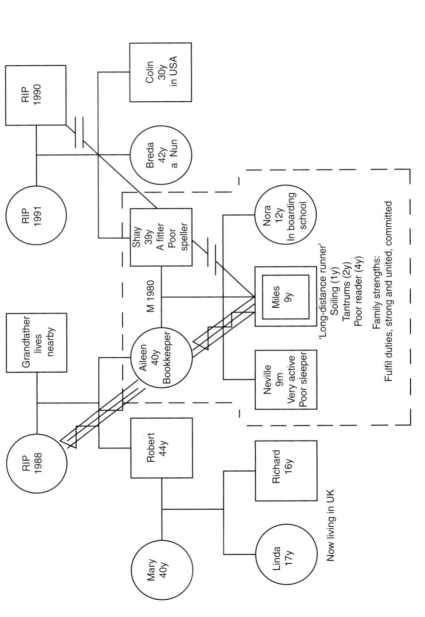

Figure 7.4 The Byrnes genogram completed in 1994

school. This event was a major loss for Miles because he has a close relationship with his sister. Miles has a close conflictual relationship with
his mother and a distant relationship with his father (a pattern that commonly maintains rather than resolves child behaviour problems) and
these relationships between Miles and his parents resemble the types of
relationships that the parents had in their families of origin. Overall, the
Byrnes have experienced a considerable build-up of life stress in the four
years prior to the referral. There have been two bereavements in father's
family of origin, the birth of a difficult temperament child and the older
daughter's departure to boarding school. The stresses may have partially compromised the parents' capacity to manage Miles' difficulties.
However, the family have a number of very significant strengths, which
suggest that Byrnes would be able to benefit from family therapy. First,
despite their multiple difficulties they continue to fulfil their duties, with
both parents holding down good jobs, running a busy household and the
two older children attending school regularly. Second, they are extremely
loyal to each other, and have a track record of being a strong united family. Third, there has never been a challenge that they had to face in the past
that they did not manage through their own determination and efforts.
Finally, all five members of the nuclear family want to use therapy as a
way of resolving their difficulties and are committed to attending therapy
for up to 10 sessions over a six-month period.

This example, and narrative summary, illustrates the way genograms
may offer a pictorial summary of significant individual developmental
and family factors in complex cases.

A complete exploration of the use of the genogram in family assessment
is given in McGoldrick, Gerson and Shellenberger's (1999) text. Numerous
interesting examples, including the genograms of Sigmund Freud, Carl
Jung and Gregory Bateson are included in this text. Web-based resources
for drawing genograms are given in Chapter 16.

Questionnaires and Rating Scales

Questionnaires and rating scales, like genograms, provide a way of routinely surveying family strengths and weaknesses. The Global Assessment of Relational Functioning (American Psychiatric Association, 2000),
presented in Figure 7.5 is a particularly useful rating scale for assessing
families' overall functioning before and after treatment. Well a designed
and standardised questionnaires and rating scales have been developed
for a number of models of family functioning that fall broadly within the
structural family therapy tradition. These models include the Beavers
Family Systems Model (Beavers & Hampson, 2000), the Circumplex Model
(Olson, 2000), the McMaster Model (Miller, Ryan, Keitner, Bishop & Epstein
2000b), the Family Process Model (Skinner, Steinhauer & Sitarenios, 2000),

and the Darlington Family Assessment System (Wilkinson, 1998). In each of these models, family functioning is conceptualised as varying along a limited number of dimensions, such as cohesion, communication or problem-solving skill, and the questionnaires and rating scales for each model allow clinicians to find out where families stand on these dimensions. Information on where to obtain these and other rating scales are

81-100 **Overall Functioning.** The family is functioning satisfactorily from clients' self-reports and from the perspective of observers.

Problem solving and communication. Agreed routines exist that help meet the needs of the family. There is flexibility for change in response to unusual demands or events. Occasional conflicts and stressful transitions are resolved through effective problem solving and communication.

Organisation. There is a shared understanding and agreement about roles and tasks. Decision-making is established for each functional area. There is recognition or the unique characteristics and merits of each partner.

Emotional Climate. There is a situationally appropriate optimistic atmosphere. A wide range of feelings is freely expressed and managed. There is a general atmosphere of warmth, caring and sharing values. Sexual relations are satisfactory.

61-80 **Overall Functioning.** The functioning of the family is somewhat unsatisfactory. Over a period of time many, but not all difficulties are resolved without complaints.

Problem solving and communication. Daily routines that help meet the needs of the family are present. There is some difficulty in responding to unusual demands or events. Some conflicts remain unresolved but do not disrupt the functioning of the family.

Organisation. Decision-making is usually competent, but efforts to control one another quite often are greater than necessary or are ineffective. There is not always recognition of the unique characteristics and merits of each partner and sometimes blaming or scapegoating occurs.

Emotional Climate. A range of feelings is expressed, but instances of emotional blocking and tension are evident. Warmth and caring are present but are marred by irritability and frustration. Sexual relations are reduced or problematic.

41-60 **Overall Functioning.** The family have occasional times of satisfying and competent functioning together, but clearly dysfunctional, unsatisfying relationships tend to predominate.

Problem solving and communication. Communication is frequently inhibited by unresolved conflicts that often interfere with daily routines. There is significant difficulty in adapting to family stresses and transitional change.

Organisation. Decision-making is only intermittently competent and effective. Either excessive rigidity or significant lack of structure is evident at these times. Individual needs are often submerged by one family member's demands.

Emotional Climate. Pain or ineffective anger or emotional deadness interferes with family enjoyment. Although there is some warmth and support between partners, it is usually unequally distributed. Troublesome sexual difficulties are often present.

21–40   **Overall Functioning.** The family is obviously and seriously dysfunctional. Forms and time periods of satisfactory relating are rare.

Problem solving and communication. Family's routines do not meet family members' needs.

They are grimly adhered to or blithely ignored. Lifecycle changes generate painful conflict and obviously frustrating failures in problem-solving.

Organisation. Decision-making is tyrannical or quite ineffective. Family members' unique characteristics are unappreciated or ignored.

Emotional Climate. There are infrequent periods of enjoyment of life together. Frequent distancing or open hostility reflects significant conflicts that remain unresolved and quite painful. Sexual dysfunction is commonplace.

1–20   **Overall. Functioning.** The family has become too dysfunctional to retain continuity of contact and attachment.

Problem solving and communication. Family routines for eating, sleeping, entering and leaving the home etc are negligible. Family members do not know each other's schedules. There is little effective communication among family members.

Organisation. Family members are not organised to respect personal boundaries or accept personal responsibilities within the family. Family members may be physically endangered, injured or sexually assaulted.

Emotional Climate. Despair and cynicism are pervasive. There is little attention to the emotional needs of others.

There is almost no sense of attachment, commitment or concern for family members' welfare.

Source: Based on American Psychiatric Association (2000). [Diagnostic and Statistical Manual of the Mental Disorders, 4th edn. Revision, DSM–IV-TR, pp. 814–816. Washington, DC: APA.]

Figure 7.5 Global Assessment of Relational Functioning Scale

contained in the list of resources in Chapter 19. A summary of research on empirical approaches to family assessment is contained in Carr (2000c).

Alliance Building

In addition to providing information, the process of assessment also serves as a way for the therapist and members of the family to build a working alliance. Building a strong working alliance is essential for valid assessment and effective therapy. *All other features of the consultation process should be subordinate to the working alliance,* since without it clients drop out of assessment and therapy or fail to make progress (Carr, 2005). The only exception to this rule is where the safety of child or family member is at risk and, in such cases, protection takes priority over alliance building.

Research on common factors that contribute to a positive therapeutic outcome and ethical principles of good practice point to a number of guidelines that therapists should employ in developing a working alliance (Sprenkle & Blow, 2004). Warmth, empathy and genuineness should characterise the therapist's communication style. The therapist should form a collaborative partnership in which family members are experts on the specific features of their own family, and therapists are experts on general scientific and clinical information relevant to family development and the broad class of problems of which the presenting problem is a specific instance.

Assessment should be conducted from a position of respectful curiosity in which the therapist continually strives to uncover new information about the problem and potential solutions and invites the family to consider the implications of viewing their difficulties from multiple different perspectives (Cecchin, 1987).

An invitational approach should be adopted in which family members are invited (not directed) to participate in assessment and treatment (Kelly, 1955).

There should be a balanced focus on individual and family strengths and resilience on the one hand and on problems and constraints on the other. A focus on strengths promotes hope and mobilises clients to use their own resources to solve their problems (Miller et al., 1996). However, a focus on understanding why the problem persists and the factors that maintain it is also important, since this information informs more efficient problem solving.

There should be an attempt to match the way therapy is conducted to the clients' readiness to change, since to do otherwise may jeopardise the therapeutic alliance (Prochaska, 1999). For example, if a therapist focuses on offering technical assistance with problem solving to clients who are still only contemplating change and needing help exploring the pros and cons of change, conflict will arise because the clients will feel coerced into action by the therapist and probably not follow through on therapeutic tasks, and the therapist may feel disappointed that the clients are showing resistance.

There should be an acknowledgement that clients and therapists inadvertently bring to the working alliance attitudes, expectations, emotional responses and interactional routines from early significant caregiving and care-receiving relationships. These transference and countertransference reactions, if unrecognised, may compromise therapeutic progress and so should be openly and skilfully addressed when resistance to therapeutic change occurs. Methods for troubleshooting resistance will be discussed below.

Formulation and Feedback

The assessment is complete when the presenting problem is clarified and the context within which it occurs has been understood; a formulation of the main problem and family strengths has been constructed following the guidelines set out in Chapter 7; and these have been discussed with the family. Detailed guidelines for presenting formulations to clients will be described in Chapter 8. Three broad principles deserve mention at this stage. First, formulations should open-up new possibilities for solving the presenting problem. Second, formulations should be complex enough to take account of important problem-maintaining behaviour patterns, beliefs and significant predisposing factors, but simple enough to be easily understood by the family. Third, formulations should fit with the information the family have discussed in the sessions, but offer a different framing of this material. The framing should be different, but not too different, from their current position. If formulations are no different from client's current position, little change will occur because there is no new information in the system. If formulations are extremely different from the family's position, then they will be rejected and so the status quo will be maintained.

STAGE 3 – TREATMENT

Once a formulation has been constructed, the family may be invited to agree a contract for treatment, or it may be clear that treatment is unnecessary. In some cases, the process of assessment and formulation leads to problem resolution. Two patterns of assessment-based problem resolution are common. In the first, the problem is reframed so that the family no longer see it as a problem. For example, the problem is redefined as a normal reaction, a developmental phase or an unfortunate but transient incident. In the second, the process of assessment releases family members' natural problem-solving skills and they resolve the problem themselves. For example, many parents, once they discuss their anxiety about handling their child in a productive way during a family assessment interview, feel released to do so. In other cases, assessment leads on to contracting for an episode of treatment. Treatment rarely runs a smooth and predictable course, and the management of resistance, difficulties and impasses that develop in the midphase of treatment require troubleshooting skills.

Setting Goals and Contracting for Therapy

The contracting process involves establishing clearly defined and realistic goals and outlining a plan to work towards those goals in light of the formulation presented at the end of the assessment stage. Clear, realistic, visualised goals that are fully accepted by all family members and that are perceived to be moderately challenging are crucial for effective therapy. Asking clients to visualise in concrete detail precisely how they would go about their day-to-day activities if the problem were solved is a particularly effective way of helping clients to articulate therapeutic goals. For example:

> *Imagine, it's a year from now and the problem is solved. It's a Monday morning at your house. What is happening? Give me a blow-by-blow description of what everyone is doing?*

> *Suppose your difficulties were sorted out and someone sneaked into your house and made a video of you all going about your business as usual. What would we all see if we watched this videotape?*

> *If there were a miracle tomorrow and your problem was solved, what would be happening in your life?*

This last question, which owes its origin to Milton Erickson, plays a central role in deShazer's (1988) solution-focused approach to therapy. He refers to it as the 'miracle question'.

Questions that ask the client to visualise some intermediate step along the road to problem resolution may help clients to elaborate intermediate goals or to clarify the endpoint at which they are aiming. Here are some questions that fall into this category:

> *Just say this problem was half-way better. What would you notice different about the way your mother/father/brother/sister talked to each other?*

> *What would be the difference between the way you argue now and the way you would argue if you were half-way down the road to solving this difficulty?*

The following goal-setting questions involve asking clients about the minimum degree of change that would need to occur for them to believe that they had begun the journey down the road to problem resolution:

> *What is the first thing I would notice if I walked into your house if things were just beginning to change for the better?*

> *What is the smallest thing that would have to change for you to know you were moving in the right direction to solve this difficult problem?*

The MRI group ask clients to set these minimal changes as their therapeutic goals. They believe that once these small changes occur and are perceived, a snowball effect takes place, and the positive changes become more and more amplified without further therapeutic intervention (Segal, 1991).

Ideally progress towards goals should be assessed in an observable or quantitative way. For many problems, progress may be assessed using frequency counts, for example, the number of fights, the number of wet beds, the number of compliments, or the number of successes. Ratings of internal states, moods and beliefs are useful ways of quantifying progress towards less observable goals. Here are some examples of scaling questions:

You say that on a scale of 1–10 your mood is now about 3. How many points would it have to go up the scale for you to know you were beginning to recover?

If you were recovered, where would your mood be on a 10-point scale most days?

Look at this line. One end stands for how you felt after the car accident. The other, for the feeling of elation you had when you were told about your promotion.

Can you show me where you are on that line now and where you want to be when you have found a way to deal with your condition?

Last week on a scale of 1–10 you said your belief in XYZ was 4. How strongly do you believe XYZ now?

Goal setting takes time and patience. Different family members may have different priorities when it comes to goal setting and negotiation about this is essential. This negotiation must take account of the costs and benefits of each goal for each family member. The costs and benefits of these may usefully be explored using questions like these:

What would each person in the family lose if you successfully achieved that goal?

What would each person in the family gain if you successfully achieved that goal?

Who would lose the most and who would gain the most if you successfully achieved that goal?

One of the major challenges in family therapy is to evolve a construction of the presenting problems that opens up possibilities where each family member's wishes and needs may be respected, when these different needs and wishes are apparently conflicting. Helping family members to articulate the differences and similarities between their positions in considerable detail, and inviting them to explore goals to which they can both agree, first, is a useful method of practice here.

Polly, a 15-year-old girl referred because of school difficulties, said that she wanted to be independent. Her parents wanted her to be obedient. Both wanted to be able to live together without continuous hassle. Detailed questioning about what would be happening if Polly were to be independent and obedient revealed that both Polly and her parents wanted her to be able, among other things, to speak French fluently. This would help Polly achieve her personal goal of working in France as an *au pair* and would satisfy the parents' goal of her obediently doing school work. Getting a passing grade in French in the term exam was set as a therapy goal. It reflected the family goal of reducing hassle and the individual goals of Polly and her parents.

After a detailed exploration of the costs and benefits of various goals, clients' acceptance of one set of goals and their commitment to them needs to be clarified. It is important to postpone any discussion of ways of reaching goals until it is clear that clients accept and are committed to them. Two key direct questions may be asked to check for acceptance and commitment.

Do you want to work towards these goals?

Are you prepared to accept the losses and hassles that go with accepting and working towards these goals?

When setting goals and checking out clients' commitment to them, it is important to give clients clear information about research on the costs and benefits of family interventions and the overall results of outcome studies (Carr, 2000a, 2000b; Sprenkle, 2002). Broadly speaking, most effective psychological interventions for families are effective in only 66–75% of cases and about 10% of cases deteriorate as a result of therapy. The more strengths a family has, the more likely it is that therapy will be effective. If therapy is going to be effective, most of the gains are made in the first 6–10 sessions. Relapses are inevitable for many types of problems and periodic booster sessions may be necessary to help families handle relapse situations. With chronic problems and disabilities, further episodes of intervention are typically offered at lifecycle transitions.

The contracting session is complete when family members agree to be involved in an episode of therapy to achieve specific goals. In these cost-conscious times, in public services or managed care services, therapeutic episodes should be time-limited to between six and ten sessions, since most therapeutic change appears to happen within this time frame.

Participating in Treatment

When therapeutic goals have been set, and a contract to work towards them has been established, it is appropriate to start treatment. Treatment may involve interventions that aim to alter problem-maintaining behaviour patterns; interventions that focus on the development of new narratives and belief-systems that open up possibilities for problem resolution; and interventions that focus on historical, contextual or constitutional predisposing factors. Detailed guidelines for these three classes of interventions are given in Chapter 9. As a broad principle of practice, it is probably most efficient to begin with interventions that aim to alter problem-maintaining behaviour patterns and the belief systems that underpin these, unless there is good reason to believe that such interventions will be ineffective because of the influence of historical family of origin issues, broader contextual factors or constitutional vulnerabilities. Only if interventions that focus on problem-maintaining behaviour patterns and belief systems are ineffective is it efficient to move towards interventions that target historical, contextual or constitutional factors. Of course, there are exceptions to this rule, but it is a useful broad principle for integrative family therapy practice (Pinsof, 1995).

Troubleshooting Resistance

It is one of the extraordinary paradoxes of family therapy, that clients go to considerable lengths to seek professional guidance on how to manage their difficulties but often do not follow therapeutic advice that would help them solve their problems. This type of behaviour has traditionally been referred to as resistance. Accepting the inevitability of resistance as part of the therapist–client relationship and developing skills for managing it, can contribute to the effective practice of family therapy (Anderson & Stewart, 1983). However, before discussing the management of resistance, the avoidance of therapist–client cooperation difficulties deserves mention.

In many instances resistance may be avoided if therapists attempt to match the way therapy is conducted to clients' readiness to change (Prochaska, 1999; deShazer, 1988). In solving any problem, clients move through a series of stages from denial of the problem, through contemplating solving the problem, to being committed to taking active steps to solve the problem, and planning and executing these steps. Later, they enter a stage where productive changes require maintenance. During the early stages of denial and contemplation, the clients' main requirement in therapy is to be given support while considering the possibility that they may have a previously unrecognised problem. Such clients are often coerced into therapy by other family members or statutory agencies.

When clients accept that they have problems and begin to contemplate the possibility of solving these, they need an opportunity to explore beliefs and narratives about their difficulties and to look at the pros and cons of change. The ambivalence of such clients may derive from demoralisation, exhaustion or fear of change. Later, during the planning and action phases of change, clients need therapists to brainstorm problem-solving strategies with them and offer technical help and support as they try to put their plan into action. Once they have made productive changes, clients may require infrequent contact to maintain these changes. If therapists do not match interventions to clients' readiness to change then resistance will arise in the therapeutic relationship. For example, if therapists offer technical assistance with problem solving to clients who are still only contemplating change and need help exploring the pros and cons of change, resistance will arise because clients will feel coerced into action by their therapists. They will probably not follow through on therapeutic tasks. In response, therapists may feel disappointed that clients are showing resistance. This disappointment may have a negative impact on the quality of the therapeutic alliance and the overall long-term effectiveness of therapy.

Despite our best efforts to match our therapeutic approach to clients' readiness to change, resistance often occurs. Resistance may occur in a wide variety of ways. Resistance may take the form of clients not completing tasks between sessions, not attending sessions, or refusing to terminate the therapy process. It may also involve not cooperating during therapy sessions. For clients to make progress with the resolution of their difficulties, the therapist must have some systematic way of dealing with resistance. Here is one system for trouble-shooting resistance. First, describe the discrepancy between what clients agreed to do and what they actually did. Second, ask about the difference between situations where clients managed to follow through on an agreed course of action and those where they did not. Third, ask what they believed blocked them from making progress. Fourth, ask if these blocks can be overcome. Fifth, ask about strategies for getting around the blocks. Sixth, ask about the pros and cons of these courses of action. Seventh, frame a therapeutic dilemma that outlines the costs of maintaining the status quo and the costs of circumventing the blocks.

When resistance is questioned, factors that underpin it are uncovered. In some instances unforeseen events – Acts of God – hinder progress. In others, the problem is that the clients lack the skills and abilities that underpin resistance. Where a poor therapy contract has been formed, resistance is usually due to a lack of commitment to the therapeutic process. Specific convictions that form part of clients' individual, family or culturally based belief systems may also contribute to resistance, where the clients' values prevent them from following through on therapeutic tasks. The wish to avoid emotional pain is a further factor that commonly underpins resistance.

Client transference and therapist countertransference may also contribute to resistance. In some instances, clients have difficulty cooperating with therapy because they transfer, onto the therapist, relationship expectations that they had as infants of parents whom they experienced as either extremely nurturing or extremely neglectful. Karpman's triangle (1968), which is set out in Figure 7.6, is a useful framework for understanding transference reactions. Clients may treat the therapist as a nurturent parent who will rescue them from psychological pain caused by some named or unnamed persecutor, without requiring them to take responsibility for solving the presenting problems. For example, a demoralised parent may look to the therapist to rescue them from what they perceive to be a persecuting child who is aggressive and has poor sleeping habits. Alternatively, clients may treat the therapist as a neglectful parent who wants to punish them and so they refuse to follow therapeutic advice. For example, a father may drop out of therapy if he views the therapist as persecuting him by undermining his values or authority within the family. In some instances, clients alternate between these extreme transference positions. When parents develop these transference reactions, it is important to recognise them and discuss once again with clients, their goals and the responsibilities of the therapist and family members within the assessment or treatment contract. In other instances, it may be appropriate to interpret transference by pointing out the parallels between clients' current relationships with the therapist and their past relationships with their parents. However, such interpretations can only be offered in instances where a strong therapeutic alliance has developed and where clients are psychologically minded.

Questioning resistance is only helpful if a good therapeutic alliance has been built. If clients feel that they are being blamed for not making progress, then they will usually respond by pleading helplessness, blaming the therapist or someone else for the resistance, or distracting the focus of therapy away from the problem of resistance into less painful areas. Blaming, distraction or pleading helplessness often elicit countertransference

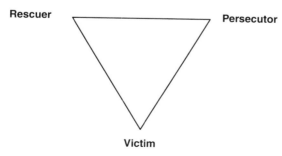

Figure 7.6 Karpman's triangle

reactions on the therapist's part, which compound rather than resolve the therapeutic impasse.

Most therapists experience some disappointment or frustration when faced with these client reactions and with resistance. These negative emotions are experienced whether the cooperation problems are due to transference or other factors. In those instances where therapists' negative reactions to cooperation problems are out of proportion to the clients' actual behaviour, they are probably experiencing countertransference. That is, they are transferring relationship-expectations based on early life experience onto current relationships with clients. As with transference reactions, Karpman's triangle (set out in Figure 7.6) offers a valuable framework for interpreting countertransference reactions. Inside many therapists there is a *rescuer*, who derives self-esteem from saving the client/*victim* from some *persecuting* person or force. Thus, in situations where a child is perceived as the victim and the parent fails to bring the child for an appointment, a countertransference reaction, which I have termed 'rescuing the child', may be experienced. With multiproblem families, in which all family members are viewed as victims, there may be a preliminary countertransference reaction of 'rescuing the family' (from a persecuting social system). If the family does not cooperate with therapy or insists on prolonging therapy without making progress, the countertransference reaction of rescuing the family may be replaced by one of 'persecuting the family'. When this countertransference reaction occurs repeatedly, burn-out occurs (Carr, 1997).

When therapists find themselves experiencing strong countertransference reactions and they act on these without reflection and supervision, they may become involved in behaviour patterns with family members that replicate problematic and problem-maintaining family behaviour patterns. For example, with chaotic families where child abuse or delinquency is the presenting problem, the countertransference reaction of persecuting the family can lead therapists to become involved in punitive behaviour patterns with clients. These may replicate the punitive family behaviour patterns that maintain the child abuse or delinquency.

STAGE 4 – DISENGAGING OR RECONTRACTING

In the final stage of therapy the main tasks are to fade out the frequency of sessions; help the family understand the change process; facilitate the development of relapse management plans; and frame the process of disengagement as the conclusion of an episode in an ongoing relationship rather than the end of the relationship.

Fading Out Sessions

The process of disengagement begins once improvement is noticed. The interval between sessions is increased at this point. This sends clients the message that you are developing confidence in their ability to manage their difficulties without sustained professional help. Here are some examples of how increasing the intersession interval may be framed so as to promote positive change:

> From what you've said today, it sounds like things are beginning to improve. It would be useful to know how you would sustain this sort of improvement over a period longer than a fortnight. So let's leave the gap between this session and the next a bit longer, say three weeks or a month?

> It seems that you've got a way of handling this thing fairly independently now. I suggest that we meet again in a month, rather than a week, and then discuss how you went about managing things independently over a four-week period. How does that sound to you?

Discussing Permanence and the Change Process

The degree to which goals have been met is reviewed when the session contract is complete or before this, if improvement is obvious. If goals have been achieved, the family's beliefs about the permanence of this change is established with questions like this:

> Do you think that ABC's improvement is a permanent thing or just a flash in the pan?

> How would you know if the improvement was not just a flash in the pan?

> What do you think your dad/mum/wife/husband/would have to see happening in order to be convinced that these changes were here to stay?

Then the therapist helps the family construct an understanding of the change process by reviewing with them the problem, the formulation, their progress through the treatment programme and the concurrent improvement in the problem.

Relapse Management

In relapse management planning, family members are helped to forecast the types of stressful situations in which relapses may occur; their probable negative reactions to relapses; and the ways in which they can use the lessons learned in therapy to cope with these relapses in a productive way. Here is an example of how the idea of relapse management may be introduced in a case where Barry, the son, successfully learned from his father, Danny, how to manage explosive temper tantrums. The following excerpt is addressed to Barry's mother.

> *You said to me that you are convinced now that Barry has control over his temper... that he has served an apprenticeship to his Dad in learning how to manage this fierce anger that he sometimes feels. OK... ? It looks like the change is here to stay also... that's what you believe. That's what I believe. But there may be some exceptions to this rule. Maybe on certain occasions he may slip... and have a big tantrum... Like when you gave up cigarettes, Danny, and then had one at Christmas in the pub... a relapse... It may be that Barry will have a temper relapse. Let's talk about how to handle relapses.*

Many relatively simple behavioural problems may be used as analogies to introduce the idea of relapse. Smoking, drinking, nail-biting, thumb-sucking and accidentally sleeping late in the morning are among some of the more useful options to consider. Once all family members have accepted the concept of relapse, then the therapist asks how such events might be predicted or anticipated.

> *If that were going to happen in what sort of situations do you think it would be most likely to occur?*
>
> *What signs would you look for, if you were going to predict a relapse?*
>
> *From what you know about the way the problem started this time, how would you be able to tell that a relapse was about to happen?*

Often relapses are triggered by similar factors to those that precipitated the original problem. Sometimes relapses occur as an anniversary reaction. This is often the case in situations where a loss has occurred and where the loss or the bereavement precipitated the original referral. More generally, relapses seem to be associated with a build-up of stressful life events. These factors include family transitions, such as: members leaving or joining the family system; family transformation through divorce or remarriage; family illness; changes in children's school situation; changes in parents' work situation; or changes in the financial status of the family. Finally, relapses may be associated with the interaction between physical environmental factors and constitutional vulnerabilities. For example, people diagnosed as having seasonal affective disorder are particularly prone to relapse in early winter and youngsters with asthma may be prone to relapse in the spring.

Once family members have considered events that might precipitate a relapse, enquires may be made about the way in which these events will be translated into a full-blown relapse:

Sometimes, when a relapse occurs, people do things without thinking and this makes things worse. Like with cigarettes... if you nag someone that has relapsed, they will probably smoke more to deal with the hassle of being nagged!! Just say a relapse happened with Barry, what would each of you do. ... if you acted without thinking... that would make things worse?

This is often a very humorous part of the consultation process, where the therapist can encourage clients to exaggerate what they believe their own and other family members' automatic reactions would be and how these would lead to an escalation of the problem. The final set of enquiries about relapse management focuses on the family's plans for handling the relapse. Here are a couple of examples.

Just say a relapse happened, what do you think each person in the family should do?

You found a solution to the problem this time round. Say a relapse happened, how would you use the same solution again?

Framing Disengagement as an Episode in a Relationship

Disengagement is constructed as an episodic event rather than as the end of a relationship. This is particularly important when working with families where members have chronic problems. Providing clients with a way of construing disengagement as the end of an episode of contact rather than as the end of a relationship is a useful way to avoid engendering feelings of abandonment. Three strategies may be used to achieve this. First, a distant follow-up appointment may be scheduled. Second, families may be told that they have a *session in the bank*, which they can make use of whenever they need it without having to take their turn on the waiting list again. Third, telephone back-up may be offered to help the family manage relapses. In all three instances, families may disengage from the regular process of consultations, while at the same time remaining connected to the therapeutic system.

Recontracting

In some instances, the end of one therapeutic contract will lead immediately to the beginning of a further contract. For example, following an episode of treatment for child-focused problems, a subsequent contract may focus on marital difficulties, or individual work for the adults in the family. Here is an example of a contract for marital work being offered to a violent family who originally came to the clinic because their son was soiling.

The main problem you wanted help with... when you first came... was Mike's soiling. And we agreed to work on that... I thought I could help you with that one. But now I know that I can't... You see... the way you describe things... with the fighting and the hitting at home... that even if you follow through on trying to manage Mike differently... he will still soil. He soils when he sees mum and dad hitting each other... But we have no agreement to discuss this issue... the violence... the hitting. This is true? But I am willing to discuss an agreement with you now, if you would like that. This agreement is a marital issue. So if you want to discuss it with me I suggest we deal with this without Mike and the girls? Just take a minute to think about that now and tell me if this is something you want or not?

Failure Analysis

If goals are not reached, it is in the clients' best interests to avoid doing *more of the same* (Segal, 1991). Rather, therapeutic failures should be analysed in a systematic way. The understanding that emerges from this is useful both for the clients and for the therapist. From the clients' perspective, they avoid becoming trapped in a consultation process that maintains rather than resolves the problem. From the therapists' viewpoint, it provides a mechanism for coping with burn-out that occurs when multiple therapeutic failures occur.

Failures may occur for a number of reasons (Carr, 1995). First, they may occur because of the engagement difficulties. The correct members of the network may not have been engaged. For example, with child-focused problems, where fathers are not engaged in the therapy process, drop out is more likely. The construction of a formulation of the presenting problem that does not open up possibilities for change or which does not fit with the family's belief systems is a second possible reason for failure. A third reason why failure occurs may be that therapy did not focus on the appropriate behaviour patterns belief systems or predisposing factors, the therapeutic alliance was poorly built, or the therapist had difficulties in offering the family invitations to complete the therapeutic tasks. Problems with handling families' reservations about change, and the resistance that this may give rise to, is a fourth and further source of failure. Disengaging without empowering the family to handle relapses is a fifth possible factor contributing to therapeutic failure. A sixth factor is countertransference. Where countertransference reactions seriously compromise therapist neutrality and the capacity to join in an empathic way with each member of the problem system, therapeutic failure may occur. Finally, failure may occur because the goals set did not take account of the constraints within which family members were operating. These constraints include: historical factors within the parents' families of origin; contextual factors in the wider social system, such as poverty; and constitutional factors, such as vulnerability to illness or disability. The analysis of treatment failure is an important way to develop therapeutic skill. Supervision for managing loss experiences associated with disengaging from both successful and unsuccessful cases is a common requirement for family therapists. Where therapy has been unsuccessful, disengagement may lead to a sense of loss of professional expertise. Loss of an important source of professional affirmation and friendship are often experienced when therapists disengage from successful cases.

SUMMARY

Family therapy may be conceptualised as a developmental and recursive process involving the stages of planning, assessment, treatment and disengagement or recontracting. In the planning stage, network analysis provides guidance on who to invite to the intake interview. The minimum sufficient network necessary for an assessment to be completed includes the customer, the person legally responsible for the problem person, the person who has a primary supportive relationship with the referred person and the referred individual. In planning an agenda, a routine interview may be supplemented by lines of questioning, which take account of hypotheses about the specific features of the case. Establishing a contract for assessment; working through the assessment agenda; dealing with engagement problems; building a therapeutic alliance and giving feedback are the more important features of the assessment stage, which may span a number of sessions. *All other features of the consultation process should be subordinate to the working alliance,* since without it clients drop out of the consultation process. The working alliance should be a collaborative partnership characterised by warmth, empathy and genuineness, respectful curiosity and an invitational approach. There should be an attempt to match the therapeutic approach to the clients' readiness to change. The inevitability of transference and countertransference reactions within the therapeutic relationship should be acknowledged. Towards the end of the assessment phase, a formulation is constructed and fed back to the family as a basis for a therapeutic contract. Inevitably, cooperation difficulties occur during therapy and case management. These may be due to a lack of skills on the client's part or to complex factors that impinge on clients' motivation to resolve their difficulties. A systematic method for analysing resistance and resolving it is required to complete case management plans. Disengagement is considered when the end of the therapeutic contract is reached. If goals have not been achieved, this should be acknowledged and referral to another agency considered. Where goals have been reached, relapse management and the options for future booster sessions are considered. In cases where further problems have emerged, a new contract for work on these issues may be offered.

FURTHER READING

Carr, A. (2000). *Special Issue: Empirical Approaches to Family Assessment.* Journal of Family Therapy, **22** (2).

McGoldrick, M., Gerson, R. & Shellenberger, S. (1999). *Genograms: Assessment and Intervention,* 2nd edn. New York: Norton.

Wilkinson I. (1998). *Child And Family Assessment: Clinical Guidelines for Practitioners,* 2nd edn. London: Routledge.

Chapter 8

FORMULATING PROBLEMS AND EXCEPTIONS

In Chapters 3, 4 and 5, we saw that the many family therapy schools and traditions may be classified in terms of their central focus of therapeutic concern and in particular with respect to their emphasis on: (1) repetitive problem-maintaining behaviour patterns; (2) constraining belief systems and narratives that subserve these behaviour patterns; and (3) historical, contextual or constitutional factors that predispose family members to adopt particular belief systems and engage in particular problem-maintaining behaviour patterns. In the same vein, hypotheses and formulations about family problems and family strengths may be conceptualised in terms of these three domains.

For any problem, an initial hypothesis and later formulation may be constructed using ideas from many schools of family therapy in which the pattern of family interaction that maintains the problem is specified; the constraining beliefs and narratives that underpin each family member's role in this pattern are outlined; and the historical, contextual and constitutional factors that underpin these belief systems and narratives are specified. For example, Charlie, aged 9, was referred because of aggression towards his siblings at home and peers at school, which had evolved over a number of years. We hypothesised that his aggression was maintained by coercive behaviour patterns with his parents and lack of coordination among parents and teachers. We hypothesised also that parents' beliefs about discipline; about parent–teacher relations; and about personal competence to deal with aggression underpinned the parents' role in the behaviour pattern. Finally, we hypothesised that family-of-origin experiences, current life stresses and lack of supports probably predisposed parents to hold these beliefs and to participate in coercive problem-maintaining behaviour. These hypotheses were checked out with lines of circular questions in the initial interview and the information obtained allowed us to make a more detailed and accurate formulation. A diagram of this formulation is presented in Figure 8.1.

For any case, a family's strengths may be conceptualised as involving exceptional interaction patterns within which the problem does not occur; empowering belief systems and narratives that inform family members'

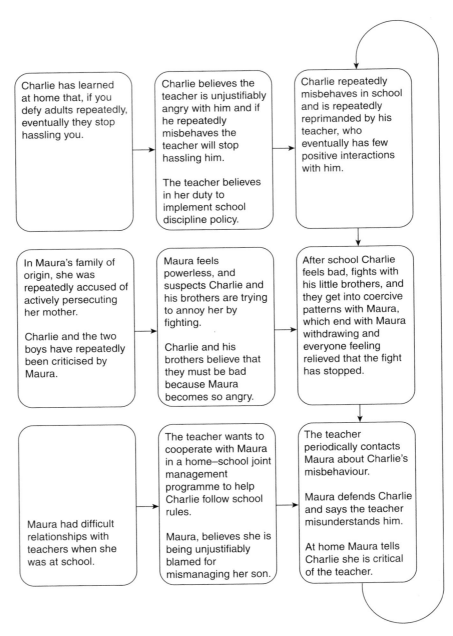

Figure 8.1 Three-column formulation of Maura and Charlie's problem

roles within these interaction patterns; and historical and contextual factors that underpin these competency-oriented belief systems and narratives and that provide a foundation for family resilience. In Charlie's case, we suspected that exceptional behaviour patterns existed in which the problem behaviour did not occur when it would have been expected. We suspected that these might be characterised by some of the following: consistent parenting; emotional connectedness between Charlie and his parents; good cooperation between parents and teachers; and clear communication among system members. We hypothesised that important beliefs about parenting underpinned these exceptional events and that these exceptions probably had their roots in positive socialisation experiences; the availability of additional support; or a reduction in family stress. These hypotheses about strengths were checked out with lines of circular questions in the initial interview and the information obtained allowed us to make a more detailed and accurate formulation of family strengths. A diagram of this formulation is given in Figure 8.2.

In light of formulations of a family's problem and strengths, a range of interventions that address interaction patterns, belief systems, broader contextual factors or constitutional vulnerabilities may be considered and those which fit best for the family and make best use of their strengths may be selected. Some interventions aim primarily to disrupt problem-maintaining interaction patterns and build on exceptional interactional patterns within which the problem does not occur. Others aim to help family members re-author their constraining narratives and evolve more liberating and flexible belief systems, often by drawing on empowering but subjugated personal and family narratives. Still others aim to modify the negative impact of historical, contextual or constitutional factors and build on contextual strengths.

In the case of Charlie, his mother Maura was a single parent with three children and she was involved in coercive behaviour patterns with all of them. These behaviour patterns were subserved by a sense of helplessness on Maura's part: a belief that much of the time her children were actively persecuting her, as, also, she believed was the school. These beliefs were underpinned by her own problematic family-of-origin experiences and negative experiences in school. The children believed that much of the time their mother was angry at them because they were inferior and this belief was subserved by repeated experiences of criticism and withdrawal by Maura.

On the positive side, during the times when her children were in classes in which they felt understood by their teacher, the children saw themselves as more competent and cooperated with both the teacher at school and Maura when they returned home. Maura tended to be more supportive of the children when they cooperated with her, and this behaviour was underpinned by a view herself as a more effective parent when this occurred. These more positive beliefs led her to deal with her children more

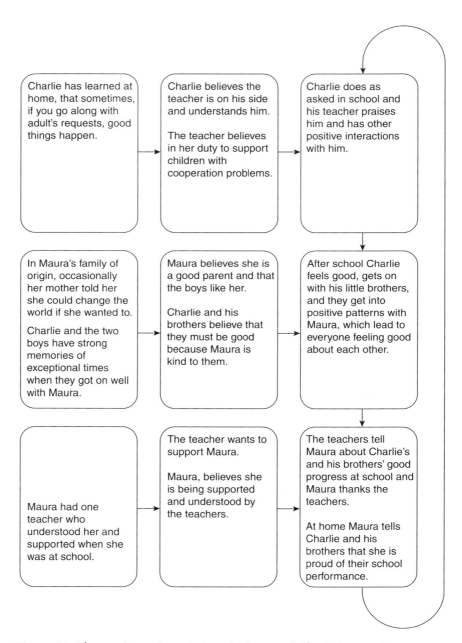

Figure 8.2 Three-column formulation of Maura and Charlie's exception

consistently. Intervention, in this case, built on the family's strengths. It focused on promoting greater cooperation between Maura and her three children's teachers, helping her to see her children's behaviour as situationally determined rather than due to intrinsic malice, and coaching her in the use of reward systems to reinforce positive behaviour and time-out to reduce the children's aggressive and uncooperative behaviour.

In this chapter, a three-column framework for formulating family problems and strengths will be described. In the next chapter, a three-column approach to conceptualising intervention options will be given.

THE THREE-COLUMN PROBLEM FORMULATION MODEL

To aid the processes of hypothesising about family problems and formulating these, ideas from many schools of family therapy have been integrated into a three-column problem formulation model, which is presented in Table 8.1.

Problem-maintaining Behaviour Patterns

Formulations and hypotheses in this style of practice must always include a detailed description of the problem and the pattern of behaviour in which it is embedded. This is placed in the right-hand column of a three-column formulation. The problem-maintaining behaviour pattern includes a description of what happened before, during and after the problem in a typical episode. Commonly, the pattern will also include positive and negative feelings. It is useful to include these emotions in the behaviour pattern since these offer a clue as to why the pattern is rigid and repeats recursively. For example, Charlie, in the previous example, when describing a typical problem behaviour pattern, said that he shouted louder when reprimanded because it made him feel better to know that eventually his mother would stop nagging him.

In making hypotheses and formulations about behaviour patterns, it is useful to draw on the wealth of theoretical ideas and research findings from the many traditions of family therapy reviewed in Chapters 1–6, and particularly those outlined in Chapter 3, concerning problematic behavioural patterns of family interaction. Some of the more important of these are listed in the right-hand column of Table 8.1. Problems may be maintained by behaviour patterns involving ineffective attempted solutions. A minor problem, such as children not doing their homework, may become a major problem, such as persistent truancy, because of the way a family tries to repeatedly solve this difficulty using ineffective solutions, such as severe punishment. Confused communication may also maintain problem behaviour, often because it leads to a lack of clarity about family members' positions, wishes, feeling and expectations. Symmetrical

Table 8.1 Three-column problem formulation model

Contexts	Belief systems	Behaviour patterns
Historical Major family-of-origin stresses 1. Bereavements 2. Separations 3. Child abuse 4. Social disadvantage 5. Institutional upbringing Family-of-origin parent–child problems 1. Insecure attachment 2. Authoritarian parenting 3. Permissive parenting 4. Neglectful parenting 5. Inconsistent parental discipline 6. Lack of stimulation 7. Scapegoating 8. Triangulation Family of origin parental problems 1. Parental psychological problems 2. Parental drug or alcohol abuse 3. Parental criminality 4. Marital discord or violence 5. Family disorganisation *Contextual* Constraining cultural norms and values Current lifecycle transitions Home–work role strain Lack of social support Recent loss experiences Bereavement Parental separation Recent illness or injury Unemployment Moving house or schools Recent bullying Recent child abuse	Denial of the problem Rejection of a systemic framing of the problem in favour of an individualistic framing Constraining beliefs and narratives about personal competence to solve the problem Constraining beliefs about problems and solutions relevant to the presenting problem Constraining beliefs and narratives about the negative consequences of change and the negative events that may be avoided by maintaining the status quo Constraining beliefs and narratives about marital, parental and other family relationships Constraining beliefs and narratives about the characteristics or intentions of other family members or network members Constraining attributional style (internal, global, stable, attributions for problem behaviour)	The problem person's symptoms and problem behaviour The sequence of events that typically precede and follow an episode of the symptoms or problem behaviour The feelings and emotions that accompany these behaviours, particularly positive feelings or pay-offs Patterns involving ineffective attempted solutions Patterns involving confused communication Symmetrical and complementary behaviour patterns Enmeshed and disengaged behaviour patterns Rigid and chaotic behaviour patterns Authoritarian and permissive parenting patterns Neglectful and punitive parenting patterns Inconsistent parenting patterns Coercive interaction patterns

Contexts	Belief systems	Behaviour patterns
Poverty	Constraining cognitive distortions	Patterns involving inadvertent reinforcement
Secret romantic affairs		
Constitutional	1. Maximising negatives	Pathological triangles and triangulation
Genetic vulnerabilities	2. Minimising positives	
Debilitating somatic states		
Early illness or injury	Constraining defence mechanisms	Patterns involving lack of marital intimacy
Learning difficulty		
Difficult temperament		
	1. Denial	Patterns involving a significant marital power imbalance
	2. Passive aggression	
	3. Rationalisation	
	4. Reaction formation	Patterns including lack of coordination among involved professionals and family members
	5. Displacement	
	6. Splitting	
	7. Projection	

interaction patterns in which, for example, aggression from one family member is responded to with aggression from another family member; or complementary behaviour patterns where, for example, increasing dependence or illness in one family member is met with increasing caretaking by another family member may also characterise problem-maintaining behaviour patterns.

Problems may be maintained by enmeshed, over-involved relationships and also by distant, disengaged relationships. Rigid repetitive interactions or chaotic unpredictable interactions may also maintain problems. Problem-maintaining behaviour patterns may involve highly authoritarian and directive parenting in which children are allowed little autonomy or by permissive parenting patterns in which children are given too much autonomy. Neglectful or punitive parenting in which the child's needs for warmth and acceptance are not met and inconsistent parenting where the child's needs for consistent routines are frustrated may maintain problem behaviour.

Coercive interaction patterns where parents and children or marital partners repeatedly engage in escalating aggressive exchanges, which conclude with withdrawal and a sense of relief for all involved, may lead to escalations in family aggression. Problems may also be maintained when other family members inadvertently reinforce problem behaviour.

Another problem-maintaining pattern, the pathological triangle, is characterised by a cross-generational coalition between a parent and a child to which the other parent is hierarchically subordinate. The pattern of alliances is covert or denied, and lip-service is paid to a strong pa·

coalition to which the child is hierarchically subordinate. Problems may be maintained by triangulation in which the triangulated individual (usually a child) is required to take sides with one of two other family members (usually the parents). Triangulation may occur when parental conflict is detoured through the child to avoid overt interparental conflict. In a detouring-attacking triad, the parents express joint anger at the child and this is associated with conduct problems. In a detouring-protecting triad, parents express joint concern about the child, who may present with a psychosomatic complaint.

Within couples, interaction patterns characterised by a lack of intimacy or a significant imbalance of power may maintain problems such as marital dissatisfaction or psychosexual problems. A lack of coordination among involved professionals including teachers, social service professional and mental health professionals may also maintain problematic behaviour.

Problem-maintaining Belief Systems

Problem-maintaining behaviour patterns may be subserved by a wide variety of constraining personal and family narratives and belief systems. Some of these, drawn from the many traditions of family therapy reviewed in Chapters 1–6 and in particular from Chapter 4, are listed in the central column of Table 8.1.

Problem-maintaining behaviour patterns may persist because family members deny the existence of the problem. For example, alcohol or drug problems may persist because the person with the problem does not accept that there is a difficulty. Problem-maintaining behaviour patterns may persist because family members reject a systemic framing of the problem and so deny their role in either maintaining the problem or contributing to its resolution. For example, parents with anorexic teenagers may reject the idea that their difficulty in cooperating so as to arrange for their youngster to eat may maintain the eating disorder. Problem-maintaining behaviour patterns may persist because family members believe that they are not competent to solve the problem. In the case of Charlie mentioned earlier, the mother Maura believed she was helpless. Problem-maintaining behaviour patterns may persist because family members have theories about the cause of the problem and the appropriate way to solve it that are not particularly useful. For example, parents who deal with school-refusal as either a reflection of defiance or serious physical illness are unlikely to help their child resolve the difficulty, because they view the appropriate solutions as being punishment or medical treatment rather than the careful management of separation anxiety.

Beliefs about the negative consequences of change and the negaments that may be avoided by supporting the status quo may also problem-maintaining behaviour. For example, a husband in a discordant marriage may persist in limiting his partner's freedom because he may believe that to treat her as an equal would involve him accepting a lower status and ultimately this would lead his wife to leave him.

There are many beliefs about marital, parental and other family relationships that can maintain problem behaviour and these beliefs often take the form:

> *A good husband/wife/mother/father/son/daughter always does X in this type of situation.*

> *If X does Y in a family then A should do B because its right, fair, or feels like the right thing to do.*

Where family members attribute negative characteristics or intentions to each other, these attributions may lead them to persist in problem-maintaining behaviour and elicit problem-maintaining behaviour in others. Such attributions include defining a family member as *bad, sad, sick* or *mad*, although often more sophisticated labels than these are used. For example, marital partners may accuse each other of being intentionally hurtful or vindictive (i.e. bad) and this can subserve coercive interaction patterns characterised by low intimacy and power imbalance, which maintains marital discord.

An attributional style where internal, global, stable, attributions are made for problem behaviour and external, specific unstable situational attributions are made for good behaviour can subserve problem-maintaining interaction patterns. For example, if parents attribute their child's misbehaviour to the fact that the child is intrinsically bad and attribute any productive behaviour he shows to the fact that it occurred in a particular situation, then these attributions may lead the parent and child to persist in a hostile, punitive interaction pattern that maintains the child's misbehaviour.

A belief system characterised by cognitive distortions, such as maximising negatives and minimising positives, may also subserve problem-maintaining interaction patterns. For example, a depressed husband who sees every glass as half empty rather than half full and every silver lining as part of a dark rain cloud, may find that this style of thinking leads him to behave in ways that prevent him from receiving the support he needs from his partner to break out of his depression.

Certain problematic defence mechanisms may be central to belief systems that maintain problematic behaviour patterns. Defence mechanisms are used to regulate anxiety that accompanies conflict due to a desire to pursue one course of action while fearing the consequences of doing so. Problematic defence mechanisms include denial as has already been mentioned and also, passive aggression, rationalisation, reaction formation, displacement, splitting and projection. With passive aggression, rather than openly talking about a conflict of interests within the family, one member passively avoids cooperating with others. With rationalisation, family members construct rational arguments to justify destructive be- haviour. For example, a parent may justify beating a child by rational- ising that it will prevent further misbehaviour. With reaction formation and displacement, rather than openly talking about a conflict of interests within the family, one family member treats those with whom he or she disagrees as if they were strongly admired and liked, but anger towards the true target of aggression may be displaced onto another family mem- ber or the same family member at a later time. For example, a mother who covertly disapproves of her teenager daughter's promiscuity may overtly permit the girl to sleep with her boyfriend, but later displace the aggres- sion by arguing with her husband or picking a fight with the teenager for coming home 10 minutes late. From this example, it may be seen that with displacement, strong negative feelings about one family member are directed towards another. With splitting and projection, the individual views other family members in black and white terms. Some family mem- bers are seen as completely good and others as wholly bad. Good quali- ties and intentions are projected onto the former while bad qualities and negative intentions are projected onto the latter. Family members defined as good are cherished and those defined as bad are scapegoated.

Problem-maintaining Contextual Factors

Problem-maintaining behaviour patterns and the belief systems and nar- ratives that subserve these may arise from predisposing factors. These pre- disposing factors may be rooted in historical family-of-origin experiences of parents or spouses; the current broader context within which the family finds itself; or constitutional vulnerabilities of individual family members. Some important factors in each of these domains are listed in the left-hand column of Table 8.1. These factors are based on theoretical insights and empirical findings from the wide variety of family therapy traditions cov- ered in Chapters 1–6, but especially those reviewed in Chapter 5.

Major family-of-origin stresses that may predispose family members to hold problematic belief systems and fall into problem-maintaining behav- iour patterns include: bereavement, particularly death of a parent; sep- arations from parents in childhood through illness or parental divorce; physical, emotional or sexual child abuse or neglect; social disadvantage and poverty; and being brought up in an institution or in multiple foster care placements. Individuals who have experienced these stresses early in life may develop personal narratives and belief systems that privilege the use of aggression, excessive interpersonal distancing, excessive inter- personal closeness or a chaotic unpredictable relational style in solving family problems.

Family-of-origin parent–child socialisation experiences that may pre- dispose individuals to hold problematic belief systems and engage in problem-maintaining behaviour patterns include insecure attachment and authoritarian, permissive, neglectful or inconsistent parenting. Included here also are parenting styles that involve little parent–child interaction and intellectual situation and family styles that involve scapegoating. All of these non-optimal socialisation experiences may give rise to the development of belief systems that in later life lead individuals to repeat these types of problematic relationships with their spouses and children.

Family-of-origin parental problems that may predispose individuals to hold problematic belief systems and engage in problem-maintaining behaviour patterns include: parental psychological problems, such as depression; parental drug or alcohol abuse; parental criminality; marital discord or violence; and general family disorganisation. All of these problematic family of origin experiences may give rise to the development of belief systems that in later life lead individuals to repeat these types of difficulties in their families of procreation.

Cultural norms and values, such as extreme patriarchy or a commitment to the use of domestic violence or corporal punishment to solve family problems, may underlie personal narratives and belief systems that subserve problem-maintaining behaviour patterns.

Lifecycle transitions, home–work role strain and a lack of social support may activate belief systems that subserve problem-maintaining behaviour patterns. Problem-maintaining belief systems may also be activated by recent loss experiences, such as bereavement, parental separation, illness, injury, unemployment, moving house or moving schools. Recent bullying or child abuse have the potential to impact on individual and family belief systems in problem maintaining ways. In families where a parent or spouse is having an ongoing secret romantic affair, the confusion caused by this may also activate belief systems that subserve problem-maintaining behaviour patterns.

Family members may be predisposed to engage in problem-maintaining behaviour patterns and the belief systems that subserve these as a result of certain constitutional vulnerabilities. Common examples of such constitutional vulnerabilities encountered in the practice of family therapy are the vulnerability to schizophrenia; the presence of diabetes, asthma or epilepsy; or disabilities arising from head injury or diseases such as AIDS. Individuals with vulnerabilities, such as difficult temperaments or learning difficulties, may also be predisposed to developing problem-maintaining beliefs and behaviour patterns. Because of the importance of child temperament in affecting both family interaction and the long-term outcome for children, a few comments on this factor will be made.

Children's temperament, and the extent to which children's temperamental characteristics fit with the parental expectations, have been found to have far-reaching effects on later adjustment. Temperament refers to those characteristic styles of responding with which a child is endowed at birth. Chess and Thomas (1995) identified three distinct and relatively common temperamental profiles. *Easy temperament children* have regular eating, sleeping and toileting habits. They approach new situations rather than avoid them and adapt to new situations easily. Their moods are predominantly positive and of low intensity. Easy temperament children have a good prognosis. They attract adults and peers to form a supportive network around them. *Difficult temperament children* have irregular eating, sleeping and toileting habits. They avoid new situations and are slow to adapt to them. Their moods are predominantly negative and of high intensity. Difficult temperament children are at risk for developing later adjustment problems. They have more conflict with parents, peers and teachers. They do better when there is a *goodness-of-fit* between their temperament and the parental expectations. Difficult temperament children need tolerant, responsive parents. *Slow-to-warm-up children* have moderately irregular eating, sleeping and eliminating habits. They are slow to adapt to new situations.

Their moods are predominantly negative but of low intensity. Children who are slow-to-warm-up require more tolerant parents than do easy temperament children. Their prognosis is more variable than those of children with the other two temperamental styles.

THE THREE-COLUMN EXCEPTION FORMULATION MODEL

To aid the processes of hypothesising about exceptions and formulating these, ideas from many schools of family therapy and findings from studies of resilience (e.g. Carr, 2004; Rutter, 1999; Walsh, 2003b) have been integrated into a three-column exception formulation model, which is presented in Table 8.2.

Exceptional Behaviour Patterns

Formulations and hypotheses about exceptions in the style of practice advocated in this text must always include a detailed description of the exception and the pattern of behaviour in which it is embedded, and this is placed in the right-hand column of a three-column exception formulation. The exceptional behaviour pattern includes a description of what happened before, during and after the problem was expected to occur but did not in a typical exceptional episode. Commonly, the exceptional pattern will also include positive and possibly negative feelings. It is useful to include these emotions in the behaviour pattern since these offer clues as to how the exceptional pattern may be strengthened. For example, Charlie, in the previous example, tended to be less aggressive at home when he was getting on well in school.

In making hypotheses and formulations about exceptional behaviour patterns, it is useful to draw on the wealth of theoretical ideas and research

Table 8.2 Three-column exception formulation model

Contexts	Belief systems	Behaviour patterns
Historical	Acceptance of the problem	The sequence of
Positive family-of-		events that occurs
origin experiences	Acceptance of a systemic	in those exceptional
Positive family-of-	framing of the problem	circumstances where
origin parent–child	Commitment to resolving	the problem does not
relationships	the problem	occur
Secure attachment		
Authoritative	Empowering beliefs	The feelings and
parenting	and narratives about	emotions that
Clear communication	personal competence to	accompany these
Flexible family	solve the problem	behaviours,
organisation	Empowering beliefs	particularly positive
Good parental	and narratives about	feelings or pay-offs
adjustment	problems and solutions	
Parents had	relevant to the	Patterns involving
good marital	presenting problem	effective solutions and
relationship	Beliefs and narratives	good problem-solving
Successful	about the advantages	skills
experiences of	of problem resolution	Patterns involving clear
coping with	outweigh beliefs	communication
problems	about the negative	
	consequences of change	Emotionally connected
Contextual	and the negative events	behaviour patterns
Empowering cultural	that may be avoided by	involving family
norms and values	maintaining the status	loyalty
Good social support	quo	Flexible behaviour
network		patterns
Low family stress	Empowering beliefs and	
Positive educational	narratives about marital,	Authoritative, consistent,
placement	parental and other	cooperative parenting
Balanced home and	family relationships,	patterns
work roles	particularly loyalty	Intimate, egalitarian
High socioeconomic	Benign beliefs and	marital interaction
status	narratives about the	patterns
	characteristics or	Patterns including good
Constitutional	intentions of other	coordination among
Physical health	family members or	involved professionals
High IQ	network members	and family members
Easy temperament	Optimistic attributional	
	style (internal, global,	
	stable, attributions for	
	productive behaviour	
	and situational	
	attributions for problem	
	behaviour)	

(Continued on next page)

Table 8.2 *(Continued)*

Contexts	Belief systems	Behaviour patterns
	Healthy defence mechanisms	
	1. Self-observation	
	2. Humour	
	3. Self-assertion	
	4. Sublimation	

findings from the many traditions of family therapy reviewed in Chapters 1–6, concerning resilience. Some of the more important of these are listed in the right-hand column of Table 8.2. Exceptions that involve effective problem-solving are often embedded in behaviour patterns characterised by clear communication and emotionally supportive relationships where there is flexibility about family rules, roles and routines. Parent–child interactions tend to be characterised by authoritative, consistent and cooperative parenting. Couples' relationships, when exceptions to problems occur, tend to involve intimacy and greater balance in the distribution of power (within the cultural constraints of the family's ethnic reference group). Exceptions tend to occur more commonly when there is good interprofessional coordination and cooperation between families and professionals.

Exceptional Belief Systems

Exceptional non-problematic behaviour patterns may be subserved by a wide variety of belief systems and narratives. Some of these, drawn from the many traditions of family therapy reviewed in Chapters 1–6, are listed in the central column of Table 8.2.

Exceptional behaviour patterns may occur because family members accept rather than deny the existence of the problem and accept responsibility for their role in contributing to its resolution. Exceptional non-problematic behaviour patterns may occur when family members become, for a time, committed to the resolution of the problem and experience themselves as competent to resolve their difficulties. When family members hold useful and empowering beliefs about the nature of the problem and its resolution, exceptions may also occur.

The occurrence of exceptions may be associated with the development of the belief that the advantages of resolving the problem outweigh the costs of change. Clients may construct personal or family narratives in which once-feared consequences associated with problem come to be seen as not so dreadful after all.

Exceptions may occur when family members construct positive and empowering beliefs and narratives about family relationships, about parenting, about marriage and about their roles in the family. This may include a realisation of how important it is to be a good mother, father, son or daughter; to be loyal to one's family; to show solidarity through thick and thin; to realise how much family members care for each other and so forth.

Exceptions may also occur when family members develop benign beliefs and narratives about the intentions and characteristics of other family members, and come to view them as good people who are doing their best in a tough situation, rather than vindictive people who are out to persecute them. An optimistic attributional style may also underpin exceptional, non-problematic behaviour patterns. Here, productive behaviour of all family members is attributed to their inherent goodness and problematic behaviour is attributed to situational factors.

When exceptional behaviour patterns occur, sometimes they are associated with the use of healthy defence mechanisms to manage anxiety arising from conflicting desires to follow a course of action but also avoid rejection or attack from others. Healthy defence mechanisms include self-observation, looking at the humorous side of the situation, being assertive about having one's needs met, and sublimation of unacceptable desires into socially acceptable channels, such as work, art or sport.

Contextual Factors Associated with Resilience

Exceptional behaviour patterns and the productive belief systems and narratives that subserve these arise from factors which foster resilience (Carr, 2004; Rutter, 1999; Walsh, 2003b). These protective factors may be rooted in the historical family-of-origin experiences of parents or spouses; the current broader context within which the family finds itself; or the characteristics of individual family members. Some important factors in each of these domains are listed in the left-hand column of Table 8.2. These factors are based on theoretical insights and empirical findings from the wide variety of family therapy traditions covered in Chapters 1–6 and research in developmental psychology.

Good parent–child relationships characterised by secure attachment, authoritative parenting and clear communication in the family of origin foster later resilience in the face of adversity and empower people to manage problems well in their families of procreation. Successful experiences of coping with problems in the family of origin, flexible organisation in the family of origin, good parental adjustment and a positive relationship between parents in the family of origin may also engender later resilience.

A good social support network including friends and members of the extended family and low extrafamilial stress enhance a family's chances of resolving the problems they bring to therapy. Where children have suitable and properly resourced educational placements and parents have well-balanced home and work roles, these enhance the family resilience.

High socioeconomic status and empowering cultural norms and values also contribute to family resilience in the face of adversity.

Important personal characteristics that contribute to family resilience are physical health, high intelligence and easy temperament.

QUESTIONS TO ASK WHEN CONSTRUCTING THREE-COLUMN FOMULATIONS

The general assessment goals for checking out specific hypotheses about problems and exceptions using the three-column formulation models set out in Table 8.1. and 8.2, are given in Table 8.3. Hypotheses and lines of questioning to check these out and achieve the general assessment goals are planned during stage 1 of the family therapy process described in Chapter 7 and presented in Figure 7.1. In conducting a first assessment session (during stage 2 of the family therapy process illustrated in Figure 7.1), broad questions about the problem and its development along with genogram construction described in Chapter 7 may throw light on hypotheses about problems and exceptions. However, certain question formats are particularly useful in checking out three-column hypotheses about problems and exceptions. Some of these are outlined below.

Questions About Problems

Questions about problems (as distinct from those about exceptions) include those about problem-maintaining behaviour patterns; problem-maintaining belief systems; and predisposing historical, contextual and constitutional factors.

Questions about Problem-maintaining Behaviour Patterns

The following are useful formats for questions to ask when interviewing about problem-maintaining behaviour patterns. They tap into the common problem-maintaining behaviour patterns listed in the right-hand column of the problem formulation model set out in Table 8.1.

Tell me, in detail, about the last time the problem occurred?

If I was watching a video of the last time the problem happened, what would I see in the lead up to it, during it and after it?

You said XYZ happened, what happened next?

You said XYZ happened, what happened just before that?

Before/during/after XYZ happened, what was each person in the family doing?

Before/during/after XYZ happened, what was each person in the family feeling?

Table 8.3 Assessment goals when conducting three-column problem and exception formulations

	Contexts	Belief systems	Behaviour patterns
Problem formulation	Explore the family-of-origin experiences that gave rise to the constraining narratives and belief systems Explore the current life contextual factors that underpin constraining narratives and belief systems Identify the constitutional characteristics of family members that contribute to them holding constraining narratives and beliefs or engaging in episodes of problem behaviour	Identify narratives and beliefs that constrain people to participate in the problem-maintaining interaction pattern Identify constraining beliefs and narratives about the problem and its solution Identify constraining beliefs and narratives about families and the roles people should take	Describe in detail everyone's behaviour during a problem episode and the ineffective solutions Describe in detail the roles taken by all involved Describe the positive and negative feelings of those involved
Exception formulation	Explore the family-of-origin experiences that gave rise to the empowering narratives and belief systems Explore the current life contextual factors that underpin empowering narratives and belief systems Speculate about the constitutional	Construct narratives and beliefs that empower people to avoid the problem-maintaining interaction pattern Construct liberating narratives and beliefs about the problem and its solution	Describe in detail everyone's behaviour during an exceptional episode when good problem solving occurs Describe in detail the roles taken by all involved Describe the positive and negative feelings of those involved

(Continued on next page)

Table 8.3 *(Continued)*

	Contexts	Belief systems	Behaviour patterns
	characteristics of family members that contribute to them holding empowering narratives and beliefs or engaging in exceptional non-problematic behaviour	Construct liberating narratives and beliefs about families and the roles people should take	

How have you tried to solve this problem?

Which solutions have worked in the past and which have not?

Which solution do you keep trying again and again?

In your recent/previous attempts to solve this problem, when A said B did you understand what he or she meant?

In your recent/previous attempts to solve this problem, when XYZ happened did you feel close to or distant from your husband/wife/mother/father/brother/sister?

In your recent/previous attempts to solve this problem, when XYZ happened did you feel like you had more power or less power than your husband/wife/mother/father/brother/sister?

In your recent/previous attempts to solve this problem, when XYZ happened, did you know what was going to happen next?

In your recent/previous attempts to solve this problem, when XYZ happened, was the outcome a good thing or a bad thing for you or your husband/wife/mother/father/brother/sister?

In your recent/previous attempts to solve this problem, when XYZ happened, who was on your team in the family?

In your recent/previous attempts to solve this problem, when XYZ happened, who was on your or your husband/wife/mother/father/brother/sister's team?

In your recent/previous attempts to solve this problem, was it clear to you what the plan was for yourself, the social worker, the doctor and the teacher? How have you tried to get a joint plan working?

Questions about Problem-maintaining Belief Systems

What follows are some useful formats for questions to ask when interviewing about belief systems that subserve problem-maintaining behaviour patterns. They tap into the common problem-maintaining belief systems and narratives listed in the middle column of the problem formulation model set out in Table 8.1.

Is there agreement within the family that there is a problem that requires a resolution?

Who holds the view most strongly that there is a problem?

Who thinks that there is no problem at all?

What explanation do you or others give for this problem?

What sort of solution goes with your explanation of the problem?

Is the problem more to do with the person or the situation?

Has the problem got worse or better since you made your appointment to come here? What explanation do you offer for this improvement, deterioration or stability?

In the past has the problem been constant or fluctuating?

How do you or others explain this stability or fluctuation?

In the future will you expect the problem to improve, deteriorate or remain stable?

What explanation do you or others give for this expected change or stability?

How does your explanation of the problem differ from that of your husband/wife/ mother/father/brother/sister, etc?

If this problem were improving, what would everybody in the family be doing differently?

If this problem were getting worse, what would everybody in the family be doing differently?

If your mother/father/grandmother/grandfather/priest/rabbi, etc. were here with us, what advice would they give us about managing this problem?

What roles should mothers/fathers/husbands/wives/doctors/social workers, etc. take in dealing with problems like these according to your mother/father/grandparents/ religion/ethnic group?

There is a downside to everything. What would be the downside to solving this problem? What would you lose?

We often do one thing to avoid another. Just say you or your mother/father/brother/ sister/husband/wife were dealing with this problem as you have been doing to avoid some other worse situation. What is it you (or they) are avoiding?

To what extent do you believe that you can control this problem and to what extent do you believe it is out of your control?

To what extent do you believe that your husband/wife/mother/father/brother/sister can control this problem and to what extent do you believe it is out of their control?

Questions about Predisposing Contextual Factors

What follows are some useful formats for questions to ask parents and spouses when interviewing about predisposing factors that may underpin problematic belief systems and problem-maintaining behaviour patterns.

They tap into the factors listed in the left-hand column of the problem formulation model set out in Table 8.1.

How would this type of situation have been handled in your family of origin?

Can you describe how a comparable situation was handled in your family of origin?

Do you believe that any of the challenges or difficulties you faced as a youngster have affected your capacity to cope with the present problem?

How would you describe your mother/father/carer's relationship with you during your childhood and adolescence?

How would you describe your mother's and father's relationship with each other during your childhood and adolescence?

How would you describe your mother/father's way of managing their lives during your childhood and adolescence?

How would you describe family life (rules, role and routines) during your childhood and adolescence?

Over the past year, what have been the main changes that have occurred for yourself and the rest of the family, that may have affected your capacity to cope with this problem?

Over the past year, what have been the main changes that have occurred for yourself and the rest of the family?

Over the past year, what have been the main pressures on you at home/work/school?

Over the past year, who has been most supportive of you and how have they shown this?

How have you juggled the demands of work and home life over the past year?

How has your health and that of other family members been over the past year?

How satisfied are you and other family members with X's school placement?

What personal characteristics of X have prevented you from resolving this problem?

Different children have different temperaments. Is your child regular and easy in his/her ways or difficult to get into a routine and difficult?

Questions about Exceptions

Questions about exceptions include those about: exceptional circumstances within which the problem does not occur; empowering belief systems and narratives that underpin these exceptions; and historical, contextual and constitutional factors, which are the foundation of family resilience.

Questions about Exceptional Behaviour Patterns

The following are useful formats for questions to ask when interviewing about exceptional behaviour patterns. They tap into the common exceptional behaviour patterns listed in the right-hand column of the exception formulation model set out in Table 8.2.

Tell me about an exceptional situation in which the problem was expected to occur but didn't?

If I was watching a video of this exception what would I see in the lead up to it, during it and after it?

You said XYZ happened, what happened next?

You said XYZ happened, what happened just before that?

Before/during/after XYZ happened, what was each person in the family doing?

Before/during/after XYZ happened, what was each person in the family feeling?

Was there a turning point during this successful exception, in which you knew that you were going to manage the problem well?

During this successful exception in which you managed the problem well, when A said B did you understand what he or she meant?

During this successful exception in which you managed the problem well, when XYZ happened did you feel close to or distant from your husband/wife/mother/father/ brother/sister?

During this successful exception in which you managed the problem well, when XYZ happened did you feel like you have more power or less power than your husband/ wife/mother/father/brother/sister?

During this successful exception in which you managed the problem well, when XYZ happened, did you know what was going to happen next?

During this successful exception in which you managed the problem well, was the outcome a good thing or a bad thing for you or your husband/wife/mother/father/ brother/sister?

During this successful exception in which you managed the problem well, when XYZ happened, who was on your team in the family?

During this successful exception in which you managed the problem well, when XYZ happened, who was on your or your husband/wife/mother/father/brother/sister's team?

During this successful exception in which you managed the problem well, was it clear to you what the plan was for yourself, the social worker, the doctor and the teacher? How did you all get a joint plan working?

Questions about Empowering Belief Systems and Narratives

What follows are some useful formats for questions to ask when interviewing about empowering narratives and belief systems that underpin exceptional non-problematic behaviour patterns. They tap into the common empowering beliefs and narratives listed in the central column of the exception formulation model set out in Table 8.2.

What is your explanation for this successful exception in which you managed the problem well?

Was your success more to do with your efforts, the efforts of other family members or the situation?

To what extent do you believe that you can make these exceptions happen again and to what extent do you believe this is out of your control?

To what extent do you believe that your husband/wife/mother/father/brother/sister can control these exceptions and to what extent do you believe that they are out of their control?

Can you give other examples from the past to show that you or your husband/wife/ mother/father/brother/sister were the main factor in managing this problem?

In the future, if you wanted to create another exceptional event in which yourself and the other family member managed the problem well, what would everyone have to do?

Questions about Predisposing Protective Factors and Resilience

What follows are some useful formats for questions to ask parents and spouses when interviewing about protective predisposing factors that underpin exceptional non-problematic behaviour patterns. They tap into the factors listed in the left-hand column of the exception formulation model set out in Table 8.2.

Can you describe a comparable situation in your family of origin. A situation where a problem was unresolved for a long time and then was managed successfully on one occasion?

If your mother/father/grandmother/grandfather/priest/rabbi, etc. were here with us, what advice would they give us about making these exceptions occur again?

What roles should mothers/fathers/husbands/wives/doctors/social workers, etc. take in making these exceptions happen again according to your mother/father/grandparents/ religion/ethnic group?

What challenges or difficulties did you face as a youngster that empowered you so that you could manage the present problem so well in this exceptional situation?

If I were watching a video of your earlier life what do you think I would see that would explain how you managed to handle the problem so well in this exceptional situation?

RECURSIVE REFORMULATION

The assessment phase of the overall therapy process involves interviewing to check out the accuracy of hypotheses made during the planning phase and modifying these in the light of the information gained in the interview. In practice, the first round of interviewing may not only lead to a modification of the preliminary hypothesis but may raise further hypotheses that need to be checked out through further interviewing. This recursive process, which characterises the assessment stage (listed Figure 7.1), is illustrated in Figure 8.3. The process comes to an end when a formulation has been constructed that fits with significant aspects of the presenting problems; with network member's experiences of the these problems; and

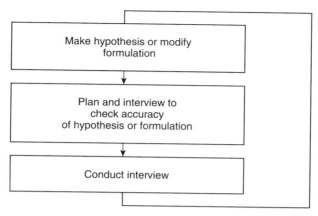

Figure 8.3 Process of recursive reformulation

with available knowledge about similar problems described in the literature. This formulation should point to a number of options for treatment.

A problem formulation is a mini-theory that explains why the presenting problems developed and why they persist. An exception or family strengths formulation, in contrast, is a mini-theory which explains why the problem does not occur in certain circumstances in which it would be expected to occur. Abstracting, classifying and combining salient points from the genogram, the history of the problem and information arising from lines of questioning based on hypotheses into coherent formulations is a demanding process, which requires both clinical acumen and a good knowledge of the literature.

The importance of formulation cannot be overemphasised. The process of constructing a formulation is the process of linking academic knowledge of theory and research to clinical practice. If the working alliance is the engine that drives the therapeutic process, formulation is the map that provides guidance on what direction to take.

Once a formulation, has been constructed, feedback is given to the family about the formulation, and options for the future management of the case are considered. The level of detail used in giving feedback needs to be matched to the family's cognitive ability to comprehend it and their emotional readiness to accept it. As part of the alliance-building process, it is usually easiest for families if the exception formulation is given first and the problem formulation second. This process of presenting the exception formulation first, highlights family strengths and generates a sense of hope. It is also important to empathise with each person's position when outlining the way in which the problem appears to have evolved. Usually family members are well intentioned but under stress, and without adequate information they inadvertently contribute to problem development or maintenance. In the process of feeding back some or all of the formulation to family members, in order to maintain a good working alliance it is useful to regularly check that the family have understood and accepted the formulation so far. Once the family have understood and accepted the formulation, broad options for treatment may be outlined. It is futile to discuss treatment options if those legally responsible for the identified client (such as parents or adults with difficulties who are legally responsible for themselves) deny the problem or refuse to accept even part of the formulation.

SUMMARY

For any problem, an initial hypothesis and later formulation may be constructed using ideas from many schools of family therapy in which the pattern of family interaction that maintains the problem is specified; the constraining beliefs and narratives that underpin each family member's role in this pattern are outlined; and the historical and contextual factors that underpin these belief systems and narratives are specified. Similarly, for any case, a family's strengths may be conceptualised as involving exceptional interaction patterns within which the problem does not occur; empowering belief systems and narratives that inform family members' roles within these interaction patterns; and historical, contextual and constitutional factors that underpin these competency-oriented belief systems and narratives and that provide a foundation for family resilience. Specific types of questions may be used to help families construct three-column formulations of problems and exceptions. In light of such formulations, a range of interventions, which address interaction patterns, belief systems, broader contextual factors or constitutional vulnerabilities, may be considered, and those which fit best for the family and make best use of their strengths may be selected. Some interventions aim primarily to disrupt problem-maintaining interaction patterns and build on exceptional interactional patterns within which the problem does not occur. Others aim to help family members re-author their constraining narratives and evolve more liberating and flexible belief systems, often by drawing on empowering but subjugated personal and family narratives. Still others aim to modify the negative impact of historical, contextual or constitutional factors and build on contextual strengths. These three classes of interventions will be considered in Chapter 9.

FURTHER READING

Wilkinson I. (1998). *Child And Family Assessment: Clinical Guidelines for Practitioners*, 2nd edn. London: Routledge.

Chapter 9

INTERVENTIONS FOR BEHAVIOUR, BELIEFS AND CONTEXTS

In Chapter 7 (Figure 7.1), we saw that treatment is the third stage of the family therapy process and is preceded by planning and assessment. Within the treatment stage clients are invited to set goals, make a contract for treatment and participate in this process. It was also noted that during treatment, cooperation difficulties (often termed 'resistance') may occur and these require careful management. Treatment goals, contracts and plans – in the integrative model of practice presented here – arise out of a clear formulation of clients' problems and strengths. The three-column models for formulating problems and exceptions to these were presented in Chapter 8. In the present chapter, the focus will be on interventions.

Interventions may be classified in terms of the particular domain they target within the three-column formulation models. Some interventions aim to directly disrupt problem-maintaining behaviour patterns or replace these with exceptional non-problematic behaviour patterns. Others aim to transform the belief systems and narratives that subserve these behaviour patterns so that clients develop more empowering narratives about themselves and their competence to manage problems. Finally, some interventions aim to modify the impact of historical, contextual and constitutional predisposing factors or mobilise protective factors or family strengths within these domains. The three-column framework given in Table 9.1 organises some of the more important therapeutic interventions from the many schools of family therapy reviewed in Chapters 3–6 in ways that facilitates integrative practice.

CRITERIA FOR SELECTING INTERVENTIONS

A number of criteria may be used in selecting interventions for particular cases. It is best to select interventions that have been shown to be effective in research studies for the type of problems with which the family presents. Some of the available evidence for the effectiveness of marital and family therapy is reviewed in the Chapter 18. It is clear from this chapter that results of research studies give little guidance on the fine

Table 9.1 Interventions to address factors within three-column formulations

Contexts	Belief systems	Behaviour patterns
Addressing family-of-origin issues Facilitating exploration of transgenerational patterns, scripts myths and relationship habits Facilitating re-experiencing, expressing and integrating emotions from family-of-origin experiences that underpin destructive relationship habits Coaching clients to reconnect with cut-off parental figures *Addressing contextual issues* Changing roles Building support Rituals for mourning losses Home–school liaison meetings Network meetings Child protection Advocacy Exploring secrets *Addressing constitutional factors* Psychoeducation about condition Facilitating adherence to medication regime Referral for medical consultation Supporting appropriate educational placement if required for individuals with learning difficulties	*Addressing ambivalence* Exploring ambivalence, beliefs about pros and cons of change, and the dilemma of change Exploring beliefs about catastrophes associated with change Exploring beliefs about powerlessness and change *Highlighting strengths* Relabelling individual actions and attributes in positive non-blaming terms Pinpointing frequently used but unacknowledged individual and family strengths *Reframing problems* Framing problems in interactional terms Framing problems in solvable terms Framing intentions in positive terms *Presenting multiple perspectives* Split messages Reflecting team practice *Externalising problems and building on exceptions* Separate the problem from the person Identify and amplify exceptions including pre-therapy improvements Involve network members Link the current life exceptions to the past and future	*Creating a therapeutic context* Contracting Laying ground rules Facilitating turn taking Managing time and space *Changing behaviour patterns in sessions* Enactment Coaching Unbalancing Boundary marking *Tasks to change behaviour patterns between sessions* Symptom monitoring Encouraging restraint Practicing symptoms Graded challenges *Skills training* Communication skills training Problem-solving skills training *Changing behavioural consequences* Reward systems Behaviour control

tuning and subtleties of clinical practice. So other criteria are required when choosing interventions in particular cases. Select interventions that fit with the three-column formulations of the family's problem and exceptional circumstances in which the problem does not occur. Select interventions that are compatible with the family's readiness to change. Where clients are ambivalent or uncommitted, then these issues rather than action planning should be the focus of treatment. Interventions that are compatible with the family's rules, roles, routines, belief systems and culture are probable preferable to those that are incompatible. Interventions that make best use of family strengths are probably better than those that do not fully exploit the family's own problem-solving and self-healing resources to the full. It is also preferable to select interventions that make best use of the therapist's or team's skills in helping the helping clients solve their problems.

There are a number of common problems in selecting interventions in particular cases. Sometimes interventions are selected because they are the current fad or fashion within the field despite a lack of evidence for their effectiveness or a rationale for their suitability for the current client. In these situations, the challenge is to develop a clear formulation and establish if the formulation provides a rationale for experimenting with a new type of intervention. In other instances, unacknowledged counter-transference reactions inform the selection of interventions. Therapists drift into inadvertently rescuing or persecuting family members and in doing so maintain the family's problems rather than contribute to their resolution. In these situations, exploring the counter-transference reactions and their impact on problem maintenance in supervision is essential for good practice.

A final difficulty in this area is where marital or family therapy is not the appropriate intervention for the clients' problem, but is offered (usually with good-will) because the therapist referred the case is a family therapist. In such cases, it is important to consider the appropriateness of the referral and explore the possibility of referral to a more appropriate service. In cases of sensory, physical, linguistic or intellectual disabilities multidisciplinary assessment is vital. Referrals to medicine, physiotherapy, speech and language therapy, occupational therapy, social work, audiology should all be considered. A referral to medicine is critical to consider if there is a suspicion that psychological symptoms may reflect an underlying organic condition, such as thyrotoxicosis (which may present as an anxiety like disorder). A referral to psychiatry is critical to consider in cases where: psychotic or hypomanic features are central to the presentation; a hospital admission may be required in cases of self-harm; or detoxification following substance abuse is required. In cases where child abuse has occurred or is suspected, national policy and local guidelines concerning interagency cooperation and reporting such cases to the statutory authorities should be followed.

BEHAVIOUR-FOCUSED INTERVENTIONS

Interventions that aim to directly disrupt or replace problem-maintaining behaviour patterns include the following:

- creating a therapeutic context as an exception to problem maintaining patterns
- changing problem-maintaining patterns in sessions using enactments
- using tasks between sessions
- skills training
- changing behavioural consequences.

Creating a Therapeutic Context

In every session the process of creating a context for therapeutic work is an intervention which disrupts, initially only temporarily, problem-maintaining behaviour patterns. In creating a therapeutic context, in every session the contract for therapeutic work and the ground rules governing this work are re-established either implicitly or explicitly. Through this process, turn taking in speaking and listening is practiced, and the therapist in collaboration with the family and the agency arranges for the session to take place for a period of uninterrupted time in an appropriate space to achieve agreed goals. However, in the first session these issues are addressed very explicitly as described in Chapter 6 in the section on contracting for assessment.

In later sessions, however, it is important to pay regular attention to creating a therapeutic context by structuring the sessions in a way that promotes collaborative problem solving and that maintains a sense of fairness. A useful structure is to open each session by inviting participants first to say how they are 'right now' and then to give a brief account of progress from their perspective. It is important for clients to say how they are 'right now', so their mood state is not misinterpreted by other family members or the therapist. For example, if a family member has just had a stressful day at school, received a parking ticket, lost their handbag, won the lottery or found out they passed their exams, all these things may cause significant mood alterations. It is important for everyone in the session to know that these sort of events have happened and that they are affecting family members' mood states. When each family member gives a brief account of progress since the last session, specific issues to be discussed in the heart of the session may be noted during this review. The heart of the session may be used for specific in-session interventions (such as those described in later sections of this chapter) focusing on behaviour, beliefs or predisposing factors. Sometimes it is helpful to take a break before concluding the session to plan how the session might most usefully be concluded. Sessions may be concluded by simply inviting participants to continue the in-session conversation in the next session. In other instances, the strengths and commitment clients have shown during the session may be highlighted. Sometimes it is useful to conclude sessions by reframing clients' problems or high-lighting multiple different perspectives. In still other instances, sessions may conclude by inviting clients to complete specific tasks for specific reasons before the next session. Specific questions and statement formats that may be used to conclude sessions in these ways are given in later sections of this chapter. Here are some questions and statements that are useful in creating a therapeutic context in the opening and middle sections of therapy sessions.

Can we open by checking how everyone is right now. What sort of a day have you had ABC. Have you been under pressure or won the lotto, or is it just a normal day?

I'm interested in what each of you remember about the last session and what has happened since then. Different people sometimes remember different things. Everyone will get a turn. Who would like to start?

One of the things about these meetings is that they have to be fair. Everybody has to get their fair say. To get their own turn so they can give their view. So let's try to all be fair and give each person a few minutes to say their piece. I will keep an eye on the clock so each person gets a fair slice of this hour. Is that OK with you?

You have a long story to tell about ABC. Lets write that down on our list of things to discuss today. We will all note that you want to tell us about that, but you have not enough time during your turn to tell us. We will come back to it when each person has had their fair turn. Is that OK with you?

There are some things you wanted to talk about today but we have run out of time. Will we put these on the list for the next day?

There are important issues and concerns that you wanted to discuss today but we have run out of time. Would you like to take some time between now and our next meeting to write them out and then read them to us all in the next session?

For this issue, my view is that it does not concern everyone in the family. May I suggest that you (to those it does not concern) take a day off therapy next week and that we (to those it does concern) meet together to talk about this specific issue?

Changing Behaviour Patterns within Sessions

Within sessions, families may be invited to try to solve their problem or some aspect of it in their usual way. Once the invitation is offered, the therapist stops talking and leaves time and space for the family to enact their usual routine for trying to solve the problem. By observing these enactments, the therapist may see first-hand an example of part or all of the behaviour pattern that maintains the problem, since often problems are maintained by ineffective attempts at their resolution. This intervention, known as enactment, is central to the practice of structural family therapy. Here is a typical invitation to engage in an enactment:

> *It sounds like this is a tough problem. But I am still not clear how it is that that you keep getting stuck when you try to solve it. I would understand this better if, right now, you tried to reach an agreement on what to do. I will sit over here and listen to how you go about this. OK start anytime your ready.*

If anyone in the family speaks directly to the therapist to try to include him or her in the family discussion, the therapist says:

> *We can talk about this later. Right now I'm just trying to watch and listen so I can understand what happens when you do this at home.*

Once the family become stuck and find that they cannot make any further progress, the therapist may then intervene in a way that frees up the family to make further progress. For example, with families containing anorexic girls, Minuchin would invite the family to enact their usual attempts to help the anorexic girl eat during a family lunch session (Minuchin et al., 1978). When the anorexic girl refused to eat despite parental requests, he would unbalance the family by siding with the parents against the girl. He would insist that they had a duty to work together to prevent their daughter's starvation. At other times, once the girl showed some recovery, he would side with her against the parents in her battle for autonomy. During enactments, directives may be given to family members to try more effective ways of solving problems, in the same way that a coach would instruct an athlete to alter his or her technique after observing the athlete's performance. For example, in families where all the members talk at the same time and no one listens, each member may be coached to take turns at listening and then talking when trying to solve a family problem. Facilitating enactments is central to the practice of structural family therapy, an approach that assumes that clear intergenerational boundaries are central to effective family problem solving. It is therefore not surprising that boundary marking, that is, supporting the maintenance of clear intergenerational boundaries, is a common aspect of coaching families who are involved in enactments. For example, parents may be invited to jointly discuss a problem and the therapist may actively prevent the children from becoming involved in this conversation.

> *I can see you are trying to be helpful by making suggestions to your parents. But, right now I want to find out what happens if just the two of them work on this problem. Can both of you ask your son to give you space until you reach an agreement on what to do?*

This boundary-marking intervention prevents a cross-generation alliance between one parent and a child from developing within the enactment. At the end of an unsuccessful enactment that did not lead to joint problem solving, the fact that it gave new information may be highlighted as a positive achievement.

> *Let's stop there. This has been really helpful. You have shown me how you try to solve this problem exactly where you usually get stuck. This is very important information. Thank you.*

At the end of an enactment that led to joint problem solving, the mastery that occurred may be highlighted.

> *Let's stop there. You have shown me that you know how to solve these sorts of problems. This seems to be one of your strengths, this way that you work together as team and make difficult decisions together.*

Tasks between Sessions

Families may be invited to complete tasks between sessions that aim to disrupt or replace problem-maintaining behaviour patterns. Among the more widely used are the following:

- symptom monitoring
- encouraging restraint
- practicing symptoms
- graded challenges.

Symptom Monitoring

For many difficulties, it is useful to invite clients to regularly record information about the main presenting problems, the circumstances surrounding their occurrence and the degree to which family members complete therapeutic homework tasks or adhere to treatment regimes if they have a primary biomedical vulnerability, such as diabetes or schizophrenia. Intensity ratings, frequency counts, durations and other features of problems or symptoms may be recorded regularly. Intrapsychic and interpersonal events that happen before, during and after problems may also be noted. When inviting clients to use a monitoring system, the chances of them cooperating is better if a simple and structured system is given, such as the form presented in Figure 9.1. Here is one way to introduce a monitoring task:

> *You have mentioned that the problem is better sometimes than others. To help us all understand this a bit better, I'm inviting you to keep a record of each time the problem happens between now and the next session. On this form (Figure 9.1) you can write*

down the time the problem happens here (in the left-hand column). Then a note of what exactly happened. If anything significant happened just before or just after the problem, there's a space for that too (pointing to columns 3 and 4). Earlier we were talking about rating the problem on a 10-point scale where 10 is the worst it's ever been and 1 is when there is no problem. You can write in your rating each time on a 10-point scale just here (pointing to column 5). Let me just check that you understand this. Can you go over the routine with me again?

NOTE EACH TIME _____ **OCCURS**				
Write down what happened before and afterwards				
Give the event a rating on a scale of 1 to 10 where				
1 means_____				
and				
10 means_____				
Day and time	**Event**	**Before**	**After**	**Rating**

Figure 9.1 Event monitoring form

Information from monitoring charts should be reviewed regularly and family members may be invited to speculate on the reasons for changes in problems and related events. Solution-focused therapists have highlighted that it is useful to phrase questions routinely about changes in positive terms (Miller et al., 1996). Here are some examples:

It looks like the problem went from 9 to 8 on the 10-point scale. What is it you were doing that made the problem improve?

The problem stayed constant at 9 all week. How did you prevent it from getting worse?

The problem went from 7 to 9 over the last week. You mentioned that in the past it has been as high as 10. How did you prevent things from completely deteriorating this past week?

Where monitoring charts show that specific factors are associated with problems, ways of eliminating these may be examined. For example, in the case of asthma, the level of dust in a child's environment may be reduced. If eliminating these factors is not possible, ways of helping clients cope with these factors may be explored. Where clear family interaction patterns are associated with problems, family members may be invited to brainstorm ways of altering these interpersonal sequences.

Encouraging Restraint

The MRI school have shown that clients' unsuccessful attempted solutions may maintain their problems (Segal, 1991). Such problem-maintaining interaction patterns may be disrupted by inviting them to stop trying to solve their problems in the way that they have been doing and postpone any new attempt at problem solving until they have thought things through carefully.

This is a complex problem. There is a danger that if you try to change things before we fully understand the problem, then it may get worse. So I am inviting you to be patient and try not to make any major changes until we have a clearer understanding of this complex problem. Is that OK with you?

Practising Symptoms

With some problems, such as children's involuntary tics, or anxious clients' tendency to ruminate, clients may be invited to practise the symptoms so as to gain control over them. The process of practice (especially if other family members support the person doing the practice) reduces anxiety about the symptoms and helps the person with the symptom begin to control them. Here is and example of how to offer such a task:

> *These tics seem to be completely outside your control at present and to be interfering with your life. To get control over them, I'm inviting you to take 10 minutes each day to practise doing them so that you can learn how to be in charge of them. It would be important for your Father/Mother to be with you during these practice sessions to give you support. Is this an invitation that you could accept?*

Graded Challenges

In cases where clients' fear and anxiety lead them to avoid particular situations, it may be appropriate to invite them to work towards facing the situation they fear most by gradually facing increasingly threatening situations. This type of intervention is appropriate where the fear is related to going out of the house, going to school, having sex, public speaking, going on airplanes, and so forth. For example, in families where a member has agoraphobia and panic attacks, it may be appropriate to invite the family to escort the person with agoraphobia on increasingly longer outings to learn how to cope with such challenges in a supportive context. For example:

> *You have mentioned that you find these situations very threatening. One way to learn how to cope with these is to start with the situations that are least threatening. To go into these with someone who you trust and you know will support you and then hang in there until your anxiety subsides. I'm wondering if that is something you would be willing to do?*

Where families contain a member who has become inactive, perhaps due to depression or schizophrenia, it may be appropriate to invite the family to engage the depressed person in increasingly more demanding pleasant activities. For example:

> *One way to improve your mood and sense of well-being is to become more active. But that's a big step to take all in one go. Some people find its easier to plan to do just one small activity each day, and when they have done this for a week, plan to do a slightly bigger activity each day and so on. This works best if someone in the family does these activities with you, so you have some support and company. Is this something you would like to consider?*

Skills Training

Clients may have difficulties communicating clearly and solving problems because they lack the skills or because intoxication, negative mood states or other factors interfere with the use of well-developed skills. Where such factors are present, therapy should focus on removing these obstacles to effective communication and problem solving. Where families have poorly developed communication and problem-solving skills, and their poorly developed skills either maintain the problem or prevent its resolution, skills training in these two areas may be appropriate. Communication and problem-solving skills training is central to the practice of behavioural family therapy (Epstein, 2003).

Communication Skills Training

Communication skills may be artificially subdivided into those used for listening and those used for telling somebody something. These skills are listed in Table 9.2. Clients need, first, to be given an intellectual understanding of these skills. Then the therapist should model the skills for the clients. Clients should at this point be invited to try using the skills to discuss a neutral topic in the session. Let the episode of communication run for 5–10 minutes, and take notes of various difficulties that occur. Then give positive feedback on those skills that were effectively used and, in the light of this, ask clients to complete the episode again.

Typical mistakes include: interrupting before the other person has finished; failing to summarise what the other person said accurately; attributing negative malicious intentions to the other person when they have not communicated that they hold such intentions; failing to check that the message was accurately sent; failing to check that the message has been accurately received; blaming; and sulking. The challenge in effective communication skills training is to help the clients avoid these mistakes, by praising them for gradual approximations to good communication. Criticising clients for making mistakes tends to threaten the integrity of the therapeutic alliance and has little impact on skill refinement.

Table 9.2 Guidelines for listening and communications skills

Specific guidelines	General guidelines
Listening skills	Make a time and place for clear
Listen without interruption	communication
Summarise key points	Remove distractions and turn off the TV
Check that you have understood	Discuss one problem at a time
accurately	Try to listen with the intention of
Reply	accurately remembering what was said
Communication skills	Try to listen without judging what is being
Decide on specific key points	said
Organise them logically	Avoid negative mind-reading
Say them clearly	State your points without attacking the
Check you have been	other person
understood	Avoid blaming, sulking or abusing
Allow space for a reply	Avoid interruptions
	Take turns fairly
	Be brief
	Make congruent 'I statements'

Once clients can use the skills to exchange views on a neutral topic, they may then be invited to use the skills to exchange views on emotionally-loaded issues, first in the session and then later at home. Communication homework assignments should be highly specific, to prevent clients from lapsing into poor communication habits. Thus, specific members of a family should be invited to find out the other person's views on a specific topic. A time and place free of distractions should be agreed and a time limit of no more than 20 minutes set for initial communication assignments and 40 minutes when skills are better developed.

Here are two useful questions to check that clients have an intellectual appreciation of the essential features of both sets of skills.

Let me check if we share the same understanding of communication skills? When you want to tell ABC something really important, first you decide what points you want to make. Then you put them in some kind of logical order and mentally rehearse them. Then you tell her what you just rehearsed and check that she has understood you. Does that sort of framework make sense to you?

Let's talk about listening skills. We hear people saying things all the time but when we really want to listen what do we do? Like, if I really want to listen to you, I hear you out, without interruption. I summarise the main points that you've made and check that is what you meant. Then, when I'm sure I've received your message accurately, I reply with what I think about it. Can you accept that sort of breakdown of listening skills? Hear the person out. Summarise. Check. Then reply?

Here is a question that can be asked to find out if clients are prepared to use communication skills at the appropriate times to break the cycle of interaction around the presenting problem, and what they perceive as the main factors that would prevent them from doing so:

I'm wondering what you see as the main things that would stop you from using these skills when you see things beginning to go wrong and you know you need to make space to discuss it?

To identify barriers to using communication skills with a particular dyad, ask them to find out what opinions they hold in common and on what points they differ in relation to a topic relevant to the presenting problem. Here is a typical invitation to complete such a task in the therapy session:

You both seem to have a good grasp of what it takes to communicate clearly. So I don't fully understand why this does not happen when you sit down to discuss this problem. Show me how you do it. I'm asking you to find out on which three or four points you agree and on which points you disagree when it comes to dealing with these difficulties. Go ahead.

Problem-solving Skills

In problem-solving training, the sequence of stages described for communication training should be followed with a progression from an explanation of the skills listed in Table 9.3 to modelling, to rehearsal in the session with the focus on a neutral topic. Positive feedback for successive approximations to good problem solving should be given during rehearsal until the skills are well developed. Criticism for mistakes should be avoided. Then clients may be invited to use the skills to solve emotionally-laden problems. When families are observed trying to solve emotionally-laden problems, often the first pitfalls they slide into is that of problem definition. Many clients need to be coached in how to translate a big vague problem into a few small, specific problems. A second pitfall involves trying to solve more than one problem at a time. A third area of difficulty is helping clients to hold off on evaluating the pros and cons of any one solution until as many solutions as possible have been listed. This is important, since premature evaluating can stifle the production of creative solutions. Often families need to be coached out of bad communication habits in problem-solving training, such as negative mind reading where they attribute negative thoughts or feelings to others, blaming, sulking and abusing others. Where families with chronic problems successfully resolve a difficulty, a vital part of the coaching process is to help them celebrate this victory.

Table 9.3 Guidelines for problem-solving skills

Specific guidelines	General guidelines
Define the problem	Make a time and place for clear communication
Brainstorm options	
Explore pros and cons	Remove distractions and turn off the TV
Agree on a joint action plan	
Implement the plan	Discuss one problem at a time
Review progress	Divide one big problem into a few small problems
Revise the original plan	
	Tackle problems one at a time
	Avoid vague problem definitions
	Define problems briefly
	Show that the problem (not the person) makes you feel bad
	Acknowledge your share of the responsibility in causing the problem
	Do not explore pros and cons until you have finished brainstorming
	Celebrate success

Here is a useful question to introduce problem-solving skills:

Tricky problems need a systematic approach. You can divide up problem solving into steps. First, state the problem specifically. Next, think about lots of different ways to solve it. It doesn't matter if some of these options are strange or unusual. Just get as many options out in the open as possible. Then look at the pros and cons of each and finally select the one that suits everybody best. So that's it. Define the problem, list the options, weigh up the pros and cons and then select the best one. I suppose some of the time you'd do something like this?

In order to check what prevents clients from using their problem-solving skills and to coach them in how to manage these resistances and blockages, the following questions may be asked:

You sometimes use a fairly systematic method for solving problems like dealing with a power cut or cooking Christmas dinner. Now the big question is, what gets in the way of you using these systematic problem-solving skills when you try to sort out this problem here?

When you ask clients to take 10 minutes to show you how they use their problem-solving skills by addressing some aspect of the presenting problem, many of the blockages and resistances will become apparent. Here is an example of the type of question that may be used to invite clients to do this:

One problem you face is finding a way to support each other so you don't get stressed out by this whole thing. Take about 10 minutes now to show me how you tackle this problem systematically and come up with a concrete plan that you can both follow through on. A plan that will provide both of you with a sense of being supported. Go ahead now.

Changing Behavioural Consequences

When families' main difficulties are child-focused behavioural or emotional problems, using reward systems and behaviour control routines are particularly useful interventions. They provide families with alternative routines to the problem-maintaining behaviour patterns in which they have become embroiled, insofar as they alter the typical consequences of the child's behaviour. Both of these interventions derive from the behavioural family therapy tradition (Epstein, 2003).

Reward Systems

Guidelines for using rewards systems are presented in Table 9.4. It is critical that the target behaviour is clearly defined, is monitored regularly,

Table 9.4 Guidelines for reward systems

Specific guidelines	General guidelines
Define the target behaviour clearly	Present the reward system to your child
Decide when and where the monitoring will occur	as a way of helping him or her learn grown-up habits
Make a smiling-face chart or points chart	All parental figures in the child's network should understand and agree to using the system
Explain to the child that they can win points or smiling faces by carrying out the target behaviour	Use a chart that is age-appropriate. Smiling faces or stars are good for children and points may be used for adolescents
Ask the child to list a set of prizes that they would like to be able to buy with their points or smiling faces	The sooner points are given after completing the target behaviour, the quicker the child will learn
Agree on how many points or faces are necessary to buy each prize	Highly valued prizes lead to faster learning
Follow through on the plan and review it for effectiveness	Try to fine tune the system so that successes are maximised
	If prizes are not being won, make the target behaviour smaller and clearer, or the cost of prizes lower, and make sure that all parent figures understand and are committed to using the system
	If the system is not working, do not criticise the child
	Always keep the number of target behaviours below five

rewarded promptly, using a symbolic system of points, tokens or stars that is age appropriate and acceptable to the child. The symbolic reward system must be backed by tangible rewards or prizes that are highly valued, so that the child may buy these with points or tokens after they have accumulated a sufficient number. When points systems are ineffective, it may be that some adult in the child's environment, such as a non-custodial parent in the case of children from separated families, is not committed to implementing the system. In other instances, the target behaviours may be ambiguous or the number of points required to win a prize too high. Trouble-shooting these difficulties is a routine part of coaching families in using reward systems.

Behavioural Control Skills

Guidelines for a behavioural control programme are set out in Table 9.5. The programme should be framed as a way for helping the child to

Table 9.5 Guidelines for behaviour-control programmes

Specific guidelines	General guidelines

Behaviour Control Programme
  Agree on a few clear rules
  Set clear consequences
  Follow through
  Reward good behaviour
  Use time-out or loss of privileges for
    rule breaking
  Monitor change visibly
 	
Time-out
  Give two warnings
  Bring the child to time-out without
    negative emotion
  After five minutes engage the child
    in a positive activity and praise
    him for temper control
  If rule-breaking continues, return
    child to time-out until 30 seconds
    of quietness occurs
  Engage in positive activity with
    child and praise for temper control
	Set out with the expectation that you
	  can teach your child one good habit
	  at a time
	Build in episodes of unconditional
	  special time into behavioural control
	  programme
	Frame the programme as learning self-
	  control
	Involve the child in filling in,
	  designing and using the monitoring
	  chart or system
	Monitor increases in positive
	  behaviour as well as decreases in
	  negative behaviour
	Do not hold grudges after episodes of
	  negative behaviour
	Avoid negative mind reading
	Avoid blaming, sulking or abusing
	Ask for spouse support when you feel
	  bad about the programme
	Celebrate success

develop self-control skills. Specific negative or aggressive behaviours are defined as targets for which time-out from reinforcement is given. When these behaviours occur, the parent gives a command to the child to stop and this may be followed up by two warnings. If children comply they are praised. If not they are brought to time-out without any display of anger or any reasoned explanation being given at that time. The time for reasoned explanation is at the outset of the programme or when it is being reviewed, not following misbehaviour. During time-out, the child sits on a chair in the corner of the kitchen, the hall or their bedroom away from family activities and interesting or reinforcing events or toys. Following a period of 2–5 minutes (depending on the child's age), the child is invited to rejoin family activities and is engaged in a stimulating and rewarding exchange with the parent. If children misbehave or protest aggressively while in time-out, they remain there until they have been compliant and quiet for 30 seconds before rejoining family activities and engaging in a stimulating interaction with the parent. Running a behavioural control programme for the first two weeks is very stressful for most families. The normal pattern is for the time-out period to increase in length gradually and then eventually to begin to diminish. During this escalation period when the child is testing out the parents' resolve and having a last binge of self-indulgence before learning self-control, it is important to help families maintain the unconditionally supportive aspect of family life. There are two important interventions that may be useful here. First, spouses may be invited to set aside special time where the focus is on mutual marital support. Second, parents may plan episodes of supportive play with the children. The important feature of spouse support is that the couple set aside time to spend together without the children to talk to each other about issues unrelated to the children. In single-parent families, parents may be helped to explore ways of obtaining support from their network of friends and members of the extended family.

Clients' intellectual understanding of the skills necessary to teach children self-control may be checked with the following type of question:

> *Let's just think about how we go about teaching children to control their tempers or how to follow rules. Everybody has strong opinions about this so I'll just talk about what scientists have found out about it when they have talked to thousands of families in different countries and followed them up over a number of years. Children learn self-control best when the rules about what they can and can't do are clear, when it's clear what will happen to them if they do or don't follow the rules, when parents always follow through and reward good behaviour but don't reward bad behaviour and when improvements in self-control over time are talked about regularly. Does that fit with what you have seen with your own children?*

The following question throws light on factors that block parents' attempts to help their children internalise rules and develop a sense of self-control:

> *When ABC has a tantrum or breaks his sister's toys you say you sometimes scream at him or spank him and other times you ignore him and occasionally you try to reason with him. Do you think that if you made a plan to do the same sort of thing each time – say like putting him in his room until he controls his temper – that you would be able to follow through…(after answer)…What would prevent you from following through?*

Many parents who have, in their opinion, *tried everything* and failed to teach their children self-control, feel powerless and have lost faith in any method for helping their youngsters control their tempers and other impulses. They usually express this sense of personal helplessness by blaming the child or the method. So, they say their child would not respond because he is intrinsically bad or because the method is useless. Other parents will admit that they would be unable to contain their own anger and frustration and would give vent to this by screaming or hitting. A vital part of dealing with these resistances is empathising with the parents' sense of exasperation and defeat without agreeing that behavioural control programmes are ineffective. Here is an example of how this was put to one parent:

It sounds like you've tried everything and got nowhere. You feel like he will never learn how to control his temper. You doubt that anything will work. I know that the programme we use here works. It takes time. It takes energy. Your boy will really test you out for a while when you try this programme so things will get worse before they get better. But in the end it works. However, you need to be ready. You need to have got your energy up and to be determined to help him avoid becoming a delinquent. I could understand it if you said you wanted to wait a while.

Once parents and children agree to become involved in a behavioural control programme, the heart of the coaching process is facilitating planning. Both parents must accept the plan and with teenagers particularly, youngsters need to play an active role in contributing to the plan to help them learn self-control. Here are some useful questions to ask or statements to make when facilitating planning a behavioural control programme:

It sounds like ABC has a number of urges that she needs to learn how to control. One is the urge to hit people, another is the urge to break things, another is the urge to stay out past bedtime. Now, of all these urges, what is the main one you want her to learn to control?

Some families like to use a chart and every time the youngster makes it through a period without losing control of his temper he gets a point on this chart. At the end of the week the points can be cashed in for a prize. Other families prefer to use a token jar. Every time an hour goes by and the youngster has controlled his temper for the hour a token goes into the jar. These can be used to get a prize at the end of the week. Which system do you think would suit your situation?

This is the way time-out works. You give two warnings first. Like this. ABC, please try to control your temper. This is your first warning. ABC, please try to control your temper. This is your second warning. Then if ABC can't control her temper, walk her to time-out (her bedroom) like this. No fuss. No shouting. Just walking. Then say: 'Take five minutes to control your temper and when you are done we will play a game of snakes and ladders' (or whatever game ABC and yourself like). If you open the door at five minutes and she shouts at you, close it for 30 seconds, then open it again if she has stopped. Keep this up until ABC can show self-control for 30 seconds. Then ask her to come out to play with you. ABC only gets out of time-out when she has shown that she can control her temper for 30 seconds after the first five-minute period. Can you run through this time out routine so I'm sure I've said it clearly?

ABC, when you go into time-out your job is to control Angry Alice (the name we gave ABC's temper) so she doesn't keep stopping you from having fun and being friends with your mum and brother. There are different things you could do. You could let Angry Alice scream and scream for five minutes. You could let Angry Alice hit the mattress one hundred times with the pillow. You could tell Angry Alice your favourite story or sing her a song. Now which of these things would you most like to do to teach Angry Alice how to control herself?

Invitations to Complete Tasks

When inviting family members to carry out tasks, such as those described so far in this chapter, it is important to keep in mind the typically low level of adherence to medical regimes. On average, patients forget about 50% of the information given to them by their doctors about their illnesses and treatment regimes and about 40% do not cooperate with their doctor's advice (Carr, 1997). Thus, almost half of the time it is reasonable to expect clients not to cooperate when invited to complete homework assignments. This level of expectation will prevent you from unnecessary self-criticism, client-criticism and other countertransference reactions. Here are 10 guidelines that make it more probable that clients will follow-through on invitations to complete tasks.

1. Design simple tasks to fulfil specific functions or goals.
2. Offer invitations to carry out tasks clearly in simple language, inviting clients to do specific things.
3. Describe tasks briefly and break complex tasks into parts.
4. Check that the clients have understood the task.
5. Give a rationale for the tasks.
6. Emphasise the importance of the task.
7. Write down complex tasks.
8. Mention any potentially negative side effects of the task.
9. State that the outcome of the task will be discussed at the next session and convey an expectation of cooperation and success.
10. Always review tasks.

INTERVENTIONS FOCUSING ON BELIEF SYSTEMS

A number of interventions that aim to transform belief systems and narratives that subserve problem-maintaining behaviour patterns are listed in Table 9.1. These include:

- addressing ambivalence
- highlighting strengths
- reframing problems
- presenting multiple perspectives
- externalising problems and building on exceptions.

All of these belief-focused interventions help clients develop more empowering narratives about themselves and their capacity to solve their problems.

Addressing Ambivalence

Making a contract to engage in any stage of family therapy is not just a discrete event, it is also an ongoing process. Different family members' commitment to the contract may fluctuate in differing ways over the course of therapy. It was noted in Chapter 7 that resistance to therapeutic progress is a common occurrence in family therapy. In some instances, this resistance occurs because family members are ambivalent about the process of change. That is, they begin to doubt that the benefits of achieving therapeutic goals outweigh the costs of change, because change inevitably entails personal costs. When this occurs, the central task in family therapy is to suspend all attempts at empowering clients to achieve their stated therapeutic goals and focus all therapeutic effort on addressing this ambivalence, no matter how long this takes. Only when clients have addressed their personal dilemmas about the costs of maintaining the status quo and the costs of changing their situation, will they be in a position to return to the process of therapeutic problem solving. The main therapeutic task is to help all family members clearly and explicitly articulate their beliefs about the costs of change and to empathise with this ambivalence. It is vital to avoid any hint of criticism, since most clients when they experience ambivalence are already engaging in covert self-criticism. Here are some questions that may be asked to help clients address ambivalence:

> After you left last week I was thinking about how difficult this problem is. I was thinking how much effort it's going to take to solve it. So today I'm wondering if you have had second thoughts about trying to sort it out?

> I sense that you believe you are between a rock and a hard place today. That you believe the costs of following through on the plans you have been making are too high. Let's take some time to talk about that today. What do you believe the downside will be for you in sorting this problem out?

> What do you think your mother/father/brother/sister believes the downside of sorting this problem out will be?

> Some people have a secret belief that some disaster will happen if they sort these types of problems out. If your mother/father/brother/sister had such a secret belief, what do you think it would be?

> Some people have a secret belief that certain relationships will suffer if they sort these types of problems out. If your mother/father/brother/sister had such a secret belief, what do you think it would be?

> I'm wondering if each of you would take a pen and paper now and list all the hassles you believe you will have to face if you take all the steps necessary to solve this problem. List the hassles you will face while solving the problem. Also when the problem is solved, imagine all the difficulties you believe this will create for you. When everyone in the family has done this, I will invite each of you to read out your list.

> To what extent do you believe that your mother/father/brother/sister's views about the downside of solving this problem are due to feelings of being powerless right now?

> Under what circumstances do you think this sense of powerlessness will be replaced by a sense of strength?

> From what you have said, it sounds like you each have good reasons to be wary of changing at this point. For you, ABC, it's the belief that change will involve

DEF. For you, GHI, it's the belief that working to solve this problem will mean that you have to do JKL. And for you, MNO, your belief that PQR will happen if this problem is resolved makes working for change a threatening affair. You all face a difficult dilemma here. The problem you have is making life difficult for everyone, but the costs of solving it are very high. My invitation to you is that we use the next couple of sessions to explore this dilemma further. Is that something you would like to do?

Highlighting Strengths

The importance of formulating exceptions and strengths as well as problems during the assessment stage was a central theme of Chapter 8. In addition to this relatively large-scale task, it is also important on a moment-to-moment basis during all stages of the therapeutic process to avail of opportunities to highlight clients' strengths. When clients have difficult or chronic problems, they become demoralised and develop beliefs that they are powerless to change their situation. Highlighting strengths reduces demoralisation and helps clients construct personal and family narratives about their ability to solve their own problems. Relabelling and pinpointing are two useful techniques for highlighting strengths.

With relabelling, the therapist routinely offers positive or optimistic labels for ambiguous behaviour as a substitute for negative or pessimistic labels or attributions. So where a parent says:

He was standing there *lazy and stupid* doing nothing, so I *told* him to get on with it,

the therapist may relabel this by saying:

When he was there *thinking through what to do next,* you *encouraged* him to start his homework.

Where a parent says:

She needs to be at home when she is this *ill,*

the sentiment may be reframed as:

While she is *recovering,* she needs to spend some time at home.

Pinpointing is a way of drawing attention to frequently used but unacknowledged individual and family strengths. Here are some examples;

The thing that really stands out for me is how carefully you are all thinking about this problem.

I'm struck by how open you each are to listening to each other's viewpoints even when you completely disagree with each other.

One thing that has arisen from this session is a sense of how much you support each other during this difficult time.

The central point to come out of this difficult session is how you are prepared to stick together against all odds, where other families would have fallen apart.

An outstanding strength that you have is this. You all feel very deeply about these issues.

In Chapter 7, in the section on genogram construction, ways in which this process can be used to pinpoint strengths are outlined.

Reframing Problems

With reframing, clients are offered a new framework within which to conceptualise a sequence of events, and this new way of conceptualising the sequence of events makes it more likely that the problem will be resolved rather than maintained (Carr, 1995). When a family therapist reframes a problem, the problem is framed in interactional terms rather than individual terms; solvable terms rather than uncontrollable or fixed terms; and family members' reasons for engaging in problem-maintaining behaviour are framed as arising from positive rather than negative intentions.

Here are a couple of examples of reframes. A distressed couple insisted that the main problem was that the other person was to blame because the other partner was a vindictive, mean selfish 'bastard' or 'bitch'. The following reframing was offered:

When you disagree with each other strongly, you both end up blaming each other and calling each other names. From what you have each said to me, the main reason you do this is because each of you feels disappointed. A deep sense of loss that your wish for your partner to meet your needs has not been met. Does that way of looking at the situation fit with your experience?

The parents of a teenager who was involved in drug-abuse and who viewed it as a sign of 'psychiatric illness' requiring hospitalisation, medication and individualised treatment were offered the following reframing.

It looks to us like your son letting you find out about his drug abuse is an important message. Since you have found out about it you have devoted a lot of time and effort to put him back on the right road. The road to maturity. The road to being grown up and making his own way in the world. For these reasons it seems important to us that you both be centrally involved in helping him recover. He needs you to help him grow up.

Presenting Multiple Perspectives

Family members with different viewpoints often become embroiled in black-and-white, either-or arguments about which viewpoint is true or right. They find it difficult to move to a cooperative both-and position where problem-solving efforts can be pooled. In such instances, especially when trying to solve complex problems, it is often very helpful for families to have access to multiple perspectives on their difficulties and multiple potential options for the resolution of these; within a frame that challenges either-or, black-and-white thinking. Presenting multiple perspectives on a problem may allow the therapist or team to empathise with a variety of family members' differing viewpoints; highlight the two sides of the dilemma the family face; underline a polarisation of viewpoints within the family, the network or the therapeutic system; and suggest that new solutions may emerge by considering and synthesising polarised positions. The idea of presenting families with multiple perspectives has evolved from the work of the original Milan systemic family therapy team (Campbell, 1999; Campbell et al., 1991), from Peggy Papp's (1983) idea of the team taking the role of a Greek Chorus, from Tom Anderson's (1991) work on the reflecting team and from the Fifth Province practice of remembering opposites (McCarthy & Byrne, 1988). From these various contributions, two distinct clinical practices may be identified: presenting families with pre-prepared split messages about their problems, and offering families the opportunity to observe a reflecting team discussing their difficulties.

Split messages are commonly prepared by a therapist with or without a team during a break towards the end of a session and then given to the family in the final part of the session. Sometimes, it is helpful (more for the therapist than the family) to write out the main points in the split message and read it to the family after the intersession break. Here is an example of a split message used to simply empathise with the viewpoints of differing family members and so strengthen the therapeutic alliance:

During the break the team have been discussing the complex and difficult problems that you face. The men on the team understand your concerns ABC as a father. You are clearly torn between your duties at work and the need you feel to be more involved at home. The women on the team were impressed by the challenges you face, DEF, as a mother. You are trying to run this household single-handed and deal with GHI's recent problems at school with little support from anyone. The youngest member of our team was struck by the courage you have been showing, JKL, as a daughter and a young woman, in trying to keep going every day, despite the huge setbacks you have faced over the last year. My own view is that the solidarity you show as a family is a good prognostic sign. It suggests that you would probably be able to use our services to solve your current difficulties. So we are inviting you to continue this process of searching for a new way to handle this difficulty. I'll answer any questions you have now.

Where families face a difficult dilemma, a perspective on the validity of each course of action may be presented as a split message, as in the following example:

> *I'm struck by the fact that there are two different ways of looking at this thing. On the one hand you could say, this problem has been with us for too long. Its really time now to plan a way out of this mess no matter what it takes. On the other hand, you could say, changing our situation. Taking on this problem. Trying to agree on a plan. And then trying to follow through is going to lead to more fighting, more conflict, more hassle. It's just not worth it. Let's pull out now to avoid further disappointment. These are two different viewpoints. Both are valid. Between now and the next session you may wish to think about each of these different positions.*

Where factions within the family or network hold polarised viewpoints and are unable to reach a consensus because they believe that one view is right and the other is wrong, then presenting multiple perspectives may help them see that all viewpoints have some validity and that the central therapeutic task is to find a shared perspective that helps resolve the problem (rather than the right answer or the one true perspective).

> *The team were impressed by the strength with which each of you hold your differing viewpoints on how best to tackle this problem. They were, however, divided in their views. Half of the team, like you Mrs ABC thought that this is a situation that requires a softly, softly approach, because they know that in the past ABC has responded to this and so may do so again. The other half of the team took your approach Mr ABC. They believed that a strict, firm but fair approach was called for. They feared the worst if the problem was not nipped in the bud. However, there was a consensus among all of us, that whichever approach you go for in the end that you will need to agree on it or it will be very confusing for your child, DEF.*

With reflecting team practice, during a break towards the end of the session, the family are invited to observe the team reflecting on the interview that has just occurred between the family and the therapist. The reflections may offer comment on the problem, explanations for it and possible solutions. In reflecting team practice it is important to use the clients' own language and avoid jargon; to frame comments respectfully and empathetically; and to highlight family strengths that may contribute to a solution. Here are some reflections from such practice where a family have a child with a chronic illness:

> (Team member 1) *One thing that went through my mind when I was listening to that conversation is how committed everyone is solving this problem that, on the face of it, seems overwhelming.*

> (Team member 2) *It occurred to me how brave ABC was being. Really brave. Having this chronic illness, but just hanging in there and keeping going. That really stood out for me. The idea that being brave and keeping going are the way to do it.*

(Team member 3) *I felt like I could see DEF's point of view very clearly. You know. The idea that sometimes it easier just to turn off. Tune out. As a sort of survival thing. Like, if you let yourself worry about this sort of stuff all the time, then it would be too much.*

(Team member 4) *I was struck by how GHI explained her sense of exhaustion and then linking that to the really busy schedule she has. And then linking that back to the demands of caring for a child with a chronic illness. In all that I was hearing a need for sharing the load a bit more.*

(Team-member 1) *Another thing that was really clear to me was the idea that there is a better way to do things. I think that was an idea mentioned by everyone especially ABC. I think these were the main themes that came up for us today. Will we leave it there? The invitation is now for ABC, DEF and GHI to discuss and reflect on our comments. To see what fits and what doesn't. Ok?*

Externalising Problems and Building on Exceptions

With externalising problems and building on exceptions the overall aim is to help clients first separate out the problem from the person; identify the effects of the problem on the person; identify and amplify situations in which the person was able to modify or avoid the problem including recent pre-therapy changes; develop a self-narrative that centralises these competencies; empower the person who has overcome the problem to let other network members know about these competencies and support their development; and develop a personal narrative that links the current life exceptions to clients' past and future. This resource-based approach to therapy has been pioneered by narrative (Freedman & Combs, 1996) and solution-focused (Miller et al., 1996) therapists.

It is common when externalising the problem with childen to give the problem a name so that it is personified. For example, with soiling, the problem may be named Sneaky Poo (following Michael White's practice); with covert problems, Mr Mischief; with aggression, the Hammerman; or with compulsions, Tidy Checker. Here is an example of a line of questioning that aims to externalise a child's difficulties in controlling aggression and build on exceptions:

Let us call the force that makes you hit people you care about the Hammerman, OK? What age were you when you first noticed the Hammerman was affecting your life?

Did the Hammerman make things between you and your mum/dad/brother/sister/ friends/teachers, better or worse?

Tell me about a time when the Hammerman was trying to make things between you and your mum/dad/brother/sister/friends/teachers go wrong, and you stopped him?

How did you stop the Hammerman, that one time?

Who was there?

What happened before you beat him?

How did you beat him?

How did you feel afterwards?

What happened then?

You beat the Hammerman that one time. Were there others?

Because you have beaten the Hammerman, what does that say about you as a person?

Does it say that you are becoming strong? Grown-up? Smarter?

Would you be interested in noticing over the next week how you will beat the Hammerman again?

Will you come back and tell me the story about how you beat him again?

When you beat him again, you will receive a certificate for beating the Hammerman and copies of this will be sent to a list of people you think should know about your victory. Will you think about who should be on that list?

With adults, it may be less developmentally appropriate to personify problems, although often people do. For example, Churchill referred to depression as his 'Black Dog'. The following line of questioning is addressed to an adult with depression and makes use of pre-session changes (which are quite common) as a way of identifying exceptions:

When did you first notice depression was coming into your life?

How long have you been fighting against depression?

How has depression been affecting your relationships with your husband/wife/son/ daughter/friends/people at work?

What feeds depression?

What starves depression?

If 10 means you are really winning the fight against depression and 1 means you are losing, right now much are you winning?

When you called for an appointment a week ago, how much were you winning on this 10-point scale?

You say you are winning more now than a week ago. You have moved from 2 up to 4 on this 10-point scale. What have you been doing to beat depression?

Take one incident when you noticed you were beating depression last week. Talk me through it as if I was looking at a video.

Who was there?

What happened before during and after this fight with depression?

You beat depression that time, what does that say about you as a person?

Does it mean that you are powerful? That you have stamina? That you are a survivor?

Would you be interested in noticing over the next week how you will overcome depression again?

Will you come back and tell me how you overcame depression again?

Who in your family or circle of friends could be on your team in this fight against depression?

Will you think about how we could connect with them. Maybe we could invite them to a session, when you have had a number of victories and they could listen to your story and offer their congratulations?

When clients begin to show change and master their problems, lines of questioning such as the following, drawn for the work of Michael White (1995), help clients consolidate new personal narratives and belief systems about themselves and their competence in managing their problems. This line of questioning links the exception to the person's past and into their future.

If I were watching you earlier in your life, what do you think I would have seen that would have helped me to understand how you were able recently to beat depression?

What does this tell you and I about what you have wanted for your life?

If you were to keep these ideas in mind over the next while, how might they have an effect on your life?

If you found yourself taking new steps towards your preferred view of yourself as a person, what would we see?

How would these actions confirm your preferred view of yourself?

What difference would this confirmation make to how you lived your life.

Of all those people who know you, who might be best placed to throw light on how you developed these ideas and practices?

INTERVENTIONS THAT FOCUS ON HISTORICAL, CONTEXTUAL AND CONSTITUTIONAL FACTORS

Interventions that aim to modify the impact of historical, contextual and constitutional predisposing factors or mobilise protective factors within these areas include the following:

- addressing family-of-origin issues
- addressing contextual issues
- addressing constitutional factors.

Addressing Family-of-origin Issues

Where parents or spouses have difficulty making progress in marital or family therapy by altering problem-maintaining behaviour patterns or the belief systems that directly underpin these in response to interventions listed in the right-hand and middle column of Table 9.1, it may be the case that unresolved family-of-origin issues are preventing them form making progress. These issues may include the following:

Major family-of-origin stresses

1. bereavements
2. separations
3. child abuse
4. social disadvantage
5. institutional upbringing.

Family-of-origin parents–child problems

1. insecure attachment
2. authoritarian parenting
3. permissive parenting
4. neglectful parenting
5. inconsistent parental discipline
6. lack of stimulation
7. scapegoating
8. triangulation.

Family-of-origin parental problems

1. parental psychological problems
2. parental drug or alcohol abuse
3. parental criminality
4. marital discord or violence
5. family disorganisation.

In such instances, it may be worth exploring transgenerational patterns, scripts and myths to help clients understand how relationship habits from their family of origin are influencing their current life situation. In some instances, it may be necessary to help clients access, express and integrate emotions that underpin destructive relationship habits. In others, it may be valuable to coach clients to reconnect with parents from whom they have become cut-off, so they can become free of triangulation in their families of origin and so stop replicating this in their families of procreation. Typically this work, which has the potential to address core identity issues and painful unresolved feelings, is done in sessions attended by couples or individuals, without their children being present.

Exploring

Clients may be invited to explore transgenerational patterns, scripts and myths relevant to their difficulties in making therapeutic progress in a wide variety of ways. Genogram construction, which was described in Chapter 7, is a useful starting point. Once the genogram is fully drawn, the client may be invited to begin exploring family-of-origin issues, relevant to resolving the presenting problem with lines of questioning like that presented below. This approach draws on the ideas and practices of transgenerational family therapy (Kerr, 2003; Nelson, 2003; Nichols, 2003; Roberto-Forman, 2002), object relations-based family therapy (Savage-Scharff & Bagini, 2002; Savage-Scharf & Scharf, 2003), approaches to family therapy that have their roots in attachment theory (Johnson, 2003a; Byng-Hall, 1995), and experiential family therapy (Volker, 2003).

I have noticed that no matter how hard you try to make sense of this problem and tackle it in a sensible way, you end up in difficulty. You have a way that you would like your relationships to be with your partner and children, but you just can't seem to get your relationships with them to work like that. Something is blocking you. One possibility is that you are carrying relationship habits from your family of origin in the back of your mind, and any time you are under stress you fall into these old habits. Would you like to explore this possibility?

The advantages of this type of exploration is that it may help you pinpoint some part of your past that is getting in the way of you living your life as you would like in the present. The disadvantage is that it may take time and effort and lead nowhere or to discoveries you would rather not have made. So are you sure this is still something you would like to explore?

Look at your genogram and think about what have been the most important relationships in your life?

What relationship habits did you learn from these relationships?

In these relationships how did you learn to live with giving and receiving care and support?

Tell me how your parents and siblings received and gave support to each other?

In these relationships, what did you learn about the way people should communicate with each other in families. How should parents and children or mothers and fathers talk to each other?

Tell me how your parents and siblings talked to each other about important issues?

In these relationships how did you learn to deal with leading and following, the whole issue of managing power?

Tell me about who was in charge in your family of origin and how others fitted in around this?

In your family of origin, how did you learn to deal with conflict?

What happened when your parents or siblings didn't agree about an important issue?

What about triangles. Did people get stuck in triangles in your family of origin?

Was anyone piggy in the middle between your parents or two other people?

Did you and your siblings fall into two camps, backing your mum or your dad in some triangle situations?

Are you still involved in a triangle in your family of origin?

Who have you stayed close to?

Who have you cut off?

Have you ever tried to reconnect from your cut-off parent?

What are you avoiding by being cut off – what is the disaster you guess would happen if you spoke intimately with the person from whom you are cut off?

What does this exploration tell you about the possible relationship habits you have learned from your parents, siblings and other family members?

When you try to do the sensible thing in solving the problem you have with your partner and children and that brought you into therapy, how do these relationship habits interfere with this?

Do you think that there are situations in which you can control the urge to follow through on these relationship habits you have received from your parents, sibling and other family members?

What is it about these situations that allows you to break these chains, these destructive relationship habits?

Would you like to explore ways of weakening their influence on you?

Before making this decision, I am inviting you to look at the downside of changing your relationship habits. One big problem is this: if you change the relationship habits you learned from your parents, you may be being disloyal to them. What are the consequences of that for you and for your relationship with them?

Lines of questioning such as this, conducted over a number of sessions, may lead in some instances to a realisation that family-of-origin issues are interfering with effective problem solving in the family of procreation. They may also lead clients to want to change these. Awareness of destructive relationship habits learned in the family of origin is rarely enough to liberate clients from slavishly following these habits when under stress.

Re-experiencing

One way to help clients weaken these relationship habits is create a context within which they can remember and re-experience the highly emotional situations in which they learned them, and integrate these forgotten and destructive experiences into their conscious narrative about themselves. Clients may be invited within therapy sessions, to close their eyes and visualise their memories of specific situations in which they learned specific relationship habits and tolerate experiencing the intense negative affect that accompanies such visualisation experiences. Clients may be invited to verbalise the self-protective emotionally charged responses that they would have liked to have made in these situations to their parents or caregivers, within therapy sessions. Such responses may be made to a visualised image of their caregiver or to an empty chair, symbolising their caregiver or parent. In addition, clients may be invited to write (but not send) detailed letters to their parents or caregivers expressing in graphic emotional terms how difficult they found their challenging early life experiences in which they learned their destructive relationship habits. These processes of re-experiencing and responding differently to early formative experiences helps clients to gain control over their destructive relationship habits.

Reconnecting

A further technique that helps clients to break free from inadvertently slipping into destructive relationship habits, is to coach them to reconnect with parents from whom they have cut off. This type of work typically follows accessing, expressing and integrating emotions that underpin destructive relationship habits. In this type of coaching, clients are invited to prepare a plan of a series of visits with the parent from whom they are cut off and talk with them in an adult-to-adult mode, and avoid slipping into their old relationship pattern of distancing and cutting-off from the parent. Initially in these visits, conversation may focus on neutral topics. However, greatest therapeutic gains tend to be made where clients can tell their parents in an adult manner, how the parent's behaviour hurt, saddened or angered the client as a child and how this led to a long period of distancing and cut off, which the client would like to end and eventually replace with a less destructive relationship. Sometimes, clients find making such statements easier if they write them out with coaching from their therapists. In other instances, clients' parents may be invited into sessions, so that the therapist can facilitate clients making this type of statement and their parents hearing them. In many instances, clients' parents mention the circumstances and constraints that led them to hurt or sadden or anger the client and a process of mutual understanding and forgiveness is set in train. Of course, this is not always possible.

Addressing Contextual Issues

Where families have difficulty making progress in therapy by altering problem-maintaining behaviour patterns or the belief systems that directly underpin these in response to interventions listed in the right-hand and middle column of Table 9.1, it may be the case that factors in the family's wider social context are preventing them from making progress. These factors include issues requiring role change such as lifecycle transitions and home–work role strain; lack of social support; recent loss experiences, such as bereavement, parental separation, illness or injury, unemployment, moving house or moving schools; recent bullying; recent child abuse; poverty; or ongoing secret romantic affairs. A range of interventions may be considered for managing these various contextual predisposing factors. These include:

- changing roles
- building support
- managing stresses
- mourning losses
- home–school liaison meetings
- network meetings
- child protection
- advocacy
- exploring secrets.

Changing Roles

During lifecycle transitions or when home–work role strain occurs, these factors can underpin problem-maintaining beliefs and behaviour patterns, and so facilitating changes in family members' roles may be appropriate. For example, when fathers are absent from family life, though work demands, separation or divorce, children are at risk for developing problems and when fathers are involved in family therapy, the outcome has been shown to be more favourable (Carr, 1997). Thus, one of the most useful role change tasks is to invite fathers to become more centrally involved in therapy and in family life. Where fathers are unavailable during office hours, it is worthwhile making special arrangements to schedule at least a couple of family sessions that are convenient for the father. Where parents are separated or divorced, it is particularly important to arrange some sessions with the non-custodial parent, since it is important that both parents adopt the same approach in understanding and managing the child's difficulties.

In families presenting with child-focused problems and in which fathers are peripheral to childcare, one role change task that may be useful is to invite fathers to provide their children with an apprenticeship to help them mature and develop skills required for adulthood. Here is an example of offering such an invitation in families where boys present with emotional or conduct problems:

> *When boys have difficulty learning to be brave and deal with fear. When boys have problems learning to cope with sadness. Or where lads have a hard time learning to control their tempers and their aggression, they need to do an apprenticeship in how to be a self-controlled young man. So, I am wondering how you might provide your son with this apprenticeship he needs. Would you be able to set aside a half an hour each day in which he tells you what he has been doing or in which you both do something that he would like to do? The other side of this is that, when he sticks to the rules, praise comes from you and when he steps over the line he would be answerable to you. How would that be for you and for everyone else in the family?*

Building Support

In many instances, families referred for therapy lack social support and this underpins problem-maintaining beliefs and behaviour patterns. This deficit can be addressed immediately in family therapy by providing a forum where clients may confide their views and feelings about their problem situation. Clients experience support when therapists relate to them in a way that is empathic, warm and genuine, and in a way that fits with their communication style and ability. So it is important to use language that clients can understand easily, especially when talking to young children or people from ethnic groups which differ from that of the therapists. Some families require no more than the additional social support afforded by regular therapy sessions to meet their needs in this area.

However, other families, particularly those with chronic problems may need a more sustained input. In some such instances, it may be possible to refer clients to self-help support groups where others with similar problems meet and provide mutual support. Some such groups provide information, ongoing weekly support, and in some instances arrange summer camps for children or special events for adults. Using a multiple family therapy format (described in Chapter 6) for chronic problems, like psychosis or chronic eating disorders, allows clients to obtain support from other families in similar circumstances.

Where nuclear families have become disconnected from their extended families and immediate community, it may be suggested that they invite members of their extended families and networks to sessions to begin to form supportive relationships with them.

For children, particularly those who have become embroiled in coercive problem-maintaining interaction patterns, an important intervention is to train parents in providing their children with support. Parents may be coached in joint sessions with their children in how to do this. The guidelines for supportive play set out in Table 9.6 are first explained. Next, the therapist models inviting the child to select a play activity and engaging in child-led play, while positively commenting on the child's activity, praising the child regularly and avoiding commands and teaching. Then the parent is invited to copy the therapist's activity and feedback is given to parents on what they are doing well and what they need to do more of. Finally, the parent and child are invited to complete a 20-minute daily episode of child-led play to increase the amount of support the child experiences form the parent.

In families with older children and teenagers where parents and children have become embroiled in coercive interaction patterns, a parent and youngster may be invited to schedule special time together, in which the child selects an activity in which the parent agrees to participate. This may increase the sense of support that the youngster experiences.

Rituals for Mourning Losses

Bereavement, parental separation, illness, injury, unemployment, moving house or moving schools are all loss experiences. Loss is an inevitable,

Table 9.6 Guidelines for supportive play

Specific guidelines	General guidelines
Set a specific time for 20 minutes supportive play per day	Set out to use the episode to build a positive relationship with your child
Ask the child to decide what he or she wants to do	
Agree on an activity	Try to use the episode to give your child the message that they are in control of what happens and that you like being with them
Participate wholeheartedly	
Run a commentary on what the child is doing or saying, to show your child that you are paying attention to what they find interesting	
	Try to foresee rule-breaking and prevent it from happening or ignore it
Make congruent 'I like it when you...' statements, to show your child you feel good about being there	Avoid using commands, instructions or teaching
Praise your child repeatedly	Notice how much you enjoy being with your child
Laugh and make physical contact through hugs or rough and tumble	
Finish the episode by summarising what you did together and how much you enjoyed it	

uncontrollable and painful aspect of the family lifecycle. In adjusting to loss, distinct processes or overlapping stages have been described in Chapter 1. These include shock; denial of the loss; futile searching for the lost person, attribute or situation; despair and sadness; anger at the lost person or those seen as responsible for the loss; anxiety about other inevitable losses including one's own death; and acceptance (Walsh & McGoldrick, 2004). These processes, which are central to the grieving process, occur as family members change their belief systems and mental models of the world so as to accommodate the loss. The grieving process is complete when family members have developed a mental model of family life and a belief system that contains the lost member as part of family history or a sustained mental or spiritual presence rather than a living physical being. Sometimes families become stuck in the mourning process. In some cases, families have tried to short circuit the grieving process and act as if they have grieved, but find that from time to time they become inexplicably and inappropriately angry or sad. In other cases, the expression of sadness or anger persists over years and so compromises family development. Prescribing morning rituals where lost members are remembered in detail and family members then bid them farewell may be liberating for families paralysed by unresolved grief. Such rituals may allow family members to alter their belief system and to accept the loss into their cognitive model of the family. This change in the belief system then frees the family to break out of the cycle of interaction that includes the stuck member's grief response and the family's reaction to it. For example, the husband and two daughters of a courageous woman who died of cancer, after two years were repeatedly involved in acrimonious fights and episodes of withdrawal, which sometimes lasted for days. As part of therapy, the daughters and the father were invited to visit the mother's grave regularly on a fortnightly basis for three months. Each of them was to recount one reminiscence during these visits. Before therapy ended they were invited to read farewell letters to their mother at the grave and then to burn them. This was the final mourning ritual. Of course this therapy did not erase the pain and grief that goes with the loss of a wife or mother, but it did unblock the grieving process and liberate the girls and their father from the treadmill of fights followed by withdrawal that led to the referral.

Home–school liaison meetings

Where factors within the school environment, particularly conflict and bullying, maintain children's problematic beliefs and behaviour at home, liaison with the school is vital if family therapy is to be effective. The most effective way to conduct school liaison is to meet with the child's teacher and parents, outline the formulation of the problem in a tentative way, check that this is accepted by the teacher and parents and then explore options for action or suggest a particular way in which the school and parents may jointly contribute to the resolution of the child's problems. For bullying, Olweus's (1993) approach, described in *Bullying At School: What We Know And What We Can Do*, offers a useful strategy for cases where victimisation of children at school prevents problem resolution. The approach aims to create a social context in which adults (school staff and parents) show positive interest and warmth towards pupils and use consistent non-aggressive sanctions for aggressive behaviour in a highly consistent way. The programme involves a high level of surveillance of children's activities and a high level of communication between parents and teachers.

Network Meetings

Where families have multiple problems and are involved with multiple agencies and professionals, network meetings for families and involved professionals are particularly important, since they provide a forum within which the family and involved professionals may share information and strive to retain a shared view of the case formulation, goals and therapy plan. Without a shared view, opportunities for using available resources effectively and synergistically may be lost. Instead members of the family and network may inadvertently drift into problem-maintaining behaviour patterns.

When convening a network meeting, particularly where difficulties have developed in the coordination and delivery of therapy and other services, set clear goals. Such goals typically include clarifying or refining the formulation and agreeing on roles and responsibilities. Open review meetings with introductions, if any team members have not met, and set the agenda and the rules for participation clearly. Make sure that everyone gets a fair hearing by helping the reticent to elaborate their positions and the talkative to condense their contributions. Summarise periodically, to help members maintain focus. Above all, retain neutrality by siding with no one, and curiously enquiring about each person's position. Use time-out, if necessary, to integrate contributions, refine the formulation and elaborate options for action. Once the meeting accepts the refined formulation, request a commitment to develop or refine the action plan. Then work towards that by examining options and agreeing on which team members are responsible for particular parts of the programme. Minute all agreements, circulate these after the meeting, and agree on further review dates.

When contributing to a network meeting, prepare points on your involvement in the case, your hypotheses and plans. Use slack time at the beginning of the meeting or during the tea break to build good working alliances with network members. Always introduce yourself before making your first contribution if you are new to the network. Outline your involvement first and hypotheses and plans later. Make your points briefly and summarise your points at the end of each major contribution. When you disagree, focus on clarifying the issue, not on attacking the person with whom you disagree. Keep notes on who attended the meeting, on the formulation and the plan agreed. If you have unresolved ambivalent feelings after the meeting, discuss these in supervision.

Child Protection

Where children's presenting problems fail to respond to family therapy interventions that target behavioural patterns and beliefs, in some instances, notably complex multiagency cases, this is because of ongoing child abuse or neglect. Where there are good reasons to suspect that intrafamilial child abuse or neglect is occurring, it is good practice to suspend therapy until a statutory investigation by a child protection agency has been conducted. Following such an investigation and related legal proceedings, therapy may in some instances be resumed. However, the terms and conditions of such input should be negotiated with the family and child protection agency. This issue is discussed more fully in Part III of this volume.

Advocacy

Where adults or children's presenting problems fail to respond to marital or family therapy interventions that target behavioural patterns and beliefs, in some instances, notably complex multiagency cases, this is because of social disadvantage, poverty, housing problems, and lack of material resources. In such cases, for therapy to be effective, it may first be necessary for the therapist to act as an advocate for the family in arranging state benefits, adequate housing, and so forth.

Exploring Secrets

When one member of a family reveals a secret to a therapist and asks that confidentiality be maintained, the therapist faces a dilemma. If this confidentiality is respected, then neutrality may be violated, particularly if the content of the secret is relevant to the maintenance or resolution of the presenting problem. In cases of child abuse, violence or self-harm, maintaining confidentiality about a secret may violate a commitment to minimising harm and maximising well-being and so be unethical. On the other hand, if the therapist maintains neutrality by telling other family members about the secret, then the promise of confidentiality is broken. This may not be justifiable in cases where, for example, one partner confides that he or she has had a secret affair. Before looking at the management of such situations, let us first consider a useful typology of secrets.

Karpel (1980) distinguishes between individual secrets held by one person only; those shared by some, but not all family members; and family secrets that are known by all family members but are concealed from the community. A distinction may also be drawn between productive and destructive secrets. Individual secrets, in the form of a private diary, may be productive insofar as they enrich the writer's sense of personal identity and autonomy. Shared secrets may be used to maintain boundaries between family subsystems. For example, many couples do not discuss the intimate details of their sexual relationship with their children. Here, shared secrets are productive by creating an intergenerational boundary. Family secrets, such as preparing a surprise party for close friends, can generate joy and wonder.

Secrets are destructive where the withholding of information leads to a sense of guilt concerning the deception, and this compromises the quality of important family relationships and leads to problem-maintaining behaviour patterns. With children and families, the most common example of this type of individual destructive secret is where a child has stolen something of particular value and concealed the theft. With couples, extramarital affairs fall into this category. Secrets are also destructive where the act of deception subjugates one or more members of the family, as in the case of intrafamilial sexual abuse. Such abuse is a typical example of a shared destructive secret. Some shared secrets, such as those related to adoptive children's parentage or a child's illegitimacy, may be maintained by parents with the best of intentions but have a destructive impact on parent–child relationships when the child suspects deception. Destructive family secrets, such as those concerning family violence, often maintain problems by cutting the family off from people or agencies in the community that may be able to help the family.

When the therapist is offered a secret in confidence by a family member, the secret and the confidence are accepted and respected as a confused plea for help (Carpenter & Treacher, 1989). The relevance of the secret to the maintenance and resolution of the presenting problems must then be established. Irrelevant secrets may be let lie. If the secret is relevant to the maintenance or resolution of the presenting problem, the implications for all family members of revealing or concealing it may be explored with the person who has revealed the secret. Here is a line of questioning that may be used in exploring, with a partner who has revealed a secret that they have had an affair, the impact of disclosing the infidelity:

> When you told me this secret, how did you think this would help to solve the presenting problem?
>
> To what extent do you believe this secret must be shared with your partner for the presenting problem to be solved?
>
> If the presenting problem can be solved without disclosing this secret, do you want to keep the secret?
>
> What will be the long-term consequences for your relationship if you keep this secret?
>
> Suppose you told your partner, straight out, that you desperately wanted to feel cared for or powerful or youthful or attractive but you couldn't find a way to do this in your marriage, so you had an affair, what do you guess would go through his or her mind?
>
> In what way would your relationship change if you told your partner about this?
>
> What is the worst thing that could happen if you told your partner about this affair?
>
> In what way would the relationship with your children change if you told your partner about the affair?
>
> Under what circumstances do you think your partner would forgive you for having this affair?
>
> How would you cope with process of atonement and forgiveness?
>
> How do you think you would cope with the increased closeness and intimacy that would follow from this process of atonement and forgiveness?

Addressing Constitutional Factors

When families have a member who has a constitutional vulnerability, they are unlikely to benefit from therapy that relies exclusively on the interventions in the right-hand and middle column of Table 9.1, which aim only to alter problem-maintaining behaviour patterns or the belief systems that directly underpin these, without directly addressing the constitutional vulnerability. Such constitutional vulnerabilities may be genetic or they may involve debilitating somatic states, sequelae of early illness or injury, learning difficulties, or difficult temperament. Families with members who have constitutional vulnerabilities require psychoeducation about the condition or vulnerability; help with ensuring the vulnerable family member adheres to the medication regime where this is appropriate; referral for medical consultation where appropriate; and support in securing an appropriate educational placement if this is required, especially in the case of individuals with learning difficulties.

Psychoeducation

In psychoeducation, families are given both general information about the problem and a specific formulation of the vulnerable family member's specific difficulties (McFarlane, 2002). Simplicity and realistic optimism are central to good psychoeducation. It is important not to overwhelm clients with information, so a good rule of thumb is to think about a case in complex terms, but explain it to clients in as simple terms as possible. Put succinctly:

Think complex – talk simple.

Good clinical practice involves matching the amount of information given about the formulation and case management plan to the client's readiness to understand and accept it. A second important rule of thumb is to engender a realistic level of hope when giving feedback by focusing on strengths and protective factors first, and referring to etiological factors later. Put succinctly:

Create hope – name strengths.

In psychoeducation, information on clinical features, predisposing, precipitating, maintaining and protective factors may be given along with the probable impact of the problem in the short and long term on cognition, emotions, behaviour, family adjustment, school adjustment and health. Details of the treatment programme should be given both orally and in written form, if appropriate, in a way that is compressible to family members. It is important to highlight family strengths that increase the probability that the vulnerable family member will respond positively to treatment. This should be balanced with a statement of the sacrifices that the child and family will have to make to participate in the treatment programme. Common sacrifices include: attending a series of consultation sessions; discussing difficult issues openly; completing homework assignments; being prepared for progress to be hampered by setbacks; learning to live with ongoing residual difficulties; accepting that episodes of therapy are time-limited; accepting that at best, the chances are only two out of three that therapy will be helpful. Psychoeducation should empower families. It should allow them to reach a position where they can give a clear account of the problems and the correct way to manage it. Family psychoeducation sessions allow the family to develop a shared understanding of the illness. Group psychoeducation offers a forum where children and parents can meet others in the same position and this has the benefit of providing additional support for family members. A psychoeducational approach to schizophrenia is given in Part IV of this volume.

Adherence to Medical Regimes

Initially, in cases where non-adherence is a problem, it is important that all family members are involved in understanding the regime and in supporting the vulnerable family member in complying with the regime. As adherence improves, more autonomous management of adherence should be encouraged. Adherence to medical regimes is maximised if the following guidelines are followed.

> *Set out the medication and medical care regime in simple language, inviting clients to do specific things.*
>
> *Describe the medication regime and medical care tasks briefly and break complex tasks into parts.*
>
> *Check that the clients have understood the regime.*
>
> *Give a rationale for the regime.*
>
> *Emphasise the importance of adherence to the regime and the positive and negative effects and side effects of both adherence and non-adherence.*
>
> *Write down complex tasks.*
>
> *State that adherence will be reviewed in every session and convey an expectation of cooperation.*
>
> *Always review adherence and respond favourably to adherence.*
>
> *Manage non-adherence in the way outlined for managing resistance in Chapter 5.*
>
> *With non-adherent children and adolescents, invite parents to use reward systems, described earlier in this Chapter, to increase adherence.*
>
> *With adherent clients, encourage autonomous management of adherence.*

SUMMARY

Interventions may be classified in terms of the particular domain they target. Some interventions aim to directly disrupt problem-maintaining behaviour patterns. Others aim to transform belief-system and narratives that subserve these behaviour patterns. Still others modify the impact of historical, contextual and constitutional predisposing factors. Ideally, classes of interventions for which there is empirical evidence of effectiveness should be used. In any given case, an attempt should be made to select specific interventions that are compatible with the three-column formulations of the family's problem; which make best use of the family's strengths; and which are compatible with the family's readiness to change. It is also preferable to select interventions that make best use of the therapist's or team's skills in helping the helping clients solve their problems and to be aware that family therapy may not be the appropriate intervention in all cases.

FURTHER READING

Carpenter, J. & Treacher, A. (1989). *Problems and Solutions in Marital and Family Therapy*. Oxford: Basil Blackwell.

Carr, A. (1995). *Positive Practice: A Step-by-Step Approach to Family Therapy*. Reading: Harwood.

Reimers, S. & Treacher, A. (1995). *Introducing User Friendly Family Therapy*. London: Routledge.

Street, E. & Downey, J. (1995). *Brief Therapeutic Consultations*. Chichester: Wiley.

Gehart, D. & Tuttle, A. (2003). *Theory-Based Treatment Planning for Marriage and Family Therapists*. Pacific Grove, CA: Brooks Cole.

Patterson, J., Grauf-Grounds, C. & Chamow, L. (1998). *Essential Sills in Family Therapy: From the First Interview to Termination*. New York: Guilford.

Pote, H., Stratton, P., Cottrell, D., Boston, P., Shapiro, D. & Hanks, H. (2000). Leeds Systemic Family Therapy Manual. University of Leeds: Leeds Family Therapy & Research Centre. Available at http://www.psyc.leeds.ac.uk/research/lftrc/index.htm

Part III

FAMILY THERAPY PRACTICE WITH CHILD- AND ADOLESCENT-FOCUSED PROBLEMS

Chapter 10

PHYSICAL CHILD ABUSE

Physical abuse refers to deliberately inflicted injury or deliberate attempts to poison a child. Physical abuse is usually intrafamilial and may occur alone or in conjunction with sexual abuse, neglect or emotional abuse (Kolko, 2002). A systemic model for conceptualising these types of problems and a systemic approach to therapy with these cases will be given in this chapter. A case example is presented in Figure 10.1. A three-column formulation of the abusive process is given in Figure 10.2. A formulation of an exception is given in Figure 10.3.

The overall prevalence of physical child abuse during childhood and adolescence is 10–25% depending on the definition used, the population studied, and the cut-off point for the end of adolescence (Wekerle & Wolfe, 2003). Community surveys in the USA, the UK and other European countries in the 1990s found that the annual incidence of physical child abuse was 5–9% (Creighton, 2004). In these surveys, physical abuse was defined as being hit with an object, punched, bitten, kicked, beaten up or attacked with a knife or gun. Only a minority of cases of physical abuse come to the attention of child protection services and are officially reported.

SYSTEMIC MODEL OF PHYSICAL CHILD ABUSE

For both clinicians and researchers, single factor models of physical abuse that focus on either characteristics of the child, characteristics of the parents or features of the family's social context, have now largely been superseded by complex systemic models (Cicchetti, 2004; Emery & Laumann-Billings, 2002; Jones, 2000; Kolko, 2002; Wekerle & Wolfe, 2003). Within such models, physical abuse is conceptualised as the outcome of a complex process in which a child with particular characteristics, which rendered him or her vulnerable to abuse, was injured by a parent involved in an ongoing problematic behaviour pattern, subserved by particular belief systems and constrained by historical, contextual and constitutional factors. For example, a child may be vulnerable to physical abuse because his difficult temperament overtaxes his parents' limited coping resources. The parent may become involved in coercive cycles of interaction with the child and come to believe that the child is purposely trying to punish the

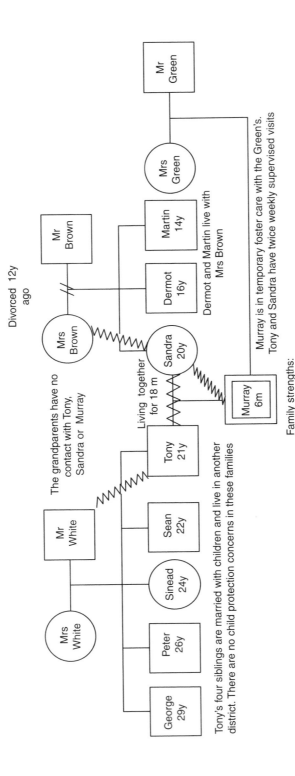

Divorced 12y ago

Mr Green

Mrs Green

Mr Brown

Martin 14y

Dermot 16y

Mrs Brown

Sandra 20y

Murray 6m

Mr White

Living together for 18 m

Tony 21y

Sean 22y

Sinead 24y

Peter 26y

George 29y

Mrs White

The grandparents have no contact with Tony, Sandra or Murray

Tony's four siblings are married with children and live in another district. There are no child protection concerns in these families

Dermot and Martin live with Mrs Brown

Murray is in temporary foster care with the Green's. Tony and Sandra have twice weekly supervised visits

Family strengths:
Sandra accepts responsibility, and shows
remorse. Sandra and Tony are open to learning parenting skills

Referral. This case was referred to a child and family mental health team by social services following a non-accidental injury, identified by the pediatrician in the district general hospital. The purpose of the referral was to see if Murray could be returned to custody of his parents. At the time of the referral, Murray was in temporary foster care with the Greens. Murray had a torn frenulum, extensive facial bruising and burn marks from an electric heater on his arm. Sandra, the mother, brought the child to casualty after the child accidentally brushed against the heater. Sandra and Tony said the torn frenulum and bruising were due to two episodes of falling down. The paediatrician said the bruises and frenulum injuries were due to recent non-accidental injury (NAI). A Place of Safety Order was taken and after medical treatment, Murray was placed in foster care with the Greens. The parents were granted twice weekly supervised access and these visits occurred at the Green's house. The mother was charged, by the police with grievous bodily harm, found guilty and put on probation. The team interviewed Tony and Sandra, observed family access visits and liaised with all involved professionals.

Assessment of the child. Murray was a difficult temperament child who reacted strongly to all new stimuli by crying and was difficult to soothe. He slept and ate at irregular times. He often vomited his food up. He did not look like a bonnie baby and probably bore little resemblance to Tony and Sandra's idea of a good baby. He had placed heavy demands on them since his birth and they were both exhausted from trying to care for him.

The mother's family history. Sandra, the mother, had a history of poor school performance. She had difficulty making and maintaining peer relationships. Her parents had a highly conflictual and violent marriage, which ended when she was eight. She had a difficult relationship with her mother. Sandra experienced episodes of low mood that bordered on clinical depression and had poor frustration tolerance.

The father's family history. Tony, the father, had a history of truancy and was the youngest child in a conflictual and chaotic family. In particular, he had a conflictual and violent relationship with his father. He also had limited skills for resolving conflicts and often resorted to violence when others disagreed with him. He had a checkered employment record. His parents disapproved of Sandra. Tony's three brothers and his sisters all had partners (either co-habitees or spouses) and children, and all lived outside of Tony's village now.

Parenting resources. Tony had little time for the baby and had few parenting skills and limited parenting knowledge. Sandra had a good knowledge of the practicalities of looking after a baby but little sense of what was developmentally appropriate for a six-month-old child. She found it difficult to interpret what his crying meant and usually attributed it to him trying to annoy her. She was unable to empathise with her child's position. She would scold him as if he were a five year old. Usually when he cried she would leave him to lie alone in the other room. Sometimes, in frustration, she would thrust his bottle at him and say 'I'll ram this down your throat if you don't shut up'.

The couple's relationship. Tony and Sandra vacillated between extreme closeness and warmth and violent rows. They had known each other about a year when Murray was born. They were unmarried and had no immediate plans to marry. They settled their differences usually by engaging in escalating shouting matches that occasionally involved mutual violence. Usually after these stormy episodes, one or both would leave the situation and one or both would get drunk. Later the issue would be dropped until the next heated exchange, when it would be brought up again.

Social support network and family stresses. Tony and Sandra were very isolated with few friends. They were unsupported by the extended family and had no regular contact with either Tony's or Sandra's parents or siblings. They were financially stressed, since neither of them worked, and relied on welfare payments to support themselves. They lived in a two-room rented flat over a shop.

The abusive incident. The abusive incident involved the following sequence of events. Murray began to cry at 3.00 a.m. and would not stop. This was typical of him as a child with a difficult temperament. Sandra interpreted the crying as Murray trying to prove she was no good as a mother and as his attempt to punish her by stopping her from sleeping. When she expressed this view to Tony, he argued with her, which further upset Murray, and then Tony went back to sleep. Sandra's anger at the child escalated, and this was fuelled by her negative attributions concerning the child's motives, her lack of empathy for Murray, her anger at Tony, and her exhaustion. She took the child's bottle and shoved it into Murray's mouth and tore his frenulum. He tried to spit it out. She hit him twice. Picked him up and then dropped him next to the heater, which he fell against. This act was influenced by her own punishment experiences as a child. Her mother had relied on corporal punishment as a routine method of control and often she was very severe. The act was also influenced by her habit of using a bottle to stop Murray from crying.

Capacity to cooperate with the team. Sandra accepted that the abuse was the result of her being unable to control her frustration in a stressful situation. She was committed to learning how to manage her child in stressful situations and to engaging in family work to learn child management skills. Sandra and Tony

(Continued on next page)

refused to accept that counselling for their personal or relationship difficulties would be of any benefit to them. Sandra was able to cooperate with the team and engaged well in the assessment. Tony found cooperation very difficult and only went along with the assessment procedures to placate Sandra.

Formulation. Three-column formulations of problematic episodes and exceptional non-problematic episodes are contained in Figures 10.2 and 10.3. The main protective factor in this case was the mother's acceptance of responsibility of the abuse and willingness to work with the team to develop parenting skills. However, an important related risk factor was the couple's refusal to acknowledge the contribution of personal and marital difficulties to the occurrence of the abuse, and the necessity of working to enhance mood regulation skills and marital communication.

Treatment. The parents were offered joint parenting skills training following the guidelines set out in this chapter. They attended some but not all sessions and had difficulty cooperating with joint homework assignments. However, feeding and sleeping routines were established and a specific role for Tony in these was negotiated. Attempts to promote increased support for Sandra from her mother were largely unsuccessful. However, support for Sandra was increased by offering her a place in a support group for mothers. The prognosis in this case was guarded because of the couple's refusal to acknowledge the role of marital factors and personal factors in occurrence of the abuse.

Figure 10.1 Case example of physical child abuse

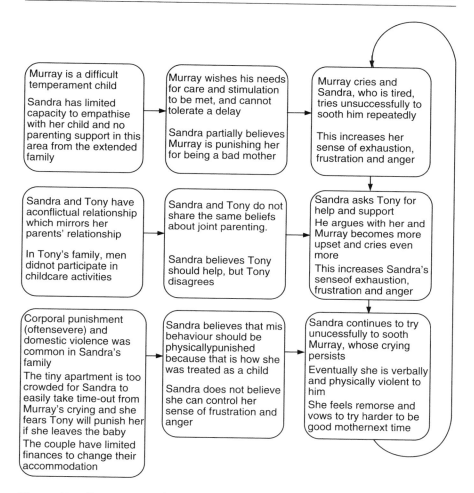

Figure 10.2 Example of a three-column formulation of physical child abuse

parent. Historical factors, such as personal abuse in childhood; contextual factors, such as high stress and low marital support; and constitutional factors, such as vulnerability to depression may constrain the parent from finding alternatives to these destructive belief systems and behaviour patterns, which ultimately culminate in the parent injuring the child.

Behaviour Patterns and Beliefs

Most abusive episodes occur in response to a triggering behaviour by the child, which the parent experiences as aversive such as crying, wetting, refusing to eat, stealing, lying or aggression. Most abusive incidents are

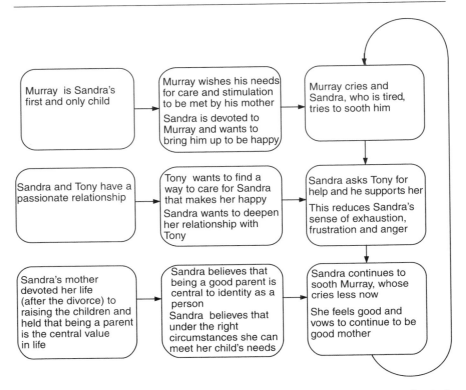

Figure 10.3 Example of a three-column formulation of an exception to physical child abuse

disciplinary encounters between parents and children, where parents use physical punishment in response to a child's trigger behaviour. The parent intends to punish the child for wrong-doing and uses physical punishment since this is their typical method of disciplining children. However, the punishment is severe because of the high level of anger and the lack of inhibition. The high level of anger, which fuels the parent's abusive act, is determined by the parent's arousal level and the parent's beliefs about the child's trigger behaviour. If the parent's level of anger before the trigger behaviour is high, then this may be displaced on to the child. Parents who have been involved in a marital conflict or a stressful conflict with someone in their work situation, extended family or community may displace their anger into their punishment of the child. In other situations, where the parents have been involved in a repetitive escalating cycle of stressful conflict with the child, the trigger behaviour may the last straw in this escalating negative interaction pattern.

Prior to an abusive act, the parent typically believes that the child's behaviour is intentionally negative and this belief system leads to the high level of anger. Parents who physically abuse their children fail to inhibit the extreme anger they experience in response to the child's trigger behaviour. Parent's who do not abuse their children empathise with the child's position or use self-talk to control their tempers. Parent's who abuse their children have difficulty empathising with children and may use self-talk to justify their anger. The escalating severity of physical punishment that precedes abuse may desensitise parents to the dangerousness of their actions, which culminate in a serious injury.

Predisposing Historical Contextual and Constitutional Factors

A range of historical, contextual and constitutional factors associated with the child, the parents, the parent–child relationship, the marriage and the family's social network may predispose families to the occurrence of physical child abuse.

Predisposing Child Factors

The following child characteristics are risk factors for physical abuse since they place additional demands upon parents: being under 5, prematurity, low birth weight, developmental delays, frequent illness, difficult temperament, and oppositional or aggressive behaviour.

Predisposing Parent Factors

Personal characteristics of the parents may place them at risk for physically abusing their children. Young parents are more likely to abuse their children than older parents. Physical abuse is more commonly carried out by mothers, but fathers may be more likely to abuse their children when considered from the point of view of opportunities; that is, acts of physical abuse per hour of time they spend in the role of the child's primary caregiver.

Parents from families with pro-aggressive attitudes are more likely to abuse their children. About a third of parents who were abused as children go on to abuse their offspring. Psychological problems including depression, borderline personality disorder and substance abuse are more common among parents who abuse their children than those that do not. Poor emotional regulation and poor empathy skills are two of the most important components of these broader psychological disorders from the point of view of increasing risk. Poor empathy skills, are a particular handicap for parents since sensitive parenting necessitates reading the child's signals and inferring the child's emotional state. Poor personal emotional regulation is also a handicap because parents may have difficulty prioritising the need to respond to the child in a way that regulates the child's emotional state since they are unable to carry out this function for themselves. Rather they find themselves descending into a pit of depression or flying into a rage of anger and feel powerless to regulate these extreme emotional states. They also have difficulty reducing stresses associated with the wider social context in which they live. These include, crowding, social isolation and financial problems.

Predisposing Historical Parent–Child Relationship Factors

The parent–child relationship in cases of physical abuse is typically conflictual. Many parents who physically abuse their children have not experienced parental sensitivity to their needs, so these parents, therefore, have no mental model to use as a basis for responding sensitively to their own children's needs. Abusive parents set unrealistically high standards for young children's behaviour and attribute their children's demanding or difficult behaviours to the child's intentional defiance.

Behaviour patterns involving parents and their abused children are typified by a high rate of egative exchanges and disciplinary encounters, which escalate in severity. Parents who abuse their children control by punishment, not praise, and the punishments, which are often severe, are out of all proportion to the child's transgression of the parent's rules for good conduct. In families where abuse occurs, children do not respond consistently to such parental control. Parents become frustrated by this ineffectiveness but have difficulty analysing why their approach to parenting is ineffective. They also have difficulty generating and testing out alternative solutions.

Predisposing Marital Factors

Conflict, instability, dissatisfaction, negative behaviour patterns, negative narratives, poor communication and ineffective problem-solving skills are the main features of marital relationships that place youngsters at risk for physical abuse. Unresolved marital conflict is very common among parents who physically abuse their children. Conflict underpins the structural instability in these relationships, which are characterised by a history of multiple separations and a low level of commitment. Low satisfaction is another feature of these relationships. Partners have difficulty meeting each other's needs for an acceptable level of intimacy and an equitable distribution of power. Conflict about intimacy often centres on the women in these relationships demanding more psychological intimacy and the men demanding more physical intimacy. Conflict about power may emerge in discussions about the division of labour within the household and about the way money is used.

These conflicts often remain unresolved because the couples lack the communication and joint problem-solving skills necessary for negotiation. These couples have difficulty conceptualising a conflict being resolved to the satisfaction of both parties (i.e. a win–win resolution). Partners in these marriages may also selectively attend to negative aspects of each other's behaviour and attribute vindictive intentions to their partners for many mildly irritating behaviours. This negative way of thinking along with the belief that in any negotiation there must be a winner and loser in turn promotes negative behaviour patterns. These patterns of interaction are characterised by blaming rather than empathy and escalating negative exchanges rather than positive exchanges. These negative exchanges may escalate into physical violence.

Violent abusive marital relationships and violent parent–child relationships may be two aspects of a violent family culture. Within this type of culture, couples are more likely to work on a short-term *quid pro quo* system, not a long-term goodwill system. Often the child is triangulated into negative exchanges between the parents. For example, a father may refuse to feed or change the child or tolerate the child's crying because the mother has not met the father's need for power or physical intimacy.

Predisposing Network Factors

Low socio-economic status, poverty, unemployment, poor housing, single parenthood and a low educational level are all risk factors for child abuse. Parental isolation and a low level of social support are also associated with physical child abuse. Parental isolation often includes isolation from the parents' families of origin. This isolation may be associated with unresolved conflicts between the parents and the grandparents of the abused child. So, it is not only the case that the grandparents may be unavailable as a source of support, but they also may be perceived as a potential threat or source of stress.

A variety of environmental stresses, most notably crowding and inadequate housing are associated with child abuse. Remaining with a crying child in a cramped living quarters requires considerable frustration-tolerance and so it is understandable that crowding may be one of the factors that sets the stage for the occurrence of abuse.

Effects of Physical Child Abuse

Physical child abuse has short- and long-term physical and psychological consequences (Cicchetti, 2004; Emery & Laumann-Billings, 2002; Jones, 2002; Kolko, 2002; Wekerle & Wolfe, 2003). The physical consequences of abuse include disfigurement, neurological damage and stunted growth. The short-term psychological consequences include developmental delays, conduct and emotional problems, and relationship difficulties. For a proportion of physically abused children, their behavioural, emotional and relationship difficulties persist into adulthood. The majority of physically abused children do not develop serious long-term problems. For those that do, the difficulties are related to the frequency and severity of abuse, the co-occurrence of neglect or emotional abuse and the number of risk factors present. These risk factors, detailed above include parental adjustment problems, child adjustment problems, problematic parent–child relationships, marital discord and high levels of family stress with low social support. Poor long-term adjustment is also associated with multiplacement experiences and protracted legal proceedings arising from involvement in statutory child protection procedures.

Protective Factors

Not all children develop serious long-term problems as a result of abuse. Children who are abused before the age of 5 and who do not sustain neurological damage tend to be more resilient, as do children with high ability levels, an easy temperament, and the capacity and opportunity to form socially supportive relationships with adults in the extended family and elsewhere despite the abuse. If parents have some capacity to empathise with their child, regulate their emotions and a willingness to develop accurate knowledge and expectations about child development, then this is also protective factor. Secure parent–child attachment and a stable satisfying marital relationship or the potential to develop these are protective factors too. Where families are embedded in social networks that provide a high level of support and place few stressful demands on family members, then it is less likely that parents' resources for childcare will become depleted and abuse will occur. The availability of a well-resourced preschool placement may also be viewed as a protective factor. Within the professional network, good coordination of multiprofessional input is an important protective factor also.

FAMILY THERAPY FOR PHYSICAL CHILD ABUSE

In families where physical child abuse has occurred, effective family therapy programmes, while premised on a broad-based assessment, focus on very specific parenting problems, with one target being tackled at time using systematic behavioural and systemic treatment principles (Azar & Wolfe, 1998; Browne, 2002; Brunk, Henggeler & Whelan, 1987; Cicchetti, 2004; Dale, 1986; Donohue, Miller, Van Hasselt & Hersen, 1998; Edgeworth & Carr, 2000; Emery & Laumann-Billings, 2002; Jones, 2002; Kolko, 2002; MacDonald, 2001; Nicol et al., 1988; Schuerman, Rzepmicki & Littem, 1994). The specific guidelines for clinical practice when working with families where physical child abuse has occurred using the approach outlined in the remainder of this chapter should be followed within the context of the general guidelines for family therapy practice given in Chapters 7, 8 and 9.

Contracting for Assessment

Family therapy may be used to help families in which physical abuse has occurred to reduce the risks of further abuse. Planning who to invite to intake interviews in such cases is a complex matter, especially where the child has been taken into statutory care following the abuse. Ideally, the statutory child-protection professional (usually a social worker) should be invited, along with the child's parents and the foster parents or childcare workers if the child is in statutory foster or residential care.

The aim of the initial contracting meeting is to form a contract for assessment. Usually, the statutory child-protection worker is the main customer for change. This worker commonly wants help with reducing the risk of further abuse, and reintegrating the child from the temporary foster care placement back into the natural family. It is not unusual for the parents to be very ambivalent about treatment and to view the family therapist as a potential threat: as another professional who is going to prevent them from retrieving custody of their child. Foster parents or care workers who are providing the child with short-term care in some instances are sympathetic towards the parents and wish to see the child re-united with them. In other instances, they are critical of the parents and want the child to remain in care for the long term. With these three different agendas running (those of the child-protection worker, the parents, and the foster parents or care workers), the potential for conflict and confusion is very high. The key to therapeutic progress is to establish a very clear contract and not to begin assessment work with the family until the contract is crystal clear.

The outcome of the contracting meeting should be that the statutory child protection worker is viewed as enlisting the aid of the family therapy agency to help the family reduce the risk of further violence, so that the child may be returned to the custody of the parents. The parents may acknowledge their ambivalence but agree to attend therapy because they want to regain custody of their child. The foster parents or childcare workers should agree to facilitate regular and frequent supervised access between the parents and the child. Finally, agreement should be made to reconvene after a family assessment has been conducted to give feedback on whether or not the family therapy service judge the family to be suitable for family treatment.

Assessment

The first aim of family assessment is to construct three-column formulations, like those presented in Figures 10.2. and 10.3, of the abusive process and exceptions to it. The second aim is to assess the family's capacity to benefit from family-based treatment. A comprehensive schedule of assessment procedures is presented in Table 10.1. The schedule includes provision for assessment of all relevant family subsystems, the wider professional network and the use of sample therapy sessions to determine the family's capacity to use marital and family therapy sessions to learn

Table 10.1 Schedule for a comprehensive family assessment package for use in cases of physical child abuse

Subsystem	Assessment procedures
Child	Individual interview with child (if the child is old enough) to assess personal strengths and resources (including assertiveness) and his or her account of the abusive incident, perception of all relevant risk factors, and wishes for the future
Parents	Individual interviews with parents to assess acceptance or denial or responsibility for abuse, parenting skills and deficits, personal resources and problems, reconstruction of the abusive incident, and perception of all relevant risk factors
Parent–child interaction	Parent–child interaction observation sessions to assess positive aspects of parenting and risk factors associated with parent–child interactions A sample session of treatment to assess responsiveness to behavioural coaching in supportive play, use of reward systems and non-violent behavioural control methods
Marital couple	Marital interview to assess marital risk factors especially joint communication and problem-solving skills for dealing with childcare issues and conflict management A sample session of treatment, to assess couples' responsiveness to coaching in joint communication and problem-solving skills for managing childcare issues
Family accommodation	Visit to family residence to assess crowding, hygiene, safety of the home for the child and opportunities for age-appropriate cognitive stimulation and play
Role of extended family	Individual interviews with other members of nuclear and extended family to assess their acceptance or denial of the abuse, their perception of risk factors, their reconstruction of the abusive incident (if appropriate), their childcare skills and deficits Joint interviews with extended family and nuclear family to observe quality of their relationship to nuclear family and assess potential for support

Subsystem	Assessment procedures
Role of other involved professionals	Individual interviews or written reports from other involved professionals in child protection, social services, health, education, and justice to obtain their expert view of risks and resources within the family and their potential future involvement in supporting the family or providing services

Joint interviews with other community-based resource people, such as the foster parents with whom the child is temporarily based, home-help, befriender, leader of mother and toddler group, director of nursery or day-care facility, etc. to observe relationship to parents and assess potential for supporting the family in future |

new skills and reduce risk. Assessment may span a number of sessions and include sessions with various subsystems of the family and aspects of the wider social network. Initially, assessment should focus on a reconstruction of the abusive incident and previous similar incidents; that is, the problem-maintaining behaviour pattern. Belief systems of parents and other family and network members that underpinned action in this cycle of violence may then be clarified. These in turn may be linked to the predisposing risk factors that have been listed above in the systemic model of physical abuse.

Contracting for Treatment

When contracting for treatment, following assessment, the statutory child-protection professional, the child's parents and the foster parents, or childcare workers if the child is in statutory foster or residential care, should be present in the contracting meeting. A summary of the family's strengths and a three-column formulation of the family process in which the abusive incident was embedded should be given. In light of this, a statement should be made about the capacity of the family to benefit from family-based treatment. The checklist set out in Table 10.2 offers a framework for assessing a family's capacity to engage in treatment. Where parents accept responsibility for the abuse, are committed to meeting their child's needs, are committed to improving their own psychological well-being and where they have the ability to change, the prognosis is good. In such cases it is worth allocating scarce resources to treatment. Where three out of four of these conditions are met the prognosis is fair. Where less than three of these conditions are met, it is unlikely that even the most skilful professional team would be able to offer a viable treatment

Table 10.2 Checklist of four conditions that predict positive treatment response in families where child abuse has occurred

1.	Acceptance of responsibility for abuse	Do the parents accept responsibility for abuse (or neglect)?
		Do parents blame the child for provoking the abuse?
		Do the parents deny that the abuse occurred?
2.	Commitment to meeting their child's needs	Do the parents accept that they have to change their parenting behaviour in order to meet their child's needs?
		Are the parents committed to using therapy to improve their parenting skills?
		Can the parents place the child's needs ahead of their own needs?
3.	Commitment to improving their own psychological well-being	Do the parents accept that their own psychological problems (depression, substance abuse, anger management problems, marital discord) compromise their capacity to meet their child's needs?
		Do the parents deny that they have psychological problems?
		Are the parents committed to using therapy to improve their psychological well-being?
4.	Ability to change	Do the parents have the ability to learn the skills necessary for meeting their child's needs?
		Do the parents have the personal flexibility to change their parenting behaviour?
		Do the parents have the emotional strength to follow through on therapeutic tasks that require considerable tolerance for frustration?
		Do the parents have the capacity to maintain a cooperative relationship with the therapy team?
	Will definitely benefit from treatment	Four conditions are met
	Will possibly benefit from treatment	Three conditions are met
	Unlikely to benefit from treatment	Two or less conditions are met

Source: Adapted from Skuse and Bentovim (1994). Physical and emotional maltreatment. In M. Rutter, E. Taylor & E. Hersov (Eds), *Child & Adolescent Psychiatry: Modern Approaches*, 3rd edn, pp. 209–229. Oxford: Blackwell.

programme. In such instances, foster care should seriously be considered as the least damaging option for the child.

If the family therapy service can offer treatment to the family because it meets the criteria for treatment suitability, then specific goals, a clear specification of the number of treatment sessions and the times and places at which these sessions will occur should all be specified in a contract. Such contracts should be written and formally signed by the parents, the family therapist and the statutory social worker. Many families in which physical child abuse occurs have both financial problems and organisational difficulties. Non-attendance at therapy sessions associated with these problems can be significantly reduced by using a home visiting format wherever possible or organising transportation if treatment must occur at a clinic.

The central aim of family therapy should be preventing the occurrence of negative cycles of interaction and promoting positive exchanges between the parents and child. Ideally this should involve intensive contact of up to three sessions per week over a three-month period (Nicol et al., 1988). It is less confusing for clients if child-focused family therapy sessions that have this overriding aim are defined as distinct from concurrent marital therapy sessions in which the focus is on couples enhancing their relationship, so that they can support each other in caring for their child.

In some instances, it may be appropriate for some sessions to be held that involve the parents with their own parents to help resolve family-of-origin difficulties and facilitate support from the extended family. Where parents have particular personal vulnerabilities, sessions that target these and aim to increase their childcare knowledge and skills and manage their own personal problems may be appropriate. Arranging intensive input for the child in a specialist day-care or nursery setting is appropriate where children have developmental delays.

Treatment

The following sections offer some guidelines for implementing different aspects of multisystemic family therapy-based intervention programmes, which include child-focused and couples-focused components along with supplementary individual and network interventions. One broad aim of treatment is for the whole family to acknowledge that the parent abused the child; is no longer denying this; wishes to atone for this injustice; and wishes to take concrete steps so no further abuse will occur.

Interventions for Parent–Child Behaviour Patterns and Belief Systems

The following principles are useful in guiding interventions that specifically aim to change destructive parent–child behaviour patterns.

Therapists should work with parents intensively (1–3 sessions per week for three months). Wherever possible, sessions should occur in the home rather than the clinic, since lessons learned in therapy sessions are more likely to generalise to routine home-life if these lessons are learned within the home. Within sessions, the therapist's role is that of a coach. The parents and child are coached in how to engage in positive exchanges and avoid negative exchanges. Between sessions, parents and children practise what has been learned in the sessions. As families successfully achieve targets, the frequency of the sessions is reduced.

The principal behaviour-focused interventions are changing behavioural consequences using reward systems and behavioural control programmes, described in Chapter 9. Target behaviours should be highly specific and easy to count so progress can be easily monitored by parents using a simple recording system. Smaller targets should be tackled before larger targets are attempted. Typical targets for families with pre-schoolers include: developing a positive parent–child play sequence and engaging in it once a day; managing episodes of crying so that they end with the child being soothed by the parent; developing a pre-sleep routine; and managing feeding time routines without fights. For every target that involves reducing a negative behaviour or exchange (such as a parent shouting at a child or a child crying), a positive target should also be selected (such as the parent cuddling the child or the child playing).

For positive behavioural targets, there should be an emphasis on developing clear daily routines involving these targets. Thus, if the target is for the parent and child to play together without conflict for 15 minutes per day using the skills for supportive play described in Chapter 9, a routine needs to be evolved where the parent and child in preparation for this 15-minute period go to a particular room at a particular time each day and run through a particular sequence of anticipatory exchanges such as: 'It's nearly playtime for Mummy and Billy. What is it? It's nearly playtime for Mummy and Billy. What is it? Yes it is…', and so forth. This sequence is appropriate for a pre-schooler. Older children will require more age-appropriate exchanges.

Parents should be coached in how to neutralise the destructive effects of negative framings of their children's behaviour and the destructive effects of marital conflict before attempting to engage in anticipatory routines leading up to a target behaviour. Reframing and relabelling, two belief-focused interventions described in Chapter 9, are the main skills parents need to be taught to break out of negative framings of their children's behaviour. Reframing involves interpreting an ambiguous behavioural sequence in a positive or empathic way rather than by attributing negative intentions or qualities to the child. For example, in a situation where a child began crying when the mother answered the phone, the mother interpreted this ambiguous sequence to reflect *the eight-month-old child's wish to prevent her from talking to her sister on the phone*. The mother was invited to reframe this situation as one in which *the child was startled by the phone ringing and disappointed at the loss of the mother's exclusive attention.*

Relabelling involves using a positive adjective to label the child rather than a negative one, if the response that led to the labelling is sufficiently ambiguous to allow this. For example, a mother who labelled her four-month-old child as a 'brat' any time he cried, was encouraged to replace this with labels, like 'you sometimes cry when your hungry, don't you?'.

Marital conflict can also interfere with setting up positive parent–child routines. Methods for working with couples will be described in more detail below. However, here it is sufficient to say that the primary caregiver's partner (who may sometimes, but not always, be the father) must be given a specific role in the anticipatory routine that precedes episodes of positive caregiver–child interaction, otherwise there is a risk that the routine will be interrupted by conflict within the couple. Such conflict is often motivated by jealousy on the part of the partner.

Coaching should be used as a central therapeutic method. That is, successive approximations to the target behaviours should be praised. The therapist should praise the parent and child for successive approximations to positive interaction. The parent should be coached in how to praise the child for successive approximations to age-appropriate positive behaviour.

The main emphasis should be on the use of a reward system and praise to shape behaviour and reach targets. Parents should be praised by therapists and parents should be trained in how to use praise, star-charts and prizes for children who accumulate a certain number of stars for engaging in positive target behaviours.

Punishment should be avoided. Parents should be coached in how to anticipate problem behaviour on the part of the child and attempt to avoid it by distracting the child or ignoring problem behaviours if they occur. Where parents are taught to use time-out routines, following the guidelines in Chapter 9, it is very important to frame these as brief episodes of no more than a couple of minutes in which the child has no access to positive interaction with the parent. Time-out periods should terminate when the child has been in time-out for about three minutes or, thereafter has stopped protesting about being in time-out for 30 seconds. Immediately after time-out, the parent must engage in a positive event with the child and re-establish positive parent–child interaction. There is always a danger that time-out will be used by stressed parents as an excuse to lock children in a room or closet for a couple of hours.

Parents should be encouraged to keep written records of progress, using monitoring charts like that given in Figure 9.1 and to celebrate success in reaching targets. There should also be an acceptance that relapses will occur. There should also be an acceptance that therapists and parents will meet patches of resistance where cooperation problems occur from time to time. These should be managed in the ways suggested in Chapters 7 and 9.

Interventions with Couples

Marital intervention may focus on helping couples solve conflicts without recourse to escalating angry exchanges, which are displaced onto the child. A full account of couples therapy is given in Chapter 14. Four components are particularly important when conducting couples work with disorganised couples following an episode of physical child abuse. These are: communication skills training; problem-solving training; behavioural exchange training; and coaching in affective self-disclosure, empathy and development of insight into relational patterns that underpin discord, violence and dissatisfaction.

Guidelines for training in communication and problem solving are given in Chapters 9 and 14. However, they will be recapped here, with specific reference to working with disorganised couples who have been involved in child abuse. The overall strategy for training couples in refining these interpersonal skills is to explain the skills and point out how necessary they are for jointly handling stressful childcare tasks. Then couples are invited to demonstrate their current level of skill development by taking a non-emotive issue and communicating or problem solving around it. The therapist then gives feedback, first indicating the couples' competencies and then pinpointing areas where improvements are required. Once the couple show competence in managing non-emotive issues, they are invited to progress to discussing emotive issues. The therapist interrupts them when they break the rules of good problem solving or communication and coaches them back on track. Homework assignments, which involve practising these skills, are also given.

In communication training, couples need to be trained in both listening to each other and sending clear messages to each other. Listening skills include giving attention without interruption, summarising key points made by their partner and checking that they have understood accurately. Skills required to send clear messages include: discussing one problem at a time; being brief; deciding on specific key points; organising them logically; saying them clearly; checking that they have been understood; and allowing space for a reply. Couple are encouraged to make congruent 'I statements', such as, 'I would like to watch *Into the West*', rather than 'you statements', such as, 'You would love *Into the West*', or declarations such as, 'Every one knows that *Into the West* is a great film'. Couples are praised for avoiding negative mind reading, blaming, sulking, name-calling or interrupting.

Problem solving involves: defining large, vague and complex difficulties as a series of smaller and clearer problems; brainstorming options for solving these smaller problems one at a time; exploring pros and cons of each option; agreeing on a joint action plan; implementing the plan; reviewing progress; revising the original plan if it was unsuccessful; and celebrating if it was successful.

Once couples have been coached in the basics of communication skills and problem-solving skills, they are invited to use them to try to solve emotive problems associated with joint childcare responsibilities, such as who should feed and change the baby on specific occasions and how personal time away from the responsibility of childcare should be organised for each person. The therapist should praise couples for using skills correctly and get them back on track if they fail to use problem solving and communications skills correctly. They should also be encouraged with emotive problems to declare that the problem (not their partner) makes them feel bad and to acknowledge their own share of the responsibility in causing the problem (rather than blaming their partner). They should be encouraged to anticipate obstacles when engaging in problem solving.

For families where child abuse has occurred, core beliefs about getting needs met are often a central obstacle to solving problems and reaching mutually acceptable agreements. Parents in these families tend to frame problems in terms of how they will get their own needs met, rather than how both members of the couple and the child can get as many needs met as possible. A common theme is that everyone cannot have their needs met, and if one person's needs are met, it must be at the expense of the needs of another not being met. A related idea is that in any negotiation about family members having their needs met there must be a winner and a loser. The idea that everyone can win if enough thought is given to solving a problem, must constantly be reintroduced by the therapist.

Destructive behavioural routines are a second set of obstacles to solving problems and reaching mutually acceptable agreements. These routines may involve attributing negative intentions to one's partner without checking these out and then either criticising, nagging, blaming, name-calling, and citing previous instances of the partner's misdemeanours on the one hand, or withdrawing, sulking or becoming intoxicated on the other. Often anger from these types of exchanges is displaced onto the abused child.

Helping partners recognise these behavioural routines and patterns, and the beliefs and feelings that underpin them, is a critical part of couples work. Once they are recognised, alternatives to them may be developed. Most of these routines are based on fears that needs related to personal power, esteem and intimacy will be thwarted, or a sense of being hurt when these needs have been thwarted. Alternative solutions to the escalating negative routines typically involve couples acknowledging and expressing feelings related to unmet needs and having their partner empathise with them about this. Therapists can help couples develop affective self-disclosure and empathy skills by interviewing them about these feelings and then empathising with them. Couples may then be coached in how to interview each other about these feelings that are rarely articulated and how to empathise with each other.

Behavioural exchange, offers a way to introduce greater positive reciprocity into a relationship marked by patterns of mutual punishment and conflict. It involves inviting the couple to list specific positive activities that their partner could carry out to show that they care for them. These items must be phrased positively rather than negatively and must not be the focus of a recent argument. The couple are invited to put the lists in a visible place in the house and to make a commitment to carry out some of the items on the list for their partner each day. However, *quid pro quo* arrangements are to be avoided. The idea is to increase the number of positive exchanges but within the context of a good-will ethic rather than a *quid pro quo* contract.

When couples engage in more positive exchanges; use communication and problem-solving skills; and engage in affective self-disclosure and empathy, solving childcare problems becomes far less stressful and far less likely to result in domestic violence.

Network Meetings

Interventions in the wider system aim to reduce stress and increase social support. Such interventions must be tailored to the ecology of the family, as mapped out during the assessment process. The following are common examples of interventions that fall into this category: work with the extended family to increase the amount of support they offer the child's primary caregiver; arranging a befriender, a home-help or a counsellor home-visiting service for an isolated parent; arranging participation in a local parent support self-help group; organising a place for the child and caregiver in a local mother and toddler group; introducing the family to a baby-sitting circle; setting up periodic relief foster care; supporting an application for housing transfer to a less cramped residence; referring family members to medical or other professional services to solve problems requiring specialist input.

Parent-focused Interventions

Individual interventions for the parents fall into two broad categories (Azar, 1989). In the first are those interventions that aim to improve parenting skills and knowledge about child development. In the second are those that aim to help parents with other psychological problems which are not exclusively associated with the parenting role, such as anger management, mood regulation and drug abuse. Parent-craft and child development classes should include a structured curriculum covering the needs and competencies of children who fall into the same age-band as the parents' children. The curriculum should be organised in such a way that parents are given a conceptual understanding of a topic followed by a practical exercise in which they plan how they will put this new knowledge into practice in caring for their child. Individual work with parents to help develop anger and mood regulation skills should offer parents a way to conceptualise how in specific situations they are likely to become apparently uncontrollably angry, sad or anxious, and then provide them with a way of controlling their emotional states in these situations.

SUMMARY

Physical abuse refers to deliberately inflicted injury or deliberate attempts to poison a child. The annual incidence of physical child abuse (excluding corporal punishment) is 5–9%, depending on the narrowness of the criterion used to define abuse. For a proportion of children, child abuse has profound negative short- and long-term physical and psychological effects. The range, severity and duration of effects depend on the nature and extent of the abuse and the balance of risk and protective factors present in any given case. Physical abuse may be conceptualised as the outcome of a complex process in which a child with particular characteristics, which rendered him or her vulnerable to abuse, was injured by a parent involved in an ongoing problematic behaviour pattern, subserved by particular belief systems and constrained by historical, contextual and constitutional predisposing factors. When cases are referred by statutory child protection agencies to family therapy services for treatment, initially a contract for comprehensive assessment should be established with the family and referrer. Assessment should involve interviews with all members of the child system and should cover relevant risk and protective factors and a verbal reconstruction of the abusive incident. A contract for treatment may be offered if the assessment shows that the parents accept responsibility for the abuse, are committed to meeting their child's needs, are committed to improving their own psychological well-being and where they have the ability to change. Treatment should be based on clear contracts to meet specific targets. Treatment and case management plans involve a central focus on improving parent–child interaction through direct work with parents and children together. This may be supplemented with couples work, interventions in the wider system and individual work for parents focusing on parent-craft and the management of personal difficulties, such as mood and anger regulation. Children may also receive input in therapeutic pre-school placements.

FURTHER READING

Browne, K. & Herbert, M. (1997). *Preventing Family Violence*. Chichester: Wiley.

Dale, P. (1986). *Dangerous Families: Assessment and Treatment of Child Abuse*. London: Tavistock.

MacDonald, G. (2001). *Effective Interventions for Child Abuse and Neglect. An Evidence-Based Approach to Planning and Evaluating Interventions*. Chichester: Wiley.

Reder, P. & Lucey, C. (1995). *Assessment of Parenting. Psychiatric and Psychological Contributions*. London: Routledge.

Chapter 11

SEXUAL ABUSE

The use of a child for sexual gratification is referred to as child sexual abuse (CSA). CSA may vary in intrusiveness (from viewing through fondling to penetration) and frequency (from a single episode to chronic abuse). A distinction is made between intrafamilial sexual abuse, such as father–daughter incest, and extrafamilial sexual abuse. In this chapter, we will be largely concerned with intrafamilial abuse. A systemic model for conceptualising these types of problems and a systemic approach to therapy with these cases will be given in this chapter. An example of a case of intrafamilial sexual abuse is presented in Figure 11.1. A three-column formulation of the abusive process is given in Figure 11.2. A formulation of exceptions to this process is given in Figure 11.3.

In international community-based self-report studies of CSA, prevalence rates in the 1990s varied from 3% to 25% in males and 8% to 42% in females (Creighton, 2004). Prevalence rates for more intrusive forms of sexual abuse involving contact were 1–16% for males and 6–20% for females. Other trends have been noted in the literature (Berliner & Elliott, 2002; Glaser, 2002; Jones, 2000; Putnam, 2003; Sequeira & Hollis, 2003; Wekerle & Wolfe, 2003). The female:male ratio for victims of CSA varies from 2.5:1 to 5:1. Less than 20% of abusers are women. CSA occurs with children of all ages but there is a peak for girls at 6–7 years and at the onset of adolescence. Estimates of the proportion of cases where CSA is intrafamilial range from about 30% to 75%. Girls are more commonly abused intrafamilially by fathers, stepfathers and siblings. Boys are more commonly abused extrafamilially by trusted family friends with authority over children. Compared with the normal population, rates of abuse are two to three times higher among children with physical and intellectual disabilities.

SYSTEMIC MODEL OF CHILD SEXUAL ABUSE

Single factor theories of sexual abuse that focus on attributes of the victim, the abuser or the social context within which the abuse occurs have been largely superseded by systemic models that conceptualise abuse as an interactional cycle of behaviour and beliefs, which involves the victim, the perpetrator and other members of the child's social system (Bentovim,

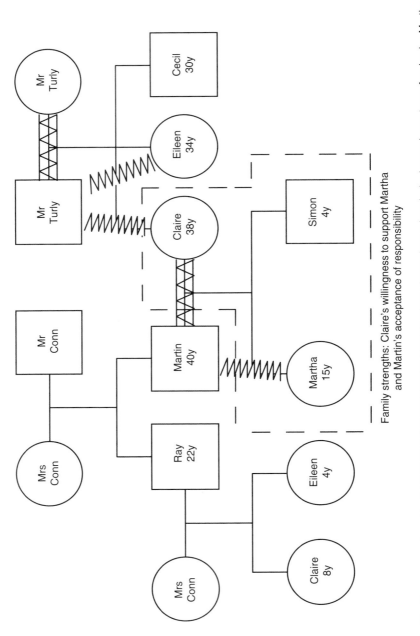

Referral. The Conns were referred by the Probation Service following Martin's release from prison, where he had served a sentence for abusing Martha over a four month period, during which his wife, Claire, was suffering from post-natal depression. Martha made the disclosure to a teacher in school and, following

Family strengths: Claire's willingness to support Martha and Martin's acceptance of responsibility subsequent legal proceedings, the father was imprisoned. Martha was aged 15 at the time of the referral, had been attending individual counselling periodically over three years since the disclosure, and was still very angry at the father, Martin. She was ambivalent about him returning home. At the time of referral he was living alone in an apartment. The mother, Claire, had been highly supportive of Martha from the start, but thought that Martin had served his sentence and deserved a chance to work towards rejoining the family. She had found it difficult to cope with the baby, Simon, over the preceding couple of years. Support offered by her brother, Cecil, and sister, Eileen, both of whom were still single, had helped her cope during Martin's imprisonment.

Assessment. The family assessment showed that Martin accepted that he had abused his daughter and wished to atone for this and work towards returning home. Claire, the mother, felt guilty that she had been unable to prevent the abuse because of her post-natal depression and felt partially responsible for it. She had made amends with her daughter and developed a strong supportive relationship with her. However, she missed Martin and wanted the family back together. The family met sufficient conditions to have a good therapeutic prognosis.

Treatment. The family engaged in a treatment programme along the lines of that described later in the chapter. Martin remained living outside the home for much of the treatment and, through marital sessions, developed a good working relationship with Claire and would visit the house regularly under Claire's supervision.

Martha never resolved her anger towards her father, despite his apology and attempts to make amends. Claire and her sister Eileen, who had a very stormy relationship with their father, during therapy hinted that they both may have been abused by him during their teens. This partial realisation helped to further deepen the protective relationship between Martha and her mother.

Figure 11.1 A case of intrafamilial sexual abuse

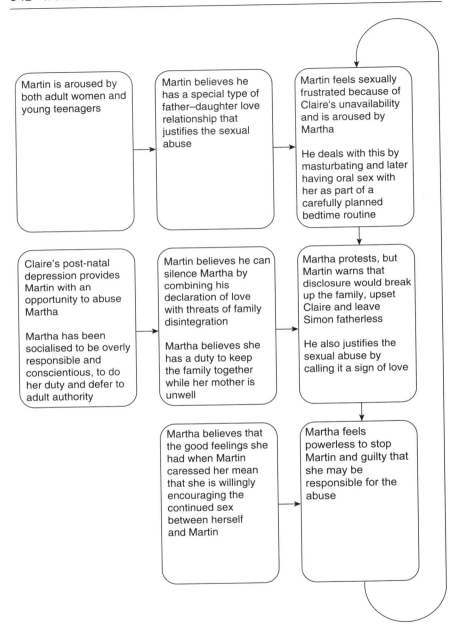

Figure 11.2 Example of a three-column formulation of child sexual abuse

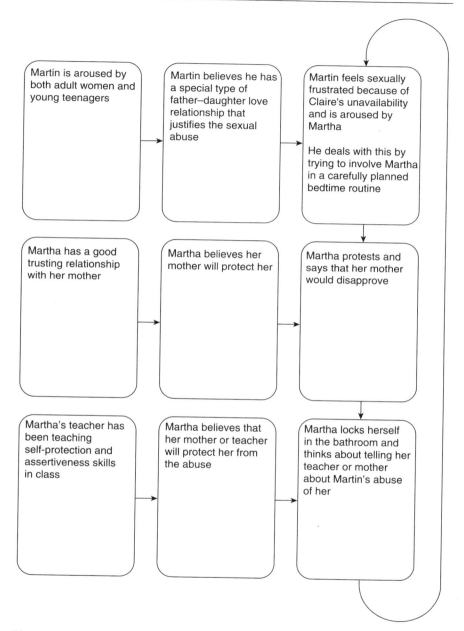

Figure 11.3 Example of a three-column formulation of an exception to sexual abuse

Elton, Hildebrand, Tranter & Vizard, 1988; Berliner & Elliott, 2002; Chaffin, Letourneau & Silovsky, 2002; Finklehor, 1984; Furniss, 1991; Glaser, 2002; Jones, 2000; Marshall, Laws & Barbaree, 1990; O'Reilly & Carr, 1998; O'Reilly, Marshall, Carr & Beckett, 2004; Putnam, 2003; Sequeira & Hollis, 2003; Trepper & Barrett, 1989; Wekerle & Wolfe, 2003). Within this cycle, children with particular characteristics, which render them vulnerable to abuse, are abused by perpetrators who are motivated for specific reasons to abuse the child and who have overcome internal and external inhibitions that would prevent the abuse occurring.

Behaviour Patterns and Beliefs

The cycle starts with the abuser reflecting on the possibility of sexually abusing a child. The abuser may engage in such reflection both because of the specific trigger situation in which he finds himself and because of a general predisposition to be motivated to abuse children. Typically, this motivation involves experiencing CSA as emotionally congruent, being aroused by children, and having access to adult partners blocked, for example, by a spouse's unavailability through illness or depression (Finklehor, 1984). The perpetrator then creates a situation in which external factors that may prevent abuse are removed or minimised. This is facilitated if the child has little parental supervision or support from a non-abusing parent and if the perpetrator and child are in a socially isolated situation. Once in a situation where there are few external inhibitors for CSA, the perpetrator overcomes personal inhibitions. He may minimise the impact of internal inhibitors, such as guilt or fear of being caught, through constructing a scenario in which the abuse in justified, its negative impact on the child is denied and the possibility of being detected is denied. Alcohol or drugs may also be used to reduce the inhibitory power of fear and guilt. The perpetrator may then coerce the child into sexual abuse by promising rewards for compliance and threatening punishment for non-compliance with the sexually abusive acts. In response to the perpetrator's coercion, the child's resistance is overcome.

The cycle may repeat the next time the perpetrator finds himself in a trigger situation. Once a pattern of abuse becomes entrenched, it may continue because children fear that their own safety or the integrity of the family will be threatened if they disclose the abuse. They may also fear reprisals from others and feel intense guilt associated with a belief that they were responsible for the abuse.

Predisposing Historical Contextual and Constitutional Factors

A range of historical, contextual and constitutional factors associated with the perpetrator, the child and the wider family context may predispose families to the occurrence of child sexual abuse.

Perpetrator Factors

A range of factors underpin perpetrators' motivation to abuse including being aroused by children, and having access to adult partners blocked, or having limited skills for making and maintaining non-coercive sexual relationships. Historically personal experience of being abused may render the perpetrator vulnerably to experiencing CSA as emotionally congruent.

Victim Factors

The child may be predisposed to being unable to resist abuse because of lack of strength, lack of assertiveness skills, fears about the consequences of not engaging in abuse, or the presence of a physical or intellectual disability. Following the abusive acts, children's resistance to further abuse may be weakened because they may believe that they were partly responsible for the abuse and because they fear the consequences of disclosure.

Family Factors

Bentovim et al. (1988) provide an important account of disorganised and over-organised patterns of family functioning that are commonly observed in cases of father–daughter incest. In disorganised families, CSA occurs because the chaotic way the family functions entails few external inhibitors for the father's or older sibling's abuse of the children. The father typically abuses a number of children and this is partially acknowledged within the family but kept secret from the public. The father bullies the family into accepting his right to abuse the children, so the abuse serves to regulate conflict within the family.

Over-organised families function in an apparently ideal fashion with an idealised marriage and apparently adequate childcare. The father typically abuses a single child and this is kept secret and remains unacknowledged within the family. Sexual dissatisfaction within the marital relationship, conflict-avoidance within the marriage, and a non-supportive relationship between the abused child and the mother characterise these families. Physical illness or psychological problems, such as depression, may contribute to the mother's involvement in an unsatisfying relationship with her partner and an unsupportive relationship with her daughter. The father and daughter may take on parental roles with respect to the ill mother, or the father may take on the role of the bully to whom both his partner and daughter are subordinate. In other instances, sexual dissatisfaction within the marriage may be associated with the father viewing himself as subordinate to his partner. In these cases, the father and daughter may both adopt child-like roles with respect to the mother.

In both over-organised and under-organised families, a central risk factor is the absence of a supportive and protective relationship between the non-abusing parent and the child.

Effects of Child Sexual Abuse

Sexual abuse has profound short and long-term effects on psychological functioning (Berliner & Elliott, 2002; Browne & Finklehor, 1986; Glaser, 2002; Jones, 2000; Kendall-Tackett, Williams & Finklehor, 1993; Paolucci, Genuis & Violato, 2001; Putnam, 2003; Sequeira & Hollis, 2003). About two-thirds of sexually abused children develop psychological symptoms. Behaviour problems shown by children who have experienced sexual abuse typically include sexualised behaviour, excessive conduct and emotional problems, school-based attainment problems and relationship difficulties. In the eighteen month period following the cessation of abuse, in about two-thirds of cases behaviour problems abate. Up to a quarter of cases develop more severe problems. About a fifth of cases show clinically significant long-term problems, which persist into adulthood.

One of the most useful models for conceptualising the intrapsychic processes that underpin the behaviour problems or symptoms that arise from sexual abuse is Browne and Finklehor's (1986) traumagenic dynamics formulation. Within this formulation, traumatic sexualisation, stigmatisation, betrayal and powerlessness are identified as four distinct yet related dynamics that account for the wide variety of symptoms shown by children who have been sexually abused.

With traumatic sexualisation, the perpetrator transmits misconceptions about normal sexual behaviour and morality to the child. These may lead the child in later life to either engage in oversexualised behaviour or to avoid sex.

With stigmatisation, the perpetrator blames and denigrates the child, and coerces the child into maintaining secrecy. Following disclosure, other members of the family or the network may blame the child for participating in the abuse. The child develops negative beliefs about the self, including the ideas of self-blame and self-denigration. These beliefs lead to self-destructive behaviours such as avoidance of relationships, drug abuse, self-harm and suicide. The child may also internalise the abuser's demand for secrecy and dissociate whole areas of experience from consciousness. These dissociated memories may occasionally intrude into consciousness later in life as flashbacks.

The dynamics of betrayal begin when the trust the child has in the perpetrator is violated and the expectation that other adults will be protective is not met. These violations of trust and expectations of protection lead the child to believe that others are not trustworthy. This loss of a sense of trust in others may give rise to a variety of relationship problems, to delinquency and to intense feelings of sadness and anger.

The dynamics of powerlessness have their roots in the child's experience of being unable to prevent the abuse because of the perpetrator's use of physical force and psychological coercion. This may be compounded by the refusal of other members of the network to believe the child or take effective professional action. The child, as a result of this experience of being powerless, may develop beliefs about generalised personal ineffectiveness and develop an image of the self as a victim. These beliefs may lead to depression, anxiety and a variety of somatic presentations. The experience of powerlessness may also lead to the internalisation of a victim–persecutor internal working model for relationships, which sows the seeds for the child later becoming a perpetrator when placed in a position where an opportunity to exert power over a vulnerable person arises. Factors associated with child protection processes, including a lack of support at disclosure, multiple investigative interviews, multiplacement experiences, extended legal proceedings and proceeding that are not child-centred or child-friendly, all contribute to the powerlessness dynamic.

Protective Factors

A number of factors have a positive influence on the outcome for children who experience CSA (Berliner & Elliott, 2002; Browne & Finklehor, 1986; Carr & O'Reilly, 2004; Glaser, 2002; Jones, 2000; Kendall-Tackett et al., 1993; Putnam, 2003; Spaccarelli, 1994). Better adjustment occurs where the CSA is less severe and less chronic and where it occurred as a single form of abuse rather than in conjunction with physical abuse or neglect. Whether the abuse was perpetrated by a family member or by someone outside the family affects the outcome because it has a bearing on the degree to which trust was violated. The less trust was violated, the better the child's adjustment following abuse. At a personal level, specific characteristics and skills of abused children are protective factors. Important protective factors include assertiveness skills, physical strength, and functional coping strategies, like seeking social support and using socially supportive relationships as opportunities for catharsis. For intrafamilial sexual abuse, a strong supportive relationship with the non-abusing parent is a critical factor for ensuring adjustment following abuse. Support for the victim from members of the extended family is also a protective factor.

FAMILY THERAPY FOR CHILD SEXUAL ABUSE

In families where CSA has occurred, effective family therapy programmes are premised on a broad-based assessment. Following the work of Trepper and Barrett (1989), Giaretto (1882) and the Great Ormond Street Group (Bentovim et al., 1988; Furniss, 1991), it is now best practice to offer family therapy following thorough assessment as the core of a multisystemic programme, which includes intensive group work and dyadic work with family subsystems. Thus, alongside regular whole family meetings, group therapy may be offered to the abused girls from a number of different families together. In parallel with this, the abusing fathers from a number of families may complete a group work programme together. Concurrently, the mothers from these families may attend a group work programme together and so also may the siblings. Concurrent mother–daughter sessions and couple sessions are also held in this multisystemic approach.

However, a contract for this type of family therapy-based multisystemic programme must be offered with an awareness that family reunification is probably an appropriate treatment goal for only a minority of cases. Bentovim et al. (1988), in a 2–6 year follow-up study of 120 cases treated with a multisystemic family therapy-based approach to father–daughter incest at Great Ormond Street Hospital, found that only 14% of abused children remained with both parents; 38% remained with one parent, 28% went to foster or residential care or relatives and the remainder left home.

The specific guidelines for clinical practice when working with families where intrafamilial child sexual abuse has occurred using the approach outlined in the remainder of this chapter should be followed within the context of the general guidelines for family therapy practice given in Chapters 7, 8 and 9.

Contracting for Assessment

A contract for assessment with the possibility of subsequent treatment using a family therapy-based, multisystemic approach may be offered to families in which father–daughter incest has occurred. Contracting for assessment in cases of CSA may take a number of meetings. Initially, it may be useful to meet with the involved statutory professionals including the referring agent. These statutory professionals may be from probation departments, child protection agencies or specialist mental health agencies. The aim of this meeting is to establish that a referral is being made from a statutory agency to a treatment agency, and the respective roles that these two agencies will adopt if the family agree to an assessment contract. Ideally, the statutory agency will agree to monitor the compliance of the family with protective living arrangements for the victim. This may include the father living out of the house or the child being in care. The statutory worker may also take the role of keeping the appropriate courts or legal authorities informed of the any non-compliance with assessment and treatment. The family therapy service, ideally, should agree to confine their input to assessment and subsequently treatment, if that is appropriate, and decline to take on any statutory responsibilities. Once the roles of the statutory referring agent and the family therapy service are clear, then a three-way meeting involving the statutory service, the family therapy service and the family may be held.

The outcome of this three-way contracting meeting should be that the statutory referring agent is viewed as enlisting the aid of the family therapy agency to help the family reduce the risk of further CSA, and to assess whether family reunification is a viable long-term therapeutic goal.

The perpetrator may acknowledge his ambivalence but agree to attend therapy because he wants to remain connected to the family and (in some jurisdictions) avoid legal sanctions. In cases where the child is in care, the foster parents or childcare workers should be invited to this contracting meeting and be asked to agree to facilitate regular and frequent supervised access between the parents and the child. Finally, agreement should be made to reconvene after a family assessment has been conducted to give feedback on whether or not the family therapy service judge the family to be suitable for family treatment.

Family therapy services should decline referrals where the victim is unprotected during family assessment and treatment, since to do so may maintain the abuse. Ideally, the father/perpetrator, not the child/victim should move out of the house, since this sends a clear message about the victim's innocence and need for protection and the perpetrator's guilt and requirement for atonement.

Assessment

The first aim of family assessment is to construct three-column formulations, like those presented in Figures 11.2. and 11.3, of the abusive process and exceptions to it. The second aim is to assess the family's capacity to benefit from family based treatment. A comprehensive schedule of assessment procedures is presented in Table 11.1. The schedule includes provision for assessment of all relevant family subsystems and their relationships with members of the wider professional network. Assessment may span a number of sessions and include sessions with various subsystems of the family and aspects of the wider social network. Initially, assessment should focus on a reconstruction of the abusive incident and previous similar incidents, that is, the problem-maintaining behaviour pattern. Belief systems of parents and other family and network members that underpinned action in this cycle of abuse and secrecy may then be clarified. Of particular importance here is the process of denial of the abuse by the perpetrator. These belief systems in turn may be linked to predisposing risk factors, which have been listed above in the systemic model of sexual abuse. In constructing a three-column formulation of exceptions to the abuse, the victim's capacity to resist the perpetrator and the capacity of the mother to protect and support the child deserve particular attention.

The abuser's response to confrontation of his denial requires careful attention during assessment. The process of confronting the denial of the abusing parent may be conducted in different ways. Some professionals confront the abuser themselves in individual interviews. Others show the abuser a videotape or transcript of the child's account of the abuse. Others favour family confrontation sessions in which the abused child

Table 11.1 Components of a comprehensive child protection assessment package for use in cases of child sexual abuse

Subsystem	Evaluation methods and areas
Child	Child's account of the abusive incidents and beliefs about these
	The location of the abuse
	The frequency and duration of the abuse
	The use of violence or threats
	The presence of other people during the abuse
	The use of drugs or alcohol by the perpetrator or the child
	Whether photographs or recordings of the abuse were made
	Impact of the abuse on the child and traumagenic dynamics of sexual traumatisation, stigmatisation, betrayal and powerlessness
	Child's perception of risk factors
	Child's perception of the non-abusing parents capacity to be protective
	Coping strategies and personal strengths and resources, particularly assertiveness
	Child's wishes for the future
The non-abusing parent(s)	Reconstruction of factors surrounding the abusive incidents
	The degree to which the parent believes the child's allegations
	The degree to which the parent aids the child's disclosure
	The degree to which the parent emotionally supports and empathises with the child
	The degree to which the parent views the abuser and not the child as solely responsible for the abuse
	The degree to which the parent pursues options that will separate the abuser from the child and protect the child
	The degree to which the parent cooperates with statutory agencies such as social services
	The degree to which the parent is prepared to discuss the abuse with other family members such as siblings or grandparents
	The degree to which the parent has protected themselves from sexual abuse
	The degree to which the parent can enlist other supports to help them
	Relevant risk factors (abusers motivation and overcoming internal and external inhibitions)
	Personal resources and problems (particularly history of personal abuse)
	Parenting skills and deficits
Abuser	Reconstructing an account of the abusive incidents
	Denial of the abuse ('it never happened')
	Denial of the frequency or severity of the abuse ('it only happened once or twice and all I did was touch her once or twice')

Subsystem	Evaluation methods and areas
	Denial of the abuser's addiction to the abusive acts ('I didn't feel compelled to do it. It was a casual thing')
	Denial of the effects of the abuse effects ('it will not do any harm')
	Denial of the abuser's responsibility for the abuse (she provoked me, she was asking for it')
	Relevant risk factors (motivation and overcoming internal and external inhibitions)
	Personal resources and problems (particularly history of personal abuse)
	Parenting skills and deficits
Marital couple	In father–daughter incest – the non-abusing parent's ability to confront the denial of the abusing parent
	In father–daughter incest – dependence of non-abusing parent on the abusing parent
	In sibling abuse – degree to which parents can set limits on abuser without scapegoating
Siblings	Possibility that they may also have been abused
	Perception of risk factors
	Perception of the non-abusing parent's capacity to be protective
	Wishes for the future
	Perception of routines of family life
Role of extended family	Acceptance or denial of the abuse
	Perception of risk factors
	Perception of the non-abusing parent's capacity to be protective
	Wishes for the future
	Perception of routines of family life
	Childcare skills and deficits
	Potential for contributing to a long-term child-protection plan
Role of other involved professionals	Health, education, social services and justice professionals' expert view of risks and resources within the family
	Potential future involvement in supporting the family and protecting the child in future
	Community resource people's potential for supporting the family and protecting the child in future

Source: Based on Trepper & Barrett (1989). *Systemic Treatment of Incest: A Therapeutic Handbook*. New York: Brunner/Mazel, Smith & Bentovim (1994). Sexual abuse. In M. Rutter, E. Taylor & L. Hersov (Eds), *Child and Adolescent Psychiatry: Modern Approaches*, 3rd edn, pp. 230–251. Oxford: Blackwell, Furniss (1991). *The Multiprofessional Handbook of Child Sexual Abuse: Integrated Management, Therapy and Legal Intervention*. London: Routledge, and Bentovim et al. (1988). *Child Sexual Abuse within the Family: Assessment and Treatment*. London: Wright.

supported by the whole family confront the abuser. Whatever method is used, the aim of this procedure is to determine the openness of the abuser to giving up denial and to do this without unduly distressing the abused child. Abusers engage in denial because giving it up may entail leaving the family home; prosecution; social stigmatisation; and personal admission of guilt. It is important to empathise with the alleged abuser about his reasons for engaging in denial, and to preface this with the statistic that in less than 10% of cases do children make false allegations (Jones & McGraw, 1987).

Furniss (1991) has developed a hypothetical interviewing style that he uses in family interviews where one or both parents deny the abuse. He explores who within the family is best and worst at bottling-up secrets (such as birthday surprises). He asks each family member what they believe would happen if the abuse had occurred and the abuser admitted to it. Who would be responsible for the abuse. Who would be responsible for protection. What would be the consequences for those who failed to protect the child. What would be the consequences for each family member of lack of trust.

For eventual partial or complete family reunification, the non-abusing parent must be able to confront the abusing parent; ask him to leave the house; and then later decide whether to work towards permanent separation or family reunification, whichever is the preferable option. To be able to follow this route, there must be sufficient differentiation within the marriage, at the time of disclosure, for the non-abusing parent to be able to confront the abuser. Observing how the mother manages these challenges and draws on professional support and support from the extended family to do so is a critical part of the assessment process.

Contracting for Treatment

When contracting for treatment, following assessment, the referring statutory professional, the family therapist or therapy team and the family should attend the contracting meeting. A three-column formation of any exceptions to the abusive patterns and a three column formulation of the family process in which the abusive incident was embedded, constructed with the family during the assessment process, should be outlined. In light of this, a statement should be made about the capacity of the family to benefit from family-based treatment. The checklist set out in Chapter 10, in Table 10.2, offers a framework for assessing a family's capacity to engage in treatment. Where the perpetrator accepts responsibility for the abuse; where both parents are committed to meeting their child's needs; where they are committed to improving their own psychological well-being; and where they have the ability to change by reducing denial and increasing protectiveness, the prognosis is good. Where less than three of these conditions are met, it is unlikely that even the most skilful professional team would be able to offer a viable treatment package. In such instances, family reunification is not a valid treatment goal.

If the family therapy service can offer treatment to the family because it meets the criteria for treatment suitability, then specific goals, a clear specification of the number of treatment sessions and the times and places at which these sessions will occur should all be specified in a contract. Such contracts should be written and formally signed by the parents, the family therapist and the statutory referrer. The treatment contract should be designed to help family members meet these specific goals and progress should be reviewed periodically. Treatment goals for sexually abused children may include:

- developing assertive self-protective skills
- developing a protective relationship with the non-abusing parent or carer
- learning to control conduct and sexualised behaviour problems
- processing intense emotions associated with the abuse and related coercion
- developing a positive view of the self
- being open to negotiating a relationship with the abuser that has appropriate boundaries.

Typical goals for non-abusing parents or carers in CSA cases are:

- learning how to offer the abused child a protective and supportive relationship
- working through the mixed feelings arising from the abuse.

Typical treatment goals for perpetrators of CSA include:

- giving up denial and accepting full responsibility for the abuse
- developing a lifestyle that does not involve sexual abuse
- demonstrating remorse and offering a full statement of responsibility and apology to the abused child and other family members.

These goals may be achieved within the context of a multisystemic intervention programme that includes regular family therapy sessions and concurrent group therapy for individual family members, with mother–daughter sessions and couple sessions scheduled as required.

Family Treatment Interventions

Ideally the abuser must live outside the family for the duration of the therapy, until the family develops protective patterns of interaction to prevent re-abuse. This may require at least a year of work. In many cases of fa-ther–daughter sexual abuse, family reunification may not be possible and therapy may aim to negotiate a protective home environment in which it is safe for the father to have periodic supervised access to the children. To conduct family therapy in situations where the abuser is still strongly locked into denial and the non-abusing parent has not yet taken a protec-tive stance towards the abused child compounds the abused child's dis-tress and should not be done.

Family therapy sessions are a forum in which the reality of sexual abuse is shared by all family members, and the three-column formulation is offered as a map that highlights the abuse-maintaining roles of all fam-ily members within this and the belief systems that allow these roles to persist. However, family sessions are also a form within which the three-column formulation of those exceptional circumstances within which abuse was expected to occur and did not may be explored further with a view to building on the family strengths inherent in these exceptions.

Each time a family session occurs and the reality of the abuse is ac-knowledged by all family members, the processes of denial, secrecy and coercion that accompanied the abuse are further weakened. Family ses-sions provide a forum where siblings can contribute to supporting a fam-ily ethos that undermines the secrecy of abuse. Where siblings have been abused or have been in danger of abuse, this may emerge in whole family meetings.

The development of a more protective relationship between the non-abusing parent and the abused child may be identified as a particular fo-cus for work to prevent the recurrence of the abuse. This work may require the child to express her anger and disappointment to the non-abusing parent and the non-abusing parent to express regret and guilt. Moth-ers, in cases of father–daughter incest, face many obstacles in reaching a position where they can wholeheartedly support their abused daugh-ters. Many mothers view supporting their daughters as synonymous with leaving their husbands. When the abused child and the non-abusing parent have expressed their views about the past and their roles in the abuse-maintaining system, the focus moves to ways in which the abused child and the non-abusing parent may spend time together to develop a supportive relationship. Often this will involve closing the emotional gap that has developed during the period of the abuse.

A difficulty with this type of work is that while the non-abusing par-ent is trying to develop this supportive relationship with the abused child, the abused child will typically be showing a range of conduct, emotional and sexualised behaviour problems. Behavioural family work on these using contingency contracts and reward systems for appropri-ate behaviour, as outlined in Chapter 9, will be required. This work, will help non-abusing parents draw a clear generational boundary between themselves and the abused child. The struggle around these issues of behavioural control may span a considerable period of time, since a lack of appropriate generational boundaries is an integral aspect of child sexual abuse. Non-abusing parents may use the forum of group therapy to seek support during these difficult struggles. Abused children may also use individual or group therapy as a forum for developing self-control skills.

Once the relationship between the abused child and the non-abusing parent has become protective and a firm integenerational boundary has been drawn, and once the abusing parent's denial has begun to decrease markedly as a result of group therapy for abusers, a series of sessions in which the abused child and the protective parent meet with the abuser may be convened. In these sessions, the abused child supported by the protective parent confronts the abuser with their experience of the abuse and forcefully expresses the anger and distress associated with abuse, the coercion and the secrecy, and requests that the abuser give up denial. It is important that in these sessions the full impact of the abuse on the child is made clear to the abuser. When the abuser says that he wishes to give up denial and apologises and makes a commitment that he will not re-abuse the child again, the more family members that are a witness to this the better. It may be appropriate to involve all siblings and members of the extended family in this apology session. Apology process can appear legitimate but be ineffective because of the way the abuser and victim are involved in the process (Crenshaw, 2004). It is important that the abused child feel no pressure to forgive the abuser. Abused children may say that they hope they will be able to forgive the abuser when he has consistently shown over a period of years that he can be true to his word. Apology sessions work best if the abuser is helped in individual sessions to construct a written apology that is read out during the apology session. There is a danger, if the apology is not written, that under pressure in the apology session the abuser will lapse into justifications for the abuse and denial of responsibility.

At this stage, a series of sessions for the mother and father may be held. These sessions may be used to help the couple work through the feelings that they have for each other arising from the abuse. Abusers may use these sessions to express guilt and remorse. Non-abusing parents may use the sessions to express anger and disappointment. There may then be a shift in focus to the present and to planning either the gradual reintroduction of the abuser into family life or separation. In either situation, the therapist coaches the couple in problem solving and communication skills, as outlined in Chapter 9, since problems in conflict management is a central difficulty for many families in which abuse occurs. Over-organised families tend to avoid conflict, and often abuse is part of a conflict avoidance behaviour pattern. Under-organised families tend to use acting-out sexually or aggressively as a way of regulating conflict.

Concurrent Group Therapy for Abused Children

Group therapy may be conducted as a short-term (12 session) programme with 5–8 group members in a closed group. For these groups to work well, it is useful if they are fairly homogeneous, with participants being the same age and having suffered either intrafamilial or extrafamilial abuse. Ideally, such groups are run jointly by a male and female therapist, who offer the child an alternative model of parenting to that offered by their own parents, marked by openness, clear communication and respect. Group work for abused children provides a forum in which they can recount and remember the traumatic abusive events and ventilate their intense mixed feelings about the abuse. These feelings include anger, sadness, anxiety, loyalty, sexual feelings and confusion. Often these intense feelings and related memories have been split-off from awareness and have not been integrated into the children's views of themselves. Through recounting and remembering, this material may be processed and integrated into the view of the self. Gradually, children may reach a situation where they explicitly recall the abuse and the feelings, both negative and positive associated with it. They must be helped to clarify that it was the abuser who was guilty and not them, although things that the abuser said may have made them feel guilty as may the pleasurable aspects of sexual arousal that they may have felt. They may be offered an opportunity to experience their anger towards the abuser, their fear of him, their sadness at the loss of the type of relationship they would have liked to have had, their anxiety that the family may spilt up for ever, and their continued loyalty to the abuser and guilt about disclosure that conflicts with their feelings of loyalty to the abuser. Anger at the non-protective parent may also be explored and sadness that the non-protective parent was unable to help.

A second function of the group is to learn to distinguish between needs for affection and care, on the one hand, and sexual needs, on the other. Abused children may have difficulty making this distinction and may therefore signal to peers or carers that they require sexual gratification when they actually want emotional support. In this context, information about normal sexual development, and the normal way people's sexual needs are met may be given. Normal heterosexual and homosexual development may be discussed. For children who have been abused by a same-sex parent, beliefs that this will effect their sexual orientation need to be addressed. Where children or teenagers engage in sexual acting-out behaviour, a behaviour modification programme in which the child is rewarded for appropriate rather than sexualised attempts to get emotional needs met may be used. This type of programme may be run in the group and at home, with the non-abusing parent monitoring the child and giving the rewards for appropriate behaviour. With teenage children, a self-control and self-reinforcement system may be used.

A third function of the group is to provide the children with peer-based social support. In this context, it is important that groups be narrowly age-banded since during childhood and adolescence children find it easier to gain social support from peers of about the same age.

A fourth function of the group is to learn to identify situations in which abuse might occur and how to mange these assertively. Role-play and rehearsal or video-feedback are useful methods for learning assertiveness skills.

A fifth function of the group is to help abused children work out what they would like to achieve in their relationships with their parents. Usually this involves finding a way to speak to their parents, particularly about intense negative feelings, so that the abused children feel heard rather than silenced or coerced into secrecy. Children can use the group to rehearse what they want to say to the family in family sessions about their anger and disappointment, their sense of betrayal, their sense of being worthless and powerless, their wish to forgive and to trust, but their difficulty in doing so.

A final function of the group is to help abused children develop a view of the self as good, worthwhile and powerful, rather than powerless.

Concurrent Group Therapy for Non-abusing Carers

Therapy for non-abusing carers ideally should be conducted in homogeneous groups. Group work should allow members to ventilate feelings of remorse and guilt and to receive support from other group members. Non-abusing carers may receive information on how to establish a protective relationship with their children and support each other during the difficult process of recovery within the group. The group is a forum in which non-abusing carers may brainstorm methods for effectively protecting their abused children in future. The group may be used as a forum for exploring how non-abusing wives may renegotiate their relationships with their abusive husbands. A final function of group work for non-abusing carers is to provide a place for dealing with issues arising from non-abusing carers own experiences of intrafamilial sexual abuse, which is not uncommon. Their children's disclosure may reawaken memories and feelings associated with this abuse, which may be processed within the group.

Concurrent Group Therapy for Abusers

Therapy with abusers has two main goals. The primary goal is to let go of denial and own up to the sexual abuse. The second goal is to accept the addictive nature of sexual abuse and to develop a lifestyle that includes strategies for managing potential relapses.

A high level of persistent confrontation coupled with empathy and support is required to help abusers give up denial because of the many important functions fulfilled by this defence. Denial wards off a sense of guilt for having hurt the abused child and allows the abuser to preserve a view of the self as good. Denial removes the fear of prosecution, punishment and loss of family relationships. Denial may also allow abusers to avoid recognition of their own abusive childhood experiences. Finally, denial allows the abuser to continue to engage in a psychologically addictive process.

For abusers to construct a lifestyle that includes strategies for avoiding relapsing into abuse, the combined problem-solving resources of a group are particularly useful, both in generating ideas and options and in critically evaluating group members' attempts to implement these experiments in new ways of living.

To achieve the goals of letting go of denial and developing a new lifestyle, a number of therapeutic approaches are useful. In the early stages of the group treatment programme, members may begin by describing to the group, the sequence of events that commonly occur in their episodes of abuse. These cycles typically begin with a specific triggering event or build-up of stresses that leads the abuser to feel tension. This in turn leads the abuser to engage in a sexual fantasy, which often involves images of abusing the child. The fantasy leads on to active planning about how to arrange the next episode of abuse. Here sexual arousal may become more intense and be the precursor of the abusive actions. The abusive act may lead to a sense of relief for the abuser and may be followed by coercive threats or bribes to retain a veil of secrecy around the abuse. Putting the abusive cycle into words is an important first step in letting go of denial.

These patterns of interaction that surround abusive episodes may occur within the context of wider patterns of interaction that involve attempts to control the abuse. From time to time, abusers may feel guilt because they recognise that the abuse is damaging their child and so they attempt to stop. Anxiety, irritability and restlessness may then be experienced, particularly when trigger events occur, and so the abuser relapses into the original pattern of abusive behaviour.

Abusers' behaviour in these cycles of interaction is often underpinned by dysfunctional internal working models of intimate or caregiving relationships, which in turn may often have their basis in predisposing early life experiences of physical or sexual abuse. Making these links between the pattern of interaction in which the abuse is embedded, the beliefs, expectations and narratives concerning relationships, and abusive early life experiences is an important part of therapy.

Typically, abusers pepper their accounts of these abusive cycles with cognitive distortions that reflect their denial of their responsibility and culpability. They may deny that the abuse happened at all; minimise the number of times it happened; minimise the degree of coercion or violence involved; minimise the effects of the abuse by claiming it will probably do little harm in the long term and minimise the degree of their wrong-doing by pointing to more severe cases of abuse. They may also attempt to reduce their guilt by maximising or exaggerating their virtues. Thus, they may point out ways in which they have been helpful or caring to the abused child, or behave like a perfect group member showing pseudo remorse and supporting the therapist in his attempts to help other group members show remorse. Denial may also find expression in projecting blame. The abused child may be blamed for provoking the abuse. Abusers may also blame outside factors for their abusive actions. For parents who sexually abuse their children, these factors may include drug or alcohol use, or the sexual difficulties that they have with their partners. This projection of blame involves defining the self as powerless to control their addictive abusive behaviour. The therapist's role is to encourage the group to confront all of these expressions of denial, while also inviting the group to support the group member and empathise with his need to engage in the denial process. Ultimately, abusers must develop the skill of self-confrontation where they recognise their own attempts to use denial as a way of warding off abuse-related guilt or avoiding the negative consequences of abusive behaviour. Towards the end of this phase of group therapy, the abuser may use a number of concurrent family therapy sessions to acknowledge the abuse to the whole family; to acknowledge the impact of the abuse on the abused child and other family members; to apologise for the abuse; and make a commitment not to re-offend.

When abusers have made marked progress in giving up denial and developed some self-confrontational skills, the focus of the group work shifts to developing lifestyles that include strategies for reducing the chances of relapses. Group members may develop profiles of high-risk situations and related fantasies, and brainstorm methods for avoiding the situations and terminating the fantasies. This may require decisions to avoid being alone with the abused child or other potential victims. In concurrent family therapy sessions, abusers may negotiate with the non-abusing family members how best to use the resources of the family to avoid re-abusing the child. This may lead on to exploring ways in which they may appropriately take on a parental role in the future. That is, how can they meet their children's needs for affection, control, increasing autonomy, intellectual stimulation, and so forth without sexualising the interactions and without introducing secrecy.

During this part of therapy, some abusers may acknowledge the impact of early abusive experiences on themselves and identify how trigger situations reactivate internal working models of abuser–victim relationships. When these internal working models are articulated, abusers may make a pact with the group, with themselves and with their families not to re-enact the abuse they experienced.

As abusers explore ways to restructure their lifestyle within the family so as to avoid future sexual abuse, the focus shifts to ways of managing their own sexual and emotional needs. This often involves addressing marital issues within marital therapy. The central concern is to help the couples develop communication and problem-solving skills, described in Chapters 9 and 14, and facilitate them in using these skill to address the way in which they sort out their mutual needs for intimacy and power sharing within the marriage.

Long-term membership of a self-help support group may be a useful way for abusers to avoid relapse. If this option is unavailable, booster sessions offered at widely spaced intervals is an alternative for managing the long-term difficulties associated with sexual offending.

SUMMARY

Prevalence rates for more intrusive forms of sexual abuse involving contact are about 1–16% for males and 6–20% for females. Most abusers are male. About two-thirds of all victims develop psychological symptoms and for a fifth these problems remain into adulthood. Children who have been sexually abused show a range of conduct and emotional problems, coupled with oversexualised behaviour. Traumatic sexualisation, stigmatisation, betrayal and powerlessness are four distinct yet related dynamics that account for the wide variety of symptoms shown by children who have been sexually abused. The degree to which children develop the four traumagenic dynamics and associated behaviour problems following sexual abuse is determined by stresses associated with the abuse itself and the balance of risk and protective factors within the child's family and social network. Case management requires the separation of the child and the abuser to prevent further abuse. A family therapy-based multisystemic programme of therapeutic intervention should help the child process the trauma of the abuse, and develop protective relationships with non-abusing parents and assertiveness skills to prevent further abuse. For the abuser, therapy focuses on letting go of denial and developing and abuse-free lifestyle.

FURTHER READING

Bentovim, A., Elton, A., Hildebrand, J., Tranter, M. & Vizard, E. (1988). *Child Sexual Abuse Within The Family: Assessment and Treatment*. London: Wright.

Crenshaw, W. (2004). *Treating Families and Children in the Child Protective System. Strategies for Systemic Advocacy and Family Healing*. New York: Brunner Routledge.

Furniss, T. (1991). *The Multiprofessional Handbook of Child Sexual Abuse: Integrated Management, Therapy and Legal Intervention*. London: Routledge.

Trepper, T. & Barrett, M. (1989). *Systemic Treatment of Incest: A Therapeutic Handbook*. New York: Brunner/Mazel.

Chapter 12

CONDUCT PROBLEMS

Families in which children have conduct problems may be referred for family therapy. In pre-adolescent children, these problems may include refusal to follow parental instructions; aggression directed to parents and siblings; destructiveness including damaging objects within the home; lying; and theft from the home. In adolescents, conduct problems may include all of these difficulties and more extreme rule violations, which extend beyond the confines of the home into the school and wider community. Adolescent conduct problems often occur within the context of deviant peer groups. Because adolescent conduct problems affect the wider community, juvenile justice, social services, special education and mental health professionals often become involved. Family disorganisation and parental criminality or adjustment problems, which occur in a proportion of these cases, also contribute to multiagency involvement. For example, professionals from adult mental health services and probation may have regular contact with the parents of children with conduct problems. Within diagnostic systems, such as the DSM-IV-TR and ICD-10, conduct problems are referred to as oppositional defiant disorder and conduct disorder, with the former reflecting a less pervasive disturbance than the latter and possibly being a developmental precursor of conduct disorder (American Psychiatric Association, 2000; World Health Organisation, 1992). A systemic model for conceptualising these types of problems and a systemic approach to therapy with these cases will be given in this chapter. A case example is given in Figure 12.1 and three-column formulations of problems and exceptions are given in Figure 12.2. and 12.3.

Overall prevalence rates for conduct problems range from 4% to 14%, depending on the criteria used and the population studied (Carr, 1993; Meltzer, Gatward, Goodman & Ford, 2000). These problems are more than twice as common as emotional difficulties in children and adolescents. Conduct disorders are more prevalent in boys than in girls with male: female ratios varying from 2:1 to 4:1. Comorbidity for conduct problems and other problems, such as ADHD, emotional disorders, developmental language delay, and specific learning disabilities is quite common, particularly in clinic populations.

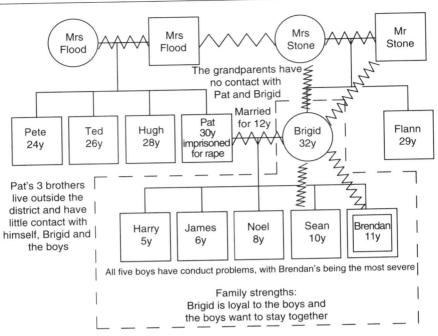

Referral. The Floods were referred by a social worker following an incident where, Brendan, aged 11, had assaulted neighbours by climbing up onto the roof of his house and thrown rocks and stones at them. He also had a number of other problems according to the school headmaster, including academic underachievement, difficulty in maintaining friendships at school and repeated school absence. He smoked, occasionally drank alcohol, and stole money and goods from neighbours. His problems were long-standing but had intensified in the six months preceding the referral. At that time, his father, Pat, was imprisoned for raping a young girl in the small rural village where the family lived.

Family history.   From the genogram it may be seen that Brendan was one of five boys who lived with his mother at the time of the referral. The family lived in relatively chaotic circumstances. Prior to Pat's imprisonment, the children's defiance and rule breaking, particularly Brendan's, was kept in check by their fear of physical punishment from their father. Since his incarceration, there were few house rules and these were implemented inconsistently, so all of the children showed conduct problems but Brendan's were by far the worst. Brigid had developed intense coercive patterns of interaction with Brendan and Sean (the second eldest). In addition to the parenting difficulties, there were also no routines to ensure that bills were paid, food was bought, washing was done, homework completed or regular meal and sleeping times were observed. Brigid supported the family with welfare payments and money earned illegally from farm-work. Despite the family chaos, she was very attached to her children and would sometimes take them to work with her rather than send them to school because she liked their company.

Brigid had a long-standing history of conduct and mood problems, beginning early in adolescence, and was being treated for depression. In particular, she had conflictual relationships with her mother and father which were characterised by coercive cycles of interaction. In school, she had academic difficulties and peer relationship problems.

Pat, the father, also had long-standing difficulties. His conduct problems began in middle childhood. He was the eldest of four brothers, all of whom developed conduct problems, but his were by far the most severe. He had a history of becoming involved in aggressive exchanges that often escalated to violence. He and his mother had become involved in coercive patterns of interaction from his earliest years. He developed similar coercive patterns of interaction at school with his teachers, at work with various gangers and also in his relationship with Brigid. He had a distant and detached relationship with his father.

Brigid had been ostracised by her own family when she married Pat, who they saw as an unsuitable partner for her, since he had a number of previous convictions for theft and assault.

Pat's family never accepted Brigid, because they thought she had 'ideas above her station'. Brigid's and Pat's parents were in regular conflict, and each family blamed the other for the chaotic situation in which Pat and Brigid had found themselves. Brigid was also ostracised by the village community in which she lived. The community blamed her for driving her husband to commit rape.

Formulations.   Formulations of Brendan's conduct problems and exceptions to these are given in Figure 12.2 and 12.3. Protective factors in the case included the mother's wish to retain custody of the children rather than have them taken into foster care; the children's sense of family loyalty; and the school's commitment to retaining and dealing with the boys rather than excluding them for truancy and misconduct.

Treatment.   The treatment plan in this case involved a multisystemic intervention programme. The mother was trained in behavioural parenting skills to break the coercive behaviour patterns that maintained Brendan's conduct problems. A series of school liaison meetings between the teacher, the mother and the social worker were convened to develop and implement a plan that ensured regular school attendance. Occasional relief foster care was arranged for Brendan and Sean (the second eldest) to reduce the stress on Brigid.

Figure 12.1 Case example of conduct problems

SYSTEMIC MODEL OF CONDUCT PROBLEMS

Single factor models of conduct problems, which explain the difficulties in terms of characteristics of the child, the parents, the family, the peer group or broader sociocultural factors, have been largely superseded by multisystemic models (Henggeler et al., 1998; Rutter, Giller & Hagell, 1998; Sexton & Alexander, 1999, 2003). These complex models view conduct problems as arising in vulnerable youngsters who are involved in problematic parent–child relationships, within the context of disorganised families, in which parents have personal adjustment problems and marital difficulties and these families may be situated within disadvantaged communities. In addition, negative peer and school influences may contribute to the difficulties, as may uncoordinated multiagency involvement.

Behaviour Patterns

Coercive family process is central to the development and maintenance of conduct problems (Patterson, Reid & Dishion, 1992). A coercive parenting style has three main features. First, parents have few positive interactions with their children. Second, they punish children frequently, inconsistently and ineffectively. Third, the parents of children with conduct problems negatively reinforce antisocial behaviour by confronting or punishing the child briefly and then withdrawing the confrontation or punishment when the child escalates the antisocial behaviour, so that the child learns that escalation leads to parental withdrawal. The other side of this interaction is that the child coaches the parent into backing down from escalating exchanges by withdrawing each time the parent gives in. This withdrawal brings the parent a sense of relief.

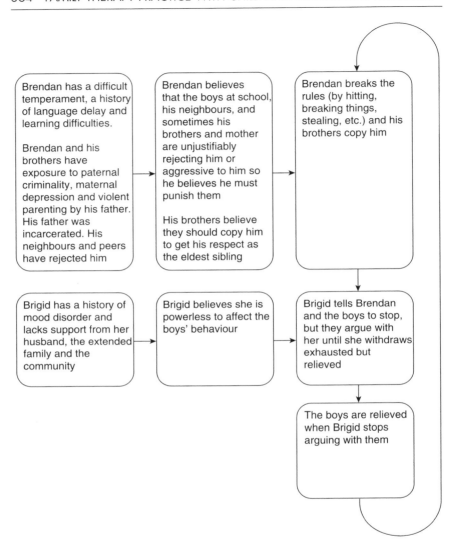

Figure 12.2 Example of a three-column formulation of conduct problems

Families containing youngsters with conduct problems often become involved with multiple agencies such as child and adult mental health, special education, juvenile justice, probation and so forth. A lack of interprofessional coordination, cooperation and consistency may reinforce the family's disorganised approach to managing their children's conduct problems and so exacerbate them.

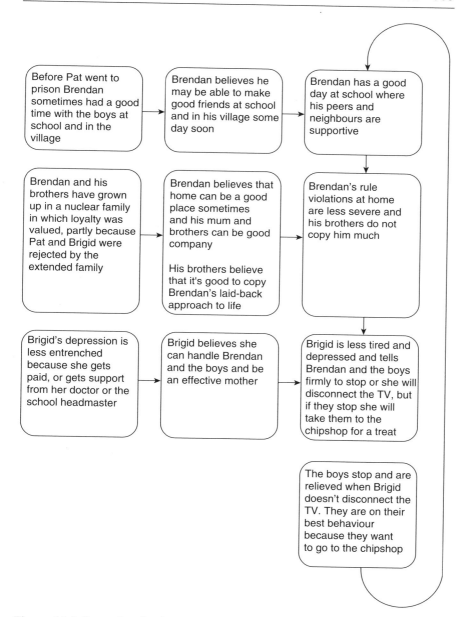

Figure 12.3 Example of a three-column formulation of an exception to conduct problem

Belief Systems

The coercive behaviour pattern just described is associated with problematic belief systems. Children come to expect that, if they persist with aggressive behaviour long enough, their parents will stop hassling them. Parents come to believe that, if they give in to their children's aggression, they will leave them in peace. Two other sets of beliefs common in families where conduct problem are the main concern also deserve mention.

Parents of children with conduct problems may treat them punitively because they attribute their children's misbehaviour to negative intentions rather than to situational factors. That is, they may hold the belief that their children are intrinsically bad or deviant rather than seeing the misbehaviour as a transient response to a particular set of circumstances from a child who is intrinsically good.

Children with conduct problems, probably because of their chronic exposure to punishment (albeit ineffective punishment) develop a belief that threatening social interactions are highly probable. Thus, they become biased in the way they construe ambiguous social situations such that they are more likely to interpret these as threatening than benign. Because of this they are more likely to respond negatively to their parents, teachers and peers.

Predisposing Factors

A wide variety of developmental, contextual and constitutional factors may predispose parents and children to become involved in behaviour patterns and to develop belief systems that maintain conduct problems. These include early parent–child relationship factors; characteristics of the child and the parent; characteristics of the marriage and the family; and features of the school, peer group and wider community.

Early Parent–Child Relationship Factors

Abuse, neglect and lack of opportunities to develop secure attachments are important aspects of the parent–child relationship that place youngsters at risk for developing conduct disorder. Disruption of primary attachments through neglect or abuse may prevent children from developing internal working models for secure attachments. Without such internal working models, the development of prosocial relationships and behaviour is problematic. With abuse, children may imitate their parent's behaviour by bullying other children or sexually assaulting them.

Child Factors

Youngsters with difficult temperaments and attention or overactivity problems are at particular risk for developing conduct disorder because they have difficulty regulating their strong negative emotions and so require very consistent and firm parenting coupled with warmth to help them sooth their negative mood states. Providing this type of parenting would be a challenge even for a resourceful and well-supported parent.

Parental Factors

Youngsters who come from families where parents are involved in criminal activity, have psychological problems, who abuse alcohol, or who have limited information about child development are at risk for developing conduct problems. Parents involved in crime may provide deviant role models for children to imitate. Psychological difficulties, such as depression or borderline personality disorder, alcohol abuse, inaccurate knowledge about child development and management of misconduct, may constrain parents from consistently supporting and disciplining their children.

Marital Factors

Marital problems contribute to the development of conduct problems in a number of ways. First, parents experiencing marital conflict or parents who are separated may have difficulty agreeing on rules of conduct and how these should be implemented. This may lead to inconsistent disciplinary practices and triangulation of the child. Second, children exposed to marital violence may imitate this in their relationships with others and display violent behaviour towards family, peers and teachers. Third, parents experiencing marital discord may displace anger towards each other onto the child in the form of harsh discipline, physical or sexual abuse. This in turn may lead the child, through the process of imitation, to treat others in similar ways. Fourth, where children are exposed to parental conflict or violence, they experience a range of negative emotions, including fear that their safety and security will be threatened, anger that their parents are jeopardising their safety and security, sadness that they cannot live in a happy family, and conflict concerning their feelings of both anger towards and attachment to both parents. These negative emotions may find expression in antisocial conduct problems. Fifth, where parents are separated and living alone, they may find that the demands of socialising their child through consistent discipline in addition to managing other domestic and occupational responsibilities alone, exceeds their personal resources. They may, as a result of emotional exhaustion, discipline inconsistently and become involved in coercive problem-maintaining patterns of interaction with their children.

Family Disorganisation Factors

Factors that characterise the overall organisation of the family may predispose youngsters to developing conduct problems. Middleborn children, with deviant older siblings in large, poorly organised families, are at particular risk for developing conduct disorder. Such youngsters are given no opportunity to be the sole focus of their parents' attachments and attempts to socialise them. They also have the unfortunate opportunity to imitate the deviant behaviour of their older siblings. Overall family disorganisation with chaotic rules, roles and routines; unclear communication and limited emotional engagement between family members provides a poor context for learning prosocial behaviour, and it is therefore not surprising that these, too, are risk factors for the development of conduct problems.

School-based Factors

A number of educational factors, including the child's ability and achievement profile and the organisation of the school learning environment, may maintain conduct problems (Rutter, Maughan, Mortimore & Ouston, 1979). In some cases, youngsters with conduct problems truant from school, pay little attention to their studies and so develop achievement problems. In others, they have limited general abilities or specific learning difficulties and so cannot benefit from routine teaching practices. In either case, poor attainment, may lead to frustration and disenchantment with academic work and this finds expression in conduct problems, which in turn compromise academic performance and future employment prospects.

Schools that are not organised to cope with attainment problems and conduct problems may maintain these difficulties. Routinely excluding or expelling such children from school allows youngsters to learn that if they engage in misconduct, then all expectations that they should conform to social rules will be withdrawn. Where schools do not have a policy of working cooperatively with parents to manage conduct difficulties, conflict may arise between teachers and parents that maintains the child's conduct problems through a process of triangulation. Typically the parent sides with the child against the school and the child's conduct problems are reinforced. The child learns that if he misbehaves, and teachers object to this, then his parents will defend him.

These problems are more likely to happen where there is a poor overall school environment. Such schools are poorly physically resourced and poorly staffed so that they do not have remedial tutors to help youngsters with specific learning difficulties. There are a lack of consistent expectations for academic performance and good conduct. There may also be a lack of consistent expectations for pupils to participate in non-academic school events such as sports, drama or the organisation of the school. There is typically a limited contact with teachers. When such contact occurs there is lack of praise-based motivation from teachers and a lack of interest in pupils developing their own personal strengths.

Peer-group Factors

Non-deviant peers tend to reject youngsters with conduct problems and label them as bullies, forcing them into deviant peer groups. Within deviant peer groups, antisocial behaviour is modelled and reinforced.

Community Based Factors

Social disadvantage, low socioeconomic status, poverty, crowding and social isolation are broader social factors that predispose youngsters to developing conduct problems. These factors may increase the risk of conduct problems in a variety of ways.

Low socioeconomic status and poverty put parents in a position where they have few resources on which to draw in providing materially for the family's needs and this in turn may increase the stress experienced by both parents and children. Coping with material stresses may compromise parents' capacity to nurture and discipline their children in a tolerant manner.

The meaning attributed to living in circumstances characterised by low socioeconomic status, poverty, crowding and social isolation is a second way that these factors may contribute to the development of conduct problems. The media in our society glorify wealth and the material benefits associated with it. The implication is that to be poor is to be worthless. Families living in poverty may experience frustration in response to this message. This frustration may find expression in violent antisocial conduct or in theft as a means to achieve the material goals glorified by the media.

Stressful Life Events and Lifecycle Transitions

Conduct problems may have a clearly identified starting point associated with the occurrence of a particular precipitating lifecycle transition or stress, or they may have an insidious onset where a narrow pattern of normal defiance and disobedience mushrooms into a full-blown conduct disorder. This latter course is associated with an entrenched pattern of ineffective coercive parenting, which usually occurs within the context of a highly disorganised family.

Major stressful life events, particularly changes in the child's social network, can precipitate the onset of a major conduct problem through their effects on both children and parents. Where youngsters construe the stressful event as a threat to safety or security, then conduct problems may occur as a retaliative or restorative action. For example, if a family move to a new neighbourhood this may be construed as a threat to the child's security. The child's running away may be an attempt to restore the security that has been lost by returning to the old peer group. Where parents find that life stresses, such as financial problems, drain their psychological resources, then they may have insufficient energy to consistently deal with their children's misconduct and so may inadvertently become involved in coercive patters of interaction that reinforce the youngster's conduct problems.

The transition to adolescence may precipitate the development of conduct problems largely through entry into deviant peer groups and associated deviant recreational activities, such as drug abuse or theft. With the increasing independence of adolescence, the youngster has a wider variety of peer-group options from which to choose, some of which are involved in deviant antisocial activities. Where youngsters already have developed some conduct problems in childhood, and have been rejected by non-deviant peers, they may seek out a deviant peer group with which to identify and within which to perform antisocial activities, such as theft or vandalism. Where youngsters, who have few pre-adolescent conduct problems, want to be accepted into a deviant peer group they may conform to the social pressure within the group to engage in antisocial activity.

Outcome

Children who become involved in coercive family processes with their parents by middle childhood develop an aggressive relational style which leads to rejection by non-deviant peers. Such children, who often have specific learning difficulties, typically develop conflictual relationships with teachers and consequent attainment problems. In adolescence, rejection by non-deviant peers and academic failure make socialising with a deviant delinquent peer group an attractive option.

Conduct problems are the single most costly child-focused problem (Kazdin, 1995). For more than half of all children with conduct problems, the delinquency of adolescence is a staging post on the route to adult antisocial personality disorder, criminality, drug abuse and conflictual, violent and unstable marital and parental roles, and progeny with conduct problems (Burke et al., 2002; Farrington, 1995; Kazdin, 1995; Loeber et al., 2000; Rutter et al., 1998). The greater the number of systemic risk factors mentioned in the preceding sections, the poorer the prognosis. In addition, youngsters who first show conduct problems in early childhood and who frequently engage in many different types of serious misconduct in a wide variety of social contexts including the home, the school and the community have a particularly poor the prognosis.

Protective Factors

For conduct problems, protective factors within the family system include positive parent–child and marital relationships, and good communication and problem-solving skills. For children, an easy temperament and the capacity to make and maintain new friendships are important personal protective factors. A supportive and well-resourced educational placement that can deal flexibly with youngsters' special needs, such as learning difficulties or school-based conduct problems, may be seen as protective educational factors. A non-deviant support network and pro-social role model are important peer group protective factors. Low stress and a high level of social support within the extended family and social network are protective factors also. Good interprofessional and interagency communication and coordination is a protective factor insofar as it may lead to a more positive response to treatment.

FAMILY THERAPY FOR CONDUCT PROBLEMS

For pre-adolescent conduct problems, parent training, where parents are coached to use reward systems and behavioural control programmes, has been shown in many studies to be a particularly effective treatment (Behan & Carr, 2000). For adolescent conduct problems, the results of empirical studies show that functional family therapy, multisystemic family therapy, and combining family therapy with temporary treatment foster care are the most effective available treatments (Brosnan & Carr, 2000). The specific guidelines for clinical practice when working with youngsters with conduct problems using these approaches outlined in the remainder of this chapter should be followed within the context of the general guidelines for family therapy practice given in Chapters 7, 8 and 9.

Contracting for Assessment

Contracting for assessment with families containing a pre-adolescent with home-based conduct problems is relatively straightforward, since it is commonly the parents who are the customers for change. It is sufficient in such instances for the parents and child to attend the initial contracting session. In some instances, the school is the main customer, and the parents have been advised to secure counselling for their child or the child will either be excluded from school or not permitted to return if the child has already been excluded. In these instances, a representative of the school, the parents and the child may be invited to the contracting meeting. In cases where an adolescent has been involved in serious acts of delinquency and has been placed in care because he is beyond the control of his parents, contracting is a more complex process. In such cases, in the contracting meeting it is important to include the referring agent, a statutory professional from the child protection or juvenile justice agency since these are potential agents of social control representing the state; foster parents or childcare workers from the youngsters temporary care placement; the parents; and the child.

Within the contracting meeting, the therapist invites the main customers to outline what the main conduct problems are that need to be resolved and why they think family therapy is necessary. The possible positive outcomes of family therapy deserve discussion and these may be framed in different ways depending on the customer and the context of the referral. With cases where the parents are the customer, the parents and child may find it useful to see family therapy as a way of helping everyone in the family to get along better. Where the school is the main customer, family therapy may be offered in cooperation with school staff to prevent a child from being excluded from school or to enable an excluded child to return. Where a statutory child protection or juvenile justice agency is the customer and the child is in temporary care, family therapy, when conducted in cooperation with the statutory agency, may provide an avenue for the child to be reunited with the family.

The more complex the case, the more likely it will be that contracting may take a couple of sessions. If families cannot reach a decision about whether to make a contract or not, then it is preferable to invite them to take a week to think about it and come back and discuss it again. Proceeding to conduct a family assessment without a clear contract is a recipe for resistance. It is also unethical.

Assessment

The first aim of family assessment is to construct three-column formulations, such as those presented in Figures 12.2. and 12.3, of a typical episode in which a conduct problem occurs and an exceptional episode in which a conduct problem is expected to occur but does not. When enquiring about conduct problems and family interaction patterns that maintain these, the coercive family process is a useful hypothesis with which to start. Belief systems that underpin action in this cycle may then be clarified. These in turn may be linked to predisposing risk factors, which have been listed above in the systemic model of conduct problems. With multi-problem families where there is multiagency involvement, assessment is typically conducted over a number of sessions and involves meetings or telephone contact with family members, foster parents or care staff who have regular contact with the referred child, involved school staff, and other involved professionals.

Contracting for Treatment

When contracting for treatment, following assessment, if the assessment has proceeded without cooperation problems then only the family need to attend the session in which a contract for treatment is established. However, in complex cases where there have been cooperation problems such as failure to attend for appointments, then school staff, statutory child-protection or juvenile justice professionals, foster parents and care staff, or other key customers for change, should be invited to the contracting meeting. A summary of the family's strengths and a three-column formulation of the family process in which the conduct problems are embedded should be given.

Specific goals, a clear specification of the number of treatment sessions and the times and places at which these sessions will occur should all be specified in a contract. In statutory cases, such contracts should be written and formally signed by the parents, the family therapist and the statutory professional. Many families in which conduct problems occur have organisational difficulties. Non-attendance at therapy sessions associated with these problems can be significantly reduced by using a home visiting format wherever possible or organising transportation if treatment must occur at a clinic.

The central aim of family therapy should be preventing the occurrence of coercive cycles of interaction and promoting positive exchanges between the parents and children. Sessions addressing these issue are the core of family therapy in cases where the main contract focuses on the reduction of conduct problems. It is less confusing for clients if child-focused family therapy sessions that have this overriding aim are defined as distinct from supplementary adult-focused or marital therapy sessions, in which the focus is on improving parental adjustment or couples enhancing their relationship, so that they can support each other in caring for their child. In some instances it may be appropriate for some sessions to be held which involve the parents with their own parents to help resolve family-of-origin difficulties and foster support from the extended family.

Treatment

For most cases where conduct problems are the main concern, a chronic-care rather than an acute-care model is the most appropriate to adopt. Episodes of treatment should be offered periodically over an extended time period (Kazdin, 1995). Effective family-based treatments are tailored to the developmental stage of the child and the complexity of the family difficulties with the most intensive therapy being offered to complex families with multiple problems (Behan & Carr, 2000; Brosnan & Carr, 2000). For home-based conduct problems, occurring within the context of a family with few risk factors, weekly sessions over two or three months may be sufficient. For pervasive severe conduct problems, occurring within the context of a family with multiple risk factors, two or three sessions per week with the family and members of the professional network over a period of year may be required, and in the most sever cases it may be necessary to combine this with treatment foster care (Chamberlain, 1994).

In all cases, treatment should involve interventions that help families to develop new belief systems about conduct problems and alter the pattern of interaction around the problem. These include: monitoring and reframing; externalising and building on exceptions; coaching in supportive play and scheduling special time; and developing reward systems and behavioural control systems. Where deficits in communication and problem-solving skills compromise the family's capacity to follow through with these types of tasks then communication and problem-solving skills training in these areas may be appropriate. Where the problems occur in multiple contexts, such as the home, the school, and a residential care placement, it is important to hold network or liaison meetings involving the family and staff in these other settings to ensure that reward and behaviour control programmes are being well coordinated and run consistently across multiple contexts. In circumstances where marital or personal difficulties, high extrafamilial stress and low support prevent parents following through on child-focused therapeutic tasks, parent-focused interventions may be necessary. These include couples therapy, parent counselling, referral to support groups and advocacy. For severe conduct problems occurring within the context of families with multiple risk factors and few protective factors, family therapy may be conducted within the context of treatment foster care. All of these interventions have been described in detail in Chapter 9, and so will only be briefly recapped here with particular reference to conduct difficulties.

Monitoring and Reframing

Parents may be helped to shift towards more useful ways of viewing their children's misconduct by observing and monitoring the impact of antecedents and consequences on their child's behaviour. A form for monitoring target behaviour problems is given in Chapter 9 (Figure 9.1). Through reframing, parents are helped to move from viewing the child's conduct problems as proof that he is *intrinsically* bad to a position where they view the youngster as a *good child with bad habits* that are triggered by certain situations and reinforced by certain consequences. When parents bring their child to treatment, typically they are exasperated and want the psychologist to take the child into individual treatment and *fix* him. Through reframing the parents are helped to see that the child's conduct problems are maintained by patterns of interaction within the family and wider social network, and therefore family and network members must be involved in the treatment process.

Externalising and Building on Exceptions

Externalising the conduct problem involves personifying the conduct problem as an external agent (such as Angry Alice or the Hammerman), which the parents and child must work together to defeat. Ideas about how to do this may come from an exploration of those exceptional circumstances in which the conduct problem was expected to occur but did not. Such explorations may lead to solutions such as: eliminating or reducing the conditions that commonly precede aggressive behaviour; reducing children's exposure to situations in which they observe aggressive behaviour; and reducing children's exposure to situations which they find uncomfortable or tiring, since such situations reduce their capacity to control aggression. In practice, such solutions often involve helping parents to plan regular routines for managing daily transitional events, such as: rising in the morning or going to bed at night; preparing to leave for school or returning home after school; initiating or ending leisure activities and games; starting and finishing meals; and so forth. The more predictable these routines become, the less likely they are to trigger episodes of aggression or other conduct problems. Within therapy sessions or as homework, parents and children may develop lists of steps for problematic routines, write these out and place the list of steps in a prominent place in the home until the routine becomes a regular part of family life.

Supportive Play and Special Time

Parents and young children may be coached in the principles of supportive play (described in Chapter 9) and with older children and adolescents, parents may be invited to schedule special time with their youngsters. Both of these interventions allow parents and children to replace negative interaction with regular periods of positive interaction. Where fathers have become peripheral to childcare tasks, inviting them to schedule regular periods of special time or supportive play with their children has the positive effect of both increasing positive interaction with the child and reducing childcare demands on their partners. Parents need to be coached in how to finish episodes of supportive play and special time by summarising what the parent and child did together and how much the parent enjoyed it. It is productive to invite parents to view these episodes as opportunities for giving the child the message that they are in control of what happens and that the parent likes being with them. Advise the parent to foresee rule-breaking and prevent it from happening. Finally, invite parents to notice how much they enjoy being with their children.

Reward Systems

Reward systems, which are described in detail in Chapter 9, involve agreeing a small number of target positive behaviours and a system for

Table 12.1 Points chart for an adolescent

For these target behaviours you can earn points	Points that can be earned
Up by 7.30 am	1
Washed, dressed and finished breakfast by 8.15	1
Made bed and standing at door with school bag ready to go by 8.30	1
Attend each class and have teacher sign school card	1 per class (max 8)
Good report for each class	1 per class (max 8)
Finish homework	1
Daily jobs (e.g. taking out dustbins or washing dishes)	1 per job (max 4)
Bed on time (9.30)	1
Responding to requests to help or criticism without moodiness or pushing limits	2
Offering to help with a job that a parent thinks deserves points	2
Going to time-out instead of becoming aggressive	2
Apologising after rule-breaking	2
Showing consideration for parents (as judged by parents)	2
Showing consideration for siblings (as judged by parents)	2
Cash in points for privileges and accept fines without arguing	2

monitoring and rewarding these regularly. With pre-adolescents, star charts may be used as part of such programmes and when the child accumulates a certain number of stars these may be exchanged for a tangible and valued reward, such as a trip to the park or an extra bedtime story. With teenagers, a points system may be used. Here points may be acquired by carrying out specific behaviours and points may be lost for rule breaking. On a daily or weekly basis, points may be exchanged for an agreed list of privileges. An example of such a point system is set out in Tables 12.1 and 12.2.

The impact of formal reward systems may be increased by inviting parents to use coaching to help their children gradually develop habits that more and more closely approximate cooperative behaviour. Parents are shown how to be a role model for cooperative behaviour and routinely to give immediate praise to their children when their behaviour approximates cooperative behaviour.

Table 12.2 Adolescents privileges and fines

You can buy these privileges with points	Points	You must pay a fine for breaking these rules	Points
Can watch TV for 1 hour	10	Not up by 7.30 am	1
Can listen to music in bedroom for an hour	5	Not washed, dressed and finished breakfast by 8.15	1
Can use computer for 1 hour	5	Not made bed and standing at door with school bag ready to go by 8.30	1
Can stay up an extra 30 minutes in bedroom with light on	5	Not attend each class and not have teacher sign school card	1 per class
Can stay up an extra 30 minutes in living room	10	Bad report for each class	1 per class
Can have a snack treat after supper	20	Not finish homework within specified time	1
Can make a phone call for 5 minutes	10	Not do daily jobs (e.g. taking out dustbins or washing dishes)	1 per job
Can have a friend over for 2 hours	25	Not in bed on time (9.30)	10
Can visit a friend for 2 hours	30	Respond to requests to help or criticism with moodiness, sulking, pushing limits or arguments	5
Can go out with friend to specified destination for 1 afternoon until 6.00pm	35	Swearing, rudeness, ignoring parental requests	10 per event
Can go out with friend to specified destination for 1 evening until 11.00	40	Physical aggression to objects (banging doors, throwing things)	20 per event
Can stay over at friend's house for night	60	Physical aggression to people	30–100
		Using others things without permission	30–100

(Continued on next page)

Table 12.2 *(Continued)*

You can buy these privileges with points	Points	You must pay a fine for breaking these rules	Points
		Lying or suspicion of lying (as judged by parent)	30–100
		Stealing or suspicion of stealing at home, school or community (as judged by parent)	30–100
		Missing class or not arriving home on time or being out unsupervised without permission	30–100

Behaviour Control

With behaviour control programmes, which are described in detail in Chapter 9, parents select a small number of target negative behaviours and set clear consequences for engaging in these, the final consequence being time-out or deprivation of privileges. With behaviour control programmes, and time-out in particular, parents need to be told that initially the child will show an escalation of aggression and will offer considerable resistance to being asked to stay in time-out. However, this resistance will reach a peak and then begin to decrease quite rapidly. Attempts to help families with children who have conduct problems through exclusive reliance on behavioural control programmes, without any attempt to improve the relationships between parents and children in ways outlined in preceding sections tend to fail. Children find it easier to respond to behaviour control programmes when concurrently their relationships with their parents is enhanced through reframing, exception amplifying, scheduling supportive play and special time, and reward systems.

Behavioural control programmes are more acceptable to children if it is framed as a game for learning self-control or learning how to be *grown up*, and if the child is involved in designing and using the reward chart. Parents should be encouraged not to hold grudges after episodes of negative behaviour and time-out, and also to avoid negative mind reading, blaming, sulking or abusing the child physically or verbally during the programme. Implementing a programme like this can be very stressful for parents since the child's behaviour often deteriorates before it improves. Parents need to be made aware of this and encouraged to ask their spouses, friends or members of their extended family for support when they feel the strain of implementing the programme. Finally, the whole family should be encouraged to celebrate success once the child begins to learn self-control.

Throughout the programme, all adults within the child's social system (including parents, step-parents, grandparents, childminders, etc.) are encouraged to work cooperatively in the implementation of the programme, since these programmes tend to have little impact when one or more significant adults from the child's social system does not implement the programme as agreed. Parents may also be helped to negotiate with each other so that the demands of disciplining and coaching the children is shared in a way that is as satisfactory as possible for both parents.

Running a behavioural control programme for the first two weeks is very stressful for most families. The normal pattern is for the time-out period to increase in length gradually and then eventually to begin to diminish. During this escalation period, when the child is testing out the parents resolve and having a last binge of self-indulgence before learning self-control, it is important to help parents to be mutually supportive. The important feature of spouse support is that the couple set aside time to spend together without the children to talk to each other about issues unrelated to the children. In single-parent families, parents may be helped to explore ways for obtaining support from their network of friends and members of the extended family.

Communication and Problem-solving Training

To deal with adolescent conduct problems, parents must share a strong alliance and conjointly agree on household rules, roles and routines that specify what is and is not acceptable conduct for the child or teenager. Consequences for violating rules or disregarding roles and routines must be absolutely clear. Once agreed, rewards and sanctions associated with rules, roles and routines must be implemented consistently. The fine tuning of these types of programmes requires parents and youngsters to be able to communicate clearly with each other and solve problems about the details of running the programme in effective and systematic ways. Where parents lack these skills, communication and problem-solving training should be incorporated into treatment.

In multiproblem families where adolescents have pervasive conduct disorders, training in communication skills must precede problem-solving skills training and negotiation of rules and consequences. It is not uncommon for such families to have no system for turn-taking, speaking and listening. Rarely is the distinction made between talking about a problem so that all viewpoints are aired and negotiating a solution that is acceptable to all parties.

The aim of communication skills training is to equip parents and teenagers with the skills required to take turns at speaking clearly and presenting their viewpoint in an unambiguous way, on the one hand, and listening carefully so that they receive an accurate understanding of the other person's viewpoint, on the other. Coaching family members in communication skills may follow the broad guidelines set out in Chapter 9. The roles of speaker and listener are clearly distinguished. The speaker is invited to present their viewpoint, uninterrupted, and when they have finished the listener summarises what they have heard and checks the accuracy of their recollection with the speaker. These skills are taught using non-emotive material, using modelling and coaching. Then family members are shown how to list problems related to the adolescent's rule breaking and discuss them one at a time, beginning with those that are least emotionally charged, with each party being given a fair turn to state their position or to reply. When taking a speaking turn, family members should be coached in how to decide on specific key points that they want to make; organise them logically; say them clearly and unambiguously; and check that they have been understood. In taking a turn at listening, family members should be coached to listen without interruption; summarise key points made by the other person and check that they have understood them accurately before replying. Wherever possible, 'I statements' rather than 'you statements' should be made. For example, 'I want to be able to stay out until midnight and get a cab home on Saturday' is an 'I statement'. 'You always ruin my Saturday nights with your silly rules' is a 'you statement'. There should be an agreement between the therapist and the family that negative mind reading, blaming, sulking, abusing and interrupting will be avoided and that the therapist has the duty to signal when this agreement is being broken.

Problem-solving skills training may follow the guidelines set out in Chapter 9. Family members may be helped to define problems briefly in concrete terms and avoid long-winded vague definitions of the problem. They should be helped to subdivide big problems into a number of smaller problems and tackle these one at a time. Tackling problems involves brainstorming options; exploring the pros and cons of these; agreeing on a joint action plan; implementing the plan; reviewing progress and revising the original plan if progress is unsatisfactory. However, this highly task-focused approach to facilitating family problem solving needs to be coupled with a sensitivity to emotional and relationship issues. Family members should be facilitated in their expression of sadness or anxiety associated with the problem and helped to acknowledge their share of the responsibility in causing the problem but their understandable wish to deny this responsibility. Premature attempts to explore pros and cons of various solutions motivated by anxiety should be postponed until brainstorming has run its course. Finally, families should be encouraged to celebrate successful episodes of problem solving.

Home–School Liaison Meetings

Many adolescents with conduct problems, engage in destructive school-based behaviour and have co-morbid learning difficulties. School interventions should address both conduct and academic problems. School-based conduct problems may be managed by arranging a series of meetings involving a representative of the school, the parents and the adolescent. The goal of these meeting should be to identify target conduct problems to be altered by implementing a programme of rewards and sanctions, run jointly by the parents and the school, in which acceptable target behaviour at school is rewarded and unacceptable target behaviour at school leads to loss of privileges at home. In Figure 12.4, an example of a daily report card for use in home–school liaison programmes is presented. A critical aspect of home–school liaison meetings is facilitating the building of a working relationship between the parents and the school representative, since often with multiproblem families containing a child with conduct problems family–school relationships are antagonistic. The psychologist should continually provide both parents and teachers with opportunities to voice their shared wish to help the child develop good academic skills

Name_____Date_____

For his or her performance today, please rate this child in each of the areas listed below using this 5-point scale

1 Very poor	2 Poor	3 Fair	4 Good	5 Excellent

	Class 1	Class 2	Class 3	Class 4	Class 5	Class 6	Class 7	Class 8
Paying attention								
Completing classwork								
Following rules								
Other								
Teacher's initials								

Figure 12.4 Daily report card

and control over their conduct problems. Where youngsters also have academic underachievement problems, it is important for the therapist to advocate for the family and take the steps necessary to arrange remedial tuition and study skills training. Guidelines for convening and participating in network meetings are given in Chapter 9.

Network Meetings

Adolescents with pervasive conduct problems that occur in family, school and community settings typically become involved with multiple agencies and professions in the fields of health, education, social services and law enforcement. In addition, other members of their families commonly have connections to multiple agencies and professionals. Coordinating multisystemic intervention packages and cooperating with other involved agencies for these multiproblem youngsters, from multiproblem families with multiagency involvement is a major challenge. First, it is important to keep a list of all involved professionals and agencies and to keep these professionals informed of your involvement. Second, arranging periodic coordination meetings is vital so that involved professionals and family members share a joint view of the overall case management plan. In particular, where children or adolescents are in temporary or relief residential or foster care, it is important to hold liaison meetings with foster parents or childcare staff so that behavioural control and reward system programmes agreed in family therapy are also conducted in the residential or foster care settings.

Parent-focused Interventions

Marital or personal difficulties, high stress and low support may prevent parents from engaging effectively in child-focused therapeutic tasks. In such instances, parent-focused interventions may be necessary. These include couples therapy, parent counselling, referral to parent support groups and advocacy to help parents secure state benefits, adequate housing, health and education entitlements. The art of effective family therapy with multiproblem families where children present with conduct problems is to keep a substantial portion of the therapy focused on resolving the conduct problem by altering the pattern of interaction between the child and the parents that maintains the conduct difficulties, and only deviate from this focus into parent-focused issues when it is clear that the parents will be unable to maintain focus without these wider issues being addressed. Where parents have personal or marital difficulties and require individual or marital counselling or therapy, ideally separate sessions should be allocated to these problems. Other members of the involved professional network may be designated to manage them or a referral to another agency may be made. Common problems include maternal depression, social isolation, financial difficulties, paternal alcohol and substance abuse and marital crises. A danger to be avoided in working with multiproblem families is losing focus and becoming embroiled in a series of crisis intervention sessions, which address a range of family problems in a haphazard way.

Treatment Foster Care

Older adolescents with chronic pervasive conduct problems may require treatment foster care, which is a particularly intensive approach to treatment (Chamberlain, 1994). Initially, the child with the conduct disorder is placed with trained foster parents who implement a behavioural programme to reduce conduct problems. Concurrently and afterwards a multisystmeic therapy package is offered to the youngster and his natural family with the aim of the adolescent returning home once his conduct problems have become manageable. The child returns for increasingly longer visits to the natural family, who use their parenting training and support from the foster parents to implement behavioural programmes to modify the child's conduct problems and improve the quality of parent–child relationships. Placement typically is for about nine months. For cases receiving multisystemic therapy and treatment foster care, small case loads not exceeding 5–10 cases per keyworker and 24-hour on-call availability for crisis intervention is an important feature of effective programmes. Follow-up multisystemic therapy or family therapy over a number of years is essential in complex cases.

SUMMARY

Conduct problems are the most common type of referral to child and family outpatient clinics. Children with conduct problems are a treatment priority because the outcome for more than half of these youngsters is very poor in terms of criminality and psychological adjustment. Up to 14% of youngsters have significant conduct problems and these difficulties are far more common among boys. The central clinical features are defiance, aggression and destructiveness; anger and irritability; and pervasive relationship difficulties within the family, school and peer group. A systemic model of conduct problems highlights the role of relationships and characteristics of members of the family and the wider social connunity in the development and maintenance of conduct problems. Treatment of conduct problems should be based on thorough multisystemic assessment. In all cases, treatment should involve interventions that help families to develop new belief systems about conduct problems and alter the pattern of interaction around the problem. Where deficits in communication and problem-solving skills compromise the family's capacity to follow through with therapeutic tasks then communication and problem-solving skills training in these areas may be appropriate. Where the problems occur in multiple contexts, such as the home, the school and a residential care placement, it is important to hold network meetings involving the family and staff in these other settings to ensure that therapeutic interventions are applied consistently across multiple contexts. In circumstances where marital or personal difficulties, high extrafamilial stress and low support prevent parents following through on child-focused therapeutic tasks, parent-focused interventions may be necessary. These include couples therapy, parent counselling, referral to support groups and advocacy. In extreme cases, treatment foster care may be combined with family therapy.

FURTHER READING

Alexander, J. & Parsons, B. (1982). *Functional Family Therapy*. Montereny, CA: Brooks Cole.

Alexander, J., Barton, C., Gordon, D., Grotpeter, J., Hansson, K., Harrison, R., Mears, S., Mihalic, S., Parsons, B., Pugh, C., Schulman, S., Waldron, H. & Sexton, T. (1998). *Blueprints for Violence Prevention, Book Three: Functional Family Therapy (FFT)*. Boulder, CO: Centre for the Study and Prevention of Violence. Available at http://www.colorado.edu/cspv/publications/blueprints.html

Chamberlain, P. (1994). *Family Connections: A Treatment Foster Care Model For Adolescents With Delinquency*. Eugene OR: Castalia.

Henggeler, S., Mihalic, S., Rone, L., Thomas, C. & Timmons-Mitchell, J. (1998). *Blueprints for Violence Prevention, Book Six: Multisystemic Therapy (MST)*. Boulder, CO: Centre for the Study and Prevention of Violence. Available at http://www.colorado.edu/cspv/publications/blueprints.html

Henggeler, S., Schoenwald, S., Bordin, C., Rowland, M. & Cunningham, P. (1998). *Multisystemic treatment of Antisocial Behaviour in Children and Adolescents*. New York: Guilford.

Herbert, M. (1987). *Behavioural Treatment of Children with Problems*. London: Academic Press.

Sexton, T. L., & Alexander, J. F. (1999). *Functional Family Therapy: Principles of Clinical Intervention, Assessment, and Implementation*. Henderson, NV: RCH Enterprises.

FURTHER READING FOR PARENTS

Barkley, R. (1998). *Your Defiant Child: Eight Steps to Better Behaviour*. New York: Guilford.

Fogatch, M. & Patterson, G. (1989). *Parents & Adolescent Living Together. Part 1. The Basics*. Eugene, OR: Castalia.

Fogatch, M. & Patterson, G. (1989). *Parents & Adolescent Living Together. Part 2. Family Problem Solving*. Eugene, OR: Castalia.

Forehand, R. & Long, N. (1996). *Parenting the Strong-Willed Child: The Clinically Proven Five Week Programme for Parents of Two to Six Year Olds.* Chicago, IL: Contemporary Books.

Webster-Stratton, C. (1992). *Incredible Years: Trouble-Shooting Guide for Parents of Children Aged 3–8.* Toronto: Umbrella Press.

Sharry, J. (2002). *Parent Power: Bringing Up Responsible Children and Teenagers.* Chichester, UK: Wiley.

Chapter 13

DRUG ABUSE IN ADOLESCENCE

Habitual drug abuse in adolescence is of particular concern because it may have a negative long-term effect on the adolescent and an intergenerational effect on their children. Drug abuse is not always a unidimensional problem and it may occur as part of a wider pattern of life difficulties. A systemic model for conceptualising these types of problems and a systemic approach to therapy with these cases will be given in this chapter. A case example is given in Figure 13.1 and three-column formulations of problems and exceptions are given in Figure 13.2. and 13.3.

Experimentation with drugs in adolescence is common (Chassin, Ritter, Trim & King, 2003; Weinberg, Harper & Brumback, 2002). Major US and UK surveys concur that by 19 years of age, approximately 80% of teenagers have drunk alcohol; 60% have tried cigarettes; 50% have used cannabis; 20% have tried other street drugs, such as solvents, stimulants, hallucinogens or opiates; and 20–40% have used multiple drugs. Between 5% and 10% of teenagers under 19 have drug problems serious enough to require clinical intervention.

SYSTEMIC MODEL OF DRUG ABUSE IN ADOLESCENCE

Single factor models of drug abuse that offer explanations in terms of biological factors, intrapsychic processes, and various characteristics of the child, the parents, the family, the peer group or society have been largely superseded by multisystemic models (Chassin et al., 2003; Cormack & Carr, 2000; Crome et al., 2004; Hawkins, Catalano & Miller, 1992; Liddle, 2005; Liddle & Hogue, 2001; Myers, Brown & Vik, 1998; Pagliaro & Pagliaro, 1996; Rowe & Liddle, 2003; Rutter, 2002; Stanton & Heath, 1995; Stanton & Todd, 1982; Szapocznik & Kurtines, 1989; Szapocznik, Hervis & Schwartz, 2002; Vik, Brown & Myers, 1997; Weinberg et al., 2002). These complex models view drug abuse as arising in vulnerable youngsters who are involved in problematic family relationships, problematic peer group relationships, and within communities where drugs are available and opportunities and other pathways self-fulfillment are blocked.

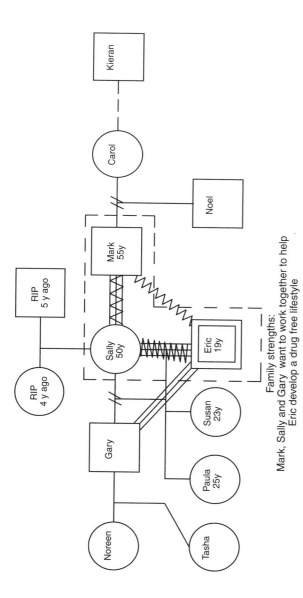

Family strengths:
Mark, Sally and Gary want to work together to help
Eric develop a drug free lifestyle

Referral. Eric and his father, Gary, sought treatment for Eric's polydrug abuse. At the time of the referral, Eric had taken a decision to stop using hard drugs, completed an outpatient detoxification programme to get off heroin, but knew that without counselling and family support he would quickly relapse as he had done on numerous previous occasions.

Assessment. Eric was living with his mother and stepfather. His drug abuse was a source of extreme conflict within the home, although he still felt partially supported by his mother. At the end of the first meeting it was agreed that Gary and Eric would invite Sally and Mark to the next appointment. The assessment led to the development of the formulations set out in Figures 13.2 and 13.3. and to a contract for treatment.

Treatment. Treatment focused on helping Gary, Sally and Mark, put their differences to one side and cooperate in helping Eric take steps to enter college, regularly attend Nar-anon meetings, and avoid the drug-using peer group of which he had been part for a few years. When relapses occurred, over the 12-month period following discharge, booster sessions were offered, and the thrust of these was helping the three adults pull together in supporting Eric's new drug-free lifestyle.

Figure 13.1 A case of polysubstance abuse

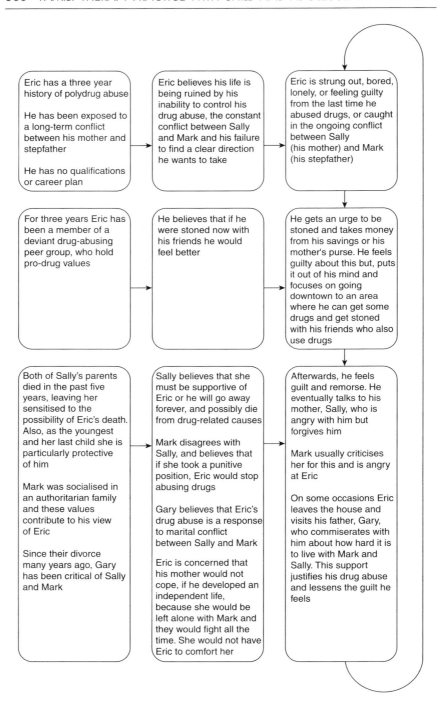

Figure 13.2 Example of a three-column formulation of drug abuse

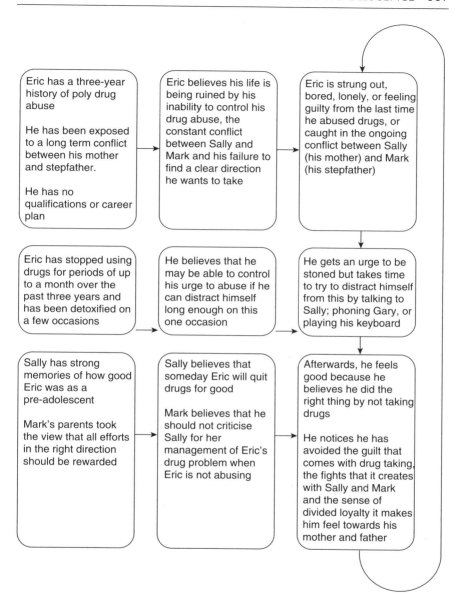

Figure 13.3 Example of a three-column formulation of an exception to an episode of drug abuse

Development of Drug Abuse

Adolescent drug abuse in western society tends to follow a progression from early use of cigarettes and alcohol, to problem drinking to the use of soft drugs to polydrug abuse (Wills & Filer, 1996). Not all adolescents progress from one stage to the next. Progression is dependent on the quality of family relationships, peer relationships, school factors and personal characteristics. However, at all stages availability of drugs is a precipitating factor when coupled with some personal wish, such as the desire to experiment to satisfy curiosity; the wish to conform to peer pressure; or the wish to control negative mood states. These negative mood states may arise as a response to recent life stresses, such as problematic family relationships, negotiating a family lifecycle transition, such as the transition to adolescence or the transition to adulthood, physical or sexual child abuse, bullying, academic failure, loss of peer friendships, parental separation, bereavement, illness, injury, parental unemployment, moving house or financial difficulties.

Involvement in a deviant peer group, parental cigarette and alcohol use and minor delinquent activities are the main risk factors that precede initial cigarette and alcohol use. Progression to problem drinking is more likely to occur if the adolescent develops beliefs and values favouring excessive alcohol use. A further progression to the use of soft drugs such as cannabis requires the availability of such drugs and exposure to peer use. A variety of family, peer group, school-based and personal factors affect the progression towards the final step of polydrug abuse, and the more of these factors that are present the more likely the adolescent is to progress to polydrug abuse.

Personal Factors

Certain personal factors may place youngsters at risk of drug abuse and, once drug taking occurs, particular personal behaviour patterns and personal beliefs and narratives may maintain drug abuse.

Predisposing Personal and Constitutional Factors

Personal factors that place youngsters at risk for drug abuse include a propensity for risk taking and positive attitudes concerning drug use. Difficult temperament and later conduct problems may predispose youngsters to drug abuse insofar as these personal characteristics may lead to involvement in a deviant peer group with a drug-using subculture. Emotional problems and low self-esteem may lead to drug abuse insofar as youngsters may use drugs to alleviate emotional distress. Specific learning disability is another personal characteristic that may place youngsters at risk for drug abuse. Drug abuse may lead to a sense of personal fulfilment that youngsters with learning disabilities are unable to obtain through academic achievement because of their disability.

Personal Beliefs and Behaviour Patterns

Once youngsters become involved in drug abuse it may be maintained by physical and psychological dependence and by a wish to regulate negative mood states that arise from physical, economic and psychosocial complications of drug abuse. Thus drug abuse may be maintained by depressed mood or anxiety arising from hepatitis, HIV infection, lack of money, relationship problems, academic and vocational difficulties, involvement in the justice system for drug-related crimes, and so forth. Drug abuse may be maintained by various belief-systems and personal narratives, such as the belief that the youngster cannot be effective in controlling drug use or by denial of the severity of the problems or the degree of dependence.

Family Factors

Certain family factors may place youngsters at risk of drug abuse and, once drug taking occurs, particular family behaviour patterns and family beliefs and narratives may maintain drug abuse.

Predisposing Family-based Risk Factors

Poor relationship with parents, little supervision from parents and inconsistent discipline, parental drug abuse, and family disorganisation with unclear rules, roles and routines are some of the family factors that may place youngsters at risk for drug abuse. Parental criminality or psychological problems, marital discord or the presence of deviant or drug-abusing siblings within the family home are other possible family-based risk factors.

Family Beliefs and Behaviour Patterns

Once youngsters begin abusing drugs, this drug abuse may be maintained by parental modelling of drug abuse, expressing positive attitudes about drug abuse, reinforcement of drug abuse through failing to consistently prohibit drug use, and failing to adequately supervise youngsters. Drug abuse may also be maintained by a process of triangulation. Here, parental conflicts are detoured through the child, so the parents chronically and inconclusively argue about how to manage the drug abuse rather than resolving their dissatisfactions with each other and then working as a cooperative co-parental team. In these instances the adolescent may engage in a covert alliance with one parent against the other. Such patterns of parenting and family organisation may be partially maintained by parental personal psychological difficulties. Parents may also become involved in drug-abuse maintaining interactions with their children if they have inaccurate knowledge about adolescent drug abuse and its management.

Network Factors

Certain network factors may place youngsters at risk of drug abuse and once drug taking occurs, particular behaviour patterns and beliefs within the wider network may maintain drug abuse.

Contextual Risk Factors within the Social Network

High levels of stress, limited support and social disadvantage within the family's wider social system may predispose youngsters to developing drug abuse, since these features may deplete parents' and children's personal resources for dealing constructively with the drug problem.

Behaviour Patterns and Beliefs within the Network

Within the professional helping network around families in which adolescents have chronic drug problems, a lack of coordination and clear communication among involved professionals including family physicians, paediatricians, psychiatrists, drug treatment counsellors, nurses, teachers, psychologists, and so forth, may maintain the adolescent's drug problems. It is not unusual for various members of the professional network to offer conflicting opinions and advice on the nature and management of drug problems to adolescents and their families. These may range from viewing the adolescent as mentally or physically ill and therefore not responsible for drug-using behaviour, on the one hand, to seeing the youngster as healthy but deviant and deserving punitive management, on the other.

Under-resourced educational placements that cannot provide a suitable learning environment for youngsters with specific learning disabilities and attainment difficulties may maintain drug abuse insofar as youngsters in such settings may cope with educational failure and achieve a sense of personal fulfilment through using drugs. Educational placements, where teaching staff have little time to devote to home–school liaison meetings and closely supervising youngsters so that they do not abuse drugs at school, may also maintain drug problems.

Drug problems may be maintained through the adolescent's attachment to a deviant peer group in which drug abuse and positive attitudes towards drugs are part of the peer group's subculture. Adolescents are more likely to continue to use drugs if they live in an area where there is high availability, a high crime rate, few alternatives to drug abuse and few employment opportunities.

Protective Factors

The probability that a treatment programme will be effective is influenced by a variety of personal and contextual protective factors. At a biological level, physical health and the absence of drug-related conditions, such as HIV infection or hepatitis, may be viewed as protective factors that may contribute to recovery. A high level of ability, an easy temperament, high self-esteem, and a capacity to make and maintain non-deviant peer friendships are all important personal protective factors.

Within the family, good relationships between parents and adolescents, a flexible family structure in which there is clear communication, high marital satisfaction and where both parents share the day-to-day tasks of caring for, and supervising the adolescent are important family-based protective factors. Accurate knowledge about drug abuse is also a protective factor.

Protective factors within the broader social network include the lack of availability of drugs, high levels of support, low levels of stress and a well-resourced educational placement. Where families are embedded in social networks that provide a high level of support and place few stressful demands on family members, then it is less likely that parents' and children's resources for dealing with drug-related problems will become depleted. Well-resourced educational placements where teachers have sufficient time and flexibility to meet children's special learning needs, attend home–school liaison meetings and offer close supervision to prevent drug taking at school contribute to positive outcomes for adolescents with drug-related problems.

Within the treatment system, cooperative working relationships between the treatment team and the family, and good coordination of multiprofessional input are protective factors.

Recovery, Readiness to Change and Relapse

When recovering from drug abuse, youngsters vary in their readiness to change and this has implications for conducting family therapy in these types of cases. Prochaska (1999) has identified five stages of therapeutic change through which individuals with drug problems progress when considering treatment: pre-contemplation, contemplation, preparation, action and maintenance. Extensive research has shown that specific techniques are maximally effective in helping clients make the transition from one stage of change to the next.

In the pre-contemplation stage, the provision of support creates a climate within which clients may ventilate their feelings and express their views about their drug problem and life situation. Such support may help clients move from the pre-contemplation phase to the contemplation phase. By facilitating an exploration of belief systems about the evolution of the drug problem and its impact on the youngster's life, the youngster may be helped to move from the contemplation to the planning stage. In the transition from planning to action, the most helpful role for the therapist to adopt is that of consultant to the clients' attempts at problem solving. This role of consultant to the clients' attempts at behavioural change is also appropriate for the transition from the action phase to the maintenance phase where the central is relapse prevention.

When youngsters have recovered from drug abuse, maintaining this recovery is influenced by their capacity to manage situations in which there is a high risk of relapse. Marlatt & Gordon (1985), in extensive research, have found that in high relapse-risk situations, individuals who have given up drug abuse and who have well-rehearsed coping strategies find that when they use these, their beliefs about their capacity to control their drug use become stronger. Consequently, they are less likely to relapse in futures similar situations. Those who have poor coping strategies for dealing with risky situations are driven to relapse by their weak beliefs in their ability to control their drug use. This leads to the abstinence violation effect (AVE), where guilt and a sense of loss of control predominate. This failure experience in turn leads to an increased probability of relapse. Thus, in the final stage of family therapy in cases of adolescent drug abuse, a central component of treatment based on this model is the development and rehearsal of coping strategies for managing situations where there is a high risk of relapse and also managing the AVE, so that a minor slip like taking drugs on one occasion, does not snowball into a major relapse.

FAMILY THERAPY FOR DRUG ABUSE IN ADOLESCENCE

Available evidence indicates that a family therapy-based multisystemic approach is the most effective available treatment for adolescent drug abusers (Cormack & Carr, 2000; Rowe & Liddle, 2003). Multisystemic family-based approaches have been shown to be effective for engaging abusers and their networks in therapy; for reducing drug abuse; for improving associated behaviour problems; for improving overall family functioning; and for preventing relapse. Effective family-based treatment programmes for adolescent drug abuse has been shown to involve the following processes: contracting and engagement; becoming drug free; facing denial and creating a context for a drug-free lifestyle; family reorganisation; and disengagement (Stanton and Heath, 1995). These processes are central to the guidelines given below. The specific guidelines given in this chapter for clinical practice when working with cases of drug abuse should be followed within the context of the general guidelines for family therapy practice given in Chapters 7, 8 and 9.

Contracting for Assessment

In cases of chronic adolescent drug abuse, engagement and contracting for treatment is a process that may span a number of sessions and involve contact with a variety of members of the adolescent's family and network. When contracting for assessment, the goal is to develop a strong working alliance with a sufficient number of family members to help the adolescent engage in treatment and change his or her drug-using behaviour. The engagement process begins with whoever comes for therapy concerned that the adolescent stop using drugs. From their account of the drug abuser's problem and the pattern of interaction in which it is embedded, other family members who are central to the maintenance of the problems or who could help with changing these problem-maintaining patterns may be identified. The therapist may then ask about what would happen if these other people attended treatment. This line of questioning throws light on aspects of resistance to engagement in treatment.

Often those family members who attend initially (for example, the mother or the drug abuser or the sibling) are ambivalent about involving other family members in treatment. They fear that something unpleasant will happen if other family members join the treatment process. Adolescents may fear that their parents will punish them. Mothers may fear that their husbands will not support them or that they will punish the adolescent. Fathers may fear that their wives will mollycoddle the adolescent and disregard their attempts at being firm. The task of the therapist is to frame the attendance of other family members in a way that offers reassurance that the feared outcome is unlikely to occur. The seriousness of the problem may always be offered as a reason why other family members will not do that which is feared. So the therapist may say:

> ABC isn't here. But from what you say, at some level, he is very concerned about this drug problem too, because we all know that there is a risk of death here. Death from overdose, AIDS, or assault is very, very common. Most families I work with are like you and ABC. They put their differences to one side to prevent the death of one of their own. So let's talk about the best way to invite ABC to come in.

The discussion then turns to the most practical way to organise a meeting. This may involve an immediate phone call, a home visit, an individual appointment for the resistant family member outside office hours or a letter explaining that the therapist needs the family member's assistance to prevent further risk to the drug-abusing adolescent.

In each meeting with each new member of the network, the therapist adopts a non-blaming stance and focuses on building an alliance with that family member and recruiting them into treatment to help deal with the drug abuse. Many parents are paralysed by self-blame and view family-based treatment as a parent-punishing process. Often this self-blame is heightened as it becomes apparent that patterns of family interaction are maintaining the drug-using behaviour. The therapist must find a way to reduce blame while at the same time highlighting the importance of the family being engaged in treatment. Here is one way to do this:

You asked me are you to blame for ABC's addiction. No you are not. Are there things you could have done to prevent it ? Probably. But you didn't know what these were. If you don't know this part of Dublin and you park below the bridge and when you go back to your car, there is a dent in it. Are you to blame for the dent? No. Because you didn't know it's a rough area down there. But the next time, you are responsible, because you know parking there is bad news. Well it's the same with drug abuse. You're not to blame for what happened. But you are partly responsible for his recovery. That's a fact. Drug abuse is a family problem because your child needs you to help recover. You can help him recover. You can reduce the risk of his death. I know you sense this and that's why you're here.

In cases where treatment is court mandated, the professional from the juvenile justice or child protection agency empowered by the court to oversee the treatment should be invited to a contracting meeting with the family. Within this meeting, the family therapy service should clarify their willingness to accept responsibility for assessment and later treatment if that is appropriate, but decline to accept statutory responsibility for ensuring treatment attendance. This responsibility may be left for the statutory agency to negotiate with the family.

The engagement phase concludes when important family members have agreed to participate in a time-limited assessment contract.

Assessment

The first aim of family assessment is to construct three-column formulations, like those presented in Figures 13.2 and 13.3, of a typical episode of drug abuse or unsuccessful attempts at its prevention occur and an exceptional episode in which drug abuse is expected to occur but does not. Belief systems that underpin family member's roles in these episodes may then be clarified. These in turn may be linked to predisposing risk factors, which have been listed in the systemic model of drug abuse presented above. With multiproblem families where there is multiagency involvement, assessment is typically conducted over a number of sessions and involves meetings or telephone contact with family members, involved school staff, and other involved professionals.

A routine medical evaluation of the adolescent is also advisable for the identification and treatment of drug-related physical complications and to determine if conditions such as hepatitis or HIV infection are present. Awareness of the extent of physical problems may have an important motivating effect for the youngster and family to become fully engaged in treatment. Regular urinalysis provides reliable information on relapse, which is critical for effective treatment of habitual but not experimental drug abusers.

In assessing the families of youngsters with drug problems, child protection issues should be kept in mind. Parents who abuse drugs act as deviant role models for their children and expose their children to a variety of other life stresses (Coleman & Cassell, 1995). These include psychological unavailability due to intoxication or drug-related illnesses especially AIDS; neglect and unresponsive parenting; poverty due to the costs of maintaining their drug abuse; exposure to aggression associated with bad debts or anger regulation problems while intoxicated or in withdrawal; exposure to criminal activities, such as prostitution; and physical child abuse due to poor frustration tolerance. Teenagers who abuse drugs and have children may require assessment from a child protection viewpoint, and reference should be made to Chapters 10 and 11 in conducting such assessments. These chapters may also be consulted in cases where the parents of referred children are engaged in habitual drug abuse that compromises the child's parenting environment.

Contracting for Treatment

When contracting for treatment, following assessment, if the assessment has proceeded without cooperation problems then, only the family need to attend the session in which a contract for treatment is established. However, in complex cases where there have been cooperation problems, such as failure to attend for appointments, then school staff, statutory child-protection or juvenile justice professionals, or other key customers for change should be invited to the contracting meeting. A clear position should be reached on whether the drug problem reflects transient experimentation or a more entrenched pattern of habitual drug abuse. A summary of the family's strengths and a three-column formulation of the family process in which the drug abuse is embedded should be given.

In light of the formulation, a treatment plan may be offered. This plan should aim to modify the youngster's pattern of drug abuse primarily by addressing significant maintaining factors and building on personal and family strengths. Specific goals, a clear specification of the number of treatment sessions and the times and places at which these sessions will occur should all be specified in a contract. In cases where treatment is court mandated, such contracts should be written and formally signed by the parents, the family therapist and the statutory professional. Many families in which drug abuse occurs have organisational difficulties. Non-attendance at therapy sessions associated with these problems can be significantly reduced by using a home-visiting format wherever possible, or organising transportation if treatment must occur at a clinic.

Family Treatment Focused on Becoming Street-drug-free

Once the family agree to participate in treatment, the therapist states that for treatment to be effective, drug use must stop first and once that has happened, alternatives to a drug-based lifestyle may be discussed, not visa versa. It is made clear that if alternatives to a drug-based lifestyle and changes in family relationships are discussed first with the expectation that this will lead to drug abuse stopping, then treatment will probably fail.

If the adolescent is not physically dependent on drugs, then a date for stopping should be set in the near future and a drug-free period of 10 days after that date set during which the parents take responsibility for round the clock surveillance of the adolescent, to both comfort him or her and prevent drug use. If the adolescent is physically dependent on drugs, plans for detoxification should be made. Home-based detoxification with medical back-up may be possible in some cases. Home-based detoxification requires the family to agree a 24-hour rota to monitor the adolescent and administer medication periodically under medical direction. Alternatively, hospital-based detoxification may be arranged. However, home-based detoxification has the advantage of giving the family a central role in the recovery process. Following home-based detoxification, family members will be less likely to become involved in patterns of behaviour that maintain drug abuse in the future. They will also be less likely to blame the treatment team when relapses occur during the recovery process and more likely to take some responsibility for dealing with these relapses.

In some instances, where opiate-dependent drug abusers are unwilling to become drug-free, participation in a methadone maintenance programme is an alternative to detoxification. Methadone is typically prescribed for people addicted to heroin as an alternative to either detoxification or continued use of street drugs. Family-based treatment in conjunction with methadone maintenance has been shown to lead to a significant reduction in the use of street drugs in comparison with methadone maintenance alone (Stanton & Todd, 1982). However, a problem with methadone maintenance is that drug dependence (albeit prescribed-drug dependence) continues to be central to the adolescent's lifestyle and to the organisation of the family.

Confronting Denial and Creating a Context for a Drug-free Lifestyle

Where adolescents have developed a drug-oriented identity and lifestyle, concurrent participation in self-help programmes, such as Nar-Anon, can contribute greatly to the effectiveness of family therapy. These programmes provide the unique combination of peer-support and confrontation required to erode denial that characterises many adolescents who have become habitual drug users. Such drug users deny their physical and psychological dependence on drugs; the impact of their drug-related behaviour on their emotional and social development; the impact of their drug-related behaviour on their family relationships; and their drug-related crimes.

If access to a self-help group is unavailable, such groups may be set up and facilitated by a family therapist. In this type of group, each member must begin by stating congruently and honestly their experience of being dependent on drugs and not in control of their lives. Members must describe repeatedly and congruently the ways in which their use of drugs has effected their relationships with all significant people in their lives and their evaluation of themselves. They must make an inventory of everyone they have wronged as a result of their drug abuse and make reparation. They must make commitment to an alternative drug-free lifestyle. The role of the facilitator is to encourage group members to confront each other's denial when they engage in various distortions, minimisation's and rationalisations for their drug-related behaviour. The facilitator must also encourage members to support each other when they have shown courage and honesty in owning up to the destructive drug-related behaviour for which they have been responsible.

As group members give up denial and accept the support of the group, unresolved personal issues related to emotional development and identity formation may emerge. These include unresolved grief associated with losses and bereavements or reactions to trauma such as physical or sexual abuse.

Adolescents who have experimented with drugs or been involved in mild recreational drug use, usually do not require group work where the focus is on denial. Rather, they require individual or group work to help them develop assertiveness skills for avoiding peer-pressure to engage in further drug use or social anxiety management training to help them deal with social pressure if this underpins their recreational drug taking.

Family Reorganisation

The central task in family reorganisation is to help the family disrupt the patterns of interaction that have evolved around the adolescent's drug-related behaviours. These drug-related behaviours include obtaining money and resources to get drugs; antisocial actions carried out when under the influence of drugs; and conduct problems, such as breaking rules about curfew times, school non-attendance, homework non-completion, theft, destruction of property and so forth. To alter interactional patterns around drug abuse and drug-related deviant behaviour, family members must be helped to set very clear, observable and realistic goals both with respect to the adolescents behaviour and with respect to the parents' behaviour. Broadly speaking, the goals for the adolescent will amount to conforming to a set of house rules, which specify minimum behavioural standards at home. The main goal for the parents will be to retain a parental alliance with respect to enforcing the house rules. Resolving conflict about the precise behaviour expected of the adolescent, the consequences for compliance and non-compliance and the way in which both parents will work jointly to support each other is a central part of this work. Communication training, problem-solving training and the use of reward and behavioural control systems in the manner described for adolescent conduct disorders in Chapter 12 may be incorporated into this stage of treatment as appropriate.

Parents should be asked to err on the side of treating adolescents as somewhat younger than their age during the early part of this phase of treatment. They should agree to relax the house rules by negotiation, as their adolescents show that they have the maturity to remain drug-free and follow the house rules.

Concurrently, the therapist should hold a number of sessions with the parents in the absence of the teenager and siblings to help them draw a boundary around their marital system by planning time together without the children. The goal here is to foster mutual support between the parents and to detriangulate the adolescent who may have been stuck in the position of a go-between with one parent looking to the child rather than their spouse for support.

Relapse Prevention and Disengagement

Once a stable drug-free period has elapsed and new routines have been established within the family, which disrupt drug-abuse maintaining family patterns, disengagement may occur. Relapse prevention is central to the disengagement process. It involves identifying situations that may precipitate relapse, and helping the youngster and family members identify and develop confidence in their coping strategies for managing these. Dangerous situations tend to be those where there is high stress, low mood, lessened vigilance and greater opportunity for drug availability and use. Coping strategies include positive thinking, distraction, avoidance and seeking social support.

One-person Family Treatment

Not all youngsters are lucky enough to have families who are willing or able to engage in conjoint family treatment. Unfortunately individual supportive or exploratory psychotherapy is of little benefit for adolescent substance abusers and, in some instances, these types of intervention may exacerbate drug abuse by helping the adolescent find historical reasons to account for their current problems. An alternative to traditional individual approaches is one-person family treatment (Szapocznik & Kurtines, 1989). In one-person family treatment, during the engagement phase, the psychologist identifies the part of the client that wants to recover and develops an alliance with that part. Treatment goals and a time-frame for the treatment contract is agreed. Then, to clarify the patterns of interaction in which the drug-related behaviours are embedded, the therapist invites the adolescent to describe the roles other family members take with respect to him or her when they engage in drug-related behaviour. When the therapist has a good idea of what these behaviours are, the therapist can role play one or more family members and check out how the adolescent responds to their mother, father, siblings, and so forth, and which aspects of their behaviour is maintaining the drug-using behaviour. This will yield a fairly accurate description of the pattern of interaction around the presenting problem.

To change the drug-abuse maintaining patterns of family interaction, the therapist maps out these patterns on paper with the adolescent and coaches him or her to act differently at home to change the family's behaviour. For example, if a regular interaction involves the adolescent's father calling him 'a good-for-nothing junkie', and this is followed by the mother attacking the father and calling him a 'waster and a lush', the adolescent might be coached to say:

> We're all in this together. We always fight with each other. It solves nothing and I'm stopping right now.

Or, if the mother has confided to the adolescent that she knows her husband is having an affair and this hurts her deeply, the adolescent might be coached to say:

> Mum, talk to him about it. Don't bring that stuff to me.

These changes in the adolescent's behaviour, will disrupt patterns of behaviour associated with drug-using behaviour. Each treatment session begins with a review of the way in which changes in the adolescent's behaviour affected drug-using related interaction patterns within the family. For one-person family treatment to be effective, it is useful if it is coupled with attendance at a drug abusers' self-help programme, such as Nar-Anon, and regular urinalysis to monitor objectively drug abstinence.

SUMMARY

Habitual drug abuse in adolescence is of particular concern because it may have a negative long-term effect on adolescents and an intergenerational effect on their children. A conservative estimate is that between 5% and 10% of teenagers under 19 have drug problems serious enough to require clinical intervention. Because of the complex aetiology of drug abuse, a multisystemic approach to assessment and treatment is essential. Effective treatment programmes for adolescent drug abuse are typically family based and involve the processes of contracting and engagement; becoming drug-free; facing denial and creating a context for a drug-free lifestyle; family reorganisation; and disengagement.

FURTHER READING

Liddle, H. A. (2005). *Multidimensional Family Therapy for Adolescent Substance abuse.* New York: Norton. A version of this book is available at www.chestnut.org/LI/cyt/products/MDFT_CYT_v5.pdf

Szapocznik, J. & Kurtines, W. (1989). *Breakthroughs In Family Therapy With Drug Abusing Problem Youth.* New York: Springer.

Szapocznik, J., Hervis, O. & Schwartz, S. (2002). *Brief Strategic Family Therapy for Adolescent Drug Abuse.* Rockville, MD: National Institute for Drug Abuse. Available at http://www.drugabuse.gov/TXManuals/bsft/BSFTIndex.html

Part IV

FAMILY THERAPY PRACTICE WITH ADULT-FOCUSED PROBLEMS

Chapter 14

DISTRESSED COUPLES

Traditionally, therapeutic work with couples has been referred to as marital therapy since most clients in this category, in the past, have been married. However, couples therapy is appropriate for married and cohabiting couples, and both heterosexual and homosexual couples may be referred for therapy. Problems with which couples present may be classified as those that are mainly individually focused and those which are fundamentally relational.

Couples may require help with managing a problem that is culturally defined as an individual psychological or medical complaint, such as depression, anxiety, alcohol abuse, schizophrenia, cancer, heart disease or the sequelae of a major accident or trauma. Couples therapy for some of these problems is addressed in Chapters 15, 16 and 17.

However, relational issues may be the primary concerns for some couples referred for therapy. That is, one or both members of the couple may be dissatisfied with their relationship and find the relationship distressing. This distress may be associated with: couples having difficulty meeting each other's needs for intimacy, support and companionship; a fair distribution of power within the relationship; sexual gratification; fidelity and honesty; or physical safety. Thus, couples may seek therapy because they feel that they have grown apart and cannot communicate with each other; or because the way they handle family finances, work role issues, household tasks or child care seems unfair; or because they have sexual problems; or because one partner is involved in an affair; or because one partner is physically abusive to another.

The goals of therapy may be to improve the relationship or to make a decision about whether or not to remain in the relationship. The present chapter is concerned with couples therapy for these relational issues. A systemic model for conceptualising these types of problems and a systemic approach to therapy with these cases will be given in this chapter. A case example is given in Figure 14.1 and three-column formulations of problems and exceptions are given in Figure 14.2. and 14.3.

In the USA and the UK between one-third and half of marriages end in divorce (Greene et al., 2003). However, most individuals who divorce or separate, remarry or enter another stable long-term relationship. This

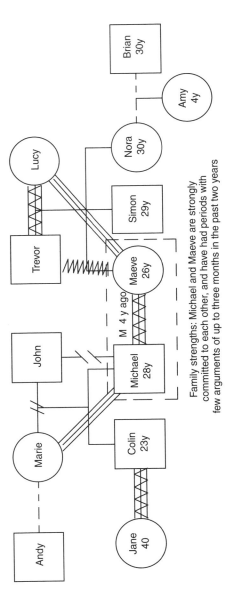

Family strengths: Michael and Maeve are strongly
committed to each other, and have had periods with
few arguments of up to three months in the past two years

Referral. Michael and Maeve sought therapy because they had been involved in repeated conflict and arguments over the preceding two years. They argued about a wide range of issues including how much time they should spend together, how much they cared for each other, sex, how they managed the house, and their finances.

Their relationship before they married and during the first year of marriage had been idyllic and they had spent all their time together, but then had begun to deteriorate. They blamed each other for the deterioration with Michael complaining that Maeve was too uptight and clingy and Maeve accusing Michael of being too laid back and distant. Their sex life had deteriorated and they now slept in separate rooms.

Formulation. Formulations of conflictual episodes and exceptional episodes where conflict was expected but did not occur are presented in Figures 14.2. and 14.3.

Therapy. In therapy it became clear that the couple had good communication and problem-solving skills but were not using them within the relationship, largely because of the impact of family-of-origin issues on their relational styles when under stress. Michael would tend to cope with his need for closeness and intimacy by becoming verbally aggressive and then withdrawing when Maeve wanted to fight with him or talk things through. This style was based on the relationship map he had acquired in his relationship with his father from whom he had now completely cut-off. Maeve's tendencies to respond with hostility or concern reflected the relationship maps she had developed in her relationships with her father and mother respectively. In therapy, they developed an understanding of the way their relationship maps from their families of origin affected the way they managed conflict in their marriage. In therapy sessions, they were helped to express the primary emotions of being hurt and misunderstood that underpinned their conflicts. They also developed regular routines for using their good communication and problem-solving skills to deal with specific issues as they arose on a day-to-day basis.

Figure 14.1 Case example of a distressed couple

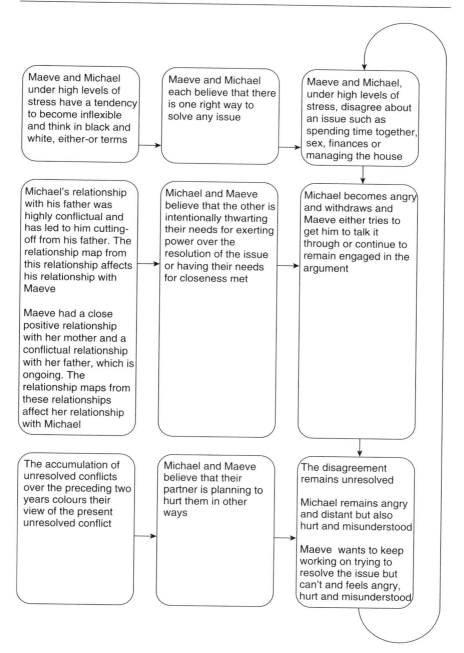

Figure 14.2 Example of a three-column formulation of relationship distress

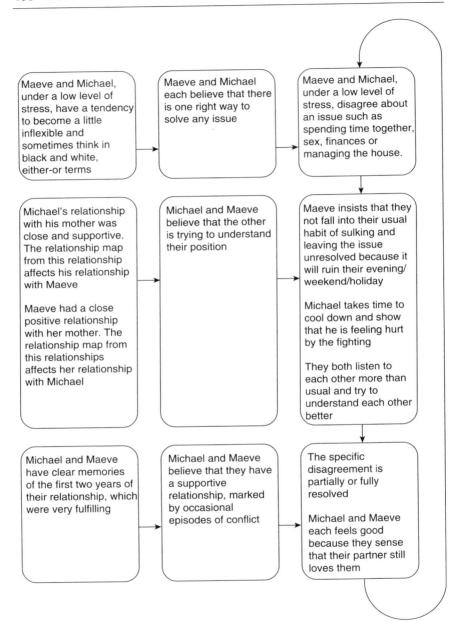

Figure 14.3 Example of a three-column formulation of an exception to relationship distress

suggests that it is not that people do not wish to maintain long-term relationships, but rather that they would like to do so but find the challenge of maintaining such relationships problematic and so fall into serial polygamy (Brody, Neubaum & Forehand, 1988). Couples therapy aims to help people with the challenge of maintaining satisfying long-term relationships.

SYSTEMIC MODEL OF DISTRESSING INTIMATE RELATIONSHIPS

Single factor models of couples problems that explain relationship difficulties exclusively in terms of behavioural patterns; belief systems; family-of-origin experiences; or wider cultural factors have made important contributions to our understanding of relationship problems, as has been shown in Chapters 1–5. However, as we saw in Chapter 6, integrative models of relationship difficulties that take account of behaviour patterns, belief systems and developmental and contextual factors offer a more comprehensive systemic framework from which to conduct couples therapy. Such an integrative approach will be adopted here.

Core Issues: Unmet Needs for Intimacy and Power

Difficulties and disagreements about communication and intimacy, on the one hand, and the power balance or role structure of the relationship, on the other, are central themes for distressed couples (Gurman & Jacobson, 2002). Underlying these difficulties are unmet needs for desired levels of intimacy and desired levels of autonomy. With respect to intimacy, usually males want greater psychological distance but more physical intimacy and females want greater psychological intimacy. With respect to power, males commonly wish to retain the power and benefits of traditional gender roles while females wish to evolve more egalitarian relationships. In disagreements about intimacy, females typically want more time spent in intimate conversation and more care and quality within the sexual relationship. Males typically want less self-disclosing conversation and more frequent sex. In disagreements over roles and power, males complain of female partners being too authoritarian and too ready to engage in nagging and fault-finding. Women complain of the constraints that the relationship places on them fulfilling their needs for personal autonomy and independence. Conversations about power often involve reference to the way the couple make financial decisions and the couple's division of labour inside and outside the home. So childcare, housework, and money are frequently mentioned in this regard. These conflicts about how couples meet each other's needs for desired levels of intimacy and power are at the heart of the problematic behaviour patterns that typify distressed couples. They are central to the beliefs that undepin these behaviour patterns. They have their roots in family-of-origin socialisation experiences and wider cultural values.

Behaviour Patterns

Observational studies of distressed couples who subsequently separate show that they gradually engage in more negative than positive interactions (Gottman, 1993; Gottman & Notarius, 2002). This escalation of negative interactions includes four linked behaviours: criticism, contempt, defensiveness and stonewalling. In meeting each other's needs, distressed couples tend to operate on a short-term *quid pro quo* basis whereas non-distressed couples tend to operate on long-term goodwill. Distressed couples also tend to control each other through punishment, whereas non-distressed couples tend to control each other less and when they do, they use positive reinforcement. Distressed couples tend to avoid each other as a way of managing conflict rather than negotiating a solution. Negotiating a solution is more aversive in the short term (particularly for men who experience far higher physiological arousal levels during verbal conflict than women) but, in the long term, negotiation as an approach to conflict resolution leads to greater marital satisfaction than withdrawal.

Beliefs

Within distressed couples, as the ratio of negative to positive interaction increases, both partners attend selectively to their spouses' negative behaviours while ignoring positive behaviours (Gottman, 1993; Gottman & Notarius, 2002). Partners in distressed marriages consistently attribute negative intentions to their spouses for negative or ambiguous behaviour but attribute their spouses' positive behaviour to situational factors. This negative belief system, coupled with the increase in negative interactions, leads to growing feelings for both partners of hurt or fear on the one hand and anger on the other. Both of these emotional states exacerbate the negative interaction patterns and negative belief systems. As these negative beliefs, emotions and behaviour patterns become more entrenched, members of the couple perceive their relationship problems as more severe and engage in more solitary rather than shared problem solving. At this stage, partners become isolated from each other and begin to live parallel lives.

In Chapter 1, two types of distressed couples were profiled in Figure 1.2 and referred to as 'conflictual' and 'disengaged'. It is probable that, eventually, conflictual couples become disengaged once they begin to live parallel lives. For a proportion of distressed couples who separate, belief systems about the marriage may undergo a final transformation. In such cases, usually following some critical incident, the most dissatisfied member of the couple reconstructs the whole history of the relationship in a negative way, which gives a rationale for the decision to separate or divorce.

Family-of-origin Experiences

Family-of-origin experiences may predispose members of distressed couples to develop problematic belief systems and behaviour patterns. Such experiences may include: triangulation between conflictual, separated or violent parents; problematic parent–child communication; enmeshed or disengaged relationships with parents; and exposure to authoritarian-critical or lax-overindulgent parenting. Such experiences may also include: neglect; physical abuse; sexual abuse; bereavement; or separation from parents for significant periods during childhood in the absence of consistent substitute carers. All of these difficulties lead individuals to develop problematic mental relationship maps (Simpson & Rholes, 1998). These problematic relationship maps guide the way they look for their needs to be met within new intimate relationships in adulthood.

In various situations, but particularly under stress, individuals experience needs for particular levels of intimacy and attachment or autonomy and power. They often look to their partners to meet these needs. The more strongly these needs are felt, the more likely it is that individuals who have had problematic family-of-origin experiences will respond to their partners in terms of their problematic relationship maps. Thus, a person who was neglected or hurt by a parent during childhood, as an adult may treat their partner as if the partner were going to neglect or hurt them when they feel a need for attachment and intimacy. In doing so, they may prompt their partner to neglect or hurt them. A person who was triangulated into their parents' conflictual marriage, when they experience conflict with their partner may triangulate in their own child, a friend or an individual or family therapist. These problematic relationship maps are commonly outside awareness, but predispose people to have beliefs, like 'my partner is intentionally trying to hurt me', and to behaviours such as criticising and stonewalling.

Most couples are unaware of these relationship maps, which are based on family-of-origin experiences. However, they are usually aware that the relationship difficulties they find themselves in are very different from their conscious relationship aspirations that they have developed as adults. Typically, these relationship aspirations include a wish for the relationship with their partner to be based on mutual respect and a commitment to meeting their partner's needs for psychological and sexual intimacy and fair power sharing and autonomy.

Wider Social and Cultural Factors and Personal Vulnerabilities

A range of wider social and cultural factors and personal vulnerabilities influence the adjustment of couples. These include cultural values, socioeconomic status, urban/rural geographical location, age at marriage, premarital pregnancy, psychological adjustment and parental divorce (Blumel, 1991; Raschke, 1987). Relationship difficulties and divorce are more common among those who come from different cultures with differing role expectations. Relationship difficulties and divorce are also more common among individuals from lower socioeconomic groups with psychological problems, who live in urban areas, and who have married before the age of 20. These problems are also common where premarital pregnancy has occurred and where parental divorce has occurred.

Outcome

Distressed couples have more physical health problems and unhappiness than non-distressed couples. They also have more difficulty with parenting and if they have children, their children have more adjustment problems.

Protective Factors

At a behavioural level, good communication and problem-solving skills and a willingness to increase the rate of positive interactions within the relationship are protective factors. In terms of beliefs, individuals who can empathise with their partner's needs and understand these are better able to develop a new and useful belief system in couples therapy. Individuals who come from families in which secure parent–child attachments were formed probably find it easier to use couples therapy to resolve relationship difficulties (Lawrence, Eldridge & Christensen, 1998). As a result of their secure attachment experiences in childhood, such individuals have relationship maps that are based on the premise that if you need a particular level of intimacy or autonomy and you ask for these needs to be met, you may trust that most of the time your partner will do their best to meet these needs. If partners do not meet these needs on every occasion, then individuals who have experienced secure attachments in childhood believe that this is not an intentional act of aggression or abandonment but a reflection that the partner may be responding to other demands on their time and energy.

With respect to sociocultural factors and personal history, similarity of cultural values and role expectations; high socioeconomic status; living in a rural area; good mental health; absence of parental divorce; absence of premarital pregnancy; and marriage after the age of 30 have all been identified as protective factors in long-term relationships (Blumel, 1991; Raschke, 1987). The lack of conflict over values associated with similarity of cultural background; the economic resources associated with high socioeconomic status; the community integration associated with rural living; the psychological resources associated with maturity; and the model of marital stability offered by non-divorced parents are the more common explanations given for the associations among these factors associated with relationship stability.

COUPLES THERAPY

For couples relationship problems, behavioural marital therapy (with and without a cognitive component), insight-oriented marital therapy, emotionally-focused couples therapy and self-control therapy have been shown to be effective interventions (Byrne et al., 2004b; Halford, 1998; Johnson, 2002b). Behavioural marital therapy involves training in communication and problem-solving skills, on the one hand, and behavioural exchange procedures, on the other (Baucom et al., 2002). When a cognitive component is added to this approach, it involves helping couples challenge destructive attributions, beliefs, assumptions and expectations that contribute to relationship distress and on replacing these with more benign alternatives. With insight-oriented marital therapy (Snyder & Schneider, 2002) and emotionally-focused marital therapy (Johnson, & Denton, 2002), the aim of therapy is to help couples express feelings of vulnerability and unmet needs (which may initially be outside awareness), and to help couples understand how these feelings and needs underpin destructive patterns of interaction within the relationship. With self-control therapy, the aim is to help couples reduce relationship distress by empowering each individual to alter their personal contribution to destructive interaction patterns (Halford, 1998). For psychosexual problems, couples therapy, which includes psychoeducational and behavioural interventions based on the seminal work of Masters and Johnson (1970), is effective in alleviating a number of common psychosexual difficulties (Baucom, Shoham, Mueser, Daiuto & Stickle, 1998; Heiman & Meston, 1998; Segraves & Althof, 2002).

In light of this evidence, a number of principles for the practice of effective couples therapy may be offered. Effective couples therapy is brief, involving about 20 sessions. This brevity may help create a focus for the couples' efforts and generate hope. Ideally, couples therapy should involve both partners, although individual assessment sessions may initially be useful. Couples therapy should facilitate the development of a shared systemic understanding of the difficulties without laying disproportionate blame on one partner. (In cases of domestic violence, the physically aggressive partner must be held accountable for their violence.) This shared understanding should allow partners to empathise with each other and see that they are both trapped in a destructive problem system to which they each make a contribution. The understanding should include reference to problematic behaviour patterns; underlying beliefs; and the role of family of origin and cultural factors in the genesis of these beliefs and behaviour patterns. At a behavioural level, effective therapy should facilitate an increase in positive exchanges and a reduction in negative exchanges. Effective couples therapy should promote the development of communication and problem-solving skills so that couples can discuss how best to meet each other's needs for desired levels of intimacy and autonomy, and develop feasible plans to do so. Communication and problem-solving skills also allow couples to support each other in managing the tasks of family life. Effective couples therapy should empower couples to renegotiate relationship roles and this in turn may lead to a more equitable distribution of power within the relationship. Where couples have psychosexual problems, effective couples therapy should provide couples with psychoeducation and homework exercises that help them to find ways to meet each other's sexual needs. Effective couples therapy should also permit couples to discuss the impact of family-of-origin issues and cultural values on current relationship functioning and this in turn may deepen empathy and psychological intimacy within the relationship. The specific guidelines for clinical practice when working with distressed couples using the approach outlined in the remainder of this chapter should be used within the context of the general guidelines for family therapy practice given in Chapters 7, 8 and 9.

Contracting for Assessment

Where both members of a couple voluntarily request couples therapy, contracting for assessment is a straightforward procedure. The couple may be invited to attend a series of sessions with a view to clarifying the main problems, and related behaviour patterns, belief systems and possible predisposing factors. The couple may be informed that once a shared understanding or formulation has been reached, then a further contract for treatment may be offered if that is appropriate.

Where both members of a couple are referred by a statutory child protection or probation agency, it is usually best practice to invite the referring agent to the contracting session, to clarify the assessment contract. For example, it may be the case that a child protection agency are making the couple's participation in therapy a prerequisite for allowing the couple to retain custody of their children. In cases of domestic violence, it may be that the probation officer is requiring a violent male to attend couples therapy during probation. In these instances, it is important to agree that statutory duties remain with the statutory agency and are not transferred to the family therapy agency. The family therapy agency may agree to offer a contract for assessment over a specific number of sessions with the goal of developing a formulation and subsequently a contract for therapy if that is appropriate.

However, it should be the statutory agency's responsibility to determine if the level of cooperation and progress is sufficient for their purposes. In these types of cases, some couples superficially cooperate with assessment initially and gradually become customers for therapy. Others never become customers for therapy and view the process as either irrelevant to their situation or a potential threat and intrusion into their privacy.

Where one member of a couple is a customer for change and the other attends reluctantly, a time-limited contract for assessment may be offered to both. The fact that a thorough assessment must focus on understanding the problem from both partner's viewpoints should be stressed, since this underlines the importance of the reluctant attender being present for the sessions. In some such cases, the process of participating in assessment and developing a formulation helps the reluctant attender to view the problem as interactional and understand that treatment is best conducted conjointly. In other instances, the reluctant attender drops out.

Where one member of a couple drops out, or where only one member of a couple attends the intake session, one-partner couple therapy may be offered where the focus is on helping the customer develop a formulation, and subsequently use this as a basis for changing his or her role within the relationship so as to influence the non-attending partner.

Assessment

The first aim of family assessment is to construct three-column formulations, like those presented in Figures 14.2. and 14.3, of a typical episode of conflict or distress and an exceptional episode in which conflict or distress is expected to occur but does not. Belief systems that underpin partners' roles in these episodes may then be clarified. These in turn may be linked to predisposing risk factors, which have been listed in the systemic model of couple's problems presented above. The second aim of assessment is to help couples develop a shared understanding of the problem and to empathise with each other's positions as they are spelled out in the formulation. During assessment sessions it is vital that the basic ground rules for therapy be strictly adhered to because these provide a model for the way the couple may eventually learn to communicate and problem solve with each other. Thus, in each session, each partner is invited to reflect on what they want to say first and then to take an uninterrupted speaking turn in response to the therapist's questions. The therapist may then summarise the response and check with the speaker that this summary was accurate. In circumstances where therapists find that they are having difficulty keeping the talking turns to approximately equal length, it is probable that triangulation is occurring. It is useful to simply make a statement that this seems to be happening and that an attempt will be made to keep each partner's turn to approximately the same duration.

Two widely used marital satisfaction inventories, that may be helpful in assessing particular areas associated with relationship distress are the *Golombok Rust Inventory of Marital State* (GRIMS, Rust, Bennun, Crowe & Golombok, 1988) and the *Marital Satisfaction Inventory-Revised* (MSI-R, Snyder, 1997).

Assessment may reveal that one partner has particular vulnerabilities, such as anxiety, depression, alcohol problems or psychosis, which need to be taken into account. Guidelines for therapy with these types of cases is described Chapters 15, 16 and 17. In this chapter, the primary concern is with cases in which relationship distress and dissatisfaction are the core issues.

Contracting for Treatment

If the assessment has proceeded without cooperation problems, only the couple need to attend the session in which a contract for treatment is offered. However, in cases referred by statutory agencies where there have been co-operation difficulties, such as failure to attend sessions, professionals representing the statutory referring agency (such as social services or probation departments) should be invited to the contracting meeting. A summary of the couples' strengths and a three-column formulation of the process in which the couples' problems are embedded should be given. Specific goals, a clear specification of the number of treatment sessions and the times and places at which these sessions will occur should all be specified in a contract for statutory cases. Such contracts should be written and formally signed by the couple, the family therapist and the statutory professional.

It is also good practice in all cases to make a statement about the probability that the couple will benefit from treatment backed up with a statement of the factors that make it likely that this is the case. Jacobson and Addis (1993), in a wide-ranging review, concluded that couples who respond best to marital therapy are younger; are less distressed at the beginning of therapy; are more emotionally engaged with each other; have less rigid gender roles; are less depressed; and do not opt for premature closure in their attempts at relationship-based problem solving. Hawton (1995), in an extensive review, concluded that therapy for couples with psychosexual difficulties is most effective for partners with good relationships, who are still attracted to each other, who have no physical or mental health problems, and in which both partners (particularly the male partners) are willing to cooperate with treatment procedures and homework exercises.

Treatment

A proportion of couples will find that the process of assessment and the developing of a shared systemic understanding of their relationship difficulties alleviates their distress and dissatisfaction. However, a proportion of couples may contract for treatment to achieve specific goals, such as increasing the frequency with which exceptional episodes of non-distressing interaction occurs; reducing the number of arguments; changing the ratio of positive to negative exchanges; improving communication; improving joint problem solving; or improving the quality of their sexual relationship. The full range of interventions described in Chapter 9 may be used in couples therapy to achieve these goals. However, some deserve particular mention because of their particular applicability and effectiveness in helping couples reduce distress and increase satisfaction. In keeping with the scheme presented in Table 9.1 in chapter 9, these may be classified as those that focus on behaviour patterns, belief systems and historical and wider contextual factors.

Interventions that Focus on Behaviour Patterns

The following interventions, which are particularly useful in couples therapy, focus largely on altering behaviour patterns.

- communication and problem-solving skills training
- increasing positive and reducing negative exchanges
- specific tasks for increasing the couples' control over regular conflicts
- self-regulation tasks
- psychosexual tasks.

Communication and Problem-solving Skills Training

Where it is suspected that lack of progress is due to communication and problem-solving skills deficits, the couple may be invited to enact their typical way of communicating and problem solving about an issue within the therapy session. This enactment may reveal their areas of difficulty with communication and problem solving. In light of this, they may be coached in communication and problem-solving skills in the way outlined in Chapter 9. With communication skills, through modelling and role play, clients may be shown how to communicate messages clearly, directly and congruently to their partners; check that one has been understood; listen in an empathic manner; paraphrase partners' messages; and check the accuracy of such paraphrases. With problem-solving skills training, clients may be coached to: define large daunting problems as a series of small solvable problems and for each problem to brainstorm solutions; evaluate the pros and cons of these; select one; jointly implement it; review progress; and modify the selected solution if it is ineffective or celebrate success if the problem is resolved. In teaching these skills, it is best to invite couples to begin with neutral non-emotive topics and when they have mastered using the skills in such situations to progress to using them with more emotive topics. Couples may be assigned homework tasks of devoting 5–10 minutes per day practising their communication or problem-solving skills. It is best for initial homework assignments to focus on non-emotive topics and for a strict time limit to be placed on these exchanges to maximise the chances of success.

Increasing Positive and Reducing Negative Exchanges

Distressed couples who have high rates of negative interaction may be invited to negotiate contracts with each other during sessions to increase the rate of positive interactions. In negotiating these, each member of the couple is invited to generate a 'wish list' of activities or events they would like to experience or they would like their partner to arrange for them. All wishes on such lists should be highly specific, positive, repeatable, realistically achievable and acceptable to both partners. An obstacle in drawing up such lists is that partners may inadvertently drift into making vague, global complaints, rather than making clear, specific, positive requests. The therapist's task is to coach clients to move from statements like 'You never spend time with me' to 'I'd like you to listen to me for five minutes each day at 6.00pm, when I come home from work, and express interest in my account of the day's happenings'. In this coaching process the therapist should praise and encourage successive approximations to specific positive statements, and avoid criticising clients for making vague complaints about their partners.

When couples have drawn up their wish lists, different types of contracts may be developed in which they are invited to plan to carry out some or all of the activities on the lists. *Quid pro quo* contracts, good faith contracts, caring days, and love days are commonly used contracts in behavioural couples therapy to increase positive and reduce negative exchanges (Sayers, 1998). With *quid pro quo* contingency contracts, couples are invited to negotiate exchanges in which one good turn begets another. For example, 'If you make dinner, I'll wash up'. Since many distressed couples operate on a short-term *quid pro quo* system, these types of contracts may not be as useful as other types of contracts. With good faith contracts, the consequences for both members of the couple of engaging in positive behaviours are specified but are not linked. For example, 'If I make dinner, I may go sailing; if you do the shopping, you may go out with friends'. In both of these types of contracts, the aim is for members of couples to be rewarded for engaging in positive behaviours or activities. With caring days, both partners agree to do more things that their partner has listed as enjoyable. With love days on *alternate* days, couples may be invited to do a range of things from their spouses list of enjoyable events and activities. With both love days and caring days, enjoyable activities are carried out at the discretion of the partner, not as a consequence for good behaviour.

Specific Tasks for Increasing the Couple's Control over Regular Conflicts

Some couples have very specific topics they routinely argue about, such as jealousy or money or sex. Where couples feel that these fights are out of their control, then a number of specific behavioural interventions may be useful in helping them get control of these battles. First, they may be invited to monitor the frequency of these events. Second, they may be advised to make haste slowly and restrain themselves from trying to change their situation too quickly, since this may have unexpected negative consequences. Third, they may be invited to set aside a designated time each day (e.g. 9.00–9.15 each evening) and confine their arguments to this period exclusively. They may be invited to do this so that they can learn to control the timing of the fights. If, their arguments escalate rapidly, they may be invited to take one long turn each of about 7 minutes in which they fully express all that they wish to say or listen to their partner doing so. This allows couples to gain control over the pacing of their fights. If they argue about a topic like jealousy, with one partner feeling particularly jealous, they may be invited during scheduled arguments over jealousy to reverse roles so that they can learn to understand each other's positions.

Where couples avoid conflict or avoid talking about couples issues and instead discuss the children, they may be invited to schedule increasingly longer conversations about couples issues each day. For example, over a 3-week period they maybe invited to lengthen their scheduled conversations from 5 to 15 minutes.

Self-regulation Tasks

Within any relationship each partner has more control over their own behaviour than that of their partner. Couples may be helped to use this insight to alter the problematic behaviour patterns in which they have become embroiled with their partners (Halford, 1998). A number of self-regulatory strategies may be used. First, they may learn to identify and state their needs more clearly as requests for specific positive actions on the part of their partners. Second, they can plan to selectively attend to their partner's positive exchanges within the relationship and use these as opportunities for responding to their partner in positive ways. Third, they can plan to avoid introducing negativity into the relationship by avoiding complaining and expressing aggression or other negative emotions within the relationship. This may involve identifying risky situations where such expressions are likely and avoiding or changing these. Fourth, they may plan to respond to negativity from their partner in ways that minimise their negative impact. For example, they may say they are taking time out, to avoid an escalating battle. Fifth, they may arrange to have needs that are unmet within the relationship, fulfilled in other relationships or situations. For example, needs for companionship may be met by arranging activities with friends. Needs for self-esteem may be based on reflecting on one's own behaviour and values rather than relying on one's partner's evaluations. Sixth, they may be invited to explore their expectations of the relationship and consider altering these, so that they more closely fit with what their partner can provide. Seventh, they may be invited to keep the option of leaving the relationship open as a possible way of reducing relationship distress.

Psychosexual Tasks

In couples where psychosexual problems occur as part of their relationship difficulties, a medical screening should be conducted. If medical causes have been outruled, the pattern of interaction in which the sexual difficulty is embedded should be explored and mapped out. Then the beliefs that underpin this may be elaborated and their roots in family-of-origin experiences and cultural values may be traced. To help couples manage psychosexual problems, it is important to provide a therapeutic context within which this type of exploration may occur, on the one hand, while, on the other, offering the couple behavioural exercises with which they can disrupt the behaviour pattern in which the psychosexual problem is embedded (Schnarch, 1991). A range of behavioural exercises, devised originally by Masters and Johnson (1970), may be used and prefaced with psychoeducation about the human sexual response in men and women (Leiblum & Rosen, 2001; Levine et al., 2003).

The central intervention for disrupting behaviour patterns that maintain sexual problems is sensate focus. Couples are advised to refrain from sexual intercourse and sexual contact except as outlined in prescribed exercises. Couples are then to give and receive pleasurable caresses along a graded sequence progressing over a number of weeks from non-sexual to increasingly sexual areas of the body and culminating in full intercourse.

For female orgasmic dysfunction, sensate focus exercises may be preceded by coaching the female partner in masturbation using sexual fantasy and imagery. Later, females may be coached in explaining masturbation techniques that they find effective to their male partners. For female dysparunia (painful sexual intercourse) and vaginismus (involuntary spasm of the outer third of the vaginal musculature) a densensitisation routine may be used. At the outset, the couple refrain from intercourse and the female partner completes a series of graduated exercises, which involve the gradual insertion of a series of dilators of increasing diameter into the vagina. This is then followed-up with the routine sensate focus exercises.

For couples in which premature ejaculation occurs, the stop-start and squeeze technique may be used to help the couple better coordinate the timing of their orgasms. With this technique, the couple are advised to have intercourse in their usual way but to stop moving and squeeze the base of the penis each time ejaculation in imminent. Over time, the man gradually learns to delay orgasm using this method. For acquired male erectile problems and impotence, the conjoint sensate focus exercise may be used, but this practice is largely being supplanted by the use of medications such as Viagra.

Interventions that Focus on Belief Systems

The following interventions, which are particularly useful in couples therapy, focus largely on transforming belief systems and narratives:

- addressing ambivalence
- pinpointing strengths
- reframing in response to triangulation
- presenting split messages
- externalising problems and building on exceptions.

Addressing Ambivalence

Ambivalence in couples therapy may arise in situations where the long-term compatibility of the couple is in question or where there is a lack of resolution within the couple after promises have been broken. In each of these instances, the couple may be ambivalent about the therapeutic process because they believe they are incompatible or that atonement and forgiveness is not possible. On the other hand, they may be avoiding addressing the issues of compatibility or forgiveness because separation may be one possible outcome of addressing these issues directly.

Compatibility   Where couples are stuck in a combative or nag–withdraw symmetrical relationship and find a relational reframing of their difficulties as an expression of connectedness (described below) does not fit with their experience, the therapist may invite the couple to explore the advantages and disadvantages of accepting the possibility that they are fundamentally mismatched or incompatible because of the expectations they have of each other. Here is one way of offering this invitation.

> *I am surprised that you have stayed together so long. It seems that the consistent conflict in which you find yourselves may be a sign that you are fundamentally mismatched, incompatible and so unable to live together without making each other thoroughly miserable. However, for good reasons you have stayed together. It may now be time to reconsider just how good these reasons are. I am inviting you to list those things that you expect of each other so that you can see clearly that it is almost impossible for you to live up to each others expectations. It may be useful for each of you then to explore the benefits of separation.*

This type of invitation may lead couples to recognise that separation is a more viable option. Indeed, some partners come to therapy looking for confirmation of this view and for permission to leave the relationship.

If this occurs, then the issue of managing separation becomes central to the assessment. However, this type of invitation may help some couples rediscover their commitment to each other and to the relationship.

Where couples continually wonder about the viability of their relationships, it may be useful to invite them to explore the pros and cons of separation, or to engage in a trial separation to get a sense of what these pros and cons might feel like in action.

When couples decide to separate, it is useful to make it clear to each member of the couple whether or not you are prepared to offer individual sessions to either of them if they request this. Some therapists do not offer such sessions because they believe that it would compromise their neutrality if the couple returned at a later date for therapy focusing on reconciliation. Other therapists take the view that this is not a risk. It is probably best to make judgments about this issue on a case by case basis, since much depends on the quality of the alliances with each partner and the availability of other therapists for the couple in the district.

Forgiveness   In relationships where one partner has wronged another through breaking a promise or through infidelity, the couple may become stuck in a pattern where the victim of the wrongdoing repeatedly punishes the villain and the villain repeatedly apologises and attempts to atone for the wrongdoing. Periodically, this pattern may be interrupted by bouts of conflict in which the villain protests that the victim is being unfair in rejecting the apology and atonement as insufficient to make up for the wrongdoing. In such circumstances, beliefs about atonement and forgiveness may be explored with a view to clarifying the circumstances under which atonement and forgiveness may be possible, if at all. Here are some ways of doing this.

> *In your own family of origin, how was the issue of making up for having done wrong and forgiveness dealt with?*
>
> *Can both of you use these ways of addressing atonement and forgiveness now in your relationship?*
>
> *What kind of things would need to happen for you to know that ABC had atoned for his/her wrong doing?*
>
> *Sometimes broken promises hurt so much that forgiveness takes a long time. In others forgiveness may be impossible. When you look into the future, say a year from now, do you imagine that things will still be as they are now or will you have moved closer to forgiveness?*

In some instances, a ritual may be constructed with the couple in which the villain reads a letter of apology to the victim and asks for forgiveness, when both members of the couple agree that the timing is right for such an event. However, it is important to keep in mind that forgiveness is sometimes impossible, and these types of interventions may well precipitate a couple's separation.

Pinpointing Strengths

Most distressed couples have a huge number of strengths of which they have lost sight. Throughout couples therapy it is important to help couples rediscover these, by drawing the couple's attention to them when things that the couple do in therapy provide evidence for their presence. Such strengths include: loyalty; sticking together through thick and thin; tolerance for distress; commitment to the idea that the relationship can improve; a shared history of a relationship that once worked well; thoughtfulness in trying to make sense of the relationship difficulties; the capacity to listen carefully to each other's viewpoints despite distress; self-control in avoiding violence; maturity in not involving the children in every marital battle; and passion for the relationship rather than apathy about it.

Reframing in Response to Triangulation

With triangulation, one or other partner in a couple overtly or covertly invites the therapist to side with him or her against their partner. In conflictual couples involved in symmetrical battles or nagging–withdrawing cycles, the request is usually for therapist to act a judge and jury and agree that one partner is right and the other wrong. In non-conflictual couples involved in complementary relationships where one member is defined as inadequate, irrational or weak and the other as competent, rational and strong, the request is usually for the therapist to take on the job of supporting the supposedly inadequate member of the relationship and take this burden off the supposedly competent member of the relationship.

The therapist may reframe all statements about one partner being right and the other wrong; or one partner being weak and the other strong in relational terms such as:

> It seems that in this relationship you have developed equally valid yet distinctive viewpoints, and discussions about which is the correct viewpoint keep you connected in frequent passionate conversations. However, at some point you may wish to explore other ways to be connected besides arguing about whose viewpoint is right and whose is wrong.

> It seems there is an acceptance that X is weaker than Y and so requires regular help and support from Y to keep going. It also seems that there is an invitation for me to assist with supporting X. I find this invitation difficult to accept because, from my vantage point, I am struck by the strength and competence that X shows in providing Y with the role of apparently being the strong and competent person in this relationship.

Presenting Split Messages to Address Polarization

Where couples have become polarised in combative symmetrical relationships or nag–withdraw relationships, they may be offered a split message that articulates and empathises with the validity of each position, while also opening up the possibility of an alternative systemic framing of their difficulties. For example:

> *I was struck by the way each of you have distinctive styles for managing situations and have discussed this with two colleagues since we last met, to obtain their expert opinions on how best to proceed. One of my colleagues was taken by ABC's style. ABC, you have shown that your own personal style is to talk straight and say what is on your mind, so if you want DEF to know you think a job needs to be done in the house, you tell him straight and don't beat around the bush. If he doesn't take notice, you tell him again. That is 'the straight talking approach'. My other colleague was impressed by your, style, DEF. You take a 'thoughtful approach'. You think things over a great deal before saying anything. This is personal style and one that reflects your careful approach to this relationship. I suppose the question that is raised for me is, how can the best of both styles be brought to bear on the difficulties and distress you are both experiencing? Perhaps you have views on this you would like to air today?*

Externalising Problems and Building on Exceptions

During the assessment stage couples are invited to construct a formulation of those exceptional circumstances in which an episode of conflict or distress was expected to occur but did not. Within this formulation, a behaviour pattern, underlying beliefs and historical or cultural factors that underpinned these are described. In treatment, couples may be invited in therapy to explore ways to recreate such exceptions and then to attempt to put this plan into action as a homework assignment.

To help couples jointly work to create positive exceptions, it is useful to externalise the force that underpins the conflict by, for example, referring to it as bad relationship habits or faulty relationship maps (White, 1995). Thus, the therapist may ask:

> *How have you both arranged from time to time to prevent these bad relationship habits/ faulty relationship maps from infecting your relationship?*

> *If I was watching a video of these exceptional episodes, what details would I see that were different from those episodes where bad relationship habits infect your relationship?*

> *How could you use this information to arrange another situation where your relationship is uninfected by these bad habits?*

They may also be invited to link together all of the non-distressing non-conflictual exceptional episodes in their relationship and construct a new narrative that frames their relationship as essentially positive with some episodes of conflict, rather than a relationship that is basically negative with some brief positive episodes:

> *It seems that all of these events are connected and reflect the degree to which you really care about each other. How do you imagine this central part of your relationship will find expression in the future? What will it look like?*

Interventions that Focus on Historical and Wider Contextual Issues

In couples work where responses to interventions focusing on beliefs and behaviour are ineffective, it is usually valuable to address family-of-origin issues in the way outlined in Chapter 9. In addition, two interventions that focus on historical and wider contextual issues and which are unique to couples therapy may be considered. These are:

- facilitating emotive expression of attachment needs
- exploring secrets.

Facilitating Emotive Expression of Attachment Needs

In couples where one partner's family-of-origin experiences included in-secure attachment, this may have a negative impact on the quality of their relationship. Usually this involves one partner responding to the other in terms of the relationship map they learned from their experience of insecure attachment in childhood. That is, they respond in a hostile and angry way because they expect that their partner will not meet their at-tachment needs for safety and security. This often elicits such behaviour from their partner, and so becomes a self-fulfilling prophecy. In such circumstances, an intervention central to emotionally-focused couples therapy is appropriate (Johnson & Denton, 2002). Couples are helped to distinguish between secondary and primary emotional responses that arise when attachment needs for safety, security and satisfaction are not met in predictable ways. Anger and resentment are secondary emotional responses. Primary emotional responses include fear, sadness, disap-pointment, emotional hurt and vulnerability. The couple's problem may be reframed as one involving the miscommunication of primary attach-ment needs and related disappointments. Members of the couple may be invited to express their attachment needs and related primary emotional responses in full and forceful ways, but not to give vent to their second-ary emotional responses through blaming or guilt induction. When this happens, the partner listening to the emotional expression of attachment needs commonly experiences empathy and is moved to go some way to-wards meeting the other's attachment needs. This transaction may come to replace that in which secondary emotional responses such as anger and resentment are responded to with rejection, if the therapist can facilitate its repetition in a number of sessions.

Exploring Secrets

In some instances, little therapeutic progress is made and the reasons for this remains obscure. When this is the case, it is worth considering that one or other member of the couple is having a secret affair. In these in-stances it is useful to ask the couple to consider the possible implications of such a hypothetical secret. Here are some useful questions to ask in such instances:

> *It seems to me that there may be some unknown factor contributing to your distress, otherwise you would be making more progress than has occurred. I don't know what this unknown factor is. My guess is that if one of you know what it is you think that it would be least hurtful if you kept it a secret. So please, hold on to your secret if you have one. For now, let us assume that one of you is having an affair with another person; or you're possibly having problems with your job, or maybe with some pastime. If that were the case how would each of you handle it. Is this something you are prepared to discuss?*
>
> *How would you react if you found out your partner was having a relationship?*
>
> *If I was watching a video of the showdown when you found out about it what would I see?*
>
> *What would it mean for your relationship if your partner were having an affair?*
>
> *If you found out your partner were having an affair and you decided to end this relationship how would that pan out? What would each of you do?*
>
> *How would you forgive your partner?*
>
> *How would you expect your partner to make up for cheating (or atone for his/her infidelity)?*

Special Problems in Couples Therapy

Three issues commonly encountered in couples therapy deserve special mention: conducting therapy with one partner in a couple; the management of domestic violence; and recovery from an episode of infidelity.

One-person Marital Therapy

Bennun (1997) has shown, through controlled empirical research, that unilateral marital therapy is as effective as conjoint marital therapy. He argues that, in the past, individually-based interventions for marital problems have yielded negative results because of their almost exclusive focus on individual issues and their lack of attention at a systemic level to relationship issues. One-person or unilateral marital therapy based on a systemic model of relationship difficulties may be appropriate in cases where only one partner is available to attend treatment; where there are dependence–independence issues in the relationship; where there are problems in sustaining intimate relationships; in cases of domestic violence; where there is a major disparity between partners' levels of self-esteem; and where one partner's unresolved family-of-origin issues contribute significantly to the couple's problems. In Bennun's (1997) approach, therapy begins with a conjoint session. During assessment, the negative impact of partners' difficulties in meeting each other's needs on each partner at an intrapsychic level and on the relationship at a systemic level is explored. In formulating the way presenting problems have emerged and are maintained, a balance is drawn between a focus on individual factors and a focus on relationship factors. Treatment targets and possible difficulties, such as resistance and relapse, are discussed with both partners at the end of the assessment session. Following assessment, in unilateral marital therapy, treatment is directed at both promoting systemic change within the relationship and the psychological development of both partners as individuals, through working with one partner only. To do this the therapist invites the attending partner (usually a female) to recount the content of each session to her partner; to engage in homework assignments with her partner; and to give the therapist feedback about the impact of these events on the relationship and psychological well-being of each partner. A good argument may be made for including self-regulatory interventions described earlier in the chapter in unilateral marital therapy.

Marital Violence

Marital violence is associated with a wide range of variables, described in Chapter 1, but particularly with skills deficits in anger control, communication and problem-solving skills and alcohol and drug abuse (Holtzworth-Munroe, Meehan, Rehman & Marshall, 2002). Only a limited number of well-controlled studies have been conducted on the effectiveness of interventions with violent marital partners and these show that court-mandated skills-training programmes are probably effective for a proportion of violent men (Davis & Taylor, 1999). Key elements of successful programmes include taking responsibility for the violence; challenging beliefs and cognitive distortions that justify violence; anger management training; communication and problem-solving skills training; and relapse prevention. In couples treatment, anger-management training focuses on teaching couples to: recognise anger cues; take time out when such cues are recognised; use relaxation and self-instructional methods to reduce anger-related arousal; resume interactions in a non-violent way; and use communication and problem-solving skills more effectively for conflict resolution (Holtzworth-Munroe et al., 2002). Stith, Rosen, McCollum and Thomsen (2004) found that a multi-couple treatment programme was more effective than a single couple programme in reducing domestic violence. Male violence recidivism rates were 25% for the multi-couple group, and 43% for the individual couple group. Conjoint marital therapy is only appropriate is cases where the aggressive male commits to a no-violence contract in which he agrees to no violence while in therapy and take steps to reduce danger, such as removing weapons from the house; and/or agrees to a temporary separation; and/or engages in treatment for comorbid alcohol and drug problems. It is essential that the female partner agree a safety plan specifying what exactly she will do and where she will go if further threats of violence occur. Where a no-violence contract and a safety plan cannot be established, it is more appropriate to treat husbands in group therapy for wife batterers, which addresses the same issues as those mentioned for conjoint therapy and for the female partner to join a support group for battered wives and receive individual treatment for post-violence trauma based on evidence-based practice guidelines for post-traumatic stress disorder.

Infidelity

About half of all males and a quarter of all females in long-term relationships or marriages have affairs, and affairs are a very frequent reason for attending couples therapy (Glass, 2002). Affairs signal relationship problems and are rarely exclusively sexually motivated. Affairs fulfil a variety of functions (Brown, 1999). Where couples continually avoid resolving conflicts within their marriage, or where one partner continually sacrifices his or her needs to care for the other, intimacy may erode and an affair provide a way for having thwarted intimacy needs met. Other couples use affairs and intense conflict about these to avoid intimacy and maintain distance within the marital relationship. In other instances, sexually addicted partners use multiple brief sexual affairs to regulate negative emotional states, much as others might use drugs or alcohol. Affairs may also be used as a way of justifying the end of a marriage – so-called 'exit affairs'. Affairs vary not only in the function they fulfil, but also in the type and degree of involvement from brief sexual encounters to sustained long-term romantic sexual relationships. Affairs have a range of effects on those involved. Betrayed partners may develop post-traumatic symptoms, including obsessive thinking, flashbacks, anxiety, depression, suicidal and homicidal thoughts. Partners involved in affairs who believe they must give up the affair to save their marriages and protect their children may experience depression associated with the loss.

Where affairs are disclosed to therapists in confidence, there is a dilemma about whether it is appropriate to offer couples therapy while keeping the affair a 'secret'. Where the affair happened a long time ago, there may be little to be gained by insisting that it be disclosed within couples sessions. However, where the affair was recent or is ongoing, it is essential that the partner who has had the affair cease contact with the person with whom they have had the affair, if conjoint couples therapy is to be effective. If this cannot be agreed, because one partner is ambivalent about giving up the affair, then each of the partners may be seen in individual therapy until the affair ends.

Gordon, Baucom and Snyder (2004), in a replicated case-study investigation of an integrative treatment for couples recovering from an affair, found the 26-session programme to be effective for four out of six couples. In the first stage of the programme, therapists assessed the impact of the affair on couple functioning, addressed immediate crises, such as suicidality or violence, contained partners' volatile emotions, and helped partners negotiate safe guidelines for interacting outside of therapy sessions. In the second stage, individual, couple and broader systemic and contextual factors that contributed to the development of the affair were explored to help the couple develop a shared understanding of how the affair occurred. In the third stage of treatment, the focus was on forgiveness and moving on. A positive outcome from this type of intervention is more likely when both partners are strongly motivated to re-invest in their marriage; where the affair involved limited emotional involvement, and where the affair occurred late in the marriage and involved the male partner.

SUMMARY

Couples may seek therapy for a wide range of problems and in this chapter the focus was on problems that are fundamentally relational in nature. These relationship problems commonly arise from difficulties in partners meeting each others' needs for desired levels of intimacy and desired levels of autonomy. These difficulties are associated with problematic behaviour patterns, which are sustained by negative belief systems and personal narratives. These behaviour patterns and belief systems may have their roots in negative family-of-origin experiences. In addition, wider contextual factors such as cultural differences or low socioeconomic status may place couples at risk for relationship problems. Therapy for couples may be conceptualised as a stage-wise process and a range of interventions targeting behaviour patterns, beliefs and historical and contextual factors have been shown to be effective in alleviating relationship distress.

FURTHER READING

Gurman, A. & Jacobson, N. (2002). *Clinical Handbook of Couple Therapy*, 3rd edn. New York: Guilford.

Halford, W. & Markman, H. (1997). *Clinical Handbook of Marriage and Couples Interventions.* New York: Wiley.

Schnarch, D. (1991). *Constructing the Sexual Crucible: An Integration of Sexual and Marital Therapy.* New York: Norton.

Leiblum, S. & Rosen, S. (2001). *Principles and Practice of Sex Therapy*, 3rd edn. New York: Guilford.

Levine, S., Risen, C. & Althof, S. (2003). *Handbook of Clinical Sexuality for Mental Health Professionals.* New York: Brunner Routledge.

FURTHER READING FOR CLIENTS

Gottman, J. & Silver, N. (1999). *The Seven Principles for Making Marriage Work*. London: Weidenfeld & Nicolson. (This guide is based on years of research by Gottman.)

Markman, H., Stanley, S. & Blumberg (1994). *Fighting for your Marriage*. San Francisco, CA: Jossey Bass. (This guide is based on a scientifically evaluated premarital programme.)

Christensen, A. & Jacobson, N. (2002). *Reconcilable Differences*. New York: Guilford.

Chapter 15

DEPRESSION AND ANXIETY

When a member of a couple develops depression or anxiety, this has a profound effect on the relationship and members of the couple may develop interaction patterns and belief systems that maintain the anxiety or depression. It is not surprising, therefore, that there is considerable evidence that couples-based treatments for depression and common anxiety disorders, such as panic disorder with agoraphobia, are particularly effective (Beach, 2002; Byrne, Carr & Clarke, 2004a). A systemic model for conceptualising these types of problems and a systemic approach to therapy with these cases will be given in this chapter. A case example is given in Figure 15.1 and three-column formulations of problems and exceptions are given in Figure 15.2. and 15.3.

The lifetime prevalence of major depression is 10–25% for women and 5–12% for men (American Psychiatric Association, 2000). Up to 15% of people with major depression commit suicide. The lifetime prevalence rates for all anxiety disorders is 10–14%, and for panic disorder with or without agoraphobia, the anxiety disorder considered in this chapter, the rate is 1.5–3.5% (American Psychiatric Association, 2000). Many people attending psychiatric services show both anxiety and depressive symptoms and often a range of other problems such as substance abuse, eating disorders and borderline personality disorder (American Psychiatric Association, 2000).

DEPRESSION

Major depression is a recurrent episodic condition involving: low mood; selective attention to negative features of the environment; a pessimistic belief-system; self-defeating behaviour patterns, particularly within intimate relationships; and a disturbance of sleep and appetite. Loss is often the core theme linking these clinical features: loss of an important relationship, loss of some valued attribute such as health, or loss of status, for example, through unemployment. In classification systems such as the DSM-IV-TR (American Psychiatric Association, 2000) and the ICD-10 (World Health Organisation, 1992), major depression is distinguished from bipolar disorder, where there are also episodes of elation, and from dysthymia, which is a milder, non-episodic mood disorder. However, 'double

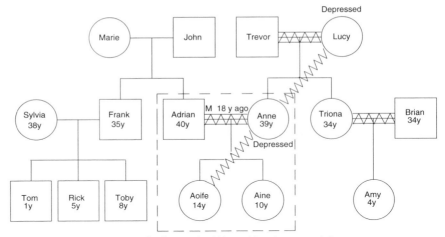

Family strengths: Adrian and Anne have prevented
depression from ending their marriage for 14 years

Referral.   Adrian and Anne originally came to therapy because of difficulties they were having with Aoife their teenage daughter, specifically the ongoing conflict between Anne and Aoife. These difficulties were addressed in an episode of child-focused family therapy, after which the couple contracted for a further episode of therapy addressing their marital problems. Since shortly after Aoife's birth they had had periodic difficulties associated with Anne's depression. Anne, like her mother Lucy was diagnosed with major depression and had been treated periodically with antidepressant medication. Like her mother, Anne found that the mood disorder created conflict in her marriage as well as in her relationship with her eldest child. Adrian found the mood disorder challenging to live with and coped by adopting a coldly efficient caregiver role with respect to Anne and the children. Periodically, however, the strain of this way of managing the situation would become too much for him to cope with and he would become highly critical of Anne and verbally aggressive towards her. This would exacerbate the depression.

Formulation.   Three-column formulations of episodes in which the depression had a profound negative impact on the relationship and exceptional episodes where such problems were expected but did not occur are given in Figures 15.2 and 15.3.

Therapy.   Therapy focused on helping the couple examine the problems that the complementary caregiver/invalid roles created in their marriage and specifically how it prevented them from meeting each other's needs for intimacy and a more balanced distribution of power. Role-reversal exercises were used with this couple to good effect, because it helped them understand the impact of the complementary roles on their partner. The couple increased opportunities for intimacy by scheduling things they like to do together on a daily basis. They also replaced reassurance requesting and giving with the CTR routine for challenging depressive beliefs and narratives described in the chapter.

Figure 15.1 Case example of depression

depression', which involves persistent dysthymia coupled with episodic major depression, characterises many chronic service users, who may be referred for couples therapy.

ANXIETY

Anxiety is distinguished from normal fear insofar as it occurs in situations that are not construed by most people as being particularly dangerous.

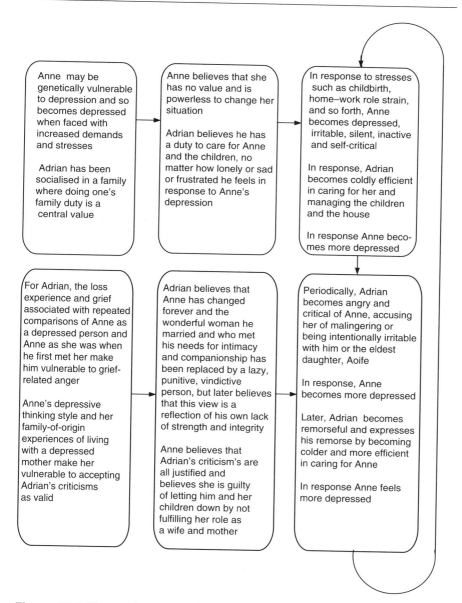

Figure 15.2 Three-column formulation of a situation in which depression damages the relationship

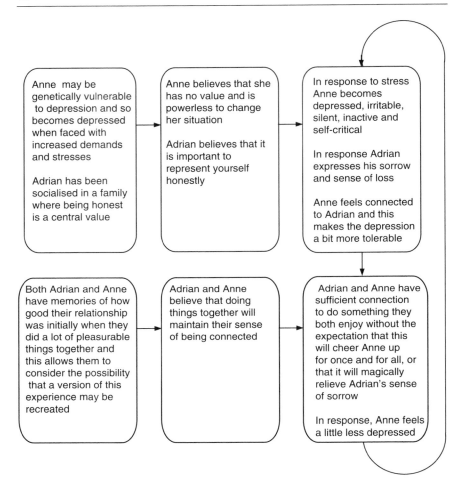

Figure 15.3 Three-column formulation of an exception to a situation in which depression damages the relationship

Within classification systems such as the DSM-IV-TR (American Psychiatric Association, 2000) and the ICD-10 (World Health Organisation, 1992), distinctions are made between a variety of different types of anxiety disorders on the basis of the types of situations that elicit anxiety, the routines people use to avoid or modify these, and the duration of episodes of hyperarousal. For example, generalised anxiety disorder, in which many situations are viewed as threatening and chronic hyperarousal occurs, is distinguished from specific phobias in which individuals only fear a discreet class of situation, such as heights or confined spaces. One of the most debilitating anxiety disorders commonly seen in outpatient clinics, and one which we will focus on in this chapter, is panic disorder with agoraphobia. With panic disorder there are recurrent unexpected panic attacks. These attacks are experienced as acute episodes of intense anxiety involving autonomic arousal and a heightened sense of being in danger. They are extremely distressing. Individuals with panic disorders come to perceive normal fluctuations in autonomic arousal as anxiety provoking, since they may signal the onset of a panic attack. Many people with panic disorder develop secondary agoraphobia where they are frightened to venture out of the safety of their own homes in case a panic attack occurs in a public setting. The idea that the world is a dangerous or threatening place is a core belief for people with anxiety disorders. They develop constricted lifestyles and many become chronically housebound.

SYSTEMIC MODEL OF ANXIETY AND DEPRESSION

Single factor models of depression or anxiety, which explain these conditions in terms of genetic vulnerabilities, biological processes, early socialisation experiences, stressful life events, intrapsychic processes and belief systems, and patterns of social interaction, have made important contributions to our understanding of depression and anxiety. However, integrative models of anxiety and depression, which take account of interactional behaviour patterns, pessimistic or threat-oriented belief systems and both genetic and developmental vulnerabilities, offer a more comprehensive systemic framework from which to conduct couples therapy (Beach, 2001, 2002; Byrne, et al., 2004a; Carr & McNulty, In Press, b; Craske & Zollner, 1995; Gollan, Friedman & Miller, 2002; Joiner & Coyne, 1999; Jones & Asen, 1999; Taylor, In Press). Such an integrative approach, based on the work just cited, will be presented below.

It should be highlighted that most of the research on integrative systemic approaches to the conceptualisation and treatment of depression and anxiety have been based on studies of white middle-class heterosexual couples in which the female partner was symptomatic and the male partner was either less symptomatic or non-symptomatic. The conceptualisation given below reflects these cultural and gender-based constraints. The conceptualisation may require modification if applied in work with cases with different cultural and gender profiles.

Predisposing Constitutional and Developmental Factors

Both genetic and environmental factors contribute to the development of anxiety and depressive conditions. For both types of disorder, the amount of stress required to precipitate the onset of an episode of depression or anxiety is proportional to the genetic vulnerability. That is, little stress may precipitate the onset of an episode in individuals who are genetically vulnerable to the condition, whereas a great deal of stress may be necessary to precipitate the disorder in individuals who have no family history of anxiety or depression.

For depression, early loss experiences such as unsupported separations, parental psychological absence through depression, bereavement and a depressive, pessimistic family culture may play a particularly important role in predisposing individuals to depression. For anxiety, anxious attachment, an inhibited temperament, excessive interpersonal sensitivity, exposure to parental anxiety and an anxiety-oriented family culture that privileges the interpretation of many environmental events as potentially hazardous may play a particularly important role in predisposing individuals to anxiety. For both depression and anxiety, negative early life experiences including abuse, neglect, multiplacement experiences, parental conflict and family disorganisation may render youngsters vulnerable to developing either condition in adulthood.

Precipitating Factors

Episodes of major depression and the onset of anxiety disorders may be precipitated by stressful life events and lifecycle transitions. Loss experiences associated with the disruption of significant relationships and loss experiences associated with failure to achieve valued goals, in particular, may precipitate an episode of depression in adulthood. Marital relationships may be disrupted through conflict and criticism, infidelity and violations of trust, physical and psychological abuse and threats of separation. Other supportive peer relationships may be disrupted through developing a constricted lifestyle or moving locality. Failure to achieve valued goals and threats to autonomy may occur with work-related performance difficulties or unemployment. Events that are perceived as dangerous or threatening to the individual's security or health may precipitate the onset of an anxiety disorder. Such events include personal or family illness or injury and victimisation or serious conflict within the marriage, wider family or the workplace. With agoraphobia in married women, one possible precipitating factor is marital conflict arising from the woman's unfulfilled need for autonomy.

Belief Systems

Both depression and anxiety are maintained by particular types of belief systems. In depression, a preoccupation with past losses, a negative view of the self as valueless and powerless, and a pessimism and hopelessness about the future are the core themes of this belief system. With anxiety, the core theme is that of danger and threat. The world is construed as a dangerous place involving multiple potential threats to health, safety and security.

Depressed individuals selectively monitor negative aspects of their own actions and those of others. Depressive belief systems are characterised by high levels of self-criticism and a belief in personal powerlessness where successes are attributed to chance and failure to personal weaknesses. This depressive belief system leads to a reduction in activities and an avoidance of participation in relationships that might disprove these depressive beliefs or lead to a sense of pleasure and optimism.

Anxious individuals are hypervigilant for danger. They may also interpret ambiguous situations as threatening or dangerous; expect that the future will probably entail many hazards, catastrophes and dangers; expect that inconsequential events in the past will probably reap dangerous threatening consequences at some unexpected point in the future; and they may believe that minor ailments or normal visceral sensations are reflective of inevitable serious illness. With panic disorder there is a conviction that fluctuations in autonomic arousal reflect the onset of full-blown anxiety attacks, which in turn are associated with a belief that death is imminent. There is also a core belief that testing out the validity of any of these beliefs will inevitably lead to more negative consequences than continuing to assume that they are true. So with panic disorder, individuals come to avoid all situations that lead to perceived fluctuations in arousal level. Since most of these occur outside the home, the belief system leads to a constricted lifestyle.

Partners of depressed and anxious individuals may develop belief systems in which they come to see their partners exclusively in terms of their problems and lose sight of other aspects of their whole personalities. Thus, non-symptomatic partners may come to construe their partners as wholly and completely depressed, anxious or incapacitated. This type of belief system give rise to excessive (and commonly futile) caregiving as described in the next section. In other instances, non-symptomatic partners may come to view their symptomatic partners as completely bad for decompensating and not fighting their condition, or as malingering and intentionally trying to control them by pretending to be more helpless than they are.

Behaviour Patterns

In marriages where one partner is depressed or anxious, the couple may become involved in destructive behaviour patterns with rigidly defined roles, which in turn maintain the anxiety or depression. In some instances, these behaviour patterns induce depression and other negative mood states in the initially non-symptomatic partner.

In one problem-maintaining behaviour pattern, the anxious or depressed partner behaves more and more helplessly and in response the other partner engages in more and more caregiving, so that the entire relationship becomes defined in terms of these two rigid complementary positions. Depressed and anxious partners have difficulty fulfilling their routine duties at home and work, and so some of these may be taken on by the non-symptomatic partner. Depressed partners typically provide and elicit little support or sexual fulfilment within their marriages, and in this sense non-symptomatic partners suffer a major loss of support when their partners develop depression. Depressed partners are less able to engage in effective joint problem solving and this is frustrating for their partners who may find that important joint decisions are left unmade or are made unsatisfactorily. Depressed partners continually seek both reassurance and confirmation of their negative views of themselves, a set of conflicting demands that is aversive for their partners and may lead to distancing.

The development of this complementary behaviour pattern greatly compromises the couple's capacity to meet each other's needs for desired levels of intimacy and autonomy. (Problems in meeting these two needs were defined as the core issues for distressed couples in Chapter 14.) Both partners experience their need for personal power and autonomy is not being met. The anxious or depressed person believes that they are helpless to change their situation because they are intrinsically powerless or because the world is too bleak or dangerous. Caregiving partners experience themselves as trapped in an endless and futile round of caregiving where nothing they do makes their partner better and yet they feel compelled to continue caregiving. This frustration of their need for autonomy gives rise to anger, which neither partner may believe is appropriate to express. The symptomatic partner may believe that it would be ungrateful to criticise their partner for excessive ineffectual caregiving. Caregiving partners may believe that it would be insensitive to criticise their symptomatic partners for not recovering.

However, periodically either partner may become so frustrated that they express their intense anger at their partner. In these instances, depressed individuals find that aggression from a previously supportive partner exacerbates their depression. Subsequently, guilt for expressing aggression may lead them to return to their previous roles of apparently grateful care-receiver or apparently dutiful caregiver. This type of behaviour pattern prevents couples from meeting each other's needs for psychological intimacy. They are only able to view each other as caregivers or receivers and unable to accept each other as people who are quite distinct from the problem and who are jointly facing the challenge of managing the anxiety or depression.

Over time, this type of caregiving and receiving behaviour pattern may deteriorate into one where more frequent verbal criticism, aggression or distancing and infidelity occur. In other cases, these hostile responses to depression or anxiety are there from the start. Verbal and physical aggression, distancing, infidelity and threatened separation all confirm the depressed or anxious partner's belief system concerning the hopelessness and dangerousness of the world and so maintain the depression or anxiety. The exacerbated symptoms may elicit further aggression or distancing from the non-symptomatic partner. However, extremely depressive and helpless behaviour has been found to inhibit non-symptomatic partners' expression of verbal or physical aggression. So in some couples, the depressed or anxious spouse learns that one way to avoid being attacked verbally or physically is to show extreme symptoms. This display of extreme symptoms also has a payoff for the non-symptomatic partner insofar as it inhibits aggression and so prevents the occurrence of the guilt that follows aggressive displays.

Wider Social and Cultural Factors and Personal Vulnerabilities

Within the wider treatment system, probably all interventions that define the symptomatic person exclusively in terms of their symptoms, rather than as a person with a wide range of attributes and competencies needing help with managing a circumscribed problem, have the potential to maintain the couple's destructive behaviour patterns. When couples attend a marital and family therapist for treatment of depression or panic disorder and agoraphobia, the majority have received individually-based treatment involving medication, psychotherapy or both. In many instances, within these programmes, they have come to be defined as their problems rather than competent people with circumscribed problems.

In Chapter 14, a range of wider social and cultural factors and personal vulnerabilities which influence the adjustment of distressed couples were discussed. It was noted that relationship difficulties are more common among couples who come from different cultures with differing role expectations; and from couples of lower socioeconomic status; who live in urban areas; who have married before the age of 20; and where premarital pregnancy has occurred.

Outcome

The average duration of a depressive episode is nine months, and half of all depressed people experience more than one episode (Carr & McNulty, In Press, b). Panic disorder with agoraphobia tends to follow a waxing and waning course (Taylor, In Press). For major depression and panic disorder with agoraphobia, approximately a third respond well to treatment; about a third show partial recovery; and about a third develop a chronically constricted lifestyle.

Protective Factors

At a behavioural level, a good marital relationship, good communication and problem-solving skills; a willingness to break out of complementary caregiver–care-receiver patterns or symmetrical aggressive patterns; and an openness to increasing the rate of positive interactions and level of activity within the relationship are protective factors. In terms of beliefs, symptomatic individuals who can challenge and test out their depressive and anxious belief systems are better able to develop new and useful belief systems in couples therapy. Non-symptomatic individuals who are flexible enough to define their partner as a competent individual with a circumscribed problem probably respond better to couples therapy.

Individuals who are able to construe couples therapy as an opportunity for making a *fresh start* are more likely to benefit from treatment.

Individuals who come from families in which secure parent–child attachments were formed probably find it easier to use couples therapy to resolve relationship difficulties.

With respect to sociocultural factors and personal history, similarity of cultural values and role expectations; high socioeconomic status; living in a rural area; absence of parental divorce; absence of premarital pregnancy; and marriage after the age of 30 have all been identified as protective factors in long-term relationships. These factors were discussed in detail in Chapter 14.

COUPLES THERAPY FOR ANXIETY AND DEPRESSION

For couples in which one member has depression or panic disorder with agoraphobia, couples-based treatment, particularly behavioural marital therapy, is as effective as other treatments such as medication or individual cognitive therapy and probably more effective in cases where there are concurrent marital difficulties (Beach, 2002; Byrne et al., 2004a). Guidelines for contracting for assessment; assessment; contracting for treatment; and treatment outlined in Chapter 14 for working with distressed couples and in Chapter 9 for family therapy may be used when working with cases of depression and anxiety. However, a number of specific procedures deserve attention when working with these cases and it to these that we now turn (Beach, Sandeen & O'Leary, 1990; Craske & Zollner, 1995; Gollan et al, 2002; Jones & Asen, 1999).

Contracting for Assessment

Where both members of a couple voluntarily request couples therapy, contracting for assessment is a straightforward procedure. The couple may be invited to attend a series of sessions with a view to clarifying the main problems, and related behaviour patterns, belief systems and possible predisposing factors. The couple may be informed that once a shared understanding or formulation has been reached, then a further contract for treatment may be offered if that is appropriate.

In the assessment contract, it may be agreed in cases where the symptomatic partner is hospitalised or housebound that the assessment be conducted in hospital or at home, but it should be mentioned that if the assessment shows that couples treatment is appropriate then some of the treatment sessions will require the symptomatic person to leave the hospital or home for some sessions and homework assignments.

Various tricyclic antidepressants and serotonin re-uptake inhibitors have been shown to have clinically significant short-term effects on both major depression and panic disorder with agoraphobia (Nemeroff & Schatzberg, 2002; Roy-Byrne & Cowley, 2002). Where symptomatic partners are on medication or are considering medication as an option, this should be encouraged. It is probable that the changes which occur during couples based interventions for anxiety and depression probably give couples the skills to maximise the effects of the medication in alleviating symptoms. These skills also help couples prevent relapse, which is commonly occurs when medication is withdrawn and couples have not received a concurrent psychosocial intervention.

When making a contract for assessment where depression is the central problem, risk of self-harm should be assessed. Where the depressed partner shows suicidal intent, statutory procedures should be followed to address this. In most jurisdictions, this involves psychiatric assessment and hospitalisation. Offering a contract for assessment should be delayed until the depressed partner is no longer actively suicidal. Where statutory procedures permit greater flexibility, members of extended family may be involved in providing a home-based 24-hour suicide watch until the depressed person's risk of self-harm recedes. Family members agree to take sitting with the suicidal person for three or four hours duration. This is a very powerful intervention since it lets the depressed person know that members of the family value and care about them sufficiently to work together 24 hours a day for as many days as it takes to keep them alive and prevent suicide.

In cases where domestic violence has occurred, an arrangement must be made that allows the couple to have continued contact without violence for the duration of the treatment programme. In extreme cases, the violent partner may need to live in a separate accommodation. In less extreme cases, an agreement to avoid all violence during assessment may be built into the contract, and a routine for using time-out to manage risky situations stipulated.

Assessment

The first aim of family assessment is to construct three-column formulations, like those presented in Figures 15.2 and 15.3, of a typical problematic episode in which the anxiety or depression is at its worst and an exceptional episode in which exacerbation was expected to occur but did not. Belief systems that underpin each partner's role in these episodes may then be clarified. These in turn may be linked to predisposing the risk factors that have been listed in the systemic model of couple's problems presented above.

One important technique for use during assessment is self-monitoring because it helps to throw light on specific situations that precipitate symptoms. It also provides a forum within which couples can learn to use 10-point rating scales, which are required for checking progress on a moment-to-moment basis in later treatment tasks, particularly with anxiety disorders. The form presented in Figure 9.1 is introduced and clients are invited to use this at times when they notice significant changes in their anxiety or depression. In particular they should note:

- the day and time
- the situation or event
- what happened before and after the change in their state of anxiety and depression
- a rating of their mood or anxiety on a 10-point scale at the end of the event.

This type of diary helps couples develop an awareness of the link between particular sequences of activity and internal states. As couples become skilled in self-monitoring they may be invited to record, not just what happened before and after each mood or anxiety changing event, but specifically:

- the activity they were doing
- the conversation they were having
- the thoughts they were having about this activity or conversation.

This self-monitoring information is useful in constructing the right-hand column and the middle column of the three-column formulation for both problematic episodes and exceptional non-problematic episodes. With depression, self-monitoring information may be used to help identify negative beliefs that need to be challenged and self-monitoring information may also be useful in constructing lists of pleasant events for couples to use to improve their mood. With anxiety, self-monitoring information may be used to help construct a hierarchy of anxiety-provoking situations, which couples must learn to cope with as homework assignments.

Contracting for Treatment

A summary of the family' strengths or exceptions and a three-column formulation of the family process in which the couples' anxiety or depression-related problems are embedded should be given when contracting for treatment. Specific goals, a clear specification of the number of treatment sessions and the times and places at which these sessions will occur should all be detailed in a contract especially in cases where one member is housebound or hospitalised. At least some of the later sessions should be conducted on a routine outpatient basis rather than in hospital or in the couple's home. It is also good practice to make a statement about the probability that the couple will benefit from treatment, backed up with a statement of the factors that make it likely that this is the case. This issue was discussed in Chapter 14.

Unless there is good reason to suspect otherwise, it is worth mentioning that in most couples in which one partner has been depressed or agoraphobic, the difficulties that this causes lead both partners to consider separation. Indeed, many couples separate once the depressed or anxious person shows any sign of recovery. For this reason, couples are invited to make a commitment to remain together for at least six months, so they may have a chance to experience what it would be like to live together once they have used therapy to remove the depression and anxiety from their relationship (Coyne, 1984). If therapy is unsuccessful (which it will be in a third of cases) or if after 6 months either partner is still dissatisfied, then separation may be seriously addressed at that point.

Particularly in cases of chronic anxiety or depression, it is important to set very small treatment goals. That is, partners are each invited to describe the minimal change that would be necessary for them to know that recovery had started. This procedure is central to practice with the MRI institutes brief therapy model (Segal, 1991) and is discussed in Chapter 3.

Treatment

Treatment for couples in which one member is depressed or anxious should aim to disrupt problematic behaviour patterns and transform the belief systems that underpin these. All of the interventions, described in some detail in Chapters 9 and 14, are appropriate for use in cases where anxiety and depression are the main concern. To avoid repetition these procedures will not be recapped in any detail here. Rather specific interventions that should be used in addition to routine interventions will be highlighted. Those appropriate for use with depression will be presented first, followed by those used in cases where anxiety is the main concern. The chapter will close with some comments on managing resistance and relapses in cases of both anxiety and depression.

Treatment of Depression

With depression, helping couples disrupt destructive behaviour patterns, scheduling pleasant events, and communication and problem-solving skills training are useful interventions for altering depressive behaviour patterns. Depressive belief systems may be addressed by coaching couples to challenge negative constructions of events. Vulnerability to depression may be addressed through psychoeducation.

Psychoeducation for Depression

The following psychoeducational intervention combines an explanation of depression, an externalisation of depression, a framing of therapy as a fresh-start experience and a rationale for treatment. The ideas in this psychoeducational input should be presented as a single spoken and written statement and but they should also be incorporated into discussions, which occur throughout the treatment sessions.

Depression is a complex condition involving changes in mood, biological functioning, beliefs and behaviour. Vulnerability to depression may be due to genetic factors or early loss experiences. Current episodes of depression arise from a build-up of recent life stress. This activates the vulnerability, which then comes to be maintained by depressed beliefs and behaviour. Genetic vulnerability may be explained as a nervous system that *goes slow* under pressure and disrupts sleep, appetite and energy. This *going slow* process leads to depressed mood.

Early loss-related vulnerability may be explained as a set of memories about loss that have been filed away, but are taken out when a recent loss occurs. The files inform the person that more and more losses will occur and this leads to depressed mood.

Treatment centres on helping the depressed person and his or her partner to learn how to challenge depressive beliefs and develop new behaviour patterns, particularly within the couple's relationship in which they do more enjoyable things together, talk together clearly, and solve problems together systematically.

Every couple who fights depression together are a problem-solving team, facing a common enemy. Depression is the common enemy.

Antidepressant medication may be used to regulate sleep and appetite and increase energy levels. However, for full recovery and to be equipped to manage situations where there is a risk of relapse, couples therapy is required.

In this sense, couple therapy can offer a fresh start, a way of beating depression and being prepared for it, if it tries to enter the couple's life again.

Disrupting Destructive Behaviour Patterns in Couples with Depression

With depression a number of interventions may be used to help couples disrupt destructive behaviour patterns.

Role Reversal

Where couples are trapped in rigid caregiving and receiving cycles, they may be invited to swap roles within the session to understand the impact of the depression on their partner. Depressed partners are invited to act completely rationally and assertively. Non-symptomatic partners are invited to fully express the sadness and sense of loss that they have felt since the depression began to destroy the relationship. Partners may need coaching in acting out these role reversals. Depressed partners may need help in practicing assertive responses. Non-depressed partners may require help remembering how good their relationship used to be, how much they have lost and how deeply that hurts them. If couples can sustain this reasonably effectively within the session they may be invited on alternate days between sessions to swap roles.

Opening Space for Recovery and Taking it Slow

Rigid caregiving and receiving cycles may be also disrupted by inviting the non-symptomatic partner to open up space for the depressed partner to recover in by not helping any more. This will mean that there will be many opportunities for the depressed partner to carry out household tasks and so forth to show that he or she is recovering. To prevent the depressed partner from feeling overwhelmed by the number of opportunities to show signs of recovery, he or she may be invited to make haste slowly.

Compliments and Statements of Affection

Non-depressed partners may be coached to refuse to offer reassurance or evaluative comments on self-critical statements, since any response to such requests will be taken to be insincere and patronising. However, they may be invited instead to identify situations when they can congruently complement their partner for doing something well and link these complements to statements of affection. These statements take the form, 'Just now you did ABC. I like the way you did that. That reminds me how much I care about you'.

Writing Positive Requests for the Future

Where partners have become embroiled in rigid mutually aggressive behaviour patterns, they may be invited whenever their partner does something to irritate them to write this down immediately in a notebook they agree to carry at all times. At the end of each day they are invited to review all their criticisms and complaints about the past day and rephrase those they still consider to be important as positive requests about future activity. For example, 'I hated it when he was complaining about my watching the TV during dinner', is rephrased as, 'I would love tomorrow to talk to you about how my day went during dinner'. Couples may be invited to set a fixed time each day to exchange these letters. Couples are invited to try to respond to those requests within the letters to which they feel it is reasonable to respond within a day of receiving the letter. However, they are invited not to discuss the contents of the letters between sessions since this may lead to them slipping back into destructive behavioural patterns.

Scheduling Pleasant Events in Depression

When one member of a couple becomes depressed, over time the couple's participation in enjoyable activities diminishes. An important intervention is to help couples list and schedule regular mutually pleasurable events. These may be graded in demandingness and degree of activity involved. As therapy progresses, couples may be invited to gradually move from low activity non-demanding tasks, like watching a sunset or reading to each other, to higher activity tasks, like taking a 20-minute walk together each day or going for a cycle ride. Physical exercise improves mood so it is important for couples to work towards increasing physical activity over the course of therapy.

Often depression disrupts normal family routines, such as times for retiring or waking, mealtimes, times for joint household chores, and so forth. Couples may be invited to reconstruct schedules for daily routines and ensure that these routines include some joint physical activity and some joint periods of supportive conversation and interaction, such as shared mealtimes.

Challenging Negative Belief Systems in Depression

Depressed individuals need to challenge their negative beliefs and gradually replace these with more positive constructions and narratives about their situation. *Challenge-test-reward* (CTR) is a simple routine for promoting this transformation. When a person challenges a self-critical belief, this involves generating an alternative positive belief. The possibility that this alternative may be true is tested by looking for evidence to support the validity of this alternative. Finally, when this task has been completed and the person has shown that there is evidence to support the positive belief, he or she engages in self-rewarding talk. Here is an example of the CTR routine:

Negative belief: 'He didn't talk to me so he doesn't like me.'

Challenging alternative: 'He didn't talk to me because he is shy.'

Test: 'He is not a loud talker and rarely speaks unless spoken to.'

Reward: 'Well done. I've found support for my positive belief.'

Both symptomatic and non-symptomatic partners may be invited to use this CTR skill in challenging situations where low mood occurs. Depressed partners may be encouraged to use this routine as an alternative to requesting reassurance or requests for agreement with negative self-criticism from their partners. Thus, a reassurance request of a partner, such as, 'Tell me things are going to work out between us', becomes a dialogue with the self:

Challenge: 'I must find one piece of evidence which suggests that things will be all right between us.'

Test: 'We watched a video last night and enjoyed being together. That means things are not all bad between us.'

Reward: 'I've done a good challenge. Well done. I've found support for the idea that things will work out OK.'

This substitution of requests for reassurance or evaluations of the self from partners with private CTR routines disrupts the depression-maintaining behaviour pattern of requesting and receiving reassurance, and replaces it with an autonomous routine that has been shown in studies of cognitive therapy to transform negative belief systems (Craighead, Hart, Wilcoxon-Craighead & Ilardi, 2002).

Communication and Problem-solving Skills Training for Depression

Communication and problem-solving skills training, following the guidelines given in Chapters 9 and 14, should be included in the treatment of couples containing a depressed partner. Communication skills once perfected may be used so that the partners can empathise with each other about positive experiences, make statements of affection linked to compliments, make highly specific requests for small positive relationship changes, and as an alternative to destructive mind-reading. Couples should be discouraged from using communication skills to empathise routinely with each other about negative experiences, since the balance of talk time will inevitably be taken up with discussions of negativity and hopelessness. Where couples have a habit of mind-reading, they should be invited, any time they fall into this habit, instead to ask their partner what they are thinking. Problem-solving skills may be used to help couples overcome the angry battles or sulky stand-offs that typically occur when they jointly try to solve a routine family problem. It should be highlighted that problem solving is a slow and painstaking process, which must be approached with the expectation of cooperation.

Treatment of Panic Disorder and Agoraphobia

Vulnerability to panic disorder with agoraphobia may be addressed initially through psychoeducation. Facilitating gradual exposure to a hierarchy of feared situations and learning coping skills to deal with these situations directly address problematic behaviour patterns. Problem-solving and communication skills training may be included in treatment, if partners have deficits in these areas that prevent them from completing the exposure exercises cooperatively.

Psychoeducation for Panic Disorder and Agoraphobia

The following psychoeducational intervention combines an explanation of anxiety, an externalisation of anxiety, a framing of therapy as a fresh-start experience and a rationale for treatment. The ideas in this psychoeducational input should be presented as a single spoken and written statement and then incorporated into discussions that occur over the course of treatment.

Fear is an adaptive response to danger because it prepares the body to respond to the dangerous situation, person or threat by fighting or fleeing. It is adaptive for the survival of the individual and, from an evolutionary perspective, it is adaptive for the survival of the species. Because of fear, our ancestors were able to detect dangers and respond to them quickly by fighting or fleeing and so they survived.

Anxiety is fear that happens in situations that are misinterpreted as dangerous. Fear and anxiety have three different parts: thoughts about being afraid; physical feelings of being afraid; and behaviour patterns that help the person avoid the situations of which they are frightened. It is the thoughts of being afraid and the *habit of interpreting situations as dangerous* that is at the root of anxiety. The physical feelings that follow from the dangerous thoughts are the second part of anxiety. The thoughts of being afraid of a dangerous situation lead to the body getting ready to fight the danger or run from it. This physical part of anxiety (autonomic hyperarousal) involves adrenaline flowing into the blood stream, the heart beating faster, a quickening of breathing and the muscles become tense. The faster breathing may lead to dizziness. The tense muscles may lead to headaches, stomach or chest pains. Sometimes these physical changes, like a racing heartbeat, dizziness or pains, are frightening themselves because they may be misinterpreted as the first signs of a heart attack, for example, and this leads to more physical changes. The thoughts of being afraid and the physical feelings that go with them lead the person to try to escape from the frightening situation or to avoid it in future. This is the third part of anxiety, the behaviour patterns that the person uses to avoid frightening situations. Many people who have had panic attacks (or nearly had them) outside in the supermarket or while queuing in the bank or on the bus may avoid these situations in future.

If the person is forced to face one of these situations that they interpret as dangerous without training, they may become so frightened that they to try to escape and leave the situation before the anxiety subsides. Unfortunately, this makes the anxiety worse. What the person needs to learn to master the anxiety is to get into training so that they can handle rising anxiety and then go into the frightening situation and use all their training to cope with it.

Treatment involves, getting into training for handling anxiety and then facing the frightening situation until the anxiety dies. The partner's role in treatment is to help the anxious person face carefully selected feared situations for specific amounts of time as homework assignments, to remind their partner to use their coping strategies to help their fear subside in these situations, and to help them celebrate each time they complete an assignment successfully.

Every couple who fight anxiety together are a problem-solving team, facing a common enemy. Anxiety is the common enemy.

Medication may be used to dampen the biological part of the fear response. However, for full recovery and to be equipped to manage situations where there is a risk of relapse, couples therapy is required.

In this sense, couples therapy can offer a fresh start, a way of beating anxiety and being prepared for it if it tries to enter the couple's life again.

Exposure and Coping Skills Training for Agoraphobia

In exposure and coping skills training for agoraphobia, the non-symptomatic partner helps the anxious partner complete homework assignments, which involved actual exposure (such as making increasingly longer excursions from the home); encourages and praises the client for exposing themselves to feared situations; and helps their partner to practise coping strategies, such as relaxation exercises or positive self-talk.

Hierarchy Construction

The process begins with the therapist inviting the anxious partner to define the most frightening and the least frightening situations. These are used as anchor points in creating a hierarchy of increasingly threatening situations. The least frightening situation (for example, sitting at home) is given a fear rating of one and the most frightening situation is given a rear

rating of 10 (for example, travelling on a train). The client is invited to select a situation to which they would give a fear rating of five (for example,
walking down the high street). Other situations are then slotted into this
hierarchy.

Highlighting Habituation

The process of habituation is then explained. The couple are informed
that anxiety may be beaten by entering these situations repeatedly, starting with the least frightening and remaining in them until the fear dies.
Eventually, habituation will occur. However, if the person leaves the situation before the fear has begun to decrease, then this may actually make
the fear worse.

Coping Skills Training

Once the hierarchy has been constructed and habituation has been
explained, the need for coping skills training is highlighted. It is pointed
out that remaining in fearful situations until anxiety dies is tough, but
there are three main strategies that can be used to make the fear die more
quickly. First, the person may use deep breathing and relaxation routines.
Second, they may use the CTR routine (described above) to challenge catastrophic beliefs, such as, 'My chest is tight. I'm going to have a heart attack'.
Third, they may use a distracting activity, such as singing along to music
on their personal stereo, to take their mind off the habituation process.

A relaxation routine and set of breathing exercises are given in Table
15.1. Couples may be coached in using these within the session and then
invited to practice them daily together at home. Relaxation skills training
with people who have panic disorder is sometimes complicated by the
fact that focusing inward on changes in muscle tension may lead to
increased tension rather than relaxation because of the tendency of people
with panic disorder to misperceive internal cues and catastrophise about
them. Where this type of problem occurs, visualisation may be used as
an alternative to progressive muscle relaxation and youngsters may be
invited to focus not on their somatic state but on relaxing imagery, such as
that suggested in Table 15.1.

In threatening situations, anxious clients misinterpret initial signs of
hypearousal as the beginning of a catastrophe, such as having a heart
attach. They may be trained to challenge such beliefs and use breathing exercises to reduce hyperarousal in the following way. Couples are
invited to enter into a state of hyperarousal by hyperventilating at a rate of
30 breaths per minute and then to wait and see if some catastrophic event
occurs (Barlow et al., 2002). When this is done on a number of occasions,
the couples learn that internal signs of arousal are not harbingers of doom.
Anxious clients may then be trained to change their breathing pattern to
regular slow deep breaths (inhale for a count of three and breath out for
a count of six). This pattern of slow breathing, contributes to relieving

Table 15.1 Relaxation exercises handout

Relaxation exercises

- After a couple of weeks' daily practice under your supervision, you will have developed enough skill to use these exercises to get rid of unwanted body tension
- Set aside 20 minutes a day to do these relaxation exercises
- Do them at the same time and in the same place every day
- Before you begin, remove all distractions (by turning off bright lights, the radio, etc.) and loosen any tight clothes (like belts, ties or shoes)
- Lie on a bed or recline in a comfortable chair with the eyes lightly closed
- Before and after each exercise breath in deeply and exhale slowly three times while saying the, word 'relax' to yourself
- At the end of each exercise praise yourself by saying 'Well done', or 'You did that exercise well', or some other form of praise
- Repeat each exercise twice
- If you decide to tape-record these instructions and listen to the tape as you do the exercises, speak in a calm relaxed quiet voice

Area	Exercise
Hands	Close your hands into fists. Then allow them to open slowly. Notice the change from tension to relaxation in your hands and allow this change to continue further and further still so the muscles of your hands become more and more relaxed
Arms	Bend your arms at the elbow and touch your shoulders with your hands. Then allow them to return to the resting position. Notice the change from tension to relaxation in your arms and allow this change to continue further and further still so the muscles of your arms become more and more relaxed
Shoulders	Hunch your shoulders up to your ears. Then allow them to return to the resting position. Notice the change from tension to relaxation in your shoulders and allow this change to continue further and further still so the muscles of your shoulders become more and more relaxed
Legs	Point your toes downwards. Then allow them to return to the resting position. Notice the change from tension to relaxation in the fronts of your legs and allow this change to continue further and further still so the muscles in the fronts of your legs become more and more relaxed Point your toes upwards. Then allow them to return to the resting position. Notice the change from tension to relaxation in the backs of your legs and allow this change to continue further and further still so the muscles in the backs of your legs become more and more relaxed

(Continued on next page)

Table 15.1 (*Continued*)

Area	Exercise
Stomach	Take a deep breath and hold it for three seconds, tensing the muscles in your stomach as you do so. Then breath out slowly. Notice the change from tension to relaxation in your stomach muscles and allow this change to continue further and further still so your stomach muscles become more and more relaxed
Face	Clench your teeth tightly together. Then relax. Notice the change from tension to relaxation in your jaw and allow this change to continue further and further still so the muscles in your jaw become more and more relaxed
	Wrinkle your nose up. Then relax. Notice the change from tension to relaxation in the muscles around the front of your face and allow this change to continue further and further still so the muscles of your face become more and more relaxed
	Shut your eyes tightly. Then relax. Notice the change from tension to relaxation in the muscles around your eyes and allow this change to continue further and further still so the muscles around your eyes become more and more relaxed
All over	Now that you've done all your muscle exercises, check that all areas of your body are as relaxed as can be. Think of your hands and allow them to relax a little more
	Think of your arms and allow them to relax a little more
	Think of your shoulders s and allow them to relax a little more
	Think of your legs and allow them to relax a little more
	Think of your stomach and allow it to relax a little more
	Think of your face and allow it to relax a little more
Breathing	Breath in...one...two...three...and out slowly...one...two...three... four...five...six...and again
	Breath in...one...two...three...and out slowly...one...two...three... four...five...six...and again
	Breath in...one...two...three...and out slowly...one...two...three... four...five...six
Visualising	Imagine you are lying on beautiful sandy beach and you feel the sun warm your body
	Make a picture in your mind of the golden sand and the warm sun
	As the sun warms your body you feel more and more relaxed
	As the sun warms your body you feel more and more relaxed
	As the sun warms your body you feel more and more relaxed
	The sky is a clear, clear blue. Above you, you can see a small white cloud drifting away into the distance
	As it drifts away you feel more and more relaxed
	It is drifting away and you feel more and more relaxed
	It is drifting away and you feel more and more relaxed
	As the sun warms your body you feel more and more relaxed

Area	Exercise
	AS the cloud drifts away you feel more and more relaxed (Wait for 30 seconds) When you are ready open your eyes ready to face the rest of the day relaxed and calm

the symptoms of hyperarousal. This type of training experience, provides couples with a sound basis for using the CTR technique (described earlier) and slow breathing exercises to challenge catastrophic beliefs and reduce hyperarousal when conducting their homework assignments.

Exposure Homework Assignments

Once the hierarchy has been constructed, habituation has been explained, and coping skills training is complete, sessions are then devoted to helping couples plan and review exposure homework assignments. Starting with the least threatening situation in the hierarchy and working upwards at a slow pace over a number of weeks, couples are invited to plan exactly how the exposure assignments will be conducted. Control over the pacing of this work should rest with the anxious partner. Couples should arrange to enter each situation on the hierarchy repeatedly until full habituation occurs, before progressing to the next situation in the hierarchy. When entering these situations, the non-anxious spouse adopts a supportive role, reminding the anxious spouse to use their coping strategies or relaxation, breathing, CTR routines, and distraction. Periodically the anxious spouse may give the non-anxious spouse ratings on a 10-point scale of their anxiety level. This allows the couple to monitor jointly the process of habituation as it occurs and to rejoice as the anxiety level begins to drop.

Communication and Problem-solving Skills Training for Anxiety

Communication and problem-solving skills training, following the guidelines given in Chapters 9 and 14, should be included in the treatment of couples containing an anxious member if a lack of these skills prevents the couples from completing exposure homework assignments.

Managing Resistance in the Treatment of Depression and Anxiety

Symptomatic partners may have difficulty cooperating because they lack energy or believe they are powerless to fight pessimism or fear. A central strategy for managing this type of resistance is for the therapist to take responsibility for inviting couples to take on assignments that were too demanding. The appropriateness of smaller assignments may then be discussed with both partners. Ways of dividing large daunting assignments into a number of smaller and less challenging assignments may be explored.

Non-symptomatic partners may have difficulty cooperating with treatment when they find that their partner's recovery reduces their autonomy and power within the relationship and increases the demands for intimacy beyond a tolerable level. If this happens both partners may be invited to explore ways that the non-symptomatic partner may be helped to tolerate a lower level of power and autonomy and a higher level of intimacy. They may also be invited to explore ways that the non-symptomatic partner's autonomy may be increased and the demands on them for intimacy decreased, without this precipitating a relapse in their previously symptomatic partner.

Members of couples in which anxiety or depression is a central concern may have unresolved family-of-origin issues that have rendered them vulnerable to anxiety or depression as adults. For example, they may have been sexually abused as children or their parents may have died when they were young. Sometimes, couples have difficulty making progress in treatment because they are preoccupied with addressing these family-of-origin issues. They believe that, if these were resolved, then the symptoms would abate. Available evidence suggests that symptomatic improvement may be achieved using the present-focused methods described above. So clients maybe invited to defer an exploration of family-of-origin issues until the symptoms have begun to improve.

Relapse Management for Depression and Anxiety

Depression and panic disorder with agoraphobia are recurrent disorders. Therefore, brief couples therapy involving up to 20 sessions must be offered within the context of a longer term care programme. Couples may be invited to identify stressful situations that may be likely to precipitate relapses and develop plans to cope with these relapses either independently or within the context of further episodes of brief couples therapy.

SUMMARY

Major depression and panic disorder with agoraphobia are debilitating conditions, which affect a significant minority of the population. Couples in which one partner, usually the woman, has one of these conditions are commonly referred to adult mental health clinics. Integrative models of anxiety and depression, which take account of problematic interactional behaviour patterns, pessimistic or threat-oriented belief systems and both genetic and developmental vulnerabilities, offer a comprehensive systemic framework from which to conduct couples therapy. Additional problem-specific intervention must be incorporated into routine couples therapy for treatment to be effective in cases where anxiety or depression are the main concern. Vulnerability to both depression and anxiety may be addressed through psychoeducation. With depression, helping couples disrupt destructive behaviour patterns, scheduling pleasant events, and communication and problem-solving skills training are useful interventions for altering depressive behaviour patterns. Depressive belief systems may be addressed by inviting couples to challenge their negative belief systems using challenge-test-reward routines. For agoraphobia, facilitating gradual exposure to a hierarchy of feared situations and coaching anxious members of couples to use coping skills to deal with these situations are central to the therapeutic process. Problem-solving and communication skills training may be included in treatment if partners have deficits in these areas which prevent them from completing the exposure exercises cooperatively. In treatment of couples with either anxiety or depression, managing resistance and planning relapse management are essential for effective treatment.

FURTHER READING

Beach, S., Sandeen, E. & O'Leary, D. (1990). *Depression in Marriage. A Model for Etiology and Treatment.* New York: Guilford.

Craske, M. & Zoellner, L. (1995). Anxiety disorders: The role of marital therapy. In N. Jacobson & A. Gurman (Eds), *Clinical Handbook of Couples Therapy,* pp. 394–411. New York: Guilford.

Gollan, J., Friedman, M. & Miller, I. (2002). Couple therapy in the treatment of major depression. In A. Gurman & N. Jacobon (Eds), *Clinical Handbook of Couples Therapy,* 3rd edn, pp. 653–676. New York: Guilford.

Jones, E. & Asen, E. (1999). *Systemic Couples Therapy for Depression.* London: Karnac.

Chapter 16

ALCOHOL PROBLEMS IN ADULTHOOD

When a member of a couple develops alcohol problems, this has a profound effect on the relationship. It is alcohol problems occuring within the context of this type of relationship that are the central concern in this chapter. A distinction is made in DSM-IV-TR (American Psychiatric Association, 2000) and ICD 10 (World Health Organisation, 1992) between alcohol dependence and alcohol abuse, with the former being characterised by a tolerance and withdrawal syndrome in the absence of alcohol and the latter, a broader condition, characterised by impaired social functioning arising from alcohol use. These two categories probably represent points on a continuum that ranges from non-problematic alcohol use, through varying degrees of abuse, to alcohol dependence accompanied by severe psychosocial and medical problems (McCrady, In Press). People at the extreme end of this continuum have traditionally been labelled as alcoholics. In clinical practice, a wide variety of people with differing types and degrees of alcohol problems are referred for treatment. A systemic model for conceptualising these alcohol problems and a systemic approach to therapy with these cases will be given in this chapter. A case example is given in Figure 16.1 and three-column formulations of problems and exceptions are given in Figure 16.2. and 16.3.

In adults over 18 years of age, the prevalence of alcohol dependence and abuse is approximately 5% (American Psychiatric Association, 2000). Alcohol problems are more common among men than women. Many people with alcohol problems also have other difficulties, such as depression, anxiety, or problems controlling aggression.

SYSTEMIC MODEL OF ALCOHOL PROBLEMS IN ADULTHOOD

Single factor models of alcohol problems, which offer explanations in terms of genetic vulnerabilities, biological processes, early socialisation experiences and related personality traits, stressful life events, intrapsychic processes and belief systems, and patterns of social interaction, have

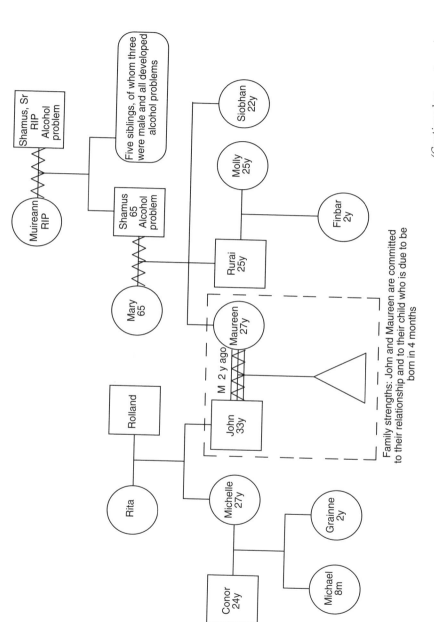

Family strengths: John and Maureen are committed to their relationship and to their child who is due to be born in 4 months

(Continued on next page)

Referral. Maureen came for therapy because of her conflict with her partner John over John's alcohol abuse. Since their marriage two years previously, John, who had always been a social drinker, had developed a habit of binge drinking on a regular basis. Maureen was particularly sensitive to alcohol-related conflict because her father and late paternal grandfather both had alcohol problems, which caused difficulties in their marriages. Maureen was seeking therapy when she did because she was due to have a baby in four months and wanted to sort out the alcohol-related conflict before the birth of the child. Maureen had spent a year in individual therapy addressing family-of-origin issues related to the impact of her father's alcohol abuse and her parents' marital conflict.

Engagement. In a series of unilateral family therapy sessions, Maureen took steps to monitor John's drinking, to withdraw from enabling and critical behaviour patterns and to create drink-free opportunities for enhancing the relationship. When some improvement had occurred in her relationship with John she invited him to therapy and he came willingly.

Formulation. Formulations of conflictual incidents and exceptions to these are given in Figures 16.2 and 16.3.

Therapy. Therapy aimed to help John develop a pattern of controlled drinking, reduce the frequency of alcohol-related conflicts. Controlled-drinking skills training for John and communication and problem-solving skills training for the couple were central to the therapy. A recurrent theme was Maureen's fear that her marriage would be a repetition of her parents' and her grandparents', and that this would ruin her child's life. The couple were helped to ritualise the statement of this concern once a week, so that it could be prevented from infecting their every waking moment. Once a pattern of controlled drinking was established, therapy focused on the lifecycle transition of planning for a baby.

Figure 16.1 Case example of couple who have conflict over alcohol abuse

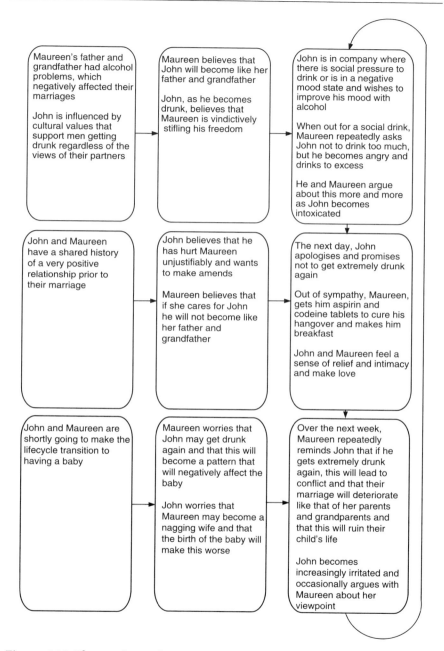

Figure 16.2 Three-column formulation of an episode of conflict over alcohol abuse

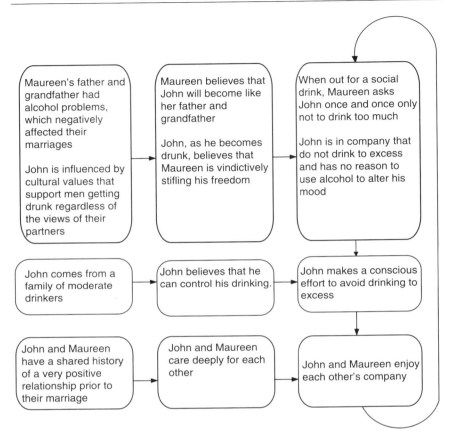

Figure 16.3 Three-column formulation of an exception to situations where conflict over alcohol is expected but does not occur

made important contributions to our understanding of problem drinking. However, integrative models of alcohol abuse that take account of behaviour patterns within which problematic drinking occurs, belief systems that underpin these patterns and constitutional, developmental and sociocultural predisposing factors offer a more comprehensive systemic framework from which to conduct couples therapy (Berg & Miller 1992; Epstein & McCrady, 2002; Finney & Moos, 2002; Hester & Miller, 2002; Kaufman & Kaufman, 1992; McCrady, In Press; O'Farrell, 1993; O'Farrell & Fals-Stewart, 2002; Steinglass, Bennet, Wolin & Reiss, 1987). Such an integrative approach, based on the work just cited, will be presented below.

Behaviour Patterns

Alcohol abuse occurs within the context of behaviour patterns which maintain it. Reduction of anxiety, depression or anger; relieving boredom or giving excitement; or relieving craving or withdrawal symptoms are some of the personal triggers that may initiate an episode of problem drinking. Inevitably, problem drinking creates difficulties for the person who drinks. Where partners of problem drinkers do things to reduce the negative consequences of their drinking, this may maintain the pattern of problem drinking. For example, arranging for a drunk partner to be carried home; cleaning them up; covering for them if they do not attend work the next day; arranging for them to have an early morning drink; arranging for them to have money to fund further bouts of drinking are common 'enabling' activities that maintain problem drinking. This complementary relationship between the caregiving and enabling sober partner and care receiving partner with a drink problem, once entrenched has the added problem of making it very difficult for couples to adequately meet each other's needs for desired levels of intimacy and autonomy. (Problems in meeting these two needs were defined as the core issues for distressed couples in Chapter 14.).

Where needs for intimacy and autonomy are frustrated, a problem drinker may use alcohol to cope with such unmet needs. Problem drinkers may feel powerless to control the deterioration of their relationship and a growing distance from their partners. Their sober partners in turn may feel helpless in the face of their partners continued drinking despite all their supportive efforts. They may also experience a growing distance within the relationship.

Sober partners may cope with this frustration by criticising, nagging, distancing and punishing their partners for drinking. In response, their partners may drink more. When couple's needs for intimacy and autonomy are frustrated and problem drinkers attempt to cope with this through further drinking, escalating patterns of verbal and sometimes physical aggression may occur during episodes of drunkenness.

After these episodes, problem drinkers usually sleep and when they awake express deep regret and remorse. In situations where sober partners forgive their partners with drink problems, and they promise to amend their ways, both partners may experience a profound sense of relief and psychological intimacy. This highly rewarding consequence to the whole cycle may be an incentive to repeat the cycle once more.

In other couples, both partners drink and their bouts of problematic drinking have the pay-off of creating a sense of cohesion and connectedness. This kind of joint drinking may also allow the couple to avoid solving difficult or complex family problems related to employment or childcare.

Where one or both members of a couple are problem drinkers, their difficulties may lead them to isolate themselves from others as the alcohol problem worsens and this in turn may make the couples problem-maintaining pattern more rigid.

Belief Systems

The behaviour patterns within which problem drinking is embedded may be sustained by a range of belief systems. For the partner with the drink problem, the behaviour may be sustained by a denial of the problem or by an acceptance of the problem but a belief that it is uncontrollable. For the partner without the drink problem, enabling behaviour may be sustained by a belief that supporting the partner with the drink problem will eventually lead to them ceasing drinking. It may also be sustained by a belief that withdrawing support may lead the partner with the drink problem to become aggressive, make self-harming or suicidal gestures, or lead to a deterioration in functioning that may result in loss of employment or other negative consequences. There may also be negative consequences for the sober member of a couple if the drinker reforms his or her ways. At the very least, it will mean that the routines of the relationship will change. However, it will probably also mean that there will be a change in the way the couple meet each other's needs for desired levels of intimacy and autonomy. A sober spouse with much power and autonomy may find that this is reduced when their drunk partner becomes sober. A spouse who cannot tolerate a high level of intimacy may find that he or she fears their partner recovering because it will mean that greater intimacy will occur within the relationship. Beliefs about these negative consequences may maintain the sober partner's enabling behaviour.

Predisposing Constitutional, Developmental and Sociocultural Factors

A person may be rendered vulnerable to developing alcohol problems because of constitutional, developmental and sociocultural factors. Of these, developmental factors and family-of-origin experiences are probably the most important. Individuals from families where alcohol abuse occurred may develop similar behaviour patterns to their parents. On the one hand, they may become involved in problem drinking like their parent with the alcohol problems. On the other hand, they may select a partner with a drink problem and adopt the role of their parent who had to cope with having a spouse with a drink problem. Where parents used alcohol to cope with stress, manage lifecycle transitions, reduce anxiety, tolerate depression or manage conflict about meeting each other's needs for particular levels of intimacy and autonomy, then their children are vulnerable to follow in their footsteps and use alcohol to solve these types of problems also. Early life experiences, which render people vulnerable to developing anxiety, depression marital distress and other difficulties discussed in preceding chapters, may render people vulnerable to developing alcohol problems, insofar as alcohol may be used to cope with these other problems.

Sociocultural factors may render people vulnerable to developing alcohol problems insofar as some cultures support a far greater level of alcohol consumption than others. For example, a high level of alcohol use is tolerated in Ireland and France but not in Iran or Iraq. Factors in the wider social system such as high levels of stress and low levels of support may also render people vulnerable to developing alcohol problems.

Constitutional factors may render people vulnerable to alcohol problems insofar as a small subgroup of people with alcohol problems are genetically vulnerable to developing alcohol dependence. It should be stressed, however, that, contrary to popular belief, this is only a small subgroup and genetic factors do not exclusively cause their alcohol problems. That is to say, extant evidence does not support the idea that for this subgroup alcoholism is a genetically caused disease. Rather, genetic factors render some individuals vulnerable to developing alcohol-related difficulties. However, for these vulnerable individuals, alcohol abuse is precipitated and maintained by other factors.

Precipitating Factors

Alcohol problems commonly develop gradually. However, they may be significantly exacerbated by a build-up of stressful life events or by life-cycle transitions.

Outcome

Outcome for people with alcohol problems is highly variable and depends on the severity and chronicity of the pattern of abuse; the rigidity of the behaviour patterns and belief systems that maintain the problem drinking; the range of risk factors present; and the readiness of the person to change their lifestyle. The worst case scenario is that chronic and severe alcohol use leads to severe physical consequences (e.g. liver failure); psychological difficulties (e.g. memory loss); career and employment problems; financial difficulties; and family disintegration with consequent negative effects on the children and spouse.

Protective Factors

At a behavioural level, a good marital relationship, good communication and problem-solving skills; a willingness to break out of complementary caregiver–care-receiver patterns or symmetrical aggressive patterns that sustain alcohol abuse; and a readiness to change to a less alcohol-focused lifestyle are protective factors. Protective belief systems involve the idea that there is a drink problem and the benefits of abstinence or controlled drinking outweigh the benefits of sustained problem drinking. Non-symptomatic individuals who are flexible enough to define their partner as a competent individual with a circumscribed problem probably respond better to couples therapy.

Individuals who come from families in which there were no alcohol or drug abuse problems and in which secure parent–child attachments were formed probably find it easier to use couples therapy to deal with problem drinking.

With respect to sociocultural factors and personal history, similarity of cultural values and role expectations; high socioeconomic status; living in a rural area; absence of parental divorce; absence of premarital pregnancy; and marriage after the age of 30 have all been identified as protective factors in long-term relationships. These factors are discussed in detail in Chapter 14.

Readiness to Change and Relapse Prevention

When recovering from alcohol abuse, couples vary in their readiness to change. DiClemente (2003) identifies five stages of therapeutic change through which individuals with alcohol problems progress when considering treatment: pre-contemplation, contemplation, preparation, action and maintenance. In helping clients make the transition from one stage of change to the next, particular techniques are maximally effective. The provision of support may help clients move from the pre-contemplation phase to the contemplation phase by creating a climate within which clients may ventilate their feelings and express their views about their alcohol abuse and life situation. By facilitating an exploration of belief systems about the evolution of the alcohol problem and its impact on the couple's relationship, the problem drinker may be helped to move from the contemplation to the planning stage. In the transition from planning to action, the most helpful role for the therapist to adopt is that of consultant to the couple's attempts at problem solving. This role of consultant to the couple's attempts at behavioural change is also appropriate for the transition from the action phase to the maintenance phase where the central issue is relapse prevention. Resistance occurs when there is a mismatch between the therapist's interventions and the clients' stage of change. For example, if clients in the precontemplation stage are offered consultation to behavioural change they will deny their problems and resist treatment.

Maintaining recovery following abstinence in abstinence-oriented treatment is influenced by a client's capacity to manage situations in which there is a high risk of relapse. In high relapse-risk situations abstinent individuals who have well-rehearsed coping strategies find that when they use these, their beliefs about their capacity to control their alcohol use become stronger (Marlatt & Gordon, 1985). Thus, they are less likely to relapse in future similar situations. Weak beliefs in their ability to control their drug use leads those who have poor coping strategies for dealing with risky situations to relapse. This leads to the abstinence violation effect (AVE) where the problem drinker believes 'If I have one drink, I will be drunk and lose all control over my drinking behaviour'. This failure experience leads to an increased probability of further relapses. A central component of the final stage of abstinence-oriented couples therapy for alcohol problems should be the development and rehearsal of coping strategies for managing situations where there is a high risk of relapse. This must involve a strategy for identifying and managing the AVE. This prevents clients from snowballing into a major relapse after a minor slip.

COUPLES THERAPY FOR ALCOHOL PROBLEMS IN ADULTHOOD

For alcohol abuse, marital and family based treatments have been shown to be particularly effective in helping people with alcohol problems and their families engage in treatment; become drug free or develop a more controlled approach to alcohol use; and avoid relapse (O'Farrell & Fals-Stewart, 2002). Guidelines for contracting for assessment; assessment; contracting for treatment; and treatment outlined in Chapter 14 for working with distressed couples and in Chapter 9 for family therapy may be used when working with couples in which one member has an alcohol problem. However, specific procedures which deserve attention when working with these cases will be outlined below.

Contracting for Assessment

Where members of a couple, in which one or both partners have an alcohol problem, voluntarily request couples therapy, contracting for assessment is a straightforward procedure. In these instances the couple may be invited to attend a series of sessions with a view to clarifying the way in which they have been managing episodes of problem and episodes or non-problematic behaviour where drinking was expected to occur but did not. The couple may be informed that once a shared understanding or formulation has been reached for each of these types of episodes, then a further contract for treatment may be offered if that is appropriate.

Where the sober member of the couple wants his or her partner to engage in therapy but the partner is denying there is a problem, then the sober partner may be invited to engage in unilateral therapy until they have been fully coached in engagement techniques, which create a context within which the chances of the partner with a drink problem entering therapy are maximized (Thomas & Ager, 1993). While unilateral family therapy and other similar interventions have been shown in research studies to be effective in facilitating engagement in therapy, this approach may be at odds with the Al-Anon family groups approach, which invites family members to detach from the person with the alcohol problem and not attempt to influence their recovery (Al-Anon Family groups, 1981).

Psychoeducation

Sober partners may be given psychoeducation about the way in which alcohol problems develop and are maintained following the systemic model outlined above. However, it should be stressed that sober partners are not responsible for the alcohol difficulties. The enabling behaviours they engage in that reinforce problem drinking are usually inadvertent. The critical and punitive measures they have taken to try to curtail their spouses drinking, which may have exacerbated it, were taken in good faith.

Reducing Enabling and Punitive Responses and Enhancing the Relationship

In light of this, the sober partner is helped to plan to reduce enabling behaviours and tolerate the possible negative consequences of this. The spouse is concurrently invited to reduce critical and punitive reactions to the drinking. The third strand of this intervention is to help spouses to plan pleasant non-drink-related events for both members of the couple to enhance the quality of the relationship when the partner with the drinking problem is not drunk. These three changes, should reduce alcohol use marginally and increase the quality of the relationship. These interventions aim to help partners with drink problems move from the pre-contemplation to contemplation stage of therapeutic change. Throughout the sober partner's use of these strategies, they are invited to monitor the amount of alcohol their partners use and note the impact of their change in behaviour on their partner's drinking.

Arranging a Physician's Appointment

When the quality of the relationship has improved sufficiently as a result of the interventions just described, the sober partner may be coached in inviting the partner with the alcohol problem to have a physical check-up with a physician. The sober partner is also coached to brief the physician before the consultation that the reason for the consultation is for the physician to advise the partner with the alcohol problem to enter treatment. This intervention is based on evidence that expert advice from a physician has a significant effect on treatment entry and recovery among problem drinkers, especially where it is given in the presence of a spouse (Thomas & Ager, 1993).

Exploring the Pros and Cons of Treatment Entry

Sober partners may be coached to invite their partners with drink problems to consider the pros and cons of maintaining their current drinking patterns or entering treatment. This intervention, aims to help partners move from the contemplating treatment to the planning or entering treatment stage of therapeutic change.

Scripted Confrontation

Where non-confrontative interventions like receiving physician's advice or exploring the pros and cons of drinking and recovery do not lead to the problem drinker entering treatment, a planned confrontation may be arranged. For the planned confrontation, the therapist helps the partner write a script for the confrontation and then to read the script to the partner in the presence of other members of the family and the therapist. The script should make the following points explicit:

- The partner wants to be heard uninterrupted.
- The partner is motivated to make this statement by love, care and concern.
- The partner states how much the drinker has been drinking and how often he or she is drunk (e.g. two full bottles of whiskey a day for a year, and is drunk most days).
- The partner gives specific examples of incidents where the drinking has hurt both members of the couple, the children or other family members.
- The effects of the drinking may be backed up by heartfelt quotations from children or grandparents who can be invited to write detailed letters saying how the drinking has hurt them.
- The partner wants the drinker to enter treatment to curtail these negative effects of drinking on the family.
- If the drinker does not enter treatment certain consequences will definitely follow (These may range from 'I will be disappointed', through 'I will not spend much time with you', to 'I will leave you').

The contents of the script must be accurate. No consequences should be stated, on which the spouse will not followed through. The therapist then helps the partner rehearse the script and plan for the drinker and other family members to attend a joint appointment where the script is read. If the partner agrees to enter therapy, a contract for assessment may be offered to the couple.

The timing and intensity of these interventions and the degree to which they are matched to the drinker's readiness to change is critical for their effectiveness. For example, to help clients engage in a scripted confrontation containing limited detail and mild consequences while the drinker is still in the pre-contemplation phase would probably increase denial and maintain problem drinking. On the other hand, a strongly scripted confrontation which occurs when the drinker has entered the contemplation stage may lead to him or her entering the preparation for action phase. There are considerable individual differences in therapist's abilities to be sensitive to these issues. Therapists who are more interpersonally skilled, more empathic and less confrontational tend to be more effective (Finney & Moos, 2002).

In the assessment contract, it may be agreed in cases where the problem drinker has become physiologically dependent on alcohol, detoxification on an inpatient or outpatient basis will be arranged.

Assessment

The first aim of family assessment is to construct three-column formulations, like those presented in Figures 16.2. and 16.3 of a typical problematic episode in which the urge to engage in problem drinking and problem drinking occurs and an exceptional episode in which an urge to engage in problem drinking occurred but the expected bout of drinking did not occur. Belief systems that underpin each partner's role in these episodes may then be clarified. These in turn may be linked to predisposing risk factors that have been listed in the systemic model of problem drinking presented above.

Monitoring Urges

One important technique for use during assessment is monitoring urges because it helps to throw light on specific situations that precipitate urges to engage in problem drinking. The form presented in Figure 9.1 is introduced and clients are invited to use this at times when they notice urges to drink occurring. In particular they should note:

- the day and time
- the situation or event
- what they were doing and thinking before and after the situation or event and whether they controlled the urge to drink
- a rating of the amount of control they felt they had over their urge to drink alcohol on a 10-point scale at the end of the event.

This urge monitoring information is useful in constructing the right-hand column and the middle column of the three-column formulation for both problematic episodes and exceptional non-problematic episodes.

A condition of assessment, which may be carried out over a number of sessions, should be that both spouses attend each session sober, since it is difficult to do effective therapeutic work with a drunk client. In some instances, spouses may be invited to make an antabuse (Disulfiram) contract to facilitate this. In such contracts, the spouse with the alcohol problem signs a contract witnessed by their spouse to take antabuse regularly.

Antabuse or Disulfiram Contracts

Antabuse or Disulfiram, which induces nausea and vomiting if alcohol is taken, has been shown to be effective in helping clients remain alcohol free during participation in psychosocial assessment and treatment programmes (O'Brien & McKay, 2002). One useful way to incorporate Disulfiram into couples therapy in which abstinence is the short- or long-term goal is in the form of a contract. The drinker agrees to take antabuse each day in the presence of his or her partner and to state that this is a sign that they wish to change their drinking habits. The other spouse agrees to thank their partner for taking the antabuse and also agrees not to mention disappointments about past drinking or apprehensions about future drinking. Both partners agree to contact the therapist if this agreement is broken on more than two consecutive days (O'Farrell, 1993). Where clinics do not have a physician on the treatment team, clients may be advised to consult their family physician and request a medical check-up with a view to assessing their suitability for a programme of antabuse. However, it is critical that the contract for taking the antabuse be made with the clinician conducting the couples therapy.

Contracting for Treatment

A summary of the family' strengths, exceptions to the problems, and a three-column formulation of the family process in which the problem drinking is embedded should be presented as a basis for the treatment contract. The treatment contract should contain a statement about whether the goal of treatment is abstinence or controlled drinking. Couples in which the pattern of problem drinking is not long-standing and severe and in which there are few risk factors and many protective factors are better suited to controlled drinking as a treatment goal. Where couples have become demoralised and state that they wish to achieve large goals like permanent abstinence or complete control over their drinking but feel powerless to achieve these, setting small preliminary goals which would show clients that they are on the right track may help them begin to develop a sense of control over their difficulties. Examples of these goals include, 'making five consecutive exceptional episodes happen in which I control the urge to drink', 'remaining abstinent for a week', or 'controlling binge drinking for two consecutive weekends'. A clear specification of the number of treatment sessions and the times and places at which these sessions will occur should all be detailed in the contract. It is also good practice to make a statement about the probability that the couple will benefit from treatment backed up with a statement of the factors that make it likely that this is the case. This issue was discussed in Chapter 14.

Treatment

Effective couples treatment programmes for alcohol problems include communication and problem-solving skills training and contracts to increase positive and reduce negative exchanges. These routine interventions have been described in Chapters 9 and 14. In addition, effective programmes for couples in which one member has an alcohol problem include a number of interventions that have been described in previous sections on contracting for assessment. These are psychoeducation; exploration of the behaviour patterns within the couple and family which maintain alcohol abuse; reducing enabling and punitive responses of the sober partner and enhancing the relationship; exploration of the positive and negative consequences of continued alcohol abuse on the one hand, and recovery on the other; and the use of antabuse or disulfiram contracts.

Additional specific interventions that typify effective couples based programmes and deserve mention here include:

- addressing belief systems that maintain alcohol abuse
- drink refusal and urge control or controlled drinking training
- facilitating the development of an alcohol-free or balanced lifestyle
- relapse prevention
- aftercare and relapse debriefing.

For most of these interventions, couples are given homework tasks to complete between sessions and, where there is a risk that these will not be completed, therapists may use phone-prompting between sessions to remind couples to complete their assignments.

Transforming Belief Systems

Transforming belief systems that underpin behaviour patterns which maintain alcohol problems is a particular challenge in couples in which the alcohol problem has been chronic and severe and led the drinker to inflict profound physical, psychological and financial hardship on the sober partner. One useful approach is to offer multiple perspectives on the various dilemmas the couple face as they try to rebuild their relationship and the drinker tries to control his or her urge to drink. Split messages from a team, multiple messages from a reflecting or two-sided messages from a single therapist, as were discussed in Chapter 9, may be offered. Here are some examples:

> *The team have taken the view that you are both still doubtful of ABC's ability to control his urge to drink and they see you both as also doubting this. However, I disagree with them. I have been impressed by the extraordinary strength you, ABC, have shown in managing your urges to drink over the past month. I have also been impressed by the way you, DEF, have been prepared to allow ABC the space to show that he can control his drinking urges and other aspects of his life. I would be very surprised if this control and the growing sense of being in charge of your own life that you are beginning to experience, ABC, did not continue to strengthen.*

> *To trust or not to trust is a difficult dilemma. The men on the team have taken the view that ABC has demonstrated through his sobriety that he is trustworthy and that he will not destroy your relationship and the family again by drinking. The women on the team argue that trust should be built slowly and ABC has not yet shown that he can be true to his word over the long term. They think that if DEF declared that the past was forgotten and she was prepared to fully trust ABC this would be a mistake. I cannot agree with either faction. My view is that your relationship will be strengthened by living with this difficult dilemma and tolerating the intense feelings of pain and hope that go with it.*

A second important intervention for transforming belief systems in cases where problem drinking is the main concern is externalising the problem and building on exceptions, previously described in Chapter 9. The urge to drink may be externalised as a problem against which both members of the couple must fight, and exceptional circumstances in which they win this battle should be explored in detail and attempts made to replicate these exceptions.

It should be noted that this approach, where the couple actively gain control over the alcohol problems, is not completely incompatible with the AA approach, where the person with the drinking problem calls on God or a higher power to help them control their alcohol problems, since invoking the aid of a higher power is in itself an act of personal control. The AA belief system is given in Table 16.1 and it is important for therapists working with alcohol problems to know this system since for many patients it is their central narrative for managing alcohol problems.

Drink Refusal and Urge Control or Controlled Drinking Training

If couples choose abstinence as a treatment goal then they need to develop skills to help them remain abstinent, specifically those necessary

Table 16.1 The 12 steps of AA

Step	Principle
1	We admitted we were powerless over alcohol and that our lives had become unmanageable
2	Came to believe that a power greater than ourselves could restore us to sanity
3	Made a decision to turn our will and our lives over to God *as we understood Him*
4	Made a searching and moral inventory of ourselves
5	Admitted to God, to ourselves and to other human beings the exact nature of our wrongs
6	Were entirely ready to have God remove all these defects of character
7	Humbly asked Him to remove our shortcomings
8	Made a list of all persons we had harmed, and became willing to make amends to them all
9	Made direct amends to such people whenever possible, except when to do so would injure them or others
10	Continued to take personal inventory and when we were wrong, admitted it
11	Sought through prayer and meditation to improve our conscious contact with God *as we understood Him* praying only for knowledge of His will for the power to carry that out
12	Having had a spiritual awakening as a result of these steps, we tried to carry this message to alcoholics, and to practise these principles in all our affairs

Source: Adapted from Alcoholics Anonymous (1986). *The Little Red Book* (1986). City Centre, MN: Hazelden.

for refusing drinks and controlling urges to drink. Problem drinkers maybe invited in couples sessions to brainstorm and then rehearse scripts that they will use to refuse drinks when offered drinks in social situation. They may also be invited to develop a list of strategies that may be useful in reducing urges such as conversation, distraction, exercise, self-talk, relaxation, or eating. Couples may be invited to make contracts in which partners whose goal is abstinence are rewarded by their spouses if they use drink refusal and urge control skills effectively.

In couples choose controlled drinking as a treatment goal then the skills required for this new form of non-problematic drinking must be acquired. These skills include placing a clear limit on the number of units of alcohol to be consumed per week, per day and per drinking occasion.

Following from this, within any drinking occasion skills necessary to reduce the rate at which alcohol is consumed must be specified and practised. Among these skills are ordering small rather than large drinks; sipping not gulping; placing the glass on the table between sips; focusing attention on conversation, eating, watching entertainment or activities other than drinking; monitoring the number of drinks taken; openly declaring to one's partner when the limit for a drinking occasion has been reached; and arranging for partners to reward the controlled drinker for using these skills to stay within agreed limits.

Facilitating the Development of an Alcohol-free or Balanced Lifestyle

For couples who select abstinence as a treatment goal and where alcohol has played a central role in their lives, couples therapy must offer a forum within which the couple plan to arrange their workdays, evenings, weekends, birthdays, celebrations and holidays in ways that do not involve alcohol. Where the partner without the drink problem wishes to continue to drink, this poses particular challenges for the couple in terms of negotiating family rules, roles and routines that do not jeopardise the sobriety of the partner with the drink problem. Where controlled drinking is the treatment goal, the challenge is to negotiate a balanced lifestyle which supports family rules, roles and routines that make limiting alcohol intake to agreed proportions feasible. In conducting these negotiations, partners are coached, where appropriate, in the communication and problem-solving skills described in Chapters 9 and 14.

Relapse Prevention

In the final stage of treatment relapse prevention is discussed. Some couples may be concerned that talking about relapses will suggest that they should happen. In fact, research shows that the opposite is the case (O'Farrell, 1993). Failure to plan relapse management is associated with relapse. In relapse prevention planning, the couple jointly draw up a list of situations in which they think there is a risk of relapse. These situations may include those where alcohol is used to control negative emotions, such as after a heavy day at work or after an argument. Couples may identify situations where there is social pressure to drink, like parties, as involving the risk of relapse. The couple is then invited to develop a relapse prevention plan that specifies how they will minimise the risk of relapse in these situations, and an relapse management plan that specifies what they will do if a relapse occurs.

Relapse prevention plans may include acknowledging risk, leaving the situation, or remaining in the situation but taking steps to use other ways to cope with negative mood states or responding assertively to social pressure. For example, going for a walk, listening to calming music, doing deep breathing exercises, talking to one's partner, or phoning a friend for a supportive conversation are all ways of managing negative mood states without using alcohol. Saying 'No thanks, I don't want a beer, but I'd like a fruit juice please' is an assertive response to social pressure to drink.

Relapse management plans include steps such as stopping after one drink, leaving the drinking situation, phoning one's partner or the therapist, detailing step by step the sequence of events that led to the relapse, agreeing to leave the relapse situation and entering a situation where there is no reason to continue drinking and opportunities for some competing activity, such as talking with friends who don't drink or doing aerobic exercises.

Aftercare and Relapse Debriefings

Family-based aftercare programmes that aim to prevent relapse or minimise the negative impact of relapse have been shown to be more effective than individually-based aftercare programmes (Edwards & Steinglass, 1995). Family-based aftercare programmes typically involve relatively infrequent marital or family sessions spread over an extended time period such as a year or two.

In aftercare sessions where couples report continued abstinence or controlled drinking, the sessions focus on highlighting the competencies of the couples in maintaining change. Here are some questions that allow couples to explore these competencies:

> Can you tell me in detail about those times when you/your partner controlled the urge to drink alcohol. What were you doing and thinking and what was your partner doing and thinking?

> Can you tell me how you have been organising your lives so that these urges to drink come less frequently now?

> During these periods when there are no urges to drink, how have you been reminding yourselves that you must be prepared for the risk of relapse?

Relapses are an inevitable part of recovery from problem drinking. It is therefore important to construct relapses, not as failures, but as staging posts on the way to recovery and as valuable learning experiences (Berg & Miller, 1992). Here are some examples of statements and questions that may be used when discussing relapses in this light:

> Why do you think it has taken you so long to relapse?

> What is it about the way you have been managing your life and your family relationships that have prevented you from relapsing before now?

In what way is this relapse different from others?

How did you break free from this relapse and stop drinking when you did?

What did you do to prevent the drink from drowning you?

What has it taught you about relapsing that will be helpful to you in managing the next risky situation?

In view of all you have learned from this relapse, what are you planning to do differently in future?

What do you need your partner/children/parents to do differently in future?

Relapses are a reminder that you are managing the recovery process. Is there any other way you or your family could remind you that you are recovering so that relapses would be less necessary?

Referral to Other Services and Family-of-origin Work

For couples who select abstinence as a treatment goal, rather than con-trolled drinking, the approach described in this Chapter is compat-ible with concurrent attendance at Alcoholics Anonymous (AA). Indeed, attendance at AA meetings may enhance the efficacy of couples therapy and be a highly feasible long-term aftercare arrangement.

A proportion of people with alcohol problems, once they develop con-trol over them and move towards a more balanced lifestyle find that they have unresolved family-of-origin issues in some instances associated with parental alcohol abuse. A contract to address these may be offered after the alcohol problem is resolved. Clients who request such work early in therapy may be advised that their efforts are better spent on addressing the alcohol problem first and the family-of-origin issues later, since there is no evidence to suggest that addressing such issues has an immediate impact on alcohol problems. However, addressing family-of-origin issues may facilitate the long-term maintenance of sobriety or controlled drink-ing. Guidelines for family-of-origin work are given in Chapters 9 and 14.

SUMMARY

The prevalence of alcohol dependence and severe abuse in adult popula-tions is approximately 5%, but in clinical practice a wide variety of people with differing types and degrees of alcohol problems are referred for cou-ples therapy. Alcohol abuse is usefully conceptualised as being maintained by behaviour patterns within which problematic drinking occurs. These behaviour patterns in turn may be viewed as being underpinned by belief systems about how to control alcohol abuse or deal with its consequences. A variety of constitutional, developmental and sociocultural predisposing factors may subserve these behaviour patterns and belief systems. When recovering from alcohol abuse, couples vary in their readiness to change and five stages of therapeutic change through which individuals with alcohol problems progress may be identified: pre-contemplation, contemplation, preparation, action and maintenance. In helping clients make the transition from one stage of change to the next, particular techniques are maximally effective. Resistance occurs when there is a mismatch between the therapist's interventions and the client's stage of change. Outcome for people with alcohol problems is highly variable and depends on the severity and chronicity of the pattern of abuse; the rigidity of the behaviour pattern and belief systems that maintain the problem drinking; the range of risk factors present; and the readiness of the person to change their lifestyle. In many instances, sober partners want their partners with alcohol problems to engage in therapy but their partners deny their drink problems. In these instances, sober partners may be invited to engage in unilateral couples therapy until they have been fully coached in engagement techniques that create a context within which the chances of the partners with drink problems entering therapy are maximised. Unilateral couples therapy involves psychoeducation; facilitating the reducing or enabling and punitive responses, and enhancing the couple's relationship; facilitating the arrangement of physician's advice to enter treatment; promoting an exploration of the pros and cons of treatment entry by the couple; and convening a scripted confrontation in which the sober spouse invites the partner with a drink problem to enter therapy. During assessment, three-column formulations are constructed of typical problematic episodes in which the urge to engage in problem drinking are not controlled and problem drinking occurs and exceptional episodes in expected bouts of drinking do not occur despite the presence of urges to drink alcohol. Clients may be invited to monitoring drinking urges during assessment and to use antabuse contracts to remain sober. Abstinence and controlled drinking are two possible long-term treatment goals and the suitability of couples for one or the other depends on the severity of the problem and the pervasiveness of the risk and maintaining factors. Effective couples treatment programmes for alcohol problems include routine communication and problem-solving skills training and contracts to increase positive and reduce negative exchanges. In addition, effective programmes for couples in which one member has an alcohol problem include addressing belief systems that maintain alcohol abuse; drink refusal and urge control or controlled drinking training; facilitating the development of an alcohol-free or balanced lifestyle; relapse prevention; and aftercare with relapse debriefing.

FURTHER READING

Berg, I. & Miller, S. (1992). *Working with the Problem Drinker: A Solution Focused Approach*. New York: Norton.

Hester, R. & Miller, W. (2002). *Handbook of Alcoholism Treatment Approaches: Effective Alternatives*, 3rd edn. Boston: Allyn Bacon.

Epstein, E. & McCrady, B. (2002). Couple therapy in the treatment of alcohol problems. In A. Gurman & N. Jacobon (Eds), *Clinical Handbook of Couples Therapy*, 3rd edn, pp. 597–628. New York: Guilford.

O'Farrell, T. (1993). *Treating Alcohol Problems: Marital and Family Interventions*. New York: Guilford.

Treatment manual for O'Farrell's behavioural couples therapy and Meyers' community reinforcement approach for problem drinkers are avaiable http://www.bhrm.org/guidelines/addguidelines.htm

Chapter 17

SCHIZOPHRENIA

Schizophrenia is conceptualised in major classification systems, such as the ICD-10 (World Health Organisation, 1992) and the DSM-IV-TR (American Psychiatric Association, 2000), as a debilitating psychological disorder. It is characterised by positive symptoms, such as delusions, hallucinations and thought disorder, and negative symptoms, such as impaired social functioning and lack of goal-directed behaviour. Subtypes of schizophrenia have been constructed on the basis of the patterning of these symptoms. Related psychotic conditions that are thought to fall along a schizophrenia spectrum, which are characterised by some, but not all of the symptoms of schizophrenia, have also been constructed.

Family-based stress has a marked impact on individual's genetically vulnerable to schizophrenia when it occurs in the absence of protective factors such as coping skills, social support and appropriate levels of antipsychotic medication (Milkowitz & Tompson, 2003). In view of this, it is not surprising that the treatment of choice for schizophrenia and related psychotic conditions is multimodal and includes antipsychotic medication coupled with psychosocial interventions, such as marital or family therapy which aim to reduce family stress, enhance coping and mobilise social support. When participation in psychoeducational family therapy programmes is combined with routine antipsychotic mediation, a significant reduction in relapse rates has been found to occur compared with cases who receive medication only. This reduction in relapse rates applies particularly to people with schizophrenia from families characterised by stressful interactions, such as excessive criticism or over-involvement (Kopelowicz et al., 2002; McFarlane, Dixon, Lukens & Lucksted, 2002; Milkowitz & Tompson, 2003).

In this chapter a systemic model for conceptualising schizophrenia and a psychoeducational approach to family therapy is presented. A case example is given in Figure 17.1 and three-column formulations of problems and exceptions are given in Figure 17.2. and 17.3.

The prevalence of schizophrenia is about 1%. For men, the onset is typically at the end of adolescence, and for women, the onset occurs in the mid-20s. Comorbid depression is common in schizophrenia and about 10% of people with schizophrenia commit suicide (American Psychiatric Association, 2000).

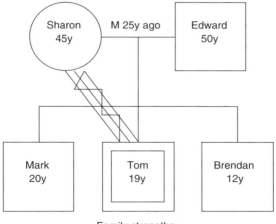

Family strengths:
Strong, united and committed to helping Tom recover

Referral.   Tom and his family were referred for family work after Tom's psychotic symptoms had been partially controlled with neuroleptic medication. He suffered residual auditory hallucinations, which were very distressing for him. He had suffered a psychotic breakdown during his first year at university where he was an exceptional student. The family history was unremarkable although there were a number of eccentric aunts and uncles on the father's side in the family. Within Tom's family there were no major health or relationship problems prior to the psychotic breakdown. Tom's development had been essentially normal. He was a popular youngster, able sportsman and good all-round student. His mother, Sharon, was devastated by her son's condition and alternated between overprotection and criticism in her conversations with him. During and after her intense interactions with him he often experienced increased auditory hallucinations, which were distressing for him and his response to these hallucinations were distressing for the family.

Formulation.   Formulations of symptom-related problematic episodes and exceptions to these are given in Figures 17.2. and 17.3.

Treatment.   Psychoeducational family-based treatment followed the protocol described in this chapter. Particularly important interventions included helping Edward take a central role in supporting Sharon as she directed her efforts to taking a less emotionally intense approach in her conversations with Tom. Mark and Brendan, who had become quite distant from their brother became more supportive. Tom and the family brainstormed ways to reduce the frequency of the auditory hallucinations, through distraction and arousal reduction. Tom eventually returned to college.

Figure 17.1   Case example of schizophrenia

SYSTEMIC MODEL OF SCHIZOPHRENIA

Single factor models of schizophrenia, which explain the condition in terms of genetic vulnerabilities, biological processes, early socialisation experiences, stressful life events, cognitive processes or deficits and belief systems, and patterns of social interaction, have made important contributions to our understanding of psychosis. However, integrative models of schizophrenia, which take account of interactional behaviour patterns, cognitive processes and belief systems, and both genetic and developmental vulnerabilities, offer a more comprehensive systemic framework

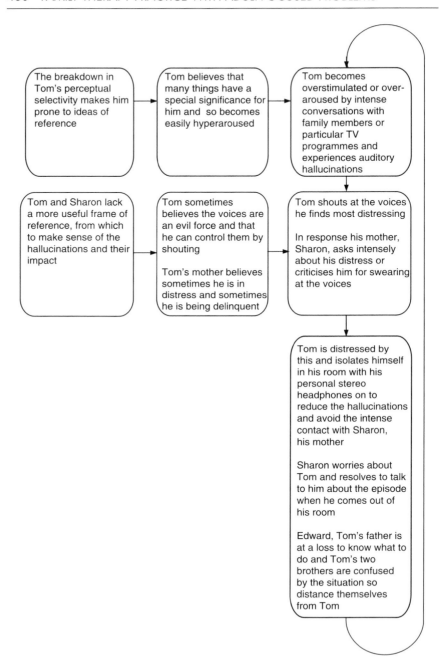

Figure 17.2 Three-column formulation of problems associated with managing psychotic symptoms

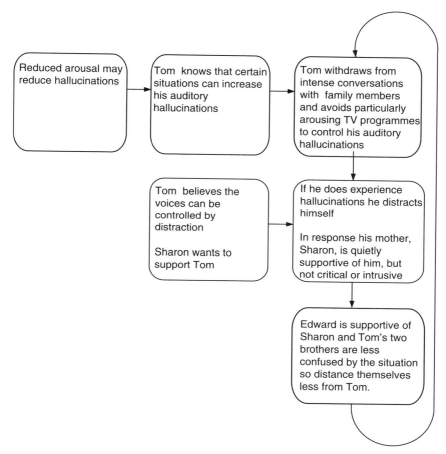

Figure 17.3 Three-column formulation of exception to problems associated with managing psychotic symptoms

from which to conduct multimodal therapy (Kopelowicz et al., 2002; Kuipers, Peters & Bebbington, In press; Milkowitz & Tompson, 2003; Murray & Castle, 2000; Zubin & Spring, 1977).

Predisposing Constitutional Factors

Genetic vulnerability as indicated by a family history of disorders on the schizophrenia spectrum may predispose youngsters to developing schizophrenia. Youngsters may also develop a vulnerability to schizophrenia as a result of intrauterine adversity as indicated by obstetric complications or maternal illness, particularly viral infection during pregnancy.

Precipitating Factors

Schizophrenia may have an acute onset or an insidious onset and prognosis in the former case is better. The onset of an episode of schizophrenia may be precipitated by a build-up of stressful life events or the occurrence of lifecycle transitions. Personal or family illness or injury or victimisation may precipitate the onset of schizophrenia. So, too, may the transition to adolescence or adulthood; leaving home; having a sibling leave home; the birth of a sibling; or bereavements within the family. Separation, moving house, changing jobs, losing friends, unemployment or increased financial hardship may all precipitate the onset of a psychotic episode. All of these events place a sudden increase in demands on the person's coping resources.

Belief Systems

People with schizophrenia have unusual perceptual experiences, and the beliefs that they develop about these may maintain their condition by sustaining either hyperarousal or hypoarousal. For example, in schizophrenia there is a disruption of perceptual selectivity and of the capacity to selectively attend to relevant events while screening out unimportant things. Thus, the experience may be that many or all things have a special significance for the person. To make sense of this, the individual may develop a delusional belief system in which they view themselves as playing a central role in some highly significant life drama, such as preventing a national disaster. In this drama, apparently innocuous things, such as a programme on the TV, or the number of milk bottles on the table, are interpreted as having special significance, such as being a signal that a catastrophe is about to occur unless some action is taken immediately. This type of belief system is very stressful and sustains hyperarousal. People with schizophrenia may also experience auditory or somatic hallucinations and develop distressing beliefs about these. For example, somatic hallucinations (tingling in the skin) may be interpreted as a sign some agency, such as the TV station or an alien spaceship, is transmitting electrical messages to them. Auditory hallucinations (hearing voices) may be interpreted as receiving instructions from the devil or an evil person who will command them to behave in distressing ways. These types of beliefs are also distressing and may lead to hyperarousal. To cope with hyperarousal, the person with schizophrenia may find that staying in bed and keeping activity to a minimum reduces their arousal significantly. This in turn may reduces their unusual perceptual experiences and the frequency with which they experience related distressing delusional beliefs.

Partners and family members of people with schizophrenia may develop belief systems in which they come to see their partners exclusively in terms of their problems and lose sight of other aspects of their whole personalities. Thus, non-symptomatic partners or parents may come to construe the person with schizophrenia as wholly and completely psychotic or incapacitated. This type of belief system give rise to excessive, intrusive caretaking. Intrusive caretaking may lead the person with schizophrenia to experience hyperarousal and this in turn may activate delusions and hallucinations. In other instances, non-symptomatic partners or parents may come to view their partner or child as completely bad for decompensating and not fighting their condition or as malingering and intentionally trying to control them by pretending to be more helpless than they are. This may frequently lead the partner or parent to criticise the person with schizophrenia. This criticism in turn may lead to hyperarousal and activate delusions and hallucinations. A widely used measure of family-based stress – expressed emotion – quantifies the amount of over-involvment and criticism present in families and this construct is associated with relapse rates in schizophrenia (Kopelowicz & Liberman, 1998).

Behaviour Patterns

From the preceding discussion of the role of belief systems in maintaining schizophrenia, it is clear that behaviour patterns, characterised by intrusive over-involvement, criticism or confused communication within the family, may maintain schizophrenia. All of these types of behaviour patterns are stressful and difficult for a person to cope with when they are in a psychotic state or recovering from psychosis. These types of interaction are more likely to occur in disorganised couples and families, distressed couples, or families where a young adult is triangulated into parental conflict, with one parent taking an over-involved stance with respect to the adolescent and the other adopting a critical position. The symptoms of schizophrenia may be maintained too, though inadvertent reinforcement by well-meaning partners or family members who respond positively to the symptomatic person's symptoms. Parents and partners may also become involved in problem-maintaining behaviour patterns with the family member who has schizophrenia if they have inaccurate knowledge about schizophrenia and are unaware of the importance of the family in creating a low-stress environment to aid recovery and prevent relapse.

Factors within the Wider Social System

Psychotic symptoms may be maintained by high levels of stress, limited support and social disadvantage within the family's wider social system, since these features may deplete family members' personal resources for dealing constructively with the psychotic condition.

Outcome

The course of schizophrenia is variable with a proportion of cases making complete recovery, a proportion showing chronic symptoms which are unresponsive to treatment and the majority of cases showing a partial response to treatment and making a partial recovery with episodic relapses.

Protective Factors

The probability that a treatment programme will be effective is influenced by a variety of protective factors. Good premorbid functioning, an acute onset and a clear precipitant are all associated with a better outcome. A better outcome occurs for females rather than males and in individuals from families in which there is little psychopathology. If there are additional affective features or a family history of affective disorders rather than schizophrenia there is a better prognosis.

Within the family, clear communication and good problem-solving skills and a non-emotive low-key approach to managing difficulties are protective factors. For families, accurate knowledge about schizophrenia is also a protective factor. A family's capacity to help the person with schizophrenia adhere to their medication regime without engaging in critical or intrusive behaviour patterns may be viewed as a protective factor also.

Within the broader social network, high levels of support, low levels of stress and membership of a high socioeconomic group are all protective factors for individuals with schizophrenia.

Within the treatment system, cooperative working relationships between the treatment team and the family and good coordination of multi professional input are also protective factors.

COUPLES AND FAMILY THERAPY FOR SCHIZOPHRENIA

For couples or families in which one member has schizophrenia, psychoeducational marital or family therapy combined with antipsychotic medication is particularly effective (Kopelowicz et al., 2002; McFarlane et al., 2002; Milkowitz & Tompson, 2003; National Collaborating Centre for Mental Health, 2003). Guidelines for contracting for assessment; assessment; contracting for treatment; and treatment outlined in Chapter 14 for working with distressed couples and in Chapter 9 for family therapy may be used when working with cases of schizophrenia. However, a number of specific procedures, outlined below, deserve attention when working with these cases (Falloon et al., 1993; Kuipers et al., 2002; McFarlane, 2002).

Contracting for Assessment

When couples or family therapy is offered in cases were psychosis is the main complaint, the offer of therapy usually occurs following a period of contact with a psychiatric service. Some cases will have had years of contact. Others will be new cases. In most cases, a thorough traditional psychiatric assessment will have been conducted. In new cases, a diagnosis of psychosis may have been given. Only after six months may a DSM-IV-TR (American Psychiatric Association, 2000) diagnosis of schizophrenia be given, since persistence of symptoms is one of the diagnostic criteria. With the ICD-10 (World Health Organisation, 1992), a diagnosis may be given after one month. In either instance, clients and their relatives will usually have been informed that their child or partner has a condition – either psychosis or schizophrenia – which is due to the interaction of a vulnerability towards the disorder with a build-up of life stress. The person with schizophrenia will typically be receiving antipsychotic medication and may have been hospitalised during the acute phase of the psychotic episode.

Treatment with first generation antipsychotic drugs, such as chlorpromazine, haloparadol, flupenthixol, or second generation antipsychotic preparations, such as clozapine, risperidone, olanzapine and sertindome, are the main approaches to pharmacological intervention for psychotic conditions (McWilliams & O'Callaghan, In Press). While first generation antipsychotic agents control the positive symptoms of schizophrenia, and the newer agents control both positive and negative symptoms, both types of drugs have short-term side effects, such as parkinsonism, which is often controlled by an anti-parkinsonism agent such as cogentin. Tardive dyskinesia, an irreversible neurological condition is one of the tragic long-term side effects of neuroleptic drug usage. For this reason, ideally the lowest possible dose of neuroleptic medication should be used.

One reason for considering psychoeducational marital or family therapy is that it may permit the person with schizophrenia to reduce their medication dosage, since lower dosages are required to control symptoms when the amount of stress in the person's family environment is minimised. Even with medication, a significant minority of people with schizophrenia continue to have residual positive and negative symptoms and to relapse periodically into episodes of full-blown psychosis. Developing ways of controlling these residual symptoms and minimising family stress so as to minimise the chances of relapse are two other reasons for considering couples or family therapy as part of a multimodal treatment programme for schizophrenia.

Where members of a couple or parents and a young person voluntarily request couples or family therapy for schizophrenia, contracting for assessment is a straightforward procedure. Contracting for assessment is also unproblematic when it is the policy of a multidisciplinary mental health team to routinely offer family therapy and antipsychotic medication as part of a multimodal treatment package. In these instances the couple or family may be invited to attend a series of sessions with a view to clarifying the way in which they have been managing episodes of symptomatic or difficult behaviour and episodes or non-problematic behaviour. The principal aim of the assessment and subsequent therapy should be framed as helping the family understand and cope with the condition. The couple or family may be informed that once a shared understanding or formulation has been reached for problematic and exceptional unproblematic episodes, then a further contract for treatment may be offered if that is appropriate. In the assessment contract, it may be agreed in cases where the symptomatic family member is hospitalised or housebound that part or all of the assessment be conducted in hospital or at home.

Where members of the family or the multidisciplinary team are ambivalent about the use of family therapy, the benefits of family therapy outlined above (reducing medication, preventing relapse, managing residual symptoms, helping the family understand and cope better) may be considered alongside the reservations of the family and other professionals. A non-blaming stance with respect to other family members is particularly important since many families inappropriately blame themselves for the occurrence of the psychotic symptoms. The core message should be, 'Family therapy provides a way for the family to help the person with schizophrenia recover'.

Assessment

The first aim of family assessment is to construct three-column formulations, like those presented in Figures 17.2. and 17.3. One formulation should focus on a typical problematic episode in which the couple or family have greatest difficulty managing one or more of the positive or negative symptoms. The other formulation should focus on exceptional episodes in which symptom-related difficulties were expected to occur but did not. Belief systems that underpin family members' roles in these episodes may then be clarified. These in turn may be linked to predisposing risk factors.

Contracting for Treatment

The formulations of problematic and exceptional episodes are discussed in the session in which a contract for treatment is offered. Family members are invited, in light of the formulations, to identify goals that they would like to achieve in therapy. The emphasis should be on clear observable achievable goals that are a step in the right direction and which indicate that significant change has begun to happen. Global vague goals should be broken down into such small achievable goals. A clear specification of the number of treatment sessions and the times and places of these should all be detailed in a contract. Stating the location of the sessions is important where the person with schizophrenia is hospitalised. At least some of the later sessions should be conducted on a routine outpatient basis rather than in hospital. It is also good practice to make a statement about the probability that the treatment will delay relapse and help the family cope better with schizophrenia. This should be backed up with a statement of the factors that make it likely that this is the case. This issue was discussed in Chapter 14.

Treatment

Effective interventions typically span 9–12 months and are usually offered in a phased format with three months of weekly sessions; three months of fortnightly sessions; three months of monthly sessions; followed by three monthly reviews and crisis intervention as required. With respect to the content and process of treatment programmes, a number of core elements typify effective family-based interventions for schizophrenia. First, emphasis is placed on blame-reduction, the positive role family members can play in the rehabilitation of the family member with schizophrenia and the degree to which the family intervention will alleviate some of the family's burden of care. These issues have been discussed above. Second, effective programmes include communication and problem-solving skills training as described in Chapters 9 and 14. Third, effective family intervention programmes for schizophrenia include psychoeducation, specifically targeting the unique difficulties that families face when coping with schizophrenia. In addition, most programmes incorporate, a variety of routine family therapy techniques, such as reframing or externalising the problem, which have been detailed in Chapters 9 and 14, to address problem-maintaining belief systems.

Psychoeducation

In psychoeducational sessions, the ideas described below may be presented. An active interactional format should be used because it leads to greater retention and understanding than a lecture format. With an active interactional format, family members are encouraged to ask questions and link the information presented to their personal experiences of coping with schizophrenia in their family. In addition, the specific actions that they can take (presented below as bullet points) should be modelled, role-played and rehearsed a number of times so family members have both an intellectual understanding or their roles in promoting recovery and a set of specific skills.

Schizophrenia is an Illness

Some people are born with the vulnerability to this illness. This vulnerability is genetically transmitted in some cases. In others, it results from pre-natal exposure to infections. Symptoms develop when a person vulnerable to schizophrenia experiences a build-up of life stress. Details of where in the brain this vulnerability is located and how it works are not known and research is being done throughout the world to answer these questions.

Incidence

One in 100 people get schizophrenia over the course of the lifetime in all countries in the world. Studies that suggested that there were more people with schizophrenia in some places – like the west of Ireland – have been shown to be wrong. In these studies, each time a person entered hospital they were counted as a new case. So if a person was hospitalized three times, the same person was counted as three cases. We now know that the rate of schizophrenia in Ireland and around the world is 1 in 100.

Family Members do not Cause Schizophrenia

They can, however, help with recovery by being supportive, reducing stress and helping with medication. In particular you can help by:

- understanding how distressing the symptoms are for the person with schizophrenia
- making home-life and family relationship calm and predictable
- helping the person with schizophrenia remember to take their medication.

One of the Symptoms of Schizophrenia is Thought Disorder

People with schizophrenia may talk a great deal but appear to lose the thread of what they are saying so that it is hard to understand what they mean. This is because they have lost the ability to control the amount of thoughts that they think and to put their thoughts in a logical order. Other times they simply stop talking abruptly. This is because they have the experience of their mind going blank. The experience of thought disorder can be confusing and sometimes very frightening. People trying to cope with it may worry a good deal about it and try to make sense of it in strange ways. They may blame someone for putting thoughts into their head. They may blame someone for robbing their thoughts. You can help by:

- acknowledging that thought disorder is confusing and distressing
- avoiding arguing about the nonsensical and illogical things the person with schizophrenia says.

Another Symptom of Schizophrenia is Auditory Hallucinations

People with schizophrenia may hear voices. This may sound like a running commentary. It may sound like two people conversing about them. It may sound like someone talking to them. This is a very frightening experience when it first happens. People may try to make sense of auditory hallucinations by attributing the voices to a transmitter, the TV, God, aliens or some other source. Sometimes people shout back at the voices to try to make them stop. Other times they feel compelled to follow instructions given by the voices. You can help by

- acknowledging that some hallucinations are distressing
- understanding that hallucinations may be partially controlled by listening to calming music, distraction or having a supportive conversation
- avoiding arguing about the reality of the hallucinations.

A Third Symptom of Schizophrenia is Delusions

People with schizophrenia may hold strong beliefs which are implausible to members of their family or community. For example, they may believe that they are being persecuted by hidden forces or by family members. They may believe that they are on a mission from God, who speaks to them. Usually delusions – these strange beliefs – are an attempt to make sense of hallucinations or thought disorder. People who hold delusions usually refuse to change these even in the face of strong evidence that their position is implausible. You can help by

- not engaging in conversations about delusional beliefs
- not agreeing with delusional beliefs
- not arguing about how ridiculous the delusional beliefs are.

Problems with Emotions May also Occur in Schizophrenia

People with schizophrenia may withdraw and show little affection or love. This withdrawal may reflect a reoccupation with hallucinations or the intense experience of a high rate of uncontrollable thought that goes with thought disorder. They may also have outbursts of laughter or anger, which appear to be inexplicable. These outbursts are often a response to hallucinations. Occasionally, people with schizophrenia realise how the condition has damaged their relationships and their lifestyle. This may result in depression. On other occasions they may deny that any changes have occurred and become inappropriately excited and optimistic. You can help by

- not trying to cheer the person up
- not criticising them for feeling as they do

- taking a matter-of-fact accepting position with respect to their emotional state.

Problems with Withdrawal, Daily Routines and Hygiene May also Occur

People with schizophrenia may have little energy, sleep a great deal, avoid the company of others and pay little attention to washing or personal hygiene. This is partly because the experiences of thought disorder and hallucinations and attempts to make sense of these experiences through delusions have left them exhausted and with the realisation that they no longer know how to fit in with other people. They may also have feelings that they cannot control and believe that they cannot direct their own behaviour. Because withdrawal, poor hygiene and a breakdown in daily routines are symptoms of an illness, it is almost impossible and probably harmful to try to persuade a person with schizophrenia to make major changes in these areas rapidly. You can help by

- making requests for small, carefully planned changes where there is a good chance of success
- praising and thanking the person for meeting these small requests
- developing a points system where the person can win points for meeting small goals and these may be traded for things they want or would like to do.

Some Symptoms are Treatable with Medication

Thought disorder, hallucinations and delusions may all become greatly reduced or disappear with medication. Some patients get their medication in pills and others get it by injection. Some patients want to stop taking medication because it has side effects, such as shaking or feeling restless. It is important to take the pills or the injection according to the doctor's or nurse's directions. Patients who stop taking their medication may feel fine for weeks or months, but then relapse because they have not enough medication in their body to keep them from relapsing. Unfortunately, medication may have long-lasting side effects, including a peculiar movement disorder called tardive dyskinesia involving strange facial movements and hand movements. These long-term side effects can be reduced if a lower dose of medication is taken. If patients live in a calm household with predictable routines, then they can usually manage on a lower dosage of medication. You can help with medication by

- finding out the person's medication regime
- reminding them to take their medication
- praising them or thanking them for managing the illness by taking medication.

Family meetings may help with Support and the Reduction of Stress

Family meetings help you to help the family member with schizophrenia to feel supported and understood. It also helps you to learn how to reduce stress in his or her life. With high support and low stress, fewer relapses will occur and less medication will be needed. The key to high support is to show you understand, communicate clearly and calmly; and follow the guidelines given above. The key to stress reduction is to make home life calm and predictable. You can help by

- making simple daily routines and following these
- making small changes in daily routines one at a time
- deciding on all changes in a calm way
- communicating clearly and simply about any changes
- avoiding criticism
- avoid letting the person with schizophrenia know that you are worrying about him or her.

Most People with Schizophrenia can Live an Independent Life

Schizophrenia is a chronic condition like diabetes. Most insulin-dependent diabetics, if they take their insulin, live relatively independent lives. The same is true for most people with a diagnosis of schizophrenia. One in four people with schizophrenia make a complete recovery from their first episode and do not relapse. The remaining three out of four live relatively independent lives but relapses occur at times of stress or when medication is stopped against medical advice.

Long-term Recovery can be Helped by Spotting Relapses before They Happen

The fewer relapses a person with schizophrenia has, the better. One important job for the whole family is to learn the signs that a relapse may be about to happen. These signs may include major stresses, like a change in family routine or forgetting to take medication. They may also include changes in the person with schizophrenia's behaviour or experiences, for example, a change in their sleep pattern, energy level, memory, capacity to concentrate, hallucinations or delusions. When you have learned relapse signs, you need to follow a relapse prevention plan as soon as these signs occur. This plan should have three parts:

1. Contact our service and request an immediate relapse prevention appointment.
2. Make sure the person with schizophrenia has taken their medication.
3. Avoid showing excessive worry or criticism.

Changing Behaviour Patterns: Communication and Problem-Solving Skills Sessions

After the psychoeducational sessions the family are invited to use further sessions to refine their ways of communicating and solving problems so that routines may be developed that make family life predictable and calm.

In communication skills training, family members are coached to follow the guidelines set out in Chapters 9 and 14. Family members may be invited to discuss a particular issue, such as how the next weekend should be spent, with view to clarifying everyone's opinion about this. As they proceed, the therapist may periodically stop the conversation and point out the degree to which the family's typical communication style conforms to or contravenes the guidelines for good communication. All approximations to good communication should be acknowledged and praised. Alternatives to poor communication should be modelled by the therapist. Typically, there are problems with everyone getting an equal share of talking time with the symptomatic family member usually getting the least. Often messages are sent in a very unclear way and listeners rarely check out that what they have understood is what the speaker intended. It is important not to criticise family members for such errors but to praise them for successive approximations to clear communication.

With problem-solving training, family members' specific goals may be listed and an order for addressing them agreed starting with the least challenging. Big problems should be broken down into smaller problems, and vague problems should be clarified before this prioritising occurs. Families have a better chance of achieving goals if they are specific, visualisable and moderately challenging. In prioritising goals it is important to explore the costs and benefits of goals for each family member so that ultimately the list of high priority goals are those that meet the needs of as many family members as possible.

Common goals for families in which young adults have schizophrenia include: arranging exclusive time that the parents can spend together without their symptomatic young adult; arranging ways in which young adults can take on some age-appropriate responsibilities, such as meeting friends, cleaning their own clothes; managing money; ensuring that they have private living space free from parental intrusion; and taking medication regularly. For couples, goals may include spending enjoyable time together with a minimum of interference from the symptoms; or reducing the degree to which the non-symptomatic partner shows their worry and concern to the partner with schizophrenia.

Family members are asked to select the least challenging goal or problem and use the guidelines for problem-solving given in Chapter 9 to solve it. This attempt is observed by the treatment team or therapist. Feedback on problem-solving skills that were well used is given and alternatives to poor problem-solving skills are modelled by the therapist.

Common pitfalls for family members include: vague problem definition; trying to solve more than one problem at a time; and evaluating the pros and cons of solutions before all solutions have been listed. The latter is an important error to correct, since premature evaluating can stifle the production of creative solutions. Often families need to be coached out of bad communication habits in problem-solving training such as negative mind reading where they attribute negative thoughts or feelings to others, blaming, sulking and abusing others. At the end of an episode of problem-solving coaching, family members typically identify a solution to the problem, they are invited to try out this solution before the next session and a plan is made to review the impact of the solution on the problem in the next session. It is always important to review such tasks that clients have agreed to do between sessions.

Once problem-solving skills have been refined they may be used to solve major structural problems. Where one parent has been shouldering the burden of care in managing a young adult with schizophrenia, problem solving may focus on helping both parents share the load more equally and strengthen the boundary between themselves and the symptomatic young adult, so that the youngster can move towards independence and the parents can spend more time with each other in a mutually supportive relationship. In single parent families, problem-solving sessions may be used to help the parent develop supportive links with members of the extended family and broader social network and strengthen the boundary between the single parent and the young adult with schizophrenia. In couples where one member has schizophrenia, problem-solving may be used to explore ways in which the couple can gradually develop strategies for creating episodes in which they minimise the intrusion of psychotic symptoms into their relationship.

Transforming Belief Systems: Reframing and Externalising Problems

Parents and partners of people with schizophrenia may believe that they are responsible for the illness and feel intense guilt. This guilt may lead them to become intrusively over-involved or highly critical of their family symptomatic member's unusual behaviour. All family members experience grief at the loss of the way the ill family member used to be before the onset of the symptoms and also a sense of loss concerning the hopes and expectations they had for the future, which must be modified.

Part of the role of therapist is to help family members express these emotions, but in such a way that the critical, over-involved or despairing presentation of the emotions is minimised. The psychoeducational sessions, by helping family members understand that much of the patient's unusual behaviour is not motivated by malicious intentions, goes some way to help parents reduce criticism. Reframing statements about emotional states made by family members is a technique that can be used to minimise the negative impact of intense emotional expression. For example, if a family member expresses criticism by saying:

> *I can't stand you. Your driving me crazy.*

this may be reframed as:

> *It sounds like you really miss the way ABC used to be and sometimes these feelings of loss are very strong.*

If a family member expresses over-involvement by saying:

> *I have to do every thing for you because you can't manage alone.*

this may be reframed by saying:

> *It sounds like you find yourself worrying a lot about ABC's future and wondering if he will be able to fend for himself.*

In response to statements like:

> *You make me so miserable with your silly carry-on. Sometimes I think what's the point.*

a reframing may be offered as follows:

> *When you see ABC's symptoms, it reminds you of how he was before all this. Then you find your mood drops and this sadness and grief is hard to live with.*

All of these reframings involve labelling the emotional experience as arising out of underlying positive feelings that the non-symptomatic family member has for the symptomatic family member. The reframings also describe the emotions as arising from the way the non-symptomatic family member is coping, rather than being caused exclusively by the symptomatic person. That is, they give the message that the non-symptomatic family member *owns* the feeling, they are not *imposed* on the non-symptomatic family member by the symptomatic family member. Reframing is a process that occurs throughout therapy rather than being covered in a couple of sessions.

Where family members lose sight of the fact much of the unusual and distressing behaviour arises from the illness – schizophrenia – not the family member, they may be invited to externalise the illness and join forces in preventing it from destroying their relationships. This is a particularly useful intervention when working with couples. Here are some questions that may be used when making this intervention.

Can you give an account of those times when you have both been stronger than the schizophrenia and prevented its symptoms from intruding into your relationship?

What ways have you found for pushing the symptoms of schizophrenia out of your relationship so you may enjoy each other's company?

Relapse Management

Signals that may herald relapse, such as the build-up of life stress or the occurrence of prodromal symptoms, may be discussed during the disengagement phase of therapy. Plans for reducing stress, increasing medication and avoiding catastrophic interpretation of symptoms may be made. Plans for booster sessions may also be discussed. A critical issue is the development of a simple and clear relapse management plan, which should involve immediate contact with the therapy service and an immediate family meeting.

SUMMARY

Schizophrenia is conceptualised in major classification systems as a debilitating psychological disorder with a prevalence of about 1%. It is characterised by positive symptoms, such as delusions, hallucinations and thought disorder, and negative symptoms, such as impaired social functioning and lack of goal-directed behaviour. Family-based stress has a marked impact on individuals genetically vulnerable to schizophrenia when it occurs in the absence of protective factors, such as coping skills, social support and appropriate levels of antipsychotic medication. In view of this, it is not surprising that the treatment of choice for schizophrenia and related psychotic conditions is multimodal and includes antipsychotic medication coupled with psychosocial interventions, such as marital or family therapy, which aim to reduce family stress, enhance coping and mobilise social support. Integrative models of schizophrenia, which take account of interactional behaviour patterns, cognitive processes and belief systems, and both genetic and developmental vulnerabilities, offer a comprehensive systemic framework from which to conduct such multimodal therapy. Good premorbid functioning, an acute onset and a clear precipitant are all associated with a better outcome. A better outcome occurs for females rather than males and in individuals from families in which there is little psychopathology. If there are additional affective features or a family history of affective disorders rather than schizophrenia there is a better prognosis. In effective marital and family therapy programmes for schizophrenia emphasis is placed on blame-reduction, the positive role family members can play in the rehabilitation of the family member with schizophrenia and the degree to which the family intervention will alleviate some of the family's burden of care. These programmes include psychoeducation, communication and problem-solving skills training and a variety of techniques, such as reframing, externalising the problem, and so forth, to address problem-maintaining belief systems. Effective programmes also include sessions on recognition of prodromal symptoms and the development of a clear relapse management plan.

FURTHER READING

Falloon, I., Laporta, M., Fadden, G. & Graham-Hole, V. (1993). *Managing Stress in Families*. London: Routledge.

Kuipers, L., Leff, J. & Lam, D. (2002). *Family Work for Schizophrenia – A Practical Guide*, 2nd edn. London: Gaskell.

Kuipers, E. & Bebbington, P. (2005). *Living with Mental Illness*, 3rd edn. London: Souvenir Press.

Part V

RESEARCH AND RESOURCES

Chapter 18

EVIDENCE-BASED PRACTICE IN MARITAL AND FAMILY THERAPY

An important question for clinicians and service funders is, 'What type of family therapy approaches and practices are effective for specific clinical problems?'. An answer to this question, based on a review of available empirical research, is provided in this chapter.

There is a growing body of empirical evidence that unequivocally supports the effectiveness of marital and family therapy in the treatment of a wide range of problems (Sexton, Alexander & Leigh-Mease, 2004; Sprenkle, 2002). A review of 12 major meta-analyses confirmed that for child-focused and adult-focused mental health problems and relationship difficulties, marital and family therapy is highly effective in a significant proportion of cases (Shadish & Baldwin, 2003). Across the 12 meta-analyses, average effect sizes of 0.65 after treatment and 0.52 at follow-up were obtained. This indicates that the average treated case fared better than 74% of untreated cases after treatment and 70% of untreated cases at follow-up. Shadish and Baldwin (2003) also concluded that for 40–50% of cases treated with marital and family therapy, the gains made during therapy were clinically significant (as well as statistically significant) and reflected important changes in the quality of clients lives. This global conclusion is important because it underlines the value of martial and family therapy as a viable intervention modality. Highlighting this overall conclusion is timely since currently increased emphasis is being placed on evidence-based practice by purchasers and providers of mental health services around the world. However, such broad conclusions are of limited value to practicing clinicians in their day-to-day work. In addition to such broad statements about the global effectiveness of family therapy, there is a clear requirement for specific evidence-based statements about the precise types of family-based interventions which are most effective with particular types of problems. The present chapter addresses this question with particular reference to a number of common child-focused and adult-focused difficulties.

In many instances reference is made in this chapter to DSM-IV-TR (American Psychiatric Association, 2000) and ICD-10 (World Health Organisation, 1992) diagnostic categories. It is recognised that these are premised on an individualistic medical model of family difficulties and so may be ideologically unacceptable to many family therapists who adopt a systemic framework and a social constructionist epistemology as a basis for practice. Elsewhere (Carr, In press), I have argued on the basis of substantial empirical evidence that both the ICD and DSM systems have reliability, coverage and comorbidity difficulties, which compromise their validity and that this is because most problems of living which come to the attention of mental health professionals, including family therapists, are not distributed within the population as disease-like categorical entities. Rather, they are more usefully socially constructed as either complex interactional problems involving identified patients and members of their social networks or as dimensional psychological characteristics or combinations of both. However, the administration and funding of clinical services and research programmes is predominantly framed in terms of the ICD and DSM systems and so, in my opinion, it is expedient to review research on the effectiveness of treatment with reference to the prevailing medical-model framework. This pragmatic approach is also taken by many family therapy training programmes (Denton, Patterson & Van Meir, 1997).

In the following sections, where possible, reference is made to important review papers and meta-analyses. When individual treatment outcome studies are cited, unless otherwise stated, these are controlled trials or comparative group outcome studies. Quantitative and qualitative treatment process studies are mentioned where they throw light on factors underpinning effective treatment of particular problems. Single case reports and single group outcome studies have been largely excluded from this review because this type of evidence is less compelling than that provided by controlled studies, meta-analyses and review papers.

The chapter is organised so that child-focused problems are considered first and adult-focused problems are addressed second. Within subsections the implications of research findings for practice and service development are given.

CHILD-FOCUSED PROBLEMS

Evidence for the effectiveness of family therapy and family-based interventions for the following problems, which occur during childhood and adolescence, will be considered in this section:

- physical child abuse and neglect
- conduct problems
- emotional problems
- psychosomatic problems.

Physical Child Abuse and Neglect

Child abuse and neglect have devastating effects on the psychological development of children (Kolko, 2002). The overall prevalence of physical child abuse during childhood and adolescence is 10–25%, depending on the definition used, the population studied, and the cut-off point for the end of adolescence (Wekerle & Wolfe, 2003). Community surveys in the USA, the UK and other European countries in the 1990s found that the annual incidence of physical child abuse was 5–9% (Creighton, 2004).

The aim of family therapy for cases in which child abuse has occurred is to restructure relationships and prevailing belief systems within the child's social system so that the interaction patterns that contributed to abuse or neglect will not recur. Significant subsystems for intervention include the child, the parents, the marital subsystem, the extended family, the school system, and the wider professional network. The results of a number of controlled trials show that effective interventions for the family and wider system within which physical child abuse and neglect occurs entail coordinated intervention with problematic subsystems based on a clear assessment of interaction patterns and belief systems that may contribute to abuse or neglect (Edgeworth & Carr, 2000). For illustrative purposes two studies will be described.

Nicol et al. (1988), in a UK study, compared the impact of social worker facilitated family-focused casework and individual child play therapy for cases at risk for physical abuse or neglect. Family casework was a home-based intervention which included behavioural family assessment and feedback followed by a programme of family-focused problem-solving therapy. This included parental instruction in behavioural child management principles, family crisis intervention and reinforcement of parents for engaging in the casework processes. As a result of the intervention, the average treated family was displaying less coercive behaviour than 76% of the untreated families.

Brunk et al. (1987) compared the effectiveness of multisystemic family therapy and behavioural parent training with families where physical abuse or neglect had occurred. Multisystemic family therapy was based on an assessment of family functioning and involved conjoint family sessions, marital sessions, individual sessions and meetings with members of the wider professional network and extended family as appropriate (Henggeler & Borduin, 1990). Interventions included joining with family members and members of the wider system, reframing interaction patterns and prescribing tasks to alter problematic interaction patterns within specific subsystems. Therapists designed intervention plans on a case-by-case basis in light of family assessment, and received regular supervision to facilitate this process. In the behavioural parent training programme, parents received treatment within a group context. The programme involved instruction in child development and the principles of behavioural management including the use of reward systems and time-out routines. Following treatment both groups showed significant improvement in parental and family stress levels but cases who received multisystemic therapy showed greater improvements in family problems and parent–child interaction.

In developing services for families in which physical abuse or neglect has occurred, programmes that begin with a comprehensive network assessment and include, along with regular family therapy sessions, the option of parent-focused and child-focused interventions should be prioritised. To maximise the impact of such programmes, given our current state of knowledge, they would probably need to run over a minimum of a six-month period. For such programmes to be practically feasible, at least two therapeutically trained staff would be required and they would need to be provided with adequate administrative support and therapeutic supervision.

Conduct Problems in Childhood and Adolescence

The effectiveness of family therapy and family-based interventions for the following four distinct but related categories of conduct problems will be considered in this section:

- pre-adolescent children with oppositional behavioural difficulties confined to the home and school
- pre-adolescent children with attentional and overactivity problems
- adolescents with pervasive conduct problems
- adolescents with drug-related problems.

Childhood Oppositional Behavioural Difficulties

Pre-adolescent children who present with oppositional behavioural problems, temper tantrums, defiance, and non-compliance confined largely to the family, school and peer group constitute a third to a half of all referrals to child and family mental health clinics, and prevalence rates for clinically significant levels of oppositional behavioural problems in the community vary from 4% to 14% (Carr, 1993; Meltzer et al., 2000). Oppositional behavioural problems are of particular concern because in the longer term they may lead to adolescent conduct problems and later life difficulties.

Oppositional behavioural difficulties tend to develop gradually within the context of coercive patterns of parent–child interaction and a lack of mutual parental support (Patterson, 1982). When coercive interaction cycles occur the child repeatedly refuses in an increasingly aggressive way to comply with parents' requests despite escalating parental demands.

Such cycles conclude with the parent withdrawing. The probability that the cycle will repeat is increased because the parent's withdrawal offers relief to both the parent and the child. The parent is relieved that the child is no longer aggressively refusing to comply with parental requests and the child is relieved that the parent is no longer demanding compliance. As the frequency of such coercive interaction cycles increases, the frequency of positive parent–child interaction decreases. Coercive parent–child interaction patterns are commonly associated with low levels of mutual parental support or extrafamilial support and may be exacerbated by high levels of family stress. Coercive interaction cycles are also associated with belief systems in which parents attribute the child's difficult behaviour to internal characteristics of the child rather than external characteristics of the situation.

For childhood oppositional behavioural problems, behavioural parent training has been shown in many studies to be a highly effective treatment (Behan & Carr, 2000). Behavioural parent training focuses on helping parents develop the skills to monitor specific positive and negative behaviours and to modify these by altering their antecedents and consequences. For example, parents are coached in prompting their children to engage in positive behaviours and preventing children from entering situations that elicit negative behaviours. They are also trained to use reward systems such as star charts or tokens to increase positive behaviours and time-out to reduce negative behaviours. Behavioural parent training is probably so effective because it offers parents a highly focused way to supportively cooperate with each other in disrupting the coercive parent–child interaction patterns that maintain children's oppositional behaviour problems. It also helps parents develop a belief system in which the child's difficult behaviour is attributed to external situational characteristics rather than to intrinsic characteristics of the child.

The impact of a variety of formats on the effectiveness of behavioural parent training have been investigated, and the results of these studies allow the following conclusions to be drawn. Behavioural parent training is most effective for families with children who present with oppositional behavioural problems when offered: intensively over at least 20 sessions; exclusively to one family rather than in a group format; and as part of a multisystemic and multimedia intervention package, which includes concurrent individual child-focused problem-solving skills training with video-modeling for both parents and children (Kazdin, 2003; Webster-Stratton & Reid, 2003). Such intensive, exclusive, multisystemic, multimedia programmes are more effective than less intensive, group-based behavioural parent training alone, child-focused problem-solving skills training alone, or video modelling alone, with minimal therapist contact. Where a primary caregiver (typically a mother) is receiving little social support from her partner, then including a component to enhance the social support provided by the partner into a routine behavioural parent training programme may enhance the programme's effectiveness (Dadds, Schwartz & Sanders, 1987).

These conclusions have implications for service development. Services should be organised so that comprehensive child and family assessment is available for cases referred where pre-adolescent conduct problems are the central concern. Where it is clear that cases have circumscribed oppositional behavioural problems without other difficulties, behavioural parent training with video modelling may be offered to parents and child-focused problem-solving training may be offered to children. Each programme should involve at least 20 sessions over a period of 3–6 months. Where there is evidence of marital discord, both parents should be involved in treatment with the focus being on one parent supporting the other in implementing parenting skills in the home situation. Where service demands greatly outweigh available resources, cases on the waiting list may be offered video modelling-based behavioural parent training, with minimal therapist contact as a preliminary intervention. Following this intervention, cases should be reassessed and if significant behavioural problems are still occurring they should be admitted to a combined 40-session programme behavioural parent training with video modelling and child-focused problem-solving training.

Childhood Attentional and Overactivity Problems

Attention deficit hyperactivity disorder is now the most commonly used term for a syndrome characterised by persistent overactivity, impulsivity and difficulties in sustaining attention (American Psychiatric Association, 2000; Barkley, 2003; World Health Organisation, 1992). The syndrome is a particularly serious problem because youngsters with the core difficulties of inattention, overactivity and impulsivity, which are usually present from infancy, may develop a wide range of secondary academic and relationship problems. Available evidence suggests that vulnerability to attentional and overactivity problems, unlike oppositional behavioural problems discussed in the preceding section, is largely constitutional, although the precise role of genetic, prenatal and perinatal factors in the aetiology of the condition are still unclear. Using DSM IV criteria for attention deficit hyperactivity disorder, a prevalence rate of about 3–7% has been obtained in community studies (American Psychiatric Association, 2000). In the UK about 1% of children, aged 5–15 years, meet the more stringent ICD-10 diagnostic criteria for hyperkinetic disorder (Meltzer et al., 2000).

Multimodal programmes are currently the most effective for children with attentional and overactivity problems (Nolan & Carr, 2000). Multimodal programmes typically include stimulant treatment of children with drugs such as methylphenidate combined with family therapy or parent training; school-based behavioural programmes; and coping skills training for children (MTA Cooperative Group,1999). Family-based multi-modal programmes are probably effective because they provide the family with a forum within which to develop strategies for managing a chronic disability. As in the case of oppositional behavioural problems discussed above, both behavioural parent training and structural family therapy help parents and children break out of coercive cycles of interaction and to develop mutually supportive positive interaction patterns. Both family therapy and parent training help parents develop benign belief systems where they attribute the child's difficult behaviour to either the disability (attention deficit hyperactivity disorder) or external situational factors rather than to the child's negative intentions. School-based behavioural programmes have a similar impact on school staffs' belief systems and behaviour. Stimulant therapy (e.g. methylphenidate/Ritalin) and coping skills training help the child to control both their attention to academic tasks and their activity levels. Stimulant therapy, when given in low dosages, helps children to both concentrate better and sit still in classroom situations. High dosage levels have a more marked impact on overactivity but impair concentration and so are not recommended. Coping skills training helps children to use self-instructions to solve problems in a systematic rather than an impulsive manner.

In cases of attentional and overactivity problems, effective family therapy focuses on helping families to develop patterns of organisation conducive to effective child management (Barkley, Guevremont, Anastopoulos & Fletcher, 1992). Such patterns of organisation include a high level of parental cooperation in problem-solving and child management; a clear intergenerational hierarchy between parents and children; warm supportive family relationships; clear communication; and clear, moderately flexible rules, roles and routines.

Parent training, as described in the previous section on oppositional behavioural problems, focuses on helping parents develop the skills to monitor specific positive and negative behaviour and to modify these by altering their antecedents and consequences (e.g. Barkley, 1997). School-based behavioural programmes in cases of attentional and overactivity problems, involve the extension of home-based behavioural programmes into the school setting through home–school, parent–teacher liaison meetings (Braswell & Bloomquist, 1991; DuPaul & Eckert, 1997). Coping skills focus largely on coaching children in the skills required for sustained attention and systematic problem solving (Baer & Nietzel, 1991; Kendall & Braswell, 1985). These skills include identifying a problem to be solved; breaking it into a number of solvable sub-problems; tackling these one at a time; listing possible solutions; examining the costs and benefits of these; selecting the most viable solution; implementing this; monitoring progress; evaluating the outcome; rewarding oneself for successful problem solving; modifying unsuccessful solutions; and monitoring the outcomes of these revised problem-solving plans.

In terms of service, multicomponent treatment packages combined with low dose stimulant therapy are the treatments of choice for youngsters with attentional and overactivity problems. In the short term, effective multicomponent treatment should probably include 30 sessions over 12 weeks, with 12 sessions for the family, 12 for the child and six liaison meetings with the school. For effective long-term treatment, it is probable that a chronic care model of service delivery is required. Infrequent but sustained contact with a multidisciplinary service over the course of the child's development should be made available to families of children with attentional and overactivity problems. It is likely that at transitional points within each yearly cycle (such as entering new school classes each autumn) and at transitional points within the lifecycle (such as entering adolescence, changing school, or moving house) increased service contact would be required.

Pervasive Conduct Problems in Adolescence

Pervasive and persistent antisocial behaviour, which extends beyond the family to the community, involves serious violations of rules or law-breaking, and is characterised by defiance of authority, aggression, destructiveness, deceitfulness, cruelty, problematic relationships with parents, teachers and peers and typically leads to multiagency involvement, is referred to as conduct disorder (American Psychiatric Association, 2000; Burke et al., 2002; Loeber et al., 2002; World Health Organisation, 1992). Conservatively estimated prevalence rates for conduct disorder range from 1% to 10% (American Psychiatric Association, 2000).

From a developmental perspective, persistent adolescent conduct problems begin during the preschool years as oppositional behavioural problems. For about a third of children, these evolve into pervasive conduct problems in adolescence and antisocial personality disorder in adulthood (Loeber & Stouthamer-Loeber, 1998). Three classes of risk factors increase the probability that preschool oppositional behaviour problems will escalate into later life difficulties, such as child characteristics, parenting practices, and family organisation problems. Impulsivity, inattention and overactivity (the core features of attention deficit hyperactivity disorder described in the previous section) are the main personal characteristics of children that place them at risk for long-term conduct problems. Coercive family processes (described previously in relation to oppositional behaviour problems), which entail ineffective monitoring and supervision of children, providing inconsistent consequences for rule violations, and failing to provide reinforcement for prosocial behaviour are the main problematic parenting practices that place children at risk for long-term conduct difficulties. The family organisation problems associated with persistence of conduct problems into adolescence and adulthood are parental conflict and violence; a high level of intrafamilial and extrafamilial stress; a low level of social support; and parental psychological adjustment problems such as depression or substance abuse.

Reviews of current outcome studies indicates that functional family therapy and multisystemic therapy are currently the most effective outpatient treatments for conduct disorders and treatment foster care is the most effective intervention for cases of conduct disorder where outpatient family-based approaches have failed (Brosnan & Carr, 2000; Henggeler & Sheidow, 2003).

Functional family therapy aims to reduce the overall level of disorganisation within the family and thereby modify chaotic family routines and communication patterns which maintain antisocial behaviour (Sexton & Alexander, 2003). Functional family therapy focuses on facilitating high levels of parental cooperation in problem-solving around the management of teenagers' problem behaviour; clear intergenerational hierarchies between parents and adolescents; warm supportive family relationships; clear communication; and clear family rules, roles and routines. Within functional family therapy it is assumed that if family members can collectively be helped to alter their problematic communication patterns and if the lack of supervision and discipline within the family is altered, then the youngster's conduct problems will improve. This assumption is based on the finding that the families of delinquents are characterised by a greater level of defensive communication and lower levels of supportive communication compared with families of non-delinquent youngsters, and also have poorer supervision practices. With functional family therapy, all family members attend therapy sessions conjointly. Initially, family assessment focuses on identifying patterns of interaction and beliefs about problems and solutions that maintain the youngster's conduct problems. Within the early therapy sessions, parents and adolescents are facilitated in the development of communication skills, problem-solving skill and negotiation skills. There is extensive use of reframing to reduce blaming and to help parents move from viewing the adolescent as intrinsically deviant to someone whose deviant behaviour is maintained by situational factors. In the later stages of therapy, there is a focus on the negotiation of contracts in which parents offer adolescents privileges in return for following rules and fulfilling responsibilities.

While, functional family therapy focuses exclusively on altering factors within the family system so as to ameliorate persistent conduct problems, multisystemic therapy in addition addresses factors within the adolescent and within the wider social system. Effective multisystemic therapy, offers individualised packages of interventions that target conduct problem-maintaining factors within the multiple social systems of which the youngster is a member (Curtis et al., 2004; Henggeler & Lee, 2003). These multiple systems include the self, the family, the school, the peer group and the community. Multisystemic interventions integrate family therapy with self-regulation skills training for adolescents; school-based educational and recreational interventions; and interagency liaison meetings to coordinate multiagency input. In multisystemic therapy it is assumed that if conduct problem-maintaining factors within the adolescent, the family, the school, the peer group and the wider community are identified, then interventions may be developed to alter these factors and so reduce problematic behaviour. Following multisystemic assessment where members of the adolescent's family and wider network are interviewed, a unique intervention programme is developed, which targets those specific subsystems that are largely responsible for the maintenance of the youngster's difficulties. In the early stages of contact, the therapist joins with system members and later interventions focus on reframing the system members' ways of understanding the problem or restructuring the way they interact around the problems. Interventions may focus on the adolescent alone; the family; the school; the peer group or the community. Individual interventions typically focus on helping youngsters develop social and academic skills. Improving family communication and parents' supervision and discipline skills are common targets for family intervention. Facilitating communication between parents and teachers and arranging appropriate educational placement are common school-based interventions. Interventions with the peer group may involve reducing contact with deviant peers and increasing contact with non-deviant peers.

In contrast to functional family therapy, which focuses exclusively on the family system, or multisystemic therapy, which addresses, in addition to family factors, both individual factors and the wider social network, treatment foster care deals with the problem of pervasive conduct problems by linking the adolescent and his or her family to a new and positive system: the treatment foster family. In treatment foster care, carefully selected and extensively trained foster parents in collaboration with a therapist offer adolescents a highly structured foster care placement over a number of months in a foster family setting (Chamberlain, 2003; Chamberlain & Smith, 2003). Treatment foster care aims to modify conduct problem-maintaining factors within the child, family, school, peer group and other systems by placing the child temporarily within a foster family in which the foster parents have been trained to use behavioural strategies to modify the youngster's deviant behaviour. Adolescents in treatment foster care typically receive a concurrent package of multisystemic interventions to modify problem-maintaining factors within the adolescent, the natural family, the school, the peer group and the wider community. These are similar to those described for multisystemic therapy and invariably the natural parents complete a behavioural parent training programme so that they will be able to continue the work of the treatment foster parents when their adolescent visits or returns home for the long term. A goal of treatment foster care is to prevent the long-term separation of the adolescent from his or her biological family so as progress is made the adolescent spends more and more time with the natural family and less time in treatment foster care.

With respect to service development, it may be most efficient to offer services for adolescent conduct problems on a continuum of care (Brosnan & Carr, 2000; Chamberlain & Rosicky, 1995). Less severe cases may be offered functional family therapy of up to 40 sessions over a one-year period. Moderately severe cases and those that do not respond to circumscribed family interventions may be offered multisystemic therapy of up to 20 hours per month over a period of up to four years. Extremely severe cases and those who are unresponsive to intensive multisystemic therapy may be offered treatment foster care for a period of up to year and this may then be followed with ongoing multisystemic intervention. It would be essential that such a service involve high levels of supervision and low case loads for front-line clinicians because of the high stress load that these cases entail and the consequent risk of therapist burn-out.

Drug Abuse in Adolescence

While experimentation with drugs in adolescence is widespread, problematic drug abuse is less common. A conservative estimate is that between 5% and 10% of teenagers under 19 have drug problems serious enough to require clinical intervention (Chassin et al., 2003; Weinberg et al., 2002). Drug abuse often occurs concurrently with other conduct problems, learning difficulties and emotional problems and drug abuse is also an important risk factor for suicide in adolescence.

Comprehensive reviews of engagement and treatment outcome studies show that family therapy is more effective than other treatments in engaging and retaining adolescents in therapy and also in reducing of drug abuse (Cormack & Carr, 2000; Rowe & Liddle, 2003; Stanton, 2004; Stanton & Shadish, 1997). Family-based therapy is more effective in reducing drug abuse than individual therapy, peer group therapy and family psychoeducation. Furthermore, family-based therapy leads to fewer drop-outs from treatment compared with other therapeutic approaches. Family therapy can also be effectively combined with other individually-based approaches and lead to positive synergistic outcomes. Thus, family therapy can empower family members to help adolescents: engage in treatment; remain committed to the treatment process; and develop family rules, roles, routines, relationships, and belief systems that support a drug-free lifestyle. In addition, family therapy can provide a context within which youngsters could benefit from individual, peer group or school-based interventions.

Family systems theories of drug abuse implicate family disorganisation in the aetiology and maintenance of seriously problematic adolescent drug-taking behaviour and there is considerable empirical support for this view (Hawkins et al., 1992; Liddle, 2005; Stanton & Heath, 1995;

Szapocznik & Williams, 2000; Szapocznik et al., 2002). Family-based interventions aim to reduce drug abuse by engaging families in treatment and helping family members reduce family disorganisation and change patterns of family functioning in which the drug abuse is embedded.

Effective systemic engagement, which may span up to eight sessions, involves contacting all significant members of the adolescent's network directly or indirectly, identifying personal goals and feared outcomes that family members may have with respect to the resolution of the adolescent's drug problems and the family therapy associated with this, and then framing invitations for resistant family members to engage in therapy so as to indicate that their goals will be addressed and feared outcomes will be avoided (Santiseban et al., 1996; Szapocznik et al., 1988). Once families engage in therapy, effective treatment programmes for adolescent drug abuse involve the following processes which, while overlapping, may be conceptualised as stages of therapy: problem definition and contracting; becoming drug-free; facing denial and creating a context for a drug free lifestyle; family reorganisation; disengagement and planning for relapse prevention (Liddle, 2005; Stanton & Heath, 1995; Szapocznik et al., 2002). The style of therapy that has been shown to be effective with adolescent drug abusers and their families has evolved from the structural and strategic family therapy traditions (Haley, 1997; Minuchin, 1974). Effective family therapy in cases of adolescent drug abuse helps family members clarify communication, rules, roles, routines, hierarchies and boundaries; resolve conflicts; optimise emotional cohesion; develop parenting and problem-solving skills; and manage lifecycle transitions.

Multisystemic ecological treatment approaches to adolescent drug abuse represent a logical extension of family therapy. They are based on the theory that problematic processes, not only within the family but also within the adolescent as an individual and within the wider social system including the school and the peer group may contribute to the aetiology and maintenance of drug abuse (Henggeler & Lee, 2003). This conceptualisation of drug abuse is supported by considerable empirical evidence. At a personal level, adolescent drug abusers have been shown to have social skills deficits, depression, behaviour problems and favourable attitudes and expectations about drug abuse. As has previously been outlined, their families are characterised by disorganisation and in some instances by parental drug abuse. Many adolescent drug abusers have experienced rejection by prosocial peers in early childhood and have become members of a deviant peer group in adolescence. Within a school context drug abusers show a higher level of academic failure and a lower commitment to school and academic achievement compared to their drug-free counterparts. Multisystemic ecological intervention programmes for adolescent drug abusers, like those for adolescents with pervasive conduct problems described earlier, have evolved out of the structural and strategic family therapy traditions (Haley, 1997; Minuchin, 1974). In each case treated with multisystemic therapy, around a central family therapy intervention programme, an additional set of individual, school-based and peer-group based interventions are offered which target specific risk factors identified in that case. Such interventions may include self-management skills training for the adolescent, school-based consultations or peer group-based interventions. Self-management skills training may include coaching in social skills, social problem-solving and communication skills, anger control skills, and mood regulation skills. School-based interventions aim to support the youngsters continuation in school, to monitor and reinforce academic achievement and prosocial behaviour in school, and to facilitate home–school liaison in the management of academic and behavioural problems. Peer group interventions include creating opportunities for prosocial peer group membership and assertiveness training to empower youngsters to resist deviant peer group pressure to abuse drugs.

With respect to service development, the results of controlled treatment trials suggest that, a clear distinction must be made between systemic engagement procedures and the process of family therapy, with resources devoted to each. Following comprehensive assessment, where there is clear evidence that factors within the individual or the wider system are maintaining the youngster's drug abuse, a multisystemic approach should be taken. If youngsters have problem-solving, social skills, or self-regulation skills deficits, training in these should be provided. Where school-based factors are contributing to the maintenance of drug abuse, school-based interventions should be offered. Where deviant peer group membership is maintaining drug abuse, alternative peer group activities should be arranged. Available evidence suggests that, to be effective, multisystemic therapy programmes should span 12–36 sessions and structural family therapy must be of at least 6–24 sessions. In those instances where adolescents have developed physiological dependence, facilities for detoxification on either an inpatient or an outpatient basis should be provided.

Emotional Problems in Childhood and Adolesence

The effectiveness of family therapy for anxiety, depression and grief following bereavement will be considered in this section.

Anxiety in Childhood and Adolescence

While all children have developmentally appropriate fears, some are referred for treatment of anxiety problems when their fears prevent them from completing developmentally appropriate tasks, such as going to school or socialising with friends. The overall prevalence for clinically significant fears and anxiety problems in children and adolescents is approximately 6–10% (Verhulst, 2001). With respect to age trends, simple phobias and separation anxiety are more common among pre-adolescents and generalised anxiety disorder, panic disorder, social phobia and obsessive compulsive disorder are more common among adolescents (Carr, In press).

Phobias The effectiveness of family-based treatments for anxiety problems has been evaluated in number of studies (Barrett & Shortt, 2003; Moore & Carr, 2000a; Northey, Wells, Silverman & Bailey, 2003). For darkness phobia, Graziano and Mooney (1980) found that a brief family-based treatment programme was effective in reducing children's fear of the dark. Parents were coached in how to prompt and reinforce their children's courageous behaviour while not reinforcing anxious behaviour. Concurrently children were given coping skills training, which focused on helping them to develop relaxation skills and to use self-instructions to enhance a sense of control and competence in managing the dark. Similar findings were obtained in another similar study (Kanfer, Karoly & Newman, 1975).

School refusal For school refusal, behavioural family therapy has been found in a number of trials to be more effective than no treatment and alternative treatments such as hospital-based multimodal inpatient programmes and a home tuition and psychotherapy programme (Heyne, King & Ollendick, 2005). Behavioural family therapy includes detailed clarification of the child's problem; discussion of the principal concerns of the child, parents and teacher; development of contingency plans to ensure maintenance of gains once the child returned to school; a rapid return to school plan; and follow-up appointments with parents and teachers until the child had been attending school without problems for a significant time period. Effective treatment is brief and intensive, spanning about a month with up to 16 sessions, some with the child alone, some with the parents alone and some conjoint meetings.

Generalised anxiety disorder For generalised anxiety disorder, cognitive behavioural family therapy conducted with individual families and groups of families has been found to be more effective than no treatment or individual treatment for about 60% of children and recovery is maintained at long-term follow-up (Hudson, Hughes & Kendall, 2004; Northey et al., 2003). In effective treatment programmes, both parents and children attend separate individual or group sessions and some concurrent family therapy sessions, and are coached in anxiety management, problem-solving and communications skills and the use of reward systems. In the anxiety management sessions, a hierarchy of anxiety-provoking situations of increasing intensity is constructed and plans are made for the child to enter these and cope with them with parental support. Parents and children also learn to monitor and challenge unrealistic catastrophic beliefs and to use relaxation exercises and self-instructions to cope with these anxiety-provoking situations. In the reward systems sessions, parents learn to reward their children's courageous behaviour and ignore their anxiety-related behaviours and children are involved setting up reward menus. In the problem-solving and communication skills sessions, coaching in speaking and listening skills occurs and families learn to manage conflict and to solve family problems systematically. A particularly user-friendly effective anxiety management programme is Paula Barrett's FRIENDS programme (Barrett & Shortt, 2003; http://www.friendsinfor.net).

Obsessive compulsive disorder   For obsessive compulsive disorder (OCD), evidence from a controlled trial shows that a family-based programme that incorporates both narrative therapy and cognitive behavioural therapy and which can be conducted with individual families or groups of families is effective (Barrett, Healy-Farrell, Piacentini & March, 2004). The programme, called FOCUS (Freedom From Obsessions and Compulsions Using Special tools) is an expanded family oriented version of March and Mulle's (1998) *How I ran OCD off my Land* programme, which is contained in their text *OCD in Children and Adolescents*. The programme begins with psychoeducation about OCD and forming an expert team, which includes the family and the therapist. In the narrative therapy externalisation component of the programme, the child and parents are helped to view obsessive compulsive disorder as a neurobehavioural disorder separate from the youngster's core identity. Children are encouraged to externalise the disorder by giving it a nasty nickname and to make a commitment to driving this nasty creature out of their lives. They then are helped to map out a graded hierarchy of situations that elicit obsessions and lead to compulsions of varying degrees and those situations in which the child successfully controlled these symptoms are noted. These situations are subsequently monitored on a weekly basis, since increases in the number of these reflects therapeutic progress. In the behavioural family therapy component of the programme children are coached in coping with anxiety by using self-instruction and relaxation skills. Parents and siblings are coached to support and reward their children through the process of facing anxiety-provoking situations from their hierarchy of such situations while avoiding engaging in compulsive anxiety-reducing rituals. This aspect of the programme is referred to as exposure and response prevention since it involves exposing oneself to situations that provoke anxiety and obsessions, and preventing oneself from engaging in compulsive behaviours. Therapists also help parents and siblings negotiate disengagement from involvement in the youngsters' compulsive rituals. The 12-session programme ends with an award ceremony, and booster sessions are offered at 1, 2, 6 and 12 months.

In developing services for children with anxiety disorders, account should be taken of the fact that the majority of anxiety disorders in children can be effectively treated in programmes ranging from 3 to 24 sessions. Core features of successful family-based programmes include creating a context within family therapy that allows the child to eventually enter into anxiety-provoking situations and to manage these through the use of personal coping skills, parental support and encouragement.

Depression and Grief in Childhood and Adolescence

Depression   Major depression is a recurrent condition involving low mood; selective attention to negative features of the environment; a pessimistic cognitive style; self-defeating behaviour patterns; a disturbance of sleep and appetite; and a disruption of interpersonal relationships (American Psychiatric Association, 2000; Goodyer, 2001; Harrington, 2002; World Health Organisation, 1992). In community samples, prevalence rates of depression in youngsters under 18 range from about 2% to 9% (Angold & Costello, 2001; Harrington, 2002).There is strong evidence that both genetic and family environment factors contribute to the aetiology of depression (Goodyer, 2001; Harrington, 2002). Parental criticism, poor parent–child communication and family discord have all been found to be associated with depression in children and adolescents. Integrative theories of depression propose that episodes occur when genetically vulnerable youngsters find themselves involved in stressful social systems in which there is limited access to socially supportive relationships. Conjoint family therapy and concurrent group-based parent and child training sessions have been found to be as effective as various individual therapies in the treatment of major depression in (Brent et al., 1997; Cottrell, 2003; Harrington et al., 1998a; Harrington, Whittaker & Shoebridge, 1998b; Lewinsohn, Clarke, Hops & Andrews, 1990; Lewinsohn et al., 1996, Moore & Carr, 2000b). Effective family therapy and family-based interventions aim to decrease the family stress to which the youngster is exposed and enhance the availability of social support to the youngster within the family context. Core features of all effective family interventions include the facilitation of clear parent–child communication; the promotion of systematic family-based problem solving; and the disruption of negative critical parent–child interactions. With respect to clinical practice the results of these studies suggest that brief family therapy, ranging from 5 to 14 sessions, is a viable intervention for depressed children and adolescents.
Grief following bereavement   Between 1.5% and 4% of children under 18 lose a parent by death (Black, 2002). Worden (1997), in a major US study of parental bereavement, found that a year after parental death 19% of children continued to show clinically significant grief-related adjustment problems. Brief family-based grief therapy programmes have been found to lead to improved adjustment in children (Black & Urbanowicz, 1987; Kissane & Bloch, 2002; Sandler et al., 1992). Such programmes focus on: engaging families in treatment; assessing and understanding the context of the loss; acknowledging the reality of the death; modifying the family's worldview so that it incorporates the loss; facilitating problem solving and reorganising the family system, and moving on. With respect

to practice, therefore, the results of these studies suggest that following parental death, brief family therapy may be offered to bereaved children who show sustained grief-related adjustment problems.

Psychosomatic Problems in Childhood and Adolesence

The effectiveness of family therapy for toileting problems, unexplained stomach aches, poorly controlled diabetes, poorly controlled asthma and anorexia nervosa in adolescence will be addressed in this section. For all of these conditions discussed, it must be highlighted that it is vital that paediatric medical screening be conducted before embarking on family therapy so that treatable medical conditions may be identified and so that clear advice on appropriate medical management and interdisciplinary collaboration may be arranged.

Toileting Problems

The development of bladder and bowel control occurs for most children during the first five years of life (Walker, 2003). The absence of bladder and bowel control by the age of four or five years has a negative impact on children's social and educational development and so may be a focus for clinical intervention. The prevalence of wetting is 5–10% among 5 year olds, 3–5% among 10 year olds, and 1% among children over 15, while the prevalence of soiling is about 1% (American Psychiatric Association, 2000).

Wetting Controlled studies concur that children benefit more from family-based psychosocial interventions which include a urine alarm than from pharmacological treatments (Hoots, 2003). Houts's (2003) programme, which is effective in 75% of cases, involves: developing a detailed treatment contract with parents, siblings and referred children; the use of a urine alarm where children are awoken immediately bed-wetting begins by a bell activated by a urine trigger pad; cleanliness training where the child cleans and remakes the bed each time the urine alarm goes off; the use of a monitoring and reward programme for tracking successes in maintaining a dry bed; daily retention control training where the child earns rewards for gradually postponing urination for a period of up to 45 minutes; over learning where the child gradually increases fluid intake to a reasonable pre-set maximum before retiring; and the facilitation of family support for the referred child.

Soiling Murphy and Carr (2000b), in a review of interventions for soiling, concluded that combined family-based behavioural therapy, laxative use and increased dietary fibre was an effective treatment for children with soiling problems. In these programmes, behavioural family therapy involved coaching the family in using reward systems so that children were rewarded by parents for following through on toileting routines negotiated during family therapy sessions. Silver, Williams, Worthington and Phillips (1998) found that a treatment programme based on Michael White's narrative therapy externalising procedure was more effective than traditional behavioural programmes for soiling (White & Epston, 1989). In this type of family therapy, the soiling problem was externalised and defined as distinct and separate from the child. The soiling problem was referred to as *Sneaky Poo*. Therapy then focused on the child, the parent and the therapist collaborating in developing a narrative in which the child and family were construed as capable of outwitting and defeating *Sneaky Poo*. In Silver's study, 63% of cases treated with narrative family therapy were not soiling at six-months follow-up, compared with 37% of those treated with behavioural procedures. In terms of service development, from this review it may be concluded that family based-urine alarm programmes and family therapy which includes externalisation procedures may effectively be used for wetting and soiling problems respectively.

Recurrent Abdominal Pain

Recurrent abdominal pains – or Monday morning stomach aches as they are colloquially known – are defined as stomach aches which have occurred on three or more occasions over a three-month period; which are severe enough to affect the child's routine activities such as going to school; and for which no specific organic cause has been found (Murphy & Carr, 2000a). Recurrent abdominal pain may occur as part of a wider constellation of complaints including nausea, vomiting, headache, limb or joint pains. Recurrent abdominal pain occurs in 10–20% of school-aged children and accounts for 2–4% of paediatric consultations (Garralda, 1999). Sanders, Shepherd, Cleghorn and Woolford (1994) found that behavioural family therapy was more effective than standard medical care in the treatment of recurrent abdominal pain. The behavioural family therapy programme included relaxation training and coping skills training for the child. Parents were trained to prompt children to use their pain control skills and to reward and praise them for doing so. The programme was offered over 10 sessions spanning six weeks. After treatment, 71% of cases treated with behavioural family therapy were recovered compared with 38% of controls. At one-year follow-up, 82% of treated cases were pain-free compared with 43% of controls. With respect to practice, such a programme may be routinely offered on an outpatient basis.

Diabetes

Juvenile-onset insulin-dependent diabetes mellitus is a complex condition which affects under 0.2% of school-aged children and adolescents (Farrell, Cullen & Carr, 2002; Mrazek, 2002). It is characterised by a deficiency in insulin production that may be corrected through careful monitoring of blood sugar levels and a regular intake of insulin. Failure to adhere to this regime may lead to a coma induced by hyperglycaemia or hypoglycaemia in the short term, and in the long term to neuropathy and retinopathy with increased risk of heart disease, kidney disease, blindness and lower limb infections leading to gangrene. A series of controlled trials has shown that psychoeducational family therapy offered to either individual families or groups of families can improve diabetic control (Farrell et al., 2002). Effective family therapy for diabetes involves: psychoeducation for the child and family; self-monitoring training; stress-management and relaxation training; family communication and problem-solving skills training; and family work aimed at helping the parents support the child in developing autonomous control over the self-care regime.

Asthma

Asthma is a chronic respiratory condition which affects 3% of children (Sarafino, 2001). In poorly controlled asthma there may be inadequate adherence to medical treatment, inadequate environmental control, and problematic family organisation. Medical treatment typically includes regular inhalation of agents, that have a long-term preventative effect (e.g. Becotide) and agents that have a short-term positive impact on respiration (e.g. Ventolin). Environmental control for asthma includes minimising the child's exposure to allergens such as dust, smoke, pollen, cold air and domestic pets. Patterns of family organisation that exacerbate asthma include: rigid enmeshed relationships between the child and a highly anxious parent; triangulation where the child is required, usually covertly, to take sides with one or other parent in a conflict; or a chaotic family environment where parents institute no clear rules and routines for children's daily activities or medication regime (Wood, 1994). Family therapy aims to alter these problematic family organisational patterns; to enhance the child's medication adherence; and to help both the parents and the child develop routines to control environmental allergens. Two controlled trials of systemic family therapy for children with poorly controlled asthma have been conducted (Lask & Matthew, 1979; Gustafsson, Kjellmon & Cederbald, 1986), along with a series of group family-based psychoeduction and relaxation training (Brinkley, Cullen & Carr, 2002). The positive results of these studies suggest that in paediatric care, asthmatic control may be fostered by short-term systemic family therapy or group family psychoeducation which aims to enhance family communication and problem solving concerning the management of children's asthma and which aims to increase children's autonomy over the management of their condition.

Anorexia Nervosa in Adolescence

Anorexia nervosa and bulimia nervosa are most common among female adolescents (Gowers & Bryant-Waugh, 2004). About 1–2% of the adolescent female population suffer from eating disorders. Anorexia is less common than bulimia. The prevalence of anorexia nervosa among teenage girls is about 0.5%. The prevalence of bulimia nervosa is about 1%. The female: male ratio for anorexia and bulimia is about 9:1 in adolescents and 4:1 in pre-adolescents. Reviews of treatment outcome studies concur that family therapy and combined individual therapy and parent counselling with and without initial hospital-based feeding programmes are effective in treating anorexia nervosa (Eisler, 2005; Mitchell & Carr, 2000). Inpatient feeding programmes must be supplemented with outpatient follow-up programmes if weight gains made while in hospital are to be maintained following discharge. Key elements of effective treatment programmes include: engagement of the adolescent and parents in treatment; psycho-education about the nature of anorexia and risks associated with starvation; weight restoration and monitoring; shifting the focus from the nutritional intake to normal psychosocial developmental tasks of adolescence; facilitating the adolescent's individuation and increasing autonomy within the family; and relapse prevention. The Maudsley family therapy model (Lock, LeGrange, Agras & Dare, 2001), behavioural family systems therapy (Robin, 2003), and structural family therapy (Minuchin et al., 1978) are the main treatment models that have been evaluated in these treatment trails. With respect to service development, available evidence suggests that for youngsters with eating disorders effective treatment involves up to 18 outpatient sessions over periods as long as 15 months. Initial hospitalisation for weigh restoration is essential where medical complications associated with weight loss or bingeing and purging place the youngster at risk.

ADULT-FOCUSED PROBLEMS

Evidence for the effectiveness of family therapy and family-based interventions for the following adult-focused problems will be considered in this section:

- marital and relationship problems
- psychosexual problems
- anxiety disorders
- mood disorders
- schizophrenia
- alcohol abuse
- chronic pain management
- family management of neurologically impaired adults.

Marital Distress

Marital distress, dissatisfaction and conflict are extremely common problems and currently in western industrialised societies a third to a half of marriages are ending in divorce (Johnson, 2003b). For couples' relationship problems, behavioural marital therapy (with and without a cognitive component), emotionally-focused couples therapy, insight-oriented marital therapy, and self-control therapy have been shown to be effective interventions (Byrne et al, 2004b; Gollan & Jacobson, 2002; Halford, 1998; Johnson, 2003b; Shadish & Baldwin, 2005). Of these, behavioural and emotionally-focused marital therapy are by far the most extensively researched. Behavioural marital therapy involves training in communication and problem-solving skills on the one hand and behavioural exchange procedures on the other (Baucom et al., 2002). The aim of behavioural marital therapy is to help couples develop the communication and problem-solving skills to maintain a fairer relationship involving more equitable social exchanges. When a cognitive component is added to the behavioural approach it involves helping couples challenge the destructive attributions, beliefs, assumptions and expectations that contribute to relationship distress and on replacing these with more benign alternatives. Integrative behavioural couples therapy, a recent refined version of behavioural marital therapy, in addition to the basic behavioural and cognitive procedures, includes a strong emphasis on building tolerance for partners' negative behaviours, acceptance of unresolvable differences and empathic joining around such problems (Dimidjian et al., 2002). To some degree, it brings behavioural marital therapy closer to the style of practice associated with emotionally-focused couples therapy. With insight-oriented marital therapy (Snyder & Schneider, 2002) and emotionally-focused marital therapy (Johnson, & Denton, 2002), the aim of therapy is to help couples express feelings of vulnerability and unmet needs (which may initially be outside awareness), and to help couples understand how these feelings and needs underpin destructive patterns of interaction within the relationship. The aim of these approaches is to help couples develop more secure attachments. Self-control therapy empowers partners to alter their personal contribution to the destructive interaction patterns that underpin marital distress (Halford, 1998).

Meta-analyses of all types of marital therapy yield an average effect size of about 0.58 indicating that the average treated couple fares better than about 71% of untreated couples (Shadish & Baldwin, 2003).

There is growing evidence that emotionally-focused couples therapy, insight-oriented marital therapy, and integrative behavioural couples therapy are more effective than traditional behavioural marital therapy (Gollan & Jacobson, 2002; Johnson, 2003b). The clinical recovery rate for emotionally-focused couples therapy is about 70%, while that for behavioural marital therapy is about 35%. Four years after treatment, 3% of cases in insight-oriented marital therapy were divorced compared with 38% of those in behavioural marital therapy. These results suggest that facilitating attachment between partners is a more effective way of reducing distress than empowering them to have fairer social exchanges.

Different factors predict a positive outcome in behavioural and emotionally-focused couples therapy (Jacobson & Addis, 1993; Johnson, 2003b). The best predictors of a successful outcome in behavioural marital therapy is initial levels of couple distress, with more distressed couples having a poorer outcome. Couples that benefit most from behavioural marital therapy are more emotionally engaged with each other and do not opt for premature closure in their attempts at relationship-based problem solving. Younger couples and couples with non-traditional values benefit most from behavioural marital therapy, which is less effective with older traditional couples that engage in distancer-pursuer interaction patterns. The best predictor of a good outcome in emotionally-focused couples therapy is the female partners' belief that her male partner still cares about her. Emotionally-focused couples therapy is effective for couples with low income and low educational levels and it is effective with young and old couples and couples with traditional and non-traditional values.

A number of common factors may underpin effective marital therapies (Bray & Jouriles, 1995). They tend to be brief and rarely exceed 20 sessions, so hope and the expectation of change is rapidly generated. They involve conjoint sessions in which clear non-defensive communication, empathy and intimacy are facilitated. They promote the development of communication and problem-solving skills. They permit couples to discuss the impact of family of origin issues on current relationship functioning and this in turn may deepen empathy and psychological intimacy within the relationship. They empower couples to renegotiate relationship roles and this in turn may lead to a more equitable distribution of power within the relationship.

Effective marital therapy may also be conducted with one partner only, under certain circumstances (Bennun, 1997). One-person or unilateral marital therapy may be appropriate in cases where only one partner is available to attend treatment; where there are dependence-independence issues in the relationship; where there are problems in sustaining intimate relationships; in cases of domestic violence; where there is a major disparity between partners' levels of self-esteem; and where one partner's unresolved family-of-origin issues contribute significantly to the couple's problems. The approach is described in Chapter 14. Bennun (1997) has shown that unilateral marital therapy is as effective as conjoint marital therapy. He argues that, in the past, individually based interventions for marital problems have yielded negative results because of their almost exclusive focus on individual issues and their lack of attention at a systemic level to relationship issues.

Under certain circumstances, marital therapy may be effective for extreme distress associated with domestic violence. Conjoint marital therapy is only appropriate is cases where the aggressive male commits to a no-violence contract and the female partner agrees a safety plan should further threats of violence occur. Stith et al. (2004) found that a multi-couple treatment programme was more effective than a single couple programme in reducing domestic violence and related marital distress. Male violence recidivism rates were 25% for the multi-couple group and 43% for the individual couple group. Key elements of treatment include: the perpetrator taking responsibility for the violence; solution-focused practices; challenging beliefs and cognitive distortions which justify violence; anger management training; communication and problem-solving skills training; and relapse prevention. Anger management training focuses on teaching couples to recognise anger cues; to take time out when such cues are recognised; to use relaxation and self-instructional methods to reduce anger-related arousal; to resume interactions in a non-violent way; and to use communication and problem-solving skills more effectively for conflict resolution.

With respect to clinical practice and service development, the findings reviewed here suggest that effective marital therapy may be offered on an outpatient basis over approximately 20 sessions.

Psychosexual Problems

Psychosexual problems while essentially relationship difficulties, have been classified in DSM IV (American Psychiatric Association, 2000) and ICD-10 (World Health Organisation, 1992) as individual male and female disorders affecting sexual desire, sexual arousal, sexual orgasm and sex-related pain. Some psychosexual problems occur in both men and women and some are gender specific. Low sexual desire, sexual aversion and painful intercourse (dysparunia) are problems that may affect both men and women. Psychosexual problems unique to women include primary and secondary female orgasmic dysfunction (the absence of orgasm during intercourse) and vaginismus (involuntary spasm of the vagina when intercourse is attempted). Psychosexual disorders unique to men include primary and secondary erectile dysfunction (absence of erection when intercourse is attempted), premature ejaculation and retarded ejaculation. Omitting premature ejaculation, which occurs in about a third of males, the overall prevalence of psychosexual problems in men and women falls between 10% and 20% (Segraves & Althof, 2002). Marital distress is extremely common where the primary complaint is a psychosexual problem (Hawton, 1995). Additional psychological problems (including depression, anxiety, eating disorders and drug abuse) occur for a proportion of people with psychosexual problems.

Most effective psychosocial treatments for psychosexual problems are based on Masters and Johnson's (1970) sex therapy (Leiblum & Rosen, 2001; Levine et al., 2003). This begins with psychoeducation about the human sexual response and exploration of the pattern of interaction and beliefs around the couple's specific problem area. Couples are advised to refrain from sexual intercourse and sexual contact except as outlined in prescribed exercises. Couples are then coached in a series of sensate focus homework exercises in which partners give and receive pleasurable caresses along a graded sequence progressing over a number of weeks from non-sexual to increasingly sexual areas of the body and culminating in full intercourse. For specific problems, additional exercises are added to this basic protocol (as outlined below). Later, sex therapists, building on the work of Masters and Johnson, have developed ways in which sex therapy and marital therapy, which addresses intrapsychic and interpersonal issues, may be effectively integrated in clinical practice (Lieblum & Rosen, 2001). The following conclusions about the effectiveness of sex therapy have been drawn for extensive literature reviews (Leiblum & Rosen, 2001; Levine et al., 2003; Segraves & Althof, 2002).

For primary female orgasmic dysfunction, partner-assisted sexual skills training has been shown to be effective in up to 90% of cases. Partner-assisted sexual skills training begins with psychoeducation; followed by coaching in masturbation using sexual fantasy and imagery; progressing to Masters and Johnson's sensate focus exercises; and later females are coached in explaining masturbation techniques that they find effective to their male partners.

For secondary female orgasmic dysfunction and hypoactive sexual desire, marital therapy (as described in the previous section) combined with Masters and Johnson's (1970) sex therapy have been found to be effective in about half of all treated cases.

For female dysparunia (painful sexual intercourse) and vaginismus (involuntary spasm of the outer third of the vaginal musculature) between 80% and 100% of cases have been shown to benefit from the densensitisation programme developed by Masters and Johnson (1970). At the outset, the couple refrain from intercourse and the female partner completes a series of graduated exercises that involve the gradual insertion of a series of dilators of increasing diameter into the vagina. This is then followed-up with the routine Masters and Johnson sensate focus sex therapy programme.

For acquired male erectile problems, the Masters and Johnson conjoint sensate focus sex therapy approach combined with couples therapy has been shown to be effective in up to 60% of cases. Sildenafil (Viagra) has been shown to be rapidly effective in alleviating acquired male erectile problems in 40–80% of cases.

For premature ejaculation, Masters and Johnson (1970) developed the stop-start and squeeze techniques where the couple cease intercourse and the base of the penis is squeezed each time ejaculation in imminent. Success rates with this method may be initially as high as 80% but may dwindle in the long-term to 25% at follow-up. Sertraline, paroxetine and clomipramine have all been shown to be rapidly effective in alleviating premature ejaculation.

Hawton (1995), in an extensive review, concluded that: motivation for treatment (particularly the male partner's motivation); early compliance with treatment; the quality of the relationship (particularly as assessed by the female partner); the physical attraction between partners; and the absence of serious psychological problems are predictive of a positive response to treatment.

With respect to clinical practice and service development, the findings reviewed here suggest that effective therapy for psychosexual problems may be offered on an outpatient basis over 10–20 sessions, depending upon the complexity of the relationship difficulties that accompany the psychosexual problems. Where members of a couple have additional difficulties such as depression, anxiety, eating disorders or drug abuse problems, the relationship between these problems and the psychosexual difficulties require careful assessment and treatment. In some instances, mood, eating or drug problems on the one hand and psychosexual difficulties on the other may reflect a difficulty with a core issue, such as managing intimacy. This core issue should be a central focus for couples therapy. In other instances, mood, eating or drug problems may precipitate and maintain psychosexual problems. In such cases, the management of the mood, eating or drug problems may be selected as the main target for treatment. A third possibility is that psychosexual problems may give rise to mood, eating or drug problems and here the main focus of treatment should probably be the psychosexual problem.

Anxiety Disorders in Adulthood

Family-based therapies have been shown to be effective for two of the most debilitating anxiety disorders – agoraphobia with panic disorder and obsessive compulsive disorder (Baucom et al., 2003; Byrne et al., 2004a; Franklin & Foa, 2002). Lifetime prevalence rates for agoraphobia with panic disorder and obsessive compulsive disorder are approximately 1.5–3.5% and 2.5% respectively, and both conditions are more common among women (American Psychiatric Association, 2000).

In agoraphobia with panic disorder, people develop constricted lifestyles and fear leaving the safety of their homes because they are apprehensive that they may have panic attacks in public places. Family members, particularly partners, come to share this belief system and become involved in patterns of interaction that maintain the constricted lifestyle of the person with agoraphobia. In the most effective family-based treatments of agoraphobia, the aim is to help all family members develop less danger-saturated belief systems, to disrupt family interaction patterns that maintain the agoraphobic person's constricted lifestyle, to enlist the aid of family members in helping the person with agoraphobia overcome their fears, and to help family members communicate more effectively.

Family-based treatment of panic disorder with agoraphobia (Byrne et al., 2004a) begins with psychoeducation about the nature of anxiety and the importance of facing feared situations and coping with these in overcoming the disorder. The person with agoraphobia is helped in couple or family therapy sessions to use self-talk, relaxation skills and support from their partner or other family members to cope with anxiety. Sessions are also used to plan a series of increasingly threatening or anxiety provoking outings for the couple to complete between sessions. In these outings, the person with agoraphobia and their partner go out to public places, which the person with agoraphobia finds anxiety provoking or threatening. In these situations, the partner supports the person with agoraphobia in using coping skills to manage the anxiety successfully. Family-based treatment of agoraphobia is often referred to as *partner-assisted exposure*, because the originators of these programmes, working within a behavioural framework, viewed the partner as assisting the therapist in helping the client become repeatedly exposed to anxiety provoking situations. In the more effective programmes, couple communication training is also conducted and couple relationship issues are addressed. Where these relationship elements are included in treatment programmes, family-based treatment is more effective than individually based cognitive-behavioural treatments (Baucom et al., 1998).

With obsessive compulsive disorder, specific situations, such as coming into contact with dirt, lead the person to experience intrusive obsessional anxiety provoking thoughts, such as the belief that contamination by dirt will lead to a fatal illness. To reduce anxiety, the person engages in compulsive rituals, such as repeated handwashing. However, these compulsive rituals only have a short-term anxiety reducing effect. Obsessional thoughts quickly return and the compulsive rituals are repeated. Family members, particularly partners, often become involved in patterns of interaction that maintain the compulsive rituals, by for example assisting with the compulsive rituals or not questioning their legitimacy. In effective family-based treatment of obsessive compulsive disorder, the aim is to disrupt family interaction patterns that maintain the obsessions and compulsive rituals and to enlist the aid of family members in helping the person with the condition overcome their obsessions and compulsions (Baucom, Starton & Epstein, 2003; Franklin & Foa, 2002).

Family-based treatment of obsessive compulsive disorder begins with psychoeducation about the nature of the condition and the importance of tolerating anxiety in situations that elicit obsessions without engaging in compulsive rituals as central to effective treatment. Within later treatment sessions, which are attended by family members with obsessive compulsive disorder and their partners, the therapist coaches partners in supporting their obsessive-compulsive spouses while they enter anxiety provoking situations (such as coming into contact with dirt) and preventing themselves from engaging in compulsive anxiety reducing responses (such as repeated handwashing). This treatment programme is often referred to as partner-assisted *exposure and response prevention* (ERP).

In some instances, it may be appropriate for family-based interventions for the two anxiety disorders discussed here to be offered in conjunction with antidepressant medication, because this has been shown to ameliorate the symptoms of panic disorder and obsessive compulsive disorder (Roy-Byrne & Cowley, 2002; Dougherty, Rauch & Jenike, 2002).

With respect to clinical practice and service development, the findings reviewed here suggest that effective family-based therapy for anxiety disorders may be offered on an outpatient basis over 10–20 sessions. Such therapy may be multimodal involving both family therapy and pharmacological interventions.

Mood Disorders in Adulthood

Effective family-based treatments have been developed for major depression and bipolar disorder (Beach, 2003; Milkowitz & Morris, 2003). Major depression is characterised by episodes of low mood, negative thinking, and sleep and appetite disturbance. Bipolar disorder is characterised in addition by episodes of mania in which elation, grandiosity, flight of ideas and expansive behaviour occur. The lifetime prevalence of major depression is 10–25% for women and 5–12% for men and the lifetime prevalence of bipolar disorder is about 1% (American Psychiatric Association, 2000).

A series of trials show that behavioural marital therapy has been shown to be effective in alleviating major depression in up to 50% of cases and in delaying relapse, particularly in couples where there is also marital distress (Beach, 2003). Behavioural marital therapy aims to improve communication and problem-solving skills and increase the rate of mutually satisfying interpersonal exchanges (Baucom et al., 2002). To achieve the first of these two goals, behavioural marital therapy includes problem-solving and communication skills training. To achieve the second goal, it includes contingency contracting, where couples negotiate increased rates of mutually satisfying exchanges.

Conjoint interpersonal therapy has been shown to be effective in alleviating depression in couples in which one partner is depressed (Foley, Rounsaville, Weissman, Sholomaskas & Chevron, 1990; Weissman, Markowitz & Klerman, 2000). Conjoint interpersonal therapy aims to alter negative interpersonal situations that maintain depression. In particular, interpersonal therapy helps couples to address unresolved difficulties in the following domains: loss, role disputes, role transitions, and interpersonal deficits.

In the UK, Leff, Asen and Jones found that systemic couples therapy with depressed patients led to lower drop-out rates and greater improvement than antidepreassants. This greater degree of improvement continued during the year following therapy. Systemic couples therapy was no more expensive in the long-term than antidepressant medication, because patients who received medication only used a range of other health services to compensate for the limited effects of antidepressants (Jones & Asen, 1999; Leff et al., 2000). Systemic couples therapy focused on helping couples move from an exclusively individual understanding of depression towards an interactional contextualisation of mood problems. It also helped them to move out of depression-maintaining interaction patterns.

Behavioural marital therapy, conjoint interpersonal therapy and systemic couples therapy probably alleviate depression and reduce the risk of relapse by reducing family-based stress and conflict and increasing marital and family support, although they employ different strategies to achieve these ends.

For bipolar mood disorders, evidence from a small number of controlled trials has shown that multimodal programmes, which include both family intervention and routine pharmacological intervention (with agents such as lithium carbonate), reduce relapse rates (Craighead et al., 2002b; Milkowitz & Morris, 2003).

Clarkin et al. (1990); (Clarkin, Haas & Glick, 1988; Clarkin, Carpenter, Hull, Wilner & Glic, 1998) found in two trials found that both inpatient and outpatient psychoeducational family therapy, when offered in conjunction with routine pharmacological treatment, led to better long-term adjustment and medication adherence than routine pharmacological treatment alone. The family therapy programme in this study provided family members with information on bipolar disorder as a chronic illness; helped them develop ways to reduce life stress and increase support for the patient; and encouraged them to maximise medication adherence.

Miller et al. (Miller, Keitner, Bishop & Ryan, 1991; Miller, Keitner, Ryan & Solomon, 2000a) in two trials found that relapse and rehospitalisation rates of patients with bipolar disorder were significantly reduced when patients were offered McMaster family therapy, either to individual families or in a group format, during hospitalisation and following discharge. The McMaster model focuses explicitly on preliminary assessment of family problem solving, communication, roles, behavioural control, affective expression, and affective involvement. Therapy aims to alter problematic functioning in each of these domains by inviting families to complete contracted home-based assignments.

Milkowitz, in a series of two studies, found that relapse rates among people with bipolar disorder were greatly reduced when routine pharmacological treatment was supplemented with a nine-month outpatient programme of family-focused treatment (Milkowitz & Morris, 2003). Family-focused treatment has distinct stages and these include: joining and alliance building; assessment of expressed emotion and family attitudes to the person with the illness; psychoeducation about bipolar disorder, pharmacological treatment; the importance of adherence to the medication regime and relapse prevention; family stress management; family communication training; and family problem-solving training.

With routine pharmacological treatment, such as lithium carbonate (Keck, & McElroy, 2002), in the absence of family therapy, people with bipolar disorder commonly relapse in response to family- and work-related stress and non-compliance with medication regimes (Craighead et al., 2002b). Inpatient family therapy, McMaster family therapy and family-focused therapy probably improve long-term adjustment by helping families address these potential relapse triggers.

With respect to clinical practice and service development, the findings reviewed here suggest that effective multimodal therapy for mood disorders may be offered on an outpatient basis over 10–20 sessions, although it is probable, because of the recurrent episodic nature of major depression and bipolar disorder, that booster sessions or therapy episodes may be required following relapses. Within such therapy programmes psycho-pharmacological therapy may be combined with family-based interventions as described above. Of course, in instances where there is a high risk of self-harm or severe impairment in social functioning brief episodes of inpatient care may be required for individuals with mood disorders.

Schizophrenia in Adulthood

Psychoeducational family-based interventions coupled with routine anti-psychotic medication have been shown in numerous controlled trials to reduce relapse rates in families characterised by high levels of expressed emotion from over 50% in cases receiving medication only, to less than 20% one year following the onset of the psychotic episode (Kopelowicz et al., 2002; McFarlane et al., 2003; Milkowitz & Tompson, 2003). Some of the controlled trials of family interventions have also shown that family-based therapy may reduce the amount of maintenance medication required and the number of days of hospitalisation required during the follow-up period.

Schizophrenia, a debilitating psychological disorder with a prevalence of about 1%, is characterised by positive symptoms, notably delusions, hallucinations and thought disorder, and negative symptoms such as impaired social functioning and lack of goal-directed behaviour (American Psychiatric Association, 2000). Exposure to life stresses, including high levels of expressed emotion (criticism and over-involvment) in family and residential settings, can adversely affect the course of schizophrenia. Stress has a marked impact on individuals genetically vulnerable to schizophrenia when it occurs in the absence of protective factors, such as social support, coping skills and appropriate levels of antipsychotic medication. In view of this, it is not surprising multimodal treatment, which includes antipsychotic medication coupled with family-based interventions that aim to reduce family stress and increase social support and family coping resources, is particularly effective in the treatment of schizophrenia.

There has been considerable variability in the format of effective family based interventions for schizophrenia (Falloon et al., 1993; Kopelowicz et al., 2002; Kuipers et al., 2002; McFarlane, 2002; McFarlane et al., 2003; Milkowitz & Tompson, 2003). However, it is clear that effective treatments involve at least some conjoint family meetings which include symptomatic and non-symptomatic family members and these meetings may involve multiple families. Relatives' support groups, which exclude patients are not particularly effective in reducing relapse rates but may reduce the burden of care experienced by family carers. Treatment intensity and attendance at treatment is associated with positive outcome. Because of this, special attention is paid in successful programmes to engaging families in treatment and reducing attrition by including the option of conducting treatment in clients' homes when engagement problems occur. Effective interventions typically span 9–12 months and are usually offered in a phased format with three months of weekly sessions; three months of fortnightly sessions; three months of monthly sessions; followed by three monthly reviews and crisis intervention as required. Briefer intensive crisis-oriented intervention may be appropriate with first episode cases. With respect to the content and process of treatment programmes, a number of core elements typify effective family-based interventions for schizophrenia. Emphasis is placed on blame-reduction, the positive role family members can play in the rehabilitation of the family member with schizophrenia and the degree to which the family intervention will alleviate some of the family's burden of care. All effective family intervention programmes for schizophrenia offer family members an explanation or framing of the condition, which provides a rationale for reducing family stress, increasing family support and active coping and arranging for the person with schizophrenia to adhere to the prescribed medication regime. A vulnerability model of the disorder is typically presented, in which the central idea is that genetically vulnerable individuals may develop schizophrenia if exposed to stress in the absence of support, coping skills and medication. Effective programmes include skills training in family stress management, family communication, family problem solving and medication management. Skills training commonly involves modelling, rehearsal, feedback and discussion.

With respect to clinical practice and service development, available evidence clearly indicates that multimodal treatment programmes should be made available to people with schizophrenia and their families. Such programmes should include both a psychopharmacological component and family-based psychoeducational therapy. During the acute phase of a psychotic episode, hospitalisation may sometimes be necessary but this is not always the case and intensive family support at this stage is another option.

Alcohol Abuse in Adulthood

The prevalence of alcohol abuse (or misuse) involving impaired social functioning arising from alcohol is approximately 5% in adults over 18 years of age (American Psychiatric Association, 2000). For alcohol abuse, family-based treatments have been shown to be particularly effective in helping people with alcohol problems and their families engage in treatment; become drug-free or develop a more controlled approach to alcohol use; and avoid relapse (Edwards & Steinglass, 1995; Finney & Moos, 2002; O'Farrell & Fals-Stewart, 2003; Stanton, 2004).

Family-based engagement techniques all involve working with non-alcoholic family members, particularly spouses, and include: family intervention (Liepman, Silvia & Nirenberg, 1989); unilateral family therapy (Thomas & Ager, 1993); community reinforcement and family training (Meyers, Smith & Miller, 1998); and the pressure to change approach (Barber & Crisp, 1995). These can help 57–86% of cases engage in treatment (either individual or family based) compared with the typical engagement rate of about 0–31% (Edwards & Steinglass, 1995; O'Farrell & Fals-Stewart, 2003). Family-based engagement techniques help non-alcoholic family members create a context within which the chances of the family member with a drink problem entering treatment are maximised. With family intervention, the therapist coaches family members over a series of sessions to stage a formal confrontation with the family member who has the alcohol problem (Liepman et al., 1989). During this confrontation, the family members describe their concerns about the drinking problem and its consequences. Unilateral family therapy includes psychoeducation; relationship enhancement training; training in avoiding enabling behaviour patterns that maintain alcohol use; preparation for confrontation, requests to reduce alcohol use and to enter treatment; coaching in maintaining treatment gains; and relapse prevention (Thomas & Ager, 1993). In cases where separation is the preferred option of the non-alcoholic spouse, then coaching in disengagement is provided. With community reinforcement and family training (Meyers et al., 1998) the spouse of the person with the alcohol problem is coached in reinforcement-based methods for avoiding physical abuse; encouraging sobriety; increasing positive relationships and communication; engaging in outside activities to reduce dependence on the relationship with the problem drinker; and encouraging the problem drinker to enter treatment. With the pressure to change approach, spouses are coached in a series of six sessions to use five gradually increasing levels of pressure on the drinker to seek help or moderate their drinking (Barber & Crisp, 1995).

Both inpatient and outpatient family-oriented treatment programmes based on systems theory and social learning theory have been shown to be effective in reducing alcohol abuse. Edwards & Steinglass (1995), in a meta-analysis of 13 studies, obtained an effect size of 0.8, which shows that up to six months following treatment, the average treated case fared better than 79% of untreated cases. The two most effective treatment packages were the community reinforcement approach (e.g. Azrin, 1976) and behavioural couples therapy (O'Farrell, 1993). Effective treatment programmes included a combination of some or all of the following components: psychoeducation; exploration of the negative consequences of alcohol abuse for all family members; exploration of the patterns of family interaction which maintain alcohol abuse; exploration of ways in which these patterns may be disrupted; enhancement of communication and problem solving within the couple and family; coaching couples in mutual contingency contracting; coaching non-alcoholic partners to reinforce their spouses for abstinence; the use of Antabuse (disulfiram) and family-based Antabuse contracts; individually-based training in drink refusal and urge control; facilitating the development of an alcohol-free lifestyle; the use of homework assignments; the use of phone-prompting between sessions; and coaching in relapse prevention. O'Farrell and Fals-Stewart (2003) concluded that effective family interventions for problem drinkers, particularly behavioural couples therapy (O'Farrell, 1993), led not only to greater sobriety or controlled drinking, but also to increased marital satisfaction, improved family functioning, reduced domestic violence and reduced hospitalisation and imprisonment, and in all of these domains it was superior to traditional individual therapeutic approaches.

Family-based aftercare programmes, which aim to prevent relapse, have been shown to be more effective than individually-based aftercare programmes (Edwards & Steinglass, 1995). Family based aftercare programmes typically involve relatively infrequent conjoint marital or family sessions spread over an extended time period.

Both client and therapists' characteristics have been shown to affect treatment outcome in cases of alcohol abuse. Family-based treatment programmes are more effective when both partners are invested in the relationship and the non-drinking spouse is highly supportive of abstinence (Edwards & Steinglass, 1995). Therapists who are more interpersonally skilled, more empathic and less confrontational tend to be more effective (Finney & Moos, 2002).

With respect to clinical practice and service development, the findings reviewed here suggest that effective multimodal therapy for alcohol abuse may be offered on an outpatient basis over an extended time period. Ideally, such treatment should be multisystemic and family based with a clear distinction made between the processes of engagement, treatment and aftercare. For individuals who are alcohol dependent, a period of inpatient or outpatient detoxification should precede therapy. To make alcohol use an aversive option disulfiram may be incorporated into a multimodal multisystemic programme.

Chronic Pain Management in Adulthood

Chronic pain, including low-back pain and rheumatoid arthritis, is only partially responsive to pharmacological interventions. Because of this, family-based interventions grounded in biopsychosocial conceptualisations of pain have been developed. For chronic low-back pain operant programmes and cognitive behavioural coping skills training programmes have both been shown to be effective and such coping skills training programmes have also been shown to be effective for rheumatic diseases (Compas, Haaga, Keefe, Leitenberg & Williams, 1998).

Operant pain management programmes entail extensive family involvement (Fordyce, 1976). They rest on the premise that much pain behaviour and sick role behaviour is inadvertently reinforced by family members. Programmes include scheduled increases in physical exercise; reduction in pain medication usage; and arranging for hospital staff and family members to avoid reinforcing pain and sick role behaviour, while concurrently offering positive reinforcement to the client for engaging in adaptive behaviour.

Traditional cognitive behavioural pain management programmes involve: psychoeducation; training in relaxation, guided imagery, activity pacing, and pleasant event scheduling; coaching in the development of cognitive coping skills; and guided practice in using cognitive and behavioural coping strategies in real-life pain management situations (Turk & Burwinkle, In press). Effective family-based and spouse-assisted cognitive behavioural training programmes have been developed for a number of conditions including rheumatoid arthritis (Radojevic, Nicassio & Weisman, 1992) and osteoarthricit knee pain (Keefe, Caldwell & Burn, 1996). Within these programmes, spouses of people with chronic pain support them in practicing and using pain management coping skills.

With respect to service development and clinical practice, family-based pain control programmes should be offered by multidisciplinary teams on an outpatient basis to patients with a variety of chronic pain disorders that are unresponsive to pharmacological interventions.

Family Management of Older Neurologically Impaired Adults

Dementia due to Alzheimer's disease or other causes is a condition characterised by multiple cognitive deficits, notably memory impairment, and an associated decline in psychosocial functioning and capacity for independent living. The prevalence of dementia in over-65 year olds is

2–4% and in those over 85 may be as high as 20% (American Psychiatric Association, 2000).

Caring for older adults with neurological problems such as Alzheimer's disease or stroke places an extraordinary psychological burden on carers and may lead to clinically significant psychological symptomatology (Campbell, 2003). Sorensen et al. (2002) concluded from a meta-analysis of 78 studies that psychoeducational interventions consistently led to significant improvement in the psychological adjustment of caregivers. Family psychoeducational groups typically involve 8–10 educational meetings offered by a health professional and are attended by a groups of caregivers. Within the meetings, caregivers learn the skills to manage the problems they face in caring for older adults with neurological problems.

With respect to service development and clinical practice, these findings suggest that psychoeducational programmes should be made available to carers of older adults with neurological impairment as a routine part of multidisciplinary care of the elderly. Such programmes may be offered on a group basis over a relatively brief time period and include 10–20 sessions.

COMMON FACTORS

While the preceding review shows that there is good evidence now for the effectiveness of specific types of marital and family therapy and systemic interventions for specific problems, Sprenkle and Blow (2004) argue that a set of common factors and mechanisms of change underpin most forms of successful psychotherapy in general, and marital and family therapy in particular, regardless of the theoretical orientations of the therapists or the specific therapeutic techniques employed. The main common factors for which there is some empirical evidence (albeit, largely from studies of individual psychotherapy) fall into the following categories:

- the therapeutic relationship
- client factors
- therapist factors
- expectancy and hope
- non-specific treatment variables common to all forms of psychotherapy
- common factors unique to systemic practice.

In marital and family therapy, a trusting and supportive therapeutic relationship with individual family members and the family as a whole is essential for effective therapy (Carr, 2005). The most important client factors are motivation to engage in treatment and readiness to change. For effective treatment, clients must be motivated to engage in therapy and ready to make changes in their lives. Factors common to most good therapists are the fact they are well adjusted themselves; they match their activity level and style to clients' expectations and preferences; they creatively find new ways to formulate and reframe clients' problems; and they offer clients credible rationales for learning new adaptive skills for resolving problems. Along with eliciting hope and the expectation of improvement, the main non-specific factors common to most forms of psychotherapy are helping clients develop more adaptive behaviour patterns; helping clients develop more adaptive ways of thinking about their problems; and helping clients regulate their emotions and make adaptive emotional connections with themselves, their family members and the therapist. There is also a developmental sequence common to most forms of psychotherapy in which interventions that support clients (such as reassurance) precede interventions that promote learning to see problems in new ways (such as reframing) and these in turn precede interventions that promote new forms of behaviour. Three common factors are unique to all forms of systemic therapy, but differentiate it from individual approaches to psychotherapy. These are: conceptualising problems as occurring within patterns of relationships; actively involving the family and social network of the identified patient in therapy; and developing a therapeutic alliance, not just with the identified patient, but also with members of their family and social network.

CLOSING COMMENTS

A number of closing comments may be made about the material reviewed in this chapter. First, well-articulated family-based interventions have been shown to be effective for a wide range of problems. Second, with respect to child-focused problems, family-based treatments have been shown to be effective for the following list of difficulties:

- child abuse and neglect
- conduct problems, including drug abuse
- emotional problems
- psychosomatic problems.

Third, family-based treatments have been shown to be effective for the following list of adult-focused difficulties:

- marital and relationship problems
- psychosexual problems
- anxiety disorders
- mood disorders
- psychotic disorders
- alcohol abuse

- chronic pain management
- family adjustment to caring for neurologically impaired adults.

Fourth, these interventions are brief and may be offered by a range of professionals on an outpatient basis in most instances but on an inpatient basis where appropriate. Fifth, for many of the interventions, useful treatment manuals have been developed which may be flexibly used by clinicians in treating specific cases. Sixth, the bulk of family-based interventions for which there is evidence of effectiveness have been developed within the cognitive-behavioural and psychoeducational psychotherapeutic traditions. However, in my view they can be incorporated into a social-constructionist, postmodern approach to practice, provided a postmodern approach is interpreted as a therapeutic positioning rather than a set of techniques. A postmodern, social-constructionist positioning entails accepting that all models of therapy and related techniques are no more than social constructions which may be more or less useful in particular cases. Seventh, in addition to the specific interventions that are effective for specific problems, a set of common factors underpins all effective systemic therapy protocols.

The findings of this review have clear implications for both practice and training. Family therapists working with clients who present with the types of problems discussed in this chapter may benefit their clients by incorporating essential elements of effective family-based treatments into their own style of practice. With respect to training, there is a strong argument to be made for family therapy training programmes, including coaching in specific practices that have been shown to be effective in their curricula. There is also a strong argument for qualified clinicians to make learning such practices a priority when planning their own continuing professional development.

Postmodern practitioners in family therapy may object to the idea of evidence-based practice, because of the unsupported claims traditionally made by modernists about the truth or objectivity of scientific knowledge. Let me close with a response to this position. The postmodern critique of scientific knowledge does not entail an abandonment of rigorous scientific methods of enquiry. Rather, it demands that we accept the limitations of the results of such enquiry. In the same vein, a commitment to social-constructionism as an overarching framework for practice does not preclude a commitment to quantitative-based research generally and evidence-based practice in particular. Diagnostic criteria, scores on individual and family-based assessment instruments, statistical formulae, rules concerning statistical and clinical significance of results are all social-constructions. These have been evolved by communities of scientists and clinicians in conversation and have been found to fit with the needs and concerns of these scientists and clinicians. That is, they have been found to be useful, the hallmark of a valid social construction. They have been found to be useful because they let us know how to bring the collective wisdom of a community of scientists and clinicians to bear on the misery and unhappiness of any specific family that is referred to a specific clinician for treatment, or indeed any specific population served by any particular agency. To turn one's back on such collective wisdom and abandon a commitment to evidence-based practice may be unethical, insofar it deprives clients of potentially useful solutions to their problems.

GLOSSARY

Clinical significance. The clinical significance of treatment-related changes is determined by comparing the number of cases who recovered in the treatment and control groups. Not all statistically significant differences are clinically significant. For example, if after family therapy the difference between the scores of the treatment group and the untreated control group is statistically significant, but the average score for each group is still within the clinical range, then the treatment cannot be said to have had a clinically significant impact.

Control group. In a randomised controlled trial, the group that receives some alternative to the treatment the efficacy of which is being tested.

Effect size. An index of the difference between two groups in a quantitative study. In meta-analysis, an effect size is calculated for each study and these are then averaged to give an overall effect size. Effect sizes of about 0.65 after treatment and 0.52 at follow-up have been obtained in meta-analyses of marital and family therapy (Shadish & Baldwin, 2002). This indicates that the average treated case fares better than 74% of untreated cases after treatment and about 70% of cases at follow-up.

Meta-analysis. A quantitative method for combining the results from many similar studies and drawing conclusions based on the overall pattern of results.

Outcome research. Scientific study of the impact of therapy on presenting problems and personal or family adjustment in which the main focus is on differences in observations made before therapy, immediately after therapy and at some follow-up point, for example six months after therapy. Outcome research addresses questions like, *'Is this type of therapy more effective than that type of therapy?'*.

Process research. Scientific study of events that occur during the process of therapy in which the main focus is on the interaction between therapists and clients. Process research addresses questions like, 'How do therapists and clients interact during therapy?'.

Qualitative research. Scientific investigation where observations are recorded as qualitative descriptions, not numerical measurements. For example, in therapy process research, clients' views on significant events within therapy sessions may be tape recorded and transcribed with a view to identifying factors that clients identify as important within the therapeutic process.

Quantitative research. Scientific investigation where observations are recorded not as qualitative descriptions but as numerical measurements or scores. For example, in randomised controlled trials of family therapy, improvements in presenting problems may be recorded as scores on questionnaires or rating scales. Average scores after therapy of treatment and control groups may then be compared to find out how effective therapy was.

Randomised controlled trial. A research study that aims to evaluate the effectiveness of a particular treatment for a particular client group in which clients with similar problems are randomly allocated to either a treatment or control group, and assessments of participants' problems are made before and after treatment and commonly at some later follow-up point.

Statistical significance. When average scores of two groups are compared after treatment to check which group improved the most, the probability that the intergroup difference was not due to chance factors may be determined with a statistical test. If the statistical test indicates that the difference was so large that it could not have occurred by chance, then the difference is statistically significant.

Treatment group. In a randomised controlled trial, the group that receives the treatment the efficacy of which is being tested.

FURTHER READING

Sprenkle, D. (2002), *Effectiveness Research in Marriage and Family Therapy.* Alexandria, VA: American Association for Marriage and Family Therapy.

Baucom, D., Shoham, V., Mueser, K., Daiuto, A. & Stickle, T. (1998). Empirically supported couple and family interventions for marital distress and adult mental health problems. *Journal of Consulting and Clinical Psychology*, **66**, 53–88.

Chapter 19

PROFESSIONAL RESOURCES

This chapter contains guidance on accessing resources for practice, training and research. The resources fall into the following categories:

- family therapy associations
- training and supervision
- ethics
- assessment instruments
- training videotapes
- web resources
- journals
- institutes, associations and websites for specific types of family therapy and systemic interventions
- written communication in therapy
- training exercises.

FAMILY THERAPY ASSOCIATIONS

Information on training, ethics, professional issues, accreditation, conferences and continuing professional development is available from professional associations. The following is a very short list of some of the major general family therapy associations. Contact details for other associations in Europe are available from the European Family Therapy Association. Details for local divisions of the American Association for Marital and Family Therapy (AAMFT) are available from the AAMFT website. Contact details for regional family therapy associations in Australia are available at the Psychotherapy and Counselling Federation of Australia. Details of specific associations for particular types of family therapy, such as solution-focused therapy, will be given later in the chapter.

- Association for Family Therapy, UK, http://www.aft.org.uk/
- Family Therapy Association of Ireland, amdps@indigo.ie
- European Family Therapy Association, http://efta-europeanfamily-therapy.com/

- American Association for Marital and Family Therapy, USA, http://www.aamft.org/
- The Psychotherapy and Counselling Federation of Australia, http://www.pacfa.org.au/
- International Family Therapy Association, http://www.ifta-family-therapy.org/

TRAINING AND SUPERVISION

Lists of accredited family therapy training programmes, and family therapy supervisor training programmes are available from national family therapy associations listed above. The following are three important sourcebooks on supervision and training:

Liddle, H., Breunlin, D. & Schwartz, R. (1988). *Handbook of Family Therapy Training and Supervision.* New York: Guilford.

Todd, T. & Storm, C. (1999). *The Complete Systemic Supervisor.* Needham Heights, MA: Allyn Bacon.

Whiffen, R. & Byng-Hall, J. (1982). *Family Therapy Supervision.* New York: Grune & Stratton

ETHICS

The practice of family therapy is guided by the professional code of ethics of the professional association of the jurisdiction within which practice is conducted. Ethics is the study of good and bad human conduct. A professional code of ethics is a statement of appropriate conduct for a professional. Codes of ethics of family therapy associations in the USA, the UK and Ireland are listed at the end of this section. Professional codes of ethics protect clients, therapists and others from bad practice. Codes of ethics for family therapy reflect the dominant morality within society, the goals and values of the profession, and current professional standards of practice. Codes of ethics also specify how breaches of these codes are to be addressed.

Ethical management of consent to treatment is a particularly important area for family therapists in training. It is currently good ethical practice to inform clients about:

- the service offered
- the qualifications of the therapists and trainees and the supervisory arrangements
- procedures for fee payment, cancellations and emergencies
- confidentiality of the content of sessions, except where maintaining confidentially would cause significant harm to the clients or others.

It is also good practice to ask for written consent from family members to videotape therapy sessions and to specify who may view the video tapes. A sample consent form covering most of these issues is given in Figure 7.2. It is good practice to obtain separate consent for the following videotape audiences: therapy team and supervisor; other therapists within the therapy facility; other therapists within the country; other therapists in other countries.

It is good practice to work within the limits of one's competence and take guidance from supervisors as appropriate, supervise trainees adequately, keep all records and notes confidential, refer clients for other services where appropriate, avoid sexual contact with clients, and prevent clients from harming themselves or others.

Common ethical dilemmas include having one family member ask that the therapist keep certain information confidential from other family members or having different values than clients about issues, such as abortion, masturbation or drug use. In making ethical decisions, therapists should specify the ethical dilemma; gather relevant information; and discuss the matter in supervision. They should then make a decision based on the professional code and in line with basic ethical principles. Such principles include doing no harm, being just, honouring commitments to others, and respecting others. Finally it is good practice to monitor the impact of the ethical decision and modify it if necessary in light of new information.

Malpractice claims may occur where therapists do not practice ethically. Common types of malpractice claims include: failure to obtain informed consent; negligent treatment; practicing outside one's area of competence; failure to supervise students adequately; failure to consult another practitioner or make a referral where this is appropriate; sexual contact with patients; and failure to prevent patients harming themselves or others.

The following are important sources on ethical issues:

Woody, J. & Woody, R. (2001). *Ethics in Marriage and Family Therapy.* Washington, DC: AAMFT.

American Association of Marital and Family Therapy, AAMFT Code of Ethics, The American Association For Marital and Family Therapy, http://www.aamft.org/. This is the main code of ethics in use in the USA.

Association or Family Therapy, AFT Code of Ethics, http://www.aft.org.uk/. This is the main code of ethics in use in the UK.

Family Therapy Association of Ireland, FTAI Code of Ethics, amdps@indigo.ie. This is the main code of ethics in use in Ireland.

ASSESSMENT INSTRUMENTS

In this era of evidence-based practice, with the increasing focus on monitoring treatment outcome, it may be helpful to use scientifically valid assessment instruments that quantify changes in marital and family functioning and symptoms of adults and children. Some advice on such instruments is given in this section.

Assessment Reference Work

Of the dozens of volumes on family assessment instruments, I have found the following two sets of books the most useful:

Corcoran, K. & Fischer, J. (2000). *Measures for Clinical Practice: A Sourcebook. Vol. 1: Couples, Families and Children*, and *Vol. 2: Adults*, 3rd edn. New York: Free Press. These books contain full copies of a wide range of very useful measures of aspects of couple and family functioning as well as measures of individual symptoms in children and adults. This is a valuable resource for busy clinicians.

Touliatos, J., Perlmutter, B. & Strauss, M. (2001). *Handbook of Family Measurement Techniques, Vols. 1, 2 and 3*. Thousand Oaks, CA: Sage. Volumes 1 and 2 include abstracts of over 1000 family measurement instruments preceded by overviews that organise and review the instruments in each chapter. Volume 3 contains full copies of 168 of the instruments abstracted in Volumes 1 and 2. The three-volume set is a useful reference work for family researchers.

Family Assessment Instruments

The following are some standardised questionnaires and rating scales that may be useful in family therapy practice and research. There are thousands of such instruments, so the following shortlist reflects an idiosyncratic selection based on my impression of scientific merit and user-friendliness. Of them all, I have found the FAD the most useful.

McMaster Family Assessment Device (FAD), McMaster Clinical Rating Scale (MCRS) and the *McMaster Structured Interview for family Functioning (McSIFF)* by I. Miller, N. Epstein, D. Bishop & G. Keitner, are available from Ivan W. Miller, PhD, Department of Psychiatry and Human Behaviour, Brown University, Potter 3, Rhode Island Hospital, 593 Eddy Street, Providence, RI 02903, USA. The FAD and MCRS measure problem-solving, communication, roles, affective responsiveness, affective involvement and behaviour control, the principal dimensions of the McMaster Model of Family Functioning. The McSIFF allows inexperienced clinicians to gather sufficient data from families to make ratings using the MCRS.

Family Assessment Measure – III (FAM III) by H. Skinner, P. Steinhauer & J. Santa-Barbara is available from Multi Health Systems: http://www.mhs.com/. It is based on the family process model. It measures task accomplishment, role performance, communication, affective expression, involvement, control, values and norms. It provides measures of these dimensions at three levels: whole family system (General Scale, 50 items), various dyadic relationships (Dyadic Scale, 42 items), and individual functioning (Self-Rating Scale, 42 items). Brief FAMs (14 items) are available for each scale as well. The FAM has been normed on 300 cases.

Family Environment Scale (FES) by R. Moos is available at http://www. mindgarden.com/products/fescs.htm. The FES yields 10 scores in three domains. In the system maintenance domain there are scores for organisation and control. In the relationship domain, there are scores for cohesion, expressiveness and conflict. In the personal growth domain there are scores for independence, achievement orientation, intellectual-cultural orientation, active-recreational orientation and moral-religious emphasis. The scale was developed and normed in the USA.

Parent Child Relationship Inventory (PCRI) by A. Gerard is available from Western Psychological Services: http://www.wpspublish.com/. It includes 70 items and measures parental support, satisfaction with parenting, involvement, communication, limit setting, autonomy, role orientation. Standardised on 1100 parents in the USA.

Beavers Interactional Scales and Self Report Family Inventory are contained in W. Beavers and R. Hampson (1990) *Successful Families: Assessment and Intervention.* New York: W.W. Norton. The rating scale and self-report instrument measure family competence and family style. They are based on the Beaver's Family System model. The scales have been normed on over 1800 families in north America.

The Family Adaptability and Cohesion Rating Scales (FACES) and the *Circumplex Model Clinical Rating Scale (CRS)* and related instruments by D. Olson are available from Life Innovations: http://www.facesiv.com/studies/fip.html. These scales measure family adaptability and family cohesion, the two principal dimensions of the Circumplex model of family functioning. They have been developed and normed in the USA.

Marital Assessment Instruments

The following are some standardised questionnaires and rating scales that may be useful in marital therapy practice and research. This short-list reflects an idiosyncratic selection based on my impression of scientific merit and user-friendliness. Of them all I have found the MSI-R the most useful.

Marital Satisfaction Inventory-Revised (MSI-R) by D. Snyder is available from Western Psychological Services: http://www.wpspublish.com/. It contains 150 items and measures affective communication, role orientation, problem-solving communication, aggression, family history of distress, time together, dissatisfaction with children, disagreement about finances, conflict over child rearing, sexual dissatisfaction, global distress. It has been developed and normed in the USA.

The Golombok Rust Inventory of Marital State (GRIMS) is available at Sales@ citypsychometrics.co.uk. The male and female versions of this 28-item questionnaire are identical and yield an overall score of marital quality for the male and female partner separately. It has been developed and normed in the UK.

The Golombok Rust Inventory of Sexual Satisfaction (GRISS) is available at Sales@citypsychometrics.co.uk. This 28-item questionnaire assesses sexual dysfunction. The female version produces scores of anorgasmia, vaginismus, non-communication, infrequency, avoidance, non-sensuality and dissatisfaction, as well as a total score. The male version produces scores of impotence, premature ejaculation, non-communication, infrequency, avoidance, non-sensuality and dissatisfaction, as well as a total score. It has been developed and normed in the UK.

Oregon Marital Assessment Instruments are available from Dr Robert L. Weiss, Oregon Marital Assessment Service, 3003 Willamette Street Suite F, Eugene, OR 97405, USA, http://www.perry-psych.com/order02.htm. This suite of instruments covers a wide range of marital issues and processes and have been developed and normed in the USA.

Adult Assessment Instruments

These two brief instruments assess a broad range of common mental health problems in adults and, as they are sensitive to change over time, they are a good way to assess changes in adult presenting problems over the course of therapy. The CORE was developed in the UK and the SCL-90 in the USA.

CORE System is available free on the CORE website: http://www.coreims. co.uk/ This main CORE instrument is a 34-item questionnaire, which yields scores for subjective well-being; problems and symptoms; personal functioning; and current risk to self or others.

The Symptom Checklist 90 (SCL-90) has been developed by Leonard Derogatis in the US to assess adult mental health problems and is available at http://www.pearsonassessments.com/tests/scl90r.htm. It yields scores for somatisation, obsessive-compulsive symptoms, interpersonal sensitivity, depression, anxiety, hostility, phobic anxiety, paranoid ideation and psychoticism. There is a parallel clinician rated version of the SCL-90-R and briefer 53- and 18-item self-report versions.

Child Assessment Instruments

These two brief instruments assess a broad range of common behavioural problems in children and, as they are sensitive to change over time, they are a good way to assess changes in child and adolescent presenting problems over the course of therapy. The SDQ was developed in the UK and the ASEBA in the USA.

Strengths and Difficulties Questionnaire (SDQ) has been developed by Robert Goodman in the UK to assess problems in children aged 5–15. The SDQ is available free at http://www.sdqinfo.com/. There are parent, teacher and self-report versions of the SDQ. Each contain about 25 items and yield scores for conduct, emotional, hyperactive and peer problems and prosocial behaviour.

Achenbach System for Empirically Based Assessment (ASEBA) has been developed by Tom Achenbach in the USA for assessing problems in children 1.5–18 years. ASEBA instruments are available at http://www.aseba.org/. There are parent, teacher, self-report and clinician versions of ASEBA instruments. Each of the ASEBA instruments contains about 110 items and yields a total problem score, scores for internalising and externalising behaviour problems; scores for up to eight empirically derived syndromes; and scores for DSM oriented scales.

TRAINING VIDEOTAPES

Family therapy was one of the first approaches to psychotherapy in which expert therapists demonstrated their techniques to those in training through the use of videotaped therapy sessions. Useful training videos and DVDs are available from the following list of sources.

AAMFT Master Series, which includes tapes by Michael White and Steve de Shazer, is available at AAMFT 112 South Alfred Street, Alexandria, VA 22314-3061, USA, http://www.audio-digest.org/cgi-bin/htmlos/0373.2.1850368359116603685

Ackerman family therapist videotapes on infertility, secrets, depression and other issues are available at Nathan Ackerman Institute of Family Therapy, 149 East 78th Street, New York, NY 10021, USA, http://www.ackerman.org/tapes.htm

Behavioural family therapy tapes are available from Research Press, 2612 N Mattis Avenue, Champaign, IL 68182, USA, http://www.research-press.com/

Doug Snyder's videotapes on couples therapy and a range of other tapes on working with coupes and sex therapy are available in the APA Videotape series 4, available at the American Psychological Association, 750 First St, NE, Washington, DC 20002-4242, USA, http://www.apa.org/videos/series4.html

Emotionally Focused Couples Therapy videotapes are available from Susan Johnson Ottawa Couple and Family Institute, 1869 Carling Avenue, Ottawa, Ontario, K2A 1E6, Canada, http://www.eft.ca/

Functional Family Therapy videotapes are available in the APA Videotape series 4 at the American Psychological Association, 750 First St, NE, Washington, DC 20002-4242, USA, http://www.apa.org/videos/series4.html

Golden triad films, associated with the Family Institute Kansas, has a series of tapes of expert family therapists including Carl Whittaker and Virginia Satir and the tapes are available at http://www.goldentriad-films.com/films/theory.htm

Insoo Kim Berg Tapes Solution-Focused Therapy Tapes for working with addiction are available at Norton Book Publishers, 500 Fifth Avenue, New York, NY 10110, USA, http://www.wwnorton.com/NPB/nppsych/cat/addict.htm

Jay Haley Videotapes on strategic therapy are available at http://members.aol.com/prizefilm/videos.htm

Monica McGoldricks videotapes are available at Multicultural Family Institute, 328 Denison St, Highland Park, NJ 08904, USA, http://www.multiculturalfamily.org/text/books_videos.shtml

Murray Bowen's archive of videotapes are available at the Bowen Centre for Study of the, Georgetown Family Centre, 4400 MacArthur Blvd NW, Suite 103, Washington, DC 20007-2521, USA, http://www.thebowencenter.org/pages/av2.html

Philadelphia Child and Family Therapy Training Centre has a range of videotapes which are available at Inc. P.O. Box 4092, Philadelphia, PA 19118-8092, USA, http://www.philafamily.com/

Psychotherapy videotapes are available at http://psychotherapy.net/

The Minuchin Centre for Family Therapy has tapes on structural family therapy at 114 East 32nd Street, New York, NY 10021, USA, http://www.minuchincenter.org/

Virginia Satir tapes are available from AVANTA, the Virginia Satir network 2104 SW 152nd St, Burien, Washington 98166-2064, USA, http://www.avanta.net/BookStore/Video/Video.htm

WEB RESOURCES

The following sites give information on web-based resources for family therapists.

General Educational Sites for Therapists

Marital and family therapy resources on the web: http://www.e-help.com/family_and_marriage_therapy.htm

History and key figures in FT. http://www.abacon.com/famtherapy/

An introductory guide to FT: http://www.guidetopsychology.com/famlytx.htm

Gregory Bateson: http://www.indiana.edu/~wanthro/bateson.htm

Genograms

Genoware genogram software for sale: http://www.genogram.org/
Genograns for personal use: http://genogram.freeservers.com/index.html

Therapy Manuals

Alexander, J., Barton, C., Gordon, D., Grotpeter, J., Hansson, K., Harrison, R., Mears, S., Mihalic, S., Parsons, B., Pugh, C., Schulman, S., Waldron, H. & Sexton, T. (1998). *Blueprints for Violence Prevention, Book Three: Functional Family Therapy (FFT)*. Boulder, CO: Centre for the Study and Prevention of Violence. Available at http://www.colorado.edu/cspv/publications/blueprints.html

Henggeler, S., Mihalic, S., Rone, L., Thomas, C. & Timmons-Mitchell, J. (1998). *Blueprints for Violence Prevention, Book Six: Multisystemic Therapy (MST)*. Boulder, CO: Centre for the Study and Prevention of Violence. Available at http://www.colorado.edu/cspv/publications/blueprints.html

Liddle, H. A. (2005). *Multidimensional Family Therapy for Adolescent Substance Abuse*. New York: Norton. A version of this book is available at www.chestnut.org/LI/cyt/products/MDFT_CYT_v5.pdf

Pote, H., Stratton, P., Cottrell, D., Boston, P., Shapiro, D. & Hanks, H. (2000). *Leeds Systemic Family Therapy Manual*. Leeds: Leeds Family Therapy & Research Centre, University of Leeds. Available at http://www.psyc.leeds.ac.uk/research/lftrc/index.htm

Szapocznik, J., Hervis, O. & Schwartz, S. (2002). *Brief Strategic Family Therapy for Adolescent Drug Abuse*. Rockville, MD: National Institute for Drug Abuse. Available at http://www.drugabuse.gov/TXManuals/bsft/BSFTIndex.html

Treatment manual for O'Farrell's behavioural couples therapy and Meyers's community reinforcement approach for problem drinkers are available at http://www.bhrm.org/guidelines/addguidelines.htm

Self-help Material for Clients

Speechmark (self-help): http://www.speechmark.net/
Smallwood (self-help): http://www.smallwood.co.uk/
Self-help resources: http://www.psywww.com/resource/selfhelp.htm

JOURNALS

The following are some of the main marital and family therapy journals and magazines. Through these, new ideas about concepts, process, practice and research are shared within local and global family therapy communities.

Australian and New Zealand Journal of Family Therapy, http://www.anzjft.com/

Contemporary Family Therapy, http://www.springeronline.com/sgw/cda/frontpage/0,11855,5-10126-70-35536948-0,00.html

Context, the UK, AFT Magazine, http://www.aft.org.uk/context/context.html

Family Process, http://www.blackwellpublishing.com/journal.asp?ref=0014-7370

Family Systems & Health, http://www.apa.org/journals/fsh/

Feedback, c/o Family Therapy Association of Ireland, amdps@indigo.ie

Human Systems: Journal of Systemic Consultation and Management, http://www.kcc-international.com/inforec/hs/index2002.htm

Journal of Couples and Relationship Therapy, http://www.haworthpress.com/store/product.asp?sku=J036

Journal of Family Psychology, http://www.apa.org/journals/fam/

Journal of Family Psychotherapy, http://www.ifta-familytherapy.org/journal.html

Journal of Family Therapy, http://www.blackwellpublishing.com/journal.asp?ref=0163-4445

Journal of Feminist Family Therapy, http://www.haworthpress.com/store/product.asp?sku=J086

Journal of Marital and Family Therapy, http://www.aamft.org/jmft/index_main.asp

Journal of Narrative Therapy and Community Work, http://www.dulwichcentre.com.au/intjournal.html

Journal of Sex and Marital Therapy, http://www.tandf.co.uk/journals/titles/0092623X.asp

Psychotherapy Networker, http://www.psychotherapynetworker.org/

Sexual and Relationship Therapy, http://www.tandf.co.uk/journals/titles/14681994.asp

The American Journal of Family Therapy, http://www.tandf.co.uk/journals/titles/01926187.asp

INSTITUTES, ASSOCIATIONS AND WEBSITES FOR SPECIFIC TYPES OF FAMILY THERAPY AND SYSTEMIC INTERVENTIONS

In this section, websites of institutes and associations have been grouped in the first instance into three categories corresponding to the divisions used in Chapters 3–5. The first section lists websites relevant to family therapy traditions that emphasise the role of problem-maintaining behaviour patterns, specifically MRI, structural, strategic, cognitive-behavioural, and functional family therapy. The second section contains websites relevant to family therapy traditions that emphasise the role of belief systems, specifically constructivisit, Milan-systemic, social constructionist, solution-focused and narrative family therapy. The third section lists websites relevant to family therapy traditions that emphasise the role of predisposing historical and contextual factors, specifically transgenerational, psychodynamic, attachment-oriented, experiential and multisystemic family therapy. Finally, lists of websites for other important institutes, associations for sex therapy, and sites that contain information on evidence-based approaches to parent training are given.

Family Therapy Traditions that Emphasise the Role of Problem-Maintaining Behaviour Patterns: MRI, Structural, Strategic, Cognitive-behavioural, and Functional Family Therapy

Mental Research Institute, Palo Alto, California, USA, http://www.mri.org/
Minuchin Family Therapy Centre, USA, http://www.minuchincenter.org/
Jose Szapocznik's strategic therapy family studies centre, http://www.cfs.med.miami.edu/
Jay Haley's Strategic therapy, http://www.jay-haley-on-therapy.com/
Cloe Madanes's Strategic Therapy, http://www.cloemadanes.com/
British Association for Cognitive and Behavioural Psychotherapies, http://www.babcp.com/
European Association for Behavioural and Cognitive Therapies, http://www.eabct.com/
Association for Advancement of Behaviour Therapy, http://www.aabt.org/
National Association for Cognitive Behavioural Therapists, http://www.nacbt.org/
Functional family therapy, jfafft@psych.utah.edu, http://www.fftinc.com/

Family Therapy Traditions that Emphasise the Role of Belief Systems: Constructivist, Milan-systemic, Social Constructionist, Solution-focused and Narrative Family Therapy

Constructivist psychology network, USA, http://www.constructivistpsych.org
European Personal Construct Association, http://www.pcp-net.org/epca/
Karnac Books-Systemic Therapy Series, http://www.karnacbooks.com/
Harlene Anderson's Houston-Galveston Institute, http://www.houston-galvestoninstitute.org/
Solution-Focused Brief Therapy Association, http://www.sfbta.org/
European Brief Therapy Association, http://www.ebta.nu/
deShazer's Solution-Focused Brief Family Therapy Centre, http://www.brief-therapy.org/people.htm
Solution-focused therapy in the UK, http://www.brieftherapy.org.uk/about_index.php
Solution-focused therapy in Ireland, http://www.brieftherapy.ie/
Miller & Duncan's solution-focused therapy, http://www.talkingcure.com/
Bill O'Hanlon's brief therapy website, http://brieftherapy.com/

Brief Therapy Institute of Sydney, http://www.brieftherapysydney.com.
au/index.html

Dulwich Centre for Narrative Therapy, Australia, http://www.dulwich-
centre.com.au/

Family Therapy Traditions that Emphasise the Role of Predisposing Historical and Contextual Factors: Transgenerational, Psychodynamic, Attachment, Experiential and Multisystemic Family Therapy

Bowen Centre, http://www.thebowencenter.org/pages/av2.html

Scharff & Scharff's International Psychotherapy Institute, which teaches
object relations-based couple and family therapy, http://iiort.velocity-
pack.com/

Emotionally Focused Couple Therapy, http://www.eft.ca/

Virgaina Satir Centre – Avanta, http://www.satir.org/

Multisystemic family therapy, http://www.mstservices.com/

Other Family Therapy Institutes

Clanwilliam Institute, Dublin, Ireland, http://www.clanwilliam.ie/

Institute for Family Therapy, UK, http://www.instituteoffamilytherapy.
org.uk/

Leeds Family Therapy and Research Centre and Peter Stratton's homep-
age, http://www.psyc.leeds.ac.uk/staff/p.m.stratton/

Ackerman Institute, USA, http://www.ackerman.org/

Monica McGoldricks Multicultural Centre, http://www.multiculturalfa-
mily.org/

Sex Therapy

British Association for Sexual and Relationship Therapy, http://www.
basmt.org.uk/

American Association for sex educators, counsellors and therapists,
http://www.aasect.org/

Parent Training for Childhood Conduct Problems

Parenting Plus, Ireland, http://www.parentsplus.ie, email:admin@parent-
splus.ie

Incredible, USA, http://www.incredibleyears.com/

Parenting Wisely, USA, http://www.familyworksinc.com/

WRITTEN COMMUNICATION IN THERAPY

Written communication may be used as a resource in family therapy. Letters may be used to help clients remember what was said during consultation, and to highlight key aspects of the sessions. Letters can provide a medium for involving other members of the system in the therapeutic process, including absent family members, the referring agent and involved professionals. Letters may be used as a medium for reframing problems. Correspondence between family members may be encouraged to help family members change roles. Children may be invited to engage in correspondence with imaginary characters as a way of receiving new ideas about how to change their situation. Letters may be used to tell youngsters parables, which may offer them a different perspective on how to cope with difficulties. Letters may also be used to address unfinished business.

Letters as Aids to Memory

Any aspect of the consultation process may be recapped in a letter. Here, the function of the letter is to help family members remember what has happened in the session. Thus, letters can be used to give family members a written account of the formulation, a summary of what has taken place in a session, details of the therapy contract, a reframing of some aspect of their problem, a summary of tasks they have been invited to complete or administrative information about appointments, other relevant services, and so forth.

Letters as a Way of Including the Referrer in the Consultation Process

Following assessment, therapists typically write to the referring agent to explain both the formulation and the direction the consultation process will take. Sufficient detail must be given so that the referring agent's interaction with clients will facilitate rather than hinder problem resolution.

Letters as a Method for Including Absent Members in the Session

Sometimes, important family members cannot attend a consultation. What follows is a letter to the father of a child whose parents were separated, asking for his views on how the next access visit should be arranged. The mother had custody of the boy and lived a considerable distance form the father. The boy's loyalty was divided between his mother and father and he was unable to commit himself to spending the Easter break with his father.

Dear Frank

Harry was referred to me recently by Dr Connors, the GP. He has been having nightmares and some problems with bullying at school. The bullying has been taken care of, but the nightmares continue. They seem to be related to a dilemma he faces this Easter.

Recently, he has said that he is in two minds about spending all of his Easter holidays at your place. On the one hand, he really wants to see you and spend as much time with you as possible because he misses you a lot. On the other, he does not want to make his mother feel lonely by staying away too long. Marion, as you know, is happy for him to spend the full two weeks with you. However, Harry fears that you will be angry if he needs to come home a few days early. This is worrying him so much, that sometimes he doubts if he should go at all and gets these bad dreams.

I cannot make a judgement about whether it would be in his best interests to go without your views. It would help me to help your son manage his nightmares if you would write an open letter that we can read in the next consultation giving your view on these matters.

I look forward to hearing from you.

Yours sincerely

Alan Carr

Frank, sent the following reply which freed Harry to make a decision to visit him with the proviso that he could come home a few days early if he felt disloyal to his mother.

Dear Alan

Harry should not be afraid to visit me. I want him to stay two weeks here. I have a new fishing rod for him and I hope that we can do that big trip we always planned. But if he has to go home to see his mother, I will not argue. I have told Marion this before but she doesn't believe me. I will not argue and Harry must understand that.

Our visits have always been good. The last time he was here we went to the lake nearly every day.

I am sorry that he was bullied in school. He needs a man to show him how to defend himself. I will show him some judo when he comes up to visit.

Tell Harry, that I will phone him soon.

Yours Sincerely

Frank

This example illustrates how letters may be used as a way of including distant family members in the consultation process.

Reframing Letters

The following letter was sent to the parents of an encopretic boy who were seen briefly at the request of a paediatrician for a consultation which was interrupted before a formulation or reframing could be given. The 11-year-old boy was referred with a five-month history of soiling. His parents were interpreting the soiling as veiled aggression. This way of making sense of the encopresis was informed by a television documentary which they had seen. The letter offers a plausible reframing of the soiling as a conditioned response to an anal fissure compounded by the later use of laxatives. Responsibility for the symptom is taken away from the boy and the parents, through this essentially mechanical reframing of the problem.

Dear Barry and Sally

Unfortunately I did not have time today to give you feedback on our session, so I am writing to you now to offer an opinion. You asked today if Bernard was soiling because he didn't want to grow up. You speculated that he wanted to remain a baby like Caris. You guessed that the soiling was his way of being angry at your attempts to encourage him to grow up. That is one viewpoint. There is another possibility. It is complicated but it seems to fit with the information I got from the GP this afternoon in addition to the ground we covered in our session this morning.

(1) Bernard unfortunately developed an anal fissure a year ago. A sore bottom. Anytime he tried to go to the toilet it was very painful. So, his unconscious told him not to. It said 'Don't go to the toilet. Its too painful'.

(2) When he didn't go for a while he got all blocked up. He developed a big faecal mass in his lower intestines and colon.

(3) Then you gave him a laxative. This melted the edge of the mass and it dribbled out.

(4) There was a fight about this and Bernard got anxious and his unconscious said to him 'Don't go to the toilet. it only leads to trouble'. The faecal mass grew even bigger.

(5) The process repeated again and again.

This process is nobody's fault. Just an unfortunate situation. I've spoken to the Paediatrician, Dr Connors, who will be happy to check the state of Bernard's faecal mass and advise on how best to get rid of it. After that we can develop a plan to prevent this happening again. You will hear from the Paediatrics Department shortly.

Yours sincerely

Dr Alan Carr

This letter was pivotal in changing the way in which the parents, Barry and Sally, viewed their son, Bernard. In the second session, which followed the receipt of the letter, the quality of the parent–child relationship had changed radically. Discussion focused on the implications of the reframing of the problem presented in the letter. The aggression, hostility and resentment, which precluded negotiation and problem-solving in the first session, dissipated. With much humour and good will, the family responded to a suggestion that an enema be arranged, in conjunction with the referring paediatrician, to remove the faecal mass, and that this be followed up with a simple star chart programme.

Letters to Facilitate Role Change

Letters can be used explicitly to facilitate changes in family members' roles. Brian, a 17-year-old boy, was referred with headaches, which were interfering with his study and sports. The headaches occurred when he overheard his parents arguing. His parents, resolved their differences through loud and dramatic arguments in which crockery was occasionally broken. As part of therapy I helped the parents, Sharon and Trevor, compose the following letter, which they read to Brian and asked him to keep it on the notice board in his room as a reminder that the arguments were a sign of their commitment to each other rather than impending divorce.

> *Brian*
>
> *We know that you have been worrying about us arguing.*
>
> *We are sorry that the worry causes you to have headaches.*
>
> *We want you to stop worrying so your headaches will go away.*
>
> *We want you to know that when we argue, this does not mean that we are going to separate. It means that we have different opinions and we need to talk about that. Arguing is a sign that we care about each other. We need to argue with each other from time to time.*
>
> *If you don't like the sound of us arguing we will not be offended if you listen to your iPod or go out for a walk.*
>
> *Thank you for worrying about us but now you deserve a break from it.*
>
> *Love*
>
> *Mum and Dad*

Letters from Imaginary Authors

Occasionally, I have enlisted the aid of imaginary authors in the treatment of children. Bozz is one of my favourite. He is an expert at helping youngsters *boss their Hammermen about*. When children have temper control difficulties and routine behavioural control programmes have not worked or the parents oppose such approaches, the aggressive impulses are personified as the *Hammerman*, or some other character. The child is then given advice on how to control the Hammerman from Bozz, a fictitious character with whom they find it easy to identify. They are encouraged to develop a correspondence with him. Below is a letter from Bozz to Tom, an eight-year-old boy referred with temper control problems. This is just one part of an ongoing correspondence, which lasted six weeks. The use of imaginary authors like Bozz allows the therapists to adopt a position where they can comment to the youngster and the parents about the correspondence their child is having with Bozz.

Dear Tom

I know that you want to keep the Hammerman from getting you into trouble. So here is what you can do. You can take him down to the end of the garden every morning at 8.15 before school and every evening at 4.00 and get him to whack the tennis ball against the wall until he's too tired to do any more. If he tries to get you into trouble with your sister say to him Hammerman hold it!

If you can't control him, ask your mum if you can go down to the end of the garden and let Hammerman whack the ball up against the wall.

Write and tell me how you got on.

Bozz

Parables

The use of parables, myths and fairy tales to help people find solutions to problems of living is a custom that has its roots in the oral storytelling tradition. Within the family therapy field, Milton Erickson has played a major part in the integration of this ancient tradition into modern clinical practice (Haley, 1973). The key to using parables in a clinical situation is to take the salient elements of the client's situation and build them into a story which arrives at a conclusion that offers the client an avenue for productive change rather than a painful cul-de-sac. The story is a metaphor for the client's dilemma, a metaphor that offers a solution. Such stories may be sent to clients as letters. The story below was sent to, Sabina, a seven-year-old girl who was referred because of recurrent nightmares in which she dreamt that her house was being burgled and her parents assaulted. The nightmares followed an actual burglary of the family's shop, over which they lived. The girl dealt with the nightmares by climbing onto the end of her parents bed when she awoke at night. She tried not to wake them and distracted herself by thinking of something other than the nightmares. During the day she refused to talk about the nightmares or the burglary. To some degree, her parents encouraged this process of denial. Sabina was in the Brownies and was learning about first aid when she was referred. Here is the letter and story I sent her.

Dear Sabina

I really liked the pictures you did today. They gave me a clear idea of the sort of stuff you have been seeing in your dreams. I like the way you draw. Just to say thank you, here is the story I told you today. If some of the words are too hard just ask your mum or dad and they will let you know what they mean. See you in two weeks.

Bye now.

Alan Carr

The Two Brownies

Two brownies were on an adventure in the woods. They decided to have a race. They were both the same height and looked alike except that one had blond hair like yours and one had dark hair. While they were racing they both tripped over the same branch at the same time and each of them cut their knee. The cuts hurt a lot and both girls felt like crying. The dark haired girl tried to stop herself from crying and her leg hurt more. The blond girl allowed herself to cry and felt relieved. The crying made her knee hurt less. Both girls went to the stream and bathed their cuts. Both girls had small first-aid kits in their pockets. The dark haired girl put a bandage from her kit on her cut straightaway. The blond girl could have done this also but she did not. She let the air get at her cut. Both girls went home for tea. After tea they went to bed. The dark haired girl couldn't sleep because the cut hurt so much. She turned on the light. She took off the bandage and noticed that the cut had become infected. It was all yellow with pus. The dark haired girl washed the cut quickly and put on another bandage over the pus. The blond girl woke in the middle of the night because her knee was hurting her. She woke her mum and her mum helped her bathe the cut in hot water to draw the pus out. This was painful, but she knew it would make her better. Three days later her cut was healed. But her friend was still wearing a bandage. Her knee still had pus in it. She still woke up in the middle of the night with the pain.

THE END

This story I sent Sabina took account of her interest in first aid and racing. A physical trauma (cutting her knee) was used as a metaphor for the psychological trauma she had suffered (being burgled). The story included one course of action taken by the dark haired girl which resembled the pattern of coping she had adopted. It also contained an alternative. This other more adaptive route was taken by the blond girl; the girl whose hair was the same colour as Sabina's. This detail was included to make it easy for Sabina to identify with her. The story reframed Sabina's dilemma from 'How can I distract myself from memories of the robbery and get rid of these nightmares so I can feel good?' to 'How can I squeeze all of this psychological pus out of my mind so the wound will heal?'. This reframing offered a new avenue for coping.

Unfinished Business

Where adults have been hurt or traumatised during childhood by their parents or others and these issues remain unresolved; or where family members have suffered bereavement and left many important things unsaid, they may be invited to write letters as a way of resolving their unfinished business. It is important that clients make a private time and place to write such letters; that they vividly imagine the other person and their feelings towards them as they write; that they express themselves in a spontaneous emotive way without mentally editing what they write; and that they know that they will never send the letter they write to the person they are writing to. These types of letters allow clients to re-experience strong emotions that have not been fully processed and to alter the way they view their relationship to those to whom they write. The letters may be read aloud with full emotional expression in therapy sessions to enhance the degree to which they facilitate processing unresolved emotional states.

TRAINING EXERCISES

The following series of five exercises offer trainers and trainees a way of developing the family therapy skills described in Chapters 7, 8 and 9. They are designed to be used over five or six half-day practical workshops. These workshops are most usefully run after the group of therapists in training have read and attended classes on Chapters 1–9 and Chapter 18.

Exercise 1 – Intake Interviewing

Ex 1. Setting up the Exercise

Required reading for this exercise is Chapters 7 and 8. To set up the exercise, invite the class to separate into a (role-play) family of four members and a therapy team (of 2–8 members). If there are more than 12 in the class, divide the class into a role-play family and a number of teams with about four members on each team. Just before the interview, randomly select one of the teams to conduct the interview and invite the other teams to be spectators.

Ask the family and team to take 20 minutes to prepare for the exercise, in separate rooms if possible. Then run the exercise for about 40 minutes. Bring refreshments (coffee, tea, soft drinks) into the session, but do not take a 20-minute break as this will cause the family to de-role, which will greatly reduce the value of the debriefing. Then do the post-session debriefing for no more than 40 minutes. If you schedule two hours, and stick strictly to this time schedule of 20 minute preparation – 40 minutes interviewing – and 40 minutes debriefing, you can let the class off 20 minutes early! If you break after the role-play, the debriefing will not work because the role-play family will have de-roled during the break.

Ask the family to get into role and ask the team to plan who will do the different parts of the interview. It's a better learning experience if as many members of the team as is practical take a turn at interviewing. However, advise the therapy team that there is no need to redo introductions each time a new team member takes on the therapist role, since this lengthens the exercise unnecessarily. Let the group role-playing the family know that the therapist will change a few times in the session and at these transitions, to save time, the family should remain 'frozen' until the new therapist takes over the interviewing. Ask the family to pretend all the interviewing is done by a single person.

In setting up the exercise don't get sidetracked into talking about the value of the exercise, how 'fake' it is, etc. Once the role-play element of the exercise beings, it takes on a life of its own.

During the planning stage of the exercise, check in with the family and the team from time to time to make sure they have understood the briefing and are completing the process of getting into role and planning the interview.

During the interview stage of the exercise, intervene as little as possible. However, it may be appropriate from time to time, to say 'freeze' as a signal that the family will pretend that time has frozen, and to use this interlude to offer 'live supervision' to the therapist and team on how to proceed. When the therapist and team are 'back on track', say 'unfreeze' and the therapist and family can pick up the interview where they left off.

Ex 1. Brief for the Family

Four people take on the roles of the family members: June is the mother, Martin is the father, Mary is the daughter and Frank is the son. (Of course you may use more ethnically appropriate names if you decide to conduct this exercise role-playing a family from another culture.) Try to complete the process of getting into role in 20 minutes. Use the skeleton roles below to get in role and decide among yourselves the patterns of interaction within which the problem occurs and the exceptional circumstances where it does not. Also develop and discuss beliefs that family members have that underpin these two different types of episodes. Then develop an imaginary family history and genogram in which there are predisposing factors or events that explain where family member's beliefs came from historically and also within the wider community in which the family have lived and are currently living.

When I facilitate this exercise with clinical psychology postgraduates at UCD, Dublin, I usually suggest the family has moved from London in the UK to Dublin in Ireland, because this is a cultural transition most postgraduates understand. However, it would be fine to conduct the exercise modelling it on a Polish family moving to Coventry, an Indian family moving to Washington, or a Maori family moving to Sydney.

In this family, the mother, June, is overwhelmed by demands of making family life work in the new town and country to which she has recently moved. She misses her own family of origin but sticks by the decision to move to this new town and country because it is best for the family's financial viability. June is very concerned about Mary. She also wishes Martin was less consumed by his work. June has certain character strengths and skills which need to be elaborated and discussed with the family as you are getting into your roles.

In this family the father, Martin, is swamped by responsibilities of a new job and there is latitude for you to make this job whatever you wish, for example, a manager; a computer programmer; a scientist; a physician; a waiter; a builder; or a train driver. It's good to choose a job you know a bit about so you can get into role more easily. Martin is good at his job and has other character strengths and skills which need to be elaborated and discussed with the family as you are getting into your roles. You wish that you had more time to spend at home, that things were happier at home, that June was more available to you, and that Mary would get a grip on the situation and put her best foot forward.

Mary, the daughter, is a 13 year old who misses the home town and country which she has recently left, her friends, her school, and her extended family, especially those people in her extended family with whom she had regular contact. You will have to make all this up to create a credible role. Mary is miserable and gets headaches very frequently, usually in response to specific triggering events. Mary also has certain strengths and skills. Work out what these are and discuss them with the role-play family as you are all getting into role. You worry about your mother, whom you have heard crying alone in the evenings when your father is still at work.

Frank, the son, is a tough survivor who mixes well and has adapted to living in this country, despite the move from another country and the fact that he has left friends, sports and his favourite school behind. You are on the football team in your new home town. You are also in karate classes and other activities. You have good friends on the street where you now live. You are having a good time. You are aware that Mary is not adjusting as well as you are, but your main focus is on keeping your new life working well and getting praise from your dad who thinks you are doing well.

In the interview, the team will sit behind the therapist. You – the family – are invited to pretend that the team is invisible. If the interviewer wants to briefly ask for help from the team to refocus the interview or for another interviewer to take over, he or she may say 'freeze' to ask you – the family – to stay frozen in time for a minute until he or she says 'unfreeze'. This device will allow the therapist to consult with the team and supervisor or make transitions with a minimum of fuss. The therapist will use this device as little as possible. Also, pretend that you are being interviewed by the same therapist all the time. This eliminates the very time consuming need for introducing yourself to each new team member who takes on the therapist role.

You may find that you want to discuss the value of the exercise with your trainer or to giggle about the role play. Ignore these tendencies as they will prevent you form getting the most out of the exercise. You will find that once the exercise gets going, it takes on a life of its own.

Ex 1. Brief for the Team

Convene a pre-session team meeting and read this letter.

Dear Colleague

Re: Mary O'Byrne. Age 13 years.

I should be grateful if you would see this 13-year-old girl. Her mother has brought her to the surgery frequently over the past six months. The main complaints are headaches and depression. The girl did not respond to antidepressants. Things seem to be getting worse. The family are originally from abroad and moved here, in the past year.

Please assess and advise.

   Yours Sincerely

   Dr B. Goode

Plan and conduct an intake interview with the whole family. In the interview, the therapist(s) must achieve the following goals:

- form a good working alliance
- construct a pattern of interaction around the problem (either headaches or depression or both)
- bring forth the beliefs of family members underpinning this pattern of interaction
- link these beliefs to predisposing factors, which you may find through doing a genogram
- construct a pattern of interaction which occurs in exceptional circumstances where the problem does not occur
- bring forth the positive beliefs underpinning this
- link these positive beliefs to predisposing factors
- make a therapy plan
- feed back the problem and exception formulations to the family and offer a contract for therapy for four further sessions.

Take 20 minutes to work out your interview plan using the material in Chapters 7 and 8. You will need to form preliminary three-column hypotheses and sets of questions to help you construct the pattern of interaction around the problem and exception and the beliefs underpinning these. You will also need to do a genogram and family history to find out the predisposing contextual factors.

Take 40 minutes to conduct the interview. Different parts of the interview may be conducted by different team members. Try to arrange for everyone to have a turn. In the interview, the team should sit behind the therapist. The family have been briefed to pretend that the team are invisible. If the interviewer wants to briefly ask for help from the team or supervisor to refocus the interview or for another interviewer to take over he or she may say 'freeze' to ask the family to stay frozen in time until he or she says 'unfreeze'. Use this device as little as possible. When a new team member takes on the therapist role, do not do introductions again. The family have been briefed to pretend that the entire interview is done by a single therapist.

You may find that you want to discuss the value of the exercise with your trainer or to giggle about the role-play. Ignore these tendencies as they will prevent you form getting the most out of the exercise. You will find that once the exercise gets going, it takes on a life of its own.

Ex 1. Debriefing Routine

When the 40-minute role-play family interview is completed, the trainer may use the following debriefing routine. Invite the family and team to bring refreshments (coffee, tea, soft drinks) into the session, but not to take a 20-minute break, since this will cause the family to de-role and so reduce the value of the debriefing. Ask everyone in the role-play family to stay in role and focus on their experience of having been in the session. Then invite each family member to describe how they feel in role right now, how they feel about their relationships with each family member, the therapist and the team. Ask them each to describe the events in the session that made them feel good, hopeful, cooperative with the therapist, and attached to family members. Also ask them which events made them feel bad, hopeless, resistant to the therapist and alienated from family members. If members of the role-play family move out of role and comment 'intellectually' on the therapy, ask them to postpone de-roling until the experiences of the family have been described 'in role' by all role-playing family members.

When all experiences of the family have been described 'in role' by all role-playing family members, ask the therapy team what they have learned from this account. Then ask the role-playing family members the same question. The sorts of lessons may include the following:

- some things therapists do improve the therapeutic alliance and others do not
- empathic statements and periodic summarising strengthen the therapeutic alliance
- neutrality can be lost from time to time, but it can be regained
- organising the interview so there is a fair distribution of talk time for all participants can help increase neutrality
- children can find aspects of family therapy difficult
- parents can find aspects of therapy difficult
- detailed hypothesis-driven curious questioning can be reassuring for parents
- aimless interviewing can be distressing for parents
- structuring the session so it has a beginning, middle and end is reassuring for all involved.

Ask the therapists who did the interviewing to self-rate the degree to which they believe they achieved each of following goals on a 10-point scale from 1 = didn't achieve this goal, to 10 = achieve this goal well:

- formed a good working alliance
- constructed a pattern of interaction around the problem
- brought forth the beliefs underpinning this

- linked these to predisposing factors
- constructed a pattern of interaction which occurs in exceptional circumstances where the problem does not occur
- brought forth the positive beliefs underpinning this
- linked these to predisposing factors
- made a therapy plan
- fed back the problem and exception formulations to the family and offered a contract for therapy.

Help interviewing therapists to avoid self-criticism. Say something like this: 'All of us in this kind of work are overly self-critical. But it is of little value when we are learning interviewing skills. So can you let us all know which of the things you set out to achieve did you actually achieve.' If the self-ratings are fair, there is no need to ask others to make rating. However, if the ratings are way out of line, ask other members of the group to remember aspects of the session which showed that the session tasks (listed above) were achieved and to offer fairer ratings. If you video the session, then you can ask members of the class as homework to review the tape to find evidence of having achieved session goals and show these to the class next week.

Exercise 2 – Enactment and Boundary Making

Ex 2. Setting up the Exercise

Required reading for this exercise is Chapters 3 and 9. To conduct this exercise it is best if the class have completed exercise 1 in which three-column formulations of the presenting problem and exceptions to it were constructed and a treatment contract was established. If this exercise is attempted without the class having done exercise 1, the supervisor/trainer must brief the role-play family and the team more extensively by providing them with three-column formulations of the problem and exception. Follow the same general procedures for this setting up this exercise as for exercise 1. This includes:

- 20 minutes for preparation, 40 minutes for role-playing, and 40 minutes for debriefing
- inviting the family and team to prepare in separate areas or rooms
- suggesting that a number of team members take turns at conducting therapy
- explaining the freeze/unfreeze device as outlined for exercise 1
- avoiding getting sidetracked into discussing the value of the exercise
- during the planning phase of the exercise, checking in with the family and the team periodically to make sure they are completing the process of getting into role and planning the interview correctly

- during the interview stage of the exercise, intervening as little as possible, and using the freeze/unfreeze device to do so.

Ex 2. Brief for the Family

Four people take on the roles of the family, as for exercise 1. Try to complete the process of getting into role in 20 minutes. Use the skeleton roles below to get in role.

In this exercise, assume that you are attending your second session. In the first session, the therapist (and team) asked about the presenting problem, the pattern of interaction around it, the beliefs underpinning it and explored possible predisposing factors by constructing a genogram with you. At the end of the first session, the therapist (and team) offered a three-column formulation of the presenting problem (Mary's headaches and low mood) and exceptions to it. Your family accepted the formulation and agreed to a treatment contract for four further sessions to resolve the presenting problems.

When getting into role, discuss what your impressions of the last session were, your memories of your relationship with the therapist and the explanation of the problems that emerged from the session. Then discuss what you will say has occurred between the first and second sessions. Imagine if you really were this family what would have gone on during this intersession interval.

In the role-play part of the exercise, the therapist will invite the family to participate in certain tasks within the session, such as discussing how to resolve the presenting problems. As a family, try to cooperate with the task, but also try to follow these role prescriptions.

If you are role-playing the mother, June, start off by working cooperatively with your husband but gradually move towards siding with your daughter, when she expresses feelings of loss and sadness at leaving her home town and country to come and live here in this town, or when your partner seems unreasonable or unsympathetic to your position. You feel lonely and overwhelmed in this new town and country. You are distraught by your daughter's condition. You miss the way your partner used to be when you lived back home.

If you are role-playing the father, Martin, start off by working cooperatively with your wife but gradually move towards siding with your son, when he says things about just getting on with life or when your partner seems unreasonable or unsympathetic. You are exhausted from working long hours and trying to get established in your new job. Things at work are very demanding, but you know you can do the job well, and in time the pressure at work will subside. When you come home you are disappointed that your wife is not more supportive. You also wish she would sort out Mary's problems instead of making them worse, by being so subtly critical of the move to this country.

If you are role-playing the daughter, Mary, and your mother and father get into a heated and potentially conflictual conversation in the session about planning what to do to help you, complain of pain, or depression or talk about stuff that is of interest to yourself and your mother but not your father. Interrupt them if you wish. Don't wait to be asked to take a turn. Just get in there, and say how things are for you. You really don't want to be in this country. You really miss all your friends. Your father is never home because of his very demanding job. Your mother is the only one who understands what it's like for you. Your father does not understand how hard it is for you or for your mother in this awful country.

If you are role-playing the son, Frank, if your mother and father get into a heated conversation in the session about planning what to do, complain about your sister and talk about stuff that is of interest to yourself and your father but not your mother. Above all, you want to get his approval as the golden boy of the family. You have done your best to fit into your new school, make new friends, and get into sports here in this new town. You want your father to say good things about you for all this.

For all of you role-playing this family, try to hold onto these extreme positions in the family interview at least for a while, but be a bit responsive to the therapist's interventions, because you trust the therapist who will in the long-term help you all adjust to your new living situation and help Mary with the headaches and sadness.

As for exercise 1:

- pretend that the team sitting behind the therapist is invisible
- pretend you are working with the same therapist throughout the session (so there is no need to reintroduce yourselves if a new team member takes the therapist role)
- pretend that time is frozen if the therapist says 'freeze' and that it has started again if the therapist says 'unfreeze'
- ignore urges to discuss the value of the exercise or to disrupt it by giggling.

Ex 2. Brief for the Team

In this exercise, assume that you are conducting the second session with this family. In the first session you asked about the presenting problem, the pattern of interaction around it, the beliefs underpinning it and explored possible predisposing factors by constructing a genogram. At the end of the first session you offered a three-column formulation of the presenting problem (Mary's headaches and low mood) and exceptions to it. The family accepted the formulation and agreed to a treatment contract for four further sessions to resolve the presenting problems.

Convene a pre-session meeting for 20 minutes to plan how to reconnect with the family; facilitate an enactment; and invite the clients when they get stuck to introduce more appropriate boundaries into their family.

To reconnect with the family, open the session by checking out how each member is right now, what they remember most vividly from the last session, and how the week has been. Use this checking-in process, to reintroduce the three-column problem formulation and formulation of exceptional circumstances where the problem is expected to occur but does not.

Plan to follow the guidelines for enactments given in Chapter 9 in the section on Changing Behaviour Patterns within Sessions (see p. 277–279). Introduce the enactment by inviting the parents to work with each other to reach agreement on what to do today, tomorrow and the next day about the problem (Mary's headaches and low mood). Ask the parents to invite the children to listen but not interrupt unless invited to do so. Invite the parents to proceed with this enactment without you intervening until they get stuck. If they try to involve you, say you just want to watch them solving the problem so you can better understand how it is that they become stuck. They may get stuck because the mother and father cannot jointly solve problems and plan without the son or daughter intervening and siding with one parent or the other. When it is clear that they are truly stuck, acknowledge this by asking them is this where they usually get stuck. Then invite the parents to jointly reach an agreement on how to proceed. Ask them to do this in a way that takes account of the youngsters' views but which is not dictated by the youngsters' views. If the parents go off track or if a child intervenes, stop them, and insist that the parents work together to reach a joint agreement on how to proceed.

About 25 minutes into the session ask the family to 'freeze'. Use the guidelines in Chapter 9 in the section on Invitations to Complete Tasks (see p. 290–291) to make a plan of how to invite the family complete these two tasks:

- The father, Martin and the Daughter, Mary, are invited to spend two 20-minute periods together during the week doing an activity of the daughter's choosing (because Mary needs her father's support at this difficult time or some other such reason).
- The couple, June and Martin, are invited to spend one evening together during the week doing something relaxing that they both enjoyed (because the couple need to spend more time together if they are to become a more effective team for helping to solve Mary's problem or some other such reason).

Ask the family to unfreeze, deliver the tasks and invite the family to attend a third session.

As for exercise 1:

- plan to conduct a 40-minute session
- plan for a few people on the team to have a turn at taking the role of the therapist to complete specific pre-planned parts of the exercise
- the family will pretend that the team sitting behind the therapist is invisible
- the family will pretend that they are working with the same therapist throughout the session (so there is no need to reintroduce yourselves each time a new team member takes the therapist role)
- the family will pretend that time is frozen if the therapist says 'freeze' and that it has started again if the therapist says 'unfreeze'
- ignore urges to discuss the value of the exercise or to disrupt it by giggling.

Ex 2. Debriefing Routine

As with exercise 1, when the 40-minute role-play family interview is completed, use the same debriefing routine as was described for exercise 1. This involves:

- inviting the class not to take a break since this will cause the family to de-role
- inviting each family member to state how they feel now about their relationships with other family members, the therapist and the team
- asking family members to specify which aspects of the session made them feel good, hopeful, cooperative with the therapist, and attached to family members
- asking them to specify what made them feel bad, hopeless, resistant to the therapist and alienated from family members
- asking the family to postpone de-roling until the experiences of the family have been described
- inviting the therapy team and family members to pinpoint what they have learned from these accounts of the family's therapy experiences.

The sorts of lessons may include the following:

- enactment can be very stressful but it does highlight the family's sticking point that is preventing them from solving their problem
- if a breakthrough occurs in enactment, it can be liberating
- inviting families to complete tasks can have a variety of immediate effects.

As with exercise 1, ask the therapists who did the interviewing to self-rate the degree to which they believe they achieved what they set out to achieve in the interview on a 10-point scale from 1 = didn't achieve this goal, to 10 = achieved this goal well, for the following items:

- reconnected with the family, checked out how each member was, what they remember from the last session, and how the week had been
- Invited the parents to reach agreement on what to do today, tomorrow and the next day about the problem with the children listening but not interrupting unless invited to do so
- let the family go at this until they got stuck
- resisted becoming sucked into the family system when the parents tried to involve you, by saying you wanted to watch them solving the problem so you can better understand how it is that they become stuck
- when the parents went off track or a child intervened, stopped them, and insisted that the parents work together to reach a joint agreement on how to proceed
- invited the family to complete two tasks and attend the next session.

As with exercise 1, if the self-ratings are unfair, invite other members of the group to remember aspects of the session which showed that the session tasks (listed above) were achieved and to offer fairer ratings. If you video the session, then you can ask members of the class as homework to review the tape to find evidence of having achieved session goals and show these to the class next week.

Exercise 3 – Addressing Ambivalence and Presenting Multiple Perspectives

Ex 3. Setting up the Exercise

Required reading for this exercise is Chapters 4 and 9. To conduct this exercise it is best if the class have completed exercises 1 and 2. In exercise 1, three-column formulations of the presenting problem (Mary's headaches and low mood) and exceptions to it were constructed and a treatment contract was established. In exercise 2, an enactment was conducted in which the therapist facilitated family problem solving and set intergenerational boundaries between the parents and the children. If exercise 3 is attempted without the class having done exercise 1, the supervisor/trainer must brief the family and the team more extensively by providing them with three-column formulations of the problem and exception. Follow the same general procedures for this setting up this exercise as for exercises 1 and 2. This includes:

- 20 minutes for preparation, 40 minutes for role-playing, and 40 minutes for debriefing
- inviting the family and team to prepare in separate areas or rooms

- suggesting that a number of team members take turns at conducting therapy
- explaining the freeze/unfreeze device as outlined for exercise 1
- avoiding getting sidetracked into discussing the value of the exercise
- during the planning phase of the exercise, checking in with the family and the team periodically to make sure they are completing the process of getting into role and planning the interview correctly
- during the interview stage of the exercise, intervening as little as possible, and using the freeze/unfreeze device to do so

Ex 3. Brief for the Family

Four people take on the roles of the family, as for exercise 1 and 2. Try to complete the process of getting into role in 20 minutes. Use the skeleton roles below to get in role.

In this exercise, assume that you are attending your third session. In the first session, the therapist (and team) asked about the presenting problem, the pattern of interaction around it, the beliefs underpinning it and explored possible predisposing factors by constructing a genogram with you. At the end of the first session the therapist (and team) offered a three-column formulation of the presenting problem (Mary's headaches and low mood) and exceptions to it. Your family accepted the formulation and agreed to a treatment contract for four further sessions to resolve the presenting problems.

In the second session you engaged in an enactment in which the parents June and Martin tried to develop a plan to deal with Mary's headaches and sadness and found that they often became stuck when the children intervened in their attempts at problem solving. At the end of the second session, the father, Martin and the daughter, Mary agreed to spend two 20-minute periods together during the week doing an activity of Mary's choosing. Also the mother, June, and the Father, Martin, agreed to spend one evening together without the children, doing something relaxing that both enjoyed.

Despite agreeing to do these tasks and knowing that the therapist would review progress with them at the start of session 3, life continued as usual in your family.

June, the mother, was scared to spend time relaxing with Martin in case it ended in a row as usual.

Martin, the father was swamped at work and didn't want the hassle of possible conflict with June or Mary and so didn't get around to doing the tasks.

Mary, the daughter, was feeling helpless and down and so did not prompt her father to do the task.

Frank, the son was uninvolved in this but saw it all happening quite clearly.

When getting into role, discuss what your impressions of the last session, your memories of your relationship with the therapist and the explanation of the problems that emerged from the session. Then discuss what you will say has occurred between the second and third sessions. Imagine if you really were this family what would have gone on in considerable detail during this intersession interval and discuss it among yourselves. Be prepared to let the therapist know that you did not do the tasks and to discuss the difficulties you may have had completing the tasks between sessions.

As for exercise 1:

- pretend that the team sitting behind the therapist is invisible
- pretend you are working with the same therapist throughout the session (so there is no need to reintroduce yourselves if a new team member takes the therapist role)
- pretend that time is frozen if the therapist says 'freeze' and that it has started again if the therapist says 'unfreeze'
- ignore urges to discuss the value of the exercise or to disrupt it by giggling.

Ex 3. Brief for the Team

In this exercise assume that you are conducting the third session with this family. In the first session you asked about the presenting problem, the pattern of interaction around it, the beliefs underpinning it and explored possible predisposing factors by constructing a genogram. At the end of the first session you offered a three-column formulation of the presenting problem (Mary's headaches and low mood) and exceptions to it. The family accepted the formulation and agreed to a treatment contract for four further sessions to resolve the presenting problems.

In the second session you facilitated an enactment in which the parents, June and Martin, tried jointly to decide how to address Mary's headaches and sadness. They tended to get stuck from time to time and the children would interrupt them, so you helped them establish a boundary between themselves and the children. At the end of the session you invited them to do two tasks and made it clear that you would review progress with the tasks in session 3. The tasks were:

- the father, Martin, and the daughter, Mary, were invited to spend two 20-minute periods together during the week doing an activity of the daughters' choosing.
- the couple, June and Martin, were invited to spend one evening together during the week doing something relaxing that they both enjoyed.

The family have come back for session 3 and will tell you that they have not completed their tasks.

Convene a pre-session meeting for 20 minutes to plan how to reconnect with the family; review the obstacles they faced in trying to carry out the tasks; address their ambivalence about completing tasks and working to solve the presenting problems; and present multiple perspectives on the dilemma they face.

To reconnect with the family, open the session by checking out how each member is right now, what they remember about the tasks they were invited to do between the last session and this session, and briefly to say how the week has been. Use this checking-in process to lead into exploring their ambivalence about changing their situation.

To address ambivalence, use the techniques in Chapter 9 in the section on Addressing Ambivalence (see p. 291–293).

About 25 minutes into the session, ask the family to 'freeze' and then work together as a team to write out a split message taking into account the multiple perspectives of various family members. Use the techniques described in Chapter 9 on Presenting Multiple Perspectives (see p. 295–297) to do this. Then ask the family to 'unfreeze' and deliver the split message to them. Conclude by inviting them to come for a fourth session.

As for exercise 1:

- plan to conduct a 40-minute session
- plan for a few people on the team to have a turn at taking the role of the therapist to complete specific pre-planned parts of the exercise
- the family will pretend that the team sitting behind the therapist is invisible
- the family will pretend that they are working with the same therapist throughout the session (so there is no need to reintroduce yourselves each time a new team member takes the therapist role)
- the family will pretend that time is frozen if the therapist says 'freeze' and that it has started again if the therapist says 'unfreeze'
- ignore urges to discuss the value of the exercise or to disrupt it by giggling.

Ex 3. *Debriefing Routine*

As with exercises 1 and 2, when the 40-minute role-play family interview is completed use the same debriefing routine as was described for exercise 1. This involves:

- inviting the class not to take a break since this will cause the family to de-role
- inviting each family member to state how they feel now about their relationships with other family members, the therapist and the team

- asking family members to specify which aspects of the session made them feel good, hopeful, cooperative with the therapist and attached to family members.
- asking them to specify what made them feel bad, hopeless, resistant to the therapist and alienated from family members
- asking the family to postpone de-roling until the experiences of the family have been described
- inviting the therapy team and family members to pinpoint what they have learned from these accounts of the family's therapy experiences.

The sorts of lessons may include the following:

- when ambivalence is addressed in the session it can lead to some family members feeling understood if it fits with individual family members' experiences
- when a multiple perspective intervention is offered to the family it can be liberating if it fits with family members' experiences.

As with exercises 1 and 2, ask the therapists who did the interviewing to self-rate the degree to which they believe they achieved what they set out to achieve in the interview on a 10-point scale from 1 = didn't achieve this goal, to 10 = achieved this goal well for the following items:

- checked out how each member was, what they remembered about the tasks they were invited to do, and asked them how the week had been
- addressed ambivalence, using the techniques in Chapter 9
- developed and presented a split message taking multiple perspectives into account using the techniques described in Chapter 9
- concluded by inviting the family to a fourth session.

As with exercises 1 and 2, if the self-ratings are unfair, invite other members of the group to remember aspects of the session which showed that the session tasks (listed above) were achieved and to offer fairer ratings. If you video the session, then you can ask members of the class as homework to review the tape to find evidence of having achieved session goals and show these to the class next week.

Exercise 4 – Externalising Problems and Building on Exceptions

Ex 4. Setting up the Exercise

Required reading for this exercise is Chapters 4 (especially the sections on solution-focused Therapy (see p. 132–135) and Narrative Therapy (see p. 135–8)) and 9 (especially the section on Externalising Problems and Building on Exceptions (see p. 297–299)). To conduct this exercise it is best if the class have completed exercise 1, and it is good if they have completes exercises 2 and 3, but not essential. In exercise 1, three-column formulations of the presenting problem (Mary's headaches and low mood) and exceptions to it were constructed and a treatment contract was established. If exercise 4 is attempted without the class having done exercise 1, the supervisor/trainer must brief the family and the team more extensively by providing them with three-column formulations of the problem and exception. Follow the same general procedures for setting up this exercise as for exercises 1 to 3. This includes:

- 20 minutes for preparation, 40 minutes for role-playing and 40 minutes for debriefing
- inviting the family and team to prepared in separate areas or rooms
- suggesting that a number of team members take turns at conducting therapy
- explaining the freeze/unfreeze device as outlined for exercise 1
- avoiding getting sidetracked into discussing the value of the exercise
- during the planning phase of the exercise, checking in with the family and the team periodically to make sure they are completing the process of getting into role and planning the interview correctly
- during the interview stage of the exercise, intervening as little as possible, and using the freeze/unfreeze device to do so.

Ex 4. Brief for the Family

Four people take on the roles of the family, as for exercise 1 and 2. Try to complete the process of getting into role in 20 minutes. Use the skeleton roles below to get in role.

In this exercise, assume that you are attending your fourth session. In the first session, the therapist (and team) asked about the presenting problem, the pattern of interaction around it, the beliefs underpinning it and explored possible predisposing factors by constructing a genogram with you. At the end of the first session the therapist (and team) offered a three-column formulation of the presenting problem (Mary's headaches and low mood) and exceptions to it. Your family accepted the formulation and agreed to a treatment contract for four further sessions to resolve the presenting problems.

In the second session you engaged in an enactment in which the parents, June and Martin, tried to develop a plan to deal with Mary's headaches and sadness and found that they often became stuck when the children intervened in their attempts at problem solving. At the end of the second session, the father, Martin and the daughter, Mary agreed to spend two 20-minute periods together during the week doing an activity of Mary's choosing. Also the mother, June, and the father, Martin, agreed to spend one evening together without the children, doing something relaxing that both enjoyed.

In the third session, the reasons why your family did not do the tasks set in the second session were explored in detail. At the end of the session, the therapist conveyed a sensitive understanding of the factors that were preventing individual family members from collectively and cooperatively solving the problems they brought to therapy.

For June, the mother, she was feeling isolated and having difficulty making connections with supportive friends. She was also missing home badly and feeling disconnected from Martin. This prevented her from working with Martin to help Mary.

For the father, Martin, he was swamped at work, frightened of further failure in this job because he failed to maintain his last job, determined to do what it takes to succeed this time, but disappointed that these obstacles were preventing him from helping his daughter and supporting his wife.

For the daughter, Mary, she was feeling helpless, sad, and worried about her mother's grief at having left her home country, and aware that fitting in here may mean accepting the loss of the old way of life. This sense of loss and worry was hard to 'snap out of', and yet she was finding it difficult to know what to do about it.

For the son, Frank, he was content to be the family survivor and to be admired by his parents, particularly his father for his adjustment to this country, but vaguely apprehensive that this role may be lost if his sister and mother begin to show better adjustment to living here.

Some of this way of looking at the problem fit with your experiences and some seemed a bit far-fetched. But the team seemed to understand your dilemma and your difficulty in overcoming the girl's depression and helping her prevent or cope with depression.

Between the last session and this session, there has been a slight easing of desperation for all of you.

June, the Mother, has begun to talk more with Martin about her loneliness and need for support.

Martin, the father, is feeling like business has turned a corner and that he will survive in his new job. He is also aware that he has really been out of touch with June and the kids and has missed them.

Mary, the daughter, met a friend in school one day and has found that this friendship is developing well. She is planning a trip to her home town in the summer to stay with old friends. She realises that she may not have to give up all connections with her old life.

Frank, the son, had row with his sister, Mary, over borrowed CDs. They nearly came to blows. They ended up fighting about how annoyed they were with each other generally over the past few months. Frank was annoyed that Mary is such a depressive influence within the family. Mary is annoyed that Frank is such a goody-two-shoes, doing everything right and getting regular praise from both parents. But then the argument developed into a quieter discussion about how good it used to be in the family's old home town, how much they both miss it, and how hard it is to be here. The children ended this episode on a positive note.

When getting into role, discuss what your impressions of the last session were, your memories of your relationship with the therapist and the explanation of obstacles to resolving the problems that emerged from the session. Then discuss what you will say has occurred between the third and fourth sessions. Imagine if you really were this family what would have gone on in considerable detail during this intersession interval and discuss it among yourselves. Be prepared to discuss exceptional circumstances in which the Mary's headaches and low mood do not occur but might be expected to occur.

As for exercise 1:

- pretend that the team sitting behind the therapist is invisible
- pretend you are working with the same therapist throughout the session (so there is no need to reintroduce yourselves if a new team member take the therapist role)
- pretend that time is frozen if the therapist says 'freeze' and that it has started again if the therapist says 'unfreeze'
- ignore urges to discuss the value of the exercise or to disrupt it by giggling.

Ex 4. Brief for the Team

In this exercise, assume that you are conducting the fourth session with this family. In the first session, you asked about the presenting problem, the pattern of interaction around it, the beliefs underpinning it and explored possible predisposing factors by constructing a genogram. At the end of the first session you offered a three-column formulation of the presenting problem (Mary's headaches and low mood) and exceptions to it. The family accepted the formulation and agreed to a treatment contract for four further sessions to resolve the presenting problems.

In the second session you facilitated an enactment in which the patents, June and Martin, tried to jointly decide how to address Mary's headaches and sadness. At the end of the session you invited them to do two tasks involving the father and daughter spending two periods together and the couple spending one evening a week together relaxing.

In the third session you found out they didn't do these tasks, explored their ambivalence about resolving their difficulties, and offered a split message in which you said you understood the obstacles each of them faced in working cooperatively to resolve their difficulties.

Convene a pre-session meeting for 20 minutes to plan the following interventions based on the section in Chapter 9 on Externalizing Problems and Building on Exceptions and the ideas of Solution-focused Therapy and Narrative Therapy presented in Chapter 4:

- Review progress and look for any evidence of positive change or exceptions where the problem was expected to occur but did not. Positive change can mean moving from 2 to 3 on scale from 1 to 10 where 10 means the problem is resolved.
- In the way you frame your questions, externalise the problem of depression as outside the girl and locate all forces for positive change inside the girl or members of her family.
- Get a detailed description of behaviours and beliefs (possibly using clues from columns 1 and 2 of the three-column exception formulation) associated with the positive changes.
- Ask the family about past similar exceptional events where positive changes occurred.
- Invite family members to thread the past and recent positive episodes together to make up a positive story about the family as a resilient team rather than a family that gets into difficulty under stress.
- Invite the family to label their strengths and project into the future how these strengths will show themselves as they continue to defeat depression and headaches.
- For homework ask them to notice instances in which their strengths come to the fore.
- Ask them to consider joining a panel of advisors for families coping with major challenges and transitions. But say a decision on this will not be required for some time.

As for exercise 1:

- plan to conduct a 40-minute session
- plan for a few people on the team to have a turn at taking the role of the therapist to complete specific pre-planned parts of the exercise
- the family will pretend that the team sitting behind the therapist is invisible
- the family will pretend that they are working with the same therapist throughout the session (so there is no need to reintroduce yourselves each time a new team member takes the therapist role)
- the family will pretend that time is frozen if the therapist says 'freeze' and that it has started again if the therapist says 'unfreeze'
- ignore urges to discuss the value of the exercise or to disrupt it by giggling.

Ex 4. Debriefing Routine

As with exercises 1 to 3, when the 40 minute role-play family interview is completed use the same debriefing routine as was described for exercise 1. This involves:

- inviting the class not to take a break since this will cause the family to de-role
- inviting each family member to state how they feel now about their relationships with other family members, the therapist and the team
- asking family members to specify which aspects of the session made them feel good, hopeful, cooperative with the therapist and attached to family members
- asking them to specify what made them feel bad, hopeless, resistant to the therapist and alienated from family members
- asking the family to postpone de-roling until the experiences of the family have been described
- inviting the therapy team and family members to pinpoint what they have learned from these accounts of the family's therapy experiences.

The sorts of lessons may include the following:

- externalising problems can be liberating
- using scaling questions to detect change can be liberating
- labelling strengths and redefining the family as strong can be liberating.

As with exercises 1 and 2 ask the therapists who did the interviewing to self-rate the degree to which they believe they achieved what they set out to achieve in the interview on a 10-point scale from 1 = didn't achieve this goal, to 10 = achieved this goal well for the following items:

- reviewed progress and looked for any evidence of positive change or exceptions where the problem was expected to occur but did not
- externalised the problem of depression as outside the girl
- obtained a detailed description of behaviours and beliefs associated with the positive changes
- identified other similar past events where positive changes occurred
- linked past and recent positive episodes together to make up a positive story about the family as a resilient team
- labelled family strengths and explored how these strengths may show themselves as the family continue to defeat depression and headaches
- invited them to notice instances in which their strengths come to the fore as a homework task
- asked them to consider joining a panel of advisors for families facing major challenges.

As with exercises 1–3, if the self-ratings are unfair, invite other members of the group to remember aspects of the session which showed that the session tasks (listed above) were achieved and to offer fairer ratings. If you video the session, then you can ask members of the class as homework to review the tape to find evidence of having achieved session goals and show these to the class next week.

Exercise 5 – Disengagment

Ex 5. Setting up the Exercise

Required reading for this exercise is Chapter 7, especially the section on Disengagement and Recontracting (see p. 242–245). To conduct this exercise, it is best if the class have completed exercises 1–4. In exercise 1, three-column formulations of the presenting problem (Mary's headaches and low mood) and exceptions to it were constructed and a treatment contract was established. In exercise 2, an enactment was conducted in which the therapist facilitated family problem solving and set intergenerational boundaries between the parents and the children. In exercise 3, the family's ambivalence about making changes required to resolve their difficulties were explored. In exercise 4, the problem was externalised and the family were helped to draw on their strengths by building on exceptions. If exercise 5 is attempted without the class having done exercise 1 and at least one of the other exercises, the supervisor/trainer must brief the family and the team more extensively by providing them with three-column formulations of the problem and exception and some relevant treatment history. Follow the same general procedures for this setting up as for exercises 1–4. This includes:

- 20 minutes for preparation, 40 minutes for role-playing and 40 minutes for debriefing
- inviting the family and team to prepared in separate areas or rooms
- suggesting that a number of team members take turns at conducting therapy explaining the freeze/unfreeze device as outlined for exercise 1
- avoiding getting sidetracked into discussing the value of the exercise
- during the planning phase of the exercise, checking in with the family and the team periodically to make sure they are completing the process of getting into role and planning the interview correctly
- during the interview stage of the exercise, intervening as little as possible, and using the freeze/unfreeze device to do so.

Ex 5. Brief for the Family

Four people take on the roles of the family, as for exercises 1–4. Try to complete the process of getting into role in 20 minutes. Use the skeleton roles below to help get into role.

In this exercise, assume that you are attending your fifth session. In the first session, the therapist (and team) asked about the presenting problem, the pattern of interaction around it, the beliefs underpinning it and explored possible predisposing factors by constructing a genogram with you. At the end of the first session the therapist (and team) offered a three-column formulation of the presenting problem (Mary's headaches and low mood) and exceptions to it. Your family accepted the formulation and agreed to a treatment contract for four further sessions to resolve the presenting problems.

In the second session, you engaged in an enactment in which the parents, June and Martin, tried to develop a plan to deal with Mary's headaches and sadness and found that they often became stuck when the children intervened in their attempts at problem solving. At the end of the second session, the father, Martin and the daughter, Mary agreed to spend two 20-minute periods together in the week doing an activity of Mary's choosing. Also the mother, June, and the father, Martin, agreed to spend one evening together without the children, doing something relaxing that both enjoyed.

In the third session, the reasons why your family did not do the tasks set in the second session were explored in detail. At the end of the session, the therapist conveyed a sensitive understanding of the factors that were preventing individual family members from collectively and cooperatively solving the problems they brought to therapy. Between the third and fourth session there were some changes in family life. Martin and June, the parents, became more mutually supportive. Mary and Frank began to talk more openly with each other. Martin's new job became less demanding. Mary made a new friend at school and begun to plan a trip back to her home town.

In the fourth session the focus was on the gains the family had made; the situations where you expected Mary to be sad or to have headaches and in fact no problems occurred; and the strengths that the family has for pulling together when tough problems occur. For homework, you were asked to notice situations where strengths come to the fore and to consider joining an expert clients panel, to advise families on managing the sorts of difficulties that you have faced.

You are aware that the fifth session is a review session because the original contract was for four sessions in addition to the intake interview. In the fifth session, you will be invited to talk about: how you are now; what important things you remember from the last session; what has happened in the past two weeks since the fourth session; whether you have noticed situations where family strengths come to the fore; if you would like to be on an expert client panel for advising other families how to manage family transitions; and to review the progress that you have made over the past two months since making your first appointment.

You all wonder if the changes you have seen are transient or permanent. You can see that gains have been made but you worry that things may become difficult again in the future. You all think that the benefits of therapy might be permanent or there may be relapses. Discuss these themes among yourselves, develop some detailed ideas about these general themes, and get into role so you have a coherent story before the interview starts. Also, there may be some things that each of you privately think about whether the changes that occurred are permanent or transitory, and you may wish to think up these private thoughts and only share them with the family in the family interview.

As for exercise 1:

- pretend that the team sitting behind the therapist is invisible
- pretend you are working with the same therapist throughout the session (so there is no need to reintroduce yourselves if a new team member take the therapist role)
- pretend that time is frozen if the therapist says 'freeze' and that it has started again if the therapist says 'unfreeze'
- ignore urges to discuss the value of the exercise or to disrupt it by giggling.

Ex 5. Brief for the Team

In this exercise assume that you are conducting the fifth session. In the first session, problem and exception formulations were constructed which were accepted by the family who agreed to a treatment contract for four further sessions to resolve the presenting problems.

In the second session, you facilitated an enactment in which the patents, June and Martin, tried to jointly decide how to address Mary's headaches and sadness. At the end of the session you invited them to do two tasks involving the father and daughter spending two periods together and the couple spending one evening a week together relaxing.

In the third session, you found out they didn't do these tasks, explored their ambivalence about resolving their difficulties, and offered a split message in which you said you understood the obstacles to them working cooperatively to resolve their difficulties.

Positive changes occurred following the third session. Martin and June, the parents, became more mutually supportive. Mary and Frank began to talk more openly with each other. Martin's new job became less demanding. Mary made a new friend as school and begun to plan a trip back to her home town. In the fourth session, the focus was on the gains the family had made, exceptional circumstances where the problem was expected to occur but did not, and the strengths the family drew on in such circumstances. For homework, the family was invited to notice situations where strengths come to the fore and to consider joining an expert clients panel for advising families on managing major life transitions.

Convene a pre-session meeting for 20 minutes to plan how to conduct this review session, which is the last session in the treatment contract. Ask family members how they are today; what important things they remember from the last session; what has happened in the past two weeks since the fourth session; whether they have noticed situations where family strengths came to the fore; and if they would like to be on an expert client panel for advising other families how to manage family transitions. Then, with reference to the section on Disengagement and Recontracting in Chapter 7, explore the following issues:

- To what degree have the goals of therapy been reached (reducing frequency and intensity of headaches and severity of their daughter's depression)?
- The degree to which family members view the positive changes as temporary or permanent.
- How the family understand the way they solved their problems over the course of the therapeutic process.
- How the family came to see the depression and headaches as part of a pattern of interaction in the family, developed an understanding of the beliefs associated with this interaction pattern and the predisposing factors.
- How the father decided to play a more central role in family life and devote less time to work.
- How the couple became more mutually supportive.
- How the daughter connected to new friends in this country and planned to retain connections with people in her home town.
- How the son chose to support his sister.
- How the family have been supporting each other while they grieve the loss of their old home and explore how to live together in this new home.

Also ask the family to forecast situations in which relapses might occur and make plans to avoid relapses or minimise their impact. Frame the end of the episode of therapy as a stage in an ongoing relationship between the family and the team and close by offering the family a clear way to reconnect with the therapy team if this is required in future.

As for exercise 1:

- plan to conduct a 40-minute session
- plan for a few people on the team to have a turn at taking the role of the therapist to complete specific preplanned parts of the exercise
- the family will pretend that the team sitting behind the therapist is invisible
- the family will pretend that they are working with the same therapist throughout the session (so there is no need to reintroduce yourselves each time a new team member takes the therapist role)
- the family will pretend that time is frozen if the therapist says 'freeze' and that it has started again if the therapist says 'unfreeze'

- ignore urges to discuss the value of the exercise or to disrupt it by giggling.

Debriefing Routine

As with exercises 1–4, when the 40-minute role-play family interview is completed use the same debriefing routine as was described for exercise 1. This involves:

- inviting the class not to take a break since this will cause the family to de-role
- inviting each family member to state how they feel now about their relationships with other family members, the therapist and the team
- asking family members to specify which aspects of the session made them feel good, hopeful, cooperative with the therapist and attached to family members
- asking them to specify what made them feel bad, hopeless, resistant to the therapist and alienated from family members
- asking the family to postpone de-roling until the experiences of the family have been described
- inviting the therapy team and family members to pinpoint what they have learned from these accounts of the family's therapy experiences.

The sorts of lessons may include the following:

- reviewing progress helps families to understand how they have used their strengths to solve their problems
- reviewing progress helps families see that they were largely responsible for therapeutic changes
- disengagement brings forth mixed feelings associated with themes like 'Therapy helped a bit, but it didn't solve everything'; 'It's sad to loose the safety net of coming to therapy sessions'; and 'I'm worried we will not be able to manage without therapy'.

As with exercises 1 and 2, ask the therapists who did the interviewing to self-rate the degree to which they believe they achieved what they set out to achieve in the interview on a 10-point scale from 1 = didn't achieve this goal, to 10 = achieved this goal well for the following items:

- reconnected with the family and reviewed homework
- checked it the goals of therapy been reached (reducing frequency and intensity of headaches and severity of daughter's depression)
- checked the degree to which clients saw their gains as temporary or permanent

- checked client's understanding of how they solved their problems during therapy
- invited the family to forecast situations in which relapses might occur and to make plans to avoid relapses or minimise their impact
- framed the end of the episode of therapy as a stage in an ongoing relationship between the family.

As with exercises 1–4, if the self-ratings are unfair, invite other members of the group to remember aspects of the session which showed that the session tasks (listed above) were achieved and to offer fairer ratings. If you video the session, then you can ask members of the class as homework to review the tape to find evidence of having achieved session goals and show these to the class next week.

CONCLUSION

Guidance on accessing resources for practice, training and research was given in this chapter with specific reference to the following areas: family therapy associations; training and supervision; ethics; assessment instruments; training videotapes; web resources; journals; institutes and associations for specific types of family therapy; written communication in therapy; and training exercises. At the end of chapters 1–18 additional resources relevant to each chapter are given.

Marital and family therapy is an effective way of helping people solve complex life problems. It is also a fascinating adventure for family therapists. Good luck.

REFERENCES

Ackerman, N. (1958). *The Psychodynamics of Family Life: Diagnosis and Treatment of Family Relationships.* New York: Basic Books.

Ackerman, N. (1966). *Treating the Troubled Family.* New York: Basic Books.

Ackerman, N. (1970). *Family Therapy in Transition.* Boston, MA: Little Brown.

Ackerman, N. (1984). *A Theory of Family Systems.* New York: Gardner.

Adams, B. (1995). *The Family: A Sociological Interpretation*, 5th edn. San Diego: Harcourt Brace.

Adams, J. (2003). Milan Systemic Therapy. In L. Hecker & J. Wetchler (Eds), *An Introduction to Marital and Family Therapy*, pp. 123–148. New York: Haworth.

Ainsworth, M., Blehar, M., Waters, E. & Wass, S. (1978). *Patterns of Attachment: A Psychological Study of the Strange Situation.* Hillsdale, NJ: Erlbaum.

Al-Anon Family groups (1981). *This is Al Anon.* New York: Author.

Alcoholics Anonymous (1986). *The Little Red Book.* City Centre, MN: Hazelden.

Alexander, J. & Parsons, B. (1982). *Functional Family Therapy.* Montereny, CA: Brooks Cole.

Alexander, J., Pugh, C., Parsons, B. & Sexton, T. (2000). *Functional Family Therapy*, 2nd edn. Golden, CO: Venture.

Alexander, P. & Neimeyer, G. (1989). Constructivism and family therapy. *International Journal of Personal Construct Psychology*, **2**, 111–121.

Amato, P. (1993). Children's adjustment to divorce. Theories, hypotheses and empirical support. *Journal of Marriage and the Family*, **55**, 23–38.

Amato, P. (2000). The consequences of divorce for adults and children. *Journal of Marriage and the Family*, **62**, 1269–1287.

Amato, P. (2001). Children of divorce in the 1990's: An update of the Amato and Keith (1991) meta-analysis. *Journal of Family Psychology*, **15**, 355–370.

Amato, P. R. & Gilbreth, J. G. (1999). Non-resident fathers and children's well-being: A meta-analysis. *Journal of Marriage and the Family*, **61**, 557–573.

American Psychiatric Association (2000). *Diagnostic and Statistical Manual of the Mental Disorders*, 4th edn. Text Revision, DSM –IV-TR. Washington, DC: APA.

Andersen, T. (1987). The Reflecting team: Dialogue and meta-dialogue in clinical work. *Family Process*, **26**, 415–428.

Andersen, T. (1991). *The Reflecting Team: Dialogues and Dialogues about the Dialogues.* New York: Norton.

Anderson, C. (2003). The diversity, strengths and challenges of single-parent households. In F. Walsh (Ed.), *Normal Family Processes*, 3rd edn, pp. 121–151. New York: Guilford.

Anderson, C. & Stewart, S. (1983). *Mastering Resistance.* New York: Guilford.

Anderson, H. (1995). Collaborative language systems: Toward a postmodern therapy. In R. Mikesell, D. Lusterman & S. McDaniel (Eds), *Integrating Family Therapy. Handbook of Family Psychology and Systems Theory*, pp. 27–44. Washington, DC: APA.

Anderson, H. (1997). *Conversation, Language and Possibilities. A Postmodern Approach to Therapy*. New York: Basic Books.

Anderson, H. (2000). Becoming a postmodern collaborative therapist: A clinical and theoretical journey, Part I. *Journal of the Texas Association for Marriage and Family Therapy*, **5** (1), 5–12.

Anderson, H. (2001). Becoming a postmodern collaborative therapist: A clinical and theoretical journey, Part II. *Journal of the Texas Association for Marriage and Family Therapy*, **6** (1), 4–22.

Anderson, H. (2003). Postmodern, social construction therapies. In T. Sexton, G. Weeks & M. Robbins (Eds), *Handbook of Family Therapy*, pp. 125–146. New York: Brunner-Routledge.

Anderson, H. & Goolishan, H. (1988). Human systems as linguistic systems: Preliminary and evolving ideas about the implications for clinical theory. *Family Process*, **27**, 371–394.

Anderson, H. & Levine, S. (1998). *Collaborative Conversations with Children: Country Clothes and City Clothes. Narrative Therapy with Children*. New York: Guilford.

Anderson, H., Goolishan, H. & Windermand, L. (1986). Problem determined systems: Toward transformation in family therapy. *Journal of Strategic and Systemic Therapies*, **5** (4), 1–14.

Angold, A. & Costello, E. (2001). The epidemiology of depression in children and adolescents. In I. Goodyer (Ed.), *The Depressed Child and Adolescent*, 2nd edn, pp. 143–178. Cambridge: Cambridge University Press.

Asen, E., Dawson, N. & McHugh, B. (2001). *Multiple Family Therapy*. London: Karnac.

Asen, E., Tomson, D., Young, V. & Tomson, P. (2004). *Ten Minutes for the Family. Systemic Interventions in Primary Care*. London: Routledge.

Atkins, D., Dimidjian, S. & Christensen, A. (2003). Behavioural couple therapy: Past, present and future. In T. Sexton, G. Weeks & M. Robbins (Eds), *Handbook of Family Therapy*, pp. 281–302. New York: Brunner-Routledge.

Atkinson, J. & Coia, D. (1995). *Families Coping with Schizophrenia: A Practitioners Guide to Family Groups*. New York: Wiley.

Azar, S. (1989). Training parents of abused children. In C. Schaefer & J. Briemaster (Eds), *Handbook of Parent Training*, pp. 414–441. New York: Wiley.

Azar, S. & Wolfe, D. (1998). Child physical abuse and neglect. In E. Mash & R. Barkley (Eds), *Treatment of Childhood Disorders*, 2nd edn, pp. 501–544. New York: Guilford.

Azrin, N. (1976). Improvements in the community based approach to alcoholism. *Behaviour Research and Therapy*, **14**, 336–348.

Baer, R. & Nietzel, M. (1991). Cognitive and behaviour treatment of impulsivity in children: A meta-analytic review of the outcome literature. *Journal of Clinical Child Psychology*, **20**, 400–412.

Banmen, J. (2002). *Special issue: Satir Today. Contemporary Family Therapy* **24** (1).

Banmen, A. & Banmen, J. (1991). *Meditations of Virginia Satir: Peace Within, Peace Between, and Peace Among*. Palo Alto, CA: Science and Behaviour Books.

Barber, J. & Crisp, B. (1995). The 'pressure to change' approach to working with the partners of heavy drinkers. *Addiction*, **90**, 269–276.

Barker, P. (1998). *Basic Family Therapy*, 4th edn. Oxford: Blackwell.

Barkley, R. (1997). *Defiant Children: A Clinician's manual for Parent Training*, 2nd edn. New York: Guilford Press.

Barkley, R. (2003). Attention deficit hyperactivity disorder. In E. Mash & R. Barkley (Eds), *Child Psychopathology*, 2nd edn, pp. 75–143. New York: Guilford.

Barkley, R., Guevremont, D., Anastopoulos, A. & Fletcher, K. (1992). A comparison of three family therapy programs for treating family conflicts in adolescents with ADHD. *Journal of Consulting and Clinical Psychology*, **60**, 450–462.

Barlow, D., Raffa, S. & Cohen, E. (2002). Psychosocial treatments for panic disorders, phobias and generalized anxiety disorder. In P. Nathan & J. Gorman (Eds), *A Guide To Treatments That Work*, 2nd edn, pp. 301–336. New York: Oxford University Press.

Barrett, P. & Shortt, A. (2003). Parental involvement in the treatment of anxious children. In A. Kazdin & J. Weisz (Eds), *Evidence Based Psychotherapies for Children and Adolescents*, pp. 101–119. New York: Guilford.

Barrett, P., Healy-Farrell, L., Piacentini, J. & March, J. (2004). Obsessive-compulsive disorder in childhood and adolescence: Description and treatment. In P. Barrett & T. Ollendick (Eds), *Handbook of Interventions that Work with Children and Adolescents: Prevention and Treatment*, pp. 187–216. Chichester: Wiley.

Barrowclough, C. & Tarrier, N. (1992). *Families of Schizophrenic Patients – Cognitive Behavioural Intervention*. London: Chapman Hall.

Barton, C. and Alexander, J. (1981). Functional family therapy. In A. Gurman, & D. Kniskern (Eds), *Handbook of Family Therapy*, pp. 403–443. New York: Brunner/Mazel.

Bateson, G. (1972). *Steps to an Ecology of Mind*. New York: Ballentine.

Bateson, G. (1979). *Mind and Nature: A Necessary Unity*. New York: Dutton.

Bateson, G. (1991). *A Sacred Unity*. New York: Harper Collins.

Bateson, G. & Bateson, C. (1987). *Angels Fear*. New York: Macmillan.

Bateson, G. & Ruesch, J. (1951). *Communication: The Social Matrix of Psychiatry*. New York: Norton.

Baucom, D. & Epstein, N. (1990). *Cognitive Behavioural Marital Therapy*. New York: Brunner Mazel.

Baucom, D., Shoham, V., Mueser, K., Daiuto, A. & Stickle, T. (1998). Empirically supported couple and family interventions for marital distress and adult mental health problems. *Journal of Consulting and Clinical Psychology*, **66**, 53–88.

Baucom, D., Epstein, N. & LaTaillade, J. (2002). Cognitive behavioural couple therapy. In A. Gurman & N. Jacobson (Eds), *Clinical Handbook of Couples Therapy*, 3rd edn, pp. 86–117. New York: Guilford.

Baucom, D., Stanton, S. & Epstein, N. (2003). Anxiety disorders. In D. Snyder & M. Whisman (Eds). *Treating Difficult Couples. Helping Clients with Co-existing Mental and Relationship Disorders* (pp. 57-87). New York: Guilford.

Beach, S. (2001). *Marital and Family Processes in Depression*. Washingtin, DC: APA.

Beach, S. (2002). Affective disorders. In D. Sprenkle (Ed.), *Effectiveness Research in Marital and Family Therapy*, pp. 289–310. Alexandria, VA: American Association for Marital and Family Therapy.

Beach, S. (2003). Affective disorders. *Journal of Marital and family Therapy*, **29** (2), 247–262.

Beach, S., Sandeen, E. & O'Leary, D. (1990). *Depression in Marriage. A Model for Aetiology and Treatment.* New York: Guilford.

Beavers, R. & Hampson, R. (2000). The Beavers Systems Model of Family Functioning. *Journal of Family Therapy,* **22** (2), 128–143.

Behan, J. & Carr, A. (2000). Oppositional defiant disorder. In A. Carr (Ed.), *What Works With Children And Adolescents? A Critical Review Of Psychological Interventions With Children, Adolescents And Their Families,* pp. 102–130. London: Routledge.

Behar-Mitrani, V. & Perez, M. (2000). Structural-strategic approaches to couple and family therapy. In T. Sexton, G. Weeks & M. Robbins (Eds), *Handbook of Family Therapy,* pp. 177–200. New York: Brunner-Routledge.

Bennun, I. (1997). Systemic marital therapy with one partner: A reconsideration of theory, research and practice. *Sexual and Marital Therapy,* **12,** 61–75.

Bentovim, A., Elton, A., Hildebrand, J., Tranter, M. & Vizard, E. (1988). *Child Sexual Abuse Within The Family: Assessment and Treatment.* London: Wright.

Bentovim, A. & Kinston, W. (1991). Focal family therapy. Joining systems theory with psychodynamic understanding. In A. Gurman & D. Kniskern (Eds), *Handbook of Family Therapy, Vol. 11,* pp. 284–324. New York: Brunner Mazel.

Berg, I. (1994). *Family Based Services: A Solution-Focused Approach.* New York: Norton.

Berg, I. & Dolan, Y. (2000). *Tales of Solutions. A Collection of Hope Inspiring Stories.* New York: Norton.

Berg, I. & Kelly, S. (2000). *Building Solutions in Child Protective Services.* New York: Norton.

Berg, I. & Miller, S. (1992). *Working with the Problem Drinker: A Solution Focused Approach.* New York: Norton.

Berg, I. & Reuss, N. (1997). *Solutions Step-by-Step: A Substance Abuse Treatment Manual.* New York: Norton.

Berliner, L. & Elliott, D. (2002). Sexual abuse of children. In J. Myers, L. Berliner, J. Briere, C. Hendrix, C. Jenny & T. Reid (Eds), *APSAC Handbook on Child Maltreatment,* 2nd edn, pp. 55–78. Thousand Oaks, CA: Sage.

Bertalanffy, L. von (1968). *General System Theory.* New York: Braziller.

Bion, W. (1948). Experience in groups. *Human Relations,* **1,** 314–329.

Black, D. (2002). Bereavement. In M. Rutter & E. Taylor (Eds), *Child and Adolescent Psychiatry: Modern Approaches,* 4th edn, pp. 299–308. London: Blackwell.

Black, D. & Urbanowicz, M. (1987). Family intervention with bereaved children. *Journal of Child Psychology and Psychiatry,* **28** (3), 467–476.

Blumel, S. (1991). Explaining marital success and failure. In S. Bahr (Ed.), *Family Research: A Sixty Year Review, 1930–1990,* pp. 1–114. New York: Lexington.

Boscolo, L. & Bertrando, P. (1992). The reflexive loop of past present and future in systemic therapy and consultation. *Family Process,* **31,** 119–133.

Boscolo, L. & Bertrando, P. (1993). *The Times of Time: A New Perspective in Systemic Therapy and Consultation.* New York: Norton.

Boscolo, L., Cecchin, G., Hoffman, L., & Penn, P. (1987). *Milan Systemic Family Therapy.* New York: Basic Books.

Boszormenyi-Nagy, I. (1987). *Foundations of Contextual Therapy: Collected Papers of Ivan Boszormenyi-Nagy.* New York: Brunner Mazel.

Boszormenyi-Nagy, I. & Krasner, B. (1987). *Between Give and Take: A Clinical Guide to Contextual Therapy.* New York: Brunner Mazel.

Boszormenyi-Nagy, I. & Spark, G. (1973). *Invisible Loyalties: Reciprocity in Intergenerational Family Therapy*. New York: Harper & Row.

Boszormenyi-Nagy, I., Grunebum, J., & Ulrish D. (1991). Contextual therapy. In A. Gurman & D. Kniskern (Eds), *Handbook of Family Therapy, Vol. 11*, pp. 200–238. New York: Brunner Mazel.

Bott, D. (2001). Client-centred therapy and family therapy: A review and commentary. *Journal of Family Therapy*, **23**, 361–377.

Bowen, M. (1978). *Family Therapy in Clinical Practice*. Northvale, NJ: Jason Aronson.

Bowlby, J. (1969). *Attachment and Loss. Volume 1*. London: Hogarth Press.

Bowlby, J. (1973). *Attachment and Loss. Volume 2*. London: Hogarth.

Bowlby, J. (1980). *Attachment and Loss. Volume 3*. London: Hogarth.

Bowlby, J. (1988). *A Secure Base: Clinical Applications of Attachment Theory*. London: Hogarth.

Braswell, L. & Bloomquist, M. (1991). *Cognitive Behaviour al therapy for ADHD Children: Child, Family and School Interventions*. New York: Guilford.

Bray, J. & Hetherington, M. (1993). Special Section: Families in Transition. *Journal of Family Psychology*, **7**, 3–103.

Bray, J. & Jouriles, E. (1995). Treatment of marital conflict and prevention of divorce. *Journal of Marital and Family Therapy*, **21**, 461–473.

Brent, D., et al. (1997). A clinical psychotherapy trial for adolescent depression comparing cognitive, family and supportive treatments. *Archives of General Psychiatry*, **54**, 877–885.

Breunlin, D., Schwartz, R. & MacKune-Karrrer, B. (1997). *Metaframeworks: Transcending the Models of Family Therapy* (Revised and updated). San Francisco, CA: Jossey Bass.

Brinkley, A., Cullen, R. & Carr, A. (2002). Prevention of adjustment problems in children with asthma. In A. Carr (Ed.), *Prevention: What Works with Children and Adolescents? A Critical Review of Psychological Prevention Programmes for Children, Adolescents and their Families*, pp. 222–248. London: Routledge.

British Crime Survey (2000). *Home Office Statistical Bulletin. Issue 18/00*. Croydon: Home Office.

Broderick, C. & Schrader, S. (1991). The history of professional marital and family therapy. In A. Gurman & D. Kniskern (Eds), *Handbook of Family Therapy, Vol. 11*, pp. 3–41. New York: Brunner Mazel.

Brody, G. Neubaum, E. & Forehand, R. (1988). Serial marriage: A heuristic analysis of an emerging family form. *Psychological Bulletin*, **103**, 211–222.

Bronfenbrenner, U. (1979). *The Ecology of Human Development: Experiments by Nature and Design*. Cambridge MA: Harvard University Press.

Brosnan, R. & Carr, A. (2000). Adolescent conduct problems. In A. Carr (Ed.), *What Works With Children And Adolescents? A Critical Review Of Psychological Interventions With Children, Adolescents And Their Families*, pp. 131–154. London: Routledge.

Brothers, D. (1991). *Virginia Satir: Foundational Ideas*. Binghampton, NJ: Haworth.

Brown, E. (1999). *Affairs. A Guide to Working Through the Repercussions of Infidelity*. San Francisco, CA: Jossey Bass.

Browne, A. & Finklehor, D. (1986). The impact of child sexual abuse: A review of the research. *Psychological Bulletin*, **99**, 66–77.

Browne, K. (2002). Child protection. In M. Rutter & E. Taylor (Eds), *Child and Adolescent Psychiatry*, 4th edn, pp. 1158–1174. Oxford: Blackwell.

Browne, K. & Herbert, M. (1997). *Preventing Family Violence.* Chichester: Wiley.

Browning, S. & Green, R. (2003). Constructing therapy: From strategic to systemic to narrative models. In G. Sholevar (Ed.), *Textbook of Family and Couples Therapy: Clinical Applications,* pp. 55–76. Washington, DC: American Psychiatric Press.

Bruner, J. (1986). *Actual Minds/Possible Worlds.* Cambridge: Harvard University Press.

Bruner, J. (1987). Life as Narrative. *Social Research,* **54,** 12–32.

Bruner, J. (1991). The narrative construction of reality. *Critical Inquiry,* **18,** 1–21.

Brunk, M., Henggeler, S. & Whelan, J. (1987). Comparison of multisystemic therapy and parent training in the brief treatment of child abuse and neglect. *Journal of Consulting and Clinical Psychology,* **55,** 171–178.

Buckley, W. (1968). *Modern Systems Research for the Behavioural Scientist: A Sourcebook.* Chicago: Aldine.

Burke, J., Loeber, R. & Birmaher, B. (2002). Oppositional defiant disorder and conduct disorder: A review of the past 10 years, part II. *Journal of the American Academy of Child & Adolescent Psychiatry,* **41** (11), 1275–1293.

Burnham, J. (1986). *Family Therapy.* London: Routledge.

Byng-Hall, J. (1995). *Rewriting Family Scripts. Improvisation and Change.* New York: Guilford.

Byrne, M., Carr, A. & Clarke, M. (2004a). The efficacy of couples based interventions for panic disorder with agoraphobia. *Journal of Family Therapy,* **26** (2), 105–125.

Byrne, M., Carr, A. & Clark, M. (2004b) The efficacy of behavioural couples therapy and emotionally focused therapy for couple distress. *Contemporary Family Therapy,* **26,** 361–387.

Cade, B. & O'Hanlon, W. (1993). *A Brief Guide to Brief Therapy.* New York: Norton.

Campbell, D. (1999). Family therapy and beyond. Where is the Milan systemic approach today. *Child Psychology and Psychiatry Review,* **4** (2), 76–84.

Campbell, D. & Draper, R. (1985). *Applications of Systemic Therapy: The Milan Approach.* London: Grune Stratton.

Campbell, D., Draper, R. & Huffington, C. (1988a). *Teaching Systemic Thinking.* London: Karnack.

Campbell, D., Reder, P. Draper, R. & Pollard, D. (1988b). *Working With the Milan Method: Twenty Questions.* London: Institute of Family Therapy.

Campbell, D., Draper, R. & Huffington, C. (1989a). *A Systemic Approach to Consultation.* London: Karnack.

Campbell, D., Draper, R. & Huffington, C. (1989b). *Second Thoughts on the Theory and Practice of the Milan Approach.* London: Karnack.

Campbell, D., Draper, R. & Crutchley, E. (1991). The Milan systemic approach to family therapy. In A. Gurman & D. Kniskern (Eds), *Handbook of Family Therapy, Vol. 11,* pp. 325–362. New York: Brunner Mazel.

Campbell, T. (2003). The effectiveness of family interventions for physical disorders. *Journal of Marital and family Therapy,* **29** (2), 263–282.

Carpenter, J. (1997). Special Issue on Brief Solution Focused Therapy. *Journal of Family Therapy,* **19** (2) (whole issue).

Carpenter, J. & Treacher, A. (1989). *Problems and Solutions in Marital and Family Therapy.* Oxford: Basil Blackwell.

Carr, A. (1991) Milan systemic family therapy: A review of 10 empirical investigations. *Journal of Family Therapy,* **13,** 237–264.

Carr, A. (1993). Epidemiology of psychological disorders in Irish children. *Irish Journal of Psychology*, **14** (4), 546–560.

Carr, A. (1995). *Positive Practice: A Step-by-Step Approach to Family Therapy.* Reading: Harwood.

Carr, A. (1997). *Family Therapy and Systemic Consultation.* Lanham, MD: University Press of America.

Carr, A. (2000a). Research update: Evidence based practice in family therapy and systemic consultation, I. Child focused problems. *Journal of Family Therapy, 22*, 29–59.

Carr, A. (2000b). Research update: Evidence based practice in family therapy and systemic consultation. II. Adult focused problems. *Journal of Family Therapy, 22*, 273–295

Carr, A. (2000c). *Special Issue: Empirical Approaches to Family Assessment. Journal of Family Therapy, 22* (2).

Carr, A. (Ed.) (2000d). *Clinical Psychology in Ireland, Volume 4. Family Therapy Theory, Practice and Research.* Lampeter: Edwin Mellen Press.

Carr, A. (2004). *Positive Psychology. The Science of Happiness and Human Strengths.* London: Brunner-Routledge.

Carr, A. (2005). Research on the therapeutic alliance in family therapy. In. C. Flaskas, B. Mason & A. Perlesz (Eds), *The Space Between. Experience, Context and Process in the Therapeutic Relationship*, pp. 187–199. London: Karnac.

Carr, A. (In Press). *Handbook of Child and Adolescent Clinical Psychology*, 2nd edn. London: Routledge.

Carr, A. & McNulty, M. (In Press, a). Systemic couples therapy. In A. Carr & M. McNulty (Eds), *Handbook of Adult Clinical Psychology: An Evidence Based Practice Approach.* London: Brunner-Routledge.

Carr, A. & McNulty, M. (In Press, b). Depression. In A. Carr & M. McNulty (Eds), *Handbook of Adult Clinical Psychology: An Evidence Based Practice Approach.* London: Brunner-Routledge.

Carr, A. & O'Reilly, G. (2004) *Clinical Psychology in Ireland Volume 5: Empirical Studies of Child Sexual Abuse.* Lampeter: Edwin Mellen Press.

Carter, B. & McGoldrick, M. (1999). *The Expanded Family Lifecycle. Individual, Family and Social Perspectives*, 3rd edn. Boston: Allyn & Bacon.

Cassidy, J. & Shaver, P. (1999). *Handbook of Attachment.* New York: Guilford.

Cecchin, G. (1987). Hypothesizing, circularity and neutrality revisited: An invitation to curiosity. *Family Process*, **26**, 405–413.

Cecchin, G., Lane, G. and Ray, W. (1992). *Irreverence: A Strategy for Therapist Survival.* London: Karnac.

Cecchin, G., Lane, G. & Ray, W. (1993). From strategising to non-intervention: Toward irreverence in systemic practice. *Journal of marital and Family Therapy*, 2, 125–136.

Cecchin, G., Ray, W. & Lane, G. (In Press). *Power Struggles: Managing Escalations in Psychotherapy.* London: Karnac.

Chaffin, M., Letourneau, E. & Silovsky, J. (2002). Adults, adolescents, and children who sexually abuse children: A developmental perspective. In J. Myers, L. Berliner, J. Briere, C. Hendrix, C. Jenny & T. Reid (Eds), *APSAC Handbook on Child Maltreatment*, 2nd edn, pp. 205–232. Thousand Oaks, CA: Sage.

Chamberlain, P. (1994). *Family Connections: A Treatment Foster Care Model For Adolescents With Delinquency.* Eugene OR: Castalia.

Chamberlain, P. (2003). *Treating Chronic Juvenile Offenders: Advances Made Through the Oregon Multidimensional Treatment Foster Care Model*. Washington, DC: American Psychological Association.

Chamberlain, P. & Rosicky, J. (1995). The effectiveness of family therapy in the treatment of adolescents with conduct disorders and delinquency. *Journal of Marital and Family Therapy,* **21**, 441–459.

Chamberlain, P. & Smith, D. (2003). Antisocial behaviour in children and adolescents. The Oregon multidimensional treatment foster care model. In A. Kazdin & J. Weisz (Eds), *Evidence Based Psychotherapies for Children and Adolescents*, pp. 281–300. New York: Guilford.

Chassin, L., Ritter, J., Trim, R. & King, K. (2003). Adolescent substance use disorders. In E. Mash & R. Barkley (Eds), *Child Psychopathology*, 2nd edn, pp. 199–230. New York: Guilford.

Chess, S. & Thomas, A. (1995). *Temperament in Clinical Practice*. New York: Guilford.

Cicchetti, D. (2004). Odyssey of Discovery: Lessons Learned through Three Decades of Research on Child Maltreatment. *American Psychologist. Special Awards Issue 2004*, **59**, 731–741.

Clarkin, J., Haas, G. & Glick, I. (1988). *Affective Disorders and the Family*. New York: Guilford.

Clarkin, J., et al. (1990). A randomized clinical trial of inpatient family intervention, V. Results for affective disorders. *Journal of Affective disorders*, **18**, 17–28.

Clarkin, J., Carpenter, D., Hull, J., Wilner, P. & Glic, I. (1998). Effects of psychoeducational intervention for married patients with bipolar disorder and their spouses. *Psychiatric Services*, **49**, 531–533.

Colapinto, J. (1991). Structural family therapy. In A. Gurman & D. Kniskern (Eds), *Handbook of Family Therapy, Vol. 11*, pp. 417–443. New York: Brunner Mazel.

Coleman, R. & Cassell, D. (1995). Parents who misuse drugs and alcohol. In P. Reder & C. Lucey (Eds), *Assessment of Parenting: Psychiatric and Psychological Contributions*, pp. 182–193. London: Routledge.

Coleman, J. & Hendry, L. (1999). *The Nature of Adolescence*, 3rd edn. London: Routledge.

Compas, B., Haaga, D., Keefe, F., Leitenberg, H. & Williams, D. (1998). Sampling of empirically supported psychological treatments from health psychology: Smoking, chronic pain, cancer and bulimia nervosa. *Journal of Consulting and Clinical Psychology*, **66**, 89–112.

Cooper, J. & Vetere, A. (2005). *Domestic Violence And Family Safety: A Systemic Approach to Working With Violence in Families*. London: Routledge.

Cormack, C & Carr, A. (2000). Drug abuse. In A. Carr (Ed.), *What Works With Children And Adolescents? A Critical Review Of Psychological Interventions With Children, Adolescents And Their Families*, pp. 155–177. London: Routledge.

Cottrell D. (2003). Outcome studies of family therapy in child and adolescent depression. *Journal of Family Therapy*, **25** (4), 406–416.

Coyle, A. & Kitzinger, C. (2002). *Lesbian and Gay Psychology: New Perspectives*. Malden, MA: Blackwell.

Coyne, J. (1984). Strategic therapy with depressed married persons.: Initial agenda, themes and interventions. *Journal of Marital and Family Therapy*, **10**, 53–62.

Craighead, E., Hart, A., Wilcoxon-Craighead, L. & Ilardi, S. (2002a). Psychosocial treatments for major depression. In P. Nathan & J. Gorman (Eds), *A Guide To*

Treatments That Work, 2nd edn, pp. 245–262. New York: Oxford University Press.

Craighead, E., Miklowitz, D., Frank, E. & Vajk, F. (2002b). Psychosocial treatments for bipolar disorder. In P. Nathan & J. Gorman (Eds), *A Guide To Treatments That Work*, 2nd edn, pp. 263–276. New York: Oxford University Press.

Craske, M. & Zollner, L. (1995). Anxiety disorders: The role of marital therapy. In N. Jacobson & A. Gurman (Eds), *Clinical Handbook of Couple Therapy*, pp. 394–411. New York: Guilford.

Creighton, S. (2004). *Prevalence And Incidence of Child Abuse: International Comparisons*. NSPCC Information Briefings. UK: NSPCC Research Department. Available at www.nspcc.org.uk/inform

Crenshaw, W. (2004). *Treating Families and Children in the Child Protective System. Strategies for Systemic Advocacy and Family Healing*. New York: Brunner Routledge.

Crome, I., Ghodse, H., Gilvarry, E. & McArdle, P. (2004). *Young People and Substance Misuse*. London: Gaskell.

Curtis, N. M., Ronan, K. R. & Borduin, C. M. (2004). Multisystemic treatment: A meta-analysis of outcome studies. *Journal of Family Psychology*, **18**, 411–419.

Dadds, M., Schwartz, S. & Sanders, M. (1987). Marital discord and treatment outcome in behavioural treatment of child conduct disorders. *Journal of Consulting and Clinical Psychology*, **55**, 396–403.

Dale, P. (1986). *Dangerous Families: Assessment and Treatment of Child Abuse*. London: Tavistock.

Dallos, R. (1991). *Family Belief Systems, Therapy and Change*. Milton Keynes: Open University Press.

Dallos, R. (1997). *Interacting Stories: Narratives, Family Beliefs and Therapy*. London: Karnac.

Dallos, R & Aldridge, D. (1985). Handing it on: Family constructs, symptoms and choice. *Journal of Family Therapy*, **8**, 45–49.

Darling, N. & Steinberg, L. (1993). Parenting styles as context: An integrative model. *Psychological Bulletin*, **113**, 487–496.

Dattilio, F. (1997). *Integrative Cases in Couples and Family Therapy. Cognitive-Behavioural Perspective*. New York: Guilford.

Dattilio, F. & Epstein, N. (2003). Cognitive-behavioural couple and family therapy. In T. Sexton, G. Weeks & M. Robbins (Eds), *Handbook of Family Therapy*, pp. 147–176. New York: Brunner-Routledge.

Dattilio, F. & Padesky, C. (1990). *Cognitive Therapy with Couples*. Sarasota, FL: Professional Resource Exchange.

Davis, R. & Taylor, B. (1999). Does batterer treatment reduce violence. A synthesis of the literature. In L. Feder (Ed.), *Women and Domestic Violence*, pp. 69–93. Binghampton, NY: Haworth.

DeJong, P. & Berg, I, (2000). *Interviewing for Solutions*, 2nd edn. New York: Brooks Cole.

Denton, W., Patterson, J. & Van Meir, E. (1997). Use of the DSM IV in family therapy programmes: Current practices and attitudes. *Journal of Marital and Family Therapy*, **23**, 81–86.

Derrida, J. (1981). *Positions*. Chicago, IL: University of Chicago Press.

deShazer, S. (1982). *Patterns of Brief Family Therapy*. New York: Norton.

deShazer, S. (1985). *Keys to Solutions in Brief Therapy*. New York: Norton.

deShazer, S. (1988). *Clues: Investigating Solutions in Brief Therapy*. New York: Norton.

deShazer, S. (1991). *Putting Difference to Work*. New York: Norton.

deShazer, S. (1994). *Words were Originally Magic*. New York: Norton.

deShazer, S., Berg, I., Lipchik, E., Nunnally, E., Molnar, A., Gingerich, W., & Weiner-Davis, M. (1986). Brief therapy, focused solution development. *Family Process*, **25**, 207–222.

Diamond, G., Siqueland, L. & Diamond (2003). Attachment-based family therapy for depressed adolescents: programmatic treatment development. *Clinical Child and Family Psychology Review*, **6** (2), 107–27.

Dicks, H. (1963). Object relations theory and marital status. *British Journal of Medical Psychology*, **36**, 125–129.

Dicks, H. (1967). *Marital Tensions: Clinical Studies Toward a Psychoanalytic Theory of Interaction*. London: Routledge.

DiClemente, C. (2003). *Addiction and Change*. New York: Guilford.

Dimidjian, S., Martell, C. & Christensen, A. (2002). Integrative behavioural couple therapy. In A. Gurman & N. Jacobson (Eds), *Clinical Handbook of Couples Therapy*, 3rd edn, pp. 251–280. New York: Guilford.

Doane, J. & Diamond, D. (1994). *Affect and Attachment in the Family: A Family Based Treatment of Major Psychiatric Disorder*. New York: Basic Books.

Donohue, B., Miller, E., Van Hasselt, V. & Hersen, M. (1998). An ecobehavioural approach to child maltreatment. In E. Van Hasselt & M. Hersen (Eds), *Handbook of Psychological Treatment Protocols for Children and Adolescents*, pp. 279–356. Mahwah, NJ: Lawrence Erlbaum.

Dougherty, D., Rauch, S. & Jenike, M. (2002). Pharmacological treatments for obsessive compulsive disorder. In P. Nathan & J. Gorman (Eds), *A Guide To Treatments That Work*, 2nd edn, pp. 387–410. New York: Oxford University Press.

Ducommun-Nagy, C. & Schwoeri, L. (2003). Contextual therapy. In G. Sholevar (Ed.), *Textbook of Family and Couples Therapy: Clinical Applications*, pp. 127–146. Washington, DC: American Psychiatric Press.

Duhl, B. (1983). *From the Inside Out and Other Metaphors: Creative and Integrative Approaches to Training in Systems Thinking*. New York: Bruner Mazel.

Duhl, B. & Duhl, F. (1981). Integrative family therapy. In A. Gurman & D. Kniskern. (Eds), *Handbook of Family Therapy*, pp. 483–516. New York: Bruner Mazel.

Duncan, B., Miller, S., Sparks, J. (2003). Interactional and solution-focused brief therapies: Evolving concepts of change. In T. Sexton, G. Weeks & M. Robbins (Eds), *Handbook of Family Therapy*, pp. 101–124. New York: Brunner-Routledge.

Dunn, J. (2004). *Children's Friendships: The Beginnings of Intimacy*. Oxford: Blackwell.

DuPaul, G. & Eckert, T. (1997). The effects of school-based interventions for attention deficit hyperactivity disorder: A meta-analysis. *School Psychology Review*, **26**, 5–27.

Edgeworth, J. & Carr, A. (2000). Child abuse. In A. Carr (Ed.), What Works With Children and Adolescents? A Critical Review of Psychological Interventions With Children, Adolescents and Their Families, pp. 17–48. London: Routledge.

Edwards, M. & Steinglass, P. (1995). Family therapy treatment outcomes for alcoholism. *Journal of Marital and Family Therapy*, **21**, 475–509.

Eisler, I. (2005). The empirical and theoretical base of family therapy and multiple family day therapy for adolescent anorexia nervosa. *Journal of Family*, **27** (2), 104–131.

Elizur, J. & Minuchin, S. (1989). *Institutionalising Madness. Families, Therapy and Society*. New York: Basic Books.

Emery, R. & Laumann-Billings, L. (2002). Child abuse. In M. Rutter & E. Taylor (Eds), *Child and Adolescent Psychiatry*, 4th edn, pp. 325–339. Oxford: Blackwell.

Emery, R. & Sbarra, D. (2002). Addressing separation and divorce during and after couple therapy. In A. Gurman & N. Jacobson (Eds), *Clinical Handbook of Couples Therapy*, 3rd edn, pp. 508–533. New York: Guilford.

Epstein, E. & McCrady, B. (2002). Couple therapy in the treatment of alcohol problems. In A. Gurman & N. Jacobson (Eds), *Clinical Handbook of Couples Therapy*, 3rd edn, pp. 597–628. New York: Guilford.

Epstein, N. (2003). Cognitive behavioural therapies for couples and families. In L. Hecker & J. Wetchler (Eds), *An Introduction to Marital and Family Therapy*, pp. 203–254. New York: Haworth.

Epstein, N., Schlesinger, S. & Dryden, W. (1988). *Cognitive Behavioural Therapy with Families*. New York: Brunner Mazel.

Epston, D. (1989). *Collected Papers*. Adelaide: Dulwich Centre Publications.

Epston, D. (1998). *Catching up with David Epston: A Collection or Narrative Practice Based Papers Published Between 1991 and 1996*. Adelaide: Dulwich Centre.

Epston, D. & White, M. (1992). *Experience, Contradiction, Narrative and Imagination*. Adelaide: Dulwich Centre Publications.

Erikson, E. (1959). *Identity and the Life Cycle*. New York: International University Press.

Fairburn, W. (1952). *An Object Relations Therapy of Personality*. New York: Basic Books.

Fairburn, W. (1963). Synopsis of an object relations theory of personality. *Journal of Psychoanalysis*, **44**, 224–225.

Falicov, C. (1995). Training to think culturally: A multidimensional comparative framework. *Family Process*, **34**, 373–388.

Falicov, C. (2003). Culture in family therapy: New variations on a fundamental theme. In T. Sexton, G. Weeks & M. Robbins (Eds), *Handbook of Family Therapy*, pp. 37–58. New York: Brunner-Routledge.

Falloon, I. (1988). *Handbook of Behavioural Family Therapy*. New York: Guilford.

Falloon, I. (1991). Behavioural family therapy. In A. Gurman & D. Kniskern (Eds), *Handbook of Family Therapy, Vol. 11*, pp. 65–95. New York: Brunner Mazel.

Falloon, I. (2003). Behavioural family therapy. In G. Sholevar (Ed.), *Textbook of Family and Couples Therapy: Clinical Applications*, pp. 147–172. Washington, DC: American Psychiatric Press.

Falloon, I. Laporta, M., Fadden, G. & Graham-Hole, V. (1993). *Managing Stress in Families*. London: Routledge.

Farrell, E., Cullen, R. & Carr, A. (2002). Prevention of adjustment problems in children with diabetes. In A. Carr (Ed.), *Prevention: What Works with Children and Adolescents? A Critical Review of Psychological Prevention Programmes for Children, Adolescents and their Families*, pp. 249–266. London: Routledge.

Farrington, D. (1995). The twelfth Jack Tizard Memorial Lecture. The development of offending and antisocial behaviour from childhood: Key findings of the Cambridge Study of Delinquent Development. *Journal of Child Psychology and Psychiatry*, **36**, 929–964.

Faust, K. & McKibben, J. (1999). Marital Dissolution: Divorce, Separation, Annulment, and Widowhood. In M. Sussman, S. Steinmetz & G. Peterson (Eds), *Handbook of Marriage and the Family*, 2nd edn. New York: Kluwer-Plenum.

Feixas, G. (1990a). Approaching the individual, approaching the system: A constructivist model for integrative psychotherapy. *Journal of Family Psychology*, **4**, 4–35.

Feixas, G. (1990b). Personal construct theory and the systemic therapies. Parallel or convergent trends? *Journal of Marital and Family Therapy*, **16**, 1–20.

Feixas, G. (1995a). Personal construct approaches to family therapy. In G. Neimeyer & R. Neimeyer (Eds), *Advances in Personal Construct Psychology*, Vol. 2, pp. 215–255. Greenwich, CT: JAI Press.

Feixas, G. (1995b). Personal constructs in systemic practice. In R. Neimeyer & M. Mahoney (Eds), *Constructivism in Psychotherapy*, pp. 305–337. Washington, DC: APA.

Feixas, G., Procter, H. & Neimeyer, G. (1993). Convergent lines of assessment: Systemic and constructivist contributions. In G. Neimeyer (Ed.), *Casebook in Constructivist Assessment*, pp. 143–178. Newbury Park, CA: Sage.

Finklehor, D. (1984). *Child Sexual Abuse: New Theory and Research*. New York: Free Press.

Finney, J. & Moos, R. (2002). Psychosocial treatments for substance alcohol use disorders. In P. Nathan & J. Gorman (Eds), *A Guide To Treatments That Work*, 2nd edn, pp. 157–168. New York: Oxford University Press.

Fisch, R. (2004). So what have you done lately? MRI Brief Therapy. *Journal of Systemic Therapies*, **23** (4), 4–10.

Fisch, R. & Schlanger, R. (1999). *Brief Therapy with Intimidating Cases. Changing the Unchangeable*. San Francisco, CA: Jossey Bass.

Fisch, R., Weakland, J. & Segal, L. (1982). *The Tactics of Change: Doing Therapy Briefly*. San Francisco: Jossey Bass.

Fishman, C. (1988). *Treating Troubled Adolescents: A Family Therapy Approach*. New York: Basic Books.

Fishman, C. (1993). *Intensive Structural Family Therapy: Treating Families in their Social Context*. New York: Basic Books.

Fishman, C. & Fishman, T. (2003). Structural family therapy. In G. Sholevar (Eds), *Textbook of Family and Couples Therapy: Clinical Applications*, pp. 35–54. Washington, DC: American Psychiatric Press.

Fitzpatrick, M. (1988). *Between Husbands And Wives: Communication In Marriage*. Newbury Park, CA: Sage.

Flaskas, C. (2002). *Beyond Postmodernism. Practice Challenges Theory*. London: Brunner Routledge.

Folberg, J., Milne, A. & Salem, P. (2004). *Divorce and Family Mediation: Models, Techniques, and Applications*. New York: Guilford.

Foley, S., Rounsaville, B., Weissman, M., Sholomaskas, D. & Chevron, E. (1990). Individual versus conjoint interpersonal therapy for depressed patients with marital disputes. *International Journal of Family Psychiatry*, **10**, 29–42.

Fordyce, W. (1976). *Behavioural Methods of Chronic Pain and Illness*. St Louis, MO: Mosby.

Foucault, M. (1965). *Madness and Civilisation: A History of Insanity in the Age of Reason*. New York: Random House.

Foucault, M. (1975). *The Birth of the Clinic: An Archaeology of Medical Perception*. London: Tavistock.

Foucault, M. (1979). *Discipline and Punish. The Birth of the Prison.* New York: Random House.

Foucault, M. (1980). *Power/Knowledge. Selected Interviews and Other Writings.* New York: Pantheon Books.

Foucault, M. (1982). The subject and power. In H. Dreyfus & P. Rainbow (Eds), *Michael Foucault: Beyond Structuralism and Hermeneutics.* Chicago, IL: University of Chicago Press.

Foucault, M. (1984). *The History of Sexuality.* Middlesex, NJ: Peregrine Books.

Franklin, M. & Foa, E. (2002). Cognitive behavioural treatments for obsessive compulsive disorder. In P. Nathan & J. Gorman (Eds), *A Guide To Treatments That Work,* 2nd edn, pp. 367–386. New York: Oxford University Press.

Freedman, J. & Combs, G. (1996). *Narrative Therapy: The Social Construction of Preferred Realities.* New York: Norton.

Freedman, J. & Combs, G. (2002). Narrative couple therapy. In A. Gurman & N. Jacobson (Eds), *Clinical Handbook of Couples Therapy,* 3rd edn, pp. 308–334. New York: Guilford.

Freeman, J., Epston, D. & Lobovits, D. (1997). *Playful Approaches to Serious Problems: Narrative Therapy with Children and Families.* New York: Norton.

Friedman, E. (1991). Bowen theory and therapy. In A. Gurman & D. Kniskern (Eds), *Handbook of Family Therapy, Vol. 11,* pp. 134–170. New York: Brunner Mazel.

Friedman, L. & Pearce, J. (1980). *Family Therapy: Combining Psychodynamic and Family Systems Approaches.* New York: Grune & Stratton.

Frude, N. (1990). *Understanding Family Problems.* Chichester: Wiley.

Furniss, T. (1991). *The Multiprofessional Handbook of Child Sexual Abuse: Integrated Management, Therapy and Legal Intervention.* London: Routledge.

Garralda, M. (1999). Practitioner review: Assessment and management of somatisation in childhood and adolescence: A practice perspective. *Journal of Child Psychology and Psychiatry,* **40,** 1159–1167.

Geertz, C. (1983). *Local Knowledge: Further Essays in Interpretative Anthropology.* New York: Basic Books.

Gelles, R. (1995). *Contemporary Families: A Sociological View.* Thousand Oaks, CA: Sage.

George, E., Iveson, C. & Ratner, H. (1999). *Problem to Solution. Brief Therapy with Individuals and Families,* revised edn. London: Brief Therapy Press.

Gergen, K. (1991). *The Saturated Self.* New York: Basic Books.

Gergen, K. (1994). *Realities and Relationships. Soundings in Social Constructionism.* Cambridge, MA: Harvard University Press.

Giaretto, H. (1982). A comprehensive child sexual abuse treatment programme. *Child Abuse and Neglect,* **6,** 263–278.

Gingerich, W. & Eusengart, S. (2000). Solution focused brief therapy: A review of the outcome research. *Family Process,* **39,** 477–498.

Glaser, D. (2002). Child sexual abuse. In M. Rutter & E. Taylor (Eds), *Child and Adolescent Psychiatry,* 4th edn, pp. 314–358. Oxford: Blackwell.

Glass, S. (2002). Couple therapy after the trauma of infidelity. In A. Gurman & N. Jacobson (Eds), *Clinical Handbook of Couples Therapy,* 3rd edn, pp. 488–507. New York: Guilford.

Goffman, E. (1961). *Asylums.* New York: Doubleday.

Goffman, E. (1986). *Frame Analysis.* Boston: North-Eastern University Press.

Gollan, J., Friedman, M. & Miller, I. (2002). Couple therapy in the treatment of major depression. In A. Gurman & N. Jacobson (Eds), *Clinical Hanbook of Couples Therapy*, 3rd edn, pp. 653–676. New York: Guilford.

Gollan, J. & Jacobson, N. (2002). Developments in couple therapy research. In H. Liddle, D. Santisteban, R. Levant & J. Bray (Eds). *Family Psychology. Science Based Interventions*, pp. 105–122. Washington, DC: American Psychological Association.

Goodyer, I. (2001). *The Depressed Child & Adolescent*, 2nd edn. Cambridge: Cambridge University Press.

Goolishian, H. & Anderson, H. (1987). Language systems and therapy: An evolving idea. *Psychotherapy*, **24**, 529–538.

Gordon, K. C., Baucom, D. H., & Snyder, D. K. (2004) An integrative intervention for promoting recovery from extramarital affairs. *Journal of Marital & Family Therapy*, **30**, 213–231.

Gorrell-Barnes, G. (2004). *Family Therapy in Changing Times*, 2nd edn. Basingstoke: Palgrave-Macmillan.

Gottman, J. (1993). The roles of conflict engagement, escalation and avoidance in marital interaction: A longitudinal view of five types of couples. *Journal of Consulting and Clinical Psychology*, **61**, 6–15.

Gottman, J. & Notarius, C. (2002). Marital research in the 20th century and a research agenda for the 21st century. *Family Process*, **41**, 159–197.

Gould, R. (1981). *Transformations: Growth and Change in Adult Life*. New York: Simon Schuster.

Gowers, S. & Bryant-Waugh, R. (2004). Management of child and adolescent eating disorders: the current evidence base and future directions. *Journal of Child Psychology and Psychiatry*, **45**, 63–83.

Graziano, A. & Mooney, K. (1980). Family self-control instruction and children's night time fear reduction. *Journal of Consulting and Clinical Psychology*, **48** (2), 206–213.

Green, R. & Mitchell, V. (2002). Gay and lesbian couples in therapy. Homophobial, relational ambiguity and social support. In A. Gurman & N. Jacobson (Eds), *Clinical Handbook of Couples Therapy*, 3rd edn, pp. 546–568. New York: Guilford.

Green, S. & Flemons, D. (2004). *Quickies: The Handbook of Brief Sex Therapy*. New York: Norton.

Greenberg, L. & Johnson, S. (1988). *Emotionally Focused Therapy for Couples*. New York: Guilford.

Greene, S., Anderson, E., Hetherington, E., Forgatch, M. & DeGarmo (2003). Risk and resilience after divorce. In F. Walsh (Ed.), *Normal Family Processes*, 3rd edn, pp. 96–120. New York: Guilford.

Grinder, J., Bandler, R. & Satir, V. (1976). *Changing with Families*. Palo Alto, CA: Science and Behaviour Books.

Grove, D. & Haley, J. (1993). *Conversations on Therapy*. New York: Norton.

Guerin, P. (1976). Family therapy: The first twenty-five years. In P. Guerin (Ed.), *Family Therapy: Theory and Practice*, pp. 1–30. New York: Gardner Press.

Gurman, A (2002). Brief integrative marital therapy: A depth behavioural approach. In A. Gurman & N. Jacobon (Eds), *Clinical Handbook of Couples Therapy*, 3rd edn, pp. 180–120. New York: Guilford.

Gurman, A. & Jacobson, N. (2002). *Clinical Handbook of Couple Therapy*, 3rd edn. New York: Guilford.

Gurman, A. & Fraenkel, P. (2002). The history of couple therapy: A millennial review. *Family Process*, **41**, 199–259.

Gustafsson, P., Kjellmon, N., & Cederbald, M. (1986). Family therapy in the treatment of severe childhood asthma. *Journal of Psychosomatic Research*, **30**, 369–374.

Guttman, H. (1991). Systems theory, cybernetics and epistemology. In A. Gurman & D. Kniskern (Eds), *Handbook of Family Therapy, Vol. 11*, pp. 41–64. New York: Brunner Mazel.

Haley, J. (1963). *Strategies of Psychotherapy*. New York: Grune & Stratton.

Haley, J. (1967a) Towards a theory of pathological Systems. In G. Zuk and I. Boszormenyi Nagi (Eds), *Family Therapy and Disturbed Families*. Palo Alto, CA: Science and Behaviour.

Haley, J. (1967b). *Advanced Techniques of Hypnosis and Therapy: Selected Papers of Milton H. Erickson, MD*. New York: Grune & Stratton.

Haley, J. (1973). *Uncommon Therapy*. New York: Norton.

Haley, J. (1976a). *Problem Solving Therapy*. San Francisco: Jossey Bass.

Haley, J. (1976b). Development of a theory: A historical review of a research project. In C. Sluzki & D. Ramson (Eds), *Double Bind: The foundation of the Communicational Approach to the Family*, pp. 1–32. New York: Grune and Stratton.

Haley, J. (1984). *Ordeal Therapy*. San Francisco: Jossey Bass.

Haley, J. (1985a). *Conversations with Milton H. Erickson, MD: Volume 1. Changing Individuals*. New York: Norton.

Haley, J. (1985b). *Conversations with Milton H. Erickson, MD: Volume 2. Changing Couples*. New York: Norton.

Haley, J. (1985c). *Conversations with Milton H. Erickson, MD: Volume 3. Changing Children and Families*. New York: Norton.

Haley, J. (1996). *Learning and Teaching Therapy*. New York: Guilford.

Haley, J. (1997). *Leaving Home: The Therapy of Disturbed Young People*, 2nd edn. Philadelphia, PA: Brunner-Mazel.

Haley, J. & Richeport-Haley, M. (2003). *The Art of Strategic Therapy*. New York: Brunner Routledge.

Halford, W. (1998). The ongoing evolution of behavioural couples therapy: Retrospect and prospect. *Clinical Psychology Review*, **18**, 613–634.

Halpern, D. (2000). *Sex Differences in Cognitive Abilities*, 3rd edn. Hillsdale, NJ: Erlbaum.

Hardy, K. & Laszloffy, T. (2002). Couple therapy using a multicultural perspective. In A. Gurman & N. Jacobson (Eds), *Clinical Handbook of Couples Therapy*, 3rd edn, pp. 569–596. New York: Guilford.

Harrington, R. (2002). Affective disorders. In M. Rutter & E. Taylor (Eds), *Child and Adolescent Psychiatry*, 4th edn, pp. 463–485. Oxford: Blackwell.

Harrington, R., et al. (1998a). Randomized trial of a home based family intervention for children who have deliberately poisoned themselves. *Journal of the American Academy of Child and Adolescent Psychiatry*, **37**, 512–518.

Harrington, R., Whittaker, J. & Shoebridge, P. (1998b). Psychological treatment of depression in children and adolescents. A review of treatment research. *British Journal of Psychiatry*, **173**, 291–298.

Haskey, J. (1999). Divorce and remarriage in England and Wales. *Population Trends*, **95**, 18–22.

Hatfield, A. (1994). *Family Interventions in Mental Illness*. San Francisco, CA: Jossey Bass.

Hawkins, J., Catalano, R. & Miller, J. (1992). Risk and protective factors for alcohol and other drug problems in adolescence and early adulthood: Implications for substance use prevention. *Psychological Bulletin,* **112**, 64–105.

Hawton, K. (1995). Treatment of sexual dysfunctions by sex therapy and other approaches. *British Journal of Psychiatry,* **17**, 307–314.

Hecker, L., Mims, G. & Boughner, S. (2003). General systems theory, cybernetics and family therapy. In L. Hecker & J. Wetchler (Eds), *An Introduction to Marital and Family Therapy,* pp. 39–62. New York: Haworth.

Heiman, J. & Meston, C. (1998). Empirically validated treatments for sexual dysfunction. In K. Dobson & K. Craig (Eds), *Empirically Supported Therapies: Best Practice in Professional Psychology,* pp. 259–304. Thousand Oaks, CA: Sage.

Henggeler, S. (1999). Multisystemic therapy; An overview of clinical procedures, outcomes and policy implications. *Child Psychology and Psychiatry Review,* **4** (1), 2–10.

Henggeler, S. & Borduin, C. (1990). *Family Therapy and Beyond: A Multisystemic Approach to Treating the Behaviour Problems of Children and Adolescents.* Pacific Grove, CA: Brooks Cole.

Henggeler, S. & Lee, S. (2003). Multisystemic treatment of serious clinical problems. In A. Kazdin & J. Weisz (Eds), *Evidence Based Psychotherapies for Children and Adolescents,* pp. 301–324. New York: Guilford.

Henggeler, S., Schoenwald, S., Bordin, C., Rowland, M. & Cunningham, P. (1998). *Multisystemic Treatment of Antisocial Behaviour in Children and Adolescents.* New York: Guilford.

Henggeler, S.W., Schoenwald, S.K., Rowland, M.D. and Cunningham, P.B. (2002). *Serious Emotional Disturbance In Children And Adolescents: Multisystemic Therapy.* New York: Guilford Press.

Henggeler, S. & Sheidow, A. (2003). Conduct disorder and delinquency. *Journal of Marital and Family Therapy,* **29** (4), 505–522.

Hester, R. & Miller, W. (2002). *Handbook of Alcoholism Treatment Approaches: Effective Alternatives,* 3rd edn. Boston: Allyn Bacon.

Hetherington, E. & Kelly, J. (2002). *For Better or for Worse: Divorce Reconsidered.* New York: Norton.

Heyne, D., King, N. & Ollendick, T. (2005). School refusal. In P. Graham (Ed.), *Cognitive Behaviour Therapy for Children and Families,* 2nd edn, pp. 320–341. Cambridge: Cambridge University Press.

Hoffman, L. (1993). *Exchanging voices: A Collaborative Approach to Family Therapy.* London: Karnac.

Hoffman, L. (2001). *Family Therapy: An Intimate History.* London: Karnack.

Hoffman, L. (2002). *Family Therapy: An Intimate History.* New York: Norton.

Holtzworth-Munroe, A., Meehan, J., Rehman, U. & Marshall, A. (2002). Intimate partner violence. An introduction for couple therapists. In A. Gurman & N. Jacobson (Eds), *Clinical Handbook of Couple Therapy,* 3rd edn, pp. 441–465. New York: Guilford.

Houts, A. (2003). Behavioural treatment for enuresis. In A. Kazdin & J. Weisz (Eds), *Evidence-Based Psychotherapies for Children and Adolescents,* pp. 389–406. New York: Guilford Press.

Howe, R. & von Foerster, H. (1974). Cybernetics at Illinois. *Forum,* **6**, 15–17.

Hoyt, M. (2001). *Interviews with Brief Therapy Experts.* Philadelphia, PA: Brunner-Routledge.

Hoyt, M. (2002). Solution focused couple therapy. In A. Gurman & N. Jacobson (Eds), *Clinical Handbook of Couples Therapy*, 3rd edn, pp. 335–373. New York: Guilford.

Hudson, J., Hughes, A. & Kendall, P. (2004). Treatment of generalized anxiety disorder in children and adolescents. In P. Barrett & T. Ollendick (Eds), *Handbook of Interventions that Work with Children and Adolescents: Prevention and Treatment*, pp. 115–144. Chichester: Wiley.

Hudson, P. & O'Hanlon, W. (1994). *Rewriting Love Stories: Brief Marital Therapy*. New York: Norton.

Imber-Black, E. (1988). *Families and Larger Systems: A Family Therapist's Guide Through the Labyrinth*. New York: Guilford.

Imber-Black, E. (1991). A family larger system perspective. In A. Gurman & D. Kniskern (Eds), *Handbook of Family Therapy, Vol. 11*, pp. 583–605. New York: Brunner Mazel.

Ingoldsby, B. & Smith, S. (2005). *Families in Global and Multicultural Perspective*, 2nd edn. New York: Sage.

Jackson, D. (1965). Family rules: The marital quid pro quo. *Archives of General Psychiatry*, **12**, 589–594.

Jackson, D. (1968a). *Human Communication Volume 1. Communication, Family and Marriage*. Palo Alto, CA: Science and Behaviour.

Jackson, D. (1968b). *Human Communication Volume 2. Communication and Change*. Palo Alto, CA: Science and Behaviour.

Jacobson, N. & Addis, M. (1993). Research on couples and couple therapy: What do we know? *Journal of Consulting and Clinical Psychology*, **61**, 85–93.

Jacobson, N. & Christensen, A. (1996). *Integrative Behavioural Couple Therapy*. New York: Norton.

Jacobson, N. & Margolin, G. (1979). *Marital Therapy; Strategies Based on Social Learning and Behavioural Exchange Principles*. New York: Brunner Mazel.

Jenkins, A. (1990). *Invitations to responsibility: The Therapeutic Engagement of Men who are Violent and Abusive*. Adelaide: Dulwich Centre Publications.

Jewell, T., McFarlane, W., Dixon, L. & Milkowitz, D. (2005). Evidence-based family services for adults with severe mental illness. In C. Stout & R. Hayes (Ed.), *The Evidence-Based Practice: Methods, Models, And Tools For Mental Health Professionals*, pp. 56–84. New York: Wiley.

Johnson, S. (1996). *The Practice of Emotionally Focused Marital Therapy: Creating Connection*. New York: Brunner Mazel.

Johnson, S. (2002a). *Emotionally Focused Couple Therapy with Trauma Survivors: Strengthening Attachment Bonds*. New York: Guilford.

Johnson, S. (2002b). Marital problems. In D. Sprenkle (Ed.), *Effectiveness Research in Marital and Family Therapy*, pp. 163–190. Alexandria, VA: American Association for Marital and Family Therapy.

Johnson, S. (2003a). Emotionally focused couple therapy: Empiricism and art. In T. Sexton, G. Weeks & M. Robbins (Eds), *Handbook of Family Therapy*, pp. 263–280. New York: Brunner-Routledge.

Johnson, S. (2003b). The revolution in couple therapy: A practitioner-scientist perspective. *Journal of Marital and family Therapy*, 29 (3), 365–384.

Johnson, S. & Denton, W. (2002). Emotionally focused couple therapy: Creating secure connections. In A. Gurman & N. Jacobson (Eds), *Clinical Handbook of Couples Therapy*, 3rd edn, pp. 221–250. New York: Guilford.

Johnson, S. & Whiffen, V. (2003). *Attachment Processes in Couple and Family Therapy.* New York: Guilford.

Joiner, T. & Coyne, J. (1999). *The Interactional Nature of Depression.* Washington, DC: APA.

Jones, D. (2000). Child abuse and neglect. In M. Gelder, J. Lopez-Ibor & N. Andreasen (Eds), *New Oxford Textbook of Psychiatry*, Vol. 2, pp. 1825–1834. Oxford: Oxford University Press.

Jones, D. & McGraw, J. (1987). Reliable and fictitious accounts of sexual abuse to children. *Journal of Interpersonal Violence*, 2, 27–45.

Jones, E. (1993). *Family Systems Therapy: Developments in the Milan Systemic Therapy.* Chichester: Wiley.

Jones, E. & Asen, E. (1999). *Systemic Couples Therapy for Depression.* London: Karnac.

Kanfer, F., Karoly, P. & Newman, A. (1975). Reduction of children's fear of dark by competence related and situational threat-related verbal cues. *Journal of Consulting and Clinical Psychology*, **43** (2), 251–258.

Kaplan, H. (1974). *The New Sex Therapy.* New York: Quadrangle.

Kaplan, H. (1995). *The Sexual Desire Disorders.* New York: Brunner Mazel.

Karpel, M. (1980) Family Secrets: I. Conceptual and ethical issues in the relational context. II. Ethical and practical considerations in therapeutic management. *Family Process*, **19**, 295–306.

Karpman, S. (1968) Fairy tales and script drama analysis. *Transactional Analysis Bulletin*, **7** (26), 39–44.

Kaslow, F. (1980). History of family therapy in the united states: A kaleidoscopic view. *Marriage and Family Review*, **3**, 77–111.

Kaufman, E. & Kaufman, P. (1992). *Family Therapy of Drug and Alcohol Abuse*, 2nd edn. Boston: Allyn & Bacon.

Kazdin, A. (1995). *Conduct Disorders in Childhood and Adolescence*, 2nd edn. Thousand Oaks, CA: Sage.

Kazdin, A. (1995). *Conduct Disorders in Childhood and Adolescence.* (Second edition). Thousand Oaks, CA: Sage.

Kazdin, A. (2003). Problem-solving skills training and parent management training for conduct problems. In A. Kazdin & J. Weisz (Eds), *Evidence Based Psychotherapies for Children and Adolescents*, pp. 241–262. New York: Guilford.

Keck, P. & McElroy, S. (2002). Pharmacological treatment of bipolar disorder. In P. Nathan & J. Gorman (Eds), *A Guide To Treatments That Work*, 2nd edn, pp. 277–300. New York: Oxford University Press.

Keefe, F., Caldwell, D. & Burn, P. (1996). Spouse assisted coping skills training in the management of osteoarthritic knee pain. *Arthritis Care and Research*, **9**, 279–291.

Keeney, B. & Sprenkle, D. (1982). Ecosystemic epistemology: Critical implications for the aesthetics and pragmatics of family therapy. *Family Process*, **21**, 1–19.

Keim, J. & Lappin, J. (2002). Structural-strategic marital therapy. In A. Gurman & N. Jacobson (Eds), *Clinical Handbook of Couples Therapy*, 3rd edn, pp. 86–117. New York: Guilford.

Kelly, G. (1955). *The Psychology of Personal Constructs*, Vols. 1 and 2. New York: Norton.

Kelly, J. (2000). Children's adjustment in conflicted marriage and divorce: A decade review of research. *Journal of the American Academy of Child & Adolescent Psychiatry*, **39** (8), 963–973.

Kempler, W. (1973). *Principles of Gestalt Family Therapy*. Salt Lake City: Dessert Press.

Kempler, W. (1991). *Experiential Psychotherapy within Families*, 2nd edn. Oslo: Kempler Institute.

Kendall, P. & Braswell, L. (1985). *Cognitive Behavioural Therapy for Impulsive Children*. New York: Guilford.

Kendall-Tackett, K., Williams, L. & Finklehor, D. (1993). Impact of sexual abuse on children. *Psychological Bulletin*, **113**, 164–180.

Kenny, V. (1988). *Special edition: Constructivism. Irish Journal of Psychology*, **9**.

Kerr, M. (2003). Multigenerational family systems theory of Bowen and its application. In G. Sholevar (Eds), *Textbook of Family and Couples Therapy: Clinical Applications*, pp. 103–126. Washington, DC: American Psychiatric Press.

Kerr, M. & Bowen, M. (1988). *Family Evaluation*. New York: Norton.

Kirschner, D. & Kirschner, S. (1986). *Comprehensive Family Therapy: An Integration of Systemic and Psychodynamic Models*. New York: Brunner Mazel.

Kissane, D. & Bloch, S. (2002). *Family Focused Grief Therapy: A Model of Family-centred Care during Palliative Care and Bereavement*. Buckingham, UK: Open University Press.

Kohut, H. (1984). *How Does Analysis Cure?* Chicago, IL: Chicago University Press.

Kolko, D. (2002). Child physical abuse. In J. Myers, L. Berliner, J. Briere, C. Hendrix, C. Jenny & T. Reid (Eds), *APSAC Handbook on Child Maltreatment*, 2nd edn, pp. 21–54. Thousand Oaks, CA: Sage.

Kopelowicz, A. & Liberman, R. (1998). Psychosocial treatments for schizophrenia. In P. Nathan & J. Gorman (Eds), *A Guide To Treatments That Work*, pp. 190–211. New York: Oxford University Press.

Kopelowicz, A., Liberman, R. & Zarate, R. (2002). Psychosocial treatments for schizophrenia. In P. Nathan & J. Gorman (Eds), *A Guide To Treatments That Work*, 2nd edn, pp. 201–228. New York: Oxford University Press.

Korsybski, A. (1933). *Science and Sanity*. New York: Scientific Press.

Kuhn, T. (1962). *The Structure of Scientific Revolutions*. Chicago, IL: University of Chicago Press.

Kuipers, E., Peters, E. & Bebbington, P. (In Press). Schizophrenia. In A. Carr & M. McNulty (Eds), *Handbook of Adult Clinical Psychology: An Evidence Based Practice Approach*. London: Brunner-Routledge.

Kuipers, L., Leff, J. & Lam, D. (2002). *Family Work for Schizophrenia*, 2nd edn. London: Gaskell.

Kupersmidt, J. & Dodge, K. (2004). *Children's Peer Relations: From Development to Intervention*. Washington, DC: American Psychological Association.

Laing, R. (1965). *The Divided Self*. London: Tavistock.

Laird, J. (2003). Lesbian and gay families. In F. Walsh (Ed.), *Normal Family Processes*, 3rd edn, pp. 176–209. New York: Guilford.

Laird, J. & Green, R. (1996). *Lesbians and Gays in Couples and Families: A Handbook for Therapists*. San Francisco, CA: Jossey-Bass.

Lankton, S. & Lankton, C. (1991). Ericksonian family therapy. In A. Gurman & D. Kniskern (Eds), *Handbook of Family Therapy, Vol. 11*, pp. 239–283. New York: Brunner Mazel.

Lask, B. & Matthew, D. (1979). Childhood asthma: A controlled trial of family psychotherapy. *Archives of Diseases in Childhood*, **55**, 116–119.

Lawrence, E., Eldridge, K. & Christensen, A. (1998). The enhancement of traditional behavioural couples therapy: Consideration of individual and dyadic factors. *Clinical Psychology Review*, **18**, 745–764.

Lebow, J. (2003). Integrative approaches to couple and family therapy. In T. Sexton, G. Weeks & M. Robbins (Eds), *Handbook of Family Therapy*, pp. 201–228. New York: Brunner-Routledge.

Leff, J., et al. (2000). The London Depression Intervention Trial. Randomised controlled trial of antidepressants versus couple therapy in the treatment and maintenance of people with depression living with a partner: clinical outcomes and costs. *British Journal of Psychiatry*, **177**, 95–100.

Leiblum, S. & Rosen, S. (2001). *Principles and Practice of Sex Therapy*, 3rd edn. New York: Guilford.

Leon, K. (2003). Risk and protective factors in young children's adjustment in parental divorce: A review of the research. *Family Relations: Interdisciplinary Journal of Applied Family Studies*, **52**, 258–270.

Lethem, J. (2002). Brief solution focused therapy. *Child and Adolescent Mental Health*, **7**, 189–192.

Leupnitz, D. (1988). *The Family Interpreted. Psychoanalysis, Feminism and Family Therapy*. New York: Basic Books.

Levine, S., Risen, C. & Althof, S. (2003). *Handbook of Clinical Sexuality for Mental Health Professionals*. New York: Brunner Routledge.

Levy, G. & Fivush, R. (1993). Scripts and gender: A new approach for examining gender role development. *Developmental Psychology*, **13**, 126–146.

Lewin, K. (1951). *Field Theory in Social Science*. New York: Harper.

Lewinsohn, P., Clarke, G., Hops, H. & Andrews, J. (1990). Cognitive behavioural group treatment of depression in adolescents. *Behaviour Therapy*, **21**, 385–401.

Lewinsohn, P., et al. (1996). A course in coping: A cognitive behavioural approach to the treatment of adolescent depression. In E. Hibbs & P. Jensen (Eds), *Psychosocial Treatments for Child and Adolescent Disorders*, pp. 109–135. Washington DC: American Psychiatric Association.

Liddle, H. A. (2005). *Multidimensional Family Therapy for Adolescent Substance Abuse*. New York: Norton. A version of this book is available at www.chestnut.org/LI/cyt/products/MDFT_CYT_v5.pdf

Liddle, H. A. & Hogue, A. (2001). Multidimensional family therapy for adolescent substance abuse. In E. F. Wagner & H. B. Waldron (Eds), *Innovations in Adolescent Substance Abuse Interventions*, pp. 229–261. London: Elsevier.

Lidz, T. C., Cornelison, A., Fleck, S. & Terry, D. (1957a). The intrafamilial environment of the schizophrenic patient: The father. *Psychiatry*, **20**, 329–342.

Lidz, T. C., Cornelison, A., Fleck, S. & Terry, D. (1957b). The intrafamilial environment of the schizophrenic patient: Marital schism and marital skew. *American Journal of Psychiatry*, **114**, 126–132.

Liepman, M., Silvia, L. & Nirenberg, T. (1989). The use of family behaviour loop mapping for substance abuse. *Family Relations*, **38**, 282–287.

Lipchik, E. (2002). *Beyond Technique in Solution-Focused Therapy*. New York: Guilford.

Lock, J., LeGrange, D., Agras, W. & Dare, C. (2001). *Treatment Manual for Anorexia Nervosa. A Family Based Approach*. New York: Guilford.

Loeber, R., Burke, J., Lahey, B., Winters, A. & Zera, M. (2000). Oppositional defiant and conduct disorder: A review of the past 10 years, Part I. *Journal of the American Academy of Child & Adolescent Psychiatry*, **39** (12), 1468–1484.

Loeber, R. & Stouthamer-Loeber, M. (1998). Development of juvenile aggression and violence: Some common misconceptions and controversies. *American Psychologist*, **53**, 242–259.

Luthar, S. (2003). *Resilience and Vulnerability: Adaptation in the Context of Childhood Adversities.* Cambridge: Cambridge University Press.

MacDonald, G. (2001). *Effective Interventions for Child Abuse and Neglect. An Evidence-based Approach to Planning and Evaluating Interventions.* Chichester: Wiley.

Madanes, C. (1981). *Strategic Family Therapy.* San Francisco, CA: Jossey Bass.

Madanes, C. (1984). *Behind the One-way Mirror: Advances in the Practice of Strategic Therapy.* San Francisco, CA: Jossey Bass.

Madanes, C. (1990). *Sex, Love and Violence.* New York: Norton.

Madanes, C. (1991). Strategic Family Therapy. In A. Gurman & D. Kniskern (Eds), *Handbook of Family Therapy, Vol. 11*, pp. 396–416. New York: Brunner Mazel.

Madanes, C. (1994). *The Secret Meaning of Money.* San Francisco, CA: Jossey-Bass.

Madanes, C. Keim, J. & Smelser, D. (1995). *The Violence of Men.* San Francisco, CA: Jossey-Bass.

Magna., A., Goldstein, M., Karno, M., Miklowitz, D., Jenkins, J. & Falloon, I. (1986). A brief method for assessing expressed emotion in relatives of psychiatric patients. *Psychiatry Research, 17*, 203–212.

Malik, N. & Furman, W. (1993). Practitioner review: Problem in children's peer relations: What can the clinician do. *Journal of Child Psychology and Psychiatry, 34*, 1303–1326.

Malley, M. & Tasker, F. (1999). Lesbians, gay men and family therapy; A contradiction in Terms. *Journal of Family Therapy, 21*, 3–29.

March, J. & Mulle, K. (1998). *OCD in Children and Adolescents: A Cognitive Behavioural Treatment Manual.* New York: Guilford.

Marcia, J. (1981). Identity and self-development. In R. Lerner, A. Petersen & J. Brooks-Gunn (Eds), *Encyclopaedia of Adolescence, Vol. 1.* New York: Garland.

Marlatt, G. & Gordon, J. (1985). *Relapse Prevention.* New York: Guilford.

Marshall, W., Laws, D. & Barbaree, H. (1990). *Handbook of Sexual Assault: Issues, Theories, and Treatment of the Offender.* New York: Kluwer/Plenum.

Masters, W. & Johnson, V. (1970). *Human Sexual Inadequacy.* Boston: Little-Brown.

Maturana, H. (1991). Maturana's basic Notions. *Human Systems; The Journal of Systemic Consultation and Management, 2*, 71–78.

McCarthy, I. & Byrne, N. (1988) Mis-taken love: Conversations on the problem of incest in an Irish context. *Family Process, 27*, 181–199.

McCrady, B. (In Press). Alcohol and other substance use problems. In A. Carr & M. McNulty (Eds), *Handbook of Adult Clinical Psychology: An Evidence Based Practice Approach.* London: Brunner-Routledge.

McCullough, L., Kuhn, N., Andrews, S., Kaplan, A., Wolf, J., & Hurley, C. (2003). *Treating Affect Phobia: A Manual for Short term Dynamic Psychotherapy.* New York: Guilford.

McDaniel, S., Hepworth, J. & Doherty, W. (1992). *Medical Family Therapy: A Biopsychosocial Approach to Families With Health Problems.* New York: Basic.

McDaniel, S., Hepworth, J. & Doherty, W. (1997). *Medical Family Therapy.* New York: Basic Books.

McEvoy, A. & Walker, R. (2000). Antisocial behaviour, academic failure, and school climate: a critical review. *Journal of Emotional and Behavioural Disorders, 8*, 130–40.

McFarlane, W. (1991). Family psychoeducational treatment. In A. Gurman & D. Kniskern (Eds), *Handbook of Family Therapy, Vol. 11*, pp. 363–395. New York: Brunner Mazel.

McFarlane, W. (2002). *Multifamily Groups in The Treatment of Severe Psychiatric Disorders*. New York: Guilford Press.

McFarlane, W., Dixon, L., Lukens, E. & Lucksted, A. (2002). Severe mental illness. In D. Sprenkle (Ed.), *Effectiveness Research in Marital and Family Therapy*, pp. 255–288. Alexandria, VA: American Association for Marital and Family Therapy.

McFarlane, W., Dixon, L., Lukens, E. & Lucksted (2003). Family psychoeducation and schizophrenia: A review of the literature. *Journal of Marital and family Therapy*, **29** (2), 223–246.

McGoldrick, M. (2002). *Re-visioning Family Therapy. Race Culture and Gender in Clinical Practice*. New York: Guilford.

McGoldrick, M. & Carter, B. (2001). Advances in coaching: Family therapy with one person. *Journal of Marital and Family Therapy*, **27**, 281–300.

McGoldrick, M., Gerson, R. & Shellenberger, S. (1999). *Genograms: Assessment and Intervention*, 2nd edn. New York: Norton.

McLeod, J. (1997). *Narrative and Psychotherapy*. London: Sage.

McNamee, S. & Gergen, K. (1992). *Therapy as Social Construction*. Newbury Park, CA: Sage.

McWhirter, D. & Mattison, D. (1984). *The Male Couple; How Relationships Develop*. Englewood Cliffs, NJ: Prentice Hall.

Meltzer, H., Gatward, R., Goodman, R. & Ford, T. (2000). *The Mental Health of Children and Adolescents in Great Britain: The report of a survey carried out in 1999 by Social Survey Division of the Office for National Statistics on behalf of the Department of Health, the Scottish Health Executive and the National Assembly for Wales*. London: The Stationery Office.

Meyers, R., Smith, J. & Miller, E. (1998). Working through the concerned significant other: Community reinforcement and family training. In W. Miller & N. Heather (Eds), *Treating Addictive Behaviours: Processes of Change*, 2nd edn, pp. 149–161. New York: Plenum.

Mikesell, R. Lusterman, D. & McDaniel, S. (1995). *Integrating Family Therapy. Handbook of Family Psychology and Systems Theory*. Washington, DC: APA.

Milkowitz, D. J., & Goldstein, M. J. (1997). *Bipolar Disorder: A Family-Focused Treatment Approach*. New York, NY: Guilford Press.

Milkowitz, D. & Morris, C. (2003). Bipolar disorder. In D. Snyder & M. Whisman (Eds). *Treating Difficult Couples. Helping Clients with Co-existing Mental and Relationship Disorders*, pp. 114–136. New York: Guilford.

Milkowitz, S. & Tompson, M, (2003). Family variables and interventions in schizophrenia. In G. Sholevar (Ed.), *Textbook of Family and Couples Therapy: Clinical Applications*, pp. 585–617. Washington, DC: American Psychiatric Press.

Miller, D., Hubble, A. & Duncan, B. (1996). *Handbook of Solution Focused Brief Therapy: Foundations, Applications and Research*. San Francisco, CA: Jossey-Bass.

Miller, I., Keitner, G., Bishop, D. & Ryan, C. (1991). Families of bipolar patients. Dysfunction, course of illness and pilot treatment study. Paper presented at a meeting of the Association for the Advancement of Behaviour Therapy, New York, November 1990.

Miller, I., Keitner, G., Ryan, C. & Solomon, D. (2000a). Family treatment of bipolar disorder. Paper presented at a meeting of the Society for Psychotherapy Research, Braaga, Portugal, June.

Miller, I., Ryan, C., Keitner, G., Bishop, D. & Epstein, N. (2000b). The McMaster approach to families: Theory, assessment, treatment and research. *Journal of Family Therapy*, **22** (2), 168–189.

Miller, R., Anderson, S. & Kaulana-Keala, D. (2004). Is Bowen theory valid?: A review of basic research. *Journal of Marital and Family Therapy*, **30**, 453–466.

Miller, S. & Berg, I. (1995). *The Miracle Method*. New York: Norton.

Minuchin, S. (1974). *Families and Family Therapy*. Cambridge, MA: Harvard University Press.

Minuchin, S. (1984). *Family Kaleidoscope*. Cambridge, MA: Harvard University Press.

Minuchin, S. & Fishman, H.C. (1981). *Family Therapy Techniques*. Cambridge, MA: Harvard University Press.

Minuchin, S. & Nichols, M. (1993). *Family Heading: Tales of Hope and Renewal from Family Therapy*. New York: Free Press.

Minuchin, S., Montalvo, B., Guerney, B., Rosman, B., Schumer, F. (1967). *Families of the Slums*. New York: Basic Books.

Minuchin, S. Rosman, B. & Baker, L. (1978). *Psychosomatic Families: Anorexia Nervosa in Context*. Cambridge, MA: Harvard University Press.

Minuchin, S., Lee, W. & Simon, G. (1996). *Mastering Family Therapy: Journeys of Growth and Transformation*. New York: Wiley.

Mitchell, K. & Carr, A. (2000). Anorexia and bulimia. In A. Carr (Ed.), *What Works With Children And Adolescents? A Critical Review Of Psychological Interventions With Children, Adolescents And Their Families*, pp. 233–257. London: Routledge.

Mitten, T. & Cinnell, G. (2004). The core variables of symbolic-expereintial family therapy. *Journal of Marital and Family Therapy*, **30**, 467–478.

Monk, G., Winslade, J., Crocket, K., & Epston, D. (1997). *Narrative Therapy in Practice: The Archaeology of Hope*. San Faracisco, CA: Jossey-Bass.

Moore, M. & Carr, A. (2000a). Anxiety disorders. In A. Carr (Ed.), *What Works With Children And Adolescents? A Critical Review Of Psychological Interventions With Children, Adolescents And Their Families*, pp. 178–202. London: Routledge.

Moore, M. & Carr, A. (2000b). Depression and grief. In A. Carr (Ed.), *What Works With Children And Adolescents? A Critical Review Of Psychological Interventions With Children, Adolescents And Their Families*, pp. 203–232. London: Routledge.

Moreno, J. (1945). *Psychodrama*. New York: Beacon House.

Morgan, A. (2000). *What is Narrative Therapy: An Easy-to-Read Introduction*. Adelaide: Dulwich Centre.

Morris, S., Alexander, J., & Waldron, H. (1988). Functional Family Therapy. In I. Falloon (Ed.), *Handbook of Behavioural Family Therapy*, pp. 130–152. New York: Guilford.

Mrazek, D. (2002). Psychiatric aspects of somatic disease and disorders. In M. Rutter, E. & Taylor (Eds), *Child and Adolescent Psychiatry*, 4th edn, pp. 810–827. Oxford: Blackwell.

MTA Cooperative Group (1999). A 14 month randomized clinical trial of treatment strategies for attention deficit hyperactivity disorder. *Archives of General Psychiatry*, **56**, 1073–1086.

Mueser, K. & Glynn, S. (1995). *Behavioural Family Therapy for Psychiatric Disorders*. Boston: Allyn & Bacon.

Murphy, E. & Carr, A. (2000a). Paediatric pain problems. In A. Carr (Ed.), *What Works With Children And Adolescents? A Critical Review Of Psychological Interventions With Children, Adolescents And Their Families*, pp. 258–279. London: Routledge.

Murphy, E. & Carr, A. (2000b). Enuresis and encopresis. In A. Carr (Ed.), *What Works With Children And Adolescents? A Critical Review of Psychological Interventions With Children, Adolescents And Their Families*, pp. 49–64. London: Routledge.

Murray, R. & Castle, D. (2000). Genetic and environmental risk factors for schizophrenia. In. M. Gelder, J. Lopez-Ibor & N. Andreasen (Eds), *New Oxford Textbook of Psychiatry*, Vol. 1, pp. 599–605. Oxford: Oxford University Press.

Myerhoff, B. (1982). Life history among the elderly: Performance, visibility and remembering. In J. Ruby (Ed.), *A Crack in the Mirror: Reflexive Perspectives on Anthropology*, pp. 99–117. Philadelphia, PA: University of Pennsylvania Press.

Myerhoff, B. (1986). Life not death in Venice: Its second life. In V. Turner & E. Bruner (Eds), *The Anthropology of Experience*, pp. 261–285. Chicago, IL: University of Illinois Press.

Myers, M., Brown, S. & Vik, P. (1998). Adolescent substance use problems. In E. Mash & L. Terdal (Eds), *Treatment of Childhood Disorders*, 2nd edn, pp. 692–730. New York: Guilford.

Napier, A. (1987a). Early stages in experiential marital therapy. *Contemporary Family Therapy*, **9**, 23–41.

Napier, A. (1987b). Later stages in experiential marital therapy. *Contemporary Family Therapy*, **9**, 42–57.

Napier, A. & Whitaker, C. (1978). *The Family Crucible*. New York: Harper Row.

National Collaborating Centre for Mental Health (2003). *Schizophrenia: Full National Clinical Guideline on Core Interventions in Primary and Secondary Care*. London: UK: Gaskell and the British Psychological Society.

Neill, J. & Kniskern, D. (1982). *From Psyche to System: The Evolving Therapy of Carl Whitaker*. New York: Guilford.

Neimeyer, G. (1985). Personal constructs and the counselling of couples. In F. Epting & A. Landfeld (Eds), *Anticipating Personal Construct Psychology*, pp. 201–215. Lincoln, NE: University of Nebraska Press.

Neimeyer, G. (1987). Marital role reconstruction through couples group therapy. In R. Neimeyer & G. Neimeyer (Eds), *A Casebook of Personal Construct Therapy*. New York: Springer.

Neimeyer, G. & Hudson, J. (1985). Couples constructs: personal systems in marital satisfaction. In D. Bannister (Ed.), Issues and Approaches in Personal Construct Psychology, pp. 96–102. London: Academic Press.

Neimeyer, G. & Neimeyer, R. (1994). Constructivist methods of marital and family therapy: a practical précis. *Journal of Mental Health Counseling*, **16** (1), 85–104.

Neimeyer, R. & Mahoney, M. (1995). *Constructivism in Psychotherapy*. Washington, DC: APA.

Nelson, T. (2003). Transgenerational family therapy. In L. Hecker & J. Wetchler (Eds), *An Introduction to Marital and Family Therapy*, pp. 255–296. New York: Haworth.

Nemeroff, C. & Schatzberg, A. (2002). Pharmacological treatment of unipolar depression. In P. Nathan & J. Gorman (Eds), *A Guide To Treatments That Work*, 2nd edn, pp. 229–244. New York: Oxford University Press.

Neugarten, B. & Weinstein, R. (1964). The changing American grandparent. *Journal of Marriage and the Family*, **26**, 199–204.

Newman, B. & Newman, P. (2003). *Development Through Life*, 8th edn. Pacific Grove, CA: Brooks/Cole.

Nichols, W. (2003). Family-of-origin treatment. In T. Sexton, G. Weeks & M. Robbins (Eds), *Handbook of Family Therapy*, pp. 83–100. New York: Brunner-Routledge.

Nicol, A., Smith, J., Kay, B., Hall, D., Barlow, J. and Williams, B. (1988). A focused casework approach to the treatment of child abuse: A controlled comparison. *Journal of Child Psychology and Psychiatry*, **29**, 703–711.

Nolan, M. & Carr, A. (2000). Attention deficit hyperactivity disorder. In A. Carr (Ed.),*What Works With Children And Adolescents? A Critical Review Of Psychological Interventions With Children, Adolescents And Their Families*, pp. 65–102. London: Routledge.

Norcross, J. & Goldfried, M. (2005). *Handbook of Psychotherapy Integration*, 2nd edn. New York: Oxford University Press.

Northey, W., Wells, K., Silverman, W. & Bailey, E. (2003). Childhood behavioural and emotional disorders. *Journal of Marital and family Therapy*, **29** (4), 523–546.

O'Brien, C. & McKay, J. (2002). Pharmacological treatments for substance use disorders. In P. Nathan & J. Gorman (Eds), *A Guide To Treatments That Work*, 2nd edn, pp. 125–156. New York: Oxford University Press.

O'Farrell, T. (1993). *Treating Alcohol Problems: Marital and Family Interventions*. New York: Guilford.

O'Farrell, T. & Fals-Stewart, W. (2002). Alcohol abuse. In D. Sprenkle (Ed.), *Effectiveness Research in Marital and Family Therapy*, pp. 123–162. Alexandria, VA: American Association for Marital and Family Therapy.

O'Farrell, T. & Fals-Stewart, W. (2003). Alcohol abuse. *Journal of Marital and family Therapy*, **29** (1), 121–146.

O'Hanlon, W. & Bertolino, B. (2002). *Even from a Broken Web: Brief, Respectful Solution-Oriented Therapy for Sexual Abuse and Trauma*. New York: Norton.

O'Hanlon, W. & Weiner-Davis, M. (2003). *In Search of Solutions. A New Direction in Psychotherapy*. New York: Norton.

Olson, D. (2000). Circumplex Model of Marital and Family Systems. *Journal of Family Therapy*, **22** (2), 144–167.

Olweus, D. (1993). *Bullying at School: What We Know and What We Can Do*. Oxford: Blackwell.

O'Reilly, G. & Carr, A. (1998). Understanding, Assessing and Treating Juvenile and Adult Sex Offenders. Special Guest Edited Issue. *Irish Journal of Psychology*, **19** (1).

O'Reilly, G., Marshall, W., Carr, A. & Beckett, R. (Eds) (2004). *The Handbook of Clinical Intervention with Young People who Sexually Abuse*. London: Brunner–Routledge.

Pagliaro, A. & Pagliaro, L. (1996). *Substance Use among Children and Adolescents*. New York: Wiley.

Paolucci, E., Genuis, M., & Violato, C. (2001). A meta-analysis of the published research on the effects of child sexual abuse. *Journal of Psychology*, **135**, 17–36.

Papalia, D., Wendkos-Olds, S., Duskin, D. & Feldman, R. (2001). *Human Development*, 8th edn. New York: McGraw Hill.

Papero, D. (1990). *Bowen Family Systems Theory*. Needham Heights, MA: Allyn & Bacon.

Papp, P. (1982). The Greek Chorus and other techniques of paradoxical therapy. *Family Process*, **19**, 45–57.

Papp, P. (1983). *The Process of Change*. New York: Guilford.

Parke, R. (2004). Development in the family. *Annual Review of Psychology*, **55**, 365–399.

Parry, A. & Doane, R. (1994). *Story Re-visions. Narrative Therapy in the Postmodern World*. New York: Guilford.

Parsons, T. & Bales R. (1955). *Family Socialization and Interaction Process.* New York: Free Press.

Patterson, G. (1971). *Families: Applications of Social Learning to Family Life.* Champaign, IL: Research Press.

Patterson, G. (1982) *Coercive Family Process.* Eugene, OR: Castalia.

Patterson, G., Reid, J. & Dishion, T. (1992). *Antisocial Boys.* Eugene, OR: Castalia.

Penn, P. (1982). Circular questioning. *Family Process,* **21**, 267–280.

Penn, P. (1985). Feedforeward: Further questioning future maps. *Family Process,* **24**, 299–310.

Perls, F. (1973). *The Gestalt Approach and Eyewitness to Therapy.* Palo Alto, CA: Science and Behaviour.

Pinsof, W. (1994). An integrative system perspective on the therapeutic alliance: Theoretical, clinical and research implications. In A. Horvath & L. Greenberg (Eds), *The Working Alliance: Theory, Research and Practice,* pp. 173–195. New York: Wiley.

Pinsof, W. (1995). *Integrative Problem-Centred Therapy.* New York: Basic Books.

Pinsof, W. (2005). Integrative problem-centred therapy. In J. Norcross & M. Goldfried (Eds), *Handbook of Psychotherapy Integration,* 2nd edn, pp. 282–402. New York: Oxford University Press.

Pinsof, W. & Catherall, D. (1986). The integrative psychotherapy alliance: family, couple, and individual scales. *Journal of Marital and Family Therapy,* **12** (2), 137–152.

Pinsof, W., Mann, B., Lebow, J., Knobloch-Fedders, L., Friedman, G. & Zinbarg, R. (2004a). *The Integrative Therapy Session Report.* Evanston, IL: The Family Institute at Northwestern University.

Pinsof, W., Zinbarg, R., Mann, B., Lebow, J., Knobloch-Fedders, L. & Friedman, G. (2004b). *The Systemic Therapy Inventory of Change.* Evanston, IL: The Family Institute at Northwestern University.

Pirrotta, S. (1984). Milan Revisited: A comparison of the two Milan Schools. *Journal of Strategic and Systemic Therapies,* **3**, 3–15.

Pocock, D. (1995). Searching for a better story. Harnessing modern and post-modern positions in family therapy. *Journal of Family Therapy,* **17**, 149–174.

Prata, G. (1990). *A Systemic Harpoon into Family Games: Preventative Interventions in Therapy.* New York: Brunner Mazel.

Prochaska, J, (1999). How do people change and how can we change to help many more people. In Hubble, M., Duncan, B. & Miller, D. (Eds), *The Heart and Soul of Change,* pp. 227–259. Washington, DC: APA.

Procter, H. (1981). Family construct psychology: An approach to understanding and treating families. In S. Walrond-Skinner (Ed.), *Developments in Family Therapy: Theories and Applications since 1948,* pp. 350–366. London: Routledge.

Procter, H. (1985a). A construct approach to family therapy and systems intervention. In E. Button (Ed.), *Personal Construct Theory and Mental Health,* pp. 327–350. London: Croom Helm.

Procter, H. (1985b). Repertory grids in family therapy and research. In N. Beail (Ed.), *Repertory Grid Techniques and Personal Constructs: Applications in Clinical and Educational Settings,* pp. 218–239. London: Croom Helm.

Procter, H. (1995). The family construct system. In D. Kalekin-Fishman & B. Walker (Eds), *The Construct on of Group Realities. Culture and Society in the Light of Personal Construct Theory,* pp. 161–180. New York: Krieger.

Procter, H. (2003). Family therapy. In F. Fransella (Ed.), *International Handbook of Personal Construct Psychology*, pp. 431–434. Chichester: Wiley.

Putnam, F. (2003). Ten-year research update review: Child sexual abuse. *Journal of the American Academy of Child & Adolescent Psychiatry*, **42**, 269–278.

Radojevic, V., Nicassio, P. & Weisman, M. (1992). Behavioural intervention with and without family support for rheumatoid arthritis. *Behaviour Therapy*, **23**, 13–30.

Rambo, A. (2003). The collaborative language-based models of family therapy: When less is more. In L. Hecker & J. Wetchler (Eds), *An Introduction to Marital and Family Therapy*, pp. 149–172. New York: Haworth.

Raschke, H. (1987). Divorce. In M. Sussman & S. Steinmetz (Eds), *Handbook of Marriage and the Family*, pp. 348–399. New York: Plenum.

Ray, W. (2004). A tradition of inquiry: special section on the Mental Research Institute. *Journal of Systemic Therapies*, **23**, 1–3.

Reder, P. & Lucey, C. (1995). *Assessment of Parenting. Psychiatric and Psychological Contributions*. London: Routledge.

Reder, P., McClure, M. & Jolley, A. (2000). *Family Matters. Interfaces between Child and Adult Mental Health*. London: Routledge.

Reder, P., Duncan, S. & Lucey, S. (2004). *Studies in the Assessment of Parenting*. London: Routledge.

Reifman, A., Villa, L., Amans, J., Rethinam, V. & Telesca, T. (2001). Children of divorce in the 1990s: A meta–analysis. *Journal of Divorce & Remarriage*, **36**, 27–36.

Reimers, S. & Treacher, A. (1995). *Introducing User Friendly Family Therapy*. London: Routledge.

Rice, P. & Dolgin, K. (2004). *The Adolescent: Development, Relationships, and Culture*, 11th edn. New York: Allyn & Bacon.

Richardson, C., Gilleard, C., Lieberman, S. & Peeler, R. (1994). Working with older adults and their families: A review. *Journal of Family Therapy*, **16**, 225–240.

Robbins, M., Mayorga, C. & Szapoznick, J. (2003). The ecosystemic 'lens' to understanding family functioning. In T. Sexton, G. Weeks & M. Robbins (Eds), *Handbook of Family Therapy*, pp. 21–36. New York: Brunner-Routledge.

Roberto, G. (1991). Symbolic-experiential family therapy. In A. Gurman & D. Kniskern (Eds), *Handbook of Family Therapy*, Vol. 11, pp. 444–478. New York: Brunner Mazel.

Roberto, L. (1992). *Transgenerational Family Therapies*. New York: Guilford.

Roberto-Forman, L. (2002). Transgenerational marital therapy. In A. Gurman & N. Jacobson (Eds), *Clinical Handbook of Couples Therapy*, 3rd edn, pp. 118–150. New York: Guilford.

Robin, A. (2003). Behavioural family systems therapy for adolescents with anorexia nervosa In A. Kazdin & J. Weisz (Eds), *Evidence Based Psychotherapies for Children and Adolescents*, pp. 358–373. New York: Guilford.

Rogers, C. (1951). *Client-centred Therapy*. Boston: Houghton Mifflin.

Rogers, C. (1970). *On Encounter Groups*. New York: Harper.

Rogers, K. (2004). A theoretical review of risk and protective factors related to post- divorce adjustment in young children. *Journal of Divorce Remarriage*, **40** (3–4), 135–147.

Rosen, K. (2003). Strategic family therapy. In L. Hecker & J. Wetchler (Eds), *An Introduction to Marital and Family Therapy*, pp. 95–122. New York: Haworth.

Rowan, T. & O'Hanlon, B. (1999). *Solution-Oriented Therapy for Chronic and Severe Mental Illness*. New York: Wiley.

Rowe, C. & Liddle, H. (2003) Substance abuse. *Journal of Marital and Family Therapy*, 29, 86–120.

Roy-Byrne, P. & Cowley, D. (2002). Pharmacological treatment of panic disorder, generalized anxiety disorder, specific phobia and social anxiety disorder. In P. Nathan & J. Gorman (Eds), *A Guide To Treatments That Work*, 2nd edn, pp. 337–366. New York: Oxford University Press.

Ruddy, N. & McDaniel, S. (2003). Medical family Therapy. In T. Sexton, G. Weeks & M. Robbins (Eds), *Handbook of Family Therapy*, pp. 365–379. New York: Brunner-Routledge.

Rust, L., Bennun, L., Crowe, M. & Golombok, S. (1988). *GRIMS. The Golombok Rust Inventory of Marital State*. Winsor: NFER-Nelson.

Rutter, M. (1999). Resilience concepts and findings: Implications for family therapy. *Journal of Family Therapy*, **21**, 119–144.

Rutter, M. (2002). Substance use and abuse: Causal pathways considerations. In M. Rutter & E. Taylor (Eds), *Child and Adolescent Psychiatry*, 4th edn, pp. 455–462. Oxford: Blackwell.

Rutter, M., Giller, H. & Hagell, A. (1998). *Antisocial Behaviour by Young People: A Major New Review*. Cambridge: Cambridge University Press.

Rutter, M., Maughan, N., Mortimore, P., & Ouston, J. (1979). *Fifteen Thousand Hours*. London: Open Books.

Sanders, M. & Dadds, M. (1993). *Behavioural Family Intervention*. New York: Pergammon Press.

Sanders, M., Shepherd, R., Cleghorn, G. & Woolford, H. (1994). The treatment of recurrent abdominal pain in children: A controlled comparison of cognitive-behavioural family intervention and standard paediatric care. *Journal of Consulting and Clinical Psychology*, **62**, 306–314.

Sandler, I., et al. (1992). Linking empirically based theory and evaluation: The family bereavement programme. *American Journal of Community Psychology*, **20**, 491–521.

Santisteban, D., Szapocznik, J., Perez-Vidal, A., Kurtines, W., Murray, E. & LaPerriere, A. (1996). Efficacy of intervention for engaging youth and families into treatment and some variables that may contribute to differential effectiveness. *Journal of Family Psychology*, **10**, 35–44.

Santrock, J. (2003). *Lifespan Development*, 9th edn. New York: McGraw Hill Education.

Sarafino, E. (2001). *Health Psychology*, 4th edn. New York: Wiley.

Sarup, M. (1993). *An Introductory Guide to Post-structuralism and Postmodernism*. London: Harvester Wheatsheaf.

Satir, V. (1983). *Conjoint Family Therapy*, 3rd edn. Palo Alto, CA: Science and Behaviour Books.

Satir, V. (1988). *The New Peoplemaking*. Palo Alto, CA: Science and Behaviour Books.

Satir, V. & Baldwin, M. (1983). *Satir Step-by-Step. A Guide to Creating Change in Families*. Palo Alto, CA: Science and Behaviour Books.

Satir, V. & Baldwin, M. (1987). *The Use of Self in Therapy*. Binghampton, NY: Haworth.

Satir, V., Banmen, J., Gerber, J. & Gomori, M. (1991). *The Satir Model: Family Therapy and Beyond*. Palo Alto, CA: Science and Behaviour Books.

Savage-Scharff, J. (1989). *Foundations of Object Relations Family Therapy*. Northvale, NJ: Jason Aronson.

Savage-Scharff, J. (1992). *Projective and Introjective Identification and the Use of the Therapists Self*. Northvale, NJ: Jason Aronson.

Savage-Scharff, J. & Bagini, C. (2002). Object-relations couple therapy. In A. Gurman & N. Jacobson (Eds), *Clinical Handbook of Couples Therapy*, 3rd edn, pp. 59–85. New York: Guilford.

Savage-Scharff, J. & Scharff, D. (1994). *Object Relations Therapy of Physical and Sexual Trauma*. Northvale, NJ: Jason Aronson.

Savage-Scharf, J. & Scharf, D. (2003). Object relations and psychodynamic approaches to couple and family therapy. In T. Sexton, G. Weeks & M. Robbins (Eds), *Handbook of Family Therapy*, pp. 59–82. New York: Brunner-Routledge.

Sayers, S. (1998). Special issue on behavioural couples therapy. *Clinical Psychology Review*, **18**(6).

Scharff, D. (1982). *The Sexual Relationship: An Object Relations view of Sex and the Family*. Boston: Routledge.

Scharff, D. & Savage-Scharff, J. (1987). *Object Relations Family Therapy*. Northvale, NJ: Jason Aronson.

Scharff, D. & Savage -Scharff, J. (1991). *Object Relations Couple Therapy*. Northvale, NJ: Jason Aronson.

Schnarch, D. (1991). *Constructing the Sexual Crucible: An Integration of Sexual and Marital Therapy*. New York: Norton.

Schuerman, J., Rzepmicki, T. & Littem J. (1994). *Putting Families First. An Experiment in Family Preservation*. New York: Aldine de Gruytner.

Schwartz, R. (1995). *Internal Family Systems Therapy*. New York: Guilford.

Schwoeri, L. & Sholevar, G. (2003). Psychoeducational family intervention. In G. Sholevar (Eds), *Textbook of Family and Couples Therapy: Clinical Applications*, pp. 173–192. Washington, DC: American Psychiatric Press.

Schwoeri, L., Sholevar, G. & Vilarose, G. (2003). Gender-sensitive family therapy. In G. Sholevar (Ed.), *Textbook of Family and Couples Therapy: Clinical Applications*, pp. 203–224. Washington, DC: American Psychiatric Press.

Segal, L. (1991) Brief Therapy: The MRI approach. In A. Gurman & D. Kniskern (Eds), *Handbook of Family Therapy*, Vol. 2, pp. 17–199. New York: Brunner/Mazel.

Segraves, R. & Althof, S. (2002). Psychotherapy and pharmacotherapy for sexual dysfunctions. In P. Nathan & J. Gorman (Eds), *A Guide To Treatments That Work*, 2nd edn, pp. 497–524. New York: Oxford University Press.

Selvini-Palazzoli, M. (1988). *The Work of Mara Selvini Palazzoli*. New York: Jason Aronson.

Selvini-Palazzoli, M., Boscolo, L., Cecchin, G. & Prata, G. (1978) *Paradox and Counterparadox*. New York: Aronson.

Selvini-Palazzoli, M., Boscolo, L., Cecchin, G. & Prata, G. (1980) Hypothesizing – circularity – neutrality: Three guidelines for the conductor of the session. *Family Process*, **19**, 3–12.

Selvini-Palazzoli, M. & Cirillo, Selvini, M. & Sorrentino, A. (1989) *Family Games: General Models of Psychotic Processes within the Family*. New York: Norton.

Sequeira, H. & Hollis, S. (2003). Clinical effects of sexual abuse on people with learning difficulty. *British Journal of Psychiatry*, **182**, 13–19.

Serbin, L., Powlishta, K. & Gulko, J. (1993). The development of sex typing in middle childhood. *Monographs for the Society for Research in Child Development*, **58** (Serial No. 232).

Sexton, T. L. & Alexander, J. F. (1999). *Functional Family Therapy: Principles of Clinical Intervention, Assessment, and Implementation.* Henderson, NV: RCH Enterprises.

Sexton, T. & Alexander, J. (2003). Functional family therapy: A mature clinical model for working with at-risk adolescents and their families. In T. Sexton, G. Weeks & M. Robbins (Eds), *Handbook of Family Therapy*, pp. 323–350. New York: Brunner-Routledge.

Sexton, T., Robbins, M., Hollimon, A., Mease, A. & Mayorga, C. (2003). Efficacy, effectiveness, and change mechanisms in couple and family therapy. In T. Sexton, G. Weeks & M. Robbins, *Handbook of Family Therapy*, pp. 229–262. New York: Brunner-Routledge.

Sexton, T., Alexander, J. & Leigh-Mease, A. (2004). Levels of evidence for the models and mechanisms of therapeutic change in family and couple therapy. In M. Lambert (Ed.), *Bergin and Garfields Handbook of Psychotherapy and Behaviour Change*, 5th edn, pp. 543–589. New York: Wiley.

Shackleton, C. (1983). The psychology of grief: A review. *Behaviour Research and Therapy*, **6**, 183–205.

Shadish, W. & Baldwin, S. (2002). Meta-analysis of MFT interventions. In D. Sprenkle (Ed.), *Effectiveness Research in Marital and Family Therapy*, pp. 339–365. Alexandria, VA: American Associatiion for Marital and Family Therapy.

Shadish, W. & Baldwin, S. (2003).Meta-analysis of MFT interventions. *Journal of Marital and Family Therapy*, **29** (4), 547–570.

Shadish, W. & Baldwin, S. (2005). Effects of behavioural marital therapy: A meta-analysis of randomized controlled trails. *Journal of Consulting and Clinical Psychology*, **73** (1), 6–14.

Sharry, J., Madden, B. & Darmody, M. (2003). *Becoming a Solution Detective. Identifying Your Clients' Strengths in Practical Brief Therapy.* New York: Haworth.

Sheidow, A., Henggeler, S. & Schoenwald, S. (2003) Multisystemic therapy. In T. Sexton, G. Weeks & M. Robbins (Eds), *Handbook of Family Therapy*, pp. 303–322. New York: Brunner-Routledge.

Shoham, V. & Rohbaugh, M. (2002). Brief strategic couple therapy. In A. Gurman & N. Jacobson (Eds), *Clinical Handbook of Couples Therapy*, 3rd edn, pp. 5–21. New York: Guilford.

Sholevar, G. (2003). *Textbook of Family and Couples Therapy: Clinical Applications.* Washington, DC: American Psychiatric Press.

Silver, E., Williams, A., Worthington, F. & Phillips, N. (1998). Family therapy and soiling: An audit of externalizing and other approaches. *Journal of Family Therapy*, **20**, 413–422.

Simpson, J. & Rholes, S. (1998). *Attachment Theory and Close Relationships.* New York: Guilford.

Singer, M., Wynne, L. & Toohey, M. (1978). Communication disorders in the families of schizophrenics. In L. Wynne, R. Cromwell & S. Matthysse (Eds), *The Nature of Schizophrenia*, pp. 30–52. New York: Wiley.

Skinner, H., Steinhauer, P. & Sitarenios, G. (2000). Family Assessment Measure (FAM) and Process Model of Family Functioning. *Journal of Family Therapy*, **22** (2), 190–210.

Skuse, D. & Bentovim, A. (1994). Physical and emotional maltreatment. In M. Rutter, E. Taylor & E. Hersov (Eds), *Child & Adolescent Psychiatry: Modern Approaches*, 3rd edn, pp. 209–229. Oxford: Blackwell.

Skynner, R. (1981). An open-systems, group-analytic approach to family therapy. In A. Gurman & D. Kniskern (Eds), *Handbook of Family Therapy*, pp. 39–84. New York: Bruner Mazel.

Slater, S. (1995). *The Lesbian Lifecycle*. London: Free Press.

Slipp, S. (1984). *Object relations: A Dynamic Bridge Between Individual and Family Treatment*. New York: Jason Aronson.

Slipp, S. (1988). *The Technique and Practice of Object Relations Family Therapy*. New York: Jason Aronson.

Smith, M. & Bentovim, A. (1994). Sexual abuse. In M. Rutter, E. Taylor & L. Hersov (Eds), *Child and Adolescent Psychiatry: Modern Approaches*, 3rd edn, pp. 230–251. Oxford: Blackwell.

Snyder, D. (1997). *Marital Satisfaction Inventory-Revised*. Los Angeles, CA: Western Psychological Services.

Snyder, D. & Schneider, W. (2002). Affective reconstruction: A pluralistic, developmental approach. In A. Gurman & N. Jacobson (Eds). *Clinical Handbook of Couples Therapy*, 3rd edn, pp. 151–179. New York: Guilford.

Snyder, D. & Wills, R. (1989). Behavioral versus insight-oriented marital therapy: Effects on individual interspousal functioning. *Journal of Consulting and Clinical Psychology*, **57**, 39–46.

Snyder, D., Wills, R. & Grady-Fletcher, F. (1991). Long-term effectiveness of behavioural versus insight-oriented marital therapy: a 4-year follow-up study. *Journal of Consulting and Clinical Psychology*, **59**, 138–141.

Spaccarelli, S. (1994). Stress, appraisal and coping in child sexual abuse: A theoretical and empirical review. *Psychological Bulletin*, **116**, 340–362.

Sprenkle, D. (2002). *Effectiveness Research in Marital and Family Therapy*. Alexandria, VA: American Association for Marital and Family Therapy.

Sprenkle, D. H. & Blow, A. J. (2004). Common factors and our sacred models. *Journal of Marital & Family Therapy*, **30** (2), 113–129.

Sprenkle, D. H. & Wilkie, S. G. (1996). Supervision and training. In F. P. Piercy, D. H. Sprenkle & J. L. Wetchler (Eds), *Family Therapy Sourcebook*, pp. 350–391. New York: Guilford.

Stanton, M. (2004) Getting reluctant substance abusers to engage in treatment/self-help: A review of outcomes and clinical options. *Journal of Marital & Family Therapy*, **30**, 165–182.

Stanton, D. & Heath, A. (1995). Family treatment of alcohol and drug abuse. In R. Mikeselle, D. Lusterman & S. McDaniel (Eds), *Integrating Family Therapy: Handbook of Family Therapy and Systems Theory*, pp. 529–541. Washington, DC: APA.

Stanton, M. & Shadish, W. (1997). Outcome, attrition and family-couples treatment for drug abuse: A meta-analysis and review of the controlled comparative studies. *Psychological Bulletin*, **122**, 170–191.

Stanton, M. & Todd, T. (1982). *The Family Therapy of Drug Abuse and Addiction*. New York: Guilford.

Steinglass, P., Bennett, L., Wolin, S., & Reiss, D. (1987). *The Alcoholic Family*. New York: Basic Books.

Stith, S., McCollum, E., Rosen, K., Locke, L. & Goldberg, P. (2005). Domestic violence focused couples treatment. In J. Lebow (Ed.), *Handbook of Clinical Family Therapy* pp. 250–275. New York: Wiley.

Stith, S. M., Rosen, K. H., McCollum, E. E. & Thomsen, C. J. (2004). Treating intimate partner violence within intact couple relationships: Outcomes of multi-couple versus individual couple therapy. *Journal of Marital & Family Therapy*, **30**, 305–318.

Stone-Fish, L. & Harvey, R. (2005). *Nurturing Queer Youth. Family Therapy Transformed*. New York: Norton.

Storm, C., McDowell, T. & Long, J. (2003). The metamorphosis of training and supervision. In T. Sexton, G. Weeks & M. Robbins (Eds), *Handbook of Family Therapy*, pp. 431–448. New York: Brunner-Routledge.

Straus, M. & Gelles, R. (1990). *Physical Violence in American Families*. New Brunswick, NJ: Transaction.

Street, E. & Downey, J. (1995). *Brief Therapeutic Consultations*. Chichester: Wiley.

Stroebe, M., Hansson, R., Stroebe, W. & Schut, H. (2001). *Handbook of Bereavement Research: Consequences, Coping, and Care*. Washington, DC: American Psychological Association.

Stuart, R. (1969). Operant interpersonal treatment of marital discord. *Journal of Consulting and Clinical Psychology*, **33**, 675–682.

Suhd, M., Dodson, L. & Gomori, M. (2000). *Virginia Satir: Her Life and Circle of Influence*. Palo Alto, CA: Science and Behaviour Books.

Swenson, C.C., Henggeler, S.W., Taylor, I.S. & Addison, O.W. (2005). *Multisystemic Therapy And Neighbourhood Partnerships: Reducing Adolescent Violence And Substance Abuse*. New York: Guilford Press.

Szapocznik, J. & Kurtines, W. (1989). *Breakthroughs In Family Therapy With Drug Abusing Problem Youth*. New York: Springer.

Szapocznik, J. & Williams, R. (2000). Brief strategic family therapy. Twenty five years of interplay among theory, research and practice in adolescent behaviour problems and drug abuse. *Clinical Child and Family Psychology Review*, **3** (2), 117–134.

Szapocznik, J., Perez-Vidal, A., Brickman, A., Foote, F.H., Santisteban, D. & Hervis, O. (1988). Engaging adolescent drug abusers and their families in treatment: A strategic structural systems approach. *Journal of Consulting and Clinical Psychology*, **56**, 552–557.

Szapocznik, J., Hervis, O. & Schwartz, S. (2002). *Brief Strategic Family Therapy for Adolescent Drug Abuse*. Rockville, MD: National Institute for Drug Abuse. Available at http://www.drugabuse.gov/TXManuals/bsft/BSFTIndex.html

Tasker, F. & McCann, D. (1999). Affirming patterns of adolescent sexual identity: The challenge. *Journal of Family Therapy*, **21**, 30–54.

Taylor, S. (In Press). Panic disorder. In A. Carr & M. McNulty (Eds), *Handbook of Adult Clinical Psychology: An Evidence Based Practice Approach*. London: Brunner-Routledge.

Thomas, E. & Ager, R. (1993). Unilateral family therapy with spouses of unco-operative alcohol abusers. In T. O'Farrell (Ed.), *Treating Alcohol Problems: Marital and Family Interventions*, pp. 3–33. New York: Guilford.

Tomm, K. (1984a). One perspective on the Milan Systemic Approach: Part I. Overview of development theory and practice. *Journal of Marital and Family Therapy*, **10**, 113–125.

Tomm, K. (1984b). One perspective on the Milan Systemic Approach: Part II. Description of session format, interviewing style and interventions. *Journal of Marital and Family Therapy*, **10**, 253–271.

Tomm, K. (1987a) Interventive interviewing Part I. Strategising as a fourth guideline for the therapist. *Family Process*, **25**, 4–13.

Tomm, K. (1987b) Interventive interviewing Part II. Reflexive questioning as a means to enable self healing. *Family Process*, **26**, 167–183.

Tomm, K. (1988) Interventive interviewing Part III. Intending to ask linear, circular, strategic or reflexive questions. *Family Process*, **27**, 1–15.

Trepper, T. & Barrett, M. (1989). *Systemic Treatment of Incest: A Therapeutic Handbook*. New York: Brunner/Mazel.

Turk, D. & Burwinkle, T. (In press). Chronic pain. In A. Carr & M. McNulty (Eds), *Handbook of Adult Clinical Psychology: An Evidence Based Practice Approach*. London: Brunner-Routledge.

Valliant, G. (1977). *Adaptation to life: How the Best and Brightest Came of Age*. Boston: Little Brown.

Vasta, R., Haith, M. & Miller, S. (2003). *Child Psychology: The Modern Science*, 4th edn. New York: Wiley.

Vaughan, C. & Leff, J. (1976). The measurement of expressed emotion in the families of psychiatric patients. *British Journal of Social and Clinical Psychology*, **15**, 157–165.

Verhulst, F. (2001). Community and epidemiological aspects of anxiety disorders in children. In W. Silverman & P. Treffers (Eds), *Anxiety Disorders in Children and Adolescents. Research Assessment and Intervention*, pp. 273–292. Cambridge: Cambridge University Press.

Vetere, A. & Dallos, R. (2003). *Working Systemically with Families. Formulation, Intervention and Evaluation*. London: Karnac.

Vik, P., Brown, S., & Myers, M. (1997). Adolescent substance use problems. In E. Mash & R. Barkley (Eds), *Assessment of Childhood Disorders*, 3rd edn, pp. 717–748. New York: Guilford.

Visher, E., Visher, J., & Pasley, C. (2003). Remarriage families and step parenting. In F. Walsh (Ed.), *Normal Family Processes*, 3rd edn, pp. 121–151. New York: Guilford.

Volker, T. (2003). Experiential approaches to family therapy. In L. Hecker & J. Wetchler (Eds), *An Introduction to Marital and Family Therapy*, pp. 173–202. New York: Haworth.

Von Foerster, H. (1981). *Observing Systems*. Seaside, CA: Intersystems.

Walker, C. (2003). Elimination disorders. In M. Roberts (Ed.), *Handbook of Paediatric Psychology*, 2nd edn, pp. 544–560. New York: Guilford.

Wallerstein, J. (1991). The long term effects of divorce on children: A review. *Journal of the American Academy of Child and Adolescent Psychiatry*, **30**, 349–360.

Walsh, F. (2003a). *Normal Family Processes*, 3rd edn. New York: Guilford.

Walsh, F. (2003b). Resilience: A framework for clinical practice. *Family Process*, **42**, 1–18.

Walsh, F. & McGoldrick, M. (2004). *Living Beyond Loss: Death in the Family*, 2nd edn. New York: Norton.

Watzlawick, P., Beavin, J. & Jackson, D. (1967). *Pragmatics of Human Communication*. New York: Norton.

Watzlawick, P. & Weakland (1977). *The Interactional View*. New York: Norton.

Watzlawick, P., Weakland, J. & Fisch, R. (1974). *Change. Principles of Problem Formation and Problem Resolution*. New York: Norton.

Weakland, J. & Fisch, R. (1992). Brief therapy: MRI style. In S. Budman, M. Hoyt & S. Friedman (Eds), *The First Session in Brief Therapy*, pp. 306–323. New York: Guilford.

Weakland, J. & Ray, W. (1995). *Propagations: Thirty Years of Influence from the Mental Research Institute.* Binghampton, NY: Haworth.

Webster-Stratton, C. & Reid, M. (2003). The Incredible Years parents, teachers and children training series: A multifaceted treatment approach for young children with conduct problems. In A. Kazdin, & J. Weisz (Eds), *Evidence Based Psychotherapies for Children and Adolescents,* pp. 224–262. New York: Guilford.

Weinberg, W., Harper, C. & Brumback, R. (2002). Substance use and abuse: Epidemiology, pharmacological considerations, identification and suggestions towards management. In M. Rutter & E. Taylor (Eds), *Child and Adolescent Psychiatry,* 4th edn, pp. 437–454. Oxford: Blackwell.

Weiner, M. (1948–1961). *Cybernetics or Control and Communication in the Animal and the Machine.* Cambridge, MA: MIT Press.

Weissman, M., Markowitz, J. & Klerman, G. (2000). *Comprehensive Guide to Interpersonal Psychotherapy.* New York: Basic Books.

Wekerle, C. & Wolfe, D. (2003). Child maltreatment. In E. Mash & R. Barkley (Eds), *Child Psychopathology,* 2nd edn, pp. 632–684. New York: Guilford.

Wetchler, J. (2003a). Structural family therapy. In L. Hecker & J. Wetchler (Eds), *An Introduction to Marital and Family Therapy,* pp. 39–62. New York: Haworth.

Wetchler, J. (2003b). The history of marital and family therapy. In L. Hecker & J. Wetchler (Eds), *An Introduction to Marital and Family Therapy,* pp. 3–38. New York: Haworth.

Whitaker, C. & Bumberry, W. (1988). *Dancing with the Family. A Symbolic-Experiential Approach.* New York: Brunner Mazel.

Whitaker, C. & Malone, T. (1953). *The Roots of Psychotherapy.* New York: Blakinson.

Whitaker, C. & Ryan, M. (1989). *Midnight Musings of a Family Therapist.* New York: Norton.

White, M. (1989). *Selected Papers.* Adelaide: Dulwich Centre Publications.

White, M. (1995). *Re-authoring Lives.* Adelaide: Dulwich Centre Publications.

White, M. (1997). *Narratives of Therapists' Lives.* Adelaide: Dulwich Centre Publications.

White, M. (2000). *Reflections on Narrative Practice: Essays and Interviews.* Adelaide: Dulwich Centre Publications.

White, M. (2005). *Narrative Practice and Exotic Lives: Resurrecting Diversity in Everyday Life.* Adelaide: Dulwich Centre Publications.

White, M. & Epston, D. (1989). *Literate Means to Therapeutic Ends.* Adelaide: Dulwich Centre Publications. (Republished in 1990 as *Narrative Means to Therapeutic Ends.* New York: Norton.)

White, M. & Russell, C. (1997). Examining the multifaceted notion of isomorphism in marriage and family therapy supervision. A quest for conceptual clarity. *Journal of Marital and Family Therapy,* **23**, 315–333.

Whitehead, A. & Russell, B. (1910–1913). *Principia Mathematica.* Cambridge: Cambridge University Press.

Wilkinson I. (1998). *Child And Family Assessment: Clinical Guidelines for Practitioners.* Routledge, London.

Wills, T. & Filer, M. (1996). Stress-coping model of adolescent substance use. In T. Ollendick & R. Prinz (Eds), *Advances in Clinical Child Psychology,* pp. 91–132. New York: Plenum.

Wood, B. (1994). One articulation of the structural family therapy model: A biobehavioural family model of chronic illness in children. *Journal of Family Therapy*, **16**, 53–72.

Woods, M. & Martin, D. (1984). The work of Virginia Satir: Understanding her theory and technique. *American Journal of Family Therapy*, **11** (1), 35–46.

Worden, J. (1997). *Children and Grief: When A Parent Dies*. New York: Guilford.

World Health Organisation (1992). *The ICD-10 Classification of Mental and Behavioural Disorders*. Geneva: WHO.

Wortman, C. & Silver, R. (1989). The myths of coping with loss. *Journal of Consulting and Clinical Psychology*, **57**, 349–357.

Wynne, L. (1961). The study of intrafamilial alignments and splits in exploratory family therapy. In N. Ackerman, F. Beatman & S. Sherman (Eds), *Exploring the Base for Family Therapy*, pp. 30–72. New York: Family Service Association of America.

Wynne, L., Ryckoff, I., Day, J. & Hirsch, S. (1958). Pseudo mutuality in the family relationships of schizophrenics. *Psychiatry*, **21**, 205–220.

Young, J. (2002). *A Celebration of the Fifth Province Feedback*, **9** (2), special issue.

Zimmerman, J. & Dickerson, V. (1996). *The Problem Speaks: Adventures in Narrative Therapy*. New York: Guilford.

Zubin, J. & Spring, B. (1977). Vulnerability: A new view of schizophrenia. *Journal of Abnormal Psychology*, **86**, 103–126.

INDEX

Wiley Series in

CLINICAL PSYCHOLOGY

Titles published under the series editorship of:

Steven Glautier and Bob Remington (Editors)	
Carlo Perris, Willem A. Arrindell and Martin Eisemann (Editors)	Parenting and Psychopathology
Paul Dickens	Quality and Excellence in Human Services
Edgar Miller and Robin Morris	The Psychology of Dementia
Ronald Blackburn	The Psychology of Criminal Conduct: Theory, Research and Practice
Max Birchwood and Nicholas Tarrier (Editors)	Innovations in the Psychological Management of Schizophrenia: Assessment, Treatment and Services
Roger Baker (Editor)	Panic Disorder: Theory, Research and Therapy